THE HOLOCAUST IN BOHEMIA AND MORAVIA

War and Genocide
General Editors: Omer Bartov, Brown University; A. Dirk Moses, University of Sydney

There has been a growing interest in the study of war and genocide, not from a traditional military history perspective, but within the framework of social and cultural history. This series offers a forum for scholarly works that reflect these new approaches.

The Berghahn series Studies on War and Genocide *has immeasurably enriched the English-language scholarship available to scholars and students of genocide and, in particular, the Holocaust.* —**Totalitarian Movements and Political Religions**

Recent volumes:

Volume 28
The Holocaust in Bohemia and Moravia: Czech Initiatives, German Policies, Jewish Responses
Wolf Gruner

Volume 27
Probing the Limits of Categorization: The Bystander in Holocaust History
Edited by Christina Morina and Krijn Thijs

Volume 26
Let Them Not Return: Sayfo— The Genocide against the Assyrian, Syriac, and Chaldean Christians in the Ottoman Empire
Edited by David Gaunt, Naures Atto, and Soner O. Barthoma

Volume 25
Daily Life in the Abyss: Genocide Diaries, 1915–1918
Vahé Tachjian

Volume 24
Microhistories of the Holocaust
Edited by Claire Zalc and Tal Bruttmann

Volume 23
The Making of the Greek Genocide: Contested Memories of the Ottoman Greek Catastrophe
Erik Sjöberg

Volume 22
Genocide on Settler Frontiers: When Hunter-Gatherers and Commercial Stock Farmers Clash
Edited by Mohamed Adhikari

Volume 21
The Spirit of the Laws: The Plunder of Wealth in the Armenian Genocide
Taner Akçam and Ümit Kurt

Volume 20
The Greater German Reich and the Jews: Nazi Persecution Policies in the Annexed Territories 1935–1945
Edited by Wolf Gruner and Jörg Osterloh

Volume 19
The Dark Side of Nation-States: Ethnic Cleansing in Modern Europe
Philipp Ther

For a full volume listing, please see the series page on our website: http://berghahnbooks.com/series/war-and-genocide

THE HOLOCAUST IN BOHEMIA AND MORAVIA

Czech Initiatives, German Policies, Jewish Responses

Wolf Gruner

Translated from the German by Alex Skinner

berghahn
NEW YORK · OXFORD
www.berghahnbooks.com

First published in 2019 by
Berghahn Books
www.berghahnbooks.com

English-language edition
© 2019, 2022 Berghahn Books
First paperback edition published in 2022

German-language edition
© 2016 Wallstein Verlag, Göttingen

Originally published in German as
Die Judenverfolgung im Protektorat Böhmen und Mähren: Lokale Initiativen, zentrale Entscheidungen, jüdische Antworten 1939–1945

The translation of this work was funded by Geisteswissenschaften International – Translation Funding for Work in the Humanities and Social Sciences from Germany, a joint initiative of the Fritz Thyssen Foundation, the German Federal Foreign Office, the collecting society VG WORT, and the Börsenverein des Deutschen Buchhandels (German Publishers & Booksellers Association).

All rights reserved. Except for the quotation of short passages for the purposes of criticism and review, no part of this book may be reproduced in any form or by any means, electronic or mechanical, including photocopying, recording, or any information storage and retrieval system now known or to be invented, without written permission of the publisher.

Library of Congress Cataloging-in-Publication Data
Names: Gruner, Wolf, 1960- author. | Skinner, Alex, translator.
Title: The Holocaust in Bohemia and Moravia : Czech initiatives, German policies, Jewish responses / Wolf Gruner.
Other titles: Judenverfolgung im Protektorat Böhmen und Mähren. English
Description: New York ; Oxford : Berghahn books, [2019] | Series: War and genocide ; volume 28 | Includes bibliographical references and index. |
Identifiers: LCCN 2019011739 (print) | LCCN 2019012289 (ebook) | ISBN 9781789202854 (ebook) | ISBN 9781789202847 (hardback : alk. paper)
Subjects: LCSH: Antisemitism--Czech Republic--Bohemia and Moravia (Protectorate, 1939–1945)--History.
Classification: LCC DS135.C96 (ebook) | LCC DS135.C96 B59713 2019 (print)
DDC 940.53/18094371--dc23
LC record available at hdps://lccn.loc.gov/2019011739

British Library Cataloguing in Publication Data
A catalog record for this book is available from the British Library.

ISBN 978-1-78920-284-7 hardback
ISBN 978-1-80073-646-7 paperback
ISBN 978-1-78920-285-4 ebook

https://doi.org/10.3167/9781789202847

Contents

List of Illustrations	vii
Acknowledgements	ix
List of Abbreviations	xi
Introduction	1
Chapter 1 The Czechoslovak Republic and Its Minorities	23
Chapter 2 Annexation: Violence, Flight and Emigration Ban	51
Chapter 3 German Expulsion and Czech Persecution	84
Chapter 4 The War and Greater German Deportation Plans	106
Chapter 5 Reorientation, Ghettoization and Protest	134
Chapter 6 Local versus Central Persecutory Initiatives	177
Chapter 7 Isolation, Forced Labour and Opposition	204
Chapter 8 Repression, Deportation and Resistance	252
Chapter 9 Transports, Theft, Forced Labour and Flight	294

Chapter 10
Those Left Behind and the End of the War 356
Conclusion 380

Appendix 399
Bibliography 411
Index of Names 429
Index of Subjects 437

Illustrations

Figures

Figure 1.1.	Jewish girl (Margit Morawetz) on a street in Prague, 1938.	29
Figure 1.2.	Map of the Protectorate of Bohemia and Moravia.	43
Figure 2.1.	Hitler and Hácha, 14–15 March 1939.	52
Figure 2.2.	Reich Protector Konstantin Freiherr von Neurath.	55
Figure 2.3.	The synagogue in Brno destroyed in 1939.	62
Figure 3.1.	Municipal playground in Prague, 'No Admission for Jews', 1939.	94
Figure 5.1.	Park entrance in Prague. The sign reads 'No Admission for Jews' in German, but 'Admission for Jews' in Czech, the word 'No' having been removed, 1940/1941.	159
Figure 6.1.	Inmates of the Linden SS Camp working in forestry, 1940.	194
Figure 8.1.	'Exclusion of Jews from the Economy, Integration into Labour Deployment', September 1941.	259
Figure 8.2.	Protectorate administrative structure in seven chief county commissioner districts, 1941.	264
Figure 9.1.	Deportation in Pilsen, probably January 1942.	295
Figure 9.2.	Jewish forced labourers clearing snow in Prague, 1941/1942.	298

Figure 9.3.	Construction of a slit trench in Prague.	308
Figure 9.4.	Contemporary map showing the distribution of the Jewish population in the Protectorate, 15 June 1942.	318
Figure 9.5.	Furniture stored by the Trust Office in a synagogue, first half of 1944.	332
Figure 9.6.	Providing an impoverished population with meals, 1943.	335
Figure 9.7.	Sorting consignments from the provinces in Prague, 1943.	337
Figure 10.1.	Jews marked with a star engaged in roadbuilding, 1943.	362
Figures 10.2 and 10.3.	Phases in the construction of the labour camp at Hagibor Square, 1944.	364
Figure 10.4.	Phases in the construction of the labour camp at Hagibor Square, 1944.	365
Figure 10.5.	The execution of Karl Hermann Frank in Prague, 22 May 1946.	369

Tables

Table A.1.	Report by the Jewish Religious Community of Prague: 'The Jews in the Protectorate of Bohemia and Moravia, 15 March 1939 to 15 June 1942'.	399
Table A.2.	Jewish emigration from the Protectorate of Bohemia and Moravia, 15 March 1939–1 March 1941.	400
Table A.3.	Support for impoverished Jews provided by the Religious Community, 1939–42.	401
Table A.4.	Forced labour deployment of Jews in the Protectorate.	403
Table A.5.	Report by the Jewish Community of Prague on the transports of Jews in the Protectorate of Bohemia and Moravia in 1941–42.	405
Table A.6.	Report by the Council of Elders of the Jews, Prague, on the transports of Jews in the Protectorate of Bohemia and Moravia in 1942.	408

Acknowledgements

I carried out preliminary research for this book during my residency as Paul Resnick Fellow at the Center for Advanced Holocaust Studies (US Holocaust Memorial Museum) in Washington DC in 2002. After completing several interim stages in the form of essays and book chapters, I completed a first draft of the manuscript during my stay as DAAD Fellow at the Selma Stern Center for Jewish Studies Berlin-Brandenburg in the summer of 2015, so I owe a special debt of gratitude for this invitation to Stefanie Schüler-Springorum, the centre's spokesperson at the time.

My sincere thanks go to the student assistants who have supported the present work over the years, including Florian Dannecke, Berlin, who examined a number of files in the Federal Archive (Bundesarchiv) in Berlin-Lichterfelde following my move to Los Angeles in 2008, Ashley Meyer, Los Angeles, who sadly passed away far too soon and who selected and transcribed interviews with survivors of persecution from the Protectorate in the USC Shoah Foundation Visual History Archive in Los Angeles, and to Aleksandra Visser and Jasneet Aulakh (both Los Angeles), both of whom also transcribed interviews. Thanks are also due to Jan Vondráček (Wuppertal/Prague), who was kind enough to help me with translations and alerted me to a number of valuable documents and essays.

I also own a tremendous debt of gratitude to the staff of a number of archives, notably the US Holocaust Memorial Museum, Yad Vashem Jerusalem and the USC Shoah Visual History Archive. I am particularly grateful to Jörg Osterloh (Frankfurt am Main), who not only supported and encouraged this project while constantly alerting me to relevant literature and sources, but who also subjected the final version of the original German manuscript to a meticulous reading and helpful critique. My sincere thanks also to Hajo Gevers, editor at Wallstein Verlag, who was not only quick to express an interest in this study, but was willing to accept long delays, carefully read the finished German manuscript and made many useful remarks.

Alex Skinner produced a careful translation and his meticulous work helped to correct some errors in the German version. Benjamin Frommer (Evanston), who supported the book project from the beginning, also alerted me to some mistakes, enabling me to eliminate them from the English version of the study. I am very grateful to the staff of Berghahn Books, especially Soyolmaa Lkhagvadorj, Caroline Kuhtz and Chris Chappell, as well as the editors of the 'War and Genocide' series, Omer Bartov and Dirk Moses, who generously agreed to pursue the English publication of my translated study even before the original German version had won various prestigious international awards: the Sybil Halpern Milton Memorial Book Prize 2017 for the best book in Holocaust Studies in 2015–16, the 2017 Yad Vashem International Book Prize for Holocaust Research for books published in 2015 and 2016 (Finalist), and one of the prizes for most outstanding German studies in humanities and social sciences in 2017 by the Börsenverein des Deutschen Buchhandels, the Fritz Thyssen Stiftung, the VG WORT and the German Foreign Office.

Three years ago, members of the interdisciplinary German Studies Group in Los Angeles engaged in a critical discussion of the final draft of the introduction to the German version of the book. All its members shared the view that this study is not only important to the history of Jews in the Protectorate but also has far-reaching implications for the history and understanding of the Nazi persecution of the Jews in general.

Wolf Gruner, Los Angeles, April 2019

ABBREVIATIONS

AG	Aktiengesellschaft (joint stock company)
Allg.	Allgemeine,-r (general)
AS	Außenstelle (branch office)
BBC	British Broadcasting Corporation
BdS	Befehlshaber der Sicherheitspolizei und des SD (Commander of the Security Police and SD)
CdZ	Chef der Zivilverwaltung (Head of the Civil Administration)
d. J.	des Jahres (of the year)
Fa.	Firma (firm)
Fig.	figure
GDR	German Democratic Republic
HIAS	Hebrew Immigrant Aid Society
HICEM	HIAS-JCA-Emigdirect
IKG	Israelitische Kultusgemeinde (Israelite Religious Community)
JCA	Jewish Colonization Association
JDC	Joint Distribution Committee
JKG	Jüdische Kultusgemeinde (Jewish Religious Community)
JTA	Jewish Telegraphic Agency
Kdr.	Kommandeur (commander)
KZ	Konzentrationslager (concentration camp)
LBI	Leo Baeck Institute
LW	Landwirtschaft (agriculture)
n.d.	no date
n.p.	no place

ORT	(Jüdische) Gesellschaft für handwerkliche und landwirtschaftliche Arbeit ([Jewish] Society for Artisanal and Agricultural Labour)
OS	Ortsstelle (local office)
RGBl	*Reichsgesetzblatt* (Reich Law Gazette)
RM	Reichsmark
RSHA	Reichssicherheitshauptamt (Reich Security Main Office)
RV	Reichsvereinigung der Juden in Deutschland (Reich Association of Jews in Germany)
SD	Sicherheitsdienst der SS (SS Security Service)
Seg.	Segment
USSR	Union of Soviet Socialist Republics
VEJ	*Die Verfolgung und Ermordung der europäischen Juden durch das nationalsozialistische Deutschland 1933–1945* (book title)

Introduction

On the day when the 'Jewish star' (Judenstern) decree came into force in the Greater German Reich, Petr Ginz, a thirteen-year-old resident of Prague, wrote in his diary: 'It's foggy. The Jews have to wear a badge … I counted sixty-nine sheriffs on the way to school, and then mummy saw more than a hundred'.[1] So far, historical studies on anti-Jewish policies in the Protectorate of Bohemia and Moravia have viewed the introduction of the 'Jewish badge' as the application of a German law and nothing more. In fact, it had a far more interesting and complex background. The impetus for this Reich-wide decree actually came from the capital of the Protectorate in July 1941 rather than Berlin, where Goebbels merely adopted the proposal.

As we will see, however, the German Reich protector (Reichsprotektor) did not come up with this idea on his own. It was in fact proposed in earlier submissions from Czech fascists and had been discussed by the ruling Czech party. The present study thus seeks to answer a number of new questions. What was the relative importance of German and Czech persecution within the Protectorate? What scope and significance did local and regional initiatives have? How autonomous and radical were developments in the Protectorate in comparison with Germany, Austria and occupied Poland? How did discriminatory policies affect the Jewish population? And – especially important – how did the Czech Jews respond to worsening persecution?

As yet, scholars have ignored the significance of anti-Jewish policies in annexed Bohemia and Moravia both to the overall development of such measures in the Greater German Reich and their escalation. This applies not just to the initiatives of the Reich protector and other German agencies but even more to measures implemented by the Czech government, the Czech ministries and Czech organizations. After the Munich Agreement and the acquisition of the Sudeten region, the Nazi state occupied 'rump Czechoslovakia' on 15 March 1939, with Hitler declaring the newly established 'Protectorate of Bohemia and Moravia' a semi-autonomous part of the Reich. Of more than 118,000 Jews living in the Bohemian and Moravian part of what had been the Czechoslovak Republic, only around 25,000 managed to flee by October 1941. Once the occupation had begun, the German and Czech authorities quickly stepped up their anti-Jewish activities in the territory. Jews were divested of their property and – a fact rarely acknowledged – had already been partially ghettoized by 1940. Later, when plans for early deportation foundered, Jews were used as forced labour. Finally, from 1941, they were either transported east or to the Theresienstadt Ghetto; in the latter case they were deported on to other destinations. During the Holocaust, around eighty thousand Jews from Bohemia and Moravia lost their lives.[2]

Surveys of the Third Reich or the Holocaust have often included detailed accounts of anti-Jewish policies in Austria, due to the brute violence and the radical measures implemented during the first few weeks after the 'Anschluß' in 1938, their effects on the Reich government's policies and Austrians' active involvement in the annihilation of Jews.[3] Yet the persecution of Jews in the Protectorate of Bohemia and Moravia was absent from the early overviews by Raul Hilberg[4] and Uwe-Dietrich Adam[5] as well as the main studies published over the last twenty years, such as the books by Peter Longerich and (Prague-born) Saul Friedländer.[6] The 2004 book on the historiography of the Holocaust edited by Dan Stone also has virtually nothing to say about this element in the Nazi persecution of Jews. Its thematic chapters, written by international historians, include just two brief mentions of the Protectorate.[7] While Christian Gerlach's recent book on the annihilation of the Jews makes several brief references to conditions in the Protectorate to comparative ends, David Cesarani's comprehensive posthumous volume dedicates just a few pages to the topic, instead focusing on Poland.[8]

For many historians, the Nazi regime's attack on Poland just five and a half months after the establishment of the Protectorate overshadowed, indeed obliterated the history of persecution in the Czech part of what had been the Czechoslovak Republic. The mass killings by the SS (Schutzstaffel, literally Protection Squadron) task forces (Einsatzgruppen) immediately after the invasion, the extreme persecution of Jews and, finally, the establishment of the extermination camps in occupied Poland probably made events in the Protectorate of Bohemia and Moravia seem insignificant to understanding the burgeoning genocide of Europe's Jews.[9] The sheer mass of Jewish victims in Poland seems to have precluded the possibility of comparison.

In contrast to Austria and Poland, which historians generally viewed as virulently antisemitic both before and after the German occupation, Czechoslovakia appeared to be a success story in the treatment of its Jewish minority. The state, which emerged after the collapse of the Habsburg Empire, was considered to be a democracy and, from a comparative European perspective, largely free of antisemitism; if it did arise, it was immediately tackled. Recent research, however, has called this idyllic picture into question, contending that much of the legend propagated by state founder Tomáš Masaryk and embodied in the cult surrounding him was more ideal than reality.[10] And one must not overlook the fact that the short-lived Second Czechoslovak Republic, established in the autumn of 1938, had an authoritarian system of government and – as we will see – implemented antisemitic measures. In 1939, the Czech Protectorate regime absorbed a number of ministers and state president Emil Hácha from the Second Republic. They represented continuity in anti-Jewish policy rather than merely doing what the Germans told them.

These insights require us to revise a number of traditional assumptions that have moulded our understanding of the Holocaust. The persecution of Jews in the Protectorate was not solely directed from Berlin, though central plans emanating from there influenced policies in the Protectorate, on deportations for example. In line with the conclusions reached in a number of publications in the 1990s with respect to Poland and Germany,[11] the present study of the Protectorate brings out the significance of regional and local initiatives to the development and radicalization of the persecution of Jews, with non-German institutions coming prominently into play for the first time. Many officials in German and Czech government agencies participated in the design and acceleration of persecution policies, not, as is often assumed, in an attempt to enhance their power in competitive situations, as suggested by the theory of polycracy, but in light of a variety of interests, either in close cooperation with one another or independently.[12] Some of the initiatives in the Protectorate influenced policies in other annexed territories, while others even shaped the decisions made in Berlin. This was partly because of the personnel involved. Many of the key actors in the persecution of Jews in occupied Europe, including Joseph Bürckel, Adolf Eichmann and Reinhard Heydrich, worked in Prague for lengthy periods.[13]

The present study documents in detail the effects of persecution on the Jewish population in the Protectorate, their impoverishment and diminishing prospects of emigration. It proves that rather than an element in their annihilation, Jewish forced labour was a response to Jews' enforced unemployment. It was a fundamental feature of anti-Jewish persecution in which specific social and economic interests often outweighed ideological goals.[14]

This study also demonstrates how the Jewish Communities[15] in the Protectorate and their functionaries, their every move scrutinized by the Security Police (Sicherheitspolizei), actively sought to alleviate the effects of persecution by expanding welfare services, providing emigration aid and facilitating labour deployments, in part by exploiting the diverging interests of different authorities. Previously, when it comes to the Protectorate, Jewish resistance has generally been described as an underground activity involving the dissemination of prohibited literature, the acquisition of forged papers and sabotage,[16] but I instead employ a definition originally formulated by Yehuda Bauer, modified through the addition of 'individual activities'. When I refer to Jewish resistance, I mean every *individual* and collective action taken against the German and Czech authorities' anti-Jewish laws, campaigns and plans.[17] This opens up a new perspective on the actions of Jewish community representatives and the conduct of countless individuals.

Jewish Czechs' diverse acts of resistance as documented in this book place a major question mark over the traditional idea that they passively accepted Nazi persecution. All the topics discussed here with respect to the Protectorate of Bohemia and Moravia thus modify our overall view of the persecution of Jews during the Second World War in Europe.

So far, historians have discussed the Theresienstadt Ghetto as the only feature of anti-Jewish persecution in the Protectorate of general historical significance, but often only because large numbers of deported German Jews arrived there. From a German perspective, including the discipline of history in the GDR, the Protectorate generally seemed interesting either as an example of Nazi policies of Germanization or of Czech resistance to the Nazi occupation. As in most states occupied by the German Reich, after the Second World War historians tended to focus on the fate of the majority population and their war of resistance rather than the suffering of their Jewish citizens. This is because, both in Western European states and the later communist ones, their countrymen were always partly responsible for persecution, having cooperated with the Germans, involved themselves in anti-Jewish activities or acquired the property of their Jewish fellow citizens. Evidently, in the immediate postwar period the prosecution of certain perpetrators resulted in often dramatic verdicts, but it was not until the 1990s that indigenous persecution and collaboration received serious attention throughout Europe, including the Czech Republic.[18]

Historians, therefore, have been unanimous in assuming that at the time of a given annexation Germany simply extended the anti-Jewish policies then current to the new territories. At an early stage, in fact before the war had ended, in both Europe and the wider world a limited external perspective gave rise to the myth that the Germans had dictated anti-Jewish policies to the Czechs.[19] In Germany, more detailed research on the Protectorate appeared to have been rendered superfluous by Detlef Brandes's important 1969 volume on Nazi rule in the territory and his assessment that the Czechs had refused to draft anti-Jewish laws, prompting the German Reich protector for Bohemia and Moravia to do so.[20] Referring to the Protectorate of Bohemia and Moravia, Eva Schmidt-Hartmann asserted in the early 1990s that 'similar and in principle the same regulations' applied as 'in every other country occupied by Germany'.[21] Variations on this view dominate to this day.[22]

Until now, historians have ignored the possibility of autonomous developments in the Protectorate, as well as in other annexed territories, despite the fact that complex demographic constellations, varying economic conditions and the differing political interests of institutions and actors, whether German or local, must have affected the persecution of Jews. As I demonstrate in what follows, detailed analysis of anti-Jewish policies and the agents involved in them renders obsolete the assumption that Berlin or the Nazi Party (NSDAP) were solely responsible for what happened in the annexed territories.[23] Rather than the Nazi persecution of Jews becoming ever more extreme from one annexation to the next in accordance with a preset ideology emanating from Berlin, an array of German and non-German actors responded to specific economic, social, demographic and political constellations in local settings. As a result, specific measures were introduced in the various territories at quite different points in time, and in some cases not at all.[24]

Before the war was over, some contemporaries already appear to have been aware of this autonomous political development in the Protectorate. This applies to Vojta Beneš and Roderick Ginsburg in their book *10 Million Prisoners*, published in the United States in 1940, and to the volume *Racial State* published by Gerhard Jacoby in 1944, which was concerned with the occupation of the Protectorate of Bohemia and Moravia and the persecution that occurred there.²⁵ The territory also played an important role in early overviews such as *Hitler's Ten-Year War on the Jews* (1943), Raphael Lemkin's *Axis Rule in Occupied Europe* (1944) and *The Black Book: The Nazi Crime against the Jewish People* (1946).²⁶

The same time period, however, saw the emergence of the myth that the Czech government had merely done what the Reich protector told it to when it came to anti-Jewish policies. Even documented initiatives by the Czech government or local agencies were claimed to have borne a German impress. On this view, while local authorities expedited the segregation of Jews, they had always acted under pressure from the Nazi county commissioners (Landräte).²⁷

The State of the Research

Up to 1990, only a few historians had tackled the period of Nazi rule in the annexed territories, while in Germany they focused exclusively on German occupation policy.²⁸ It was not until the 1980s that studies appeared on anti-Jewish policies in these areas.²⁹ In the GDR, 1988 saw the publication of the first volume in the sourcebook series 'Europa unterm Hakenkreuz' ('Europe under the Swastika'), in which the Protectorate played an important role. The series remained uncompleted at the time of German reunification.³⁰ Work on another series of source materials, 'Die Verfolgung und Ermordung der europäischen Juden durch das nationalsozialistische Deutschland 1933–1945' ('The Persecution and Murder of the European Jews by Nazi Germany, 1933–1945'), which is to include an eventual total of sixteen volumes, began in 2005. A collaborative project involving the German Federal Archive (Bundesarchiv), the Berlin-Munich Institute for Contemporary History (Institut für Zeitgeschichte Berlin-München) and the Chair of Modern and Contemporary History (Lehrstuhl für Neuere und Neueste Geschichte) at the Albert-Ludwigs-Universität Freiburg im Breisgau, this contains key documents from German and international archives on the Protectorate of Bohemia and Moravia, relating not just to occupation policy but to the experiences of the Jewish population as well.³¹ The latter applies in particular to another sourcebook series recently published by the United States Holocaust Memorial Museum.³²

In Germany a range of studies have appeared over the last two decades that mention the Protectorate but rarely analyse it specifically. In her 2003 book on the SS Race and Settlement Main Office (Rasse- und Siedlungshauptamt), Isabel Heinemann examined its 'racial' survey in Bohemia and Moravia.³³ Recently Detlef Brandes has provided a detailed study of the Nazi regime's 'Volkstumspolitik' (ethnic policy) in the Protectorate.³⁴ 'Volkstumspolitik' and 'Jewish policy', as elements in Nazi occupation policy in Bohemia and Moravia, have also been explored in the new biographical studies by René Küpper on Karl Hermann Frank, secretary of state under the Reich protector and from 1943 minister of state in the Protectorate, and by Robert Gerwarth on Reinhard Heydrich, who carried out the functions of the Reich protector from late September 1941 until his death in early June 1942.³⁵ In a 1994 essay, meanwhile, Austrian historian Gabriele Anderl described the three central agencies for Jewish emigration of significance to the history of persecution in Vienna, Prague and Berlin.³⁶

Economic developments have been explored in more depth, with a number of texts investigating the theft of Jewish assets in Bohemia and Moravia. Initially these studies were pursued within the framework of comparative overviews or company histories and they were often the result of collaborative efforts by German and Czech scholars. More recently, Czech scholars have produced similar studies within the Czech Republic.³⁷ In addition, over the last few years researchers in a number of countries have analysed the question of national identity and the coexistence of Czechs, Germans and Jews in Bohemia and Moravia, particularly in Prague.³⁸

In the Czechoslovak Republic, meanwhile, early accounts of the policy of persecution were written by authors, such as H.G. Adler, who had themselves been among its victims,³⁹ while systematic research began in the mid 1970s thanks to the efforts of Miroslav Kárný.⁴⁰ Yet a tendency towards suppression long held sway in the field, and this seems not to have been due solely to communist historiography, as it also applies to memoirs and accounts produced beyond the Iron Curtain and (in particular) to the historiography of the Sudeten Germans.⁴¹ Since the early 1990s, the persecution of Jews has received substantially more attention, alongside the previously dominant focus on the fate of non-Jewish Czechs and their resistance to the occupation.⁴² Czech researchers, with Miroslav Kárný once again leading the way, have now published important monographs and collections of documents relating to anti-Jewish measures,⁴³ a field of research that has received new impetus from the Institut Terezínské Iniciativy (the Terezín Initiative Institute) founded in Prague in 1993.⁴⁴ Meanwhile, the Department of Jewish History at the Institute of Contemporary History of the Czech Academy of Sciences has edited, among other things, a volume of source materials and a collection of essays on the situation of Jews in the Protectorate.⁴⁵

The first major non-Czech overview of the history of Jews in the Protectorate was produced by Livia Rothkirchen in Israel in 2005. She analysed numerous reports from Jewish institutions and diplomatic missions but wrote astonishingly little about anti-Jewish policy, the situation of the Jewish population and their everyday lives.[46] Often, her account fails to clarify when anti-Jewish measures were implemented, when riots occurred and who was responsible for them.[47] Unfortunately, due to limited source materials, the research presented in Marc Oprach's *Nationalsozialistische Judenpolitik im Protektorat Böhmen und Mähren* (2006) is rather superficial.[48] So far, we have no studies analysing not just anti-Jewish policy itself but its effects on Jewish institutions and the Jewish population in Prague and the so-called provinces, and there is also a dearth of scholarship on the history of the Jewish Communities in Prague and other cities.[49]

Methodological Approach

Since 2005, the present author has published initial studies emphasizing the development of an independent anti-Jewish policy in the Protectorate as well as ascribing to the Czech government and its subordinate local authorities a substantial role in drafting and implementing this policy, alongside the German occupation authorities.[50] The existence of such autonomous regional varieties of persecution in occupied Europe, which even influenced the policies pursued by Berlin to some extent, was confirmed by the comparative research on a number of territories annexed by the Nazi state presented in the 2010 volume edited by the present author and Jörg Osterloh, *Das Großdeutsche Reich und die Juden* (published in English in 2015 as *The Greater German Reich and the Jews*).[51]

As set out in the introduction to the above volume, the Nazi state established the Protectorate of Bohemia and Moravia as part of the Reich by edict of the Führer (Führererlass) but granted it autonomy. The Czech Protectorate government was to make 'its own laws in every legal field not directly administered by the Reich', including Jewish policy. At the same time, the (German) Reich protector was directly answerable to Hitler and not subject to the directives of the Reich authorities, allowing him considerable room for manoeuvre. Every German residing in the territory immediately received citizenship of the Reich, while the non-Germans became 'members of the Protectorate' ('Protektoratsangehörige') with fewer rights.[52] It was not until 1942, when every resident was required to carry an identity card, that the

Protectorate's ambiguous constitutional position ended and it was subsumed fully into the Reich.[53]

The administration of the annexed territories required a tremendous bureaucratic effort: in the months after the various annexations, relevant laws and decrees filled the *Reich Law Gazette*. While the central offices for the various annexed territories within the Reich Ministry of the Interior, all headed by State Secretary Wilhelm Stuckart, were supposed to guarantee the effective harmonization of laws throughout the Reich, the timing and form of the various anti-Jewish measures differed significantly due to diverse local conditions and interests.[54]

In the 'Old Reich' (Altreich), from 1939, all Jews became compulsory members of the Reich Association of Jews in Germany (Reichsvereinigung der Juden in Deutschland), which – supervised by the Gestapo (Geheime Staatspolizei or Secret State Police) – had to organize Jewish schools, welfare and emigration. In the Protectorate of Bohemia and Moravia, however, beginning in 1940 the Jewish Religious Community (Kultusgemeinde) of Prague was made responsible for all Jewish Communities. Here Prague followed the example of Vienna, though the Jewish population was less concentrated in the Protectorate than in Austria, where most Jews lived in the capital. In some cases, the experiences gained through the annexation of Austria, carried out just a year earlier, led to the modified application of the policies developed there in annexed Bohemia and Moravia. At other times, negative experiences arising from the Austrian case engendered a very different approach in Prague. For example, in order to prevent 'wild' looting as in Austria and ensure that the state received its share of plundered assets, Berlin took charge of the 'Aryanization' of Jewish property in the Protectorate from the outset.[55]

Even more than the experiences of previous annexations or the direct effects of conditions in the Protectorate, it was the initiatives pursued by various institutions that moulded the persecution of Jews in Bohemia and Moravia. As in the 'Old Reich' and Austria, in the Protectorate the interaction between different agencies shaped the development of anti-Jewish policies, though in an occupied territory one might have expected there to be less room for manoeuvre, with central directives dominating. But the radicalization of anti-Jewish policies did not just result from an interplay between measures introduced by local, regional and central institutions.[56] It occurred within a fraught framework determined by four key factors: the policies of the Reich government in Berlin, the actions of the German Protectorate authorities, the steps taken by the Czech government in Prague and the restrictions imposed by an array of local and regional authorities, often leading to autonomous developments in the Protectorate.[57]

This is a new research perspective on the persecution of Jews in the Protectorate between 1939 and 1945. As we will see in this book, the Czech authorities and the Czech government, as well as the German Reich protector plus his administration and Eichmann's Central Office for Jewish Emigration (Zentralstelle für jüdische Auswanderung), operated by the SS Security Service (Sicherheitsdienst or SD), enjoyed great room for manoeuvre in formulating anti-Jewish policies on the ground. As in Germany and Austria then, here too we find that it was by no means Berlin alone or the typical institutions of persecution such as the SS and the Gestapo[58] that dominated anti-Jewish policies or directed their development.

In the Protectorate, the Czech government, the Czech ministries and the Czech municipalities on the one hand, and the Office of the German Reich Protector, the German chief county commissioners (Oberlandräte) and mayors along with Eichmann's Central Office for Jewish Emigration, founded in Prague in July 1939, on the other, all participated equally in initiating discrimination against Jews. While the Reich protector and the Security Police focused on expediting the 'Aryanization' of Jewish firms, the Czech Protectorate government, the chief county commissioners and the municipalities pressed ahead with the public segregation of the Jewish population. German and Czech antisemites perpetrated acts of violence on a near-unprecedented scale and put pressure on German and Czech authorities to intensify persecution. A number of initiatives emanating from the Protectorate influenced decision-making within the German Reich, while others had an impact on measures introduced in other occupied territories. The Protectorate, therefore, occupies a hitherto unacknowledged, important place in the radicalization of Nazi anti-Jewish policies.[59]

Chapter 1 foregrounds the situation prior to the German annexation, beginning with the birth pangs of the Czechoslovak Republic after the First World War. It deals with the social, demographic, economic and political conditions in the new state, along with the situation of Jews, Germans and Czechs. It also challenges the traditional assumption of a very low level of antisemitism there in comparison with other European countries, while examining the growing power of the German minority and its attempts to destabilize the country. The chapter concludes by analysing the politics of the Second Republic after the Munich Agreement, particularly the debate on the growing number of Jewish refugees and the anti-Jewish measures initiated by the Czech government months before the occupation.

Chapter 2 provides an account of the German occupation of March 1939, the persecution of Jews during the first few weeks and the first constitutional measures following annexation by Germany. The focus here is on anti-Jewish impulses, which – as noted earlier – did not come solely from Germany. Ethnic Germans and Czechs carried out acts of violence from the outset. The discussion centres on the institutions that initiated the first persecution measures and the fields of society affected. The chapter also examines why, surprisingly, after the occupation the Gestapo initially prohibited the emigration of Jews from the Protectorate, despite the fact that their expulsion was an avowed goal of German policy.

The territory's incorporation into the German Reich and the establishment of key institutions are the focus of chapter 3. Among other things, it discusses the following questions. Which individuals and agencies expedited anti-Jewish policies? How did anti-Jewish measures impact on Jewish communities and how did the latter respond? As we will see, many of these initiatives came from Czech actors, while the Germans focused chiefly on banishing Jews from the economic and financial spheres. Another significant topic dealt with here is the lifting of the ban on Jewish emigration and the belated establishment of Adolf Eichmann's Prague Central Office.

Chapter 4 is concerned with the radically different situation that pertained after the start of the war. For a brief period, central measures emanating from the Reich capital, Berlin, dominated: this chapter explores in detail when and why Hitler and his regime – contrary to the received wisdom – quickly made the strategic decision to deport Jews from the Greater German Reich to the occupied territories, and how Eichmann put these plans into practice through the newly established Reich Security Main Office (Reichssicherheitshauptamt) in Berlin. The chapter discusses how, after Heinrich Himmler suspended deportation in November 1939, the Protectorate authorities rethought persecution, reinstating the option of forced emigration. It also examines the activities of the Jewish Religious Community of Prague with respect to the emigration, welfare and schools of the impoverished Jewish population.

Chapter 5 assesses subsequent central policies and their root causes, such as the extension in the authority of Eichmann's Central Office from Prague to the entire Protectorate in early 1940. It also discusses the transformation of the Jewish Religious Community of Prague into an organization with compulsory membership for all 'racial Jews' (Rassejuden) that was now responsible for all the Jewish Communities in the Protectorate and explores the dissolution of Jewish associations or their incorporation into the new institution. The analysis shows how this organization actively sought to counter the burgeoning impoverishment of the Jewish population – resulting from forced unemployment and 'Aryanization' – by stepping up its provision of welfare services and organizing teams of workers for agricultural and roadbuilding duties. Other topics examined are early, little-known ghettoization measures and the first cases of Jewish resistance.

Chapter 6 investigates growing ghettoization in dozens of small towns in the Protectorate, the incipient concentration of Jews in certain districts of Prague and the Czech government's new policies of isolation within the public sphere. Both the increasingly dim prospect of forced emigration, which the German authorities nonetheless prioritized because of the now indefinite suspension of deportation, as well as their attempts to step up the centralization of Jewish policy within the Protectorate will be examined. The chapter also shows how, in the autumn of 1940, the Prague Jewish Community centralized its activities and sought to place work details with private businesses in an attempt to reduce a welfare burden spiralling out of control as resettlement and Aryanization plunged Jews ever deeper into poverty.

Chapter 7 explores why, from early 1941 onwards, the German and Czech authorities prioritized centralization and sought to adapt anti-Jewish policies to the model in Germany, for example by making the Jewish Communities responsible for the provision of welfare and terminating retraining (Umschulung) as a means of preparing Jews for emigration. The Central Office came to play a more prominent role in this process, particularly in the concentration and ghettoization of the Jewish population, which it now extended beyond Prague to other major cities. The complex political situation becomes evident in the fact that when the Czech Ministry of Social and Health Administration introduced the German model of compulsory labour deployment for Jews in 1941, it was subsequently managed by the German labour offices in the Protectorate. Many of the steps taken by the Czech government and German authorities now served the purpose of strictly separating Jews from non-Jews.

From the late summer of 1941, plans were hatched to expedite this segregation within the Protectorate by introducing the 'Yellow Star' and stepping up the process of ghettoization, as described in Chapter 8, which also discusses the increased use of forced labour, those involved in it and its main characteristics. The account will illuminate Reinhard Heydrich's assumption of power and his draconian measures, involving hundreds of death sentences and mass arrests. As we will see, these nevertheless failed to quell the opposition and resistance of many Jews, who defended themselves against the countless forms of persecution, whether by non-compliance, open refusal or flight. More and more Jews embraced such options after the resumption of mass deportations to the east and to the Theresienstadt Ghetto, which was established within the Protectorate partly as a way station on the eastward route.

The penultimate chapter highlights the work of Jewish Community representatives: how they sought to alleviate the well-nigh overwhelming burdens of persecution and how they resisted anti-Jewish measures. At this point, the study demonstrates how Eichmann's Central Office and other authorities forced the Prague Jewish Community and its branch offices to take part in many forms of persecution, whether in organizing forced labour, preparing mass deportations or processing stolen Jewish property. Surprisingly, at this late stage, individual Jews still carried out numerous acts of resistance, whether through flight, fighting restrictions or sabotage.

The final chapter deals with the years 1943 to 1945, demonstrating how the German Protectorate authorities increasingly took charge of Jewish policy, such as forced labour and the residential concentration of Jews in 'mixed marriages'. As we will see, even in the final stages of the war, Jewish resistance to persecution played a role. The chapter concludes with a look at the early postwar period, which saw the trial of perpetrators, an ambivalent attitude on the part of the new Czechoslovak state (already evident during the war), and survivors' efforts to document what had happened.

The present book thus goes beyond previous studies on the persecution of Jews within the Protectorate. Surprising new findings include the fact that before the occupation started the Czechoslovak Republic had independently expelled Jews of Polish origin and that by 1940 Czech towns had already begun to ghettoize Jews in specific streets or abandoned buildings, in much the same way as in occupied Poland.

This study, however, not only analyses the diversity and originality of anti-Jewish policies within the Protectorate, their origin and background, but also compares them with developments in Austria, Germany and Poland. This brings to light some unique characteristics with respect, for example, to forced labour. In the Protectorate, this was introduced in 1941 rather than in 1939 as in Germany and its use then increased substantially until May 1942, despite the mass deportations that greatly reduced the Jewish population from month to month. Against previous assumptions of an anti-Jewish policy laid down in Berlin, the study shows that the Protectorate authorities had room for manoeuvre until well into the war, opening up to both German and Czech officials and citizens a broad field for individual initiatives and thus personal responsibility.

The present study, however, seeks to examine the agency not just of the perpetrators but also of the victims of persecution, namely Jews themselves. In an attempt to write a truly 'integrated history of the Holocaust',[60] this account not only includes the voices of the persecuted, but also explores the direct consequences of persecution for the Czech Jews and documents the responses of Jewish organizations and Jews' resistance with the aid of new sources.

Sources

After more than a decade of intensive study of Nazi Jewish policies in Germany[61] and Austria,[62] during a lengthy research stay at the United States Holocaust Memorial Museum in 2002 I began to examine more closely conditions in the Protectorate of Bohemia and Moravia. I sought to determine whether here too municipal politics exercised an influence on the design of anti-Jewish persecution, a question rapidly answered in the affirmative by examination of copies of records from the Prague State Archive. An invitation to speak at a conference in Terezín in 2004 triggered a more intensive engagement with the topic and prompted me to write an article that amounted to a preliminary study.[63] My knowledge of the material on the Protectorate that I had found in the archive of the United States Holocaust Memorial Museum initially inspired me to write a comparative study on Jewish forced labour in Germany, Austria and Poland. One chapter in the resulting book, published in 2006, outlines for the first time the largely uncharted history of Jewish forced labour in Bohemia and Moravia.[64] The surprising results of this in-depth comparison of just one component of anti-Jewish policy in the Greater German Reich revealed the need for a comprehensive analysis. This ultimately resulted in a volume, co-edited with Jörg Osterloh, in which invited specialists – aided by a strict set of questions – examined anti-Jewish policies in every annexed territory in a comparable way.[65]

This conscious effort to integrate the Protectorate into the 'Greater German' context facilitated a more precise and also more contextualized look at conditions within this annexed territory, giving rise to the key questions I seek to answer in the present book. What consequences for anti-Jewish policies resulted from the mutual dynamics between local, regional and central institutions, between German and Czech officials and authorities, between periphery (Prague) and centre (Berlin)? Which institutions were responsible for which aspects of persecution policy in the Protectorate? Who initiated the radicalization of these measures, where, when and why? When exactly did shifts in the balance of power occur and why? Was there mutual interaction between policies in the Protectorate and those in Austria or occupied Poland? How did Berlin view persecution policies in the Protectorate, and when did the central government make decisions or intervene? What was the impact of inconsistent power structures on the Jewish population? How did Jews respond when persecution worsened?

Addressing these questions required the comprehensive study of a wide range of sources. The answers to most of them were to be found in the documents, predominantly in German, produced by a wide range of authorities, contemporary newspaper reports published in German or English and survivors' diaries, memoirs and interviews. My limited knowledge of the Czech language prevented me from describing in more detail the interaction between Jews and Czechs or the activities of the low-ranking, mostly Czech administrative personnel.[66] To a degree, this linguistic lacuna also impeded access to the untranslated results of Czech research. However, the *Theresienstädter Studien und Dokumente*, published in both Czech and German, provided me with a decent grasp of the state of Czech research. In a number of recent cases, I received help with translations.

This shortcoming, however, was more than offset by a source that furnishes us with unforeseen findings about the formation and impact of anti-Jewish policies. In 2010, in the archive of the Yad Vashem Holocaust Memorial in Israel, I discovered the weekly reports of the Prague Jewish Religious Community (which was of course responsible for the Jewish population of Prague until early 1940 and subsequently for Jews throughout the Protectorate). Previously unknown to researchers, these were produced for Eichmann and his Central Office for Jewish Emigration. The weekly reports, which inform the present study seamlessly from the summer of 1939 until late 1942 with the exception of one quarter, have enabled me to analyse for the first time not just the complex and sometimes contradictory anti-Jewish policies in the Protectorate, but above all their effects on the lives of Jews. The present study is also the first to scrutinize monthly, quarterly and annual reports composed by the Prague Jewish Community, correspondence between Jewish Communities outside Prague and the local Gestapo and other authorities, along with materials such as the records of the Jewish Religious Community in Olomouc (Olmütz) concerning summonses from the Gestapo. Other sources originate in a variety of archives: Czech ministerial records mostly in the archive of the United States Holocaust Memorial Museum (copies of documents from the Státní ústřední archiv [State Central Archive] in

Prague); reports by the chief county commissioners and other documents in the Bundesarchiv Berlin-Lichterfelde; materials produced by Jewish Communities and organizations in the Central Archives for the History of the Jewish People Jerusalem, the Central Zionist Archives Jerusalem, the Leo Baeck Institute Archive in New York, the Rossiiskii gosudarstvennyi voennyi arkhiv (Russian State Military Archive or RGVA), Moscow, and the Vojenský historický archiv (Military History Archive) in Prague. The study gained a broader perspective by analysing contemporary English- and German-language newspapers, the reports of the Jewish Telegraphic Agency, first-hand accounts in the Wiener Library and twenty-two video interviews with survivors in the USC Shoah Foundation Visual History Archive, Los Angeles. Finally, previously unknown photographs and charts from the Prague Jewish Religious Community's weekly reports also enrich the book.

Notes

1. Entry of 19 September 1941 in Petr Ginz, *The Diary of Petr Ginz 1941–1942*, ed. Chava Pressburger, trans. Elena Lappin (New York, 2007), 28 (translator's note: the English translation has been amended for style).
2. On the figures, see Miroslav Kárný, 'Die tschechischen Opfer der deutschen Okkupation', in Detlev Brandes and Václav Kural (eds), *Der Weg in die Katastrophe: Deutsch-tschechoslowakische Beziehungen 1938–1947* (Essen, 1994), 151–64, here 152–53.
3. The first general accounts of the Nazi persecution of Jews, however, failed to take account of the radicalizing influence of events in Austria and especially Vienna in the spring of 1938. See, for example, Gerald Reitlinger, *The Final Solution: The Attempt to Exterminate the Jews of Europe 1939–1945* (London, 1952); Raul Hilberg, *The Destruction of the European Jews* (Chicago, 1961); Uwe-Dietrich Adam, *Judenpolitik im Dritten Reich* (Düsseldorf, 1972). In recent accounts, by way of contrast, Austria occupies an important place, examples being Peter Longerich, *Politik der Vernichtung: Eine Gesamtdarstellung der nationalsozialistischen Judenverfolgung* (Munich, 1998) (in English as *Holocaust: The Nazi Persecution and Murder of the Jews* [New York, 2010]); Saul Friedländer, *Nazi Germany and the Jews: The Years of Persecution, 1933–1939* (New York, 1997) and *The Years of Extermination: Nazi Germany and the Jews, 1939–1945* (New York, 2007).
4. Although one chapter is entitled 'The Reich Protectorate Area', his standard work includes just a few remarks on the topic. See Hilberg, *The Destruction of the European Jews*, 106.
5. Adam, *Judenpolitik im Dritten Reich*.
6. Longerich, *Holocaust*; Friedländer, *Nazi Germany and the Jews*. See also Martin Dean, Constantin Goschler and Philipp Ther, *Robbery and Restitution: The Conflict over Jewish Property in Europe* (New York, 2007).
7. Dan Stone (ed.), *The Historiography of the Holocaust* (Houndmills, Basingstoke, 2004), 327, 428.

8. Christian Gerlach, *The Extermination of the European Jews* (Cambridge, 2016), e.g. 320–23, 343; David Cesarani, *Final Solution: The Fate of the Jews 1933–1949* (London, 2016), 225–28, 425 (536–42, 682–86 on Theresienstadt), 789.
9. On Poland, see esp. Christopher Browning, *The Origins of the Final Solution: The Evolution of Nazi Jewish Policy, September 1939–March 1942* (Lincoln, NE, 2004).
10. Andrea Orzoff, *Battle for the Castle: The Myth of Czechoslovakia in Europe 1914–1948* (New York, 2009), 24, 30, 131.
11. On occupied Poland, for example, see Dieter Pohl, *Nationalsozialistische Judenverfolgung in Ostgalizien 1941–1944* (Munich, 1996); Thomas Sandkühler, *'Endlösung in Galizien': Der Judenmord in Ostpolen und die Rettungsinitiativen von Berthold Beitz 1941–1944* (Bonn, 1996). On Germany, see Frank Bajohr, *'Aryanisation' in Hamburg: The Economic Exclusion of Jews and the Confiscation of Their Property in Nazi Germany* (New York, 2002) (German original 1997).
12. The polycracy thesis contends that the persecution of Jews intensified due to power struggles between rival institutions. The suggestive idea of a polycratic system comes from Hans Mommsen, *Beamtentum im Dritten Reich: Mit ausgewählten Quellen zur nationalsozialistischen Beamtenpolitik* (Stuttgart, 1966).
13. See Wolf Gruner and Jörg Osterloh, 'Einleitung', in Wolf Gruner and Jörg Osterloh (eds), *Das Großdeutsche Reich und die Juden: Nationalsozialistische Verfolgungspolitik in den angegliederten Gebieten* (Frankfurt a. M., 2010), 25–26. Throughout the book the citations refer to the updated and expanded English edition: Wolf Gruner and Jörg Osterloh (eds), *The Greater German Reich and the Jews: Nazi Persecution Policies in the Annexed Territories 1935–1945* (New York, 2015).
14. The idea that forced labour meant extermination from the outset can be found in Daniel J. Goldhagen, *Hitler's Willing Executioners: Ordinary Germans and the Holocaust* (New York, 1996), 283–92.
15. I capitalize the term Community throughout the book to denote the Jewish religious institution as opposed to the Jewish community in a general sense.
16. See Jiří Kosta, Jaroslava Milotová and Zlatica Zudová-Lešková (eds), *Tschechische und slowakische Juden im Widerstand 1938–45* (Berlin, 2008), 17–90.
17. Wolf Gruner, '"The Germans Should Expel the Foreigner Hitler": Open Protest and Other Forms of Jewish Defiance in Nazi Germany', *Yad Vashem Studies* 39(2) (2011), 13–53, here 18; Wolf Gruner, 'Verweigerung, Opposition und Protest: Vergessene jüdische Reaktionen auf die NS-Verfolgung in Deutschland', in Alina Bothe, Monika Schärtl and Stefanie Schüler-Springorum (eds), *Shoah: Ereignis und Erinnerung* (3. Jahrbuch Zentrum Jüdische Studien Berlin-Brandenburg) (Berlin, 2019), 11–30.
18. Gruner and Osterloh, 'Introduction', in *The Greater German Reich*, 8–9. On the historiography, see Dieter Pohl, 'Die Holocaust-Forschung und Goldhagens Thesen', *Vierteljahrshefte für Zeitgeschichte* 45 (1997), 1–48, here 3–4; Christoph Dieckmann and Babette Quinkert, 'Einleitung', in Christoph Dieckmann and Babette Quinkert (eds), *Kooperation und Verbrechen: Formen der 'Kollaboration' im östlichen Europa 1939–1945* (Beiträge zur Geschichte des Nationalsozialismus, vol. 19) (Göttingen, 2003), 9–21. For a critical discussion of the Czech research, see Stanislav Kokoška, 'Resistance, Collaboration, Adaptation ... Some Notes on the Research of the Czech Society in the Protectorate', *Czech Journal of Contemporary History* 1 (2013), 54–76.
19. For examples of this assumption, see Vojenský historický archiv (VHA) Prague, fonds 140, carton 19, no. 2, fol. 306: Report 'The Protectorate of Bohemia and Moravia in light of its daily press', carbon copy, n.d. (c. spring 1940), 20; Eugen V. Erdely, *Germany's First European Protectorate: The Fate of the Czechs and Slovaks* (London, 1942), 142–43; Institute of Jewish Affairs (ed.), *Hitler's Ten-Year War on the Jews* (New York, 1943), 56–57.

20. Brandes refers solely to the decree of 21 June 1939 while failing to cite sources or provide further evidence. Detlef Brandes, *Die Tschechen unter deutschem Protektorat*. Part 1: *Besatzungspolitik, Kollaboration und Widerstand im Protektorat Böhmen und Mähren bis Heydrichs Tod (1939–1942)*, ed. Vorstand des Collegium Carolinum, Forschungsstelle für die böhmischen Länder (Munich, 1969), 45.
21. Eva Schmidt-Hartmann, 'Tschechoslowakei', in Wolfgang Benz (ed.), *Dimension des Völkermords: Die Zahl der jüdischen Opfer des Nationalsozialismus* (Munich, 1991), 353–79, here 359.
22. Kárný writes that certain decrees came from the Reich protector, while other measures implemented by the Czech government bore a clear German thumbprint, but in many cases, he states, it is unclear whether they were issued in response to German pressure or on the initiative of the Czechs. There was, he goes on, a clear tendency on the part of the Germans to monopolize the 'Jewish question': Miroslav Kárný, 'The Genocide of the Czech Jews', in *Terezín Memorial Book: Jewish Victims of Nazi Deportations from Bohemia and Moravia 1941–1945* (Terezín, 1996), 27–88, here 37. Frommer asserts that the German occupiers rapidly took charge of anti-Jewish measures previously pursued by the Czech government: Benjamin Frommer, *National Cleansing: Retribution against Nazi Collaborators in Postwar Czechoslovakia* (New York, 2005), 17. Küpper investigates only German actors, as if there had been no Czech policies. See René Küpper, *Karl Hermann Frank (1898–1946): Politische Biographie eines sudetendeutschen Nationalsozialisten* (Munich, 2010), 178–89; Cesarani writes that the Germans quickly took control of Jewish policy, introducing a whole package of measures: Cesarani, *Final Solution*, 227.
23. An example being Diemut Majer, *'Non-Germans' under the Third Reich: The Nazi Judicial and Administrative System in Germany and Occupied Eastern Europe with Special Regard to Occupied Poland, 1939–1945* (Baltimore, 2003) (German original 1981), 204. Opposing arguments are put forward by Gruner and Osterloh, 'Conclusion', in *The Greater German Reich*, 347–49.
24. For an in-depth account, see Gruner and Osterloh, 'Conclusion', 344–61.
25. Vojta Beneš and R.A. Ginsburg, *10 Million Prisoners (Protectorate Bohemia and Moravia)* (Chicago, 1940); Gerhard Jacoby, *Racial State: The German Nationalities Policy in the Protectorate of Bohemia and Moravia* (New York, 1944).
26. Institute of Jewish Affairs, *Hitler's Ten-Year War*; Raphael Lemkin, *Axis Rule in Occupied Europe: Laws of Occupation, Analysis of Government, Proposals for Redress* (reprint of original 1944) (Clark, NJ, 2008); The Jewish Black Book Committee (ed.), *The Black Book: The Nazi Crime against the Jewish People* (New York, 1946). On early efforts at documentation, see Elisabeth Gallas, '"Facing a Crisis Unparalleled in History": Jüdische Reaktionen auf den Holocaust aus New York 1940 bis 1945', *S:I.M.O.N. Shoah: Intervention. Methods. Documentation* 2 (2014), 5–14, here 6–11.
27. See, for example, Moses Moskowitz, 'The Jewish Situation in the Protectorate of Bohemia and Moravia', *Jewish Social Studies* 4(1) (January 1942), 17–44, 19.
28. The main example being Brandes, *Die Tschechen unter deutschem Protektorat*. Part 1.
29. See the updated research overview in Gruner and Osterloh, *The Greater German Reich*, 371–86.
30. See, for example, *Europa unterm Hakenkreuz: Die faschistische Okkupationspolitik in Österreich und der Tschechoslowakei (1938–1945)*, document selection and introduction by Helma Kaden, with the assistance of Ludwig Nestler et al. (Berlin [East], 1988); *Europa unterm Hakenkreuz: Die faschistische Okkupationspolitik in Polen (1939–1945)*, document selection and introduction by Werner Röhr, with the assistance of Elke Heckert et al. (Berlin [East], 1989).

31. Of the volumes published so far, the following have proved particularly relevant to the Protectorate: *Die Verfolgung und Ermordung der europäischen Juden durch das nationalsozialistische Deutschland 1933–1945* [VEJ], vol. 2: *Deutsches Reich, 1938–August 1939*, ed. Susanne Heim (Munich, 2009); VEJ, vol. 3: *Deutsches Reich und Protektorat, September 1939–September 1941*, ed. Andrea Löw (Munich, 2012). An English translation of the whole series is underway, with the first volumes to be published in 2019. An overview of the sourcebook project can be found at: www.editionjudenverfolgung.de.
32. See, for example, Alexandra Garbarini et al. (eds), *Jewish Responses to Persecution: Vol. II 1938–1940* (Lanham, MD, 2011).
33. Isabel Heinemann, *'Rasse, Siedlung, deutsches Blut': Das Rasse- und Siedlungshauptamt der SS und die rassenpolitische Neuordnung Europas* (Göttingen, 2003).
34. Detlef Brandes, *'Umvolkung, Umsiedlung, rassische Bestandsaufnahme': NS-'Volkstumspolitik' in den böhmischen Ländern* (Munich, 2012).
35. Küpper, *Karl Hermann Frank*; Robert Gerwarth, *Hitler's Hangman: The Life of Heydrich* (New Haven, CT, 2011).
36. Gabriele Anderl, 'Die "Zentralstellen für jüdische Auswanderung" in Wien, Berlin und Prag – ein Vergleich', *Tel Aviver Jahrbuch für deutsche Geschichte* 23 (1994), 276–99.
37. See several chapters in Dieter Ziegler (ed.), *Banken und 'Arisierungen' in Mitteleuropa während des Nationalsozialismus* (Stuttgart, 2002); also Christoph Kreutzmüller and Jaroslav Kučera, 'Die Commerzbank und die Vernichtung der jüdischen Gewerbetätigkeit in den böhmischen Ländern und den Niederlanden', in Ludolf Herbst and Thomas Weihe (eds), *Die Commerzbank und die Juden 1933–1945* (Munich, 2004), 173–222; Harald Wixforth, *Die Expansion der Dresdner Bank in Europa*, with the assistance of Johannes Bär et al. (Munich, 2006), 306–50; Drahomír Jančík, Eduard Kubů and Jiří Šouša, with the assistance of Jiří Novotný, *Arisierungsgewinnler: Die Rolle der deutschen Banken bei der 'Arisierung' und Konfiskation jüdischer Vermögen im Protektorat Böhmen und Mähren (1939–1945)* (Wiesbaden, 2011).
38. Kateřina Čapková, *Czechs, Germans, Jews? National Identity and the Jews of Bohemia* (New York, 2012) (in Czech) (Prague, 2005); Ines Koeltzsch, *Geteilte Kulturen: Eine Geschichte der tschechisch-jüdisch-deutschen Beziehungen in Prag (1918–1938)* (Munich, 2012).
39. The first significant text on the Protectorate was H.G. Adler's monumental 1955 study of the Theresienstadt Ghetto: H.G. Adler, *Theresienstadt 1941–1945: Das Antlitz einer Zwangsgemeinschaft. Geschichte, Soziologie, Psychologie* (Tübingen, 1955) (English translation 2017); H.G. Adler (ed.), *Die verheimlichte Wahrheit: Theresienstädter Dokumente* (Tübingen, 1958).
40. For an overview of Kárný's oeuvre, see the 'Auswahlbibliographie der Arbeiten von Miroslav Kárný 1971–2001' in *Theresienstädter Studien und Dokumente* 2002, 33–44.
41. Eva Hahn, 'Verdrängung und Verharmlosung: Das Ende der jüdischen Bevölkerungsgruppe in den böhmischen Ländern nach ausgewählten tschechischen und sudetendeutschen Publikationen', in Brandes and Kural, *Der Weg in die Katastrophe*, 138–45. For a recent, more nuanced account, see Peter Hallama, *Nationale Helden und jüdische Opfer: Tschechische Repräsentationen des Holocaust* (Göttingen, 2015).
42. However, the latter themes continue to receive plenty of attention: Pavel Maršálek, *Protektorát Čechy a Morava: Státoprávní a politické aspekty nacistického okupačního*

režimu v českých zemích 1939–1945 [The Protectorate of Bohemia and Moravia: Constitutional and Political Aspects of the Nazi Occupation Regime in the Bohemian Lands 1939–1945] (Prague, 2002); Jan Boris Uhlíř, *Ve stínu říšské orlice: Protektorát Čechy a Morava, odboj a kolaborace* [In the Shadow of the Imperial Eagle: The Protectorate of Bohemia and Moravia, Resistance and Collaboration] (Prague, 2002). On the historiography, see also Chad Bryant, *Prague in Black: Nazi Rule and Czech Nationalism* (Cambridge, MA, 2007), 6–8; and for a critical take, see Jaroslav Kučera and Volker Zimmermann, 'Zum tschechischen Forschungsstand über die NS-Besatzungsherrschaft in Böhmen und Mähren: Überlegungen anlässlich des Erscheinens eines Standardwerkes', *Bohemia* 49(1) (2009), 164–83.

43. Miroslav Kárný, *'Konecné resení': Genocida ceských zidu v nemecké protektorátní politice*, vol. 1 (Prague, 1991); Kárný, 'The Genocide of the Czech Jews'; *Osud Židů v protektorátu 1939–1945*, ed. Milena Janišová (Prague, 1991); Helena Petrův, *Právní postavení židů v Protektorátu Čechy a Morava (1939–1941)* (Prague, 2000); Miroslav Kárný and Jaroslava Milotová (eds), *Protektorátní politika Reinharda Heydricha* (Prague, 1991); *Deutsche Politik im 'Protektorat Böhmen und Mähren' unter Reinhard Heydrich 1941–1942: Eine Dokumentation*, ed. Miroslav Kárný, Jaroslava Milotová and Margita Kárná (Berlin, 1997); Helena Krejčová, Jana Svobodová and Anna Hyndráková (eds), *Židé v Protektorátu: Hlášení Židovské náboženské obce v roce 1942. Dokumenty* (Prague, 1997).

44. *Theresienstädter Studien und Dokumente* (TSD) (Prague, 1994–2008; German edition); *Terezínské studie a dokumenty*, (Prague, 1996–2008; Czech edition).

45. Krejčová et al., *Židé v Protektorátu*; Helena Krejčová and Jana Svobodová, *Postavení a osudy židovského obyvatelstva v Čechách a na Moravě v letech 1939–1945: sborník studií* (Prague, 1998).

46. Livia Rothkirchen, *The Jews of Bohemia and Moravia: Facing the Holocaust* (Lincoln, 2005).

47. See, for example, ibid., 100–102.

48. Marc Oprach, *Nationalsozialistische Judenpolitik im Protektorat Böhmen und Mähren: Entscheidungsabläufe und Radikalisierung* (Hamburg, 2006).

49. This is a view shared by Magda Veselská, '"Sie müssen sich als Jude dessen bewusst sein, welche Opfer zu tragen sind ...": Handlungsspielräume der jüdischen Kultusgemeinden im Protektorat bis zum Ende der großen Deportationen', in Andrea Löw, Doris Bergen and Anna Hájková (eds), *Alltag im Holocaust: Jüdisches Leben im Großdeutschen Reich 1941–1945* (Munich, 2013), 151–66, here 152.

50. Wolf Gruner, 'Protektorát Čechy a Morava a protižidovská politika v letech 1939–1941', in *Terezinske Studie a Dokumenty 2005* (Prague, 2005), 25–58 (German: 'Das Protektorat Böhmen/Mähren und die antijüdische Politik 1939–1941: Lokale Initiativen, regionale Maßnahmen und zentrale Entscheidungen im "Großdeutschen Reich"', in *Theresienstädter Studien und Dokumente* 2005, 27–62); and the chapter 'Protektorat', in Gruner and Osterloh, *Das Großdeutsche Reich*, 139–73 (in updated form as 'Protectorate', in Osterloh and Gruner, *The Greater German Reich*, 99–135); see also the chapter on Jewish forced labour: 'The Protectorate of Bohemia and Moravia', in Wolf Gruner, *Jewish Forced Labor under the Nazis: Economic Needs and Racial Aims (1938–1944)* (New York, 2006), 141–76. Recently Benjamin Frommer put forward a similar hypothesis regarding the active involvement of the Czech authorities: Benjamin Frommer, 'Verfolgung durch die Presse: Wie Prager Bürokraten und die tschechische Polizei halfen, die Juden des Protektorats zu isolieren', in Löw, Bergen and Hájková, *Alltag im Holocaust*, 137–50, esp. 138, 149–50.

51. On what follows, see Gruner and Osterloh, 'Introduction' and 'Conclusion', 1–9, 340–65.

52. Minutes of the meeting of state secretaries on 25 March 1939 and appendix in VEJ/3, doc. no. 240, 574–80, here 579; appendix appears separately in *Europa unterm Hakenkreuz: Österreich und Tschechoslowakei*, doc. no. 36, 110–12. See also Decree concerning the edict issued by the Führer on the Protectorate of Bohemia and Moravia, 22 March 1939, in *Verordnungsblatt des Reichsprotektors in Böhmen und Mähren* 1939/No. 6, 32.
53. Announcement concerning the decree on identity cards, 3 March 1942, in *Reichsgesetzblatt* (RGBl.) 1942 I, 100.
54. Gruner and Osterloh, 'Introduction', 348.
55. For more detail on this, see the contributions in Gruner and Osterloh, *The Greater German Reich*.
56. Wolf Gruner, 'Die NS-Judenverfolgung und die Kommunen: Zur wechselseitigen Dynamisierung von zentraler und lokaler Politik 1933–1941', *Vierteljahrshefte für Zeitgeschichte* 48(1) (2000), 75–126; Wolf Gruner, Öffentliche Wohlfahrt und Judenverfolgung: *Wechselwirkungen lokaler und zentraler Politik im NS-Staat (1933–1942)* (Munich, 2002); Wolf Gruner, *Zwangsarbeit und Verfolgung: Österreichische Juden im NS-Staat 1938–1945* (Innsbruck, 2000); Wolf Gruner, 'Local Initiatives, Central Coordination: German Municipal Administration and the Holocaust', in Gerald D. Feldman and Wolfgang Seibel (eds), *Networks of Nazi Persecution: Bureaucracy, Business, and the Organization of the Holocaust* (New York, 2005), 269–94.
57. For some initial thoughts on this, see Gruner, 'Das Protektorat Böhmen/Mähren und die antijüdische Politik', 27–62.
58. This common misconception appeared most recently in Gerwarth, who assumes that Eichmann led Jewish policy as Heydrich's expert: Gerwarth, *Hitler's Hangman*, 220.
59. On the broader context of these developments, see Gruner and Osterloh, *The Greater German Reich*.
60. See his statement in Friedländer, *Nazi Germany and the Jews*, 2.
61. Wolf Gruner, *Der Geschlossene Arbeitseinsatz deutscher Juden: Zwangsarbeit als Element der Verfolgung 1938–1943* (Berlin, 1997); Gruner, *Öffentliche Wohlfahrt*.
62. Gruner, *Zwangsarbeit und Verfolgung*.
63. See Gruner, 'Protektorát Čechy a Morava', 25–58 (German: 'Das Protektorat Böhmen/Mähren und die antijüdische Politik', 27–62).
64. See chapter 5 in Gruner, *Jewish Forced Labor under the Nazis*.
65. Gruner and Osterloh, *The Greater German Reich*.
66. For an in-depth look at this level of persecution, see the forthcoming work by Benjamin Frommer, *The Ghetto without Walls: The Identification, Isolation, and Elimination of Bohemian and Moravian Jewry, 1938–1945*.

CHAPTER 1

THE CZECHOSLOVAK REPUBLIC AND ITS MINORITIES

Modified Maps, New States, Changed Relations

As in Germany, the First World War profoundly altered both maps and power relations in central and eastern Europe, laying the ground for subsequent developments in Bohemia (Čechy) and Moravia (Morava). The new Czechoslovak Republic (ČSR), one of the successor states to the Austro-Hungarian monarchy, comprised the majority of Czechs and Slovaks along with German, Jewish, Hungarian, Polish and Ruthenian minorities.[1] The declaration of independence of 28 October 1918 promised to furnish every section of the population, including the minorities, with equal rights and fair political representation.[2]

The government of the new republic signed the Treaty of Saint-Germain-en-Laye of 10 September 1919, incorporating its provisions on the protection of minorities into the first constitution of the Czechoslovak Republic (as Art. 128) on 29 February 1920. This included recognition of a Jewish national minority, a partly political move intended to weaken the German and Hungarian communities. However, many of the 354,000 Jews, the vast majority of them German speakers, considered themselves members of the German minority and did not declare themselves Jews.[3] More than thirteen million people lived in the republic in 1921: alongside 6,840,000 Czechs there were almost two million Slovaks and somewhat more than three million Germans, who thus represented the second largest ethnic group in Czechoslovakia.[4]

By the end of 1930, the population of the republic had grown to almost fifteen million people, most of whom lived in the west (Bohemia, Moravia and Silesia), with four million in the east (Slovakia and Carpatho-Ukraine). Nine hundred thousand people were resident in the capital city of Prague (Praha).[5] Thirty-four per cent of the Czechoslovak population worked in agriculture, a similar number in industry, and less than 10 per cent each in commerce, transportation, the civil service and other fields. In Bohemia, agriculture accounted for just 24 per cent of those in employment, while almost 42 per cent worked in industry (a larger proportion of industrial jobs than in Germany), whereas in Carpatho-Ukraine the ratio was 62 per cent to 12 per cent.[6]

In Bohemia, alongside two-thirds of Czechs, Germans made up a third of the population in 1930, while in Moravia they accounted for almost 23 per cent alongside 74 per cent of Czechs, though due to a lower birth rate Germans' share of the overall population was decreasing.[7] While Czechs and Slovaks gained cultural and political freedoms with the advent of the new republic, the Germans lost the privileged position they had enjoyed during the Habsburg era. Many formerly Germanized Czechs now professed loyalty to their republic. The overwhelming majority of Germans, on the other hand, withheld their allegiance and even called for the German-speaking Bohemian areas to become part of German-Austria. When the victorious powers prohibited this, the Sudeten Germans oriented themselves towards Germany/Berlin, again in vain.[8]

Particularly in the major cities, however, residents also chose (and changed) their nationality as they saw fit; there were Czechicized Germans and Germanized Czechs.[9] Based solely on *ius soli*, everyone born in Czechoslovakia received citizenship. Women enjoyed the equal right to vote.[10] Though the language law adopted in 1920 granted only Czech and Slovak the status of official languages, in those parts of the country in which they made up at least a fifth of the population minorities could officially use their languages, including German, when interacting with local authorities.[11] In addition, Germans were guaranteed the full range of minority rights, among other things a proportional share of parliamentary and town council seats as well as access to cultural and educational services. In 1935, 97 per cent of German children attended German schools.[12] Nevertheless, many Germans accused the Czechs and Slovaks of seeking to create a homogenous Slavic state, failing to grant them equal rights and removing Sudeten Germans from the civil service.[13]

The new emphasis on the nation in the immediate postwar period stoked an antisemitism that certainly existed in Bohemia and Moravia, though it became less visible than in the neighbouring countries.[14] The early days of the republic witnessed scattered demonstrations against Jews, as well as the looting of a small number of businesses and homes in Prague.[15] In December 1918, in the small town of Holešov (Holleschau), members of the nearby army unit, together with local residents, vandalized apartments and offices. Two Jews died as a result of the three-day pogrom. In September 1919, some nationalists among the Legionnaires, the Czech volunteers who fought in Allied armies during the First World War, called for a dictatorship under Masaryk and the dismissal of Germans and Jews from the army and state administration.[16] Students of a *völkisch* inclination demonstrated at the German University in Prague. When Samuel Steinherz was later elected its rector, the Czech education minister quickly quelled a protest against the 'Judaization of the German university', but in 1924 the university senate resolved to limit the number and rights of Jewish students.[17] With reference to the same period, however, Anny Maass, who was attending school in Moravian Ostrava (Moravská Ostrava, Mährisch-Ostrau), remembers barely any antisemitism.[18]

Later, in 1927, a fascist party on the Italian model emerged in the ČSR and antisemitic agitation gradually gained ground in the press.[19] More demonstrations and even some attacks occurred at universities in Prague. Katherine Kral, for example, had to fend off an assault by German students.[20] State founder and president Tomáš G. Masaryk, however, did everything he could to combat such tendencies.[21]

The Jewish Inhabitants of the New Republic

Of 354,000 individuals of Jewish religion or origin living in Czechoslovakia in 1921, half identified with a Jewish nationality in the census carried out at the time (11,251 of 79,777 in Bohemia, 19,016 of 45,306 in Moravia, and larger shares in the rest of the republic). The remainder saw themselves as Czechs, Germans or Hungarians.[22] Jews lived in a state of close coexistence with the other groups in Czech society in both towns and cities,[23] while political actors often instrumentalized differences between groups.[24] Many people spoke several languages. The Jews of Prague in particular were characterized by cultural hybridity[25] and multiple nationality.[26]

Alfred Dube (b. 1923), the child of a Jewish banker of Czech origin who was also a reserve lieutenant in the Czech army,[27] grew up in Pilsen

(Plzeň) in western Bohemia speaking Czech and German. He went to a German school and had Jewish and German friends. His best friend was Eddie Weck, a German.[28] Hilda Beran, born in Moravian Ostrava in 1913, spoke German at home and learned Czech at school. She first attended a Jewish educational establishment then a public high school for girls, where she experienced some antisemitism.[29] In Prague, Zuzana Podmelova, born in 1921, spoke Czech and German with members of her family and attended a German school.[30]

In the Bohemian lands, Jews' long history of settlement and their special demographic situation had made many of them highly secularized. In this respect they differed from most of their counterparts in Germany and Austria who, regardless of how integrated they were, anchored their Jewishness in religion, as they tended to do in other parts of Czechoslovakia as well. The founding of the republic sparked the rise of a Czech-Jewish movement advocating universal assimilation, alongside a Zionist movement that took a variety of forms in the different regions of Czechoslovakia.[31] Other than those of a communist persuasion, most Jews were extremely loyal to the Czech state.[32]

For Alfred Dube, who moved from Pilsen to Prague at the age of ten, religion played a significant role. His family saw themselves as Reform Jews; his father had a paid seat in the synagogue, and they went to the temple every Friday. Alfred was instructed in religion at school by a rabbi under state auspices, just as the Catholics had their weekly religious lesson.[33] Some Jews upheld traditional Jewish values, such as the well-to-do family of Anny Maass (b. 1909)[34] and that of Anna Grant (b. 1921), both resident in Moravian Ostrava. The latter grew up in what she described as a close-knit Jewish community. Her parents attended the more conservative of the city's two synagogues.[35] Others were not very religious, such as the family of Katherine Kral (b. 1909), who attended the synagogue in Moravian Ostrava only on the High Holy Days,[36] or the family of Curt Allina, who, having moved from Vienna to Prague, observed the Jewish holidays only at the homes of relatives.[37] Georgine Hyde from Prague (b. 1925) went so far as to celebrate Christmas with her employees, attended a reform synagogue solely on the High Holy Days, with the service in Czech, and participated in other festivals at most with her religious grandparents.[38] In Brno (Brünn), meanwhile, the family of Helen Blenkins (b. 1927) ignored all the Jewish holidays.[39]

The majority of Jews, however, lived in the east of the republic, in Slovakia and Carpatho-Ukraine. They accounted for 14 per cent of the inhabitants in these regions, with roughly 90 per cent of them identifying with a Jewish nationality. These often rather orthodox Jews differed in cultural, political and social terms from their largely assimilated counterparts in the west of the country.

The founding of the republic prompted the immigration of several thousand orthodox Jews from Bukovina and Galicia, who settled mainly in Prague and Moravian Ostrava, where they encountered certain reservations about refugees.[40] The immigrants' poor economic situation and different culture also sparked tensions within the Jewish communities.[41]

The legal status of the Jewish Communities was based on the Austrian law of 1890 in Bohemia and Moravia and the Hungarian agreements of 1870 in Slovakia and Carpatho-Ukraine. While a rich religious life developed in Moravia, including welfare and educational activities, in Bohemia it was Jewish Community institutions that sustained the practice of religion. After 1918, there were three Jewish umbrella organizations in Czechoslovakia, serving greater Prague, the Czech-speaking communities and their German-speaking counterparts. They banded together with the Moravian communities in 1926 to form the Supreme Council of the Jewish Religious Communities, which fostered the study of Jewish history, religion and culture. This body also supported the Prague Jewish Museum, the translation of the Five Books of Moses into Czech, the establishment of a chair in Semitic philology at the University of Prague and – unsuccessfully until 1938 – the establishment of a rabbinical seminary, in an attempt to remedy the lack of religious education.[42]

The Jewish population had been in steady decline since the turn of the century, with Jews' share of the overall population falling by 9.4 per cent in Moravia and 4.3 per cent in Bohemia between 1921 and 1931. The Prague Jewish Community lost almost 1,500 members between 1934 and 1938, with 1,130 leaving and 314 converting to Christianity.[43] Conversions played a significant role in the diminishing Jewish population as did the falling birth rate, the secularization of Czech society and the growing number of interconfessional marriages (already accounting for 30 per cent by 1933), all of which also indicate Jews' high degree of acculturation and social acceptance. According to the second census carried out in Czechoslovakia, a total of 356,830 Jews lived there in 1930, in 150 Jewish communities – 76,301 (21.5 per cent) in Bohemia and 41,250 (11.5 per cent) in Moravia and Silesia.[44] Of slightly more than ten million inhabitants of Bohemia and Moravia in 1930, the 117,551 Jews accounted for just 1 per cent. In Bohemia, just a fifth of inhabitants of Jewish religion declared themselves to be of Jewish nationality in the census, with half identifying as Czech and more than 30 per cent as German, in contrast with Moravia, where more than half described themselves as Jewish, a little under a third as German and 17 per cent as Czech. Most Jews lived in the cities; in Bohemia alone almost 50 per cent were resident in Prague (35,403), while in Moravia 25 per cent lived in Brno (11,103) and Moravian Ostrava (6,865). More than half of all Jews in the two provinces lived in the five cities with more than fifty thousand inhabitants. In addition to Prague, Brno and Moravian Ostrava, there were 2,773 Jews in Pilsen and 2,198 in Olomouc. Jews as a proportion of the overall population amounted to 4.2 per cent in Prague and Brno, 5.5 per cent in Moravian Ostrava, 2.4 per cent in Pilsen and 3.3 per cent in Olomouc. In a number of smaller towns, Jews made up more than 10 per cent of residents.[45] In much the same way as in western Europe, the majority of Czech Jews, 60 per cent, worked in trade and commerce, 14 per cent in the civil service and just a few in agriculture. While 22 per cent worked in industry and crafts in Bohemia, the figure was 28 per cent in Moravia.[46]

Alfred Dube, mentioned above, initially attended German schools: his father was determined that he be fully bilingual as a prerequisite for a career in business. Only when Hitler took power in Germany did Dube switch from a private German school to a public Czech one attended by three or four other Jewish pupils.[47] In the 1930s, Jews made up more than 10 per cent of students in higher education, half enrolling at German and half at Czech institutions. Jewish academics taught at Czech and German universities or made a living in a wide range of other fields. Many Jews achieved renown in the spheres of culture, media and art, as well as in politics and in most of the political parties of the ČSR, with ministers of Jewish origin serving in a number of coalition governments. For example, Dr Alfréd Meissner (1871–1952), one of the authors of the democratic constitution, was twice appointed both minister of justice and minister of social welfare during the 1920s and 1930s.[48]

The Jewish minority played an active part in political life, sending representatives to town councils and regional parliaments. The Zionist movement, led until 1938 by Dr Josef Rufeisen, its headquarters initially in Prague then in Moravian Ostrava, pursued the goal of a Jewish homeland in Palestine, meeting with strong opposition from the ultraorthodox camp, which regarded Zionism as heresy. In Bohemia and Moravia, Zionism failed to create a mass movement and only made a political impact when Jews began to feel the effects of the Nazi dictatorship.[49] The founding of the republic also triggered the emergence of a Czech-Jewish movement, which, under the leadership of Dr Edvard Lederer, propagated universal assimilation. It comprised two thousand members, mostly drawn from a religiously indifferent cultural elite. Its members attacked the Zionists' objectives, particularly in Prague. Orthodox Jews, meanwhile, were the numerically weakest section of the Jewish community.[50]

Figure 1.1. Jewish girl (Margit Morawetz) on a street in Prague, 1938. © USHMM Washington, Photo Archive, no. 28698.

Minorities struggled to make an electoral impact in the republic. It was not until the late 1920s that the 'Jewish Party', established in 1919, managed to get its candidates into parliament thanks to an agreement with the party of the Polish minority. The Jewish Party initially sought to improve the situation of Jews in the eastern parts of the country and fought for the recognition of Hebrew schools in Carpatho-Ukraine, while in the 1930s it sought to combat escalating Nazi agitation, local nationalists and antisemites.[51] In the western border regions, younger people in particular were increasingly excluded by German youth organizations, while older people continued to cultivate a range of relationships with the German middle class. It was particularly among the young, therefore, that the Zionists attracted support.[52]

German Shadows over Czech Politics

A heterogeneous party landscape emerged in the new republic that reflected its different cultural and social strata. Between fifteen and twenty political parties were represented in parliament, with five of them taking the lion's share of seats: the Czechoslovak Social Democratic Workers' Party, the Czechoslovak Socialist Party (from 1926 the Czechoslovak National Socialist Party), the Czechoslovak People's Party, the Czechoslovak National Democracy and the Republican Party of Farmers and Peasants (the Agrarians).[53]

The German minority was represented in parliament and on a significant scale. Three of the 'German parties' participated in government from 1926 onwards. Germans even served as ministers.[54] From the mid 1920s onwards, it was the 'Activism' propagated by the German Agrarian Party (Deutsche Agrarpartei) and the German Christian Social People's Party (Deutsche Christlich-Soziale Volkspartei) that dominated among Germans rather than the 'Negationism' of the German National Party of Bohemia (Deutsche Nationalpartei Böhmens) and German National Socialist Workers' Party (Deutsche Nationalsozialistische Arbeiterpartei). In 1929, the German Social Democratic Party (Deutsche Sozialdemokratische Partei), which had gained in strength with Czech help, sent representatives to parliament in place of the clerical politicians.[55]

Soon, however, external factors, above all the global economic crisis from 1929 and the Nazi seizure of power in Germany in 1933, altered the Czech political landscape. The global downturn and the dwindling of trade between Germany and the ČSR hit the Bohemian economy hard, particularly in the industrialized west where most Germans lived.[56] From the late 1920s onwards, the area saw the emergence among Germans of what their leader Konrad Henlein (1898–1945)[57] called a 'radical form' of National Socialism.[58]

The government in Prague tried to crush the political movement that took off in the 1930s against this background in the Sudeten region, triggering the dissolution of the radical parties. The German National Socialist Workers' Party, which was openly propagating union with Germany in 1933, and the German National Party of Bohemia pre-empted their prohibition by disbanding themselves. Many of their members, however, joined the Sudeten German Home Front (Sudetendeutsche Heimatfront), led by Konrad Henlein and founded on 1 October 1933. The National Socialists' defeat initially strengthened the 'Activists', reinforcing some Germans' allegiance to the ČSR.[59]

Hitler's 'successes', however, bolstered the Home Front, which was renamed the Sudeten German Party (Sudetendeutsche Partei or SdP) in 1935 at Prague's behest. It won more than a million votes in the parliamentary elections of 1935 and became the leading political force in the region.[60] Officially, it described itself as democratic and loyal to the Czech state, but it extolled the Führer principle and the Nazi idea of a People's Community (Volksgemeinschaft). The fact that Henlein himself declined to stand in the parliamentary election was perceived within the Czech public sphere as a failure to respect the democratic constitution. Though many Sudeten Germans became more conscious of their ties to the ČSR, from the mid 1930s onwards the Sudeten German Party presented itself as their sole representative. When the Czech government agreed to devolve greater powers to the region in response to growing political pressure, Henlein responded by calling for full autonomy for the ethnic German community, including 'race-based' forms of political representation.[61]

Arthur Löw, born in Karlsbad (Karlovy Vary, Sudetenland) in 1901, was a member of the Sudeten German Party and the Sudeten German Free Corps (Sudetendeutsches Freikorps). In 1936, in a Karlsbad café, he provocatively demanded the *Münchner Neueste Nachrichten* instead of a Czech newspaper, making critical remarks about the Czech economy for all to hear. While everything was fine in Germany, he contended, the Czechs were illiterate and incapable of governing. They must leave: 'Surely everyone can see that. The Eastern Jews come here and make themselves at home and the Czechs do nothing about it, but the Germans are oppressed'. In 1942, Löw was sentenced to three months in prison for making disparaging remarks about the Führer (for dismissing field marshal Walther von Brauchitsch). The special court that dealt with the case, however, interpreted his earlier conviction by a Czech district court as a mitigating factor: referring to him as a 'half-Jew', it nonetheless gave him a suspended sentence in light of his outstanding contribution to 'Germanity (Deutschtum) in the Sudetengau'.[62]

Austria's incorporation into Germany in March 1938 then dealt a death blow to all attempts to reach an accommodation. Henlein welcomed the establishment of 'Greater Germany' and invited every German in the

ČSR to join his big-tent party, prompting the dissolution of the Agrarian League (Bund der Landwirte) and the German Christian Social People's Party. The Socialists, meanwhile, left the cabinet. Henlein now openly propagated a programme inspired by the Nazi state and its antisemitic policies, with his new Sudeten German Party bringing together heterogeneous elements united by their dissatisfaction and by the new idea of a People's Community as extolled by Germany.[63] As the Activists among the German minority lost out to the Negationists under Henlein, the Slovakian nationalists under Andrej Hlinka gained ground in a parallel process.[64]

Anti-Jewish agitation in the ČSR had been gathering steam since the mid 1930s, with the Sudeten German Party pursuing a particularly antisemitic course.[65] Propaganda targeting Jews emanated mostly from German circles but also from right-wing Czech and Slovak groups. During this period, Fred Klein (b. 1922) suffered veiled verbal attacks in a German school and a German gymnastics club in Pilsen.[66] Mimi Berger, three years younger, also heard anti-Jewish remarks in her Prague school, but as she remembers it, they were not a dominant feature of her everyday life.[67]

Though a latent antisemitism existed among sections of the population, overall the republic was considered liberal and positively inclined towards Jews.[68] Looking back, Alfred Dube stated that Prague especially was almost entirely free of antisemitism until Hitler occupied Bohemia.[69] Jewish Communities themselves demanded that 'neither individuals nor Jewish bodies give the non-Jewish population any occasion for indignation or resentment'.[70]

Antisemitic agitation targeted 'Jewish Bolshevism' and above all the growing number of refugees from the German Reich. From 1933 onwards, thousands of victims of political and racial persecution sought refuge in Czechoslovakia. The government and general public initially gave them a warm welcome until pressure from right-wing political forces prompted the ČSR to adopt a more restrictive immigration policy.

The 'Problem' of Jewish Refugees

Thousands of those persecuted by the Nazi regime fled to Czechoslovakia, which had a long unguarded border with various parts of the German Reich. In Prague a Jewish Relief Committee (Hilfskomitee) was established to help refugees, who arrived initially from Germany, then from Austria and finally from the Sudetenland. Social democrats, communists and Czech intellectuals established similar bodies.[71] The Jewish Relief Committee was soon cooperating with the International Jewish organizations HICEM and the Joint Distribution Committee (the Joint or JDC) to help alleviate the suffering of persecuted Jews. In the mid 1930s, all the relief groups then united to form a National Coordination Committee, which obtained funds from a variety of sources: prosperous individuals, the Czechoslovak president, Quakers in the United States and the Red Aid organization in Moscow.[72]

Both the government and the general public welcomed the first refugees with open arms. But from the mid 1930s, growing pressure from right-wing political forces led to a more restrictive immigration policy, which affected Austrians in particular.[73] The Jewish Relief Committee alone helped 3,600 individuals emigrate to other states. The ČSR authorities, meanwhile, now went so far as to send some refugees rejected by other countries back to Germany. In fact, even Czech Jews feared excessive Germanization of the Czech Jewry as this would go down badly with the rest of the population.[74]

In late 1937 or early 1938, the Czechoslovak Republic evidently made a conscious decision to expel Polish Jews from its territory. In February, the Czech police forced large numbers of Jews with Polish citizenship from their homes in Moravian Ostrava, deporting them across the nearby border into Poland. As documented in one case, however, Polish border officials immediately sent the expellees back again. They turned to the Jewish Community in Moravian Ostrava, which passed them on to the local police. As a result, the Community was later accused of having failed to do enough for the Polish Jews. This caused particular acrimony in cases of former Community employees or individuals who had lived in the area for fifty years. At the time, officials of the Jewish Community had declared openly that they were unwilling to appeal to the Czech authorities to help the Polish Jews, even upon learning that they had been arrested. Apparently, they had acted on the false assumption that the 'position of the Czech Jews [could] be strengthened by the departure of the Polish Jews'.[75]

Migration, Agitation and Dictatorship: The Second Republic

Anti-ČSR propaganda intensified in Germany. In its March 1938 issue, the periodical *Volk und Reich* printed a number of antisemitic articles examining the Jewish question in relation to a number of countries in central and eastern Europe. Here Georg Hartmann, for example, fantasized about the power of Jews in Czechoslovakia, summing up his views as follows:

> In the Czechoslovak Republic there is today no sphere of life that has not somehow got into a state of dependency on the Jews, which – should it wish to have nothing to do with them – is not compelled to come to terms with them. But it is in connection with the German-Czech question that the Jewish problem is becoming particularly important to internal Germanity (Binnendeutschtum).[76]

In a general way, the periodical accused Czechoslovakia of warmongering and oppressing the Sudeten Germans.[77] The Czechoslovak Republic, with fifteen million inhabitants, one of the most modern armies in Europe, strong defences and a developed armaments industry was certainly an adversary to be taken seriously.[78] Contemporaries already suspected that the German minorities were the Trojan horse that would enable the Reich to breach the Czech bastion.[79]

As the self-proclaimed champion of the 'Greater German People's Community' (Großdeutsche Volksgemeinschaft), the Nazi state believed itself entitled to interfere in the life and politics of other states.[80] The Czechoslovak government, on the other hand, perceived this as an expression of traditional pan-Germanic imperialism.[81] The pressure on the ČSR mounted from without and within. It was not helped by its founder-president Masaryk's resignation in 1935 and death in 1937.

After the expiration of the German-Polish Accord on East Silesia, which was followed by pogrom-like riots targeting the area's Jewish population in July 1937, and the annexation of Austria in March 1938, which triggered persecution of Jews on an unprecedented scale, things came to a head in the summer. Nazi agitation, organized violence and boycotts of Jewish and Czech businesses, expedited by Henlein's troops, dominated life in the Sudetenland.[82] Many tried to flee the region, but above all from Austria, in an attempt to escape the violence. Czech officials now prevented hundreds of Jewish refugees from entering the country on a daily basis along the southern Moravian border. While 'permanent residence in the ČSR [was] unrealistic for political and economic reasons', the government in Prague pledged – following intervention by the British Foreign Office – not to deport the Jews confined in a camp in Brno for the time being.[83]

Political circles in the republic itself took advantage of this situation to step up their anti-Jewish agitation. The Czech clerical newspaper *Lydowe Listy* criticized Jews for failing to act as Czechoslovak citizens: in the Sudeten territories they still spoke German and were thus weakening Czech culture. They should 'nationalize' themselves as quickly as possible if they wanted the sympathetic response they had enjoyed in the ČSR to continue.[84]

The aggressive speech with which Hitler concluded the 'first Reich party congress of Greater Germany' in Nuremberg on 12 September 1938, in which he condemned Prague's 'criminal' oppression of Germans, triggered an upsurge in violence in the Sudetenland.[85] A report by the Security Service of the SS described how, in a number of Sudeten German localities, particularly the Egerland, some of those participating in night-time demonstrations on 13 September calling for union with Germany had smashed the windows of 'Jewish and Czech businesses', prompting Jews and Czechs to flee.[86]

In response to these developments, in mid September the Czech state declared martial law in a number of districts in the Sudeten region and northern Bohemia,[87] though Henlein's supporters carried on attacking Jewish and non-Jewish Czechs regardless. The Czech authorities liberated seventeen Jews detained by Henlein's Sturmabteilung (SA) forces in Marienbad.[88] Prominent Jews such as noted Zionist Dr Emil Margulies in Litoměřice (Leitmeritz) received death threats. Such large numbers of Jews now fled their homes that, for example, of three thousand resident in Karlsbad, two thousand sought help in Prague.[89]

The ČSR had granted the Sudeten Germans substantial freedoms, though never political autonomy. It finally offered to do so in the late summer of 1938, by which time they were already pursuing a much larger goal. In late September, the United Kingdom and France – rightly fearing war – gave in to Hitler's demands, made so openly in Nuremberg, for self-determination for the Sudeten Germans and the transfer of border regions to Germany.[90]

The Munich Diktat of 30 September 1938 de facto divided the young republic into three. The Sudeten region went to Germany while Slovakia was granted substantial autonomy, with a mutilated Czechoslovakia losing to Germany not just three-tenths of its territory (see Figure 1.2), a quarter of its population and innumerable natural resources, but also its thousand-year-old (heavily fortified) border.[91] In the following days and weeks, the Gestapo arrested tens of thousands of 'enemies of the Reich' in the annexed Sudeten region, prompting many people to flee. It ordered the expulsion of large numbers of Jews, giving them only forty-eight hours to leave in many cases.[92] Immediately after the entry of German troops, new attacks on Jewish businesses began; shops were vandalized, for example, in Karlsbad, Eger (Cheb) and Franzensbad (Františkovy Lázně). Some Jews committed suicide, as in the case of lawyer Dr Rudolf Lederer from Teplitz (Teplice), who threw himself from a tower.[93]

In the part of Moravia incorporated into Silesia, according to an SD report,

> a sudden and strong reaction had already [set in] among the Jewry following the announcement of the Munich Agreement. Even before the occupation, most Jews had left this area, some of them leaving behind substantial property and other assets. The Jews who remained were almost exclusively frail and elderly. Moreover, in the course of the occupation the provisional transfer of Jewish businesses to 'Aryan' ownership was initiated through the immediate appointment of trustees, so the implementation of the expiatory campaign [a reference to the November pogrom] in Moravia deviated significantly from that in the Old Reich, taking a less intense form.[94]

During the next few days and weeks, the trains and railway stations were full to overflowing with 'Jewish and Marxist refugees', with many individuals sleeping on the floor.[95]

The pogrom of November 1938 was organized throughout the German Reich, not excepting the Sudeten region. Synagogues were set on fire in many places, while Jews were attacked, persecuted and confined in camps.[96] A total of around seven thousand Jews had now fled to the Czech Republic.[97] Newspapers in the Sudeten region, exemplified by the front page of the *Marienbader Zeitung* of 16 November, were soon sneeringly reporting that entire towns had already declared themselves 'Jew-free'.[98]

According to the Prague Statistical Office, there were now more than 259,000 religious Jews (Glaubensjuden) living in the rump Czechoslovak state, or 252,000 minus refugees: 99,000 in Bohemia, Moravia and Silesia, 87,000 in Slovakia and 66,000 in Carpatho-Ukraine.[99] The new wave of refugees reinforced anti-German and anti-Jewish resentment among parts of the Czech population. The *CV-Zeitung* reported that the government in Prague was considering forcing some Jews to emigrate in the near future. Such goals were also propagated by the agrarian newspaper *Venko*, the *Národní politika* and other titles. Jewish spokesmen, on the other hand, emphasized that Jews had always stood loyal to the Czech Republic and were just as committed to the new state; as a sign of goodwill, one Jewish newspaper in Prague had begun to appear in Czech rather than German.[100]

The Jewish Party and the Zionists declared their loyalty to the Czech state. Meanwhile, the government under General Syrový – formed by Eduard Beneš in late September prior to his departure into exile on 15 October 1938 – was now governing the so-called Second Republic in authoritarian fashion, prohibiting the Communist Party and establishing a unified trade union. At the same time, it sent in the police to break up antisemitic demonstrations, with backing from the Catholic Church. But it yielded to an increasingly nationalistic public mood, decreeing that all those who had immigrated since 1914 had to leave the country. While the Czech government received a £10 million loan from France and the United Kingdom, partly in order to provide for the Sudeten refugees and to organize the emigration of Jews and imperilled German opponents of the Nazis, in Slovakia, the Slovak People's Party (Hlinkova slovenská ľudová strana), led by Andrej Hlinka, implemented the first anti-Jewish measures, deporting thousands of Jews in late October to those areas now allocated to Hungary.[101] Hungary then expelled Jews from its new territories. Many hundreds of Jews thus found themselves in no man's land. A similar picture prevailed in the Polish border areas. Seventeen hundred now stateless Polish-Jewish families ended up in Moravian Ostrava, just minutes away from the German and Polish borders.[102]

In late November 1938, Emil Hácha (1872–1945)[103] was elected president, while Rudolf Beran (1887–1954) formed a right-wing government. Slovakia was granted substantial autonomy, with the country now calling itself Czecho-Slovakia. While rejecting antisemitic policies, the government made a distinction between long-established Jews and recent Jewish immigrants, requiring the latter to leave the country. Nonetheless, pressure from the ethnic German groups domestically and the Nazi regime externally continued to mount.[104] A number of Czech newspapers began to publish antisemitic articles.[105] One Czech title in Brno, for example, claimed that half the students at the Agricultural University were Jews, supposedly 'arousing tremendous disquiet and outrage' among the non-Jewish students.[106]

The Jews themselves responded with great sensitivity. In a newspaper article published in early November, the president of the Jewish Community in Prague, Dr Emil Kafka, advised refugees from the Sudetenland to avoid speaking German in public and to refrain from spending too much time in cafés and restaurants in order not to irritate the Czechs.[107] Later, the Supreme Council of the Jewish Religious Communities sent a memorandum 'concerning the Jewish question' to the Czech government, addressing the refugee problem and how to guarantee Jews' civil rights and religious freedom, while rejecting any moves towards economic discrimination. Zionists, revisionists and the Czech Jews subsequently submitted their own petitions.[108]

Czech society faced a difficult social and political test, as hundreds of thousands of Czech and German refugees had to be accommodated and provided for. Hitler, conversely, had no interest in absorbing into Germany the remainder of what had been three million ethnic Germans in Czech territory. Their role was to help further destabilize the ČSR. Although the Czech government responded positively when other countries expressed concerns about its anti-Jewish policies, its own actions contradicted its official stance.[109]

In November 1938, the Czech authorities counted 68,212 displaced Czechs and Slovaks and 8,817 Germans, while the figures for December were 128,087 and 10,965.[110] During this period, all Jews had to leave the Sudetenland, some being given a deadline of five or thirty days, while others were instructed to leave by the end of January 1939.[111] In November, 4,765 Jews fled, and 6,234 in December. By religious affiliation, the Czechs counted as many as 12,392 and 15,186 Jewish refugees in these two months respectively; many of them identified as Czech nationals.[112] Contemporaries told of seventeen to twenty thousand Jews, most of them settling in Prague, Brno, Moravian Ostrava and Olomouc.[113] In smaller towns residents feared the refugees' arrival would trigger supply problems, leading to antisemitic tensions.[114]

In the Czech Republic, Jewish and leftist refugees from the Sudetenland were fearful in light of threats to send them back, which might mean detention or death. This prompted many to take their own lives.[115] Arnold Stein described the situation of his family in a journal meant for his child's later perusal:

> We had to flee from Karlsbad. We had to, though we did so of our own free will, despite being told by the good people on hundreds of occasions that nothing would happen to us ... We left my business [and] our flat there. We took mother's knitting machines with us. We have now been living here in Prague since the end of Sept. 38. First with Aunt Trude, then Serafine Novotna in Bélskeho and now, since 15 February, at 8 Nekazanka. Of our [sic] constant rushing and chasing around from office to office, every week new regulations requiring various documents, etc., a chaos in which no one knows what they're doing [and] when you've got it done the whole thing turns out to have been pointless. On top of that there's the running back and forth to the consulates.[116]

Arnold Stein's wife and child travelled on to England in March 1939.[117] More than half the refugees subsequently emigrated despite the many obstacles to doing so.[118]

The New Government's Anti-Jewish Measures

The many Jews fleeing from the Sudeten region into the ČSR contributed to growing antisemitism in the ČSR. On 22 December 1938, Czech

Education Minister Dr Jan Kapras ordered the indefinite suspension of Jewish professors at the German Charles University and the two German technical colleges in Brno and Prague. Whether thirty members of the academic staff or more would be affected by this measure was not immediately clear: it would depend on whether definitions similar to those found in the Nuremberg Race Laws were used or less strict rules. On the same day, the Czecho-Slovak Cabinet discussed the 'Jewish question'. Well-informed sources assumed that they debated anti-Jewish measures, including a *numerus clausus* in the education system, the imposing of restrictions on doctors and the purging of the civil service through early retirement. The government resolved to suspend all Jews teaching at German educational establishments, from primary schools (Volksschulen) to universities, from 1 January 1939.[119]

During the same period, the youth wing of the new Party of National Unity (Strana národní jednoty), founded by Beran, adopted a programme for the renewal of the Czechoslovak state. The Jews were not a part of the nation, it declared. Here the term 'Jew' included those with just one Jewish grandparent, even if they were fluent in a Slavic language; Jews were a 'minority of a different nationality' and their fate would be determined by a special law. They would be barred from the civil service and removed from the education system, with their participation in other fields being reorganized in accordance with their share of the population.[120]

In Prague, newspapers speculated that the Beran government was planning a 'solution to the Jewish question'. When he set out his government's plans, however, Rudolf Beran addressed the subject only in a very general way, apparently – as German newspapers suspected – due to pressure from London. Despite this, as reported in a Viennese newspaper, his government was preparing to 'register all Jews', forcing them to identify with the Jewish nation alone. A census to be held in the coming March was likely to serve as the basis for compiling such a 'register of Jews', which would make it possible to establish their share of the population. While Jews were to be removed entirely from the political sphere, civil service, education system and media, this report continued, a proportional system would be implemented in business, industry and finance. Citizenship for Jews and Jewish assets would be subject to strict scrutiny. Rather than the extreme definition demanded by the Party of National Unity's youth wing, however, the report claimed, that set out in the Nuremberg laws would apply.[121]

In early January 1939, the youth wing of the Party of National Unity held its first rally, with speakers expressing harsh criticism of the old Beneš government, while Radola Gajda, leader of the National Fascist

Community (Národní obec fašistická), founded in 1929, received a warm welcome. Although the press of the Czech nationalist youth movement had published articles declaring that the 'Jewish question must [be resolved] on a racial basis' and cries of 'Jews out' were heard at the rally on several occasions, the members of the youth wing did not in fact adopt an anti-Jewish programme.[122]

In early 1939, the *Pražsky Večer* (Evening Prague) newspaper, which was affiliated with the Party of National Unity, claimed that the government was poised to implement a systematic solution to the Jewish question and had decided to expel ten thousand Jews and other immigrants.[123] On 5 January, the *Deutsche Allgemeine Zeitung* in Berlin reported that a number of Czech ministers had been tasked with drawing up anti-Jewish ordinances.[124] Czech lawyers, meanwhile, as reported in another newspaper, had established an 'Aryan' club in Prague for legal professionals, which had attracted three hundred members. The Society of Moravian Lawyers barred Jews entirely, while its Bohemian counterpart decided not to do so.[125] The Prague Association of Czech Advocates expelled 127 Jewish members in late January, while the Všherd Lawyers' Club, a leading Czech student organization, sent a memorandum to the education minister demanding that he 'settle the Jewish question' in their profession in order to ensure better career prospects for young lawyers.[126]

Responding to letters of protest from Jewish and non-Jewish organizations abroad, the government approved a foreign currency package, drawing on the so-called Pound Loan to expedite the expulsion of the ten thousand refugees. According to the Czech newspaper *Express*, more than twenty doctors' and lawyers' associations presented a collective petition to the government demanding that Jews and half-Jews be permitted to practise medicine and law only in exceptional cases and that their participation in these fields must not exceed their share of the population. As the official newspaper of the NSDAP in Reichenberg (Liberec), *Die Zeit*, underlined, of 1,200 legal professionals in Prague more than six hundred were supposedly Jews, in Brno the figure was 110 of 235, in Moravian Ostrava 75 of 160 and in Olomouc 28 of 65; in total, Jews made up 35 per cent of lawyers in Bohemia and 46 per cent in Moravia. Jews' presence in the medical profession, the newspaper contended, was larger still: they accounted for more than 70 per cent of doctors working in the medical insurance system.[127]

The Czecho-Slovak Cabinet permitted every immigrant to acquire up to 120,000 crowns in foreign currency but at 25 per cent above the normal rate. It also established a committee 'to resolve the Jewish question' along with two subcommittees, the first comprising Agriculture Minister Dr Ladislav Feierabend, Finance Minister Josef Kalfus and

Trade Minister Dr Vlastimil Šadek, the second Interior Minister Dr Ottokar Fischer and Minister without Portfolio Dr Jiří Havelka.[128]

In mid January 1939, the Cabinet discussed a 'Jewish law'. According to press reports, this borrowed from the recently enacted 'Hungarian law' and radicalized it, featuring quotas in certain professional fields with varying deadlines.[129] A proposal put forward by the recently appointed Cabinet committee, which advocated a solution to the Jewish question on a 'racial basis', also envisaged a census centred on 'ancestry' to provide the foundation on which the government would then introduce restrictions.[130] At the same time, the general assembly of the Czechoslovak lawyer organizations was drawing up exclusionary provisions, which representatives of the Jewish Community threatened to challenge in the courts for preventing Jews from practising their professions.[131] These events demonstrate that the direct pressure applied by Hitler in a private conversation with Foreign Minister František Chvalkovský (1885–1945)[132] on 21 January 1939 was not the decisive factor in ensuring the implementation of anti-Jewish measures, as has often been claimed.[133] It was in fact discussions within the new Czech government that gave rise to these initiatives.

The government enacted two decrees on 27 January 1939. One created the basis for the expulsion of all those who had immigrated since 1914, including Czecho-Slovak nationals, while the other required checks to be carried out on citizenship granted since 1918. In addition, Jews were to be removed from the civil service, press and cultural life, while new regulations would restrict their activities within the independent professions and their influence in big business.[134]

On 9 February, the youth wing of the Party of National Unity organized antisemitic demonstrations in Prague. After gathering on Sophie Island (Slovanský Ostrov, Slawische Insel), the participants struck out from the banks of the Vltava chanting slogans such as 'Work for the workers, rope for the Jews!'. The police broke up the demonstration in front of the National Theatre. A number of demonstrators tried to continue their march to Wenceslas Square, where they encountered more police, who arrested many of them.[135]

Subsequently, on 25 February the Transport Ministry instructed national railway offices, post offices and savings banks in Prague and Brno to suspend 'employees of Jewish ancestry' unless they resigned voluntarily. A Jew, the ministry elaborated, was anyone whose parents had both practised the Jewish religion at any point in time.[136] The Interior Ministry had already issued a matching decree with reference to the public administration on 19 February.[137] The army suspended Jewish officers, while Jewish doctors were to leave their posts at public hospitals. Forty-five professors working in the German section of Charles University in Prague were pensioned off. German schools dismissed Jewish teachers while German newspapers sent home Jewish journalists. Education Minister Kapras issued an ultimatum to the University of Brno to terminate the lectures being given by professor of criminal law Jaroslav Stránský, because he was of Jewish origin. Henceforth the Association of Czech Physicians admitted 'Aryans' only.[138]

As a consequence of the above-mentioned expulsion, fourteen thousand Jews left the country, an involuntary move that saved some of their lives. Many others also sought to leave the country, besieging the Prague passport offices in ever greater numbers from November onwards. Sixty per cent of the seven hundred passports issued daily went to Jews and political emigrants, most of whom fled to South America, the United States and Scandinavia.[139]

* * *

The Czechoslovak Republic, born out of the consequences of the First World War, was considered less antisemitic than its neighbours. Most of its approximately 350,000 Jewish inhabitants, particularly in Bohemia and Moravia, were well integrated if not assimilated into society. Many had rich relationships with their Czech or German neighbours, spoke several languages and played an important role in the political and cultural life of the new state.

Nonetheless, nationalistic fervour led to antisemitic attacks as the new state came into being. Some regarded the Jews as an impediment to the emergence of the new Czechoslovak nation, because many of them were considered members of the German minority. In the 1930s, Czech nationalist and fascist groups as well as German National and National Socialist circles intensified their anti-Jewish propaganda. However, anti-Jewish incidents were the exception, with state founder Masaryk in particular consistently prosecuting those responsible until his resignation in 1935.

When a growing number of political and Jewish refugees arrived in the Czechoslovak Republic as a result of repression within the Nazi state, the annexation of Austria and the separatist movement in the Sudeten region, the government's attitude hardened, supposedly due to growing social tensions. Subsequently, after the loss of the Sudetenland in the wake of the Munich Diktat, a new authoritarian government took charge of the new state of Czecho-Slovakia. Led by Rudolf Beran, it introduced the first anti-Jewish measures, expelling Jews who had not lived in the territory before 1914 and dismissing Jews from the civil service. Czech professional associations also began to exclude those of

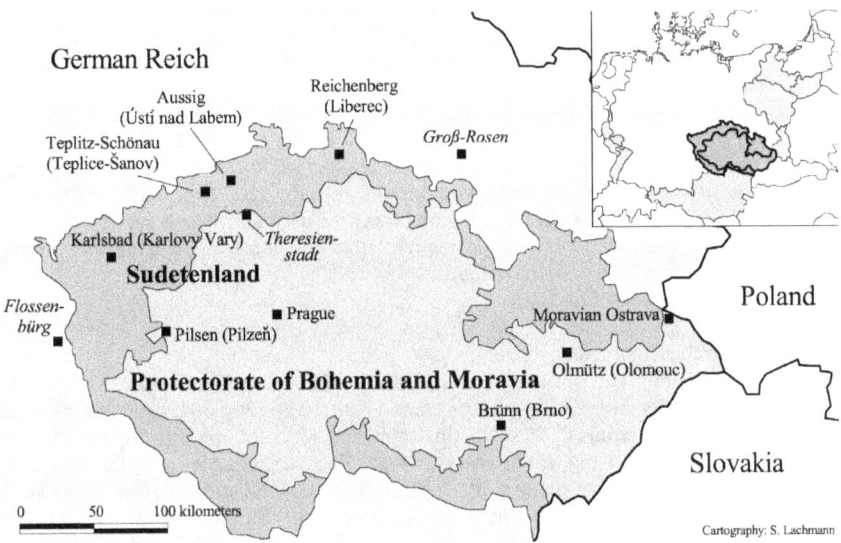

Figure 1.2. Map of the Protectorate of Bohemia and Moravia. Courtesy Sabine Lachmann.

Jewish faith. These anti-Jewish measures were independent developments influenced by radical Czech circles and had little to do with any direct pressure imposed by Hitler, who was already drawing up plans to forcefully annex the beleaguered state.

Notes

1. On the debates carried on by Czech but also German nationalists, see Peter Haslinger, *Nation und Territorium im tschechischen politischen Diskurs 1880–1938* (Munich, 2010).
2. Rothkirchen, *Jews*, 26–28; Jeremy King, *Budweisers into Czechs and Germans: A Local History of Bohemian Politics, 1848–1948* (Princeton, 2005), 159–63.
3. Jörg Osterloh, 'Religionsgemeinschaft oder Nation? Der Weg zur Anerkennung einer jüdischen Nationalität in den böhmischen Ländern', in Martin Schulze Wessel, Kristina Kaiserová and Eduard Nižňanský (eds), *Religion und Politik: Deutsche, Tschechen und Slowaken im 20. Jahrhundert* (Essen, 2015), 91–109; see also Kristina Kaiserová, Eduard Nižňanský and Martin Schulze Wessel (eds), *Religion und Nation: Tschechen, Deutsche und Slowaken im 20. Jahrhundert* (Essen, 2015); King, *Budweisers*, 159–63.
4. Rothkirchen, *Jews*, 29. See also Konrad Henlein, 'The German Minority in Czechoslovakia', *International Affairs* 15(4) (1936), 561–72, here 563.
5. Emanuel Čapek, 'Racial and Social Aspects of the Czechoslovak Census', *The Slavonic and East European Review* 12(36) (1934), 596–610, here 596 and 605.
6. Ibid., 606; see also *Das Protektorat Böhmen und Mähren im deutschen Wirtschaftsraum: Überreicht von der Deutschen Bank* (Berlin, 1939), 12.

7. Čapek, 'Racial and Social Aspects', 598. On Bohemia, see Nancy Wingfield, *Flag Wars and Stone Saints: How the Bohemian Lands Became Czech* (Cambridge, MA, 2007).
8. Robert William Seton-Watson, 'The German Minority in Czechoslovakia', *Foreign Affairs* 16(4) (1938), 651–66, here 655–57; Emil Sobota, 'Czechs and Germans: A Czech View', *The Slavonic Review* 14(41) (1936), 301–20, here 304. See also King, *Budweisers*, 154–57. German-Austria was initially the term for the German-speaking areas of Austria-Hungary, and was then used for the new republic in 1918. Following the Treaty of Saint-Germain in 1919, the name, and the idea of unifying with Germany, had to be abandoned.
9. Bryant, *Prague in Black*, 21.
10. Ibid., 20.
11. Rothkirchen, *Jews*, 31.
12. Seton-Watson, 'The German Minority', 654–57; Elizabeth Wiskemann, 'Czechs and Germans after Munich', *Foreign Affairs* 17(2) (1939), 291–304, here 297; Sobota, 'Czechs and Germans', 304. On this topic and what follows, see Bryant, *Prague in Black*, 18–20; King, *Budweisers*, 154–57; Rothkirchen, *Jews*, 31; for a detailed account, see Jaroslav Kučera, *Minderheit im Nationalstaat: Die Sprachenfrage in den tschechisch-deutschen Beziehungen 1918–1938* (Munich, 1999); or Michaela Marek, Dusan Kovác, Jirí Pesek et al. (eds), *Kultur als Vehikel und als Opponent politischer Absichten: Kulturkontakte zwischen Deutschen, Tschechen und Slowaken von der Mitte des 19. Jahrhunderts bis in die 1980er Jahre* (Essen, 2010).
13. Henlein, 'The German Minority', 563.
14. See Michal Frankl, *'Prag ist nunmehr antisemitisch': Tschechischer Antisemitismus am Ende des 19. Jahrhunderts* (Berlin, 2011); Helena Krejčová and Alena Mišková, 'Anmerkungen zur Frage des Antisemitismus in den Böhmischen Ländern Ende des 19. Jahrhunderts', in Jörg K. Hoensch et al. (eds), *Judenemanzipation – Antisemitismus – Verfolgung in Deutschland, Österreich-Ungarn, den Böhmischen Ländern und in der Slowakei* (Essen, 1999), 55–62; also Helena Krejčová and Alena Mišková, 'Die antijüdischen bzw. antideutschen Kundgebungen und Demonstrationen in Böhmen und Mähren (1899)', in ibid., 63–84. See also the special issue of *Judaica Bohemiae* 46(2) (2011), which is dedicated to the antisemitic essays published by prominent writer Jan Neruda (1834–91) in a major daily newspaper and their historical context, and several essays in Michael Brenner, Andreas Gotzmann and Yfaat Weiss (eds), 'Germans – Jews – Czechs: The Case of the Czech Lands', special issue, *Bohemia* 46(1) (2005).
15. For an in-depth account, see Ines Koeltzsch, 'Antijüdische Straßengewalt und die semantische Konstruktion des "Anderen" im Prag der Ersten Republik', *Judaica Bohemiae* 46(1) (2011), 73–99.
16. Martin Zückert, *Zwischen Nationsidee und staatlicher Realität: Die tschechoslowakische Armee und ihre Nationalitätenpolitik 1918–1938* (Munich, 2006), 104–5.
17. Jörg Osterloh, '"… gegen den jüdischen Rektor Steinherz": Antisemitische Proteste an der Deutschen Universität in Prag 1922/23', in Pavel Kocman, Milan Řepa and Helmut Teufel (eds), *'Avigdor, Beneš, Gitl' – Juden in Böhmen, Mähren und Schlesien im Mittelalter: Samuel Steinherz zum Gedenken (1857 Güssing–1942 Theresienstadt)* (Essen, 2016), 415–26.
18. USC Shoah Foundation/Visual History Archive (USC SF/VHA), video interview, Anny Maass, tape 1, min. 18:00–18:15.
19. Rothkirchen, *Jews*, 27, 45–46; Heidrich Bodensieck, 'Das Dritte Reich und die Lage der Juden in der Tschecho-Slowakei nach München', *Vierteljahrshefte für Zeitgeschichte* 9(3) (1961), 249–61, here 249.

20. USC SF/VHA, video interview, Katherine Kral, tape 2, min. 6:15–10:00.
21. Martin Schulze Wessel, 'Czech Anti-Semitism in the Context of Tensions between National and Confessional Programs, and the Foundation of the Czechoslovak National Church', *Bohemia* 46(1) (2005), 102–7. On Masaryk's political views and ideas, see Eva Schmidt-Hartmann, *Thomas G. Masaryk's Realism: Origins of a Czech Political Concept 1882–1914* (Munich, 1984); Valentina von Tulechov, *Tomas Garrigue Masaryk: Sein kritischer Realismus in Auswirkung auf sein Demokratie- und Europaverständnis* (Göttingen, 2011). For a recent critique of the democratic myth embodied by Masaryk and the associated rejection of antisemitism, see Orzoff, *Battle for the Castle*.
22. *Čechoslovakische Statistik*, vol. 9, series VI (Census 1), part I: Census in the Czechoslovak Republic of 15 February 1921 (Prague, 1924), 86–97. For an in-depth examination of the problem of individuals' self-perception and on what follows, see Čapková, *Czechs, Germans, Jews?*
23. Kateřina Čapková, 'Czechs, Germans, Jews – Where Is the Difference? The Complexity of National Identities of Bohemian Jews, 1918–1938', *Bohemia* 46(1) (2005), 7–14, here 10–11; Čapková, *Czechs, Germans, Jews?*, 14–25. On the Jews in Bohemia, see Hillel J. Kieval, *The Making of Czech Jewry: National Conflict and Jewish Society in Bohemia, 1870–1918* (New York, 1988). On Prague, see Koeltzsch, *Geteilte Kulturen*.
24. Dimitry Shumsky, 'Introducing Intellectual and Political History to the History of Everyday Life: Multiethnic Cohabitation and Jewish Experience in Fin-de-Siecle Bohemia', *Bohemia* 46(1) (2005), 39–67.
25. Scott Spector, 'Mittel-Europa? Some Afterthoughts on Prague Jews, "Hybridity", and Translation', *Bohemia* 46(1) (2005), 28–37, here 30.
26. Čapková, 'Czechs, Germans, Jews – Where Is the Difference?', 10–11.
27. On the army, see Zückert, *Zwischen Nationsidee und staatlicher Realität*.
28. USC SF/VHA, video interview, Alfred Dube, tape 1, min. 10:09–14:05.
29. She later escaped on the last ship to Shanghai. USC SF/VHA, video interview, Hilda Beran, tape 1, min. 15:27–20:00; tape 2, min. 1:00–9:50; tape 3, min. 9:17.
30. USC SF/VHA, video interview, Zuzana Podmelova, tape 1, seg. 3.
31. On the Zionists, see the recent work by Tatjana Lichtenstein, *Zionists in Interwar Czechoslovakia: Minority Nationalism and the Politics of Belonging* (Bloomington, IN, 2016). See also Čapková, *Czechs, Germans, Jews?*, 169–240.
32. Čapková, 'Czechs, Germans, Jews – Where Is the Difference?', 10–11.
33. USC SF/VHA, video interview, Alfred Dube, tape 1, min. 10:09–14:05.
34. USC SF/VHA, video interview, Anny Maass, tape 1, min. 5:18–8:41, 15:44–16:53.
35. USC SF/VHA, video interview, Anna Grant, tape 1, min. 7:31–9:45.
36. USC SF/VHA, video interview, Katherine Kral, tape 1, min. 11:01.
37. USC SF/VHA, video interview, Curt Allina, tape 2, seg. 52.
38. USC SF/VHA, video interview, Georgine Hyde, tape 1, min. 4:00–15:17.
39. USC SF/VHA, video interview, Helen Blenkins, tape 1, min. 4:39–6:05.
40. Čapek, 'Racial and Social Aspects', 603; Rothkirchen, *Jews*, 29; Jörg Osterloh, *Nationalsozialistische Judenverfolgung im Reichsgau Sudetenland 1938–1945* (Munich, 2006), 48.
41. Rothkirchen, *Jews*, 30.
42. Ibid., 34–35.
43. Moskowitz, 'The Jewish Situation', 32.
44. *Čechoslovakische Statistik*, vol. 98, series VI (Census 7), part I: Census in the Czechoslovak Republic of 1 December 1930 (Prague, 1934), 82–99. See Rothkirchen, *Jews*, 34–36.

45. Moskowitz, 'The Jewish Situation', 31–35.
46. Rothkirchen, *Jews*, 32–39.
47. USC SF/VHA, video interview, Alfred Dube, tape 1, min. 10:09–14:05.
48. Rothkirchen, *Jews*, 38–39; Beneš and Ginsburg, *10 Million Prisoners*, 134.
49. On the Zionists from 1918 onwards, see Tatjana Lichtenstein, '"Making" Jews at Home: Zionism and the Construction of Jewish Nationality in Inter-War Czechoslovakia', *East European Jewish Affairs* 36(1) (2006), 49–71; Tatjana Lichtenstein, 'Racializing Jewishness: Zionist Responses to National Indifference in Interwar Czechoslovakia', *Austrian History Yearbook* 43 (April 2012), 75–97; Lichtenstein, *Zionists in Interwar Czechoslovakia*; Martin J. Wein, 'Zionism in Interwar Czechoslovakia: Palestino-Centrism and Landespolitik', *Judaica Bohemiae* 44(1) (April 2009), 5–47.
50. For a general account, see Čapková, *Czechs, Germans, Jews?* Cf. Rothkirchen, *Jews*, 32–35.
51. Later, in 1935, it cooperated with the Social Democratic Party. Because the latter promised only seats but no coalition, some of the party's leaders were vehemently opposed to cooperation, such as party chairman Dr Emil Margulies, who was outvoted and stood down. On the Jewish Party, see Čapková, *Czechs, Germans, Jews?*, 221–25; Rothkirchen, *Jews*, 31–32; Wein, 'Zionism in Interwar Czechoslovakia', 30–32.
52. Čapková, 'Czechs, Germans, Jews – Where Is the Difference?', 14.
53. Rothkirchen, *Jews*, 30.
54. Bryant, *Prague in Black*, 22–25; Henlein, 'The German Minority', 564. For a more detailed account, see Jörg Osterloh, *Nationalsozialistische Judenverfolgung*, 66–77.
55. Seton-Watson, 'The German Minority', 659–60; Sobota, 'Czechs and Germans', 308.
56. Bryant, *Prague in Black*, 22.
57. Konrad Henlein, teacher, founded the Sudeten German Home Front (Sudetendeutsche Heimatfront) in 1933, joined the SS in 1938, was Reich commissioner (Reichskommissar) for the Sudeten German territories in 1938–39, Gauleiter from 1938, Reich governor (Reichsstatthalter) of the Sudetenland from 1939, joined the NSDAP, was appointed chief of civil administration (Chef der Zivilverwaltung or CdZ) of Bohemia in 1939, Reich defence commissioner (Reichsverteidigungskommissar) for the Sudetenland from 1942 to 1945, SS senior group leader (Obergruppenführer) in 1943, and took his own life in an American internment camp; see VEJ/3, 569.
58. Henlein, 'The German Minority', 564. On the situation and politics of the Sudeten Germans, see Volker Zimmermann, *Die Sudetendeutschen im NS-Staat: Politik und Stimmung der Bevölkerung im Reichsgau Sudetenland (1938–1945)* (Essen, 1999); Ralf Gebel, *'Heim ins Reich!': Konrad Henlein und der Reichsgau Sudetenland (1938–1945)* (Munich, 1999); Christoph Boyer, *Nationale Kontrahenten oder Partner? Studien zu den Beziehungen zwischen Tschechen und Deutschen in der Wirtschaft der ČSR (1918–1938)* (Munich, 1999); Kučera, *Minderheit im Nationalstaat*.
59. See the documents in Boris Celovsky, *Germanisierung und Genozid: Hitlers Endlösung der tschechischen Frage. Deutsche Dokumente 1933–1945* (Dresden, 2005), 62–63; Seton-Watson, 'The German Minority', 660–61; Osterloh, *Nationalsozialistische Judenverfolgung*, 80–89.
60. For a detailed account, see Birgit Vierling, *Kommunikation als Mittel politischer Mobilisierung: Die Sudetendeutsche Partei (SdP) auf ihrem Weg zur Einheitsbewegung in der Ersten Tschechoslowakischen Republik (1933–1938)* (Marburg, 2014).

61. Seton-Watson, 'The German Minority', 661–64; Sobota, 'Czechs and Germans', 314–17. On this and what follows: Caitlin E. Murdock, *Changing Places: Society, Culture, and Territory in the Saxon-Bohemian Borderlands, 1870–1946* (Ann Arbor, 2010), 181–99; Bryant, *Prague in Black*, 23–25; Osterloh, *Nationalsozialistische Judenverfolgung*, 89–100. On the views of German diplomats, see the following sources: Manfred Alexander, *Deutsche Gesandtschaftsberichte aus Prag: Innenpolitik und Minderheitenprobleme in der Ersten Tschechoslowakischen Republik. Teil III: Von der Regierung unter Svehla bis zum Vorabend der nationalsozialistischen Machtergreifung in Deutschland 1926–1932* (Munich, 2009); Heidrun Dolezel and Stephan Dolezel (eds), *Vom Vorabend der Machtergreifung in Deutschland bis zum Rücktritt von Präsident Masaryk 1933–1935: Berichte des Gesandten Koch, der Konsuln von Bethusy-Huc, von Druffel, von Pfeil und des Gesandtschaftsrates von Stein. Deutsche Gesandtschaftsberichte aus Prag*, Part 4 (Munich, 1991). On German and Sudeten German politics, see also the documents in Celovsky, *Germanisierung und Genozid*, 55–128.
62. Landesarchiv Berlin, A Rep. 355, no. 5140 Löw, Arthur (29 March 1901): Transcript of verdict reached by Special Court II, 14 May 1942.
63. Osterloh, *Nationalsozialistische Judenverfolgung*, 136–84. See also Seton-Watson, 'The German Minority', 661–65; Sobota, 'Czechs and Germans', 314–17; Bryant, *Prague in Black*, 23–25.
64. Rothkirchen, *Jews*, 50–51.
65. Osterloh, *Nationalsozialistische Judenverfolgung*, 100–108.
66. USC SF/VHA, video interview, Fred Klein, tape 1, min. 10:00–12:00.
67. USC SF/VHA, video interview, Mimi Berger, tape 1, min. 6:30–7:10.
68. Rothkirchen, *Jews*, 49–50, 56–59.
69. USC SF/VHA, video interview, Alfred Dube, tape 2, min. 00:37. For similar views, see USC SF/VHA, video interview, Georgine Hyde, tape 1, min. 19:42–20:40; video interview, Gertrude Pfeiffer, tape 1, min. 20:00–21:00.
70. Yad Vashem (YV) Jerusalem, M 58/JM 11813, fol. 347: Circular Dr. Popper (Jewish community of Loštice), 23 March 1933.
71. Kateřina Čapková and Michal Frankl, *Unsichere Zuflucht: Die Tschechoslowakei und ihre Flüchtlinge aus NS-Deutschland 1933–1938* (Vienna, 2013) (Czech original 2008), 105–13.
72. Bryant, *Prague in Black*, 23–25; Rothkirchen, *Jews*, 46–77.
73. On this and what follows, see Čapková and Frankl, *Unsichere Zuflucht*; Michal Frankl, 'Prejudiced Asylum: Czechoslovak Refugee Policy, 1918–60', *Journal of Contemporary History* 49(3) (2014), 477–90.
74. Rothkirchen, *Jews*, 53–54 and 73–77.
75. YV Jerusalem, M 58/JM 11816, fol. 231–32: Herman Tafel-Traubner, Krakau, to Jewish Religious Community of Moravian Ostrava, 20 February 1938; ibid., fol. 240–42: Herman Tafel-Traubner, Krakau, to Jewish Religious Community of Moravian Ostrava, 28 April 1939.
76. Georg Hartmann, 'Die Judenfrage in der Tschechoslowakei', *Volk und Reich: Politische Monatshefte*, edited by Friedrich Heiß, 14(3) (1938), 180–98, here 198.
77. See various articles in *Volk und Reich* 14 (1938), issues 5–6 and 9–11.
78. George E.R. Gedye, *Fallen Bastions: The Central European Tragedy*, 7th ed. (London, 1940), 371–73.
79. Seton-Watson, 'The German Minority', 666. On the year 1938 and the situation and politics of the Sudeten Germans, see Detlef Brandes, *Die Sudetendeutschen im Krisenjahr 1938* (Munich, 2008); Osterloh, *Nationalsozialistische Judenverfolgung*, 136–84.

80. Max Hildebert Boehm in *Volkstheorie und Volkstumspolitik der Gegenwart* (1935), quoted in Sobota, 'Czechs and Germans', 312.
81. Sobota, 'Czechs and Germans', 312; Wiskemann, 'Czechs and Germans after Munich', 303 f.
82. Osterloh, *Nationalsozialistische Judenverfolgung*, 136–65; Rothkirchen, *Jews*, 60–61; Murdock, *Changing Places*, 199–201.
83. RGVA Moscow, 500-1-967zII, no. 79, fol. 362: SD Main Office, Office III, status report 'Jewry', 6 August 1938.
84. Ibid.
85. On the relevant passages in Hitler's speech, see Max Domarus (ed.), *Hitler: Reden und Proklamationen 1932–1945*. Vol. I, 2nd half-volume 1935–1938 (Munich, 1965), 900–906. On the speech and the ensuing riots in the Sudetenland, see Osterloh, *Nationalsozialistische Judenverfolgung*, 168–76.
86. RGVA Moscow, 500-1-967zII, no. 79, fol. 56–58: Report by SD Main Office, Office III, 28 September 1938 along with travel report by colleague SS Senior Leader (Oberführer) Tittmann and enclosure I, 'Effects of the shift of ethnic group leadership to the Reich within the Sudeten German community'.
87. 'Standrecht in 16 Bezirken', *Egerer Zeitung*, 17 September 1938, 5.
88. 'Jews Flee from Sudetenland', *The Jewish Chronicle*, 7 October 1938, 12; for a German translation, see VEJ/2, doc. 102, 301–2.
89. 'Jews Leave Sudetenland: Mass Exodus Follows Riots', *The Jewish Chronicle*, 23 September 1938, 22.
90. For an account of the historical background from the perspective of a critical British journalist, see Gedye, *Fallen Bastions*, 381–508. Hitler had been preparing for war with Czechoslovakia since November 1937; see Memorandum on the meeting of 5 November 1937, in Celovsky, *Germanisierung und Genozid*, 120–23.
91. See Jürgen Zarusky and Martin Zückert (eds), *Das Münchener Abkommen von 1938 in europäischer Perspektive* (Munich, 2013).
92. For a detailed account, see Osterloh, *Nationalsozialistische Judenverfolgung*, 185–232.
93. 'Jews Flee from Sudetenland', *The Jewish Chronicle*, 7 October 1938, 12; for a German translation, see VEJ/2, doc. 102, 301–2.
94. Otto Dov Kulka and Eberhard Jäckel (eds), *The Jews in the Secret Nazi Reports on Popular Opinion in Germany, 1933–1945* (New Haven, CT, 2010) (German original 2004), CD doc. no. 2775: SD Higher Section (Oberabschnitt) South-East II 112, Report for 1938 'Jewry', Breslau, 21 January 1939.
95. RGVA Moscow, 500-1-967zII, no. 79, fol. 113–14: SD Main Office, Office III, to RFSS, 8 October 1938, plus ČSR Status Report no. 43.
96. For a detailed account of the pogroms, see Osterloh, *Nationalsozialistische Judenverfolgung*, 203–32.
97. Bodensieck, 'Das Dritte Reich', 249–50. A telegram sent by the American League in Prague on 23 November 1938 reported 91,632 registered refugees, including 6,700 Jews; Rothkirchen, *Jews*, 78. On this and what follows, see Bryant, *Prague in Black*, 25–26.
98. *Marienbader Zeitung*, 16 November 1938, 1, printed in VEJ/2, doc. 158, 462–63. On Asch, see *Leitmeritzer Zeitung*, 23 November 1938, 16.
99. Bodensieck, 'Das Dritte Reich', 255–57.
100. *CV-Zeitung* 42, 20 October 1938.
101. Bodensieck, 'Das Dritte Reich', 252–53; Rothkirchen, *Jews*, 75–83; Bryant, *Prague in Black*, 25. Of the loan granted in January 1939, £4 million was to be used for refugees; there were also donations from various British organizations, some of which

were collected immediately after the occupation of the Sudetenland; Peter Heumos, 'Flüchtlingslager, Hilfsorganisationen, Juden im Niemandsland: Zur Flüchtlings- und Emigrationsproblematik in der Tschechoslowakei im Herbst 1938', *Bohemia* 25(2) (1984), 245–75, here 254.

102. Report Marie Schmolka (HICEM), 27 November 1938, in Heumos, 'Flüchtlingslager', 272. See also Rothkirchen, *Jews*, 69.
103. Dr Emil Hácha, jurist, translator, president of the Czecho-Slovak Republic from 1938 to 1939, president of the Protectorate of Bohemia and Moravia from 1939 to 1945. Arrested on 13 May 1945, he died shortly afterwards in a prison hospital in Prague; see VEJ/3, 567.
104. Beneš and Ginsburg, *10 Million Prisoners*, 14; Bodensieck, 'Das Dritte Reich', 255–61; Rothkirchen, *Jews*, 75–90; Bryant, *Prague in Black*, 25.
105. Beneš and Ginsburg, *10 Million Prisoners*, 14–15.
106. Deutsches Nachrichtenbüro (German news service), 13 December 1938, 1, http://www.theeuropeanlibrary.org/tel4/newspapers (accessed 29 June 2015).
107. Rothkirchen, *Jews*, 83.
108. Ibid., 87.
109. Ibid., 88–89.
110. Heumos, 'Flüchtlingslager', 246–52; Rothkirchen, *Jews*, 80 f. For a general account of flight and forced migration from the annexed territories, see Jan Benda, 'Okupace pohraničí a nucená imigrace v letech 1938–1939', *Český Časopis Historický* 110(2) (2012), 329–47.
111. Letter from Walter Schwartz (WJC) to Paris, 18 December 1938, printed in English translation in Garbarini et al., *Jewish Responses*, vol. II, 92.
112. Heumos, 'Flüchtlingslager', 246–52; Rothkirchen, *Jews*, 80 f.
113. Arieh Tartakower and Kurt R. Grossmann, *The Jewish Refugee* (New York, 1944), 37. According to a report by the Joint of 28 November 1938 there were seventeen thousand; Rothkirchen, *Jews*, 78.
114. Rothkirchen, *Jews*, 78.
115. Heumos, 'Flüchtlingslager', 251.
116. Leo Baeck Institute Archives, New York, ME 1536: Baby's diary, 1927–1939, entry 18 February 1939, http://www.lbi.org/digibaeck/results/?term=Arnold+Stein&qtype=basic&stype=contains&paging=25&dtype=any (accessed 3 March 2019). Entry reprinted in English in Garbarini et al., *Jewish Responses*, 53–54.
117. LBI/A New York, ME 1536: Baby's diary, 1927–1939, entry 14 March 1939, http://www.lbi.org/digibaeck/results/?term=Arnold+Stein&qtype=basic&stype=contains&paging=25&dtype=any (accessed 3 March 2019).
118. Heumos, 'Flüchtlingslager', 252; Rothkirchen, *Jews*, 80–81.
119. YV Jerusalem, O 7/15, n.p.: *The Times*, London, 23 December 1938 (Zeitungs-Ausschnitt-Büro Metropol-Gesellschaft); ibid.: *Breslauer Neueste Nachrichten*, 23 December 1938; Sächsisches Hauptstaatsarchiv Dresden, News Office of the State Chancellery-News Clippings Collection, Czechoslovakia, 1 November 1938–14 August 1939, n.p.: *Der Freiheitskampf*, 25 December 1938.
120. YV Jerusalem, O 7/15, n.p.: *Hamburger Fremdenblatt*, 24 December 1938 (Zeitungs-Ausschnitt-Büro Metropol-Gesellschaft).
121. A person was declared a Jew if he or she had three Jewish grandparents; YV Jerusalem, O 7/15, n.p.: *Neues Wiener Tagblatt*, 29 December 1938 (Zeitungs-Ausschnitt-Büro Metropol-Gesellschaft); ibid.: *Schlesische Tageszeitung*, 29 December 1938.
122. YV Jerusalem, O 7/15, n.p.: *Hannoverscher Kurier*, 4 January 1939 (Zeitungs-Ausschnitt-Büro Metropol-Gesellschaft); ibid.: *Vogtländischer Anzeiger*, Plauen, 4 January 1939.

123. YV Jerusalem, O 7/15, n.p.: *Breslauer Neueste Nachrichten*, 5 January 1939 (Zeitungs-Ausschnitt-Büro Metropol-Gesellschaft).
124. YV Jerusalem, O 7/15, n.p.: *Deutsche Allgemeine Zeitung*, 6 January 1939 (Zeitungs-Ausschnitt-Büro Metropol-Gesellschaft).
125. YV Jerusalem, O 7/15, n.p.: *Wiener Neueste Nachrichten*, 5 January 1939 (Zeitungs-Ausschnitt-Büro Metropol-Gesellschaft); ibid.: *Deutsche Allgemeine Zeitung*, 6 January 1939.
126. *Brünner Tagesbote*, 29 January 1939, 7.
127. YV Jerusalem, O 7/15, n.p.: *Die Zeit*, Reichenberg, 11 January 1939 (Zeitungs-Ausschnitt-Büro Metropol-Gesellschaft).
128. YV Jerusalem, O 7/15, n.p.: *Friedländer Zeitung*, 14 January 1939 (Zeitungs-Ausschnitt-Büro Metropol-Gesellschaft).
129. YV Jerusalem, O 7/15, n.p.: *Neue Freie Presse*, Vienna, 13 January 1939 (Zeitungs-Ausschnitt-Büro Metropol-Gesellschaft).
130. YV Jerusalem, O 7/15, n.p.: *Wiener Neueste Nachrichten*, 13 January 1939 (Zeitungs-Ausschnitt-Büro Metropol-Gesellschaft).
131. YV Jerusalem, O 7/15, n.p.: *Deutsche Allgemeine Zeitung*, Berlin, 28 January 1939 (Zeitungs-Ausschnitt-Büro Metropol-Gesellschaft).
132. František Chvalkovský, jurist, Czecho-Slovak foreign minister 1938–39, envoy of the Protectorate of Bohemia and Moravia in Berlin 1939–45, died during an aerial attack on Berlin; VEJ/3, 581.
133. As expressed, for example, in Rothkirchen, *Jews*, 91; for similar views, see also VEJ/3, 582, fn 5.
134. YV Jerusalem, O 7/15, n.p.: *Berliner Börsenzeitung*, 28 January 1939 (Zeitungs-Ausschnitt-Büro Metropol-Gesellschaft); ibid.: *Neues Wiener Tagblatt*, 29 January 1939; ibid.: *Wiener Neueste Nachrichten*, 2 February 1939.
135. YV Jerusalem, O 7/15, n.p.: *Wiener Neueste Nachrichten*, 9 February 1939 (Zeitungs-Ausschnitt-Büro Metropol-Gesellschaft); ibid.: *Nordische Rundschau*, Kiel, 9 February 1939.
136. United States Holocaust Memorial Museum/Archives (USHMM) Washington, RG 45.005M, reel 1 (Prague State Archive, Transport Ministry), no. 31, n.p.: copy of Transport Minister Peška's ordinance of 25 February 1939, 1–4.
137. USHMM Washington, RG 45.005M, reel 1 (Prague State Archive, Interior Ministry), no. 1, n.p.: List of the legal regulations issued by the Interior Ministry relating to Jews or Jewish half-breeds (Mischlinge), 25 September 1940, 1.
138. Beneš and Ginsburg, *10 Million Prisoners*, 15; Bodensieck, 'Das Dritte Reich', 257–61; Rothkirchen, *Jews*, 91–93; Bryant, *Prague in Black*, 25. On discrimination against Jews and Roma and growing chauvinism during this period, see also Mary Heimann, *Czechoslovakia: The State That Failed* (New Haven, CT, 2011), 100 f.
139. YV Jerusalem, O 7/15, n.p.: Pester Lloyd, Budapest, 4 January 1939 (Zeitungs-Ausschnitt-Büro Metropol-Gesellschaft); Beneš and Ginsburg, *10 Million Prisoners*, 15; Bodensieck, 'Das Dritte Reich', 257–61; Rothkirchen, *Jews*, 91–93; Bryant, *Prague in Black*, 25.

CHAPTER 2

ANNEXATION: VIOLENCE, FLIGHT
AND EMIGRATION BAN

The Occupation of 'Rump Czechoslovakia'

The Wehrmacht had been planning the occupation of Czechoslovakia since autumn 1937. On 21 October 1938, shortly after the annexation of the Sudeten region, Hitler gave the German armed forces specific instructions to ready themselves to 'deal with rump Czechoslovakia' by force of arms.[1] The Nazi leadership expected the planned annexation to trigger military resistance and war.

On 1 March 1939, the Reich Ministry of the Interior thus discussed with the Wehrmacht, Security Police, Order Police and the head of the Concentration Camps Inspectorate (Chef der Inspektion der Konzentrationslager) the possibility of 'Jewish service in case of war'. All Jewish men between eighteen and fifty-five years of age would be liable for this 'service', which the ministry envisaged as a form of forced labour. This demographic group was estimated to number around two hundred thousand of a total of six hundred thousand Jews in the German Reich and the territories slated for annexation. These Jews would be deployed 'in the manner of work gangs, separated from workers of German blood' to help build roads and work in quarries. The meeting participants intended to intern these Jewish forced labourers 'in special camps', though it was yet to be decided whether the Wehrmacht, the Concentration Camps Inspectorate or the Labour Administration (Arbeitsverwaltung) ought to finance, establish and maintain the camps. Presumably, the Security Police would play the lead role in forcing Jews to work.[2] However, Berlin shelved these plans for Jewish wartime labour in the Greater German Reich for the time being because Germany managed to occupy the territory of Czecho-Slovakia unchallenged.

On 15 March 1939, the short life of the second Czecho-Slovak Republic came to an end. The Slovak part of the country had already split off the previous day and declared its independence under German protection.[3] Hitler had summoned president Hácha, who was suffering from serious heart problems, and his foreign minister Chvalkovský to Berlin (see Figure 2.1); here, at around two in the morning, under extreme psychological pressure, they acceded to a German ultimatum and agreed to allow the occupation to go ahead unopposed.[4] Just a few hours later the German army marched into what was left of the territory of the Czecho-Slovak Republic. The Wehrmacht had already occupied Moravian Ostrava and Frýdek-Místek (Friedeck) the evening before, the order to invade having been issued on 14 March at 10 p.m.[5]

It was a grey and foggy morning, with snow flurrying along Prague's frozen streets. The first German troops moved in around nine in the

Figure 2.1. Hitler and Hácha, 14–15 March 1939. © Bundesarchiv Berlin, B 145 Bild-F051623-0206.

morning, as tanks, artillery and field kitchens rumbled across the bridges over the Vltava. In the centre of the rapidly occupied capital, at the corner of Na příkopě (the Graben) and Wenceslas Square, a surging mass of people soon congregated, scarcely held in check by chains of police. Among the crowd was sixteen-year-old Curt Allina. He saw people in tears and as a Jew he suddenly felt like a caged animal, with no prospect of escape.[6]

On the mood among the Czechs, Camill Hoffmann (1878–1944), a former Czech diplomat, noted:

> Loud, lengthy bouts of mass whistling, then Kde domov můj[7] again, fists in the air. If this goes on, I tell myself, blood is going to be spilt. The tension is tremendous, the mood gloomy. Otherwise, the crowd is astonishingly disciplined. One person is said to have died. ... Many suicides among Jews, many arrests. ... In the evening, the surprising news spreads that Hitler arrived at Prague Castle at 7.40pm. The Führer's standard above the Hradschin.[8]

Hitler immediately stamped his authority on occupied Prague. Following his journey by train and state carriage, he was welcomed at Prague Castle, the swastika flag now flying above it, by Heinrich Himmler, Kurt Daluege and Joachim von Ribbentrop, all of whom had arrived before him, along with Prague National Socialists. He spent the night at the Hradschin. Reich Minister of the Interior Wilhelm Frick and his State Secretary Wilhelm Stuckart arrived in occupied Prague by plane the next day.[9]

On 16 March 1938, Hitler issued a Führer's decree declaring that 'the Bohemian-Moravian lands' had been part of the 'living space [Lebensraum] of the German people' for one thousand years. He had to delve deep into the historical past in an attempt to construct a claim to a territory in which – in what was by then a considerable list of annexations – for the first time no German majority existed.[10] In light of his 'sincere desire to serve the true interests of the peoples living in this Lebensraum, to safeguard the national way of life of the German and Czech people, to advance peace and the social welfare of all', Hitler explained, from now on this territory would form part of the Greater German Reich, enjoying its protection as the 'Protectorate of Bohemia and Moravia'.[11] He left Prague the same evening, spending the night on a special train en route, via Olomouc, to Brno. There, as in Prague, he was welcomed by rapturous crowds of Germans, as well as Joseph Bürckel, Reich commissioner for the reunification of Austria with the Reich (Reichskommissar für die Wiedervereinigung Österreichs mit dem Reich) and Gauleiter of Vienna, who had arrived earlier, and Reich Governor (Reichsstatthalter) Arthur Seyß-Inquart.

Hitler's long-term plan was to fully Germanize the Bohemian-Moravian region by settling it with German farmers.[12] As he had openly declared before Nazi Party functionaries as early as 1932, the Czechs were to be relocated to Siberia or elsewhere in Russia.[13] With tremendous symbolism, after the occupation of Prague Hitler ordered the Golden Bull issued by Charles IV, Holy Roman emperor, composed in 1356, to be removed from a Czech regional archive and taken to Nuremberg, site of the Reich party congresses.[14]

Thus, the primary objective was to strengthen Germanity (Deutschtum). Through the Führer's decree of 16 March 1939, German residents of the Protectorate automatically received German citizenship and were subject solely to German laws. 'The provisions on the protection of German blood and German honour thus apply to them as well.' As subjects of the Protectorate, Czechs and Jews, even those of German origin, were now second-class citizens with fewer rights.[15] The Germans in the Protectorate, conversely – much as in the case of the reintegration of the Saarland and incorporation of the Sudetenland – were granted representation in the Greater German Reichstag.[16] At the suggestion of Reich Minister and Nazi Party Parliamentary Leader Frick, on 25 April Ernst Kundt, Prag-Podol, Dr Rudolf Meckel, Gau student leader (Gaustudentenführer), Prag 2, Dr Raimund Siegel, acting Nazi Party county leader (Kreisleiter) in Jihlava (Iglau), Ing. Karl Foltar, party county leader in Brno, and Hans Westen, manufacturer and acting party county leader in České Budějovice (Budweis), were appointed 'as representatives of the ethnic Germans in the Protectorate of Bohemia and Moravia' on the basis of § 2 of the law on the 'representation of the German national comrades [Volksgenossen] resident in the Protectorate of Bohemia and Moravia'.[17]

Over the short term, however, Germanization could not be an option, as Hitler was still pursuing a cautious foreign policy course.[18] As a result, the Nazi leadership integrated the Czech areas into the German Reich but granted them a degree of political autonomy. Hitler had discussed this step with Goebbels on the eve of the invasion, the latter noting: 'We go through the new statute for Bohemia and Moravia; they have the status of Reich protectorate. Retain their own administration. Czechs are not to be Germanized, but enjoy the protection of the Reich. Common military, foreign and economic policy. Otherwise autonomy'.[19] In line with this, article 3 of the Führer's decree stipulated that: '(1) The Protectorate of Bohemia and Moravia is autonomous and administers itself. (2) It exercises the sovereign rights to which it is entitled within the framework of the Protectorate in line with the political, military and economic interests of the Reich. (3) These sovereign rights are safeguarded through its own organs and its own authorities with their own officials'.[20]

On 16 March, however, Hitler also created the position of 'Reich protector in Bohemia and Moravia', with an official residence in Prague, as the 'custodian of Reich interests'. 'As the representative of the Führer and Reich chancellor and as the agent of the Reich government, his task [is to] ensure that the political guidelines laid down by the Führer and Reich chancellor are respected' and to confirm the appointment of 'members of the Protectorate government'. The Reich protector was 'entitled to be informed about all the measures implemented by the Protectorate government and to give it advice'; he could 'raise objections' to any steps 'likely to damage the Reich', and to laws, ordinances and legal rulings.[21] On 18 March, as General Johannes Blaskowitz, commander of the occupying troops, held a military parade in the heart of the Czech capital, Hitler, who had now arrived in Vienna, appointed former Foreign Minister Konstantin Freiherr von Neurath to the post of Reich protector (see Figure 2.2).[22]

Figure 2.2. Reich Protector Konstantin Freiherr von Neurath. © Bundesarchiv Berlin, N_1310_Bild-135,_Konstantin_von_Neurath.

Initially, however, it was the German army that held executive power. Tellingly, Sudeten German Konrad Henlein functioned as chief of the civil administration (Chef der Zivilverwaltung or CdZ) of the army in Bohemia, with Josef Bürckel holding the same post in Moravia; Reich commissioner in Vienna at the time, his stint as Reich commissioner for the reintegration of the Saarland (Reichskommissar für die Rückgliederung des Saarlandes) had endowed him with valuable experience of the incorporation of territory into the Reich. The pair were tasked with the development of a German administration and were to monitor what was left of the Czech authorities. They also held authority over the police. The Gestapo and SS, therefore, were initially subordinated to the army command.[23]

Hot on the heels of the Wehrmacht, a so-called Task Force of the Security Police and SS Security Service (Einsatzgruppe der Sicherheitspolizei und des Sicherheitsdienstes SS) moved into Bohemia under the leadership of Dr Otto Rasch, formerly Gestapo head in Frankfurt am Main and Linz and then inspector of the Security Police and SD in Kassel. Another proceeded into Moravia under the command of Dr Franz Walter Stahlecker, previously Gestapo head in Stuttgart and Breslau and now Inspector of the Security Police and SD in Vienna; Stahlecker had already served as leader of a task force in the Sudetenland.[24] Later, in the occupied Soviet Union, both headed the notorious SS-Einsatzgruppen (task forces) that carried out the systematic mass murder of Jews.[25]

SS-Totenkopfverbände (Death's Head Units) had also marched into the Protectorate. Waiting on standby and confined to their barracks at the Sachsenhausen concentration camp since 11 March, they received their marching orders on 14 March at 8.20 p.m. – before Hitler's conversation with Hácha. Their journey first took them to Flossenbürg, where they were joined by the 'Upper Bavaria' 1st SS Death's Head Regiment (Totenkopfstandarte) from Dachau. The battalions finally reached the Protectorate on 16 March. After arriving in Prague, SS group leader Theodor Eicke immediately met with Himmler at the Hradschin and was instructed to continue on to Brno, where Hitler was expected. Two motorized Death's Head battalions then proceeded via Jihlava to Brno, where they cordoned off the streets for Hitler's reception on 17 March.[26] Although sent into the Protectorate for this sole purpose, on 22 March Himmler ordered both battalions to station themselves on a long-term basis in the Moravian capital of Brno, a city of three hundred thousand people.[27]

In Berlin, on 22 March 1939, Hitler personally appointed State Secretary Wilhelm Stuckart head of the Central Office for the Implementation of the Decree for the Protectorate of Bohemia and

Moravia (Zentralstelle zur Durchführung des Erlasses für das Protektorat Böhmen und Mähren). He was responsible, as in his earlier role in Austria and the Sudetenland, for coordinating the work of the Reich bureaucracy and its regional counterpart. To this end, he travelled to the annexed territories, where he informed himself about the occupation policy and the integration of the indigenous administrations. In addition, the Reich Ministry of the Interior supervised the selection of administrative staff for the occupied territories.[28] Although all measures had to be agreed with the Reich Interior Ministry as the central authority, in the Protectorate the ministry played only a reduced role: here, in contrast to Austria and the Sudetenland, the goal was not to introduce Reich law but to bring the 'self-administration of the Protectorate' into 'line with the general interests of the Reich'. In this context, Hitler thus rejected Hermann Göring's request for an exception to this rule.[29]

On 5 April 1939, the Wehrmacht officially transferred authority to von Neurath as Reich protector; however, he acquired executive power only ten days later, on 16 April, when Hitler had released the supreme commander of the army from his responsibilities.[30] Other leading National Socialists, such as Goebbels, were sceptical about Hitler's cautious decision to appoint a cultivated, internationally recognized diplomat to this post.[31]

As state secretary, Karl Hermann Frank (1898–1946) de facto became vice Reich protector. Deputy chairman of the Sudeten German Party since 1937, he seemed of a quite different calibre than von Neurath. Born in Karlsbad into a family with Greater German ambitions, Frank had fought in the First World War. After breaking off his law degree and studying commerce in Prague, he worked in the municipal administration of Vítkovice (Witkowitz) until 1920, and later as an independent bookseller. A member of the German National Party before 1933, he became a full-time staff member of the Sudeten German Party in Eger in 1934. In addition, on 28 April 1939, Himmler appointed the radical antisemite Frank senior SS and police chief (Höherer SS- und Polizeiführer) in the Protectorate.[32]

In order to ensure that the new German authority enjoyed a 'powerful position vis-à-vis the autonomous agencies of the Protectorate', the Reich Ministry of the Interior asked the Reich authorities to identify an appropriate consultant for each of the different sections within the Office of the Reich Protector.[33] The new body in Prague was subdivided into a central administration and four departments: I Administration, Justice and Education, II Economy and Finances, III Transport, and IV Cultural Policy. The offices of the Commander of the Security Police and the SD (Befehlshaber der Sicherheitspolizei und des SD or BdS) and of the Order Police also formed part of the new agency. Otto Rasch initially served as BdS in Prague, but after just five weeks he was replaced by Stahlecker, who had earned his stripes in Vienna dealing with Austria's incorporation into the Reich.[34]

The thirty-five chief county commissioners (Oberlandräte), who had been appointed by the supreme army commander to monitor the low-level Czech administrative authorities, district offices (Bezirksämter) and the associated district heads (Bezirkshauptmänner), were now transformed into regional agents of the Reich protector.[35] Every head of department in the Office of the Reich Protector came from the Old Reich, as did twenty-four of the thirty-five chief county commissioners, with another four from Austria and seven from the Sudeten region.[36]

The Nazi Party created no separate organization in the newly occupied territory. The local Nazi Party heads in the Protectorate were subordinate to the Gauleiters of the adjoining administrative party districts (Gaue) in the Sudetenland, the Bavarian Eastern March (Bayerische Ostmark), Upper Danube (Oberdonau) and Lower Danube (Niederdonau).[37]

In contrast to Austria and the Sudetenland, therefore, the Protectorate retained its own legal status and government, though the latter was closely monitored by the Reich protector. The Protectorate administered itself, with the exception of foreign policy, military matters, transport and communication. Czech law continued to apply to the extent that it did not infringe Reich regulations.[38]

Above all, however, a Czech government remained in office, albeit one under the watchful eye of the Reich protector. Czechs continued to run the Ministries of the Interior, Finance, Education and Culture, Justice, Public Works, Agriculture, Commerce and Crafts, and Health and Welfare, including a number of ministers from the Second Republic, such as Agriculture Minister Feierabend, Finance Minister Kalfus (in office since 1936, no less) and Transport Minister Havelka.[39] President Emil Hácha, also still in office, had dissolved the Czech parliament on 21 March 1939. Hácha, a conservative Catholic, thus symbolized the definitive abandonment of democratic structures. He backed anti-Jewish measures, while simultaneously remaining in contact with the Czech underground and confidants of Beneš in exile.[40]

Before the end of March 1939, Hácha had founded a new National Partnership (Národní souručenství); as a unified movement, this was intended to replace the Czech parties and function as both National Assembly and political organization. It barred Jews and women from membership. National Partnership soon had more than two million members, 98.5 per cent of all Czech men in the Protectorate. This outcome countered German efforts to register as many Czechs as possible as Germans.[41] Instead of an elected parliament, a 92-member committee appointed by the president and intended to act as an advisory body to the Czech government was installed in the parliament building. National Partnership saw itself as the 'custodian and champion of the rights and demands of the Czech people'.[42]

On 27 April 1939, Hácha carried out a reshuffle, with General Alois Eliáš (1890–1942)[43] – approved by the Reich protector – taking over as prime minister from Rudolf Beran. While the political views of Eliáš, previously a delegate to the League of Nations and most recently transport minister under Beran, were similar to those of Hácha (he cultivated contacts with exiles on his behalf), Justice Minister Jaroslav Krejčí (1892–1956), who continued in post, was an enthusiastic supporter of Nazi rule.[44]

In addition to the Reich protector, the Czech government and the chief county commissioners, local authorities played an important role in anti-Jewish policy as well.[45] In Prague, where a substantial portion of the Protectorate's Jewish inhabitants lived, Otakar Klapka remained in office as mayor – known as the primator from late 1939 onwards. By 16 March 1939, however, Josef Pfitzner (1901–45), a historian and Sudeten German politician, had been made his deputy.[46] The Czech regional president (Landespräsident) appointed Pfitzner – who publicly proclaimed, in January 1940, that the Prague authorities had been treating the German community unfairly for three generations – government commissioner (Regierungskommissar) as well as deputy primator. These roles endowed Pfitzner with considerable influence on the relatively autonomous politics of Prague. From late 1939 onwards, he was entitled to request reports from all city authorities and had to countersign all the primator's decisions.[47]

Violence and Terror in the Wake of the Occupation

Reacting to the demonstrations triggered by the entry of German troops into Prague, Propaganda Minister Joseph Goebbels remarked acerbically in his diary: 'And Prague still has too many Jews and Marxists. We'll soon smoke them out'.[48] At this point, in the remnant of the former Czech state, now annexed by Germany, there lived 118,310 Jews (possibly more), organized in 136 Communities (see Table A.1 in the appendix).[49] Operation Gitter ('Bars'), in whose framework the Czech police too carried out raids, claimed numerous Jewish victims, particularly in Prague. Within a week, on the basis of carefully drawn-up lists, the Gestapo arrested more than a thousand people; soon this figure climbed to more than 4,600 communists, social democrats, legionnaires and German refugees, of whom a quarter, mostly Jews who had earlier emigrated to Czechoslovakia, ended up in concentration camps.[50]

As in Vienna during the first few days after the 'Anschluß', Jewish institutions were closed or placed under the control of the Gestapo.[51] The Gestapo also shut down the Prague office of HICEM, a federation of international Jewish relief organizations that had focused mainly on facilitating the emigration of Jews from the Czech Republic.[52] One of the many people arrested was Dr Marie Schmolka (1890–1940),[53] head of both the Prague Jewish Community's Refugee Relief Programme and HICEM Prague. The Gestapo confiscated the money the Relief Programme had collected for the Sudeten German Jews.[54]

During the occupation, anti-Jewish riots broke out in a number of locations. Germans and evidently Czechs as well burnt down the local synagogues in Olomouc and Vsetín (Wsetin).[55] The town of Jihlava banned Jews from using trams and forced them to clear snow, while the local synagogue went up in flames in late March.[56] Akin to the SS and SD, the Wehrmacht preferred to seize villas owned by Jews, converting them to their own ends.[57] Synagogues were also destroyed in Moravian Ostrava and Kynšperk nad Ohří (Königsberg an der Eger). In a number of cases, the local Czech population was responsible for anti-Jewish attacks. In Klatovy (Klattau), a town of fourteen thousand people, mayor František Biček submitted his resignation when he failed to quell the riots.[58]

As a consequence of these events, vast numbers of Jews sought to flee. Katherine Kral's father was arrested immediately after the German forces' arrival in Moravian Ostrava; her mother helped her brother to escape, but guards detained him at the Polish border.[59] The brothers of Hilda Beran from Moravian Ostrava also attempted to flee in this way, but were sent back by Polish border guards under a rain of blows. It took a second attempt for them to successfully get away.[60] On 25 March, at the border with the Sudetenland, a customs patrol arrested merchant Leopold Polak and sales representative Rudolf Polak, when they sought to cross the border at an unauthorized point en route from Prague to Belgium. As they were carrying more than the permitted quantity of Reichsmarks, a court of lay assessors (Schöffengericht) in Mährisch-Schönberg (Šumperk) sentenced the pair to three months in prison and fined them 1,000 RM for 'currency smuggling'.[61]

Many Czech Jews from other localities sought to escape to Poland, mostly across the border near Moravian Ostrava, as Bohemia and Moravia were encircled on their other sides by the Sudetenland or bordered Slovakia, a client state of the German Reich with its own anti-Jewish laws (see Figure 1.2). Many Jews tried to evade the border controls by hiding in trains or coal wagons or made their way through the forest with the help of paid or unpaid escape helpers. One secure route led underground. The shafts of the coal mines in the vicinity of Moravian Ostrava often originated from the period before the map was redrawn after the First World War, so certain connections still existed, as for example between the Ludwig shaft near Radvanice (Radwanitz) and the Hedwig shaft in Poland. As an act of resistance, Artur Radvanský, who had grown up in the area and was himself Jewish, repeatedly guided Jews sent his way through the shafts to Poland.[62]

Before the Gestapo's net began to close in, some Jews even sought refuge in clinics or sanatoria if they failed to make it over the border. Reports of suicides among the Jewish population soon began to pile up. During the first week of the occupation, thirty to forty Jews took their own lives in Prague on a daily basis. Four hundred individuals lay in hospitals following attempted suicides.[63]

For want of central directives, the various authorities responded quite differently to the chaotic circumstances. By 19 March, Dr Curt von Burgsdorff (1886–1962),[64] undersecretary of state to the Reich protector, was already reporting to Reich Commissioner Bürckel, as CdZ with responsibility for Moravia, that the 'main synagogues in Brno', the synagogue in Olomouc, and the synagogue and Rabbi's house in Vsetín had been burned down (see Figure 2.3). He had, he stated, prevented the second synagogue in the Moravian capital from being set on fire. Shops, meanwhile, had been daubed with 'graffiti such as "Jud" [Jew] and "Saujud" [Jewish swine]'. Curt von Burgsdorff complained: 'Though it is quite right for Jewish businesses to be marked, this must be done in an orderly fashion and not with graffiti'. He had, he went on, given instructions to that effect to the acting police chief of Brno, Pg. (Parteigenosse, 'party comrade') Dr Schwabe, who had been personally appointed by Himmler. The undersecretary of state also criticized the spread of 'unruly attempts at Aryanization'. A very large number of Jewish businesses, he noted, already bore notices declaring them to be 'under commissarial administration'. In an attempt to rein in the commissarial system, on the basis of a 'decree issued by Field Marshal Göring, provisionally conveyed [to him] in verbal form, according to which all interference in Jewish businesses is prohibited', he intended to promulgate an ordinance outlawing the sale of Jewish businesses, 'because ninety-nine times out of a hundred the sale is made under pressure'.[65]

The same day, Chief County Commissioner Dr Oskar Grazer (1906–91)[66] informed his subordinate district heads in Moravské

Figure 2.3. The synagogue in Brno destroyed in 1939. © YV Jerusalem, Photo Archive, no. 933_14_6.

Budějovice (Mährisch-Budwitz), Třebíč (Trebitsch) and Hrotovice (Hrottowitz) that he intended to ensure 'uniform regulation of all issues relating to Jews in the districts assigned to me'. 'Individual actions against Jews' as well as the closure by the authorities of 'existing Jewish businesses' were therefore to be prohibited. He would leave it to 'the general public [to avoid] Jewish businesses as they see fit'. These were immediately to be distinguished by signs 'measuring 20 x 50 cm' bearing the words 'Jewish business' in German and Czech.[67]

On 21 March, the chief county commissioner in Vsetín, on the other hand, ordered the district authorities in Vsetín, Holešov and Valašské Meziříčí (Walachisch-Meseritsch) to immediately remove 'the graffiti daubed on Jewish businesses such as "Jude ['Jew' in German], Žid ['Jew' in Czech], and Judengeschäft [Jewish business]"'.[68] The chief county commissioner in Kroměříž (Kremsier) instructed the district authorities in Kroměříž, Vyškov (Wischau) and Kyjov (Gaya) to do the same. Nonetheless, he wished to mark 'Aryan' businesses owned by

Czechs and Germans, so he commissioned a local printer to produce bilingual signs.⁶⁹ Abroad, the Jewish Telegraphic Agency soon published reports on the branding of non-Jewish businesses in Prague.⁷⁰

Conflicting Interests, Clashing Plans

The Czech government initiated the first national anti-Jewish measure while Rudolf Beran was still prime minister. Two days after the occupation, on 17 March 1939, it issued a decree stripping Jewish doctors and lawyers of their licence to practice, removed Jews from key posts in industry and social organizations and made preparations to visibly identify 'Aryan' businesses. More far-reaching plans were also discussed.⁷¹ In a parallel development, the representatives of all Czech doctors' associations held a conference, at which they resolved to propose to the relevant authorities that 'Jewish doctors and advocates be banned from practising their professions'.⁷²

On 25 March, the Czech finance minister froze all bank accounts held by Jews in the Protectorate. Henceforth, Jews were permitted to open bank safes and deposits only in the presence of government officials and could draw a weekly maximum of 1,500 crowns from their own deposits, while the banks drew up lists of accounts held by individuals of Jewish faith. In August 1939, the Reich Ministry of the Economy was to copy this method, extending it so that all Jews in the Reich were forced to get by with just one 'security account' (Sicherungskonto).⁷³

According to German estimates, around thirty thousand Jewish businesses existed in the Protectorate. In fact, the figure was probably closer to twenty thousand.⁷⁴ A number of important metals firms, such as the Witkowitzer Eisenwerke (Witkowitz Ironworks), and coal mines, such as those in Ostrava-Karvinná, were owned by Jews.⁷⁵ By 20 March, the Czech government had already decreed that the authorities could appoint trustees to manage businesses if this was in the 'public interest'. The fact that the district authorities had to prepare lists of Jewish businesses liable for 'Aryanization' made the government's objectives abundantly clear.⁷⁶

But Jewish property in the Protectorate was also claimed by the Reich. The Wehrmacht set the tone. As it entered Prague it immediately issued a directive: 'Jewish assets are now the property of the people (Volksgut)'.⁷⁷ Within the Reich, Prime Minister Hermann Göring, who was in charge of the Four Year Plan, was eager to prevent confusion over the division of responsibilities and instances of arbitrary private gain (as had occurred the year before in Vienna when Austria was incorporated into Germany). He immediately took steps to ensure that all stolen property went directly to the Reich. On 16 March 1939, in an express letter to the chiefs of the civil administrations, Henlein and Bürckel, who were subordinate to the Wehrmacht, he reserved for himself 'decision-making power with respect to all core economic issues'. From now on, the express letter declared, within the Protectorate major changes of ownership (for example in the case of real estate or business enterprises) would require Göring's approval; the Reich minister of the economy was to guarantee the duty of disclosure and the requirement for official approval (Genehmigungsvorbehalt). Point 4 in the letter stated that unruly attempts at Aryanization must be prevented. The timing, scale and pace of any de-Judaization measures (Entjudungsmaßnahmen) would be determined by Göring himself. Further, there was to be no 'appointing of trustees' to manage businesses.[78]

Four days later, Göring decreed that the sale, transfer and gifting of Jewish property required his approval.[79] In the Protectorate, the chiefs of the civil administrations for Moravia and for Bohemia respectively, Henlein and Bürckel, immediately issued corresponding directives. On 20 March 1939, they outlawed the appointing of commissioners and administrators to manage individual businesses.[80] By the end of March, they had banned Jews from selling businesses and real estate.[81] The German state thus seemed to have set the stage for the orderly 'Aryanization' of Jewish property in the Protectorate.

Unexpected obstacles, however, soon piled up. There was still no consensus on who ought to determine the nature of anti-Jewish policies in general and in specific fields henceforth. Between 22 and 26 March, in what was clearly an orchestrated move, various regional and local offshoots of the Czech fascist organizations Gajda and Vlajka (Flag) telegraphed Hitler, urging him to pursue a 'radical resolution of the Jewish question in our country on the model of Germany'.[82]

However, at a meeting of state secretaries chaired by Stuckart in the Reich Interior Ministry on 25 March 1939, that is, ten days after the occupation, it was concluded that the Nazi state had no interest in any 'racial cultivation (Rassenpflege) intended to protect the Czech people'. 'In principle it would be possible to leave it up to the Protectorate government whether to take action against Jews and in what way.' The 'Jewish question' would 'likely develop in its own way in the Protectorate'. Hitler still set the course: he had decided that 'the Jews will be eliminated from the public life of the Protectorate'. However, the 'execution of this task will be down to the Protectorate government rather than the direct responsibility of the Reich'. The Reich protector would recommend to the government in Prague that it:

take the necessary steps. These would include: a) withdrawal of the right to vote and the right to be elected, b) exclusion from public office, c) elimination from the press, broadcasting and other activities with an influence on public opinion, d) elimination from the technical associations to be established to maintain internal security and order (art. 7 of the Führer's Decree), e) a ban on owning weapons and further ban on the manufacture of and trade in weapons.

In the first instance the Reich would implement no special measures relating to the economy. 'Instead [it would] be left to the Protectorate government itself to tackle the economic side of the elimination of Jewry'. This decision fit with the Protectorate's ambiguous constitutional position as a semiautonomous component of the Greater German Reich, a status that was discussed in more detail at the meeting of state secretaries. The Reich, the meeting participants concluded, had the final say, yet the Protectorate was constitutionally independent and thus, through its government, enjoyed the autonomy 'to make its own laws in every legal field not directly administered by the Reich'. At the same time, within the hierarchy of the German state the Reich protector enjoyed tremendous latitude, for he was subordinate only to Hitler; the Reich authorities could not tell him what to do. As the report on the meeting produced by the Reich Interior Ministry also laid bare, 'the provisions of the Blood Protection Law (Blutschutzgesetz), that is, the prohibition on marrying Jews in particular' already applied to the ethnic German population. This law targeted 'Jews within the Protectorate to the benefit of the German members of the Reich', as did the Marriage Health Law (Ehegesundheitsgesetz) and the Law for the Prevention of Hereditarily Diseased Offspring (Gesetz zur Verhütung erbkranken Nachwuchses).[83]

In its quarterly status report, the SS Security Service thus observed: 'With respect to the Jewish question, the creation of the Protectorate of Bohemia and Moravia has brought about a situation in which around 87,000 additional Jews have been placed within the borders of the Greater German Reich. There has, however, been no immediate engagement on the part of the Reich to solve the Jewish problem in Bohemia and Moravia'.[84]

Terror and Emigration after the Occupation

Regardless of Berlin's restraint, the anti-Jewish measures implemented by the Czech government and the German authorities rapidly put the Jewish population of the Protectorate in a difficult position. Czech organizations, such as the Central Council of Businessmen, followed by the associations of lawyers and physicians, made their own contributions to the exclusion of Jews; over the next few months they were joined by other associations, societies and clubs.[85] Opportunism and compliance dominated among the economic elites; at the end of the day, anti-Jewish policy ensured the elimination of numerous competitors. Much the same applied across broad swathes of the Czech civil service, the police force and the remnant of the army, which had been reduced to seven thousand men.[86]

In early April 1939, the Gestapo reversed the closure of Jewish institutions. The Jewish Social Institute (Jüdisches Soziales Institut) in Prague was 'unsealed' and resumed its work. Its staff began to provide the poor with support once again on 12 April, their first priority being to alleviate the desperate situation that had arisen since the institute's closure. It helped not just locals in need but also many refugees from the Old Reich, Austria and the Sudeten region.[87] On 17 April, the chairmen of seven religious associations in Prague agreed to join forces in an attempt to get on top of the crisis.[88] It was only after a request from the Czech welfare minister to the German authorities that the Gestapo released Marie Schmolka, head of the Refugee Relief organization in Prague, towards the end of May.[89]

On 31 May 1939, Jews receiving welfare benefits in Prague comprised 2,500 local poor (Ortsarme), 731 emigrants, 2,694 refugees, 502 repatriates and 354 transitory migrants (Durchwanderer). Half the support for the 'local poor' came from the Jewish Social Institute, half from the Jewish Communities. A report written by Dr Emil Kafka and František Weidmann for the Jewish Religious Community of Prague stated:

> The number of people in need of support is growing day by day. Jewish white-collar workers are being dismissed, the Jewish middle class, on which the entire system of social work and the Jewish Communities rely, is becoming steadily impoverished, the rich Jews have left the national territory, and within a very short period of time the local Jewry will be incapable of meeting its welfare needs itself. In the absence of copious foreign aid our system of social welfare will be unable to function over the long-term.[90]

As US diplomat George Kennan observed in the rapidly Nazified border town of Moravian Ostrava, the expropriation of Jewish property was already well advanced by the end of April. While the Gestapo had moved into a villa formerly owned by the richest local Jewish businessman, Jews had been banned from all public spaces. According to Kennan, since the beginning of the occupation, a period of just over a month, one doctor had recorded thirty-three suicides among Jews.[91]

In a parallel process, Jews and their institutions increasingly suffered attacks from Czech fascists, which were in part an attempt to challenge President Hácha. Violent demonstrations, however, failed to spark a positive response among many Czechs. During the second half of May 1939, fascists harassed Jews in cafes or attacked them on the street, chiefly in Brno and Prague. The president deployed the police to tackle such behaviour.[92] In late May, a bomb exploded in a historic building at 17 Pariser-Gasse (Pařížská ulice) in Prague, which formed a complex together with the Hoheschul-Synagogue and the Jewish city hall opposite the Old-New Synagogue in the heart of the city – an act of which most Czechs strongly disapproved. A fire destroyed the synagogue in Vítkovice near Moravian Ostrava. *Die Zeit*, a Nazi Party newspaper in the Sudetengau, reported in late May that Falkenau (Falknov nad Ohří) was among the places recently rendered 'Jew-free'. The Jewish population, consisting of several hundred people, the paper reported, had been forced to leave the city. The synagogue had been burned down, while twenty-eight houses and thirty shops owned by Jews could be considered 'Aryanized'.[93] In May and June, synagogues in Brno, Olomouc, Uherský Brod (Ungarisch-Brod), Chlumec (Kulm), Náchod (Nachod) and Pardubice (Pardubitz) fell victim to arson. In the early hours of 9 June, Germans set fire to two synagogues in the vicinity of Moravian Ostrava. A total of six synagogues are said to have been set alight in this region in rapid succession during this period. On 17 June, a bomb exploded in a restaurant in Prague owned by a Jew and frequented by many Jewish customers. Thirty-nine individuals were recorded as injured, as the American consul reported. Several attacks targeted the historic Old-New Synagogue in Prague.[94]

In its bulletin, the most radical Czech fascist and antisemitic organization, the so-called Czech National Socialist Camp – 'Vlajka', was already calling for the ghettoization of Jews.[95] Under the leadership of the 'Czech Julius Streicher', Jan Roszevac Rys, this small group, comprising just thirteen thousand members at the time, had only recently split off from General Gajda's fascist organization. Even before the establishment of the Protectorate, courts had jailed Rys on several occasions for bomb attacks on Jewish businesses.[96] Before and after the occupation, Vlajka members also set off bombs in Jewish cemeteries.[97] In the early hours of 16 July, Czech fascists attempted to blow up the ceremonial hall of the new Jewish cemetery in Kroměříž, Moravia, with one of the assailants losing his life when the bomb went off early.[98]

In mid June 1939, the Jewish Telegraphic Agency reported that, according to confidential sources in Prague, synagogues were being set on fire in the Protectorate almost every day. The most recent case was in Zabrek (presumably Zábřeh [Hohenstadt] in Moravia), where the SA broke into the local synagogue in the evening, doused the pews and Torah ark with petrol, set everything on fire and threw the Torah scrolls into the flames. In general, the report went on, responding fire brigades in the Protectorate were instructed to prevent the spread of these fires but not to put them out, just as during the November pogrom. In Kladno, the authorities ordered the Jewish Community to pay most of the damages imposed following the murder of a German policeman, despite the fact that the community consisted of just two hundred mostly poor members.[99] In České Budějovice, in early June, the Gestapo closed the Jewish Community Hall and the synagogue, shut down all Jewish organizations and arrested members of the B'nai B'rith lodge. In Hradec Králové (Königgrätz), by way of contrast, the recently established 'National Aryan Cultural Union' (Národní arijská kulturní jednota), which propagated a race-based antisemitism, failed in its attempts to hold a meeting. Local Czechs protested against their plans, while the 'Sokol' ('Falcon') Gymnastics Club and other Czech associations, as well as individuals, refused to let the 'National Aryan Culture Union' use their premises.[100]

The German occupation and growing antisemitism rapidly marred relations between non-Jews and Jews. Many Germans, and many Czechs as well, broke off contact with those of Jewish faith, with just a few sticking by them.[101]

Time and again, Jews paid the price for attempts to resist the occupation. In late April, when German soldiers were jeered at in a tram in Pilsen, the occupying authorities arrested 150 alleged Marxists and 150 Jews, either in their homes or in cafes. On 17 May, the Gestapo sent twenty-two Jews to the Dachau concentration camp. The above-mentioned murder of the German policeman in Kladno in June triggered a similar outcome.[102] Many Jews were arrested for other reasons and placed in concentration camps. Some died there, while others took their own lives.[103]

A growing number of people now wished to emigrate. It was not just mounting poverty that prevented them from doing so, but initially – in contrast to normal practice in the Reich and Austria – the Security Police itself. In Prague, the Gestapo occupied the large residence formerly owned by Jewish banker Julius Petschek as its new headquarters.[104] In early May 1939, 'as a guideline for the approach to the Jewish question to be adopted by the Prague Special Command Unit (Sonderkommando)', Heydrich had instructed the Security Police under his command to 'prevent the emigration of Jews' as far as possible. For the time being, therefore, he had no plans to establish a Central Office for Jewish Emigration as in Vienna.¹⁰⁵ On 12 May, the Security Service held a meeting in Prague, at which those present made a categorical decision to prohibit further emigration from the Protectorate, because this would be at the expense of the immigration quotas for Germany, for example those adopted by the United States, since the Protectorate now counted as part of Germany. Approval for emigration could be given only in cases of total destitution.¹⁰⁶ Contemporary observers soon noticed that in the major cities the Gestapo was now preventing Jews from leaving.¹⁰⁷

Initiatives towards a 'Judengesetz' (Jew Law)

When it came to anti-Jewish policy, in principle the approach to the relationship between the Reich government, Reich protector and Czech government laid down by Hitler continued to apply. Hitler reiterated this to von Neurath in early May 1939 in person: 'The Reich protector spoke to the Führer about the introduction of the Nuremberg laws. The Führer decreed that the Czechs must resolve the Jewish problem themselves and that we should avoid meddling. Otherwise the Reich protector takes the view that ultimately, given the prevailing dynamics, the Jewish problem will be solved in line with the Nuremberg laws'.¹⁰⁸

Such a dynamic did not yet exist, but various actors worked to change this. By the end of March 1939, the 'Aryan Union' had already called on President Hácha to bar Jews by law from holding Protectorate citizenship. A Jew, the Union declared, was anyone who adhered to the Jewish faith, maintained social contact with Jews or had offended against the nation or the 'Aryan race'. Jews must also be compelled to bear an identifying mark.¹⁰⁹ Internally, in the context of the November pogrom of 1938, the SS Security Service had proposed the use of such branding in Germany, but Hitler nixed the idea in light of the likely reaction abroad.¹¹⁰ A few weeks later, National Partnership proposed that the government deprive Jews of various rights and introduce an official definition of the term Jew based on religious affiliation.¹¹¹

Both National Partnership and the Czech government had appointed special commissions to 'resolve the Jewish issue'.¹¹² On 11 May 1939, General Eliáš informed the Reich protector that the Czech government was already giving its 'utmost attention to drafting a government decree on the Jewish question'. Since this was an 'extremely important and urgent problem', one 'whose speediest resolution and a [related] announcement in the near future' would serve the Protectorate's orderly development, he proposed 'direct communication' between personally authorized representatives on both sides, in order to agree the details prior to Cabinet approval.[113] According to the draft document, Jews would not be full-fledged citizens of the Protectorate. A Jew was a person with four Jewish grandparents, but not if he or she was not a member of a Jewish religious Community after 1918. In addition, the draft included comprehensive restrictions on Jews in public life under threat of punishment, in the legal, medical and veterinary professions for example, and provided for the elimination of Jews from public agencies, corporations and schools, the administrative system, courts, stock exchanges, the art world, health system and National Partnership.[114]

Two days later in Prague, while giving representatives of the Czech press a brief overview of his government programme, Prime Minister General Eliáš publicly announced that a solution to the Jewish problem would soon be found.[115] In his introductory remarks, he had explained that the Protectorate government was 'responsible for ensuring open communication with the Office of the Reich Protector, in order to align [the government's] activities with the interests and needs of Reich policy. The main problem facing the Czech people is the problem of work'. The government would consider the introduction of an obligation to work and would intervene in the economy to guide its development. With respect to the 'Jewish problem', the general remarked: 'Its resolution will reflect the interests of public life and the need for undisturbed economic development and will bring the current transitional state to an end. The relevant decree will be published shortly'.[116]

A Cabinet committee had completed the draft law, which the government planned to discuss a few days later. As the Jewish Telegraphic Agency reported, the law, which ran to forty paragraphs, would exclude Jews from public life and numerous professions. While the Czech daily newspapers disseminated anti-Jewish propaganda in order to ensure public approval for the law, according to the Jewish Telegraphic Agency this had little effect on most Czechs.[117] The *Manchester Guardian* reported that the planned law took 'Jew' to mean only those not baptized after 1918 and with four Jewish grandparents. In addition, Hácha retained the right to except individual Jews from the law. The newspaper underlined that the non-introduction of the Nuremberg laws in the Protectorate constituted a major concession wrung from the Germans.[118]

Things were to turn out differently, however. The planned Czech 'Jewish decree' turned into the first test of the autonomy Hitler had granted. While there could be 'no negotiations on the definition of the term', as Hitler had decided that this must 'remain reserved to the Protectorate government', on 22 May 1939 representatives of every division in the Office of the Reich Protector discussed the Czech proposal, judging its definition of the term Jew to be far too mild and too 'out of sync with the German regulations'.[119] Stahlecker, Commander of the Security Police, also criticized the draft law in a letter to State Secretary Frank on 1 June: 'As experience has shown, it is the rich and influential Jews that are most likely to have abandoned the Mosaic faith, so according to the draft law they would not be treated as Jews'.[120]

Subsequently, the Reich protector started to restrict the Czech government's freedom of action. On 30 May, the Reich Protectorate authorities decreed that firearms licences would no longer be issued to Jews.[121] Rather than continue the already protracted negotiations with the Czech government, a month later the Reich protector pre-empted it with a more radical definition of the term Jew.[122] On 21 June 1939, his decree, published in German and Czech, 'on Jewish assets' laid down that in the Protectorate – as in the 'Nuremberg racial laws' – a Jew was anyone with three grandparents of Jewish faith, regardless of their actual religious affiliation. Those who had two Jewish grandparents, but who were either members of a Jewish Community at the time of the Protectorate's establishment or were married to a Protectorate citizen, were also considered Jews. This officially created three classes of resident: German Reich citizens, Czech citizens of the Protectorate and Jews.[123] This new definition chiefly served to restrict Jews' control over their own assets, which were estimated to amount to a total of seventeen billion crowns.[124] Alongside the crown, since 1939 the Reichsmark had been legal tender in the Protectorate, at a compulsory rate of ten crowns to one Reichsmark.[125]

As had applied since April 1938 in Germany and Austria, Czech Jews too now had to disclose their assets or face punishment. They had to register real estate with the chief county commissioners and precious metals, jewellery and art objects at the Czech National Bank, or at locations it stipulated, by 31 July 1939. With retroactive effect from 17 March, Jews, Jewish firms and Jewish organizations were no longer allowed to dispose of their property without approval from the authorities; previously this had pertained only in the case of sale or liquidation. They were no longer permitted to acquire real estate, securities or enterprises, lease immovable property or establish new businesses. The decree also defined which firms the Germans considered to be 'Jewish'. It endowed the Reich protector with the right to appoint trustees to manage Jewish firms or dismiss administrators who had already been installed. The directives issued on the basis of the previous decrees promulgated by the chiefs of the civil administrations as well as the trustees appointed by the chief county commissioners were not affected.[126]

This early demonstration of the Reich protector's power placed severe restrictions on Jews' economic activities and ended the clearly visible conflict of interest with respect to the 'Aryanization' of Jewish businesses. This had been smouldering since the Czech and German parallel measures of March 1939, because the March decrees issued by the chiefs of the civil administrations had by no means annulled the Czech government directive issued the same month.[127]

Czech and German 'Efforts at Aryanization'

At the instigation of the Prague headquarters of National Partnership, since May 1939 its local branches had been compiling lists of Jewish businesses. In places such as Olomouc this clearly occurred in cooperation with the local Chamber of Commerce and the municipal authorities in an attempt to install Czech trustees wherever possible. In Olomouc, both key Czech actors and the German occupation authorities appointed compulsory administrators to manage Jewish firms around this time. As a consequence of intervention by the police authorities, furthermore, 'non-Aryans' had to vacate the boards of directors and give up their posts as managers of joint-stock companies in the city.[128]

In mid April, the president of the Anglo-Czechoslovak & Prague Credit Bank, Bohuslav Kučera, had urged the Czech finance minister to expedite 'Aryanization' in the national Czech interest.[129] One member of the Banking Council (Bankenrat) of the Czech National Bank, sugar manufacturer Robert Mandelík, had already been forced to resign on 'racial grounds' in March. The German authorities had concurrently dispatched a special plenipotentiary to the Czech National Bank, which was soon to play a multifaceted role in 'Aryanization'.[130] The hopes cultivated by a fair number of Czechs, that they alone would profit from Jewish assets, quickly emerged as a naïve fallacy that failed to factor in the Germans.[131]

Beginning on 29 March 1939, an SD special command unit launched an initiative intended to remove 'Jewish assets from the Czech sphere of influence with the help of the banks under German influence' and place them 'in German hands'.[132] Major German banks also sent representatives to carve out a slice of the action: by April, the Dresdner Bank had already taken control of the Böhmische Escompte-Bank, without owning a single share. The Gestapo arrested senior officials of Jewish origin, while more junior Jewish employees were dismissed.[133]

The Deutsche Bank, meanwhile, took charge of the Böhmische Union-Bank.[134] The Dresdner Bank and Deutsche Bank would subsequently process the lion's share of Aryanization transactions, thus enabling them to access a new clientele.[135]

By the summer, the main German actors had stepped up the pressure to 'Aryanize' Jewish businesses in a range of ways. Within the Reich Protectorate administration, Group VII 'Trade and Industry' (Gewerbliche Wirtschaft), led by Erich von Wedelstädt, established a Department for 'De-Judaization'. This was initially headed by Senior Government Counsellor (Oberregierungsrat) Siegfried Ludwig, who had been sent from the Reich Ministry of the Economy and was well-versed in 'Aryanization issues'. In the autumn of 1939, he was replaced by Dr Rudolf Stier from the corresponding division of the Reich Commissar's Office in the Sudetenland. The Department of De-Judaization now dealt with applications, proposed applicants to the Finance Bureau (Vermögensamt) within the Office of the Reich Protector and had purchase prices checked by the Deutsche Revisions- und Treuhand-Gesellschaft (German Auditing and Trust Company) in Prague. The head of the Trade and Industry group saw 'Aryanization' not just as a means of acquiring property but also as a way of Germanizing the Protectorate.[136]

In line with this, on 9 June 1939 the Olomouc county commissioner wrote to the Přerov (Prerau) District Authority that the Czech trustees must cease their work if they wished to avoid arrest by the Gestapo. This prompted the county vice president (Landesvizepräsident) in Brno to inform the Czech minister for trade and industry that under these conditions it was impossible to comply with the instructions issued by the government in March.[137] Through the ordinance of 21 June, the Reich protector secured his power over economic matters: trustees could now be appointed to manage non-Jewish companies as well. In response, President Hácha lodged a protest with the Reich protector, assailing this 'instrument of Germanization under the guise of Aryanization'.[138]

* * *

On 15 March 1939, the German army moved into Prague, closely followed by the SS Task Forces, SS Death's Head Units and the Security Police. When Hitler arrived in Prague, Himmler and other leading Nazis were already there waiting for him. He established the Protectorate of Bohemia and Moravia and granted it substantial autonomy, including the power to formulate anti-Jewish policies, because unlike Austria this was a territory with a majority non-German population. Hence, the Czech government continued to exist, as did the Czech state administration and Czech law.

To enhance its control, Germany quickly established a parallel German bureaucracy. Those responsible for creating it drew on the experience of earlier annexations. Joseph Bürckel, who had served in the Saarland and in Austria as Reich commissioner for reunification with the Reich, now introduced the first anti-Jewish measures as chief of the civil administration in Moravia. He had also brought his staff from Vienna, including von Burgsdorff, who had already worked for him in the Austrian capital and was soon playing a key role as under-secretary of state in the Office of the Reich Protector. A similar trend is evident in the appointment of Stahlecker as Commander of the Security Police in Prague.

Although the de jure power of the German Security Police in the Protectorate of Bohemia and Moravia seemed likely to outstrip the authority it had enjoyed in Austria, in reality a number of parties persecuted Jews from the outset: the Office of the Reich Protector, the Security Police, the chief county commissioners, the Czech government and its ministries, the district authorities and the municipalities.

By March 1939, while Beran was still prime minister, the Czech government had already implemented the first anti-Jewish measures to eliminate Jews from the state apparatus and public life. While the Gestapo focused on arresting prominent Jews and closed all Jewish institutions, during the first few weeks after the annexation ethnic Germans and Czechs attacked synagogues and Jewish institutions in a number of places. Synagogues went up in flames, bombs went off, and businesses were daubed with anti-Jewish slogans. Czech fascist circles were already calling for the segregation of Jews. The German chief county commissioners, who were tasked with monitoring the Czech local authorities, responded in a variety of ways: some prohibited the marking of Jewish businesses, while others opted for the supposedly less politically sensitive visible identification of 'Aryan' businesses.

In May, the Czech Cabinet, with input from the German authorities, drew up a comprehensive law to eliminate Jews from public life. Disregarding the autonomy on 'Jewish policy' personally granted by Hitler to the Czech government, in June 1939 the Reich protector issued a decree that entailed a stricter definition of the term Jew, one in compliance with the Nuremberg laws, but whose main goal was the 'Aryanization' of Jewish property. Particularly after the negative experiences of 'unruly Aryanization' in Austria, Göring made an early intervention from Berlin in an attempt to monitor and steer the sale of firms, banks and businesses.

Many Jews lost their jobs and income. They were left with few options. While the Jewish Communities attempted to mitigate the impact of terror and anti-Jewish directives, in May 1939 Heydrich actually stopped Jews from leaving the Protectorate, as this would be at the expense of Jewish emigration from Germany. This hopeless situation sparked panic among Jews, with many fleeing across the unguarded border into Poland, while others committed suicide.

Notes

1. Domarus, *Hitler*, vol. I, 2nd half-volume, 960.
2. Konrad Kwiet, 'Forced Labour of German Jews in Nazi Germany', *Leo Baeck Institute Year Book* XXXVI (1991), 389–407, annex, 408–10: Note Dr. Best (CdS), 1 March 1939. See Gruner, *Jewish Forced Labor*, 141–43.
3. Beneš and Ginsburg, *10 Million Prisoners*, 22–23; Bryant, *Prague in Black*, 28.
4. Note Office Weizsäcker on coming visit of 14 March 1939 and Note Hewel on meeting with Hácha on 15 March 1939, in Celovsky, *Germanisierung und Genozid*, 200–203; Lemkin, *Axis Rule in Occupied Europe*, 133–34, fn 13. Cf. the portrayal of Vladislav Klumpar, minister of social and health administration, in Wilhelm Dennler, *Die Böhmische Passion* (Freiburg im Breisgau, 1953), 95–98. Dennler is likely to have written his 'diary' after the war in an attempt to justify his own actions. A senior official in the Protectorate authority and later deputy minister in the Czech government, Dennler presents himself as critical of the Nazi leadership, yet makes no mention whatsoever of the persecution of Jews and describes the German treatment of the Czechs as friendly, with the exception of a few 'excesses'. He denied the existence of forced labour; the Czechs had been only too keen to join the 'Reich'.
5. Hitler's decree, 14 March 1939, facsimile in Hans-Ludwig Grabowski and Wolfgang Haney (eds), *Kennzeichen 'Jude': Antisemitismus – Entrechtung – Verfolgung – Vernichtung. Dokumentation basierend auf Belegen der zeitgeschichtlichen Sammlung Wolfgang Haney* (Regenstauf, 2014), 196–97. Cf. documents in Celovsky, *Germanisierung und Genozid*, 200–202. Frýdek-Místek was the scene of one of the very few armed clashes, but the Czech infantry regiment involved surrendered after a brief exchange of fire; Gerald Mund (ed.), *Deutschland und das Protektorat Böhmen und Mähren: Aus den deutschen diplomatischen Akten von 1939 bis 1945* (Göttingen, 2014), doc. 29, 81.
6. USC SF/VHA, video interview, Curt Allina, tape 2, seg. 119. See also ibid., video interview, Georgine Hyde, tape 2, min. 9:56–10:28.
7. Czech: 'Where Is My Home?', the Czech national anthem.
8. Diary entry by Camill Hoffmann, 15 March 1939, in VEJ/3, doc. 235, 567–68. See also *New York Times*, 19 March 1939. Camill Hoffmann (1878–1944), diplomat, journalist, writer, editor of the *Dresdner Neueste Nachrichten* 1912–19, head of the press office of the Czechoslovak legation in Berlin 1921–38, principal in the Czechoslovak Foreign Ministry 1927, retired 1939, deported to Theresienstadt 1942, deported to Auschwitz 1944 where he was murdered.
9. Beneš and Ginsburg, *10 Million Prisoners*, 30; Max Domarus (ed.), *Hitler: Reden und Proklamationen 1932–1945*, vol. II, 1st half-volume 1939–1940 (Munich, 1965), 1097–98; *New York Times*, 19 March 1939. See also Ernst Frank, *Karl Hermann Frank: Staatsminister im Protektorat*, 2nd expanded ed. (Heusenstamm, 1971), 76.

10. This rendered obsolete attempts to legitimize annexations by underlining Germans' right to self-determination, so often evoked by Hitler; Mark Mazower, *Hitler's Empire: Nazi Rule in Europe* (New York, 2008), 40–63.
11. Decree issued by the Führer and Reich chancellor on the Protectorate of Bohemia and Moravia, 16 March 1939, RGBl. 1939 I, 485–86; in German and Czech in *Verordnungsblatt für Böhmen und Mähren* 1939/no. 2, 7–10. Reprinted in Mund, *Deutschland und das Protektorat*, doc. 1, 59–61.
12. According to Hermann Rauschning, *Gespräche mit Hitler* (New York, 1940, 42); Petr Němec, 'Das tschechische Volk und die nationalsozialistische Germanisierung des Raumes', *Bohemia* 32(2) (1991), 424–55, here 426. On the policy of Germanization in Bohemia, see Brandes, *Umvolkung, Umsiedlung, rassische Bestandsaufnahme*.
13. According to Rauschning, *Gespräche mit Hitler*, 42, quoted in Němec, 'Das tschechische Volk', 426.
14. Rothkirchen, *Jews*, 99.
15. Führer's decree, 16 March 1939, in RGBl. 1939 I, 486.
16. See Joachim Lilla, 'Die Vertretung des "Reichsgaus Sudetenland" und des "Protektorats Böhmen und Mähren" im Großdeutschen Reichstag', *Bohemia* 40(2) (1999), 436–71, here 444.
17. Deutsches Nachrichtenbüro (German news service), 25 April 1939, 1. See the law of 13 April 1939, in RGBl. 1939 I, 762.
18. Statement by Karl Hermann Frank in a memorandum discussing how best to deal with the 'problem of the Czechs', quoted in Němec, 'Das tschechische Volk', 434.
19. *Die Tagebücher von Joseph Goebbels. Part I: Aufzeichnungen 1923–1941*, ed. Elke Fröhlich, vol. 6, *August 1938–June 1939*, ed. Jana Richter (Munich, 1998), 286: entry of 15 March 1939.
20. Führer's decree of 16 March 1939, in RGBl. 1939 I, 486. For a general account, see Patrick Crowhurst, *Hitler and Czechoslovakia in World War II: Domination and Retaliation* (London, 2013).
21. Führer's decree of 16 March 1939, in RGBl. 1939 I, 486. See also Joint circular sent by Frick and Lammers to the Reich ministers and supreme Reich authorities (Oberste Reichsbehörden), 1 April 1939, in Mund, *Deutschland und das Protektorat*, doc. 101, 177–79.
22. Domarus, *Hitler*, vol. II, 1100–102. See Beneš and Ginsburg, *10 Million Prisoners*, 30; Rothkirchen, *Jews*, 99; Frank, *Karl Hermann Frank*, 76. On von Neurath, see Lars Lüdicke, *Constantin von Neurath: Eine politische Biographie* (Paderborn, 2014) (on his appointment: 508–13). Lammers sent the letter of appointment to von Neurath on 20 March; Mund, *Deutschland und das Protektorat*, doc. 67, 114.
23. Hans Umbreit, *Deutsche Militärverwaltungen 1938/39: Die militärische Besetzung der Tschechoslowakei und Polens* (Stuttgart, 1977), 34–56.
24. Klaus Michael Mallmann, 'Menschenjagd und Massenmord: Das neue Instrument der Einsatzgruppen und -kommandos 1938–1945', in Gerhard Paul and Klaus-Michael Mallmann (eds), *Die Gestapo im Zweiten Weltkrieg: 'Heimatfront' und besetztes Europa* (Darmstadt, 2000), 291–316, here 292–94; Oldřich Sládek, 'Standrecht und Standgericht: Die Gestapo in Böhmen und Mähren', in ibid., 317–39, here 322–26.
25. For a general account of this, see Michael Wildt, *An Uncompromising Generation: The Nazi Leadership of the Reich Security Main Office* (Madison, 2009) (German original 2002).
26. Vojenský historický archiv (VHA) Prague, Fonds Leaders SS Death's Head regiments and concentration camps, cat. 12, no. 89a, fol. 14–15RS: Diary 'Companies

Moravia and Bohemia. 15 March 1939', entries of 11, 14 and 16 March 1939, 1–4; ibid., fol. 8: Copy 'Mission report on the Bohemia and Moravia mission' produced by motorized squadron (Kraftfahrstaffel) 2nd SS Death's Head Regiment 'Brandenburg', 2 May 1939, 1; ibid., fol. 15: Copy 'Progress report on the Bohemia and Moravia mission produced by the 1st SS Death's Head Regiment Upper Bavaria', n.d.

27. VHA Prague, Fonds Leaders SS Death's Head regiments and concentration camps, cat. 12, no. 89a, fol. 96: Telephone report from SS regiment leader Simon, 23 March 1939. On the number of inhabitants, see *Der Neue Tag. Tageszeitung für Böhmen und Mähren*, 8 October 1941, 9.
28. Hans-Christian Jasch, *Staatssekretär Wilhelm Stuckart und die Judenpolitik: Der Mythos von der sauberen Verwaltung* (Munich, 2012), 140–44.
29. BA Berlin, R 43II/1329a, fol. 2: Göring to the Reich interior minister, 21 March 1939; ibid., fol. 8–13: Draft circular order sent by the Reich interior minister to the supreme Reich authorities, March 1939 (n.d.); ibid., fol. 14RS: Note on personal report to Hitler, 25 March 1939; Joint circular sent by Frick and Lammers to the Reich ministers and supreme Reich authorities, 1 April 1939, in Mund, *Deutschland und das Protektorat*, doc. 101, 177–79.
30. VHA Prague, Fonds Leaders SS Death's Head regiments and concentration camps, cat. 12, no. 89a, fol. 2: Copy Circular sent by the supreme commander of the army to all Reich authorities, 14 April 1939. See Umbreit, *Deutsche Militärverwaltungen*, 59.
31. Bryant, *Prague in Black*, 33.
32. Karl Hermann Frank, Member of the National German Association of Commercial Employees (Deutschnationaler Handlungsgehilfenverband), subsequently an accountant at the Dux-Bodenbacher Eisenbahn company in Karlsbad, apprentice bookseller at the Wandervogel publishing house in Hartenstein, Saxony, from 1923 onwards, independent bookseller in Elbogen (Loket) near Karlsbad from 1926 and in Karlsbad from 1931, member of the German National Party until its dissolution in 1933, later established the local branch of the Sudeten German Home Front in Karlsbad, worked full-time from 1934 in Eger in the upper echelons of the Sudeten German Party (Sudetendeutsche Partei or SdP) as head of publicity and organization, SdP deputy in Prague in 1935, deputy SdP chair from 1937, also deputy Nazi Party Gauleiter in Reichenberg from 1938, state secretary to the Reich protector from spring 1939, minister of state for Bohemia and Moravia from August 1943, condemned as a war criminal and executed in Prague after the war. For a detailed account, see Küpper, *Karl Hermann Frank*. For an apologia, see Frank, *Karl Hermann Frank*.
33. BA Berlin, R 43II/1329a, fol. 102: Circular RMdI (State Secretary Pfundtner) to the supreme Reich authorities, 3 April 1939.
34. Sládek, 'Standrecht und Standgericht', 322–26. See also Livia Rothkirchen, 'The Protectorate Government and the "Jewish Question", 1939–1941', *Yad Vashem Studies* 27 (1999), 331–62, here 336. On the very similar structure that existed in 1940, see BA Berlin, R 43II/1329a, fol. 137: Organizational plan produced by the Reich protector authority, 1 October 1940.
35. Sládek, 'Standrecht und Standgericht', 322–26. See also Rothkirchen, 'The Protectorate Government', 336.
36. Detlef Brandes, 'Nationalsozialistische Tschechenpolitik im Protektorat Böhmen und Mähren', in Brandes and Kural, *Der Weg in die Katastrophe*, 39–56, here 52.
37. Ibid., 43.
38. Führer's decree of 16 March 1939, in RGBl. 1939 I, 486–87.

39. Rothkirchen, 'The Protectorate Government', 336; Jan Björn Potthast, *Das jüdische Zentralmuseum der SS in Prag: Gegnerforschung und Völkermord im Nationalsozialismus* (Frankfurt a. M., 2002), 56–60.
40. Bryant, *Prague in Black*, 42.
41. VHA Prague, fonds 140, carton 19, no. 2, fol. 299–300: Report 'The Protectorate of Bohemia and Moravia in Light of its Daily Press', undated copy (c. spring 1940), 12–13; Beneš and Ginsburg, *10 Million Prisoners*, 67–68; Moses Moskowitz, 'Three Years of the Protectorate of Bohemia and Moravia', *Political Science Quarterly* 57(3) (September 1942), 353–75, here 372; King, *Budweisers*, 180; Bryant, *Prague in Black*, 45.
42. VHA Prague, fonds 140, carton 19, no. 2, fol. 299: Report 'The Protectorate of Bohemia and Moravia in Light of its Daily Press', undated copy (c. spring 1940), 12.
43. Alois Eliáš, career soldier, politician, as divisional general the commanding general of the 5th Army Corps in 1938 at the time of the Munich Conference, then deputy to the minister for national defence in the Sirovy Cabinet, transport minister in the new Beran Cabinet from 1 December 1938, prime minister of the Protectorate of Bohemia and Moravia 1939–41, condemned to death and executed in 1941 for treason in light of his contacts with the Czechoslovak government in exile; VEJ/3, 593; Helmut Heiber, 'Zur Justiz im Dritten Reich: Der Fall Eliáš', *Vierteljahrshefte für Zeitgeschichte* 3 (1955), 275–96, here 279.
44. Brandes, 'Nationalsozialistische Tschechenpolitik', 42; Bryant, *Prague in Black*, 44; Rothkirchen, *Jews*, 100, 141.
45. On this and what follows, see Gruner, 'Das Protektorat Böhmen/Mähren und die antijüdische Politik'.
46. Josef Pfitzner, b. 24 March 1901 in Petersdorf (Silesia, now Piechowic in Poland), executed on 6 September 1945 in Prague, gymnasium in Opava (Troppau), study of history at the German University in Prague, doctorate, professor at the Chair of Eastern European History at the age of twenty-nine shortly after his habilitation in 1930, member of the Sudeten German Party since the mid 1930s, represented the SdP in the Prague city government from May 1938; Vojtěch Šustek, 'Die nationalsozialistische Karriere eines sudetendeutschen Historikers', in Alena Míšková and Vojtěch Šustek, *Josef Pfitzner a protektorátní Praha v letech 1939–45* [Josef Pfitzner and Prague under the Protectorate, 1939–1945], vol. 1 (Prague, 2000), 71–109. On his biography, see Detlef Brandes and Alena Míšková (eds), *Vom Osteuropa-Lehrstuhl ins Prager Rathaus: Josef Pfitzner 1901–1945* (Essen, 2013). On Pfitzner's political activities, see Detlef Brandes, 'Bemühungen um die Germanisierung Prags während der NS-Okkupation: Aus den Berichten des Stellvertretenden Primators Josef Pfitzner', in Monika Glettler, Ľubomir Lipták and Alena Míšková (eds), *Geteilt, besetzt, beherrscht. Die Tschechoslowakei 1938–1945: Reichsgau Sudetenland, Protektorat Böhmen und Mähren, Slowakei* (Essen, 2004), 53–66. On the university, see Pavel Kolár, 'Die Geschichtswissenschaft an der Deutschen Universität Prag 1882–1938: Entwicklung der Lehrkanzeln und Institutionalisierung unter zwei Regimen', in Hans Lemberg (ed.), *Universitäten in nationaler Konkurrenz: Zur Geschichte der Prager Universitäten im 19. und 20. Jahrhundert* (Munich, 2003), 85–114.
47. Brandes and Míšková, *Vom Osteuropa-Lehrstuhl ins Prager Rathaus*, 186–87, 230, 234. On the Germanization of the Prague municipal administration carried out by him, see ibid., 228–76; VHA Prague, fonds 140, carton 19, no. 2, fol. 296: Report 'The Protectorate of Bohemia and Moravia in Light of its Daily Press', undated copy (c. spring 1940), 9. See chief county commissioner Watter to Gies (aide to Frank), 17 May 1940 with letter to Reich protector, in Vojtěch Šustek, *Josef Pfitzner a protek-*

torátní Praha v letech 1939–45, vol. 2 (Prague, 2001), 152–56. See also Moskowitz, 'Three Years of the Protectorate', 362.
48. *Die Tagebücher von Joseph Goebbels*. Part I: *Aufzeichnungen 1923–1941*, vol. 6, 289: entry of 17 March 1939.
49. *Deutsche Politik im 'Protektorat Böhmen und Mähren' unter Reinhard Heydrich 1941–1942: Eine Dokumentation*, ed. Miroslav Kárný, Jaroslava Milotová and Margita Kárná (Berlin, 1997), doc. 23, 125: Report by the Central Office, 2 October 1941, appendix: table 1. For a critical view of these figures, see Miroslav Kárný, 'Zur Statistik der jüdischen Bevölkerung im sogenannten Protektorat', *Judaica Bohemiae* 22(1) (1986), 9–19; and Schmidt-Hartmann, 'Tschechoslowakei', 358; Rothkirchen, *Jews*, 116.
50. Rothkirchen, *Jews*, 100 and 217; Bryant, *Prague in Black*, 34.
51. Report by Dr Franz Friedmann, 'Legal position of the Jews, Protectorate, as at 31 July 1942', in Krejčová, Svobodová and Hyndráková, *Židé v Protektorátu*, doc. 15, 234. See also Rothkirchen, *Jews*, 99–100. On Vienna, see Gruner, *Zwangsarbeit und Verfolgung*, 23–25.
52. YV Jerusalem, O 7/53, fol. 2: Weekly report of the Jewish Religious Community of Prague, 23 July–29 July 1939, 1.
53. Dr Marie Schmolka (Schmolkova), b. Eisner, association official, head of refugee relief at the Jewish Community and HICEM in Prague, representative of the Czechoslovak Relief Committee at the League of Nations, chair of the Comité national Tchéco-Slovaque pour les réfugiés provenant d'Allemagne 1933–38, two months in jail from March 1939, emigrated to the United Kingdom after the start of the war, where she was involved in the establishment of the National Council of the Czechoslovak Jews; see VEJ/3, 584. See also Martin Wein, 'The Czechoslovak Exile in London and the Jews 1938–1945', in Jan Láníček and James Jordan (eds), *Governments-in-Exile and the Jews during the Second World War* (Middlesex, 2013), 135–50, here 137–38.
54. Account by a Dutchman, Prague, spring 1939, in VEJ/3, doc. 241, 581–84, here 584.
55. Josef Bartož, 'Die Arisierung jüdischen Vermögens in Olmütz im Jahre 1939', in *Theresienstädter Studien und Dokumente* 2000, 282–96, here 283; Rothkirchen, *Jews*, 101.
56. Jens Hampel, 'Das Schicksal der jüdischen Bevölkerung der Stadt Iglau 1938–1942', in *Theresienstädter Studien und Dokumente* 1998, 70–99, here 74; Rothkirchen, *Jews*, 101.
57. Hampel, 'Schicksal', 79. In fact, the German Defence Service Law prohibited the requisition of private homes; only public buildings were supposed to be used. See Umbreit, *Deutsche Militärverwaltungen*, 53.
58. Rothkirchen, *Jews*, 101. On the population figure, see *Der Neue Tag*, 8 October 1941, 9.
59. USC SF/VHA, video interview, Katherine Kral, tape 1, min. 25:05–27:00.
60. USC SF/VHA, video interview, Hilda Beran, tape 2, min. 11:45–13:00.
61. *Brünner Tagesbote*, 22 April 1939, 9.
62. Ina Boesch, *Grenzfälle: Von Flucht und Hilfe. Fünf Geschichten aus Europa* (Zürich, 2008), 64–79.
63. Report by a Dutchman, Prague, spring 1939, in VEJ/3, doc. 241, 581–84, here 584.
64. Curt von Burgsdorff, administrative official, joined the Nazi Party 1933, SA group leader, Ministerialdirektor and head of department in the Saxony Interior Ministry 1933–1936, head of the Office of the Reich Governor in Vienna 1938/39, undersecretary of state to the Reich protector 1939–42, governor of the District of Krakau

1943–45, sentenced to three years in prison in Poland 1948, released 1949; VEJ/3, 571.
65. Report by undersecretary of state von Burgsdorff, Brno, to Gauleiter Bürckel, Vienna, 19 March 1939, in VEJ/3, doc. 239, 571–73.
66. Oskar Grazer, jurist, joined Nazi Party 1932, SA 1933, full-time SA employee 1933–36; at Bavarian State Ministry of the Interior 1937/38, acting district head October 1938 to August 1939, then county commissioner in Znojmo (Znaim), Moravia, subsequently in Mikulov (Nikolsburg), then in Tulln, Austria 1940 to 1942, moved to the Party Chancellery 1942, Gau hauptmann in Salzburg 1944, founded Dr. Grazer & Co., Vienna 1954; VEJ/3, 571.
67. USHMM Washington, RG 45.005M, reel 1 (Prague State Archive, Chief of the Civil Administration), carton 2, no. 23, n.p.: Letter from the chief county commissioner of Moravské Budějovice to district heads in Moravské Budějovice, Třebíč and Hrotovice, 19 March 1939. Reprinted in VEJ/3, doc. 238, 571.
68. USHMM Washington, RG 45.005M, reel 1 (Prague State Archive, Chief of the Civil Administration), carton 2, no. 19, n.p.: Circular issued by the chief county commissioner in Vsetín, 21 March 1939.
69. Ibid., no. 20, n.p.: Circular issued by the chief county commissioner in Kroměříž, 23 March 1939.
70. Jewish Telegraphic Agency report, 3 April 1939, reprinted in English in Garbarini et al., *Jewish Responses*, 88.
71. Mentioned in USHMM Washington, RG 48.005M, reel 5 (Prague State Archive), I 3b-5800 carton 387, no. 18, n.p.: Cabinet Office (Ministerratspräsidium) to Office of the Reich Protector, 24 July 1940; see Rothkirchen, 'Protectorate Government', 340; Kárný, 'The Genocide of the Czech Jews', 34.
72. Deutsches Nachrichtenbüro (German news service), 18 March 1939, 1.
73. Martin Dean, *Robbing the Jews: The Confiscation of Jewish Property in the Holocaust, 1933–1945* (Cambridge, 2008), 136–37.
74. Jörg Osterloh and Harald Wixforth, 'Die "Arisierung" im Protektorat Böhmen und Mähren: Rahmenbedingungen und gesetzliche Vorgaben', in Wixforth, *Die Expansion der Dresdner Bank*, 306–48, here 306.
75. Rothkirchen, *Jews*, 106.
76. Bartož, 'Arisierung', 285; Kreutzmüller and Kučera, 'Commerzbank', 199. On this and what follows, see Osterloh and Wixforth, '"Arisierung" im Protektorat'; Miroslav Kárný, 'Die Protektoratsregierung und die Verordnungen des Reichsprotektors über das jüdische Vermögen', *Judaica Bohemiae* XXIX (1993), 54–66.
77. Quoted in Rothkirchen, *Jews*, 144–45.
78. Reprinted in full in VEJ/3, doc. 237, 569–70; and in *Europa unterm Hakenkreuz: Österreich und Tschechoslowakei*, doc. no. 32, 106. See also Drahomír Jančik, 'Die "Arisierungsaktivitäten" der Böhmischen Escompte Bank im Protektorat Böhmen und Mähren 1939–1945', in Ziegler, *Banken und 'Arisierungen'*, 143–73, here 145.
79. Bryant, *Prague in Black*, 82.
80. Osterloh and Wixforth, '"Arisierung" im Protektorat', 307.
81. USHMM Washington, RG 48.005M, reel 1 (Prague State Archive, Land Office [Bodenamt]: Regulations on Jews), no. 3, n.p.: Decree issued by chief of the civil administration for Moravia, 20 March 1939; ibid., reel 1 (Prague State Archive, Land Office: Regulations on Jews), no. 2, n.p.: Decree issued by chief of the civil administration for Bohemia, 29 March 1939. See Jaroslava Milotová, 'Die Zentralstelle für jüdische Auswanderung in Prag: Genesis und Tätigkeit bis zum Anfang des Jahres 1940', in *Theresienstädter Studien und Dokumente* 1997, 7–30, here 20; Potthast, *Das jüdische Zentralmuseum*, 60.

82. BA Berlin, R 43II/1324, fol. 40–44: telegrams of 22–26 March 1939; quotation fol. 40.
83. NA Prague, URP, ST 1005/1, 109/1/87–107 or USHMM Washington, RG 48.008M, reel 96, or SUA, fonds AA, carton 10, 195974–195989: Minutes of state secretaries' meeting, 25 March 1939 and enclosure, quoted in reprint in VEJ/3, doc. 240, 574–80, here 579. See reprint of enclosure only in *Europa unterm Hakenkreuz: Österreich und Tschechoslowakei*, doc. no. 36, 110–12; Miroslav Kárný and Jaroslava Milotová (eds), *Anatomie okupační politiky hitlerovského Německa v 'Protektorátu Čechy a Morava': Dokumenty z období říšského protektora Konstantina von Neuratha* (Prague, 1987), 13 f., docs. 1 and 2. See also Milotová, 'Zentralstelle', 7; Potthast, *Das jüdische Zentralmuseum*, 62; Umbreit, *Deutsche Militärverwaltungen*, 54.
84. Kulka and Jäckel, *Jews*, CD doc. no. 2851: SD Main Office II 1, Report for January, February and March 1939, Berlin, n.d.
85. Beneš and Ginsburg, *10 Million Prisoners*, 135.
86. Rothkirchen, *Jews*, 102.
87. BA Berlin, R 58/6401, fol. 231–34: Letter from Böhme (SD Central Office in Prague) to head of the Main Security Office, 8 June 1939 with report from the JKG Prague of 1 June 1939.
88. Rothkirchen, *Jews*, 117.
89. Jewish Telegraphic Agency (JTA), 'Czechs Indignant over Bombing of Historic Jewish Building', 31 May 1939. All JTA citations can be found at www.jta.org.
90. BA Berlin, R 58/6401, fol. 231–34: Letter from Böhme (SD Central Office in Prague) to head of the Security Main Office, 8 June 1939 with report from the Jewish Community Prague of 1 June 1939.
91. Report (confidential) by George Kennan, Moravian Ostrava, 26–27 April 1939, in VEJ/3, doc. 244, 590–92.
92. Rothkirchen, *Jews*, 101; Bryant, *Prague in Black*, 44.
93. JTA, 'Czechs Indignant over Bombing of Historic Jewish Building', 31 May 1939.
94. Beneš and Ginsburg, *10 Million Prisoners*, 136–37; Rothkirchen, *Jews*, 101–2; Bryant, *Prague in Black*, 44; Jan Machala, '"Unbearable Jewish Houses of Prayer": The Nazi Destruction of Synagogues Based on Examples from Central Moravia', *Judaica Bohemiae* 49(1) (2013), 59–87, here 67.
95. On Vlajka and its views, see VHA Prague, fonds 140, carton 19, no. 2, fol. 308–11: Report 'The Protectorate of Bohemia and Moravia in Light of its Daily Press', undated copy (c. spring 1940), 22–25.
96. JTA, 'Czech Anti-Semitic Extremists Split off from Gajda Group', 6 June 1939. On the membership figure, see Frommer, *National Cleansing*, 8.
97. For example on 7 March 1939 in Pilsen and 16 July 1939 in Kroměříž; RGVA Moscow, 1488-1-7, fol. 126: Cabinet Office to Reich Protector, 30 January 1940, appendix 'Nationales Faschistenlager', 24. I thank Jörg Osterloh, Frankfurt a. M., for alerting me to RGVA holding 1488.
98. Machala, '"Unbearable Jewish Houses of Prayer"', 67.
99. JTA, 'Synagogues Put to Torch Almost Daily in Nazi Protectorate', 13 June 1939.
100. JTA, 'Gestapo Seals Jewish Buildings in Czech City', 9 June 1939.
101. Rothkirchen, *Jews*, 109.
102. Kim Wünschmann, *Before Auschwitz: Jewish Prisoners in the Prewar Concentration Camps* (Cambridge, MA, 2015), 218.
103. Beneš and Ginsburg, *10 Million Prisoners*, 141.
104. Rothkirchen, *Jews*, 103.
105. BA Berlin, R 58/6401, fol. 260: Note SD II 112 Dannecker of 10 July 1939 based on Note Hagen of 2 May 1939; ibid., fol. 243–45: Note Hagen of 16 June 1939 for

submission to Head II (Six). On this and what follows, see Gruner, 'Das Protektorat Böhmen/Mähren und die antijüdische Politik', 34–37. See also Hans Safrian, *Eichmann's Men* (Cambridge, 2009) (German original 1993), p. 50.
106. BA Berlin, R 58/6401, fol. 243–45: Note Hagen of 16 June 1939 for submission to Head II (Six); and ibid., fol. 260: Note II 112 Dannecker of 10 July 1939.
107. Report by Camill Hoffmann, n.d. (summer 1939), in VEJ/3, doc. 249, 598. On the emigration of the Czech Jews and on the role of the various institutions, including the Jewish Community, see Laura Brade, 'Networks of Escape: Jewish Flight from the Bohemian Lands, 1938–1941', Dissertation (University of North Carolina-Chapel Hill, 2017).
108. USHMM Washington, RG 48.005M, reel 5 (Prague State Archive), I 3b-5803 carton 388, no. 3, n.p.: Note Reich protector (von Burgsdorff), 2 May 1939; reprinted in VEJ/3, doc. 245, 592. Also quoted in Milotová, 'Zentralstelle', 8.
109. Draft law quoted in Beneš and Ginsburg, *10 Million Prisoners*, 136.
110. Michael Wildt (ed.), *Die Judenpolitik des SD 1935–1938: Eine Dokumentation* (Munich, 1995), 60.
111. King, *Budweisers*, 181. Abroad, the Jewish Telegraphic Agency discovered soon afterwards that on the occasion of a discussion between President Emil Hácha and Reich Protector Konstantin von Neurath on a planned anti-Jewish law, the 'Commission of the National Partnership Party on the Jewish Question' had been dissolved and a new committee appointed; JTA, 'Czechs Indignant over Bombing of Historic Jewish Building', 31 May 1939.
112. VHA Prague, fonds 140, carton 23, no. 97, fol. 10: Report 'The Jewish Question', n.d., 3.
113. USHMM Washington, RG 48.005M, reel 5 (Prague State Archive), I 3b-5803 carton 388, no. 5, n.p.: Chairman of the government to protector with the draft, 11 May 1939, reprinted in VEJ/3, doc. 246, 593.
114. USHMM Washington, RG 48.005M, reel 5 (Prague State Archive), I 3b-5803 carton 388, no. 4, n.p.: Draft of the Czech government decree, 11 May 1939, 1–22. See also Rothkirchen, *Jews*, 144.
115. *New York Times*, 14 May 1939, mentioned in Moskowitz, 'Three Years of the Protectorate', 357. See *Manchester Guardian*, 15 May 1939, 15.
116. Deutsches Nachrichtenbüro (German news service), 13 May 1939, 1.
117. JTA, 'Anti-Jewish Law Drafted, Czechs Unmoved by Anti-Jewish Agitation', 15 May 1939.
118. *Manchester Guardian*, 15 May 1939, 15.
119. USHMM Washington, RG 48.005M, reel 5 (Prague State Archive), I 3b-5803 carton 388, no. 2, n.p.: Draft of the minutes of the meeting at the Reich Protector's Office on 22 May 1939, (no date, May 1939), 1–3.
120. Letter from the BdS, 1 June 1939, quoted in 'Einleitung', in VEJ/3, 24.
121. News brief, Report from Prague, 30 May; JTA, 31 May 1939, 4.
122. Whether this really came as a surprise, as is often stated in the literature, is an open question. In any case, it took more than a month for the decree to come into force. On this reading, see, for example, Rothkirchen, *Jews*, 144. The decree, however, was not introduced by Eichmann and – as we will see shortly – had nothing to do with the establishment of the Central Office, as Christiane Kuller assumes; Christiane Kuller, *Bürokratie und Verbrechen: Antisemitische Finanzpolitik und Verwaltungspraxis im nationalsozialistischen Deutschland* (Munich, 2013), 377.
123. *Verordnungsblatt des Reichsprotektors in Böhmen und Mähren*, 1939/no. 6, 45–48, reprinted in VEJ/3, doc. 247, 593–96. Also reprinted in Walther Utermöhle and

Herbert Schmerling, *Die Rechtsstellung der Juden im Protektorat Böhmen und Mähren* (n.p., 1940), 8–14. See also BA Berlin, R 58/6401, fol. 255: SD Central Office Prague B 1 (Böhme) to CdS, 23 June 1939. On the decree, see Jaroslava Milotová, 'Zur Geschichte der Verordnung Konstantin von Neuraths über das jüdische Vermögen', in *Theresienstädter Studien und Dokumente* 2002, 75–115. For a general account of the legislation, see John G. Lexa, 'Anti-Jewish Laws and Regulations in the Protectorate of Bohemia and Moravia', in A. Dagan (ed.), *The Jews of Czechoslovakia: Historical Studies and Surveys*, vol. 3 (Philadelphia, 1984), 75–103.

124. *New York Times*, 22 June 1939, 1.
125. Grabowski and Haney, *Kennzeichen 'Jude'*, 201.
126. The decree explicitly invalidated the directives issued by the chiefs of the civil administration in Brno of 20 March 1939, the CdZ decree concerning prohibition of the sale of Jewish property in Moravia of 22 March and the decree issued by the chiefs of the civil administration in Prague concerning Jewish property of 29 March; *Verordnungsblatt des Reichsprotektors in Böhmen und Mähren* 1939/no. 6, 45–48, reprinted in VEJ/3, doc. 247, 593–96. On the economic aspects, see Eduard Kubů, 'Die Verwaltung von konfisziertem und sequestriertem Vermögen – eine spezifische Kategorie des "Arisierungs-Profits": Die Kreditanstalt der Deutschen und ihre Abteilung "F"', in Ziegler, *Banken und 'Arisierungen'*, 175–210, here 179; Kreutzmüller and Kučera, 'Commerzbank', 200–201.
127. See Kubů, 'Die Verwaltung von konfisziertem und sequestriertem Vermögen', 177–78.
128. Ibid., 177–78; Bartož, 'Arisierung', 286–88.
129. Osterloh and Wixforth, '"Arisierung" im Protektorat', 307.
130. Jiří Novotný and Jiří Šouša, 'Die Nationalbank in den Jahren 1939–1945 und die "Arisierung" im Protektorat Böhmen und Mähren', in Ziegler, *Banken und 'Arisierungen'*, 119–42, here 125–27.
131. Erdely, *Germany's First European Protectorate*, 146–47.
132. According to a report produced by the SD Central Office for Bohemia and Moravia in Prague (Böhme), this initiative was considered to have run its course in light of the decree issued by the Reich protector in Bohemia and Moravia on Jewish assets of 21 June 1939. The campaign had yielded around 440 million crowns' worth of cash assets, securities, foreign currency claims and real estate; BA Berlin, R 58/6401, fol. 263: RFSS-SD/SD Central Office for Bohemia and Moravia in Prague to CdS Berlin, 28 June 1939; see also Celovsky, *Germanisierung und Genozid*, 209.
133. Jančik, '"Arisierungsaktivitäten" der Böhmischen Escompte Bank', 143–44.
134. Lothar Gall et al., *Die Deutsche Bank 1870–1995* (Munich, 1995), 369. See also Harold James, *The Deutsche Bank and the Nazi Economic War against the Jews: The Expropriation of Jewish-Owned Property* (New York, 2001).
135. Erdely, *Germany's First European Protectorate*, 147.
136. Osterloh and Wixforth, '"Arisierung" im Protektorat', 307–8.
137. Bartož, 'Arisierung', 288–89.
138. Quoted in Osterloh and Wixforth, '"Arisierung" im Protektorat', 309. See also Jaromír Balcar, *Panzer für Hitler – Traktoren für Stalin: Großunternehmen in Böhmen und Mähren 1938–1950* (Munich, 2014), 67–75, here 71.

CHAPTER 3

GERMAN EXPULSION AND CZECH PERSECUTION

The Establishment of the Prague 'Central Office for Jewish Emigration'

While many Jews were keen to leave the Protectorate sooner rather than later, it was not just growing poverty that impeded emigration but, initially, the Security Police itself. On 21 June 1939, however, the day of issuance of the fateful Neurath decree, which was intended to exclude Jews from economic life, Heydrich decided to establish a 'Central Office for the Facilitation of Jewish Emigration' in Prague after all. As in Vienna, the Office was to expedite emigration. But in Prague, in a compromise between German and Czech interests and with the help of Czech funds, it was also to ensure that German Jews left the territory. Hence, over the next few weeks the ground was laid for the establishment of a Central Office on the Austrian model.[1]

The decision to establish the Central Office, however, was not made autocratically but in consultation with the Czech government. Stahlecker discussed every aspect with Prime Minister Eliáš, who declared that while the 'emigration of Jews from the Protectorate was desirable, he must reserve the right for the Cabinet to decide the [government's] final position'. On 19 July, Stahlecker, as Commander of the Security Police, convened a meeting in the Petschek building at which representatives of the Czech Interior and Finance Ministries, the National Bank and the Reich Protector Office discussed the issue. Both sides agreed to establish an institution in which the SD would share authority with autonomous staff dispatched by the Czech ministries. In light of this, on 20 July the Czech government gave its blessing to the creation of the new agency.[2]

Reich Protector von Neurath established the 'Central Office for Jewish Emigration' in Prague, by official decree, on 15 July 1939.[3] It was initially subordinate to the Security Main Office in Berlin and combined certain responsibilities held by the Gestapo and SD. Intended to function as a central hub to tackle all 'issues involved in the emigration of Jews', in concrete terms the agency was supposed to 'facilitate emigration through negotiations on entry permits with the relevant emigration organizations', acquire the foreign currency necessary for emigration, establish and supervise retraining facilities, and work with travel agencies and shipping companies to speed up emigration. The Central Office was to monitor the 'Jewish political and other emigration organizations' and cooperate 'with all German agencies and the agencies of the Protectorate government of relevance to the exodus of Jews from the Protectorate'. It was also tasked with the 'standardized and expeditious acquisition' of all 'certificates [necessary for emigration] – while maintaining the different departments' jurisdiction' and ensuring 'close cooperation between the German agencies and the relevant agencies of the Protectorate government'. Stahlecker, SS Senior Group Leader and Commander of the Security Police, was to head the Central Office for Jewish Emigration in Prague, henceforth the essential point of contact for 'Jews wishing to emigrate from the Protectorate'. The Office would acquire the certificates necessary for emigration and supervise the final emigration itself, a provision that would initially apply to Prague and the surrounding areas. The Czech government would potentially issue directives, 'particularly with respect to the secondment of the civil servants required by the agencies of the Protectorate government for the departmental processing of Jewish emigration and with respect to the referral of all applications for emigration to the Central Office for Jewish Emigration in Prague'.[4]

Stahlecker summoned Eichmann from Vienna to Prague,[5] the latter bringing along his experienced assistants Hans Günther and Alois Brunner.[6] From 23 July 1939 onwards, as in Vienna, the Jewish Community of Prague had to provide Eichmann with weekly, monthly and quarterly reports on its work and all matters relating to the Jewish population.[7] The Central Office for Jewish Emigration, meanwhile, began its work on Monday 31 July in an 'Aryanized' villa at 11 Dělostřelecka, Prague-Střešovice (Schillstraße 11, Prag-Streschowitz).[8]

At the time, the SD was engaged in internal discussions on whether to establish a second Central Office in Brno, as the newly established institution was responsible only for Prague and the surrounding areas.[9]

The Organization of Forced Emigration

According to official sources, between October 1938 and late July 1939, 24,131 individuals emigrated, of whom 20,684 were Jews, including many German and Austrian refugees.[10] In late July 1939, as one of its first official acts, the Central Office informed the Jewish Religious Community of Prague that a further thirty thousand Jews must leave the Protectorate by the end of the year.[11] Adolf Eichmann summoned Dr Kafka and Dr Weidmann of the Religious Community and Dr Franz Friedmann of the Zionist Federation (Zionistische Vereinigung) to tell them this terrible news.[12] In fact, by the summer of 1940, as the Jewish Telegraphic Agency reported, no fewer than seventy thousand Jews, more than half the Protectorate's Jewish population, were supposed to emigrate.[13]

With immediate effect, two hundred Jews a day had to leave the Protectorate in order to comply with Eichmann's demands. Concurrently, to lay the ground for emigration, Jews from the provinces were to be concentrated in Prague, again at the rate of two hundred people per day. In České Budějovice, Bohemia, as reports indicated, the authorities had already mandated the relocation of Jews to Prague.[14] In response, as president of the Prague Religious Community and member of the Protectorate's Council of the Jewish Communities, in August Dr Emil Kafka gathered together representatives of the provincial Communities for an urgent meeting, during which he informed them that Eichmann had mandated that all Jews must leave the Protectorate. Never in the thousand-year history of the Czech Jewry, he stated, had there been a more bitter moment.[15] In parallel, on behalf of the Prague Community, Jakob Edelstein wrote to the provincial Communities describing the new situation and calling for unity among Jews as they set about their tragic task.[16]

Prior to the occupation, the HICEM office in Prague had organized emigration. Because the Gestapo had immediately closed its bureau, the Central Office now instructed the Prague Religious Community to establish an emigration department with a staff of ninety in short order.[17] By 20 July, Eichmann had sent officials from the Prague Community to Vienna to gain relevant first-hand experience. Taking the Vienna institution as their guide, they were to help organize Jewish emigration in the Protectorate.[18] In the Palais Rothschild in Vienna they thus familiarized themselves with the procedures developed by the Central Office to this end.[19] In the second week of August, meanwhile, specialists from the Vienna Religious Community visited Prague to help the Jewish functionaries create an effective organization.[20]

Emil Kafka travelled to Paris, where he spoke with representatives of international Jewish relief organizations such as the Joint Distribution Committee, the HIAS-JCA Emigration Association and the World ORT Federation along with other Jewish bodies. On behalf of the American Jews, Morris C. Troper, European chair of the JDC, pledged to provide aid, as did Baron Robert de Rothschild in the name of the French Jewry. On 24 July, Kafka also discussed the 'pressing problem of emigration' in the Protectorate with representatives of Jewish organizations in London.[21]

Two months before the opening of the Central Office, in mid May 1939, Jakob Edelstein, head of the Prague Palestine Office (Palästinaamt), had already been compelled to travel to Palestine, at the behest of the SD, to sound out emigration options for Czech Jews in consultation with all relevant authorities and 'to secure an appropriate share of certificates for the Protectorate territory through in-depth negotiations'. He was clearly successful in this, securing 20 per cent of the certificates available for the entire world for Jews in the Protectorate. They received a total of 902 certificates, covering 1,593 individuals. Edelstein also received 'assurances of indirect emigration to Palestine' for another 1,500 Jewish individuals 'via vocational training in various states'. The Palestine Office now felt able to 'ensure the emigration of more than 3,000 people from Protectorate territory' by 30 September.[22]

The Prague Religious Community now set up three emigration departments, one for all countries apart from Palestine, one for Palestine, organized by the Palestine Office, and another to facilitate the emigration of non-Community members. The Religious Community took over the responsibilities of the HIAS-JCA, which had by now been disbanded in the Protectorate.[23]

The emigration departments obtained documents for Jews who were already in a position to leave the country. Eichmann ordered the Prague Religious Community to transfer a daily total of 250 and later 300 applicants to the Central Office, virtually unachievable targets. The fact that the Central Office could only approve emigration for residents of the capital made a difficult situation even worse, with Jews from the provinces willing to emigrate having to relocate to Prague first.[24] On 29 July 1939, the Religious Community sent the first 148 applicants to the Central Office to obtain exit documents, 931 the following week and

897 in mid August, but just 489 and 477 in the following two weeks as emigration options were rapidly exhausted.[25]

On 26 and 27 July, when Czech ministerial officials visited the Central Office for Jewish Emigration in Vienna, Eichmann asserted that the latter was 'intended only for those Jewish emigrants who voluntarily present themselves for purposes of emigration'. Crucially, he explained, the Central Office concentrated 'all specialized fields relating to Jewish emigration in one place'. In this way, he went on, it expedited bureaucratic procedures, prevented the omission of important steps and controlled 'Jewish emigration'. Each individual must 'obtain an application form [from the Central Office], fill out two copies and attach the appropriate certification'. Clerks at the Jewish Religious Community's Document Procurement Office (Dokumentenbeschaffungsstelle) would initially check this application to make sure all the necessary documents had been included, such as birth certificate, residence certificate (Heimatschein), home registration certificate (Wohnungsmeldezettel) and identity card (Kennkarte). The applicant would then go to the Central Office and submit his application to a clerk, who would assign it a number and seal it in an envelope. The emigrant would subsequently request a variety of certificates from officials at a number of different institutions, such as a character reference, passport, and the residence permit required for a visa.

> Along with the other documents, the application is then forwarded to the following divisions: the Criminal Investigation Division (Kriminalabteilung), the State Security Divisions (Abteilungen für Staatssicherheit), the Foreign Currency and Economic Police (Devisen- und Wirtschaftspolizei), the Penal Register (Strafregister), the Investigation Division (Ermittlungsabteilung), the divisions of the Public Prosecutor's Office (Staatsanwaltschaft) and the Central Offices for Combating Trafficking in Girls (Zentralstelle für den Kampf gegen Mädchenhandel) and Registering Refusal to Work and Prostitution (Zentralstellen für die Erfassung von Arbeitsverweigerung und der Prostitution).

The application's passage through these offices was meant to take four to five hours. Each division noted on the envelope whether all necessary documents were present and whether they had any objections to emigration. Finally, the 'exit fee' was calculated[26] and the passport and documentation issued. The aspiring emigrant was given an 'exit deadline' of up to two months. With the certificates now in his possession, he could acquire an entry visa for the country in question and tickets for his journey. As Eichmann explained to the Czech officials, if the emigrant was unable to leave by the date specified and could provide no adequate explanation, he would be 'sent to a Jewish concentration camp'. Eichmann was referring here to so-called retraining camps of the kind run by the Austrian SS in Doppl and Sandhof.[27] There, according to Eichmann, such Jews were 'subjected to a relentless regime of strenuous physical exercise'. If they still failed to comply with the order to emigrate, they would be 'sent to a regular concentration camp'. In accordance with the Vienna model, the Prague Central Office too intended 'to force the emigrants to leave the country by sending them to concentration camps. Where and how these concentration camps [were to be] established' would be the subject of a joint discussion on 31 July in the Prague Central Office. While procedures in Vienna must have appeared smooth and efficient to the Czech visitors, who included officials from the Czech Ministry for Social and Health Administration, the reality was quite different.[28]

Like its counterpart in Vienna, in the Jewish community the Prague Central Office soon became an object of fear and notoriety. Long queues of Jews willing to emigrate waited outside the building. Men were forced to wait with their heads uncovered. If they put their hands in their pockets, they were struck. Despite waiting for hours, applicants were banned from leaning on the wall. According to contemporary accounts, Central Office staff treated them like dogs.[29]

By this time, Czech Jews' passports were reportedly marked with a 'J'.[30] In early August 1939, as the Jewish Telegraphic Agency learned, the Gestapo prohibited the emigration of Jewish doctors under forty-five years of age and it was keen to extend this ban to scientific chemists, possibly in preparation for war. In Prague this necessitated reallocation of forty Palestine Certificates already earmarked for Jewish doctors. Jews wishing to benefit from the transfer agreement and the British fund for Czech emigration now had to deposit 450,000 crowns in order to transfer 1,000 pounds; prior to the occupation, the same sum had garnered 3,240 pounds. Those in possession of Palestine Capitalist Immigration Certificates (Palästina-Kapitalisteneinwanderungszertifikate) had to deposit 300,000 crowns at the National Bank plus 150,000 crowns for the Reich Flight Tax (Reichsfluchtsteuer) and other fees to gain approval for the monetary transfer.[31] In the Protectorate, the government introduced an 'emigration tax' – akin to the German Reich Flight Tax, originally enacted in 1931 – to prevent emigrants from transferring large amounts of capital. This applied to assets in excess of 200,000 crowns, which attracted a tax of 25 per cent.[32]

The Prague Religious Community did all it could to help, establishing new departments to provide advice on emigration and forging contacts abroad. In late August, for example, it registered candidates for a 'Children's Transport' (Kindertransport) to France in collaboration with the 'Comité Israélite pour les enfants venant d'Allemagne et de l'Europe central' in Paris.³³ The Jewish Communities stepped up their retraining programmes. While such Hachshara camps had existed before, as in Germany there were very few of them.³⁴ By the spring of 1939, the intensified 'redeployment of Jews in agriculture' had already begun, specifically to prepare them for emigration. In late August, there were 550 of these mostly young people, though numbers tailed off later for seasonal reasons.³⁵

Attempts to Concentrate Jews in Prague

It seems that shortly after Eichmann's arrival, the Prague Central Office, emulating its Austrian counterpart, issued a directive to the Jewish Communities to concentrate Jews from the provinces in the capital as a first step towards their total resettlement abroad.³⁶ For the first time, the Religious Community's weekly reports provide us with more detail on this. At the first meeting of representatives from 130 provincial Communities, held in Prague in late July 1939, Weidmann began by explaining the newly decreed priorities, namely emigration assistance, welfare and schooling, and above all the reorganization of emigration. Further, at the meeting he informed the ninety-five representatives from seventy-seven Religious Communities that Jews in Německý Brod (Deutsch-Brod, modern-day Havlíčkův Brod) and České Budějovice had received notice that they must leave their homes within a month and move to Prague. The Prague Religious Community asked Eichmann's Central Office to suspend these measures until its complete reorganization: it was already overburdened by the general influx of Jews from the provinces and was struggling to accommodate them.³⁷ The Jews in the places mentioned now lived in the grip of despair.³⁸

In response the Central Office declared that for now only household heads from the provinces making preparations for emigration should settle in Prague.³⁹ The received view so far has been that this plan was put on ice after intervention by the Czech local authorities and the minister for industry and trade, who underlined the economic difficulties it would entail.⁴⁰ Yet on 13 August, with the Gestapo's approval, a further meeting of the heads of the provincial Communities took place in Prague. There they learned that the Central Office had mandated that all Community members be instructed to take up residence in the Protectorate capital. The Community heads were also to submit, without delay, statistics on membership figures, organizations and retraining courses to the Prague Religious Community, which would collate it and forward it to the Central Office.⁴¹

Subsequently the Gestapo forced Jews to relocate to Prague from a number of districts, including Německý Brod, Pelhřimov (Pilgram), Kamenice nad Lípou, Humpolec (Humpoletz), Ledeč nad Sázavou, České Budějovice and other places. This move triggered a mood of panic among the Jewish population as it destroyed many families' means of subsistence.⁴²

Doing its best to provide for destitute Jews from the provinces, the Prague Community was completely overwhelmed. In its weekly report of 20–25 August, it asked the Central Office to at least grant the expellees time to liquidate their assets.⁴³ By 25 August, the Community had allocated ten apartments and more than ninety rooms to Jews newly arrived in Prague.⁴⁴ In the period between 27 August and 1 September, it registered 174 cases of resettlement from the provinces requiring its assistance. The Community again asked the Central Office to at least suspend forced resettlement in order to give those affected a chance to 'Aryanize' their assets, that is, sell off their property, even if at a minimal price.⁴⁵

Expulsion from Associations and Organizations

When the Reich interior minister transferred responsibility for restructuring all existing organizations to the Reich protector in June 1939, the latter established a bespoke agency, namely the Commissioner for Organizations (Beauftragter für die Organisationen) in Prague. This institution, integrated into the Office of the Protector as Group 21, was headed by Albert Hoffmann, a fanatical National Socialist born in 1907 who had previously held the post of Liquidation Commissar (Stillhaltekommissar) in Austria and the Sudetenland.⁴⁶ The establishment of a Liquidation Commissar in Austria in 1938 had created a novel institution with no German role model, one subsequently emulated in the Sudetenland and the Protectorate.⁴⁷ Whenever territory was incorporated into the Reich, the respective Liquidation Commissar undertook a 'tacit Reich reform', which applied to both Jewish and non-Jewish organizations. Rather than focusing on the 'coordination' (Gleichschaltung) of associations as in the Reich, the Liquidation Commissar simply dissolved most of them and/or created new ones in order to exclude political opponents and the racially persecuted. Ultimately, the priorities here were to adjust structures, steal assets, secure hegemony and ensure the efficacy of Nazi rule.⁴⁸

In the Protectorate, on 29 July the new authority, renamed the Commissioner for the Organizational System (Beauftragter für das Organisationswesen), demanded the 'registration of all Jewish associations, federations, organizations and association-like entities' within fourteen days. In addition to registering in duplicate, they had to submit a list of assets and a copy of their articles of association.[49] This also applied to foundations and burial fraternities (Beerdigungsbruderschaften).[50] Later, on 9 September, this ordinance was reissued and the deadline extended to mid September.[51]

On 1 August 1939, the Jewish Telegraphic Agency reported that this was the deadline for the general registration of private Jewish property. According to the Agency, over the last few days hundreds of Jews had queued up outside the doors of the Czech National Bank from the early hours of the morning to register their property and valuables. Apparently, even silver buttons worth ten cents were to be reported. The Prague press estimated that around one hundred thousand applications had been filed, yet underlined that Jewish assets that had once been worth fourteen billion crowns had fallen first to a value of seven and now to three billion, the equivalent of 120 million dollars.[52]

Czech Initiatives in Anti-Jewish Policy

Regardless of their expulsion ordinance, Eichmann and the Central Office by no means set themselves up as the sole authority on anti-Jewish policy, as has often been claimed.[53] Nor, contrary to Bryant's assertions, did Reich Protector von Neurath take sole charge of these matters through his decree of 21 June.[54] In reality, a range of German and Czech authorities continued to compete.[55]

In late June, the Czech Schools Ministry prohibited the admittance of 'non-Aryan' pupils or students wishing to transfer to Czech-language educational establishments from schools where another language was spoken, starting from the coming 1939/40 academic year. Those affected included children expelled from German schools. The Ministry also limited the uptake of new Jewish pupils and students to 4 per cent of those in a given academic year.[56] At the behest of the Reich protector, on 12 July the Czech Ministry of Education then prohibited all private schools and educational establishments owned by Jews from admitting 'German-Aryan' children.[57] On 4 July 1939, the Czech government issued a comprehensive decree on the exclusion of Jews from judicial and administrative roles, the civil service and public offices, as well as the independent professions, which affected doctors, lawyers, judges, teachers and editors.[58]

In a report of early August 1939, the Jewish Telegraphic Agency wrote that, despite the strenuous efforts of National Socialists and Czech fascists, anti-Jewish movements were attracting little support within Czech society; just two such movements existed, the fascist Vlajka group and the 'Aryan Culture Union', both just a few hundred strong. It was, the report went on, widely recognized that the Czech authorities were introducing anti-Jewish measures only due to pressure from the Germans, while most Czechs regarded them as an aspect of their own oppression. In an attempt to eliminate this impression, the Agency underlined, the Czech newspapers printed every proclamation issued by the two organizations, such as one from the Aryan Culture Union propagating the separation of Jews and non-Jews in trams and buses. Vlajka, meanwhile, had demanded that discussions of the 'Jewish problem' be incorporated into daily radio broadcasts.[59]

Though outside observers well-disposed towards the Czechs wished to believe the latter were acting solely due to German pressure when it came to the Jewish question, many actually did so of their own accord. In Prague, members of the 'Aryan Czechs' carried out raids on swimming pools, ordering Jews to leave the premises over megaphones.[60] On 29 July 1939, at an event in Pardubice, František Drázda, spokesman for the 'National Aryan Cultural Association' (Národní arijská kulturní jednota), demanded that Jews and Jewish freemasons be excluded from national life, indeed annihilated entirely.[61] The Pilsen police ordered bilingual signs bearing the words 'Jewish business' to be hung on all shops owned by Jews, while in Prague the Czech 'Aryan Union' demanded that the police issue matching ordinances. The Union also wished to bar Jews from 'Aryan' restaurants, cafes and public baths.[62] In addition, in a petition to the city government, it demanded the complete exclusion of Jews from trams and buses in the Protectorate capital.[63] Apparently, as the Jewish Telegraphic Agency reported in London on 6 August, the 'Aryan Union' had now received permission from the Prague Police Directorate to mark all non-Jewish businesses. Furthermore, the Agency stated, the Union was pressing the government to issue a decree forcing the Jewish Communities to pay back state funding officially received since 1923, a total of more than twenty-two million crowns. Ironically, the 'Aryan Union' highlighted the Protectorate budget, which earmarked just 685 crowns for this purpose in 1939.[64] A few days before, on 31 July, it had declared war on 'white Jews', in other words individuals who were friendly towards Jews. The Union, which opposed Hácha's National

Partnership, wanted to see the same kind of strict segregation of Jews and 'Aryans' as in Germany.[65]

The division of powers in anti-Jewish policy became clear on 3 August 1939 when the separation of the Jewish population within the Protectorate was ushered in not by an ordinance from the new Central Office or the Reich protector, but by a decree from the Presidium of the Czech Interior Ministry. This government decree responded to local initiatives and attempted to synchronize them. It stated that some authorities had developed their own regulations on cohabitation with the Jewish population; in order to standardize this policy, in future local administrations must regulate visits to public establishments (inns [Gasthäuser], restaurants, coffee houses and wine taverns) in such a way that patrons did not constantly encounter Jews; they were also to ensure general segregation in public baths and institutions (such as hospitals and sanatoria) and mark all Jewish businesses.[66]

Subsequently, on 5 August 1939, the Presidium of the State Authority (Landesbehörde) in Prague decreed that Jews could patronize hospitality businesses (Gaststättenbetriebe) only if they had special rooms set aside for them.[67] Soon afterwards, on 14 August, the Prague Police

Figure 3.1. Municipal playground in Prague, 'No Admission for Jews', 1939. © Bildarchiv Preussischer Kulturbesitz, no. 30025479.

Directorate expanded on this regulation by announcing that Jews would be prohibited from patronizing public establishments on Sophie Island and other places. Restaurants were to hang up signs declaring 'no admission for Jews', while Jewish establishments and craft businesses (Handwerksbetriebe) were to bear the sign 'Jewish business'. Privately run public swimming pools had to reserve a section for Jews and mark them accordingly, or introduce special 'Jews' hours'. Henceforth, Jews were to be banned from municipal swimming schools and swimming pools, while hospitals, sanatoria and poorhouses had to provide separate accommodation for them.[68]

The Police Directorate of Hradec Králové, meanwhile, prohibited Jews from patronizing certain inns, cafés and hotels, as well as all public reading rooms (Lesehallen). It permitted them to use the swimming pool only on Tuesdays between 4 p.m. and 8 p.m. Businesses owned by Jews had to be marked as 'Jewish'. Violation of these ordinances would result in a fine of five thousand crowns or fourteen days in prison.[69] In Pardubice at around the same time, the city government expropriated the local synagogue, turning it into a market hall.[70] These examples demonstrate how local authorities, whether Police Directorates, city governments or chief county commissioners, actively pursued their own interests through their anti-Jewish policies.

The Reich protector reacted to this new situation by issuing a decree informing the chief county commissioners of the Czech government ordinance and ordering them to provide him with reports on the local policies implemented by the Police Directorates. The chief county commissioners, however, were not to intervene or attempt to influence local initiatives.[71]

The Germanization of the Administrative System

By now the power structure had shifted in towns with a large German population. By late March 1939, the Reich Interior Ministry had already discussed whether special arrangements ought to be made for the 'administration of the German language islands'. Brno, with around sixty thousand German inhabitants, Jihlava with twenty-five thousand and Olomouc with twenty thousand, were regarded as language islands, while another roughly thirty thousand German citizens lived in the vicinity of Moravian Ostrava.[72]

President Hácha had allowed ethnic Germans to opt either for German or Protectorate citizenship, the disadvantages of the former being conscription into the Wehrmacht and the dominance of a Nazi worldview. As late as spring 1939, the chief county commissioner in the Olomouc region perceived the imminent disappearance of Germanity: only twenty ethnic Germans had registered for Reich citizenship. Just a year later, however, focused efforts to Germanize the district had resulted in the appointment of German mayors, the opening of a German theatre and expansion of the German school system.[73]

In May 1939, the Wehrmacht local commander (Ortskommandant) disbanded the Olomouc City Council, demanding that the Czech Interior Ministry appoint a German commissar (Kommissar) and two German assistants. Though the city was 72 per cent Czech, just one assistant was to represent this group. In Prague, the municipal government protested against the dissolution of the elected City Council but its pleas fell on deaf ears.[74]

On 3 July 1939, the Reich protector officially dissolved the city councils in Brno, Jihlava, Moravian Ostrava, Olomouc and České Budějovice, all of them major cities with a large German population.[75] With the exception of České Budějovice, where one Czech commissar remained in office, after the Reich protector put pressure on President Hácha every city received German commissars appointed by the Reich protector, supposedly in revenge for the dissolution of German authorities following the foundation of Czechoslovakia.[76] Germans were also appointed to leading posts within the police force in these places, while streets and trams were given German names. In Brno, with a German population of 22 per cent, this prompted the Czechs to boycott the 'German' trams, just as their counterparts in Prague had done.[77]

Since the summer of 1939, the Protectorate of Bohemia and Moravia had been divided into nineteen chief county commissioner districts, twelve in Bohemia and seven in Moravia, but by late 1940 this had been reduced to fifteen. The chief county commissioners, subordinate to the Reich protector, were responsible for those authorities that had been placed under the administration of the Reich and were also in charge of the German police; they constituted a new, active player in anti-Jewish policy that supervised the Czech authorities in their districts.[78]

In late July 1939, meanwhile, twenty-three labour offices with eighty-five branch offices were established at the behest of the Reich protector. These were subordinate to the Czech Ministry for Social and Health Administration under Dr Vladislav Klumpar, their directors appointed with the Reich protector's approval. In areas with a significant German population (Brno, České Budějovice, Jihlava, Moravian Ostrava and Olomouc), the directors of the new labour offices formed personal unions with the directors of the Department for Labour Issues (Abteilung für Arbeitsfragen), a division of the chief county commissioner offices.[79] In contrast to Germany and Austria, however, in the Protectorate of Bohemia and Moravia the ordinance issued by the Reich Labour Administration on 20 December 1938 concerning the forced deployment of unemployed Jews in segregated work units did not yet apply. Nonetheless, following their exclusion from the independent professions and state apparatus, from the summer of 1939 onwards, Jews had little option but to engage in manual labour. A total of 25,458 men and 24,028 women were between eighteen and forty-five years of age and thus 'able to work'.[80]

On 10 August 1939, State Secretary Stuckart informed Reich Protector von Neurath – with copies of his letter going to the Security Police Main Office and SD Main Office – about the Reich Interior Ministry's current thinking on the 'treatment of Jews in the Protectorate'. Supposedly, a

> large part of the Czech population [wanted to see] the Jewish question resolved as rapidly and radically as possible, in line with the measures implemented in the Old Reich. It will be imperative to bring these efforts into alignment with the interests of the Reich as a whole. To the extent that the Jewish question is a biological problem, in the first instance I do not consider it to be in the immediate interest of the Reich to implement special measures to the benefit of the Czech people.[81] ... Conversely, the Reich has a considerable interest in ensuring that the Jews living in the Protectorate do not exercise an influence on the Protectorate's general relationship with the Reich or the Protectorate's internal political development. I therefore consider it necessary for Jews to be excluded from the public life of the Protectorate. It will be the responsibility of the Protectorate government to carry out this task. I suggest that you recommend to the Protectorate government that it implement the necessary measures. These would include 1. Withdrawal of the right to vote and stand in elections. 2. Exclusion from public offices. 3. Exclusion from the press, broadcasting and the other institutions exercising an influence on public opinion. 4. Exclusion from Czech associations (article 7 of the Führer's Decree). 5. Complementing point 4, a ban on the possession of weapons and supplementary ban on manufacturing and trading in weapons. The Reich also has an interest in ensuring that the resolution of the Jewish question in the Protectorate is not rushed. Experiences in the Old Reich have made it abundantly clear that due to their deep integration into every area of life, the exclusion of the Jews can only be carried out without injury to the general population if it is done in a methodical way and at a reasonable pace.

Stuckart expressed reservations about the draft government decree, which he had received from the Reich protector on 30 May and had been drawn up earlier that month, as it might have a negative effect on economic development: 'I consider a step-by-step approach to be the only appropriate one. The exclusion from public life referred to above would be the first step. After implementing these measures a decision would have to be made on which area to tackle next. One particularly important question will be whether it is possible to remove Jews from leading positions in the economy as well'. The objective of Jewish policy, he contended, was emigration. Excessive measures would be apt merely to 'hamper the achievement of this goal'. As the representative of the Reich Ministry of the Interior, Stuckart also requested that he always be involved in draft decrees and measures relating to the Jewish question in the Protectorate. He set great store by ensuring the consistency of Jewish policy, of which he claimed ultimate control in the Protectorate and elsewhere.[82]

Jewish Responses to the New Anti-Jewish Measures

While there was evidently a need for coordination, Stuckart's guidance did not signify any shift of power towards the Germans or Berlin. The institutional quadrangle of anti-Jewish measures, consisting of Berlin, the Reich protector, the Czech government and the local authorities, remained intact. One indirect response to Stuckart's ideas came in the shape of new Czech initiatives, undertaken both by public agencies and private organizations: in Prague, Jews could now patronize just one special cinema, while the Sokol Gymnastics Club and the Czech Red Cross dismissed their Jewish members on 26 August.[83] While the Sokol had officially been 'Aryanized' for months, some of its branches had refused to exclude Jews.[84]

Measures such as the one implemented by the Prague Police Directorate on 14 August, featuring restrictions on Jews in public, along with similar directives in the provinces, made the 'seriousness of the situation' clear to many Jews, reinforcing their desire to leave the Protectorate.[85] On 17 August, moreover, the resettlement of Jews from the provinces in Prague was initiated, and a housing department established by the Prague Jewish Community began organizing shelter for them.[86]

The more intensive and comprehensive anti-Jewish policy became, the more the Protectorate's Jewish community was gripped by hopelessness and poverty. In late July 1939, the Jewish Religious Community's Social Institute provided for 3,564 individuals in greater Prague, and for 3,869 by early August. In mid August, as a result of rapidly growing emigration, this figure sank to 2,989, but then climbed rapidly again to 3,305 by 19 August. In late July, the soup kitchens offered the needy 4,214 weekly lunches, in early August 4,387, then in mid August 4,749 and on 19 August no fewer than 5,178, an increase probably due mainly to worsening poverty and the influx from the provinces.[87] In total, the

Prague Community provided for 14,858 people and distributed 25,321 meals in August. In late August, the Religious Community incorporated the Social Institute as the new Social Department (Sozialabteilung). The Health Service (Krankenfürsorge), which included an Out-Patient Clinic (Ambulatorium), was also integrated. The Social Department now catered to a weekly total of 3,926 individuals and provided 5,281 lunches.[88]

In an attempt to meet the growing challenges as effectively as possible, the Prague Religious Community also incorporated schools into its administrative structure. Because many public schools no longer taught Jewish children, the Religious Community planned to greatly expand the existing Jewish primary school (Volksschule), while also establishing a new secondary school (Bürgerschule) for school-age adolescents. A total of 141 men and 39 women were now attending the Community's retraining courses.[89]

Emulating an earlier directive issued in Berlin in November 1938, later copied in Vienna, as its supervisory authority the Gestapo now ordered the Jewish Religious Community of Prague to publish a newspaper, which was supposed to function as its 'official organ'.[90] In reality, however, it served to inform Jews about the growing number of anti-Jewish measures, particularly Gestapo directives. Eichmann's Central Office increasingly imposed its will on the Jewish Community, as evident in the former's demand that the latter surrender all its bank deposits. Subsequently, of its total assets, which amounted to somewhat more than 1.2 million crowns, the Central Office released funds on a weekly basis. While the Religious Community had an income of slightly more than 63,000 crowns in the week from 20 to 25 August, it spent the same amount solely on welfare services. But it disbursed another 27,000 crowns facilitating emigration.[91] Between 17 August and 1 September 1939, meanwhile, the Community recorded an income of 117,000 crowns, but it had to spend 143,000 on welfare services and 82,000 on emigration aid.[92] Soon, with the beginning of the war, the parameters of its work were to shift once again, from one day to the next.

* * *

On 21 June 1939, as Chief of the Security Police and the SD, Heydrich implemented a change of policy, annulling the ban on emigration for Czech Jews. In an attempt to expedite emigration while also guaranteeing strict control, he now favoured a Central Office on the Vienna model after all. Instituted by the Reich protector in coordination with the Czech government, it operated according to the same assembly line system, bringing all essential administrative operations together under one roof. Like the Central Office in Vienna, Eichmann and Stahlecker headed its Prague counterpart. Representatives of the Jewish Religious Community of Prague and seconded Czech officials from various ministries were sent to Vienna to gain first-hand experience before the Central Office took up its work.

Eichmann now informed the Prague Jewish Community that by the end of 1939, thirty thousand Jews had to emigrate, while a total of seventy thousand had to leave by the following summer. Because the Central Office was responsible only for Prague and the surrounding areas, Jews from the provinces were instructed to relocate to the Protectorate capital so the authorities could better organize their forced emigration. Subsequently, more than six cities expelled Jewish residents as local authorities exploited this state of affairs.

The expulsion of such a large number of Jews was a sign of the advancing programme of Germanization in the Protectorate. The Reich authorities set about bolstering the German administration in the 'German language islands' in particular, replacing most senior staff in the relevant cities with Germans, with Czech approval. While this enabled the Reich to pursue Germanization more effectively, it did not automatically give it a greater influence on 'Jewish policy'.

Despite the establishment of the Central Office, the previous power structure remained in place, with the German government, the Reich protector, Berlin and the local authorities in the Protectorate all playing distinct roles. While the Germans showed more interest in finances and 'Aryanization', the Czech government and its ministries, under increasing pressure from Czech fascists, began to segregate Jews in public spaces, such as businesses, restaurants and schools.

The decree issued by the Czech government in July 1939, which excluded Jews from various professions, resulted in widespread impoverishment and hopelessness among the Jewish population. The Jewish Religious Community of Prague did everything it could to alleviate these burdens. Responding to rapidly worsening poverty and the influx of large numbers of Jews from the provinces, but also to the stricter financial control imposed by Eichmann's Central Office, the Community absorbed into its own structures the formerly separate agencies responsible for Jewish emigration, welfare and schools, in an attempt to coordinate their work more effectively.

Notes

1. BA Berlin, R 58/6401, fol. 249–50: Circular Head SD Office II (Six), 16 June 1939; ibid., fol. 243–45: Note Hagen, 16 June 1939 for submission to Head II (Six); ibid., fol. 261: Note SD II, 22 June 1939; see also ibid., fol. 260+RS: Note II 112 Dannecker, 10 July 1939.
2. USHMM Washington, RG 48.005M, reel 4 (Prague State Archive), I 3b-5811 Central Office, no. 5, n.p.: Note Reich protector I 3 on meeting of 19 July 1939, 9 August 1939, 1–2. For more detail, see Gruner, 'Das Protektorat Böhmen/Mähren', 36; and Milotová, 'Zentralstelle', 10–15.
3. On the establishment of the Prague Central Office in July 1939, see Milotová, 'Zentralstelle', 7–30; Anderl, 'Die "Zentralstellen für jüdische Auswanderung"'. On the Central Office in Vienna, see Gabriele Anderl and Dirk Rupnow, *Die Zentralstelle für jüdische Auswanderung als Beraubungsinstitution*, with the editorial assistance of Alexandra-Eileen Wenck (Vienna, 2004).
4. USHMM Washington, RG 48.005M, reel 4 (Prague State Archive), I 3b-5811 Zentralstelle, no. 1, n.p.: Circular order issued by Reich protector Freiherr von Neurath with letter from Neurath to prime minister in Prague, 15 July 1939, 1–5, reprinted in VEJ/3, doc. 252, 609–10.
5. At this point, in late June 1939, Eichmann was not yet head of the Jewish Division (Judenreferat) in the RSHA, which was established in September 1939. For an example of this erroneous belief, see Rothkirchen, *Jews*, 145.
6. David Cesarani, *Becoming Eichmann: Rethinking the Life, Crimes and Trial of a 'Desk Murderer'* (Cambridge, 2004), 74–76.
7. YV Jerusalem, O 7/53, fol. 1: List of weekly reports 1939. On the use of the Vienna IKG-reports, scattered across several archives, as a source, see Gruner, *Zwangsarbeit und Verfolgung*.
8. On date and location: USHMM Washington, RG 45.005M, reel 1 (Prague State Archive, Interior Ministry), no. 10, n.p.: Ministry of the Interior and the state authorities in Prague and Brno, 1 August 1939, 1–2, and VEJ/3, 616. The identity of the owner of the villa is contested; he was either a Jewish wine wholesaler or Mark Rosenthal. See Beneš and Ginsburg, *10 Million Prisoners*, 138; or Rothkirchen, *Jews*, 103.
9. USHMM Washington, RG 48.005M, reel 1 (Prague State Archive, Interior Ministry: Jewish regulations), no. 10, n.p.: Copy MdI to state authorities in Brno and Prague, 1 August 1939; ibid., reel 4 (Prague State Archive), I 3b-5811 Central Office, no. 1, n.p.: Copy circular order issued by Reich protector Freiherr von Neurath with letter from Neurath to prime minister in Prague, 15 July 1939, 1–5. According to Veselská, a second Central Office was in fact established in Brno in late 1940: Veselská, '"Sie müssen sich als Jude dessen bewusst sein, welche Opfer zu tragen sind …"', 155.
10. JTA, 'Gestapo Orders Emigration of 70,000 Jews from "Protectorate" in Year', 27 July 1939. See Tartakower and Grossmann, *The Jewish Refugee*, 37.
11. Ibid.
12. *Manchester Guardian*, 11 August 1939, 9.
13. JTA, 'Gestapo Orders Emigration of 70,000 Jews from "Protectorate" in Year', 27 July 1939.
14. *Manchester Guardian*, 11 August 1939, 9.
15. According to Otto Dov Kulka, 'History and Historical Consciousness: Similarities and Dissimilarities in the History of the Jews in Germany and the Czech Lands

1918–1945', *Bohemia* 46(1) (2005), 68–86, here 68. On other meetings during this period, see Rothkirchen, *Jews*, 145–46.
16. YV Jerusalem, M 58/JM 11813, fol. 614–19: Letter Jakob Edelstein, carbon copy, n.d. (c. August 1939), 1–5. On the relationship between the Prague Jewish Community and the provincial Communities, which changed frequently until the deportations, their subordinate status and communication between the two, see Veselská, '"Sie müssen sich als Jude dessen bewusst sein, welche Opfer zu tragen sind ..."', 151–66.
17. YV Jerusalem, O 7/53, fol. 2: Weekly report Jewish Religious Community of Prague, 23–29 July 1939, 1; see ibid., fol. 168: Monthly report Jewish Religious Community of Prague, 1–30 July 1939, 1.
18. YV Jerusalem, O 7/53, fol. 2: Weekly report Jewish Religious Community of Prague, 23–29 July 1939, 1.
19. Milotová, 'Zentralstelle', 17.
20. YV Jerusalem, O 7/53, fol. 6: Weekly report Jewish Religious Community of Prague, 6–12 August 1939, 1.
21. JTA, 'Kafka Prague Jewish Leader in London for Emigration Aid Talks', 24 July 1939.
22. Report Edelstein in Letter from the SD Central Office Prague (B1, Wo/Zb) to the head of the Security Main Office, Special Agency for Bohemia and Moravia, Berlin, 7 July 1939, in VEJ/3, doc. 250, 601–2. Despite being urged to stay in Palestine, Edelstein returned to Prague; Margalit Shlain, 'Jakob Edelsteins Bemühungen um die Rettung der Juden aus dem Protektorat Böhmen und Mähren von Mai 1939 bis Dezember 1939', in *Theresienstädter Studien und Dokumente* 2003, 71–94, here 74–77.
23. JTA, 'Gestapo Orders Emigration of 70,000 Jews from "Protectorate" in Year', 27 July 1939. See also Tartakower and Grossmann, *The Jewish Refugee*, 37.
24. VHA Prague, fonds 140, carton 23, no. 97, fol. 12: Report 'The Jewish Question', n.d., 5.
25. YV Jerusalem, O 7/53, fol. 2: Weekly report Jewish Religious Community of Prague, 23–29 July 1939, 1; ibid., fol. 4: Weekly report Jewish Religious Community of Prague, 30 July to 5 August 1939, 1; ibid., fol. 6: Weekly report Jewish Religious Community of Prague, 6–12 August 1939, 1; ibid., fol. 10: Weekly report Jewish Religious Community of Prague, 13–19 August 1939, 1; ibid., fol. 12: Weekly report Jewish Religious Community of Prague, 20–25 August 1939, 1.
26. As in Germany, the emigrant was required to pay a wealth tax (separate from the Reich Flight Tax, which was introduced in the Protectorate later) of between 0.5 and 20 per cent. The funds raised were supposedly used to help destitute Jews, but were in fact pocketed by the Central Office; VHA Prague, fonds 140, carton 23, no. 97, fol. 12–13: Report 'The Jewish Question', n.d., 5–6.
27. For more detail, see Gruner, *Zwangsarbeit und Verfolgung*, 177–87.
28. Report, signed by Dr Balaž, section counsellor (Sektionsrat) at the Interior Ministry, and Karel Herr, government counsellor (Regierungsrat) in the State Police Service (staatlicher Polizeidienst), 28 July 1939, in VEJ/3, doc. 255, 612–16. Quoted in Milotová, 'Zentralstelle', 17. See also Anderl and Rupnow, *Die Zentralstelle für jüdische Auswanderung*, 334–35.
29. Beneš and Ginsburg, *10 Million Prisoners*, 138.
30. Report by an unidentified Dutchman, Prague, spring 1939, in VEJ/3, doc. 241, 581. See Circular sent by Head of Division (Referatsleiter) Passrecht, 19 June 1940, in Mund, *Deutschland und das Protektorat*, doc. 255, 385.
31. JTA, 'Gestapo Bans Emigration of Young Jewish Doctors from "Protectorate"', 8 August 1939.

32. Mentioned in VHA Prague, fonds 140, carton 19, no. 2, fol. 305: Report 'The Protectorate of Bohemia and Moravia in Light of its Daily Press', carbon copy, n.d. (c. spring 1940), 19.
33. YV Jerusalem, O 7/53, fol. 13: Weekly report Jewish Religious Community of Prague, 20–25 August 1939, 2.
34. The HeHalutz Jewish youth movement ran six non-urban centres attended by seventy-seven pupils in 1932; YV Jerusalem, M 58/JM 11813, fol. 580: *Der Hechaluz in der ČSR* (author's edition 1932), 3.
35. Report by the Jewish Religious Community of Prague, 'Work' (n.d., mid 1942), in Krejčová, Svobodová and Hyndráková, *Židé v Protektorátu*, doc. 5, 111.
36. As asserted without supporting evidence in Rothkirchen, *Jews*, 145. On Austria, see Gruner, *Zwangsarbeit und Verfolgung*, 41.
37. YV Jerusalem, O 7/53, fol. 4–5: Weekly report Jewish Religious Community of Prague, 30 July to 5 August 1939, 1–2. See also Veselská, '"Sie müssen sich als Jude dessen bewusst sein, welche Opfer zu tragen sind ..."', 158.
38. Rothkirchen, *Jews*, 146.
39. YV Jerusalem, O 7/53, fol. 6: Weekly report Jewish Religious Community of Prague, 6–12 August 1939, 1.
40. Rothkirchen, *Jews*, 146.
41. YV Jerusalem, O 7/53, fol. 10: Weekly report Jewish Religious Community of Prague, 13–19 August 1939, 1.
42. Ibid., fol. 15: Weekly report Jewish Religious Community of Prague, 20–25 August 1939, 4.
43. Ibid., fol. 15: Weekly report Jewish Religious Community of Prague, 20–25 August 1939, 4.
44. Ibid., fol. 17: Weekly report Jewish Religious Community of Prague, 20–25 August 1939, 6.
45. Ibid., fol. 24 and 26–27: Weekly report Jewish Religious Community of Prague, 27 August to 1 September 1939, 5 and 7–8.
46. Verena Pawlowsky, Edith Leisch-Prost and Christian Klösch, *Vereine im Nationalsozialismus: Vermögensentzug durch den Stillhaltekommissar für Vereine, Organisationen und Verbände und Aspekte der Restitution in Österreich nach 1945* (Vienna, 2004), 43–44, 97–101.
47. See Osterloh, *Nationalsozialistische Judenverfolgung*, 263–99.
48. See the contributions in Gruner and Osterloh, *The Greater German Reich and the Jews*. Cf. Pawlowsky, Leisch-Prost and Klösch, *Vereine im Nationalsozialismus*, 79–80.
49. YV Jerusalem, M 58/JM 11810, fol. 148: Circular, signed by SS Sturmbannführer Lothar Schröder, Reich protector in Bohemia and Moravia/Commissioner for the Organizational System, 29 July 1939; ibid.: date stamp on circular.
50. Ibid., fol. 149–51: Articles of association of the Launer Poor People's, Sickness and Burial Fraternity, Prague 1877.
51. YV Jerusalem, M 58/JM 11814, fol. 142: Copy directive Reich protector/Commissioner for the Organizational System, 9 September 1939.
52. JTA, '100,000 Jews List Wealth in "Protectorate"; Czechs Hostile to Anti-Semitism', 1 August 1939.
53. For an example of this belief, see Schmidt-Hartmann, 'Tschechoslowakei', 359; Anderl, 'Die "Zentralstellen für jüdische Auswanderung"', 279. Rothkirchen too believes that while the Czech government continued to issue numerous anti-Jewish decrees, it now played virtually no role in the decisions being made: Rothkirchen, *Jews*, 145, see also 299. See also Miroslav Kárný, 'Die "Judenfrage" in der nazistischen Okkupationspolitik', *Historica* 21 (1982), 137–92.

54. See Bryant, *Prague in Black*, 50.
55. For the first discussion of this, see Gruner, 'Das Protektorat Böhmen/Mähren', 27–62.
56. USHMM Washington, RG 48.005M, reel 3 (Prague State Archive, Ministry for Schools and National Education: Jewish regulations), no. 5, n.p.: Ministry to the State School Offices (Landesschulämter) in Prague and Brno, 24 June 1939.
57. Ibid., no. 9, n.p.: Circular sent by the Ministry to the State School Boards (Landesschulräte) in Prague and Brno and the state authorities in Prague and Brno, 12 July 1939.
58. Utermöhle and Schmerling, *Die Rechtsstellung der Juden im Protektorat Böhmen und Mähren*, 47–54. See also Institute of Jewish Affairs, *Hitler's Ten-Year War*, 57.
59. JTA, '100,000 Jews List Wealth in "Protectorate"; Czechs Hostile to Anti-semitism', 1 August 1939.
60. Beneš and Ginsburg, *10 Million Prisoners*, 139.
61. Rothkirchen, *Jews*, 103.
62. JTA, 'Gestapo Orders Emigration of 70,000 Jews from "Protectorate" in Year', 27 July 1939.
63. JTA, 'Czech Fascists Seek Ban on Use of Prague Street Cars by Jews', 31 July 1939.
64. JTA, 'Czech "Aryan" Union Would Have Jews Repay Religious Grants of 16 Years', 6 August 1939.
65. JTA, '"Aryan" Union Declares War on "White Jews"', 1 August 1939.
66. USHMM Washington, RG 48.005M, reel 1 (Prague State Archive, Interior Ministry: Jewish regulations), no. 11, n.p.: Decree MdI Prague, 3 August 1939; ibid., no. 38, n.p.: Print compilation of the laws and decrees of the Protectorate of Bohemia and Moravia, 21 April 1940. Reprinted in VEJ/3, doc. 256, 616–18. See also 'Bericht eines Reisenden', in *Deutschland-Berichte der Sozialdemokratischen Partei Deutschlands (Sopade) 1934–1940*, ed. Klaus Behnken, vol. 7 (1940) (Salzhausen, 1989), 262–64.
67. Friedmann, 'Rechtsstellung', in Krejčová, Svobodová and Hyndráková, *Židé v Protektorátu*, 245.
68. Ibid., 246. See Brandes and Míšková, *Vom Osteuropa-Lehrstuhl ins Prager Rathaus*, 276; Lexa, 'Anti-Jewish Laws', 78.
69. USHMM Washington, RG 48.005M, reel 4 (Prague State Archive), Office of the Reich Protector, Jewish regulations, no. 3, n.p.: Announcement Königgrätz Police Directorate, 8 August 1939.
70. JTA, '100,000 Jews List Wealth in "Protectorate"; Czechs Hostile to Anti-Semitism', 1 August 1939.
71. USHMM Washington, RG 48.005M, reel 4 (Prague State Archive), Office of the Reich Protector, Jewish regulations, no. 4, n.p.: Circular order Reich protector to the county commissioners (Landräte), 29 August 1939, 1–2.
72. Minutes of the meeting of state secretaries, 25 March 1939, enclosure; reprinted in VEJ/3, 574–80, here 577–78.
73. This was to lead to more applications for Reich citizenship in the summer of 1940, including among Czechs. Czechs who took German citizenship benefited directly from anti-Jewish policies; Bryant, *Prague in Black*, 52–53, 67–72. On the efforts to promote German culture, see Volker Mohn, *NS-Kulturpolitik im Protektorat Böhmen und Mähren: Konzepte, Praktiken, Reaktionen* (Essen, 2014).
74. Beneš and Ginsburg, *10 Million Prisoners*, 122.
75. According to Bryant, the Reich protector barely intervened in Czech politics until the beginning of the war; Bryant, *Prague in Black*, 41.
76. Moskowitz, 'Three Years of the Protectorate', 360; Brandes, *Die Tschechen unter deutschem Protektorat*, part I, 165–66; Petr Němec, 'Die Lage der deutschen

Nationalität im Protektorat Böhmen und Mähren unter dem Aspekt der "Eindeutschung" dieses Gebiets', *Bohemia* 32(1) (1991), 39–59, here 56.
77. Beneš and Ginsburg, *10 Million Prisoners*, 121; Bryant, *Prague in Black*, 39.
78. Decree on the structure of the administration and on the German Security Police in the Protectorate of Bohemia and Moravia, 1 September 1939; RGBl. 1939 I, 1681–82. See excerpt in *Europa unterm Hakenkreuz: Österreich und Tschechoslowakei*, doc. no. 51, 128–29. See also Moskowitz, 'Three Years of the Protectorate', 359; Bryant, *Prague in Black*, 31; Lemkin, *Axis Rule in Occupied Europe*, 135.
79. Wilhelm Dennler, *Sozialpolitik im Protektorat Böhmen und Mähren* (Berlin, 1940), 4.
80. Report by the Central Office, 2 October 1941, appendix: Table 1, in *Deutsche Politik im 'Protektorat Böhmen und Mähren'*, doc. no. 23, 125. For general information on the deployment of Jews in segregated work units in Germany, Austria and the Protectorate, see Gruner, *Jewish Forced Labor*.
81. This was a reference to the application, not planned at the time, of the Nuremberg laws to Protectorate citizens, such as a prohibition on marriage and sexual relations between Jewish and non-Jewish Czechs.
82. BA Berlin, R 58/6401, fol. 274–75: Stuckart (RMdI) to Reich protector B/M for the attention of County Commissioner Fuchs, 10 August 1939.
83. Beneš and Ginsburg, *10 Million Prisoners*, 139.
84. JTA, '100,000 Jews List Wealth in "Protektorate"; Czechs Hostile to Anti-Semitism', 1 August 1939.
85. YV Jerusalem, O 7/53, fol. 10: Weekly report Jewish Religious Community of Prague, 13–19 August 1939, 1.
86. Ibid., fol. 11: Weekly report Jewish Religious Community of Prague, 13–19 August 1939, 2.
87. Ibid., fol. 2: Weekly report Jewish Religious Community of Prague, 23–29 July 1939, 1; ibid., fol. 4: Weekly report Jewish Religious Community of Prague, 30 July to 5 August 1939, 1; ibid., fol. 6: Weekly report Jewish Religious Community of Prague, 6–12 August 1939, 1; ibid., fol. 10: Weekly report Jewish Religious Community of Prague, 13–19 August 1939, 1.
88. Ibid., fol. 172: Monthly report Jewish Religious Community of Prague, 1–31 August 1939, 5.
89. Ibid., fol. 16: Weekly report Jewish Religious Community of Prague, 20–25 August 1939, 5; ibid., fol. 23: Weekly report Jewish Religious Community of Prague, 27 August to 1 September 1939, 4.
90. Ibid., fol. 16–17: Weekly report Jewish Religious Community of Prague, 20–25 August 1939, 5–6.
91. Ibid., fol. 16–17: Weekly report Jewish Religious Community of Prague, 20–25 August 1939, 5–6.
92. Ibid., fol. 25–26: Weekly report Jewish Religious Community of Prague, 27 August to 1 September 1939, 6–7.

CHAPTER 4

THE WAR AND GREATER GERMAN DEPORTATION PLANS

New Borders, New Plans

On 1 September 1939 the German Reich invaded Poland. When the war began, the Gestapo was granted supreme policing powers in the Protectorate ahead of all other agencies, including the Czech ones. By decree, all German authorities in the Protectorate, with the exception of the Wehrmacht, were now formally subordinate to the Reich protector. He also supervised the Czech 'autonomous administration' as a whole. The state secretary functioned as his deputy. The Reich, however, now absorbed the Gestapo and parts of the Criminal Police (Kriminalpolizei) in the Protectorate, previously under the Reich protector. Within the Protectorate, the Gestapo was tasked with investigating and combating 'all activities directed against state and people'. In addition, the Reich protector, as well as the SS Reichsführer and head of the German police in conjunction with the Reich protector, were henceforth empowered to take all steps necessary to ensure order and security in Bohemia and Moravia, even outside the law, as set out in the Göring decree.[1]

Evidently, as a result the authorities initially regarded the work of the Prague Central Office, opened just one month earlier, as superfluous, so it was wound up.[2] Because most borders had been closed since the start of the war and those wishing to leave the country now had few transportation options, the number of emigrants soon fell sharply. Only a small number of Jews had obtained visas for neutral countries. Seventy per cent of those who still managed to leave the Protectorate now went to Palestine.[3] Due to the many impediments to emigration, the authorities considered efficient coordination particularly important, prompting the Prague Central Office to resume its work after all, eleven days after its closure.[4]

On 6 September, the SS Reichsführer imposed an 8 p.m. curfew on the Jewish population and ordered the construction of separate air-raid shelters for Jews.[5] The Prague Jewish Community announced the Reich-wide decree promulgating the curfew through the 'snowball system' (that is, informing some members rather than issuing a circular to all of them, with those in the know then passing on the information, and so on). The local police and the Prague city authorities, clearly uninformed, questioned the directive, but the Prague Jewish Community referred them to the Central Office for Jewish Emigration. To give the German authorities an overview of the number of Jews and their utility, the Prague Community, like the Jewish Communities in the Old Reich, had to submit to the Gestapo updated statistics on the Jews still living in the Protectorate along with their distribution by age and profession, statistics based on the 1930 census for want of other data.[6]

On 7 September, as chief of the Security Police and SD, Heydrich ordered the arrest of all Polish Jewish men of seventeen years of age and above in the Reich.[7] The Jewish Community of Prague now had to report to the Central Office all Jews of Polish or formerly Polish citizenship of whom it was aware. The speedy arrest of around one thousand individuals greatly unsettled the Jewish community in both Prague and the Czech provinces.[8]

The strains on the Prague Jewish Community greatly intensified as a result of the long-standing involuntary influx from the provinces initiated by the Gestapo, which was accompanied by a growing voluntary inflow of Jews wishing to emigrate.[9] In the first week of September 1939 alone, eighty-six families relocated to Prague.[10] In Jihlava, the Gestapo informed all Jewish residents that they had to leave within three weeks. Because this was detrimental to the ongoing 'Aryanization negotiations' in the town, Chief County Commissioner Fiechtner complained to Reich Protector Neurath in Prague.[11] Though its efforts to provide for the incomers had brought the Prague Jewish Community to the brink of financial collapse, it was not until mid September that the Gestapo halted the forced relocation of Jews from the provinces to Prague – presumably in connection with new plans drawn up after the occupation of Poland.[12]

New Decisions Following the Victory over Poland

After the Nazi state's surprisingly rapid occupation of Poland, political conditions in the Protectorate changed fundamentally, including with respect to 'Jewish policy'. On 18 September 1939, at a meeting in Moravian Ostrava, SS Oberführer Dr Stahlecker and Government Counsellor Hermann discussed the 'evacuation of several thousand Jews to Galicia': the registration of '8,000 Jews' was underway, while homes were being seized and held in trust.[13] The Jews at issue here were from Moravian Ostrava and the surrounding area – a portent of new, more radical plans. Reflecting this shift, on 21 September Heydrich informed the Security Police that Hitler had approved the general 'deportation of Jews' to a soon-to-be-established foreign-language Gau on Polish territory.[14] The first convoys were to be sent from the annexed territories to occupied Poland.[15]

To this end, throughout the German Reich the authorities made a fresh effort to register the Jewish population, including in the Protectorate.[16] On 22 September 1939, the Prague Jewish Community initiated the registration process. It now had to record the name, address, age, gender, religious affiliation and 'approximate wealth' of all 'racial Jews' in the Protectorate within three days. This was no easy task given that it lacked information on non-members of the religious Communities.[17] Most members of staff, including those working in the Community's Emigration Department, schools and welfare services, had to down tools and help out with the campaign of registration. Including voluntary helpers, 1,300 individuals contributed to the collection of the relevant data or the confiscation of radios, which was carried out in parallel.[18] This registration drive revealed that on 1 October 1939, 90,147 Jews still lived in the Protectorate, including 80,139 religious Jews. Around 28,000 individuals, therefore, had managed to flee the Protectorate since its establishment. A total of 46,170 Jews now lived in Prague, meaning that somewhat more than half the Protectorate's Jewish population was already concentrated there.[19]

On 6 October 1939, before the German Reichstag, Hitler publicly heralded the ethnic reorganization of Europe and the 'solving of the Jewish problem'.[20] The same day, Gestapo Chief Heinrich Müller instructed SS Hauptsturmführer (captain) Adolf Eichmann, who would later organize the deportations, to initiate the expulsion ('Abschiebung') of Jews from the Kattowitz (Katowice) area and the 'Moravian Ostrava region' across the Vistula. The main objective here was to 'acquire experience' of relevance to 'the evacuation of large numbers of people'. Daily reports on the execution of this task were to be submitted to Müller at the newly established Reich Security Main Office,[21] which now united the Gestapo and the SS Security Service under one roof.[22]

So far, historians have viewed the events that followed either as a local test-run or as an instance of Eichmann going it alone.[23] Until recently they had consistently overlooked a revealing document: on 6 October, Eichmann made detailed preparations for the 'removal' of Jews from the German Reich, including the Protectorate, not in Vienna, Prague or Moravian Ostrava, but at his workplace in the newly established Reich Security Main Office in Berlin. On the basis of the new statistics and other data provided by the Jewish Communities, on that date he wrote: '1. Organize lists of all registered Jews and assign to Old Reich, Protectorate and Eastern March (Ostmark [Austria]). Divide these up in turn according to Religious Communities ... on the basis of the maps submitted by the Jewish organizations. 2. Disclose assets of destitute Jews to be deported (Ausziehen des Vermögens der zum Abschub gelangenden mittelosen Juden)'.[24] The first convoys were slated to depart from East Upper Silesia (Ostoberschlesien), which had now been incorporated into the 'Old Reich', the Protectorate and Austria in mid October 1939. In the rest of the 'Old Reich', the convoys would begin in the first or second week of November.[25]

A leaflet from October 1939 informed the relevant State Police headquarters that initially 'destitute Jews of German, Polish and Czech citizenship along with stateless Jews' were being registered by name. The relevant Jewish Communities, the instruction sheet went on, were each assembling groups of one thousand individuals and preparing the transports. 'The relocating Jews [could take with them] up to 50 kg of appropriately sized items per capita' plus provisions for eight days. 'Prior to the departure of the transport, the J.[ewish] Communities are to ensure that each Jew (assigned for deportation) carefully fills out a personal questionnaire of the kind typically used by the Central Offices for Jewish Emigration (two photographs).' The deportees had to hand over their personal documents and cash, their money was converted into zloty and a 1 per cent levy was imposed on their assets. Jews waiting to be transported were to be 'concentrated' in appropriate premises near the railway stations. For the time being, 'the seriously war-disabled, the industrially disabled and the seriously ill' would be excepted. The Gestapo was to notify the Wehrmacht High Command (Oberkommando der Wehrmacht) of the transports, with the trains being escorted either by the police (Schutzpolizei) or Gestapo.[26]

These two documents prove that at this early stage authorities in Berlin were making meticulous preparations for the mass deportation of Jews from the Greater German Reich. They had to provide Himmler with a progress report on the first deportations from the annexed territories, a copy of which would be submitted to the Führer. At this point, Hitler had not yet decided to remove all Jews from the Reich; instead, he 'ordered the relocation of 300,000 impecunious Jews from the Old Reich and the Eastern March'.[27] Nonetheless, impecunious Jews, that is, impoverished Jews regarded as incapable of emigration, made up the majority of the Jewish population: the number of religious Jews in Germany, Austria and the Protectorate was 326,000, while so-called racial Jews numbered 430,000. Hence, the fate of the Jews in the Greater German Reich, including the Protectorate, was clearly sealed at this early stage.

Consonant with the planned deportations, on 3 October the German state implemented the 'Decree on the Deprivation of Citizenship of the Protectorate of Bohemia and Moravia' (Verordnung über die Aberkennung der Staatsangehörigkeit des Protektorats Böhmen und Mähren), which applied to individuals who were living abroad and committing acts hostile to the state. Their assets were forfeited to the Reich rather than the Protectorate.[28] In the Reich, laws already introduced in 1933 made it possible to strip Germans who were living or had fled abroad of their citizenship and, consequently, their property. The same regulations had been introduced in Austria in July 1939.[29]

The Reich now planned similarly drastic measures against the remaining Jews to forestall any resistance. Just one day after the Decree on the Deprivation of Citizenship, the Reich interior and finance ministers authorized the Reich protector to seize the assets of individuals and organizations that had supported 'actions hostile to the Reich'. Such property could thus be confiscated before an individual had been stripped of citizenship. Associations whose assets had been seized were considered dissolved. The administration of the confiscated property was the responsibility of the Reich protector in consultation with the Reich Finance Ministry.[30] In August 1939, two months prior to the decree, in a circular to the Gestapo on behalf of the Reichsführer SS, Dr Werner Best had defined all anti-German acts by Jews as hostile to the state, even those carried out before the establishment of the Protectorate.[31] In another circular, Heydrich adopted the same definition of 'hostility to the Reich' (Reichsfeindlichkeit) in the decree issued in October.[32] Representatives of the Reich Chancellery and the other ministries had already reached agreement on this definition and its application to Jews in the Protectorate, among others, at a meeting on 23 September 1939.[33]

The First Deportations

Evidently, by now the Reich protector had given Stahlecker the green light to deport Jews from the Protectorate.[34] However, Eichmann did not plan the first deportations solely behind his new desk in the capital of the Greater German Reich. Making use of the detailed knowledge he had acquired from his time in Vienna and Prague, he personally supervised their implementation on the ground. He travelled first to Moravian Ostrava, where, on 9 October, he announced that

> in accordance with the order issued by SS Oberführer Müller of the Secret State Police Office (Geheimes Staatspolizeiamt), Berlin, one Jewish transport from Moravian Ostrava and one from Kattowitz must be put together as soon as possible, in such a way that these transports may, as it were, be deployed as an advance party in the territories earmarked to receive the first transports, for example in the Rozwadow [Rozwadów]-Annopol-Krasinik [*sic*., actually Krasnik (Kraśnik)] region south-west of Lublin. It will be the task of this Jewish advance party to erect a makeshift village, which is intended to function as a transit camp for all subsequent transports.

The first transports were to be 'composed [exclusively] of less well-off Jewish men fully capable of work', whereas later gender and age would no longer be relevant.[35]

At the same time, Eichmann gave the order to bring Jewish Community officials Storfer, Boschan, Friedmann, Murmelstein, Edelstein and Grün from Vienna and Prague to Moravian Ostrava, as they were to accompany the first transport to occupied Poland. The Central Offices in Prague and Vienna were to ensure that the Jewish officials reported to SS-Hauptsturmführer Günther in Moravian Ostrava on 16 October with four weeks' worth of clothing.[36] The Jewish Community in Vienna was informed of this on 10 October.[37] In response it sent Richard Friedmann, an official of the Vienna Community still working in Prague, along with the head of the Prague Palestine Office, Jakob Edelstein, to help prepare the transports to Moravian Ostrava.[38]

Eichmann flew to Krakau on 12 October. Apparently after discussions with the leadership of the General Government that had just been established, he informed Moravian Ostrava that Nisko, on the San River, was to be the transports' destination.[39] On 14 October, the Jewish Community of Moravian Ostrava submitted the first lists of names to the local Gestapo, identifying 362 Jewish men between the ages of eighteen and thirty-five and 1,014 between the ages of thirty-six and sixty.[40] On 16 October, Eichmann seemed to expect a steady flow of deportations henceforth: 'Regular transports are now going routinely, for the time being from Vienna in the Eastern March, from Moravian Ostrava in the Protectorate and from Kattowitz in formerly Polish territory'.[41]

Public notices initially appeared in the local daily newspapers[42] summoning all Jewish men from Moravian Ostrava between the ages of seventeen and seventy to the local riding school at 8 a.m. on 17 October. Shortly before the day of the first transport, the Jewish Community then distributed a leaflet providing more detail on the arrangements. Because men would be selected for transport only at the specified location, they were to turn up fully prepared between 7 and 7.30 a.m. with provisions for two to three days, a rucksack and suitcase. They could bring cash to a value of up to three hundred Reichsmarks or three thousand crowns. The men must bring with them their identity cards, along with their birth and citizenship certificates, and submit them to the transport organizers. Talking was strictly prohibited in the riding hall. After they had been transported to the 'retraining camp', which, the leaflet emphasized, was not a forced labour camp, the men's wives were to inform the local police of their departure and report to the Jewish Community the next day with evidence that they had done so. Relatives were strictly prohibited from turning up outside the riding hall or at the train station.[43] Some men, such as Yehudah Bakon's father, evaded the transport thanks to a doctor's certificate.[44]

On 18 October, when the first transport was about to leave Moravian Ostrava, Czechs and Jewish women – despite being banned from doing so – stood by the road leading up to the railway station, calling out expressions of support for the deportees. This remarkable incident even gained a mention in the SS Security Service's *Meldungen aus dem Reich* (Reports from the Reich).[45] Among Jews in Prague, 'rumours of the establishment of work camps beyond the borders of the Protectorate' had begun to spread. Anxious Jewish residents bombarded the Jewish Community with enquiries.[46]

This first train, with 901 men from Moravian Ostrava on board, left Czech territory the same day.[47] It comprised twenty-two passenger carriages and twenty-nine freight carriages loaded with building materials, tools and victuals and it was escorted as far as eastern Poland by border police along with SS men from the Vienna and Prague Central Offices.[48] Eichmann was there to see this first transport from the Protectorate arrive in Nisko.[49]

Suspension of Deportations or Shifting of Priorities?

In Moravian Ostrava, confusion briefly reigned about the next transports from that city and from Kattowitz, planned for the week of 22–28 October, due to a telex from Müller that arrived while the first transport was still being boarded. Here he underlined that deportations to the territory of what would become the rump Polish state required 'central guidance', in other words that every train required approval from Berlin.[50] But this did not mean that the Jews' 'removal' was halted because it was an arbitrary act by Eichmann, as some authors have claimed. The 'Jewish relocation campaigns' were in fact kicked off by 'command of the Chief of the Security Police and SD'.[51]

The next day, 19 October, the Gestapo ordered the Jewish Religious Community in Moravian Ostrava to assemble Jewish women with children by Saturday, while single Jewish females and married women without children would travel on the next transport.[52] This instruction provoked panic among Jews and new protests by non-Jewish residents. On 20 October the Jewish Community called an information meeting. Czech women blocked the entrance, 'calling out to the Jewish women that the plan was to deport the Jews first, then it would be the Czechs' turn'. Subsequently, many Jewish women fled to Prague with their children.[53]

The next transport, on 21 October, took 875 Jews from Kattowitz, Königshütte (Chorzów) and Bielitz (Bielsko). The Gauleiter, Chief of the Civil Administration, Border Guard (Grenzschutz) and SD were informed about this and told that 'soon another transport of Jews, which may include women, is likely to depart from Kattowitz and Moravian Ostrava'.[54] The same day, in Moravian Ostrava, Günther phoned the Gestapo Headquarters (Staatspolizeileitstelle) in Brno in response to a telex it had sent the day before:

> Government Counsellor Hermann informed me that on the basis of instructions issued by the Reich Security Main Office, which he had learned about from Government Counsellor Maurer, all deportations of Jews are to cease. He was unable to confirm whether this directive applies to the entire territory of the Reich. When I enquired as to whether the second planned transport of Jews from Moravian Ostrava to Poland, which to my knowledge SS Oberführer Müller and SS Hauptsturmführer Eichmann have already discussed, could depart, Government Counsellor Hermann intimated that this transport cannot be carried out either. When I suggested that I might make enquiries with the Gestapa (Geheimes Staatspolizeiamt Berlin or Secret State Police Office, the Gestapo's national headquarters), he asked me to keep him apprised at all times.[55]

This directive has been misunderstood as ushering in the complete cessation of the deportation programme, yet on the same day, 21 October, a transport from Vienna was dispatched from Moravian Ostrava carrying 912 Jewish men.[56] Berlin clarified the situation on 24 October, officially decreeing that 'initially, the Protectorate is not to be included in the evacuation campaign, in order that the de-Judaization of Vienna can be carried out as rapidly as possible'.[57] The same day, phoning Moravian Ostrava from the Reich Security Main Office in Berlin, Eichmann merely clarified that 'for the time being the deportation of Jews from the Protectorate for the purposes of retraining (Umschichtung) [must] cease until further notice'. 'For now the women registered for the next transport are not to be deported', he went on, though he stated that he was unable to give the reasons for this by telephone. The Gestapo in Moravian Ostrava explained that 'preparations for the next transport are already at a fairly advanced stage in Moravian Ostrava and a large number of Jews, eager to make a hasty escape from the city, have now been arrested', asking Eichmann if it might therefore be permitted to 'carry out at least one transport of the available men' in order to help

> the local State Police save [face]. SS Hauptsturmführer Eichmann agreed that up to 400 Jewish males might be deported. The plan is to attach this part-transport to the one leaving from Kattowitz on Friday 27 October 1939. SS Oberführer Müller has issued instructions that every transport is to be reported to the Gestapa two days before departure, along with details of the exact number of people, number of carriages, transport leader and escort, as well as station of departure. With immediate effect, the Krakau SD Task Force Unit (Einsatzkommando) is to inform Nisko that it will be the destination of every transport, regardless of whether it departs from Moravian Ostrava, Kattowitz or Vienna.[58]

The authorities thus had no plans to discontinue the transports but instead sought to coordinate them more effectively, prioritizing Austria over the Protectorate.[59] A telex from Brno reached Moravian Ostrava on 24 October 1939, stating that another transport, carrying three hundred individuals, would be departing from the former for the latter on the coming Thursday.[60] The next day, Günther informed the authorities in Krakau that a train from Moravian Ostrava carrying four hundred Jewish men was slated to make the journey to Kattowitz on 26 October, where it would be joined up with carriages carrying a further one thousand Jews to create a special train; this would depart from Kattowitz on 27 October.[61] The second transport would thus leave Moravian Ostrava on 26 October. At this point in time, the deportation process in that city had ensnared a number of Jews above the age of sixty-five.[62]

On 28 October 1939, Berlin then confirmed once again that the Wehrmacht High Command had informed the Secret State Police Office that it was untrue 'that the High Command [had] prohibited all transports to the region south of Lublin until mid November'. Due to the 'bringing in of the root crop harvest', there were currently restrictions on transports to the occupied Polish territories, but this did not exclude the possibility of 'squeezing in a few transports of Jews from Vienna, to the extent that this is compatible with the prisoner transports'. As head of the Berlin Gestapa, Müller recommended that the regional authorities 'contact the Transport Headquarters (Transportkommandantur) [directly] to ensure that the Jewish transports are incorporated into the prisoner transports'. If 'the problems cannot be satisfactorily resolved in this way', then the RSHA must be informed. 'Immediate consultation' with the Reich Railway Headquarters (Reichsbahndirektion) revealed that it would 'not be possible to squeeze in a Jewish transport from Vienna' until 4 November, as Brunner telexed Müller from Vienna. Brunner asked that both the RSHA Berlin and the Gauleitung (the regional Nazi Party office) in Vienna ensure this transport take place. Should the Vienna transport leave on 31 October, he underlined, the authorities in Moravian Ostrava must be informed in good time.[63]

The 'prisoner transports' mentioned here are probably a reference to the deportation of the formerly Polish Jews who were arrested in Austria and the other annexed territories when the war began. So far, the literature has failed to fully acknowledge that these competed with the 'Jewish transports' or even took priority over them.[64]

In Prague itself the Gestapo had already arrested 304 stateless Jews in September, many of Polish origin and held in Pankraz Prison under SS guard. In his memoirs, Wilhelm Hechter, born in Moravian Ostrava in 1903, describes how this group of men were accommodated in a hall. For several weeks they spent the nights crammed together on the floor, sleeping in shifts due to the overcrowding. On 27 October they were ordered to inform their families that they would be deported from Prague and that their nearest and dearest should bring some food and clothing to the institution. The men were transported to Moravian Ostrava the same night.[65] Before the train left, the Prague Jewish Community did what it could to provide this group with warm clothing, food and shoes, at a cost of more than sixty-four thousand crowns.[66] In Prague, the transfer of Jews from the District Court to the Wilson Railway Station sparked protests. Thirty Jewish women initially demonstrated against the deportation, which 'in turn caused Czech passers-by to form a crowd, which was ultimately dispersed by the Czech police'.[67]

The next – but for the time being last – goods train was made ready for dispatch on 1 November 1939 in Moravian Ostrava. It carried the more than three hundred Jews who had arrived from Prague on 28 October, whom the SD referred to as 'prisoners'.[68] On the train, rumours circulated that the transport was headed for Oświęcim, where a camp was supposedly to be established in a horse hospital dating from the First World War. Finally, the authorities in Prague ordered the train to proceed initially to Sosnowitz in East Upper Silesia.[69] There the detainees, escorted by the Gestapo and police, were accommodated in a factory, where they had to sleep on straw mats or the concrete floor. Moshe Merin, chairman of the local Jewish Community, sought to help the Jews from Prague by supplying them with provisions and, as Wilhelm Hechter recalls, made 'genuinely moving' efforts to look after them.[70]

On the Suspension and Significance of the First Transports

Before the transport from Moravian Ostrava continued its journey, it was in fact supposed to integrate another group of Jews in Sosnowitz. Additional transports were evidently planned as well.[71] Yet this particular transport stayed put in Sosnowitz: since early November, it had become impossible to reach the planned area of Jewish settlement near Lublin due to the 'bridges over the San [that had been] washed away'.[72] As a result, Reichsführer SS Heinrich Himmler personally suspended the 'emigration operation to Poland until February of next year', after far in excess of five thousand people had been deported from the Protectorate, Vienna and East Upper Silesia.[73]

The Gestapo subsequently contacted the chief county commissioner in Moravian Ostrava by telephone. He was informed that:

> this is the first attempt in the entire Reich to carry out the resettlement of Jews or their settlement in certain reserves in Inner Poland as planned by the Reichsführer SS. 1,341 Jewish men have been deported to Poland. The removal of the women and children has not yet taken place, having had to be postponed for the time being on the instructions of the Reichsführer SS, Berlin, due to poor weather and a lack of potential shelter.[74]

Thus, the Nisko deportation – as it has often been called due to its destination – was neither a local Eichmann operation nor an attempt to cleanse the annexed territories of Polish Jews. It was in fact the beginning of the 'total relocation', planned shortly after the start of the war, of the Jewish population in the Protectorate, Austria, East Upper

Silesia and the 'Old Reich'. The goal was to 'cleanse' the border areas first, which is why Moravian Ostrava and Kattowitz were affected as well as the cities with the largest Jewish communities in the annexed territories of the Greater German Reich, namely once again Moravian Ostrava, along with Prague, Brno and Vienna.[75] The transportation of the prisoners, that is, those Jews of formerly Polish citizenship who had been arrested since the beginning of the war, merely occurred in parallel to these 'Jewish relocation operations'. As late as 19 December 1939, an internal note composed in advance of a meeting of division heads in the Reich Security Main Office stated that with respect to a 'Jewish reserve [to be established] in Poland', the 'administration [was to be left] under Security Police leadership' until such time as 'the [re-]settlement of the Jews from Reich territory, the Eastern March and Bohemia/Moravia has been carried out'.[76] The Müller decree of 21 December, sent to Gestapo offices throughout the Reich, also underlines once again the intended scale of the first deportation programme. It announced that 'until further notice [Himmler has] prohibited the removal of Jews from the Old Reich, including the Eastern March and the Protectorate, to the occupied Polish territories'.[77]

Even 'hostile' countries had got wind of these far-reaching plans. The *New York Times* reported that the deportation of all Jewish families in Český Těšín (Teschen) to Poland, already announced for 25 November – which would, the report stated, have completed the removal of Jews from the Protectorate – had been terminated for the time being. This, it went on, was part of the German plan to resettle all Jews from the Greater German Reich, a total of two million people, in occupied Poland, namely in a reservation south-east of Lublin. While the newspaper greatly overstated the progress of the deportations, which, as indicated above, it believed to be almost complete, it was right about the scale of the operation, which encompassed the Old Reich, the Protectorate, Austria and the annexed areas of western Poland. According to its German sources, the project was to be completed by April 1940.[78]

Thus, the RSHA in Berlin had directed and controlled these transports. The Vienna Central Office bore the costs of the transports from the Eastern March and East Upper Silesia, while the Prague Central Office paid for those from the Protectorate.[79] These first deportations following the occupation of Poland represented a new, more radical form of persecution. Rather than being forced to emigrate or driven across the border, Jews from Greater Germany were to be forcibly resettled in a region under German domination while being stripped of their property and any real prospect of a regular income.[80] Over the short and medium term, meanwhile, the planning and suspension of the mass transports exercised a major influence on the development and shape of anti-Jewish measures in the Protectorate.

Jews' Situation since the First Transports

Shaken by his personal experience of the Nisko deportation, by 9 November 1939 Jakob Edelstein had returned from eastern Poland to Prague, where he informed the Jewish Community that the 'resettlement operation [had been] postponed until February 1940'. In the meantime, he emphasized, the priority must be to do everything possible to help Jews emigrate and thus avoid future transports.[81]

In the meantime, Jewish officials were still trying to negotiate with a range of foreign states and private organizations in order to facilitate emigration (see Table A.2 in the appendix for the destination countries). They also paid for tickets and procured passports, with dozens of Jews managing to leave the Protectorate in October.[82] After contacting Eichmann and Reich Bank Counsellor (Reichsbankrat) Untermöhle, the Religious Community deposited hundreds of thousands of crowns at the Böhmische Escomtebank in order to acquire foreign currency for emigrants, enabling them to pay for ship passage, for example. Negotiations with the American Joint on the provision of another $47,000 were still ongoing in mid October 1939.[83] Between early October and early November, the Jewish Community provided aspiring emigrants with more than $29,000, which equated to more than three million crowns, while receiving from the latter just $13,000 or 1.4 million crowns.[84]

During these few weeks, the Jewish Community referred hundreds, possibly thousands of aspiring emigrants to the Central Office. On 10 November, shortly after the suspension of the transports to Poland, Eichmann summoned the heads of the Prague Jewish Community and Palestine Office, pressing them not only to continue referring a daily contingent of 120 people to the Central Office to resolve their emigration issues but to greatly increase this figure. The Jewish representatives highlighted the lack of foreign currency impeding this goal. Both subsequently travelled to Vienna to discuss emigration options with the relevant officials.[85]

During the next week, the Jewish Community stepped up its efforts to meet the target set by the Central Office, preparing 339 individuals for departure, 172 of them to China, 28 of whom were destined for Shanghai, and 90 to Chile. The Community sent a daily total of around seventy individuals to the Central Office and negotiated with the authorities on the provision of agricultural courses.[86] Thus, despite the obstacles thrown up by war, in November emigration increased once again. A total of 811 Jews left the Protectorate: 472 men, 270 women and 69 children. A third of them went to China, Ecuador and Shanghai, which was under a shared international authority independent of China.[87] In December, 940 Jews – 561 men, 329 women and 50 children – emigrated, more than half of them travelling to Peru and Ecuador.[88]

While most Jews now regarded emigration as their last hope, war, impoverishment and persecution presented formidable obstacles. From the outset, the Jewish Community made a great effort to provide its members with legal advice, often relating to emigration. In the third week of November alone, 134 individuals sought advice from the Community; in eleven cases it or its lawyers entered into contact with various authorities on their behalf, also composing seven petitions for poor members.[89] In the second week of December, the number of those seeking advice had risen to 210; the Community intervened in fifteen cases and filed six petitions for impoverished Jews.[90] In mid November, the Community noted a 'deterioration in Jews' legal situation in the Protectorate', particularly in the wake of new decrees imposing minimum periods of notice for Jewish white-collar workers and regulating rental income from Jewish-owned buildings or land. Henceforth, Jews had to pay such income into blocked accounts at specific banks and could no longer dispose of it as they saw fit.[91]

Many of the anti-Jewish measures introduced since the establishment of the Protectorate had deprived Jews of work and income. The Central Jewish Employment Office (Zentrales Jüdisches Arbeitsamt), run jointly by the Jewish Community and the Palestine Office, had registered 934 individuals by early November. For the first time, the Jewish Community's weekly reports reveal that the Employment Office increasingly found work for unemployed Jews within the Protectorate by establishing Jewish work details, for example dispatching sixty men to the Kostelec nad Černými lesy district and thirty to Německý Brod to work in forestry.[92] A total of 1,026 individuals had already registered for placement by mid November, and 1,392 by the end of the month.[93] In an attempt to enhance Community members' prospects of emigration, the Office negotiated with the Association of Large Landowners (Verband der Großgrundbesitzer) regarding the leasing of a property for retraining purposes, but was referred to the Czech Agriculture Ministry. The Jewish Community spoke to forest owners to facilitate the deployment of Jews in forestry.[94] Here the Jewish representatives built on previous experience in Germany and Austria, where the Reich Association of Jews in Germany and the Vienna Jewish Community had developed comprehensive 'camp programmes' during the preceding months.[95]

Some Jews tried to secure training or jobs on their own. Alfred Dube, for example, was employed by a sculptor, who even paid his social security contributions.[96]

Due to growing unemployment, the forced resettlement of Jews from the provinces and the decline in emigration, the Prague Jewish Community had to cater to the needs of an increasing number of destitute Jews. The public Soup Kitchen (Volksküche) was expanded, enabling it to feed a daily total of 1,500 individuals. The Community established a Central Purchasing Centre (Zentraleinkaufsstelle) because, in addition to the expanded Soup Kitchen, it operated three old people's homes, a children's home, two orphanages, two hostels for apprentices and a hospital. By this stage, the Community's weekly outgoings of 236,000 crowns substantially exceeded its income of 166,000 crowns. Forced to eat into its reserves, it teetered on the brink of ruin.[97]

Because 'Aryanization' in the Protectorate was also proceeding apace, the Prague Jewish Community estimated that soon the majority of Jews would be dependent on its support: to save money, it discussed switching its welfare services solely to the provision of food.[98] Jews' impoverishment, and thus the need for the Jewish Community to provide them with relief (see Table A.3 in the appendix), increased exponentially.[99] In total, the Jewish Community helped 16,713 individuals in September and distributed 25,891 meals, while in October it was already supporting 22,983 individuals and providing 37,073 lunches.[100] The Community geared up for a winter aid campaign to counter the growing poverty.[101] In the second week of October, the Housing Office (Wohnungsamt) did what it could to help Jewish families from Prague districts III and IV who had lost their homes.[102]

Among the needy were many refugees from Germany and Austria, some of whom now tried to draw on the property and assets they had left behind. To take just one example, the Gestapo detained Ludwig Beer, 'formerly of Bergreichenstein', because 'in contravention of the regulations on foreign currency, he arranged for the money he had deposited in the Old Reich to be sent to the Protectorate of Bohemia and asked an Aryan in the Reich to cross an unfenced area of the border in order to bring him the money'.[103]

At this point in time, the Jewish Community had a weekly income of around 212,000 crowns, but was spending more than twice this amount.[104] In total, in November 1939 the Community provided 25,996 individuals with more than 541,000 crowns and distributed 47,203 meals, 10,000 more than in the previous month (see also Table A.3 in the appendix).[105] The Clothing Service (Kleiderkammer) helped provide a monthly total of around 350 families with shoes, clothing and furniture. In December, this number grew rapidly, as Jews no longer received clothing coupons. In early September, before the introduction of wartime rationing, just forty people had sought help from the Clothing Service.[106]

As in the rest of the Reich, when the war began Jewish associations were disbanded or integrated into the Prague Jewish Community.[107] The Jewish Community of Moravian Ostrava referred to this imposed process as the 'centralization of the Jewish associations', during the course of which it asked the Jewish Women's Association (Jüdischer Frauenverein) in Přívoz to provide details, as soon as possible, of the date of its most recent audit and general meeting and to present its cash books.[108] Many of the now liquidated organizations had been engaged in charitable activities. While the Jewish Community took over their responsibilities and expenditure, it had to deposit their assets at Eichmann's Central Office.[109]

Impoverishment, poor housing conditions and an abysmal diet impaired Jews' health, particularly that of children. The Children's Clinic (Kinderambulanz) informed the Jewish Community that most children were 'undernourished, weakly and [exposed to] infections of every kind', with almost half suffering from tuberculosis.[110] At this point in time, the Jewish Community was stepping up its efforts to identify buildings in which it might establish new children's and old people's homes.[111] On 1 December, it opened a Jewish hospital in rented premises.[112]

A newly established news bulletin, the *Jüdisches Nachrichtenblatt*, urged its readers to reach out a helping hand in these tumultuous times and make sacrifices in aid of the Jewish community. At this point in history, the bulletin underlined, this meant more than just making donations.[113]

The *Jüdisches Nachrichtenblatt*

The history of the founding of the *Jüdisches Nachrichtenblatt* in Prague points up the selective influence of central planning on anti-Jewish policy in the Protectorate while also shedding light on the power relations within it. As mentioned earlier, before August was over, the Gestapo had ordered the Prague Jewish Community to produce a Jewish newsletter. This, however, required approval from the Czech government.[114] The Prague Police Directorate initially blocked publication, prompting the Jewish Community to protest to the State Office (Landesamt) in October.[115] In the third week of October, the authorities were still refusing to give their approval; anticipating the Jews' removal, they apparently felt a Jewish newspaper was no longer necessary.[116] However, things moved rapidly when the deportations from the Greater German Reich were halted. By the second week of November, the Jewish Community of Prague had presented the Central Office with material for the first issue.[117]

Six months after the German occupation but just a few weeks after the suspension of the transports to Poland, on 24 November 1939, a Jewish news bulletin was published in Prague for the first time. Evidently, the Protectorate authorities now expected Jews to remain over the medium term and thus recognized the need to inform them about anti-Jewish regulations. As had already occurred in the Reich, the weekly publication subsequently detailed all anti-Jewish laws and Gestapo directives.[118]

In contrast to the versions produced in Berlin and Vienna, this was a bilingual publication appearing under the name *Jüdisches Nachrichtenblatt – Židovské Listy*. Despite being censored by the Gestapo, for some time it was regarded as the only newspaper in the Protectorate largely free of outside control. Dr Oskar Singer, formerly editor of the *Prager Tagblatt*, later chronicler of the Łódź ghetto, was in charge of the publication, with a number of well-known journalists on his staff. The first issue, with a print run of nine thousand, declared that the key tasks for the future were emigration, welfare and providing for young people.[119] Later, the newsletter promoted retraining in manual labour and the skilled trades, highlighting Jewish traditions and the enhanced prospects of emigration in this context.[120]

At the end of the year, the authorities reiterated to Jewish representatives in Prague that every Jew under sixty years of age had to leave the Protectorate by the end of 1940. In fact, men below the age of thirty-seven were only given until 28 February 1940 to depart, regardless of the destination. Otherwise they faced the prospect of being sent to concentration camps. Meanwhile, the plan to establish a reservation in the Lublin region, which prompted the World Jewish Congress (WJC) to protest to the Polish exile government, appeared to have been abandoned. A number of those who returned from the area stated that because it was impossible to make a living there, many deportees had fled to the Soviet Union.[121]

Resistance to the Occupation

As clearly evident in protests against deportations, non-Jewish Czechs' growing sense of solidarity with the Protectorate's Jewish residents was anchored in intensifying anti-German sentiment.[122] Regardless of propaganda evoking a German 'city on the Moldau', even during the occupation fewer than twenty thousand Germans lived in Prague, alongside hundreds of thousands of Czechs. The Czech language dominated on the street and in businesses, restaurants and theatres.[123] Mass anti-German or pro-Czech demonstrations were held on 28 October 1939, the twenty-first anniversary of the founding of the Czechoslovak Republic; in many places people wore badges, armbands or caps featuring the three national colours, with many singing the Czech national anthem. Large crowds gathered in the centre of Prague, in front of the Gestapo offices for example, chanting slogans such as 'German police – German pigs!' and 'We want our freedom!'. When the Germans shot two Czech police officers who were trying to calm the crowds on Zitna Street, Czechs began to tear down the German signs on the trams and remove anti-Jewish slogans from shops.[124]

Over the next few weeks a spate of attacks targeted the railways. From late August 1939, such acts of sabotage had incurred the death penalty.[125] In Kladno, Czechs demonstrated in protest against performances of Leni Riefenstahl's film on the Olympics on 8 November. When a Czech police officer failed to intervene, the Germans initiated proceedings against him.[126] During the demonstrations in Prague, Jan Opletal, a medical student at Charles University, was shot in the stomach and died three days later. In mid November, three thousand individuals then took part in student demonstrations marking Opletal's funeral procession and lying in state. Some protesters berated German passers-by. Only after an hour and a half did the Czech police intervene.[127]

The occupying power took vigorous action to quell the opposition. On 18 November 1939, the state presidents (Landespräsidenten) of Bohemia and Moravia imposed martial law on the Czech population in greater Prague and three adjoining districts. The SS and the police had already occupied Prague University and a number of student residences the night before. At daybreak the SS executed nine alleged Czech ringleaders, and later another three for attacking a German. For the next three years, Czech institutions of higher education, including the Agricultural College in Brno and a seminary in Olomouc, were closed, and more than 1,200 students arrested.[128] Given that Jews had been prohibited from attending German schools and universities since September at the latest, this also meant the end of higher education for the Jewish population.[129]

On 19 November, a transport carrying 1,140 Czech university students arrived at the Sachsenhausen concentration camp near Berlin, where eighteen of them later died. A number of Jews were among them.[130] While martial law was lifted on 21 November, in early 1940, as deputy to the Reich protector, State Secretary Frank gave a public speech warning residents of the Protectorate that 'from now on, we will take the strongest possible action, without warning. You are either with us or against us. Those who are against us will be crushed'.[131]

The majority of Germans in the Protectorate, conversely, are likely to have welcomed the crackdown. Some of them, in fact, felt the authorities ought to do more to deter the Czechs from resisting, as reported by Chief County Commissioner Volkmar Hopf in Zlín (Zlin), home to the headquarters of Bata, one of the world's leading shoe firms. The deep hatred between ethnic Germans and Czechs, Hopf contended, was preventing peaceful coexistence, at least among members of the present generation.[132] At the same time, the Germans in the Protectorate complained about their supposedly poor economic situation, as wages failed to keep pace with the rising cost of living.[133] Tensions had sprung up between Reich Germans (Reichsdeutsche) and Germans from the Czech territories: thanks to the strong Reichsmark, the former were emptying shops in the Protectorate of goods while also occupying all the best positions in the Protectorate administration. The latter, on the other hand, made up the majority of trustees.[134]

The repressive measures triggered a shift in the public mood in the Protectorate. As a result of the university closures, which blocked access to education for the great bulk of the Czech people, Czech attitudes towards the Germans hardened and calls for freedom grew louder.[135] At the same time, non-Jewish Czechs felt an increasing sense of solidarity with Jews in the Protectorate. Initially, some Czechs helped Jews flee across the border and later to hide from the authorities, often for several years. Church members played a significant role here.[136]

According to SD reports, the Czech Jews emphasized their 'common ground with the Czechs' and hoped for Soviet diplomatic intervention.[137] On attitudes among the Jewish community, the *Meldungen aus dem Reich* contended that 'the Jews have cast off fears that they might suffer adverse consequences from the Munich assassination attempt [against Hitler in November 1939] and are exhibiting their traditional insolence. This is particularly noticeable in many Jewish pubs in Prague, which are also frequented by many members of the Czech semi-intelligentsia'.[138]

Some Jews were actively involved in the Czech resistance. One newspaper reported that 'the Jew Bauer, together with Protectorate citizen Kulka [had carried out] acts of sabotage' and created a secret ammunition dump. Appeals for clemency having been rejected, both were condemned to death for treason by a court martial and executed in Brno on 31 January 1940.[139]

* * *

After Germany occupied Poland, it radicalized its plans for the Jewish population in the Greater German Reich. Measures emanating from the political centre, such as the curfew, briefly predominated. In the Protectorate, the German police alone were now responsible for the Jews, with all German administrative agencies being subordinated to the Reich protector. In Berlin – in light of the rapid victory over Poland and after the Jewish Communities had carried out an initial statistical survey – in mid September Hitler and his senior staff made the decision to expel all less well-off Jews, which meant most of them, from the Greater German Reich to the east of the occupied Polish territories. This required all so-called racial Jews in the Greater German Reich, including the Protectorate, to register with the Jewish Communities by the end of September, necessitating the deployment of more than one thousand helpers in Prague alone.

The first mass transports, coordinated by Eichmann in the Reich Security Main Office, were tasked with moving Jews from the border area between the Protectorate and Upper Silesia, as well as the cities in the Protectorate and Austria, to Nisko in eastern Poland. This did not mean that Eichmann acted on his own; in fact, he helped to implement a radicalized central plan. However, after the first transport had departed from Moravian Ostrava, inspiring protests from the local Czech residents, the transports from Vienna took precedence over those from the Protectorate, a shift of priority that historians have often wrongly construed as the termination of the deportations. Yet further part-transports from Brno and Prague left the Protectorate. In early November, when Himmler suspended the deportations until February 1940 for technical reasons, a total of five thousand Jews had been deported since 18 October 1939.

Over the medium term, this temporary suspension influenced the planning of Jewish policies in the Protectorate. The Prague Central Office, which had been reopened following its brief closure at the start of the war, once again prioritized the forced emigration of Jews from the Protectorate, repeating its threat to expel all Jews by the summer of 1940. Meanwhile, the authorities had been planning to establish the *Jüdisches Nachrichtenblatt* since summer 1939, but delayed doing so when the war began. It is no coincidence that publication began two weeks after the transports had stopped: an organ providing the Jewish population with information seemed necessary over the medium term.

While the Reich Security Main Office in Berlin was in charge of all deportations, including those from the Protectorate, other fields of

Jewish policy in the occupied Czech territories remained the responsibility of local or regional agencies. The Jewish Communities responded to the impoverishment engendered by mass unemployment by attempting to organize their work more efficiently. Organizations and institutions were incorporated into the Prague Jewish Community, which organized help for the needy, children, old people and new arrivals from the provinces, now spending more than twice its income to this end.

Notes

1. Decree on the structure of the administration and on the German Security Police in the Protectorate of Bohemia and Moravia, 1 September 1939, RGBl. 1939 I, 1681–82. See also Moskowitz, 'Three Years of the Protectorate', 357.
2. USHMM Washington, RG 45.005M, reel 1 (Prague State Archive, Interior Ministry), no. 14, n.p.: Letter Interior Ministry to state authorities in Prague and Brno, 1 September 1939, 1.
3. YV Jerusalem, O 7/53, fol. 38: Weekly report Jewish Religious Community Prague, 16–22 September 1939, 1.
4. USHMM Washington, RG 45.005M, reel 1 (Prague State Archive, Interior Ministry), no. 15, n.p.: Interior Ministry to the state authorities in Prague and Brno, 11 September 1939, 1.
5. StA Freiburg i. Br., Mühlheim County Commissioner's Office (Landratsamt), P. 365 No. 243, n.p.: Telex decree issued by the RFSS, 6 September 1939 in circular decree from the Karlsruhe State Police Headquarters, 10 September 1939.
6. The Prague Community was to make the regulation on the construction of separate air-raid shelters public only after their completion; YV Jerusalem, O 7/53, fol. 35: Weekly report Jewish Religious Community of Prague, 9–15 September 1939, 4. On events in the Old Reich, see Gruner, *Der Geschlossene Arbeitseinsatz*, 110.
7. Reprinted in VEJ/3, doc. 3, 93–94.
8. YV Jerusalem, O 7/53, fol. 35: Weekly report Jewish Religious Community of Prague, 9–15 September 1939, 4. On the arrests and the dreadful conditions in which detainees were held, see Lukáš Přibyl, 'Das Schicksal des dritten Transports aus dem Protektorat nach Nisko', in *Theresienstädter Studien und Dokumente* 2000, 297–342, here 300–305.
9. YV Jerusalem, O 7/53, fol. 25–26: Weekly report Jewish Religious Community of Prague, 27 August to 1 September 1939, 6–7.
10. Ibid., fol. 29: Weekly report Jewish Religious Community of Prague, 2–8 September 1939, 2.
11. According to Jihlava administrative report; Bryant, *Prague in Black*, 112.
12. YV Jerusalem, O 7/53, fol. 31: Weekly report Jewish Religious Community of Prague, 2–8 September 1939, 4; ibid., fol. 33: Weekly report Jewish Religious Community of Prague, 9–15 September 1939, 2.
13. BA Berlin, R 70/9, n.p.: Wagner, Brno Gestapo, Moravian Ostrava Border Police Station (Grenzpolizeikommissariat), to Brno Gestapo, 19 September 1939.
14. RSHA memorandum, 27 September 1939 concerning meeting on 21 September 1939, in *Europa unterm Hakenkreuz: Polen*, 119, doc. no. 12.
15. For a detailed account of what follows, see Wolf Gruner, 'Von der Kollektivausweisung zur Deportation der Juden aus Deutschland (1938–1945): Neue Perspektiven

und Dokumente', in Beate Meyer and Birthe Kundrus (eds), *Die Deportation der Juden aus Deutschland: Pläne, Praxis, Reaktionen 1938–1945* (Beiträge zur Geschichte des Nationalsozialismus, vol. 20) (Göttingen, 2004), 21–62. With a somewhat different tenor, see also Longerich, *Holocaust*, 132–50. On the deportations in general, see H.G. Adler, *Der verwaltete Mensch: Studien zur Deportation der Juden aus Deutschland* (Tübingen, 1974); Alfred Gottwaldt and Diana Schulle, *Die 'Judendeportationen' aus dem Deutschen Reich 1941–1945: Eine kommentierte Chronologie* (Wiesbaden, 2005).

16. YV Jerusalem, O 7/53, fol. 43: Weekly report Jewish Religious Community of Prague, 16–22 September 1939, 6. See also Gruner, 'Kollektivausweisung', 31; Gruner, *Der Geschlossene Arbeitseinsatz*, 110.

17. Report Jewish Religious Community of Prague, 'Evidence on the Jews, Registration, Transports' (n.d., mid 1942), in Krejčová, Svobodová and Hyndráková, *Židé v Protektorátu*, doc. 10, 166. See also Veselská, '"Sie müssen sich als Jude dessen bewusst sein, welche Opfer zu tragen sind ..."', 159.

18. YV Jerusalem, O 7/53, fol. 45–51: Weekly report Jewish Religious Community of Prague, 23–29 September 1939, 1–7.

19. Institute of Jewish Affairs, *Hitler's Ten-Year War*, 55. With slightly different figures (80,391 religious and 9,828 non-religious Jews), see Alena Hájková, 'Erfassung der jüdischen Bevölkerung des Protektorats', in *Theresienstädter Studien und Dokumente* 1997, 50–62, here 53.

20. Quoted in Götz Aly, *'Final Solution': Nazi Population Policy and the Murder of the European Jews* (London, 1999) (German original 1995), 34. See also Longerich, *Holocaust*, 150.

21. The RSHA was created as a result of an RFSS decree of 27 September 1939. On the staff and history of this institution, see Michael Wildt, *An Uncompromising Generation: The Nazi Leadership of the Reich Security Main Office* (Madison, 2009) (German original 2002).

22. YV Jerusalem, O 51/91 (Prague State Archive), fol. 3: Note, 6 October 1939. Excerpt in Adler, *Der verwaltete Mensch*, 128.

23. For the idea that he acted on his own, see above all Seev Goshen, 'Eichmann und die Nisko-Aktion im Oktober 1939', *Vierteljahrshefte für Zeitgeschichte* 29(1) (1981), 74–96, here 84; Browning, *The Origins of the Final Solution*, 36–43; Cesarani, *Final Solution*, 258–59. Longerich deviates from these interpretations. He states that Eichmann expanded on existing policies, but not without backing from Berlin; Longerich, *Holocaust*, 151–55. For a similar analysis, see also Jonny Moser, *Nisko: Die ersten Judendeportationen* (Vienna, 2011). Adler, on the other hand, refers to central government action: Adler, *Der verwaltete Mensch*, 128–40; much the same goes for Safrian, *Eichmann's Men*, 50–56; Gruner, *Zwangsarbeit und Verfolgung*, 137–42. On these issues, the new documents that have come to light and the reinterpretation that follows here, see Gruner, 'Kollektivausweisung', 30–37.

24. YV Jerusalem, O 51/91 (Prague State Archive), fol. 4: Note, 6 October 1939. The first to highlight this document was Longerich, *Holocaust*, 151–52. After Longerich, other authors did so too, such as Wildt, *An Uncompromising Generation*, 237 and especially footnote 167. A recent example is Moser, *Nisko*, 34.

25. BA Berlin, R 70/9, n.p.: Telex Eichmann to Gestapo Branch Office Moravian Ostrava, for the attention of Günther, 16 October 1939. See also Safrian, *Eichmann's Men*, 54; Longerich, *Holocaust*, 152.

26. BA Berlin, R 70/9, n.p.: Leaflet (unsigned, n.d.), 1–4.

27. YV Jerusalem, O 51/91, n.p.: Eichmann's meeting in Kattowitz, 9 October 1939; ibid.: Note Günther, 28 October on meeting of 9 October 1939. See also Moser,

Nisko, 35. Goshen, meanwhile, believes that the Führer's order, with the figure of three hundred thousand, was Eichmann's invention, a means of initiating the transports in Kattowitz: Goshen, 'Eichmann', 85.
28. Decree, 3 October 1939, RGBl. 1939 I, 1997. See VHA Prague, fonds 140, carton 19, no. 2, fol. 303: Report 'The Protectorate of Bohemia and Moravia in Light of its Daily Press', carbon copy, n.d. (c. spring 1940), 16.
29. Decree, 11 July 1939, RGBl. 1939 I, 1235.
30. Decree on the confiscation of assets in the Protectorate of Bohemia and Moravia, 4 October 1939, RGBl. 1939 I, 1998–99. The draft of this decree stated that the property of individuals who had supported activities hostile to the Reich would be confiscated to the benefit of the Reich and administered by the Reich protector; BA Berlin, R 43II/1325, fol. 118: Draft decree on the confiscation of assets in the Protectorate of Bohemia and Moravia, n.d. See also Lemkin, *Axis Rule in Occupied Europe*, 137.
31. BA Berlin, R 43II/1325, fol. 170–72: Circular decree (copy) RFSSuChdtPol, by order of Dr. Best, 8 August 1939.
32. Ibid., fol. 186+RS: Circular decree (copy) RFSSuChdtPol, Heydrich, 22 January 1940.
33. Ibid., fol. 137: Note Reich Chancellery, 1 February 1940.
34. Moser, *Nisko*, 36.
35. BA Berlin, R 70/9, n.p.: Note Dannecker, 11 October regarding meeting on 9 October 1939 in Moravian Ostrava, 1–2.
36. YV Jerusalem, O 30/82, n.p.: Note Gestapo Moravian Ostrava, 13 October 1939. On Vienna, see Moser, *Nisko*, 44.
37. YV Jerusalem, O 30/82, n.p.: Note Israelite Religious Community of Vienna, 11 October 1939.
38. YV Jerusalem, O 7/53, fol. 70–71: Weekly report Jewish Religious Community of Prague, 7–13 October 1939, 8–9. See Shlain, 'Jakob Edelsteins Bemühungen', 80–81.
39. Safrian, *Eichmann's Men*, 52–53.
40. BA Berlin, R 70/9, n.p.
41. Ibid.: Telex Eichmann to Gestapo Moravian Ostrava (Günther), 16 October 1939. See Safrian, *Eichmann's Men*, 54–55.
42. YV Jerusalem, O 7/38, n.p.: Notice (in Czech), Community Head Salo Krämer, n.d.
43. Ibid.: Leaflet, Salo Krämer, Community Head Moravian Ostrava, n.d.
44. USC SF/VHA, video interview, Yehudah Bakon, tape 1, min. 24:50–28:00.
45. BA Berlin, R 58/144, n.p.: Report no. 6, 20 October 1939, 15. Reprinted in *Meldungen aus dem Reich 1938–1945: Die geheimen Lageberichte des Sicherheitsdienstes der SS*, ed. and with an introduction by Heinz Boberach, vol. 2 (Herrsching, 1984), 380–81.
46. YV Jerusalem, O 7/53, fol. 78–79: Weekly report Jewish Religious Community of Prague, 14–20 October 1939, 7–8.
47. The names of the deportees can be found in Mečislav Borák, *Transport to TMY: První deportace evropských Židů* (Ostrava, 1994), 199–211. Among them were Jews from Moravian Ostrava; by no means were the great majority of them Polish Jews as asserted by Gerhard Wolf in *Ideologie und Herrschaftsrationalität: Nationalsozialistische Germanisierungspolitik in Polen* (Hamburg, 2012), 113.
48. YV Jerusalem, O 51/91 (Prague State Archive), fol. 22: Note for Eichmann, 18 October 1939; see also ibid., Daily report SD Office (Dr. Heinrich) Moravian Ostrava, 18 October 1939. On the process of selection and removal, see Přibyl, 'Das Schicksal des dritten Transports', 298.

49. Goshen, 'Eichmann', 90. On events in Nisko, see USC SF/VHA, video interview, Oskar Felcer, tape 1, seg. 6–7. See also Adler, *Der verwaltete Mensch*, 135–40.
50. YV Jerusalem, O 30/82, n.p.: Handwritten note Blumenfeld on telex Müller, 18 October [1939]; ibid.: Note SD Moravian Ostrava, n.d.
51. Ibid.: Eichmann, Central Office for Jewish Emigration, Vienna, to Moravian Ostrava Border Police Station, 1 December 1939. Same doc. in BA Berlin, R 70/9, n.p.
52. BA Berlin, R 70/9, n.p.: Daily report, 19 October 1939, 3.
53. Ibid.: Note, 23 October 1939. Quoted in Wolf Gruner, *Widerstand in der Rosenstraße: Die Fabrik-Aktion und die Verfolgung der 'Mischehen' 1943* (Frankfurt a. M., 2005), 40. See also Moser, *Nisko*, 58–59.
54. BA Berlin, R 70/9, n.p.: Note G/Z Moravian Ostrava, 21 October 1939.
55. Ibid.: Note G/Z Moravian Ostrava, 21 October 1939 in telephone conversation.
56. Ibid.: Note Günther, 21 October 1939.
57. ÖStA/AdR Vienna, Bürckel-Mat, no. 2315/6, fol. 22: Note for District President Barth, 25 October 1939; see also Central Zionist Archives (CZA) Jerusalem, S 26, no. 1191g, n.p.: Report Israelite Religious Community of Vienna, 19 May 1938-1944/45, 17. On events in Vienna, see Gruner, *Zwangsarbeit und Verfolgung*, 137–42; Moser, *Nisko*, 34–41.
58. BA Berlin, R 70/9, n.p. Excerpt in Adler, *Der verwaltete Mensch*, 134.
59. For a recent example of a text contending that the transports were discontinued and that Eichmann acted autonomously, see Moser, *Nisko*, 75.
60. BA Berlin, R 70/9, n.p.
61. Ibid.: Telex Günther, Moravian Ostrava to Krakau, 25 October 1939.
62. The names of the deportees can be found in Borák, *Transport to TMY*, 199–211.
63. BA Berlin, R 70/9, n.p.: Telex Brunner, 28 October 1939, 10.05 p.m., Danube SD to Stapo Field Office, for the attention of Eichmann.
64. Only Gerhard Wolf has pointed this out, though he construes the first deportations as an element in policies targeting Polish Jews rather than Jews throughout the Greater German Reich: Wolf, *Ideologie und Herrschaftsrationalität*, 113–20.
65. YV Jerusalem, O 3/1107, n.p.: Eyewitness account Wilhelm Hechter, 2. See Přibyl, 'Das Schicksal des dritten Transports', 305–6.
66. YV Jerusalem, O 7/53, fol. 82: Weekly report Jewish Religious Community Prague, 21–28 October 1939, 3; ibid., fol. 92: Weekly report Jewish Religious Community Prague, 28 October to 2 November 1939, 6.
67. BA Berlin, R 30/56 (Investigation Regional Court Düsseldorf), fol. 45: RFSS/SD Central Office for Bohemia and Moravia, Daily report no. 129 Prague, 28 October 1939, 5. Also quoted in Gruner, *Widerstand in der Rosenstraße*, 41; Gruner, 'Das Protektorat Böhmen/Mähren', 38.
68. YV Jerusalem, O 51/91 (Prague State Archive), fol. 38: Telex, 3 November 1939 with Daily Report (Dannecker) to Central Office Vienna for 1 and 2 November 1939. See Moser, *Nisko*, 77.
69. YV Jerusalem, O 3/1107, n.p.: Eyewitness account Wilhelm Hechter, 3.
70. Ibid. The conditions in this camp were dreadful, and the Gestapo beat the detainees. Thirty to forty of them fled to Krakau; ibid., 4. Following an intervention by the Sosnowitz Community, most of the remaining Jews were taken to a camp in Vyhne, Slovakia, in early 1940 as a 'Jewish emigrant group'. Initially they were supposed to remain there prior to emigration, but in 1941 it was turned into a work camp. For a detailed account, see Přibyl, 'Das Schicksal des dritten Transports', 314–30; see also Eduard Nižnansky, 'Die Aktion Nisko, das Lager Sosnowiec (Oberschlesien) und die Anfänge des Judenlagers in Vyhne (Slowakei)', *Jahrbuch*

für Antisemitismusforschung 11 (2002), 325–35, and YV Jerusalem, O 3/1107, n.p.: Eyewitness account Wilhelm Hechter, 4–6.
71. BA Berlin, R 70/9, n.p.: Telex, 3 November 1939.
72. YV Jerusalem, O 51/91 (Prague State Archive), fol. 38: Telex, 3 November 1939 with Daily Report (Dannecker) to Central Office Vienna, for 1 and 2 November 1939.
73. ÖStA/AdR Vienna, Bürckel-Mat, no. 2315/6, fol. 22: Note Dr. Becker, 13 November 1939; ibid., fol. 25: Himmler to Bürckel, 9 November 1940.
74. BA Berlin, R 30/4a, fol. 99: Administrative report, 2 October 1939 (in fact 2 November), 2. See ibid., fol. 94–95: Draft of the administrative report; and ibid., fol. 141: Note on Gestapo information, n.d. See also Gruner, 'Kollektivausweisung', 34.
75. See BA Berlin, R 70/9, n.p.: Notes 6 October to 3 November 1939.
76. BA Berlin, R 58/544, fol. 218: RSHA/II 112 to Head II, 19 December 1939.
77. USHMM Washington, RG 11.001M.04, reel 72 (OSOBI Moscow 503-1-324), n.p.: Circular decree RSHA IV, 21 December 1939. Reprinted in VEJ/3, doc. 40, 148. See BA Berlin, R 58/1074 (microfiche), fol. 65: List of Security Police decrees 1936–1942.
78. 'Respite Granted to Teschen Jews', *The New York Times*, 27 November 1939, 7.
79. BA Berlin, R 70/9, n.p.: Telex Central Office Vienna (Eichmann) to Moravian Ostrava Border Command (Grenzkommando), 1 December 1939; and YV Jerusalem, O 51/91 (Prague State Archive), fol. 38: Note SD II B 4 Moravian Ostrava, 25 January 1940.
80. Gruner, 'Kollektivausweisung', 35. However, when the plan fell through, dozens of those deported from Moravian Ostrava were driven across the border into the Soviet Union, where they later lived in a variety of locations; YV Jerusalem, O 7/38, n.p.: Several lists of names with addresses in the Soviet Union, n.d.; ibid.: Copy letter Leo Silbiger from Apkaschewo, 10 August 1940; *Manchester Guardian*, 30 December 1939, 7. For a detailed account of the deportees' fate, see Moser, *Nisko*, 85–166.
81. YV Jerusalem, O 7/53, fol. 101: Weekly report Jewish Religious Community Prague, 3–9 November 1939, 8; Shlain, 'Jakob Edelsteins Bemühungen', 81–85.
82. YV Jerusalem, O 7/53, fol. 63–65: Weekly report Jewish Religious Community Prague, 7–13 October 1939, 1–3.
83. Ibid., fol. 73: Weekly report Jewish Religious Community Prague, 14–20 October 1939, 2.
84. Ibid., fol. 95: Weekly report Jewish Religious Community Prague, 3–9 November 1939, 2.
85. Ibid., fol. 112: Weekly report Jewish Religious Community Prague, 10–16 November 1939, 11.
86. Ibid., fol. 113 and 117: Weekly report Jewish Religious Community Prague, 17–23 November 1939, 1 and 5.
87. Ibid., fol. 184: Monthly report Jewish Religious Community Prague, 1–30 November 1939, 2; ibid., fol. 188: Appendix, Statistical overview of emigration, 1–30 November 1939.
88. Ibid., fol. 195: Monthly report Jewish Religious Community Prague, 1–31 December 1939, Appendix, Statistical overview of emigration, 1–31 December 1939.
89. Ibid., fol. 115: Weekly report Jewish Religious Community Prague, 17–23 November 1939, 3.
90. Ibid., fol. 146: Weekly report Jewish Religious Community Prague, 8–14 December 1939, 4.
91. Ibid., fol. 111–12: Weekly report Jewish Religious Community Prague, 10–16 November 1939, 10–11. See Decree on the dismissal of Jewish white-collar workers

in the Protectorate of Bohemia and Moravia (Verordnung über die Entlassung jüdischer Angestellter im Protektorat Böhmen und Mähren), 23 November 1939, published 11 November 1939, in *Verordnungsblatt des Reichsprotektors in Böhmen und Mähren 1939*/no. 34, 281–82. On rental income, see *The New York Times*, 15 November 1939, 3.

92. YV Jerusalem, O 7/53, fol. 98: Weekly report Jewish Religious Community Prague, 3–9 November 1939, 5.
93. Ibid., fol. 106: Weekly report Jewish Religious Community Prague, 10–16 November 1939, 5; ibid., fol. 161: Weekly report Jewish Religious Community Prague, 22–29 December 1939, 3.
94. Ibid., fol. 156: Weekly report Jewish Religious Community Prague, 15–21 December 1939, 5.
95. Gruner, *Jewish Forced Labor*, 45–50 and Gruner, *Zwangsarbeit und Verfolgung*, 93–97.
96. USC SF/VHA, video interview, Alfred Dube, tape 1, min. 21:00–29:07, tape 2, min. 9:08–10:30.
97. YV Jerusalem, O 7/53, fol. 40–43: Weekly report Jewish Religious Community Prague, 16–22 September 1939, 3–6.
98. Ibid., fol. 44: Weekly report Jewish Religious Community Prague, 16–22 September 1939, 7.
99. Ibid., fol. 13: Weekly report Jewish Religious Community Prague, 20–25 August 1939, 2; ibid., fol. 29: Weekly report Jewish Religious Community Prague, 2–8 September 1939, 2.
100. Ibid., fol. 176: Monthly report Jewish Religious Community Prague, 1–30 September 1939, 3; ibid., fol. 180: Monthly report Jewish Religious Community Prague, 1–31 October 1939, 2.
101. Ibid., fol. 55 and 61: Weekly report Jewish Religious Community Prague, 30 September to 6 October 1939, 3 and 9; ibid., fol. 66: Weekly report Jewish Religious Community Prague, 7–13 October 1939, 4.
102. Ibid., fol. 67: Weekly report Jewish Religious Community Prague, 7–13 October 1939, 5.
103. District President Lower Bavaria and Upper Palatinate, Report for October 1939, Regensburg, 8 November 1939, in Kulka and Jäckel, *Jews*, CD doc. no. 3009.
104. YV Jerusalem, O 7/53, fol. 121: Weekly report Jewish Religious Community Prague, 17–23 November 1939, 9.
105. Ibid., fol. 184–85: Monthly report Jewish Religious Community Prague, 1–30 November 1939, 2–3.
106. Ibid., fol. 126: Weekly report Jewish Religious Community Prague, 24–30 November 1939, 4; ibid., fol. 135: Weekly report Jewish Religious Community Prague, 1–7 December 1939, 4; ibid.: fol. 29: Weekly report Jewish Religious Community Prague, 2–8 September 1939, 2; ibid., fol. 194: Monthly report Jewish Religious Community Prague, 1–31 December 1939, 6.
107. Ibid., fol. 70: Weekly report Jewish Religious Community Prague, 7–13 October 1939, 8; ibid., fol. 78: Weekly report Jewish Religious Community Prague, 14–20 October 1939, 7.
108. YV Jerusalem, M 58/JM 11815, fol. 227: Letter from the Jewish Religious Community Moravian Ostrava, 6 October 1939. However, the association had already ceased its activities in June 1939; ibid., fol. 228: Handwritten letter from Ella Förster (association secretary) to the Moravian Ostrava Jewish Community, 13 October 1939.
109. YV Jerusalem, O 7/53, fol. 92: Weekly report Jewish Religious Community Prague, 28 October to 2 November 1939, 6.

110. Ibid., fol. 89–90: Weekly report Jewish Religious Community Prague, 28 October to 2 November 1939, 2–3.
111. Ibid., fol. 118: Weekly report Jewish Religious Community Prague, 17–23 November 1939, 6.
112. Ibid., fol. 136: Weekly report Jewish Religious Community Prague, 1–7 December 1939, 5.
113. Article, 28 December 1939, reprinted in English in Garbarini et al., *Jewish Responses*, 292–93.
114. YV Jerusalem, O 7/53, fol. 27: Weekly report Jewish Religious Community Prague, 27 August to 1 September 1939, 8.
115. Ibid., fol. 65: Weekly report Jewish Religious Community Prague, 7–13 October 1939, 3.
116. Ibid., fol. 79: Weekly report Jewish Religious Community Prague, 14–20 October 1939, 8.
117. Ibid., fol. 106: Weekly report Jewish Religious Community Prague, 10–16 November 1939, 5.
118. See YV Jerusalem, O 7/55, fol. 40: Weekly report Jewish Religious Community Prague, 27 April to 3 May 1940, 4.
119. Rothkirchen, *Jews*, 118. For a general account, see Ruth Bondy, 'Chronik der sich schließenden Tore: Jüdisches Nachrichtenblatt – Židovské Listy (1939–1945)', in *Theresienstädter Studien und Dokumente* 2000, 86–103.
120. See *Jüdisches Nachrichtenblatt*, Prague edition, article, 15 December 1939. Reprinted in English in Garbarini et al., *Jewish Responses*, 290–91.
121. 'Order to Jews. Must Leave the Protectorate', *Manchester Guardian*, 30 December 1939, 7; 'Jewish Reservation in Poland is Scored', *The New York Times*, 7 December 1939, 12.
122. For a general take on non-Jewish Czechs' attitudes towards the Jews, see Livia Rothkirchen, 'Czech Attitudes toward the Jews during the Nazi Regime', *Yad Vashem Studies* 13 (1977), 287–329.
123. Dennler, *Böhmische Passion*, 6.
124. VHA Prague, fonds 140, carton 19, no. 2, fol. 289: Report 'The Protectorate of Bohemia and Moravia in Light of its Daily Press', carbon copy, n.d. (c. spring 1940), 2; ibid., fol. 366: Report 'Statement by the Czechoslovak Student Union for November 17th', n.d. (early November 1941), 1; Status report SD, 28 October 1939, in Celovsky, *Germanisierung und Genozid*, 218–19; Beneš and Ginsburg, *10 Million Prisoners*, 155. For a detailed description of the demonstrations, see Brandes, *Die Tschechen unter deutschem Protektorat*, part I, 83–95.
125. Los Angeles Museum of the Holocaust/Archive (LAMOTH/A), RG-66.87, n.p.: Poster showing decree issued by Reich protector von Neurath, 26 August 1939.
126. BA Berlin, R 58/144, n.p.: Report no. 17, 17 November 1939, 14. Reprinted in *Meldungen aus dem Reich*, vol. 3, 474.
127. References to the date of these demonstrations as 15 November 1939 can be found in: diary entry of 18 November 1939 in William L. Shirer, *Berlin Diary: The Journal of a Foreign Correspondent 1934–1941* (London, 1942), 199; SD status report, 20 November 1939, in Celovsky, *Germanisierung und Genozid*, 222; Beneš and Ginsburg, *10 Million Prisoners*, 156–57; Sládek, 'Standrecht und Standgericht', 329. They are reported as having occurred on 16 November 1939 in BA Berlin, R 58/144, n.p.: Report no. 17, 17 November 1939, 14. Reprinted in *Meldungen aus dem Reich*, vol. 3, 474.
128. VHA Prague, fonds 140, carton 19, no. 2, fol. 289–90: Report 'The Protectorate of Bohemia and Moravia in Light of its Daily Press', carbon copy, n.d. (c. spring 1940),

2–3; ibid., fol. 366: Report 'Statement by the Czechoslovak Student Union for November 17th', n.d. (early November 1941), 1; Entry of 18 November 1939, in Shirer, *Berlin Diary*, 199; SD status report, 20 November 1939, in Celovsky, *Germanisierung und Genozid*, 222; Beneš and Ginsburg, *10 Million Prisoners*, 156–57; Percival Knauth, '10,000 S. S. Guards Sent to Garrison Czech Capital; City is Reported Quiet', *Washington Post*, 18 November 1939, 1; 'More Czechs Shot', *The New York Times*, 19 November 1939, 1; Sládek, 'Standrecht und Standgericht', 330.

129. USHMM Washington, RG 48.005M, reel 3 (Prague State Archive, Ministry for Schools and Public Education: Jewish regulations), no. 13, n.p.: Copy of letter from Ministry to the German State School Boards in Bohemia and in Moravia, 24 June 1939.
130. Information provided to the present author by Anna Milarch (Archive of the Sachsenhausen Concentration Camp Memorial), 27 January 2009.
131. VHA Prague, fonds 140, carton 19, no. 2, fol. 290–91: Report 'The Protectorate of Bohemia and Moravia in Light of its Daily Press', carbon copy, n.d. (c. spring 1940), 3–5. See LAMOTH/A Los Angeles, RG-23.06.07, n.p.: Poster announcing the Prague State Authority's lifting of martial law, 21 November 1939. On Frank's uncompromising attitude towards the demonstrations, see Küpper, *Karl Hermann Frank*, 212–21.
132. According to the report for December 1939, in Brandes, 'Nationalsozialistische Tschechenpolitik', 55.
133. BA Berlin, R 58/144, n.p.: Report no. 17, 17 November 1939, 14. Reprinted in *Meldungen aus dem Reich*, vol. 3, 475.
134. Bryant, *Prague in Black*, 46–48.
135. Dennler, *Böhmische Passion*, 11.
136. Rothkirchen, *Jews*, 114, 217–23.
137. BA Berlin, R 58/144, n.p.: Report no. 6, 20 October 1939, 15. Reprinted in *Meldungen aus dem Reich*, vol. 2, 380.
138. BA Berlin, R 58/144, n.p.: Report no. 17, 17 November 1939, 14. Reprinted in *Meldungen aus dem Reich*, vol. 3, 474.
139. VHA Prague, fonds 140, carton 19, no. 2, fol. 292: Report 'Das Protektorat Böhmen und Mähren im Lichte seiner Tagespresse', carbon copy, n.d. (c. spring 1940), 5.

CHAPTER 5

REORIENTATION, GHETTOIZATION AND PROTEST

Strategic Changes in the Reich's Anti-Jewish Policy

Stahlecker, Commander of the Security Police in the Office of the Reich Protector, expected to see the resumption of the deportations that had been discontinued until February 1940. On 29 January, he thus extended the jurisdiction of the Central Office for Jewish Emigration, now located at Artilleriestraße 11, Prague XVIII, from the capital to the entire territory of the Protectorate.[1] It may have been in this context that on 1 February the Czech Interior Ministry recommended to the state authorities in Prague and Brno that they require Jews to assume the additional first names of Sara and Israel, as already mandatory in the rest of the Greater German Reich.[2] Shortly afterwards, the ministry also informed both these state authorities of the Central Office's new powers.[3]

On 19 February 1940, however, in conversation with Göring, Heydrich re-evaluated the goals of anti-Jewish policy. To expedite the deportation of Jews from the annexed Polish territories over the short term, 'Jews living in Reich territories, including the Protectorate of Bohemia and Moravia, cannot be evacuated to the General Government at this time'.[4] As a result, the focus of anti-Jewish policy shifted back to the Protectorate, with emigration taking priority once again. That the extension of the Central Office's supervisory powers to all Jewish Communities did not mean it was in sole charge of the 'Jewish question' within the Protectorate, as a number of researchers have assumed,[5] is evident in the events of the first half of 1940.

By order of the Reich Security Main Office, on 5 March 1940 Dr Franz Weidmann, senior secretary of the Prague Jewish Community, and Jakob Edelstein, head of the Palestine Office, made an overnight trip to Berlin to meet with representatives of the Reich Association, the Vienna Jewish Community and its Palestine Office. Their discussion is likely to have centred on how best to accelerate emigration, given that the mass deportations had again been postponed, this time with no deadline for their resumption.[6] In the Protectorate, coordinating negotiations with provincial Jewish Communities had already taken place in early December 1939 in an attempt to bolster the emigration process. The Jewish Communities, meanwhile, were required to disclose their assets, which equated to just under twenty-three million crowns, to the Central Office.[7] Its jurisdiction over the entire Protectorate immediately simplified procedures: now Jews from the provinces no longer had to move to Prague in order to submit their applications for emigration.

At the same time, the authorities had recently imposed significant restrictions. In the third week of February 1940, the Prague Central Office had informed the Jewish Community of the fateful decision to impose 'a ban on emigration for men between 18 and 45 years of age' in the Protectorate. This prompted the Community to submit a memorandum to the Central Office underlining that this restriction on men of working age would bring the entire emigration process 'to a standstill' and render every project, from the 'Bolivian campaign' to the settlement in Santo Domingo, null and void.[8] Even in its weekly report to Eichmann, normally composed in a strictly neutral tone, the Jewish Community urged him to lift the ban.[9]

Elimination from the Economy

Quite apart from the wartime closure of borders and negligible opportunities for transportation, new anti-Jewish measures drastically curtailed individuals' ability to finance migration, while also having a deleterious effect on the finances of the Jewish Community, whose budget depended on individual contributions.

Since the start of the year, Jews' financial activities, both individual and collective, private and public, had been subject to strict controls. In the wake of a decree issued by the Czech Finance Ministry on 23 January 1940, payments to both Jews and Jewish businesses could only be made to so-called security accounts at specified banks. Jews could withdraw a weekly total of just 1,500 crowns from these 'Jewish blocked accounts', a procedure that was subject to strict supervision.[10]

By this point the German authorities had taken the initiative in the economic sphere. On 26 January 1940, the Reich protector in Bohemia and Moravia issued a further ordinance on the 'elimination' of Jews from economic life. Henceforth it would be permissible to deny Jews senior roles in business enterprises.[11] On the same day, an implementing decree prohibited Jews from running businesses in the textile, shoe, leather goods and retail trades. Jews also had to cease involvement in peddling and itinerant trade. Jewish firms, meanwhile, had to provide the authorities with details of their domestic and foreign assets (as at end 1939) by 15 March 1940.[12] International observers viewed these measures as an attempt to definitively eliminate Jews from the economic life of the Protectorate. In the Protectorate itself, many opined that the Jews had failed to understand the warning of June 1939, otherwise they would have emigrated.[13]

As late as November 1939, in his administrative report the chief county commissioner in Moravian Ostrava complained that while the 'Aryanization' of Jewish property was proceeding apace, the question of jurisdiction remained unresolved. For example, he went on, following a meeting in Prague the Gestapo had asserted that it could act alone, in other words appoint sequestrators. He suggested that the German authorities in Prague ought to harmonize their instructions to the chief county commissioners and Gestapo.[14] On 9 February 1940, the Office of the Reich Protector now provided the chief county commissioners with more detail on how to implement the ordinance of 26 January. In the introduction to its guidelines on the 'elimination' of Jews from economic life, the Office stated that 'the decree is crucial to the progress of de-Judaization in the Protectorate. It enables the de-Judaization of the Protectorate's economy and the transfer of previously Jewish firms into non-Jewish hands by force of law'. Jews could now be prohibited from running businesses in entire branches of the economy and individual firms, or they could be compelled to 'convert [their firms] into non-Jewish property'. Liquidation or 'Aryanization' was determined by 'the perspectives of Volkstum policy'. In 'German fields of interest' it was thus possible, 'despite existing overcrowding in a given branch of the economy, [to order] a firm to be placed in German hands in the interest of the German Volkstum'. For Jews, from the day they received the order to liquidate a business, the disposition of all assets was subject to approval. In cases of 'Aryanization', 'conditions [may be] imposed with respect to the person of the desired purchaser'. Trustees were essentially ruled out as purchasers. The 'payment accruing to the Jew', which '[shall] as a rule be no higher than the liquidation value', had to be paid into a blocked account. The Office of the Reich Protector reserved the right to lower the purchase price and 'impose a compensatory levy, which [would] generally [amount] to 70% of the difference between the liquidation value and market value on the day of the sale'. Factoring goodwill into the calculation of a company's market value was not permitted.[15] Often under threat of violence or arrest, firms changed hands for a fraction of their true value. For example, in March 1940 a German acquired a Prague coal business worth four million crowns for just 400,000, but deposited just 130,000 crowns at the bank.[16]

Against the background of these measures, in February the Czech constabulary began to close Jewish retail businesses in the textile and leather industries in a number of locations. This, as the Prague Jewish Community complained to the Central Office and the Secret State Police, contravened the ordinance of 26 January, which was supposed to facilitate the declaration of property.[17] The fourth implementing decree relating to the decree issued by the Reich protector on 7 February 1940 regulated the declaration of all firms' assets.[18] Once again, this required Jews to provide information on the assets of all their businesses, including craft enterprises, as well as registering real estate, shares and investments.[19] In late March, the Reich protector barred Jews from the Protectorate's film industry.[20]

One year after Jews in Germany and Austria had been forced to hand over all the precious metals and jewels in their possession for sale at public pawn offices,[21] the fifth implementing decree relating to Reich Protector von Neurath's decree on Jewish assets was issued on 18 March 1940. It forced all Jewish citizens of the Protectorate, but also 'Jewish' businesses and associations, to deposit shares, securities, items of precious metal, precious stones and pearls in their possession or ownership at a foreign exchange bank within two weeks. They were permitted to keep only gold teeth and wedding rings. In its weekly report to the Central Office, the Prague Jewish Community requested that the religious objects found in synagogues be excepted from the compulsory deposit scheme.[22] Jews could no longer sell precious metals, except (with official approval) at HADEGA GmbH in Prague.[23]

The Forced Organization of the Jewish Communities in the Protectorate

During this period, the Security Police also restructured the entire organization of the Jewish Communities in the Protectorate. The initial plan was to align the compulsory regulations with those pertaining to the Reich Association of Jews in Germany.[24] Since July 1939, it had been compulsory for all 'racial' Jews to take up membership in the Reich Association. This organization, controlled by the Gestapo, organized a separate Jewish welfare and school system and compulsory emigration.[25] On 7 December, the Czech Cabinet approved a draft government ordinance on the 'forcible amalgamation of the Jews', presumably as a medium-term response to the interruption of the mass transports. The draft document on the establishment of an 'Association of Jews headquartered in Prague' was modelled on the Reich Association. Like its counterpart in Berlin, as a legal person the Prague Association was to be subordinate to the Interior Ministry, in this case the Czech one, and organize the Jewish schools and welfare system as well as compulsory emigration. To this end it would impose a levy on its compulsory members, that is, all Jewish citizens of the Protectorate along with Jews residing there, as defined by the provisions in the Neurath ordinance of 21 June 1939. All Jewish 'legal entities' that still existed, in other words Communities, foundations and organizations, had to be incorporated into the Association by a certain date, with failure to do so resulting in liquidation. With respect to 'schooling', under the supervision of the Czech Education Ministry a sufficient number of schools were to be established, while existing institutions would be taken over by the planned Association. When it came to welfare, the Association was to 'provide its members with the support that their home Communities and states would otherwise be obliged to provide'.[26] As had applied in Germany since November 1938, in 1940 the Jewish Communities in the Protectorate were now to be saddled with the state's duty of care.[27] The Office of the Reich Protector, however, criticized some aspects of the draft document. Among other things, the Association was not clearly described as a *Verein*, meaning a registered society under German law.[28]

In the end the Reich protector withheld approval, believing the planned Czech government ordinance contradicted the ordinance on the status of the Central Office for Jewish Emigration. Furthermore, it failed to declare the Jewish Communities compulsory organizations. The Reich protector thus planned to issue his own ordinance. At a meeting on 9 January 1940 chaired by Ministerial Counsellor Dr Mokry and attended by BdS Stahlecker, it was decided that the latter would draw up this ordinance on the model of Austria, given the success of its emigration policy. The Reich protector would be in charge of the compulsory organization in Prague, while the emigration levy would be used to establish a 'fund for Jewish emigration'.[29] The Commander of the Security Police had already submitted the draft document to the Reich protector by 23 January 1940.[30]

On the Austrian model but with certain modifications, on 5 March 1940 Reich Protector von Neurath thus issued a decree pertaining to the Protectorate. It stipulated that, henceforth, the Jewish Communities had to provide for all persons considered Jews according to paragraph 6 of the decree of 21 June 1939, that is, not just for their current members. They could raise taxes to do so. From now on, all Jewish Communities and organizations in the Protectorate must comply with the demands of the Prague Jewish Community. According to the decree, the Jewish Religious Communities – now officially designated as compulsory organizations – as well as all other Jewish organizations and foundations, would be supervised by the Central Office, which received its instructions from the Reich protector. An emigration fund would be established for Bohemia and Moravia as the property of the Central Office for Jewish Emigration. The Central Office, which would be authorized to liquidate Jewish organizations, could transfer the property of dissolved Communities or organizations to the fund.[31]

The Liquidation of Associations and Other Consequences of Forced Organization

The weekly report produced by the Prague Jewish Community stated that the ordinance of 5 March 1940, published on 8 March, had 'created the basis for the centralization of all Jewish activities'. While the Central Office would be in charge of all Jewish organizations, the report went on, the Prague Jewish Community was authorized to instruct all provincial Communities and organizations in the Protectorate, legalizing the state of affairs that had pertained hitherto.[32] On 18 March, Eichmann gave Weidmann, as senior official of the Jewish Community, and Edelstein, as head of the Palestine Office, instructions regarding the implementation of the Protectorate ordinance on the 'supervision of the Jews and Jewish organizations'. One day later, a letter from the Central Office appointed Weidmann head of the Jewish Community and Edelstein his deputy. Both subsequently worked to reorganize the

Prague Jewish Community and the provincial Communities in line with the instructions issued by the Central Office.[33]

On 21 March 1940, the Prague Community arranged a meeting to consider these issues with the heads of the Jewish Communities and representatives of associations from the districts of Prague, Kolín (Kolin), Mladá Boleslav (Jungbunzlau), Pilsen and Louny (Laun).[34] By the end of the month, a number of such meetings had been held with the officials of other provincial Communities to discuss the changed situation in the wake of the ordinance and the dissolution of all associations outside Prague. The representatives of the associations were required to sign a declaration affirming their associations' voluntary disbandment and the transfer of their assets to the Prague Jewish Community. The Prague Community's Provincial Department (Provinzabteilung) played an important role in planning the reorganization of the provincial Communities and in drawing up the new regulations on membership fees. Meanwhile, the Central Office's first step was to dissolve Prague's suburban Communities and incorporate them into the Prague Jewish Community.[35]

This continued a trend that had already begun, for the Jewish Community had already liquidated six associations in the last week of February, their assets transferred to the 'Central Office for Jewish Emigration, Subaccount Organizations' at the Böhmische Union-Bank.[36] Meanwhile, in late March the provincial associations and burial fraternities received requests from Prague to draw up statements of assets.[37]

The process of disbanding associations, therefore, began before an official ordinance had been issued, as apparent in the case of the self-dissolution of the chevra kadisha in Hranice. The representatives of this burial association met in the local Community hall one week after receiving a letter from the Prague Jewish Community of 29 March 1940 and resolved to disband their association, which had existed since 1876. Its assets, to the tune of twenty-one thousand crowns, initially went to the Prague Jewish Community, which was also supposed to take over its functions.[38]

By late May 1940, at the behest of the Central Office, the Prague Jewish Community's Associations Department (Vereinsreferat) had drawn up a statement of assets covering all 183 provincial associations, of which 106 were in Bohemia and 77 in Moravia. However, the Community still lacked guidelines setting out the liquidation process.[39]

Within the Jewish Community, a Central Registry (Zentralevidenz), consisting of a Central Records Unit (Zentralkartei) and a Research Service (Recherchedienst), took up its work, collating 'the data of all Jews living in the Protectorate of Bohemia and Moravia'.[40] Towards the end of May, by order of SS Hauptsturmführer Günther, the Central Records Unit then entered into contact with the Central Registration Office (Zentralmeldeamt), which henceforth informed the Prague Jewish Community daily of applications to register and notices of departure from all individuals in the greater Prague area, for whom the Jewish Community was responsible.[41]

On 16 March, as instructed by the Central Office for Jewish Emigration, the Jewish Community had established the 'Division for Non-Mosaic Jews' (Abteilung für nichtmosaische Juden), which immediately set about registering all non-religious Jews in the Protectorate based on the incoming registration forms.[42] In the second week of March, every newspaper in the Protectorate published the Central Office's call for all non-religious Jews to report to the Jewish Communities.[43] According to the ordinance issued by the Reich protector on 2 April 1940, individuals considered Jews under the Nuremberg laws were obliged to register with the Jewish Communities, which could impose taxes on them.[44] By late April, the Division had registered 10,490 individuals, 8,740 in Bohemia and 1,750 in Moravia,[45] who now had to pay a welfare levy to the Community.[46] The officials at the Division for Non-Mosaic Jews attempted to facilitate their emigration through negotiations with Christian organizations, while also arranging for them to receive assistance from the Jewish Community's welfare services.[47]

Radicalization and Ghettoization

When the Germans centralized the control of Jewish institutions and accelerated the elimination of Jews from the economy, they also placed limits on their freedom of movement. The Czech Interior Ministry informed the state authorities in Prague and Brno that the Gestapo had prohibited Jews from frequenting public places after 8 p.m., concurrently solving, as the Ministry underlined, the problem of Jews' presence in entertainment venues. All theatres and cinemas were to put up prohibitory signs, had they not done so already.[48] On 10 February, the Gestapo raided Prague cafés and restaurants with Jewish owners. Officials escorted three hundred of them to the Gestapo headquarters, where they were issued with fines and given to understand that the sooner they emigrated, the better.[49]

In late February 1940, police stations began to mark the 'citizen's ID cards (Bürgerlegitimationen)', which had been issued to Jews in 1939 to replace their passports, 'with a "J"', evidently in order to better monitor compliance with the restrictions.[50]

In early March 1940, the authorities announced a general ban on attendance at the Czech theatre for Jews.[51] At the same time, President Hácha had approved the programme propagated by National Partnership, which aspired to be a 'national-social movement', supposedly anchoring its nationalism in a millennium-old Czech consciousness. It hoped the Germans would recognize the autonomy of Czech nationalism. According to this organization, within the Czech lands the 'idea of the People's Community (Volksgemeinschaft)' demanded 'the elimination of elements alien to the people (volksfremd), particularly the Jews'. Its exponents would dedicate themselves to 'preserving the foundations of the Czech People (des tschechischen Volksbodens)' and cleansing the economy of 'alien elements'.[52]

By this point in time, the Reich protector had received petitions calling for the introduction of a Jewish badge. Individual petitioners proposed, for example, a Star of David to be worn on clothing, while the 'National Aryan Cultural Association' in Prague suggested a strip of yellow cloth bearing the label 'Jew'.[53] This sparked a debate in the Office of the Reich Protector on the introduction of a badge. The Security Police, however, stated that higher authorities were not yet in favour of such an insignia – as in the territory of the Reich and in contrast to occupied Poland.[54]

In the housing industry too, a number of agencies adopted more radical policies.[55] In the third week of April 1940, the Prague city government gave all Jews in municipal housing eviction notices.[56] In May, the Jewish Telegraphic Agency reported that Jews in the Protectorate forced to abandon their homes were also required to pay a special levy of one thousand crowns for the cleaning of the premises, which was cynically referred to as 'de-Judaization'.[57]

In parallel to Jewish renters' loss of tenancy in Prague, the authorities in towns began to force Jews into ghettos. In the second half of June, in Mladá Boleslav, Turnov (Turnau), Semily (Semil) and Jičín (Jitschin), the Jewish Communities were tasked with 'clearing [all] accommodation occupied by Jews and concentrating the Jews in one street'.[58] In Hořice v Podkrkonoší (Horschitz) and Nové Benátky (Neu-Benatek), the local Jews had to congregate in 'specific groups of houses or certain buildings',[59] as was also the case in Mnichovo Hradiště (Münchengrätz). In Mladá Boleslav, the local Jews were housed in an old castle, in other places in 'even less appropriate' accommodation, as the Prague Jewish Community highlighted in its official report to the Central Office.[60] In late June, the head of the Prague Jewish Community's Provincial Department visited the town of Lysá nad Labem (Lissa), where the authorities had instructed 'Jews to concentrate in a factory building'; he discussed arrangements for this 'resettlement' with local officials. The Prague Jewish Community lodged an appeal against the ghettoization recommended by District Offices in the area under the jurisdiction of the Jičín Chief County Commissioner's Office and composed a number of petitions.[61] On 13 July, in Mladá Boleslav, the head of the Provinces Department and a physician examined the living quarters of the families now accommodated in the old castle, along with their sanitary conditions and health.[62]

Much as with the establishment of 'Jews' houses' (Judenhäuser) in Germany, in the Protectorate a number of local authorities were quick to ghettoize Jews in order to seize their homes and relieve the strain on the local housing market.[63] The scale and radical nature of their approach, however, were more reminiscent of occupied Poland.[64]

The Prague Jewish Community's Response

At the beginning of 1940, the Prague Jewish Community had 496 employees. As its responsibilities steadily increased, however, it rapidly expanded its staff through the appointment of additional teachers and other personnel. In January, in an attempt to function more effectively, under Central Office supervision the Prague Community incorporated all suburban Communities, absorbing their staff and taking charge of their finances. By the end of January, the Community had a staff of 546.[65]

On 8 February 1940, however, the Central Office prohibited the Prague Jewish Community from appointing staff without its approval. The Office directly controlled the Community's finances and thus its staffing budget as well.[66] Nonetheless, by the end of March the Prague Jewish Community already had a staff of 637 people, while the Central Zionist Union (Zionistischer Zentralverband) employed a further ninety-five individuals in the Palestine Office. Most of the Community's new staff members had originally worked in the thirty-six associations and organizations that had been disbanded in the preceding weeks.[67] The Central Office now controlled not just the appointment but also the remuneration of employees, for which the Jewish Community had to request the release of funds on a monthly basis.[68]

In response to the special challenges imposed by the impoverishment of its members, the Prague Jewish Community created new divisions in an attempt to provide for poor, sick and old individuals whose families could no longer support them.[69] In total, it soon employed 2,600 staff members in thirty-two divisions.[70]

In the first week of 1940, the Jewish Community's Welfare Division (Fürsorgeabteilung) provided support for 5,567 individuals at a cost of 276,600 crowns, while by late January this number had already increased to 7,139 people at a cost of 293,000 crowns. In the first week of January, the Community distributed 9,422 lunches at a cost of more than 78,000 crowns, already increasing to 10,004 lunches and 3,665 evening meals by the end of the month.[71] In January 1940, a total of more than 32,000 needy individuals received support to a value of almost 1.5 million crowns from the Prague Jewish Community. The Clothing Service provided clothing, shoes and furniture to a value of 470,000 crowns.[72] Expenditure on welfare thus made up almost half of the Jewish Community's monthly outgoings of around five million crowns, while it spent one million supporting emigrants. Of the almost 4.9 million crowns total income for January, nearly 2.8 million came from a Protectorate-wide fundraising collection entitled 'Sacrifice – Construct – Live'.[73]

In the month of March, a total of 32,148 individuals received support to a value of more than 1.1 million crowns.[74] In the final week of that month, the Welfare Department alone provided for 6,999 individuals at a cost of more than 272,400 crowns, while the Soup Kitchen distributed 9,621 lunches and 4,592 evening meals to a value of more than 35,000 crowns (see Table A.3 in the appendix). The Child Welfare Service (Kinderfürsorge) distributed more than four hundred food parcels, underlining the privation suffered by many Jewish families in the capital with no income.[75] The number of Jews registered by the Jewish Community as receiving welfare support grew from 5,277 in January to 7,070 in late March, while the Social Department spent the same monthly total of around 1.3 million crowns despite catering to a growing number of needy individuals.[76]

In the first quarter of 1940, the Jewish Community had a total budget of 21.6 million crowns, generated by the following sources: grants from the Joint, the 'Sacrifice – Construct – Live' fundraising collection and religious taxes. The collection alone brought in 7.7 million crowns, despite advancing 'Aryanization' and the fact that most Jewish businesses were under commissarial administration. Its expenditure in this quarter, however, was twenty-five million crowns, chiefly on emigration and welfare. The Jewish Community now had thirty-five properties at its disposal, ten of its own, seven belonging to foundations and eighteen buildings taken over from disbanded associations.[77]

Since March 1939, 21,724 Jews had left the Protectorate, 1,982 had died and just 137 had been born. The Jewish population thus fell from 103,389 to 79,820 by 31 March 1940. The mortality rate outstripped the birth rate by a factor of ten, highlighting the fragile social situation and extreme ageing of the Czech Jewish population as a result of intensifying persecution.[78]

Meagre but steady emigration, particularly of young people, caused huge problems, as ever more elderly people and individuals in need of care remained in Prague with no relatives to turn to. Over the previous months, the Jewish Community had already expanded its support services. In early March 1940, it asked the Central Office for permission to establish a special home for the one hundred most urgent cases, at a cost of seventy thousand crowns, a sum the Community duly requested.[79] Towards the end of the same month, the Jewish Community operated ten juvenile homes with 395 residents and five old people's homes housing 231 individuals, all of which came under the remit of the Community's so-called institutional support services (geschlossene Fürsorge). In total, the Jewish Community provided for 625 individuals in sixteen institutions. The Jewish 'Home for the Feeble-Minded' (Schwachsinnigenheim) in Hloubětín (Tiefenbach) cared for forty-one individuals, with sixty-two in the 'Provisional Infirmary' (provisorisches Siechenhaus).[80] However, in late March 1940, there were 416 outstanding applications for a place in an old people's home, so the Jewish Community planned to expand the building in Prague XI to house eighty-four individuals, open another home for forty residents in Prague II, Leihamtsgasse 3, and convert the children's home in Libeň (Lieben) into a home for fifteen old people.[81]

The housing market was also a source of rapidly growing problems as an increasing number of 'Aryan' landlords were no longer willing to admit Jews, so individuals' attempts to find a home were frequently unsuccessful. Many Jews thus sought refuge at the Jewish Community's Housing Office (Wohnungsamt).[82] In March, its staff worked flat out to draw up a register of 'all Jewish homeowners in greater Prague'.[83] In early April, in its weekly report, the Jewish Community warned Eichmann's Central Office that the situation on the Prague housing market for Jews looking to rent would soon assume 'disastrous proportions', as ever more Jews faced the termination of their rental contracts.[84] Two weeks later, the Prague City Government cancelled the contracts of all Jewish tenants in city-owned housing, affecting more than fifty families in small flats, most of them living in a state of poverty.[85] In early May, the Housing Office provided these families with advice on finding accommodation and lodged protests against the notices to quit with the Prague city authorities and the municipal Social Institute.[86]

In response to the decrees of February and March 1940, the Prague Jewish Community established an Economic Advisory Centre (Wirtschaftsberatungsstelle).[87] Its officials provided information on the forced deposit and sale of precious metals, the 'liquidation' of leather, shoe, textile and retail businesses and the topic of blocked accounts.[88] On 24 April 1940, the government decree of 4 July 1939 appeared in the Compendium of Laws and Decrees of the Protectorate (Sammlung der Gesetze und Verordnungen des Protektorates), which introduced new regulations on the status of Jewish doctors, advocates, technicians, engineers and other members of the free professions. This, the Jewish Community feared, would force all Jewish doctors and lawyers to abandon their practices, leaving hundreds of families with no income.[89] In late April, the Community contacted the Czech Ministry of Justice directly to protest against the treatment of Jewish legal professionals.[90] Meanwhile, the Reich protector evidently excluded Jews from peddling and itinerant trade with effect from 30 April.[91] In the month of April alone, the Community's Legal Department (Rechtsabteilung) lodged 112 protests and composed forty-five petitions or appeals.[92]

In the first week of April 1940, the number of individuals receiving non-institutional welfare (offene Fürsorge) from the Jewish Community had already climbed to 7,204, costing the Social Department 293,000 crowns. For example, in addition to providing the destitute with clothing, the Community distributed 412 food parcels to children. In the same week, the Community's institutional support services catered to 651 individuals living in seventeen institutions.[93] By early May, there were 733 needy individuals living in the expanded total of eighteen institutions, while the Community provided 431 children with food parcels and 613 individuals received emigration support.[94] By early June, 7,353 Jews were benefiting from various forms of non-institutional support (see Table A.3 in the appendix). A total of 699 people in need and ninety-eight old people were now living in eighteen homes.[95]

In June 1940, the Prague Jewish Community spent just over four million crowns, of which 1.4 million paid for welfare.[96] In late June, impoverished Jews in Prague received more than 11,945 lunches and 7,688 evening meals. To cut costs, the Community had placed many of those in need in homes. More than five hundred children and young people lived in eleven children's homes, while 253 elderly individuals were accommodated in five old people's homes. At the instruction of the Central Office, from now on the elderly and those in need of care from throughout Bohemia were to be concentrated in Prague. Almost five thousand people were candidates for accommodation within the framework of the Community's services for the elderly, more than three thousand of them in Bohemia outside Prague. Five hundred were in desperate need of accommodation in one of the Community's institutions.[97] In addition, illnesses proliferated due to poverty and shortages of basic necessities. The number of those suffering from tuberculosis was ten times the central European average.[98]

Attempts to Emigrate

In early January 1940, the Jewish Community of Prague transferred around thirty individuals daily to the Central Office for Jewish Emigration to arrange for their emigration. Almost five hundred received advice from the Jewish Community in the first week of January, and 637 in the third week.[99] During this month, a total of 950 individuals managed to leave the Protectorate, of whom 527 were men, 353 women and 70 children. Officially, 12 moved to Palestine, the same number to Bolivia, 187 to Ecuador, 245 to Shanghai or China, 249 to Peru and just 59 to the United States. A dozen went to Hungary and a similar number to Yugoslavia, while the rest were divided between more than thirty countries. Seventy-five went to Slovakia.[100] In the latter case, these were chiefly so-called 'Rückwanderer' or returnees, in other words Slovakian Jews.[101] In February, with the help of the Prague Community, which was now supporting Jews from the provinces as well, 853 individuals emigrated, more than half of them to China and Shanghai, while the figure for March was 910.[102]

In the first quarter of 1940, the Jewish Community and Palestine Office faced an increased workload not just because anti-Jewish measures had intensified the pressure to emigrate, but also because of the growing number of enquiries from the provinces. In total, 67,394 individuals received advice on emigration in person, while Jewish officials dealt with almost twenty thousand cases by letter.[103]

The Jewish Community advised more than 670 individuals a week in mid February, with 137 leaving the city of Prague, more than half of them for Shanghai or Ecuador, as in the preceding weeks.[104] Increasingly, Prague Community staff helped advise and process entire groups from other locations. For example, in early March two groups of emigrants from Olomouc and one from Uherský Brod made the trip to Prague, submitting their emigration applications to the Central Office, while groups from smaller towns had already informed the Community that they would travel to the capital in the near future. Sixty-four of the 122 individuals who emigrated in the first week of March went to Shanghai, while twenty-one sought refuge in Slovakia.[105] Often, child emigrants in particular rapidly grew apart from their parents or failed to contact them for weeks, including the son of Lotte Meissner from Třešť (Triesch), who lived in Denmark.[106]

The Prague Jewish Community maintained constant contact with its Vienna counterpart and the Reich Association in Berlin to resolve general emigration issues but also to advance specific projects.[107] Of one hundred candidates for the Santo Domingo resettlement project, the Prague Community approved ninety-six applicants, of whom, in addition to nineteen from Austria and thirty-six from the Old Reich, twenty individuals from the Protectorate were selected for the first transport.[108] If it considered them essential to expediting emigration, the Central Office gave approval for Prague Community officials to travel for meetings with the Berlin and Vienna Communities.[109]

Providing support for destitute Jews – paying for costly passage aboard ships, for example – proved a particular challenge. Even with the help of the Joint, the Community was able to respond positively to only just over half of the three hundred requests for help in the first quarter of 1940, due to the exorbitant cost of the requisite foreign currency. In order to open up new options for emigration, the Prague Emigration Advisory Service (Auswanderungsberatung) negotiated with the United States – among other things – to obtain student visas, with Shanghai to arrange employment contracts, with Santo Domingo in relation to settlement projects, and with sixteen consulates. The Palestine Office organized so-called 'special group transports' (Sondergruppentransporte) to Palestine, selecting 650 Jews out of a large number of applicants.[110]

In order to expedite emigration, Community representatives discussed retraining Jews who had lost their jobs in the free professions as a result of persecutory measures. Together with the Jewish Employment Office, the HeHalutz sounded out the potential to communicate with the Real Estate Office (Bodenamt) in Prague and big landowners concerning the leasing of manors for educational purposes.[111] Towards the end of January, the Jewish Community organized training and retraining courses attended by a total of 472 individuals in fields such as car mechanics, electrical wiring, precision engineering, optics, locksmithing, clockmaking, shoemaking, *Lackiererei* (metal lacquering, mostly for vehicles), joinery, English, nursery school teaching, infant care, cooking, tailoring, ladies' hairdressing, beauty treatment, manicure, nursing, psychotechnics (Psychotechnik) and pedicure.[112] In mid February, the Community was providing a total of twenty-nine courses, run by fifty-nine trainers and now with more than 569 participants. New classes taught fountain pen repair and jointless flooring. Sixteen additional new courses were in the pipeline.[113] By March, the Community already ran thirty courses featuring fifty-four working teams and with 779 participants.[114]

Since the foundation of the Protectorate, the Jewish Community had 'retrained' 6,233 Jews: 2,220 in agriculture, 52 as harvest hands and 1,473 as craftsmen.[115] Despite problems finding sites for agricultural training, the HeHalutz managed to increase the number of those employed in agriculture, above all younger Jews, from 138 in January 1940 to 700, in almost eighty locations, by the end of June. This occurred partly through cooperation with labour offices and chief county commissioners, in the vast majority of cases in the form of employment measures. Eventually, Eichmann's Central Office aired the prospect of establishing a training estate to facilitate an education in farming as preparation for emigration.[116] In June, 1,078 retrainees, including 160 in agriculture and livestock breeding, 175 in metalworking and electrical engineering, and 176 in healthcare, were already attending forty-three courses run by the Jewish Community. The Community had received more than five hundred applications for subsequent courses.[117] In the first half of 1940, therefore, many new – mostly very small – groups were established for training or retraining purposes, though the prospects of emigration had diminished dramatically since the beginning of the war.

In the *Jüdisches Nachrichtenblatt* the Jewish Community regularly informed its readers about retraining and language courses and promoted new emigration options,[118] as for example in early February 1940, when it provided information on the settlement project in Santo Domingo.[119] In a variety of essays in the newspaper, the Legal Department provided details of all anti-Jewish decrees. The publication had 3,087 subscribers in January and more than 6,200 in late March, with twelve thousand copies being published. By the end of June, the number of subscribers had grown to 8,123.[120]

In the month of April, 1,024 Jews emigrated from the Protectorate, 588 to Shanghai and China, 214 to Peru, 71 to Slovakia, 26 to Santo Domingo and 18 to the United States. Of these, 580 were men, 401 women and 43 children.[121] When Bolivia blocked entry in May, visas valid until July that had already been issued became obsolete, as the sea route via Genoa had been cut off and the journey via Yokohama took more than eight weeks. Meanwhile, the Prague Jewish Community attempted to open up a land route via the Soviet Union to facilitate emigration to Shanghai.[122]

In May, 1,075 individuals left Bohemia and Moravia, 914 of them headed for Shanghai, 22 for the United States, 43 for Peru and 39 for Slovakia,[123] while in June the figure was 1,087, 933 of whom were bound for Shanghai. For the latter month, the emigrants comprised 536 men, 411 women and 140 children, so the under-representation of females had been mitigated to a degree over the course of the previous six months.[124]

In early June, when Italy entered the war, the sea route via the Italian ports ceased to be viable.[125] Together with the Reich Association in Berlin, the Prague Jewish Community now tried to open up the land route to East Asia in order to facilitate travel to South America. The Community invested more and more effort in organizing the so-called special group transports, dealing with temporary obstacles by placing candidates for these journeys in retraining or work schemes.[126] The Central Office now refused to accept more applications for emigration from stateless Jews, who had previously made up 15 per cent of applicants in the Protectorate.[127]

The 'Aryanization Race'

The process of 'Aryanization' pushed by the Germans received additional impetus from the decrees of February and March. The appointment of German administrators in Jewish businesses, for example, increased the share of Germans in the various economic sectors. Meanwhile, the Jewish competition had ceased to exist, opening up new market opportunities.[128] Though Czechs seeking to become trustees were usually disappointed, German firms and banks as well as nonspecialists competed to obtain profitable properties.[129]

In the *Meldungen aus dem Reich*, the SD claimed that – in light of Czech business circles' interest in 'Aryanization' – Jews in Prague preferred German buyers, believing it would be easier to get their property back in the event of a German withdrawal. This is indirect evidence that at this time Jews and others in the Protectorate were by no means convinced that German hegemony would persist over the long term.[130]

At the same time, the Reich protector complained to the Czech Interior Ministry that various authorities and 'organs of the territorial self-administration associations (Selbstverwaltungsverbände) have approached Jewish Communities in an attempt to get them to surrender real estate; in most cases, an extremely meagre sum of money or nothing at all was offered or provided in exchange'. Yet Jewish assets, the Reich protector continued, were supposed to finance emigration; all organizations, associations and foundations, he emphasized, were subject to oversight by the Central Office, which decided whether the transfer of assets seemed desirable in the 'interest of the general public'.[131] Towns such as Čáslav (Caslau), Nový Bydžov (Neubidschow), Domažlice (Taus), Strakonice (Strakonitz) and České Budějovice had in fact put pressure on Jewish Communities in an attempt to obtain their properties, such as synagogues and other community buildings, at low cost.[132] Later, the City of Prague also bought apartment buildings and mansions from Jews at 15 per cent below their estimated value.[133]

By this point in time, the occupying power had de facto won the battle to control 'Aryanization'. At the end of June 1940, in the district of the chief county commissioner in Prague, 1,109 Germans and just ninety-six Czechs decided the fate of Jewish businesses as trustees.[134]

On 1 May 1940, the chief county commissioner in Moravian Ostrava lamented the fact that 'Aryanization' had slackened off.

> The reasons are, first, the fall in Jewish emigration as a result of the war and, second, the return of Jews from the Nisko retraining camp to their hometowns as decreed by the General Government's senior SS and police chief. The Jews are now clinging tightly to their enterprises and it has become virtually impossible to persuade them to sell voluntarily. The only solution is the appointment of sale trustees, though as a consequence of the laborious procedures involved this too is an ineffective means of accelerating Aryanization.[135]

Here the chief county commissioner was referring to the partial return of the first Jews deported to Poland. On 29 April 1940, the chief of police in Moravian Ostrava had informed the chief county commissioner that:

> On 13 April a transport carrying 516 Jews arrived at the main railway station in Moravian Ostrava from Nisko, where they had been deported for retraining in November 1939. 301 Jews remained in Ostrava, 18 were taken to Český Těšín and 197 travelled on to Vienna. The return of these Jews inspired all kinds of rumours and the underground propagandists exploited it to the hilt. Of the 301 Jewish returnees in Ostrava, only 174 are resident here and there is nothing I can do to stop them from staying. Of the other Jews, 6 were immediately arrested as they were being sought by various courts. 49 Jews are foreigners and they were denied permission to remain here. In response to these measures, 34 Jews left Ostrava voluntarily.[136]

Unemployment and Work Details (Gruppeneinsatz)

An increasing number of Jewish Czechs found themselves with no prospect of employment or income as a result of bans on practising their professions and conducting trade, along with dismissal from 'Aryanized' and other establishments, both public and private. In June 1940, the Prague Jewish Community, which had compiled statistics on men between the ages of eighteen and fifty, stated that 'Jews have been eliminated from the general labour force to an extraordinary degree within a comparatively short period of time'.[137] While 36.5 per cent of Jews between eighteen and thirty-four years of age were unemployed and 53 per cent of those between twenty-five and thirty-four, the figure was 59 per cent for the thirty-five to forty-four age group and no less than 69 per cent for those between forty-five and fifty.[138]

In September 1939, the Prague Jewish Community had to spend 533,000 crowns on welfare services, climbing to almost 2.2 million in June 1940, though this was far from sufficient.[139] The Jewish Community's Employment Office, as the Community's first six-monthly report stated, chiefly provided assistance to 'individuals in receipt of support from the Jewish Community's Social Institute', in other words those receiving welfare, in order to 'relieve the strain on the Community's coffers'.[140]

In light of the poverty afflicting the Jewish population, the Prague Community actively sought solutions to the employment crisis. Though 1,434 individuals had now registered as in search of work, in the first week of January 1940 the Community found gainful employment for just twelve of them, nine of whom were women, and twenty-two in the second week of January, all of them women this time – but only as housemaids in Jewish families. The Jewish Employment Office thus sent two voluntary assistants to the provinces, among other places to Německý Brod, Kolín (Kolin) and Kutná Hora (Kuttenberg), to look for jobs for the unemployed, mainly in agriculture. News reached the Community from the districts of Rakonitz (Rakovník) and Beroun (Beraun) that 1,400 forestry workers were needed as a result of severe forest damage caused by recent snowfalls. The Jewish Community persuaded the Free Forestry Association (Freie Forstvereinigung) to alert its members, in a circular, to the Jewish labourers available for clearing work, while also corresponding initially with individual labour offices, for example in Tábor (Tabor), which provided the addresses of farmers in need of labourers. In the second week of January, the Community Employment Office then targeted all labour offices in the Protectorate. Twenty-one sent back the addresses of interested farmers, 180 of whom the Jewish Employment Office then contacted. Great hopes were attached to these enquiries as a reference confirming an individual's employment in agriculture, even on a short-term basis, greatly improved the prospects of emigration: the governments of a number of South American countries would only admit individuals with work experience of this kind.[141] In the third week of January, Jewish Community representatives met with the Free Forestry Association in Prague, while also contacting another 150 farmers. The first batch of letters resulted in ten job offers. A number of these potential positions came to nothing, however, because applicants had to bring with them sturdy shoes and work clothes that even the Jewish Community was unable to acquire due to restrictions on Jews.[142]

By mid February, 1,715 Jews had registered with the Jewish Community of Prague as unemployed. Following intensive negotiations with labour offices and firms, the Jewish Employment Office hoped to provide jobs for large groups in agriculture and motorway and railway construction – areas in which firm undertakings had already been given – from March, when the frost period was over. Individual farmers had already offered seventy-nine positions.[143]

Large landowners were willing to employ Jews should Slovakian seasonal workers prove unable to enter the Protectorate. In early March, meanwhile, the Prague Social Institute employed a group of ten men to work in the municipal woods. By this point in time, 1,823 unemployed individuals had registered at the Jewish Employment Office, which found work for more than thirty people a week. More than half were now men, who were placed in positions in casual employment or agriculture, while women found employment exclusively in Jewish households.[144]

Only when the weather had changed did the first large landowners request a number of fairly small work details, such as the Koryčany (Koritschan, Moravia) City Council as well as construction firms, such as Ing. Šamanek, for railway construction in Tišnov (Tischnowitz). A branch of the Brno Labour Office took on the task of assembling a 'group of 5–10 navvies' for the latter work. In the second half of March, twenty labourers were employed first to renovate the Hagibor sports ground for the Prague Jewish Community, before splitting into two groups, one to work in the Jewish Cemetery and the other in the garden of the Community's old people's home. The Community also budgeted for additional groups to restore the flood-damaged Liebenauer Cemetery and for gardening work at the 'Home for the Feeble-Minded' in Hloubětín.[145] Towards the end of March, twenty-six Jews worked as seasonal staff on the large estate in Koryčany, thirteen of them women. While 1,981 unemployed persons were now registered at the Jewish Employment Office, it managed to find work for a weekly maximum of twenty-four individuals.[146]

On 19 March 1940, a government decree had reformed the system of unemployment assistance (Arbeitslosenhilfe), for which the labour offices were now responsible rather than the Czech trades unions as previously.[147] The labour offices, which were subordinate to the Czech Minister for Social and Health Administration, began to recruit Jews, vast numbers of whom were registering as unemployed, for forced labour units. Nonetheless, in contrast to Germany, Austria and Poland, in the Protectorate neither the SS nor the Labour Administration (Arbeitsverwaltung) formally introduced compulsory labour for unemployed Jews or all Jews.[148]

In early April 1940, the firm Ing. Bramberger und Ing. Frič took on sixteen Jews to work in motorway construction in Moravia, with the local branch of the Jewish Employment Office tasked with assembling the work team upon approval from the Brno Labour Office. By now, more than 2,041 jobless Jews had registered with the Jewish Employment Office in Prague, but in the first week of April it managed to find work for just eighteen individuals, ten of them women employed in Jewish households.[149] Thirty candidates for emigration to Santo Domingo gained work in forestry in Dobříš (Doberschisch), supposedly in preparation for the settlement project.[150] By the end of April, 2,304 individuals looking for work had registered at the Jewish Employment Office.[151]

During this period, the Jewish Community sent occupational questionnaires to men in Prague between the ages of eighteen and fifty.[152] The Jewish Employment Office now managed to find work for small contingents of men in beet harvesting on various farms, and in dam construction in Štěchovice (Stechowitz), while in Brno no fewer than forty-four men were despatched to Tišnov to work in railway construction.[153] In late May, the Brno Jewish Community reported that sixty-two men had already been employed in Tišnov. Twenty-four Jews gained work in the regulation of the Vltava in České Budějovice, as arranged by the local Jewish Community, while twenty-two men were employed in roadbuilding in Hulice (Hulitz).[154] The Jewish Community itself employed and paid twenty men who were put to work on earthworks and in the old Jewish cemetery.[155] In June, the Community found beet work for twenty Jews at the Schimitz estate near Kobylisy (Kobilis) in Prague and for ten in beet and poppy work on the Lothka estate near Prague, as well as procuring work for groups of men in roadbuilding and a brickyard, the latter in Třebichovice (Trebichowitz). On 15 June, 201 men were engaged in work details assembled by the Jewish Community, 2,835 people had registered as unemployed, while so far a total of 840 had been placed in work.[156]

Germanization and Administration

The Protectorate received no clear signal from Berlin as to how Germanization policy ought to proceed.[157] On 1 March 1940, 189,000

Germans lived in the Protectorate, a figure that had already risen to 245,000 by 1 September, including 40,000 Sudeten German incomers and 20,000 former Czechs of German origin, who had taken the opportunity to acquire German citizenship. Preferential treatment and massive Germanity-based propaganda ultimately prompted more Protectorate citizens to embrace their German origins. Nonetheless, Germans made up only around 3.3 per cent of the 7,380,000 inhabitants of the Protectorate. They represented 1.8 per cent of the population of Bohemia and 6.2 per cent in Moravia. In the Brno county commissioner's district, the figure was no less than 10 per cent, and 6.8 per cent in the District of Budějovice. The thirty-two thousand Germans in Prague, meanwhile, represented just 2.6 per cent of the city's inhabitants and in Zlín and Tábor Germans made up less than 1 per cent of the population. As Brno Chief County Commissioner Hofmann noted with resignation, moreover, a disproportionate share of the German population consisted of old people.[158]

Initially, the German authorities sought to establish enclosed areas of settlement in Moravia in order to create a so-called 'Volkstum bridge' between Silesia and Austria, while later they favoured dispersed settlements, around Jihlava for example. In their areas, the chief county commissioners pursued their own plans in competition with other agencies. Positive or negative effects on German Volkstum policy also played a role in the planning of army bases and industrial sites. Because the settlement of Germans from abroad seemed unrealizable during the war, meanwhile, the relevant officials in Berlin and Prague discussed the possibility of 'racially' assimilating Czechs as a route towards Germanization rather than deporting them.[159]

Because strengthening the economy was viewed as fundamental to bolstering the German Volkstum, the Office of the Reich Protector gave 'Aryanized' businesses to German Protectorate citizens on a preferential basis. The goal of full employment and the granting of public contracts to Germans were further manifestations of this policy. In an attempt to solve the housing problem, the authorities made use of Jewish or city-run accommodation, with only Germans being allowed to buy Jewish-owned houses.[160]

A concerted effort was made to expand the German authorities. Many towns with a majority German population in the Jihlava area gained new heads, often ethnic Germans, who had been appointed by the Wehrmacht or other institutions following the invasion. In places with a large German population but a Czech majority, mayors had been dismissed and replaced by German commissarial mayors. However, the chief county commissioners took the time to assess the new mayors' reliability before approaching the Czech authorities, via the Reich protector, in order to dissolve the local councils and appoint the commissarial mayors government commissars.[161] According to the still-valid Czech municipal code, the Czech Ministry of the Interior alone could vest the government commissars with powers.[162]

While the government commissars in Olomouc, Moravian Ostrava, Budějovice, Brno and Jihlava were appointed without further ado, resistance from the Czech ministry scuppered the process in other locations within the Jihlava language island. In autumn 1939, Karl Fiehler, Nazi Party Reich Leader (NSDAP-Reichsleiter) with responsibility for local government policy, reported this disapprovingly to the Deputy Führer, who had already been informed about it by the Lower Danube Gauleitung (Nazi Party organization at Gau level).[163] Fiehler, also president of the German Council of Municipalities (Deutscher Gemeindetag), sought to engage this body in order to put pressure on the Reich Interior Ministry to solve the problem, but the Council was unwilling to get involved because towns in the Protectorate were not among its members.[164] The Reich Interior Ministry confirmed the long-drawn-out nature of the process but stated that this was not due to Czech obstructionism. In fact, the ministry went on, the chief county commissioners had been waiting for the situation to stabilize and the vetting of the German candidates had then taken a long time. This was now complete in ten out of fifteen cases.[165] In early 1940, some commissarial mayors were yet to be appointed as government commissars.[166]

Ninety-five cities and towns were under German leadership in late December 1939 and 125 a year later. German mayors now headed all localities with more than twenty-five thousand inhabitants, except Prague and Pilsen; there, however, the deputy mayors were German.[167] The mayors and district chiefs, who later grew in number, particularly from 1940 onwards under Heydrich, came mostly from the Sudetenland.[168]

Since 12 December 1939, principles had held sway in Bohemia that abolished the democratic form of the elected municipal authority.[169] Around the same time, Deputy Führer Rudolf Heß created a 'Party Liaison Office' (Parteiverbindungstelle) under Gauleiter Dr Hugo Jury, in an attempt to better coordinate the 'cooperation of all the Party's offices, their divisions and associated organizations' within the Office of the Reich Protector.[170] Previously, the Reich protector had approved the attendance of party functionaries responsible for local government policy at the chief county commissioners' coordination meetings in order to enhance the commissioners' work with the German municipalities.[171] The Nazi Party, meanwhile, promoted a plan to establish an

'Association of German Municipalities in the Protectorate'. This would be headquartered in Brno and give advice to local authorities under German leadership on municipal issues, as the German Council of Municipalities had been doing since 1933. Despite support, in late 1939, from a number of chief county commissioners and the involvement, in autumn 1940, of the Deputy Führer himself, this plan came to grief due to resistance from the Reich protector.[172] He had permitted the chief county commissioners to hold working conferences but rejected the idea of a bespoke association in order to retain Prague's control.[173]

In 1941, German councillors were still arguing against the introduction of the German Municipal Code (Gemeindeordnung) of 1935 in the Protectorate, which was intended to cement the Nazi Party's influence on the municipal administrations. A small number of 'German municipalities', they underlined, were up against a majority of Czech municipalities, where the Nazi Party could play no role, and it was wrong to endow the Czech mayors with authority in accordance with the Führer principle. The district authorities, they went on, were still 'democratic' bodies made up of representatives of the old political parties, while most of the district chiefs were Czech. The dualism characteristic of the municipalities, they asserted, must be eliminated, but it was not feasible simply to appoint Germans everywhere as Czech communities would reject them 'out of hand'. While it was out of the question, they went on, for Czechs to serve as senior municipal functionaries, the Germans were dependent on the Czechs' cooperation when it came to municipal administration – for linguistic reasons, apart from anything else.[174]

In late 1939, the Reich protector decreed that so-called German municipalities were to be provided with electricity, raw materials and loans in preference to 'Czech municipalities', while expenditure would be focused to a greater degree than hitherto on strengthening Germanity, through the building of schools, theatres, roads and libraries. The chief county commissioners must make up for lost ground by focusing their efforts on 'municipal oversight'.[175] In spring 1940, Chief County Commissioner Molsen in Olomouc reported on his efforts to improve 'the situation of German trade and commerce' through the preferential provision of work units, raw materials and resources from liquidated Jewish firms as well as orders from Jewish companies held in trust and, finally, by obstructing the Czech competition. Within the process of 'Aryanization' in Olomouc, he stated, the authorities were doing their best to increase the participation of ethnic Germans, who had taken over twelve out of thirteen companies.[176]

The authorities also upped the number of Germans in the police, railways, postal service and the new authorities for labour deployment and economic oversight.[177] Prague University appointed Reich German academics as a matter of priority, such as Friedrich Klausing in 1940, who applied for the Chair in Civil, Economic and Labour Law after volunteering to serve in the war against France. Klausing, a member of the Militant League for German Culture (Kampfbund für deutsche Kultur) since 1930, had played a significant role in the purge of Jews from Frankfurt University in 1933.[178]

Since April 1939, SS Oberführer Curt von Gottberg, former head of the Settlement Office (Siedlungsamt) within the SS Race and Settlement Office (Rasse- und Siedlungsamt), had served as head of the Land Office (Bodenamt) of the City of Prague. At this early stage, from a German perspective his actions were too radically anti-Czech; he announced, for example, that in ten years' time there would be no land left in Czech hands. He was thus replaced by Theodor Groß. Later, the somewhat more moderate Groß managed to thwart attempts to dispossess the Czech nobility and transfer Jewish property to the Reich Association for National Welfare and Aid for Settlers (Reichsverein für Volkspflege und Siedlerhilfe e. V.), which had been established by the SS.[179]

In April 1940, the Reich protector decreed that all marriages between Germans and Czechs must be approved by the chief county commissioner.[180] Germanization, however, was not progressing as fast as the German authorities wanted. By this stage, the mood in the Protectorate had changed. The kind of demonstrations that had still been going on in the autumn of 1939 had become few and far between, particularly since the German victories in Western Europe in the spring of 1940.[181] While resentment towards the occupation continued to manifest itself on the individual level, some Czech fascists, such as the members of the organization known as the 'Green Czech Swastika', produced pro-German propaganda and called for the Czech lands to be fully incorporated into the Reich. In the summer, National Partnership established a district group to promote cooperation with the Germans in Moravian Ostrava.[182]

By the end of August 1940, therefore, Reich Protector Neurath and his deputy Frank had sent memoranda to Hitler. Both regarded the ultimate goal as total incorporation of the Bohemian-Moravian lands into the Reich and their settlement with Germans, though now, rather than deporting the Czechs in their entirety, they contemplated their partial assimilation.[183] In parallel and in the same vein, Undersecretary of State Curt von Burgsdorff called for the Nuremberg laws to be extended to Protectorate citizens, because hitherto, if taken literally, they could be applied solely to their German counterparts. As von Burgsdorff saw it, if the authorities wished to avoid making a strict dis-

Figure 5.1. Park entrance in Prague. The sign reads 'No Admission for Jews' in German, but 'Admission for Jews' in Czech, the word 'No' having been removed, 1940/1941. © USHMM Washington, Photo Archive, no. 07635.

tinction between Czechs and Germans in future, Protectorate citizens' offspring must be racially flawless.[184] Though the German authorities had drawn up draft plans to ban marriage between Jews and non-Jewish Protectorate citizens, Hitler decided to leave this up to the Czech government.[185]

In September 1940, Hitler then opted for an interim solution with respect to the future of the Protectorate. In his view, neither a special constitutional status nor 'total resettlement' of the Czechs was possible, the latter because it would be impossible to fill the resulting vacuum with Germans. It might be feasible to Germanize a large proportion of the Czech population, if the 'racially useless Czechs and those hostile to the

Reich were [simultaneously] discarded or subject to special treatment [Sonderbehandlung]'. This, however, would take one hundred years.[186]

Jewish Resistance and Protest

Every time a Jew violated German or Czech ordinances, he or she did so consciously and at great personal risk: the Jewish community was well informed about anti-Jewish measures. Through regular essays in the *Jüdisches Nachrichtenblatt*, the Prague Jewish Community's Legal Department enlightened readers about all relevant legislation.[187]

Like all Jews, Zdenka Fantlová's family, who lived in Rokycany (Rokitzan) near Pilsen, had to surrender their radio at the beginning of the war. The authorities imposed a blanket ban on listening to so-called enemy broadcasters, cutting Jews off almost entirely from up-to-date news. On several occasions, Zdenka's father thus took up a non-Jewish neighbour's invitation to listen to Czech-language broadcasts from the BBC in London.[188] Following a denunciation, the Gestapo arrested him, subjecting him to 'protective custody' (Schutzhaft) in the Buchenwald concentration camp. A court later sentenced him to one year in prison.[189]

Many Jews were put on trial or taken into protective custody in concentration camps for committing violations or expressing public criticism. In mid February 1940, the authorities decided that 'if there was no criminal case against them', Jews in protective custody could be made to emigrate. This prompted the Jewish Community to factor three hundred to four hundred detainees into its emigration planning.[190] Within two weeks, its officials prepared applications from 106 Jewish concentration camp detainees in such a way as to allow the Central Office to decide on their emigration.[191] Community staff, well aware of the dreadful conditions in the camps, thus proceeded with haste. In the third week of July 1940 alone, meanwhile, the Prague Community received three urns directly from crematoria, as two women had died in the Ravensbrück concentration camp, while a man had passed away in Buchenwald near Weimar.[192]

The staff of the provincial Jewish Communities also found ways to resist. Some of them, for instance, demonstratively composed their correspondence in Czech, despite repeated warnings from the Prague Community to write in German for the sake of the supervisory authority.[193]

The number of violations evidently burgeoned, prompting the antisemitic press to publish public denunciations of Jews who had defied the ban on visiting public parks, restaurants, libraries and dance halls.

The Czech Interior Ministry collated such articles, passing them on to the relevant local authorities so they could prosecute the individuals involved.[194] In December 1939 and January 1940, the *Vlajka* newspaper reported that Rudolf Beck and his son regularly frequented an inn from which Jews were barred in Prague-Smíchov. The police, spurred to action by the Provincial Office (Provinzialamt), ascertained that Beck had patronized the establishment for thirty years: prior to the occupation he had headed a local football club that used to gather in a room at the inn. Beck received a fine of one thousand crowns, while his son had to pay two hundred.[195]

Following the imposition of the evening curfew on Jews, the Prague Gestapo introduced sanctions on those who violated it, as the Jewish Community was informed in February 1940.[196] Jews ignored the curfew for a wide variety of reasons. Max Mannheimer, who was working in roadbuilding near the spa town of Luhačovice (Luhatschowitz), evaded the curfew as an act of resistance to the authorities' persecutory measures. He wrote in his diary:

> During the week my quarters are a wooden hut behind the toolshed. From there, despite the 8 o'clock curfew and the ban on entering parks, I go to the spa gardens. I count the signs declaring 'No Admittance for Jews'. There are six of them. Later, around eleven, I wrench all the signs out the ground, throwing some into the bushes, others into a stream. All my courage was in vain. The next evening all the signs were back. I couldn't pluck up the courage a second time. I'm no hero.[197]

In April 1940, the *Leitmeritzer Tagblatt* published an entire series of articles intended to highlight the legal penalties for Jews who aired public criticism. On 19 April, under the headline 'The Grumbling Jewess', the newspaper attacked one Marie Pick.[198] In accordance with the Treachery Act (the so-called Heimtückegesetz),[199] the Leitmeritz (Litoměřice) Special Court had sentenced this Protectorate citizen to seven months' imprisonment for making critical remarks. Marie Pick had become incensed when the authorities sought to sell her home in Komotau (Chomutov), which was already under commissarial administration. Tax inspector Karl Zebisch wished to buy the house, valued at 13,580 Reichsmarks; the county commissioner had already approved the transaction. Having apparently been informed of a better offer, however, Pick suddenly demanded a higher price. According to the newspaper, when Zebisch

> drew her attention to the impossibility and illegality of her demand, she heatedly declared that the Jews, and she herself, were being betrayed and

unleashed a slew of invective against the Führer. She had, as she stated, relatives in England and America and would make sure the entire world found out about the betrayal she had suffered. Furthermore, she predicted that Zebisch and all those who betrayed the Jews would face God's judgement.

In court, Pick denied making certain particularly malicious statements attributed to her concerning Hitler and official regulations, but she was 'found guilty due to the entirely credible witness statements and the fact that two married daughters of the defendant have secretly moved away from Prague and are probably overseas'.[200]

In July 1940, the Prague Special Court sentenced Berta Weiß from Klatovy, born in 1881, to six months in jail, again for slandering the Reich. She had obtained a leaflet featuring an 'abusive poem about the German Reich, the establishment of the Protectorate and President Hácha' from a non-Jewish acquaintance, with the goal of having her son Leo make copies on a typewriter. Having done so, he distributed them to non-Jewish Czechs.[201]

According to the Moravian Ostrava chief county commissioner's administrative report of September 1940, members of the German community had lodged complaints asserting that:

> the Jews are conducting themselves in an intrusive manner in public streets and squares. Ever since the Jews' return from the Polish work camp[202] and from Prague they have felt right at home in Moravian Ostrava due to their peculiar conviction that the authorities are unable to handle them. Through all kinds of tricks they manage to evade the restrictions imposed on them through legal ordinances. They frequently fail to comply with the stipulated shopping hours or get round them with the help of Aryan household staff, so harsh measures will be required. As one might expect there are a large number of Czech businessmen, particularly [female] market traders, who continue to help the Jews and send goods to their homes. In such cases the Jews then pay a surcharge to cover the 'delivery fee'. In the month of July alone, [the authorities] had to take punitive action against fifty-eight Jews for failure to comply with the regulations.[203]

The head of the Party Liaison Office complained directly to the Reich protector that in every part of the Protectorate the 'Jews are failing to comply with the shopping hours allocated to them'. Czechs, he went on, were helping them in this. If it were not possible to mark Jews across the board, he argued, ration cards ought to be stamped with the word 'Jew'.[204] In fact, however, the ration cards introduced when the war started had already been marked for several months, either with 'J' and 'Jew' or 'Ž' and 'Žid'.[205]

On 'Settling the Jewish Question'

Two months after the initial announcement, Heydrich confirmed on 24 April 1940 that 'until further notice there will be no evacuation of Jews, regardless of their citizenship, from Reich territory to the General Government'. Concurrently, for the first time he now decreed that 'whenever possible Jews capable of military service or of serving in work units are not permitted to emigrate to other European countries, and under no circumstances to the hostile European states'.[206] This partial cessation of emigration for the majority of the Jewish population signalled the start of a new phase of persecution.

Germany's conquest of parts of Western Europe took its deportation plans to a new level: the focus was no longer solely on Jews from the annexed territories or the Greater German Reich. Furthermore, deportation now took priority over emigration. On 24 June 1940, Heydrich had informed the foreign minister that the 'overall problem of the roughly 3¼ million Jews in the territories under German sovereignty ... [can] no longer be solved through emigration; a final territorial solution would be required'.[207] A day later, the Gestapo informed the Reich Association that when the war ended – as it was expected to do in the autumn – the authorities would 'seek to settle this issue once and for all by making available a colonial reservation for the Jews from Europe'. The candidates for this resettlement programme would be 'Jews from the Old Reich, the Eastern March, the Protectorate, the General Government, in addition those from Denmark, Norway, Holland, Belgium, France, Italy and possibly also ... the Jews in England'. The Reich Association must 'now give careful attention to this problem, so that if called upon it can come forward with provisional plans'.[208]

The same went for the Jewish Communities of Prague and Vienna: on 2 July 1940, at the behest of the Central Office, their head, Dr Franz Weidmann, and his deputy Jakob Edelmann, made a three-day trip to Berlin.[209] On 3 July, at a meeting with Jewish representatives from Berlin, Prague and Vienna, Eichmann explained that after the war the Reich would seek to find a 'comprehensive solution to Europe's Jewish problem', in the form of the resettlement of around four million people. Eichmann ordered them to furnish him with a memorandum listing the factors requiring consideration were the Reich to pursue such a plan.[210]

The expectation of such mass deportations was to lead to more coordination and central control of anti-Jewish policy in the Protectorate.

* * *

Eichmann's Central Office extended its jurisdiction to the entire Protectorate at the beginning of 1940, but this did not mean it took over Jewish policy in its entirety. Instead, the Office merely extended its control over the work of the Jewish Communities and their finances, an expansion that laid the ground for the resumption of the deportations in February, though Heydrich then suspended these for an unspecified period of time. This had implications for anti-Jewish policy in the Protectorate, where the authorities now worked on the assumption that the Jewish population would stay put over the medium term.

In March, therefore, the Prague Jewish Community was given a supervisory function vis-à-vis all the Jewish Communities in the Protectorate, while concurrently being transformed into a compulsory organization, which all 'racial Jews' were now required to join. So rather than the model of the Reich Association, as discussed in Prague since autumn 1939, it was a modified version of the Vienna approach to endowing a Jewish Community with responsibility that the Prague body emulated. It is likely that the extension in the Community's authority dovetailed with its own efforts to centralize the Jewish Communities' affairs. Key Jewish actors had already discussed this subject, though the observations above cast doubt on the idea that these discussions were the reason for the shift of responsibility, as assumed by Otto Dov Kulka with respect to the Protectorate (and Germany).[211]

The Prague Jewish Community was forced to establish a 'Division for Non-Mosaic Jews'. It also began to centralize Jewish welfare, educational and emigration services, which formed the background to the dissolution of Jewish associations. The Central Office, however, administered its finances. The costs of emigration grew because more and more countries in Europe were occupied and thus no longer relevant destinations. Furthermore, Heydrich had prohibited Jews capable of work from emigrating to other European countries. While the majority of Jews were eager to leave the Protectorate as rapidly as possible in light of persecution, destitution and incipient ghettoization, so that week on week the Jewish Community of Prague had to provide thousands of individuals with advice, there were ever fewer opportunities for flight. In the first six months of 1940, Shanghai was the primary target for emigration.

The renewed push to provide Jews with retraining, whether through courses in handicrafts or deployment in agricultural work teams, served not only to prepare them for emigration but also to relieve the strain on Jewish welfare services. Since spring 1940, the Prague Jewish Community had had to assume the burden of state welfare for all Jews, prompting the Jewish Employment Office to negotiate with farmers, landowners, labour offices and private businesses in an attempt to arrange work for groups of unemployed Jews. The breakup of families as a result of emigration, relocation or expulsion from provincial towns and the loss of work and income as a consequence of persecution soon impoverished many Jews in the Protectorate. The number of those receiving money and food from the Jewish Welfare Department grew week on week.

New decrees issued by the Reich protector to eliminate Jews from the economy in early 1940 exacerbated the situation. So too did 'Aryanization', the eviction of Jewish tenants residing in municipal accommodation in Prague and the first steps towards ghettoization in a number of towns, where Jews had to vacate their homes and were herded into a particular street or old factory buildings. But the authorities' pursuit of a more radical form of persecution following the suspension of the deportations also triggered greater resistance among the Jewish population and in the Jewish Communities. For criticizing the persecution or evading bans, many Jews were detained, made to stand trial and punished with custodial sentences, while others were placed in concentration camps.

Notes

1. USHMM Washington, RG 48.005M, reel 4 (Prague State Archive), I 3b-5811 Central Office, no. 2, n.p.: Circular decree Reich protector/BdS II 308/40, 29 January 1940. Contrary to Potthast's assertions, therefore, this occurred earlier than mid February; Potthast, *Das jüdische Zentralmuseum*, 76.
2. USHMM Washington, RG 45.005M, reel 1 (Prague State Archive), Ministry of the Interior, no. 23, n.p.: Copy circular decree Ministry of the Interior to the State Authorities in Prague and Brno, 1 February 1940, 1–2.
3. USHMM Washington, RG 45.005M, reel 1 (Prague State Archive), Ministry of the Interior, Jewish regulations, no. 26, n.p.: Circular decree from the Ministry of the Interior in Prague, 22 February 1940, to State Authorities.
4. Quoted in Aly, *'Final Solution'*, 49.
5. One example is Milotová, 'Zentralstelle', 23.
6. Both Prague-based officials returned after three days; YV Jerusalem, O 7/54, fol. 135: Weekly report Jewish Religious Community of Prague, 2–8 March 1940, 15.
7. YV Jerusalem, O 7/53, fol. 140–41: Weekly report Jewish Religious Community of Prague, 1–7 December 1939, 9–10.
8. On the settlement of Jews in the Dominican Republic, see Hans Ulrich Dillmann and Susanne Heim, *Fluchtpunkt Karibik: Jüdische Emigranten in der Dominikanischen Republik* (Berlin, 2009); Marion A. Kaplan, *Dominican Haven: The Jewish Refugee Settlement in Sosúa, 1940–1945* (New York, 2008). On emigration to Bolivia, see Leo Spitzer, *Hotel Bolivia: The Culture of Memory in a Refuge from Nazism* (New York, 1998); Wolf Gruner, 'Von Wien nach La Paz: Der Lebensweg von Max Schreier', in Stiftung Jüdisches Museum Berlin and Stiftung Haus der Geschichte

der Bundesrepublik (eds), *Heimat und Exil: Emigration der deutschen Juden nach 1933* (Frankfurt a. M., 2006), 161–63.
9. YV Jerusalem, O 7/54, fol. 105–6: Weekly report Jewish Religious Community of Prague, 17–23 February 1940, 15–16.
10. According to *Neuer Tag*, 28 January 1940; see Moskowitz, 'The Jewish Situation', 27; YV Jerusalem, O 7/54, fol. 257: Report by the Jewish Religious Community and the Prague Palestine Office on their activities in the first quarter of 1940, submitted to the Prague Central Office for Jewish Emigration, 35.
11. Decree, 26 January 1940, *Verordnungsblatt des Reichsprotektors Böhmen und Mähren*, 1940/no. 7, 41–43, excerpt in *Europa unterm Hakenkreuz: Österreich und Tschechoslowakei*, doc. no. 62, 139.
12. Report 'The Legal Position of Jews', in Krejčová, Svobodová and Hyndráková, *Židé v Protektorátu*, doc. 15, 251; Osterloh and Wixforth, 'Die "Arisierung" im Protektorat Böhmen und Mähren', 310; YV Jerusalem, O 7/54, fol. 257: Report by the Jewish Religious Community and the Prague Palestine Office on their activities in the first quarter of 1940, 35.
13. *The New York Times*, 11 February 1940, 39; *The Los Angeles Times*, 11 February 1940, 3; *The Washington Post*, 11 February 1940, 12; *The Manchester Guardian*, 12 February 1940, 3; Erdely, *Germany's First European Protectorate*, 144.
14. BA Berlin, R 30/4a, fol. 103: Administrative report chief county commissioner Moravia Ostrava, 2 October 1939 (in fact 2 November), 6 (II general economic issues).
15. Express letter from the Reich protector in Bohemia and Moravia (II/1/Jd 3452/40), by order of Dr Bertsch, Prague, along with the guidelines of 26 January 1940 (strictly confidential) to the chief county commissioners and the Moravia Group, 9 February 1940, in VEJ/3, doc. 269, 658–60. See also Ingo Köhler, 'Werten und Bewerten: Die "kalte" Technik der Arisierung', in Hartmut Berghoff, Jürgen Kocka and Dieter Ziegler (eds), *Wirtschaft im Zeitalter der Extreme: Beiträge zur Unternehmensgeschichte Österreichs und Deutschlands. Im Gedenken an Gerald D. Feldman* (Schriftenreihe zur Zeitschrift für Unternehmensgeschichte, vol. 20) (Munich, 2010), 316–36.
16. Erdely, *Germany's First European Protectorate*, 148–50.
17. YV Jerusalem, O 7/54, fol. 105: Weekly report Jewish Religious Community of Prague, 17–23 February 1940, 15; ibid., fol. 203: Monthly report Jewish Religious Community of Prague, 1–29 February 1940, 9.
18. *Verordnungsblatt des Reichsprotektors Böhmen und Mähren*, 1940/7, 45–47; Utermöhle and Schmerling, *Die Rechtsstellung der Juden im Protektorat Böhmen und Mähren*, 14–16. See also Moskowitz, 'The Jewish Situation', 26–27.
19. Mentioned in YV Jerusalem, O 7/54, fol. 89–90: Weekly report Jewish Religious Community of Prague, 10–16 February 1940, 13–14; see also ibid., M 58/JM 11814, fol. 31: Form for registering Jewish real estate, rights equivalent to real estate and mortgages (March 1940).
20. YV Jerusalem, O 7/54, fol. 259: Report by the Jewish Religious Community and the Prague Palestine Office on their activities in the first quarter of 1940, 37.
21. Wolf Gruner, 'The German Council of Municipalities and the Coordination of Anti-Jewish Local Policies in the Nazi State', *Holocaust and Genocide Studies* 13(2) (1999), 171–99, here 181–88. For a general account of the theft of precious metals in the annexed and occupied territories, see Ralf Banken, *Edelmetallmangel und Großraubwirtschaft: Die Entwicklung des deutschen Edelmetallsektors im 'Dritten Reich' 1933–1945* (Berlin, 2009), 286–364 and 397–475.

22. YV Jerusalem, O 7/54, fol. 167: Weekly report Jewish Religious Community of Prague, 16–22 March 1940, 16. See also *The New York Times*, 19 March 1940, 10.
23. YV Jerusalem, O 7/54, fol. 257: Report by the Jewish Religious Community and the Prague Palestine Office on their activities in the first quarter of 1940, 35. See Drahomír Jančík and Eduard Kubů, 'Ein abartiges Monopol: "Hadega" Handelsgesellschaft m. b.H. und ihr Geschäft mit Edelmetallen und Edelsteinen während des Zweiten Weltkrieges', in *Theresienstädter Studien und Dokumente* 2001, 305–72.
24. The authorities had been working on this since mid November. Letter of 12 November 1939, mentioned in USHMM, RG 48.005M, reel 4 (Prague State Archive), I-3b 5810 Forcible amalgamation of the Jews, n.p.: BdS Stahlecker to Reich protector, Group I 3 b, for the attention of Modry, 23 January 1940.
25. 10th ordinance on the Reich Citizenship Law (Reichsbürgergesetz), RGBl. 1939 I, 1097. On the Reich Association, see Esriel Hildesheimer, *Die Jüdische Selbstverwaltung unter dem NS-Regime: Der Existenzkampf der Reichsvertretung und Reichsvereinigung der Juden in Deutschland* (Tübingen, 1994); Beate Meyer, *A Fatal Balancing Act: The Dilemma of the Reich Association of Jews in Germany, 1939–1945* (New York, 2013) (German original 2011); Wolf Gruner, 'Poverty and Persecution: The Reichsvereinigung, the Jewish Population, and the Anti-Jewish Policy in the Nazi State, 1939–1945', *Yad Vashem Studies* 27 (1999), 23–60.
26. USHMM, RG 48.005M, reel 4 (Prague State Archive), I-3b 5810 Forcible amalgamation of the Jews, n.p.: Reich protector to Group I 3, 11 December 1939; ibid.: Draft government decree with handwritten alterations, 7 December 1939, 1–7; ibid.: Report (Motivenbericht), n.d., 1–3.
27. On this process in Germany, see Gruner, *Öffentliche Wohlfahrt*, 157–274.
28. USHMM, RG 48.005M, reel 4 (Prague State Archive), I-3b 5810 Forcible amalgamation of the Jews, n.p.: Reich protector to Group I 3, 21 December 1939.
29. USHMM, RG 48.005M, reel 4 (Prague State Archive), I-3b 5810 Forcible amalgamation of the Jews, n.p.: Note Reich protector (I 3 b), 17 January 1940, 1–3.
30. Ibid., BdS to Reich protector, Group I 3 b, for the attention of Modry, 23 January 1940.
31. Utermöhle and Schmerling, *Die Rechtsstellung der Juden im Protektorat Böhmen und Mähren*, 58–59. Copy of the decree in English in Moskowitz, 'The Jewish Situation', 43–44. See also Report by the Central Office, 2 October 1941, in *Deutsche Politik im 'Protektorat Böhmen und Mähren'*, 123–24, doc. no. 23; Institute of Jewish Affairs, *Hitler's Ten-Year War*, 57.
32. YV Jerusalem, O 7/54, fol. 135–36: Weekly report Jewish Religious Community of Prague, 2–8 March 1940, 15–16.
33. Ibid., fol. 167–68: Weekly report Jewish Religious Community of Prague, 16–22 March 1940, 16–17.
34. Ibid., fol. 156: Weekly report Jewish Religious Community of Prague, 16–22 March 1940, 5.
35. Ibid., fol. 173, 182 and 185a: Weekly report Jewish Religious Community of Prague, 23–29 March 1940, 4, 13 and 17; see ibid., fol. 213: Monthly report Jewish Religious Community of Prague, 1–31 March 1940, 9.
36. Ibid., fol. 114: Weekly report Jewish Religious Community of Prague, 24 February to 1 March 1940, 8.
37. YV Jerusalem, M 58/JM 11814, fol. 124: Statement of assets of the Nové Strašecí (Neu-Straschitz) Israelite Burial Fraternity (Israelitische Beerdigungsbruderschaft), 31 March 1940.
38. YV Jerusalem, M 58/JM 11812, fol. 426–27.

39. YV Jerusalem, O 7/55, fol. 63: Weekly report Jewish Religious Community of Prague, 18–24 May 1940, 6.
40. YV Jerusalem, O 7/54, fol. 214: Monthly report Jewish Religious Community of Prague, 1–31 March 1940, 10; ibid., fol. 256a: Report by the Jewish Religious Community and the Prague Palestine Office on their activities in the first quarter of 1940, 34.
41. YV Jerusalem, O 7/55, fol. 63: Weekly report Jewish Religious Community of Prague, 18–24 May 1940, 6.
42. Ibid., fol. 21: Weekly report Jewish Religious Community of Prague, 6–12 April 1940, 5; ibid., fol. 180: Report by the Jewish Religious Community and the Prague Palestine Office on their activities in the first half of 1940, 37.
43. Mentioned in YV Jerusalem, O 7/54, fol. 151: Weekly report Jewish Religious Community of Prague, 9–15 March 1940, 15.
44. According to the *Jüdisches Nachrichtenblatt*, 3 April 1940, in Moskowitz, 'The Jewish Situation', 23. See also Hájková, 'Erfassung', 54.
45. YV Jerusalem, O 7/55, fol. 113: Monthly report Jewish Religious Community of Prague, 1–30 April 1940, 6. See the contrasting statements by Rothkirchen, who believes the decree led to an increase in the number of registered Jews through the addition of 12,680 non-religious Jews: Rothkirchen, *Jews*, 116. In the summer of 1940, the Jewish Communities in the Protectorate registered 92,000 members, 5,000 more than prior to the April ordinance; Bryant, *Prague in Black*, 58.
46. YV Jerusalem, O 7/55, fol. 129: Monthly report Jewish Religious Community of Prague, 1–30 June 1940, 7.
47. Ibid., fol. 21: Weekly report Jewish Religious Community of Prague, 6–12 April 1940, 5; ibid., fol. 180: Report by the Jewish Religious Community and the Prague Palestine Office on their activities in the first half of 1940, 37.
48. USHMM Washington, RG 45.005M, reel 1 (Prague State Archive, Ministry of the Interior), no. 25, n.p.: Letter Presidium of the Ministry of the Interior to Presidium of the State Authority in Prague and Brno, 20 February 1940, 1–2.
49. *The New York Times*, 11 February 1940, 39; *The Los Angeles Times*, 11 February 1940, 3; *The Washington Post*, 11 February 1940, 12; *The Manchester Guardian*, 12 February 1940, 3; Erdely, *Germany's First European Protectorate*, 144.
50. YV Jerusalem, O 7/54, fol. 120: Weekly report Jewish Religious Community of Prague, 24 February to 1 March 1940, 14. See Hájková, 'Erfassung', 52.
51. YV Jerusalem, O 7/54, fol. 135: Weekly report Jewish Religious Community of Prague, 2–8 March 1940, 15.
52. BA Berlin, R 58/149, fol. 15: Report no. 66, 15 March 1940, 6. Reprinted in *Meldungen aus dem Reich*, vol. 4, 894. See Report by the Foreign Office representative in the Office of the Reich Protector, 6 May 1940, in Mund, *Deutschland und das Protektorat*, doc. 237, 356–58.
53. USHMM Washington, RG 48.005M, reel 4 (Prague State Archive), Designation of Jews, carton, I-3b-5851, no. 1, n.p.: Handwritten petition (Rudolf Pitzak) to Office of the Reich Protector (February 1940); ibid., no. 6: Národní arijská kulturní jednota Prague to Reich Protector von Neurath, 12 June 1940.
54. Ibid., no. 3, n.p.: Reich protector/BdS to Group I/3, Office of the Reich Protector, 5 March 1940.
55. On anti-Jewish housing policies, see Sedláková. Sedláková, however, assumes that pressure began to mount in summer 1940 as a result of the resettlement of Jews in Prague. See Monika Sedláková, '"Burza" s židovskými byty – součást protektorátní bytové politiky', in *Documenta Pragensia XXVI. Evropská velkoměsta za druhé světové války Každodennost okupovaného velkoměsta. Praha 1939–1945 v*

evropském srovnání (Prague, 2007), 205–20, here 207. My thanks to Jan Vondráček (Wuppertal/Prague) for alerting me to Sedláková's chapter and translating it.

56. YV Jerusalem, O 7/55, fol. 33: Weekly report Jewish Religious Community of Prague, 20–26 April 1940, 5; *The New York Times*, 23 April 1949, 4.
57. JTA, 'Jews in Protectorate Must Pay Fee when Evicted from Homes', 21 May 1940.
58. YV Jerusalem, O 7/55, fol. 98: Weekly report Jewish Religious Community of Prague, 15–21 June 1940, 8.
59. Ibid., fol. 106: Weekly report Jewish Religious Community of Prague, 22–28 June 1940, 8.
60. Ibid., fol. 183: Report by the Jewish Religious Community and the Prague Palestine Office on their activities in the first half of 1940, 40.
61. YV Jerusalem, O 7/56, fol. 7: Weekly report Jewish Religious Community of Prague, 29 June to 5 July 1940, 6.
62. Ibid., fol. 32: Weekly report Jewish Religious Community of Prague, 13–19 July 1940, 8.
63. On Germany, see Marlies Buchholz, *Die hannoverschen Judenhäuser: Zur Situation der Juden in der Zeit der Ghettoisierung und Verfolgung 1941 bis 1945* (Hildesheim, 1987); Susanne Willems, *'Der entsiedelte Jude': Albert Speers Wohnungsmarktpolitik für den Berliner Hauptstadtbau* (Berlin, 2002). For a comparative look at different cities, see Gruner, 'Local Initiatives, Central Coordination', 275–76.
64. On ghettoization in Poland, see Browning, *The Origins of the Final Solution*, 111–68.
65. YV Jerusalem, O 7/54, fol. 12: Weekly report Jewish Religious Community of Prague, 1–6 January 1940, 10–11; ibid., fol. 25: Weekly report Jewish Religious Community of Prague, 7–12 January 1940, 12; ibid., fol. 38: Weekly report Jewish Religious Community of Prague, 13–19 January 1940, 12; ibid., fol. 61: Weekly report Jewish Religious Community of Prague, 27 January to 2 February 1940, 10.
66. Ibid., fol. 71–72: Weekly report Jewish Religious Community of Prague, 3–9 February 1940, 10–11.
67. Ibid., fol. 256: Report by the Jewish Religious Community and the Prague Palestine Office on their activities in the first quarter of 1940, 33.
68. YV Jerusalem, O 7/54, fol. 185: Weekly report Jewish Religious Community of Prague, 23–29 March 1940, 16.
69. On comparable developments in Germany and Austria, see Gruner, *Öffentliche Wohlfahrt*; Gruner, *Zwangsarbeit und Verfolgung*.
70. Rothkirchen, *Jews*, 120.
71. YV Jerusalem, O 7/54, fol. 5: Weekly report Jewish Religious Community of Prague, 1–6 January 1940, 4; ibid., fol. 17: Weekly report Jewish Religious Community of Prague, 7–12 January 1940, 4; ibid., fol. 31: Weekly report Jewish Religious Community of Prague, 13–19 January 1940, 5; ibid., fol. 56: Weekly report Jewish Religious Community of Prague, 27 January to 2 February 1940, 5.
72. Ibid., fol. 189: Monthly report Jewish Religious Community, 1–31 January 1940, 2–4.
73. Ibid., fol. 192: Monthly report Jewish Religious Community of Prague, 1–31 January 1940, 2–7.
74. Ibid., fol. 208: Monthly report Jewish Religious Community of Prague, 1–31 March 1940, 4.
75. Ibid., fol. 174: Weekly report Jewish Religious Community of Prague, 23–29 March 1940, 5.
76. Ibid., fol. 246a: Report by the Jewish Religious Community and the Prague Palestine Office on their activities in the first quarter of 1940, 22.

77. Ibid., fol. 249–53: Report by the Jewish Religious Community and the Prague Palestine Office on their activities in the first quarter of 1940, 26–29.
78. Ibid., fol. 231: Report by the Jewish Religious Community and the Prague Palestine Office on their activities in the first quarter of 1940, 11.
79. Ibid., fol. 135: Weekly report Jewish Religious Community of Prague, 2–8 March 1940, 15.
80. Ibid., fol. 174–75: Weekly report Jewish Religious Community of Prague, 23–29 March 1940, 5–6.
81. Ibid., fol. 246h: Report by the Jewish Religious Community and the Prague Palestine Office on their activities in the first quarter of 1940, 23.
82. Ibid., fol. 22: Weekly report Jewish Religious Community of Prague, 7–12 January 1940, 9.
83. Ibid., fol. 161: Weekly report Jewish Religious Community of Prague, 16–22 March 1940, 10.
84. YV Jerusalem, O 7/55, fol. 11: Weekly report Jewish Religious Community of Prague, 30 March to 5 April 1940, 10.
85. Ibid., fol. 33: Weekly report Jewish Religious Community of Prague, 20–26 April 1940, 5.
86. Ibid., fol. 46: Weekly report Jewish Religious Community of Prague, 4–10 May 1940, 4.
87. YV Jerusalem, O 7/54, fol. 204: Monthly report Jewish Religious Community of Prague, 1–29 February 1940, 10.
88. YV Jerusalem, O 7/55, fol. 30: Weekly report Jewish Religious Community of Prague, 20–26 April 1940, 2.
89. Ibid., fol. 35–36: Weekly report Jewish Religious Community of Prague, 20–26 April 1940, 7–8.
90. Ibid., fol. 41: Weekly report Jewish Religious Community of Prague, 27 April to 3 May 1940, 5.
91. Mentioned in YV Jerusalem, O 7/54, fol. 89–90: Weekly report Jewish Religious Community of Prague, 10–16 February 1940, 13–14.
92. YV Jerusalem, O 7/55, fol. 110: Monthly report Jewish Religious Community of Prague, 1–30 April 1940, 3.
93. Ibid., fol. 7: Weekly report Jewish Religious Community of Prague, 30 March to 5 April 1940, 7.
94. Ibid., fol. 45: Weekly report Jewish Religious Community of Prague, 4–10 May 1940, 3.
95. Ibid., fol. 77: Weekly report Jewish Religious Community of Prague, 1–7 June 1940, 4.
96. Ibid., fol. 169–70: Report by the Jewish Religious Community and the Prague Palestine Office on their activities in the first half of 1940, 26–27.
97. Ibid., fol. 160–63: Report by the Jewish Religious Community and the Prague Palestine Office on their activities in the first half of 1940, 20–22.
98. Ibid., fol. 167: Report by the Jewish Religious Community and the Prague Palestine Office on their activities in the first half of 1940, 25.
99. YV Jerusalem, O 7/54, fol. 15: Weekly report Jewish Religious Community of Prague, 7–12 January 1940, 2; ibid., fol. 28: Weekly report Jewish Religious Community of Prague, 13–19 January 1940, 2.
100. Ibid., fol. 187–88: Monthly report Jewish Religious Community of Prague, 1–31 January 1940, 2–3.
101. Ibid., fol. 186: Monthly report Jewish Religious Community of Prague, 1–31 January 1940, 1.

102. Ibid., fol. 196: Monthly report Jewish Religious Community of Prague, 1–29 February 1940, 2; ibid., fol. 207: Monthly report Jewish Religious Community of Prague, 1–31 March 1940, 3.
103. Ibid., fol. 223: Report by the Jewish Religious Community and the Prague Palestine Office on their activities in the first quarter of 1940, 4.
104. See, for example, ibid., fol. 77–78: Weekly report Jewish Religious Community of Prague, 10–16 February 1940, 1–2.
105. Ibid., fol. 121: Weekly report Jewish Religious Community of Prague, 2–8 March 1940, 1.
106. Letter by Lotte Meissner, 21 March 1940, reprinted in English in Garbarini et al., *Jewish Responses*, 303.
107. YV Jerusalem, O 7/55, fol. 23: Weekly report Jewish Religious Community of Prague, 13–19 April 1940, 1; ibid., O 7/56, fol. 7: Weekly report Jewish Religious Community of Prague, 29 June to 5 July 1940, 6.
108. Ibid., fol. 23: Weekly report Jewish Religious Community of Prague, 13–19 April 1940, 1.
109. Ibid., fol. 138: Report by the Jewish Religious Community and the Prague Palestine Office on their activities in the first half of 1940, submitted to the Central Office for Jewish Emigration, Prague, 4.
110. YV Jerusalem, O 7/54, fol. 224–26: Report by the Jewish Religious Community and the Prague Palestine Office on their activities in the first quarter of 1940, 5–7.
111. Ibid., fol. 8: Weekly report Jewish Religious Community of Prague, 1–6 January 1940, 7.
112. Ibid., fol. 46: Weekly report Jewish Religious Community of Prague, 20–26 January 1940, 7.
113. Ibid., fol. 83: Weekly report Jewish Religious Community of Prague, 10–16 February 1940, 7.
114. Ibid., fol. 143: Weekly report Jewish Religious Community of Prague, 9–15 March 1940, 7.
115. YV Jerusalem, O 7/53, n.p.: Report by the Jewish Religious Community and the Prague Palestine Office on their activities in the first quarter of 1940, chart: Retraining activities, 15 March 1939 to 1 April 1940.
116. See YV Jerusalem, O 7/54, fol. 177: Weekly report Jewish Religious Community of Prague, 23–29 March 1940, 7; ibid., O 7/55, fol. 155, 155a and 156: Report by the Jewish Religious Community and the Prague Palestine Office on their activities in the first half of 1940, 15, 16 and chart: 'Agricultural retraining by the HeHalutz'.
117. YV Jerusalem, O 7/55, fol. 94: Weekly report Jewish Religious Community of Prague, 15–20 June 1940, 4; ibid., fol. 155b and 157: Report by the Jewish Religious Community and the Prague Palestine Office on their activities in the first half of 1940, 17 and chart: 'Retraining courses in Prague'.
118. YV Jerusalem, O 7/54, fol. 229: Report by the Jewish Religious Community and the Prague Palestine Office on their activities in the first quarter of 1940, 9.
119. Ibid., fol. 71: Weekly report Jewish Religious Community of Prague, 3–9 February 1940, 7.
120. Ibid., fol. 229: Report by the Jewish Religious Community and the Prague Palestine Office on their activities in the first quarter of 1940, 9; ibid., O 7/55, fol. 152–53: Report by the Jewish Religious Community and the Prague Palestine Office on their activities in the first half of 1940, 13–14.
121. YV Jerusalem, O 7/55, fol. 109: Monthly report Jewish Religious Community of Prague, 1–30 April 1940, 2.

122. Ibid., fol. 74: Weekly report Jewish Religious Community of Prague, 1–7 June 1940, 1.
123. Ibid., fol. 116: Monthly report Jewish Religious Community of Prague, 1–31 May 1940, 2.
124. Ibid., fol. 124: Monthly report Jewish Religious Community of Prague, 1–30 June 1940, 2.
125. Ibid., fol. 83–84: Weekly report Jewish Religious Community of Prague, 8–14 June 1940, 1–2.
126. Ibid., fol. 147: Report by the Jewish Religious Community and the Prague Palestine Office on their activities in the first half of 1940, 10.
127. Ibid., fol. 83–84: Weekly report Jewish Religious Community of Prague, 8–14 June 1940, 1–2.
128. According to a report on the chief county commissioners' successful efforts to promote Germanity, 5 October 1940, cited by Němec, 'Das tschechische Volk', 451.
129. For a detailed account, see Osterloh and Wixforth, 'Die "Arisierung" im Protektorat Böhmen und Mähren', 307, 310–31. See also Kárný, '"Judenfrage"', 142, 150 and 167; Rothkirchen, *Jews*, 107 f. Most recently, see Jančík, Kubů and Šouša, *Arisierungsgewinnler*; cf. Drahomír Jančík and Eduard Kubů, *'Arizace' a arizátoři: Drobný a střední židovský majetek v úvěrech Kreditanstalt der Deutschen (1939-1945)* ['Aryanization' and Aryanizers: Small- and Medium-Sized Jewish Property in the Loans Issued by the Kreditanstalt der Deutschen] (Prague, 2005); and Balcar, *Panzer für Hitler*, 67–75.
130. BA Berlin, R 58/149, n.p.: Report no. 63, 8 March 1940, 20. Reprinted in *Meldungen aus dem Reich*, vol. 3, 864.
131. USHMM Washington, RG 45.005M, reel 1 (Prague State Archive, Ministry of the Interior), no. 37, n.p.: Copy Minister of the Interior General Ježek to the Presidium of the State Authorities in Prague and Brno, 17 April 1940, 1–4.
132. Ibid., reel 3 (Prague State Archive, Ministry for Schools and Public Education: Jewish regulations), no. 31, n.p.: Ministry to Jewish Community, 5 April 1940; YV Jerusalem, O 7/55, fol. 178: Report by the Jewish Religious Community and the Prague Palestine Office on their activities in the first half of 1940, 35.
133. Brandes and Míšková, *Vom Osteuropa-Lehrstuhl ins Prager Rathaus*, 281.
134. Osterloh and Wixforth, 'Die "Arisierung" im Protektorat Böhmen und Mähren', 307; Rothkirchen, *Jews*, 108.
135. BA Berlin, R 30/4b, fol. 121–22: Administrative report chief county commissioner Moravian Ostrava, 1 May 1940, 5–6.
136. Ibid., fol. 115–16: Police chief, status report April 1940 Moravian Ostrava, 29 April 1940, to the chief county commissioner, 4–5.
137. YV Jerusalem, O 7/55, fol. 142: Report by the Jewish Religious Community and the Prague Palestine Office on their activities in the first half of 1940, 7.
138. The lower figures for the younger age groups were no doubt due to higher levels of participation in retraining schemes; ibid., fol. 142a: Report by the Jewish Religious Community and the Prague Palestine Office on their activities in the first half of 1940, chart 'Elimination of Jews from the economic process'.
139. Ibid., fol. 143: Report by the Jewish Religious Community and the Prague Palestine Office on their activities in the first half of 1940, 8.
140. Ibid., fol. 158: Report by the Jewish Religious Community and the Prague Palestine Office on their activities in the first half of 1940, 18; ibid., O 7/54, fol. 99: Weekly report Jewish Religious Community of Prague, 17–23 February 1940, 9.

141. Ibid., fol. 8–9: Weekly report Jewish Religious Community of Prague, 1–6 January 1940, 7–8; ibid., fol. 20–21: Weekly report Jewish Religious Community of Prague, 7–12 January 1940, 7–8.
142. Ibid., fol. 34: Weekly report Jewish Religious Community of Prague, 13–19 January 1940, 8. On the problem of work clothes, see ibid., fol. 96: Weekly report Jewish Religious Community of Prague, 17–23 February 1940, 6.
143. Ibid., fol. 84–85: Weekly report Jewish Religious Community of Prague, 10–16 February 1940, 8–9; see ibid., fol. 99: Weekly report Jewish Religious Community of Prague, 17–23 February 1940, 9.
144. Ibid., fol. 114–15: Weekly report Jewish Religious Community of Prague, 24 February to 1 March 1940, 8–9.
145. Ibid., fol. 144: Weekly report Jewish Religious Community of Prague, 9–15 March 1940, 8; ibid., fol. 159–60: Weekly report Jewish Religious Community of Prague, 16–22 March 1940, 8–9.
146. Ibid., fol. 179: Weekly report Jewish Religious Community of Prague, 23–29 March 1940, 10.
147. Dennler, *Sozialpolitik*, 4 and 9.
148. For a general account of forced labour units, see Gruner, *Der Geschlossene Arbeitseinsatz*. On the topic of forced labour in the Protectorate between 1939 and 1945, see the detailed account in chapter 5 of Gruner, *Jewish Forced Labor*.
149. YV Jerusalem, O 7/55, fol. 10: Weekly report Jewish Religious Community of Prague, 30 March to 5 April 1940, 9.
150. Ibid., fol. 33: Weekly report Jewish Religious Community of Prague, 20–26 April 1940, 5.
151. Ibid., fol. 40: Weekly report Jewish Religious Community of Prague, 27 April to 3 May 1940, 4.
152. Ibid., fol. 49–50: Weekly report Jewish Religious Community of Prague, 4–10 May 1940, 6–7.
153. Ibid., fol. 55: Weekly report Jewish Religious Community of Prague, 11–17 May 1940, 4.
154. Ibid., fol. 61: Weekly report Jewish Religious Community of Prague, 18–24 May 1940, 4.
155. Ibid., fol. 78: Weekly report Jewish Religious Community of Prague, 1–7 June 1940, 81.
156. Ibid., fol. 87: Weekly report Jewish Religious Community of Prague, 8–14 June 1940, 5; ibid., fol. 94: Weekly report Jewish Religious Community of Prague, 15–20 June 1940, 4.
157. For a range of views on Germanization, see the documents in Celovsky, *Germanisierung und Genozid*, 236–49. On this and for general information on what follows, see Brandes, 'Umvolkung, Umsiedlung, rassische Bestandsaufnahme'.
158. Brandes, 'Nationalsozialistische Tschechenpolitik', 52; Němec, 'Die Lage der deutschen Nationalität', 39–40. See also Report by the Foreign Office representative in the Office of the Reich Protector, 5 July 1940, in Mund, *Deutschland und das Protektorat*, doc. 263, 394–95.
159. Němec, 'Das tschechische Volk', 443 f.; Němec, 'Die Lage der deutschen Nationalität', 43–55; Bryant, *Prague in Black*, 116–25.
160. Němec, 'Die Lage der deutschen Nationalität', 50–55.
161. BA Berlin, NS 25/725, fol. 13: Copy Reich Ministry of the Interior, Pfundtner, to Deputy Führer, Ministerial Director Sommer, Munich, 24 November 1939.

162. Ibid., fol. 4–5: Nazi Party Reich Directorate (NSDAP-Reichsleitung), Main Office for Local Government Policy, Karl Fiehler, Munich, to Deputy Führer, Munich, 26 September 1939.
163. Ibid.
164. Ibid., fol. 4: Handwritten note on Nazi Party Reich Directorate, Main Office for Local Government Policy, Karl Fiehler, Munich, to Deputy Führer, Munich, 26 September 1939; ibid., fol. 10: Nazi Party Reich Directorate, Main Office for Local Government Policy, Munich, to the German Council for Municipalities, Berlin, 2 October 1939; ibid., fol. 11: German Council for Municipalities, Councillor Schlüter, Berlin, to Nazi Party Reich Directorate, Main Office for Local Government Policy, Munich, 10 October 1939.
165. Ibid., fol. 13–14: Copy Reich Interior Ministry, Pfundtner, to Deputy Führer, Ministerial Director Sommer, Munich, 24 November 1939.
166. Ibid., fol. 15: Nazi Party Reich Directorate, Main Office for Local Government Policy, Munich, to the Lower Danube Gauleitung, Gau Office for Local Government Policy (Gauamt für Kommunalpolitik), Vienna, 6 February 1940.
167. Brandes, *Die Tschechen unter deutschem Protektorat*, part I, 165–66.
168. Brandes, 'Nationalsozialistische Tschechenpolitik', 52. In the Sudeten region itself, meanwhile, most of the mayors were Reich Germans; Sudeten Germans were sent to the Protectorate, chiefly due to their linguistic abilities. See Osterloh, *Nationalsozialistische Judenverfolgung*, 237.
169. Moskowitz, 'Three Years of the Protectorate', 357.
170. BA Berlin, NS 25/774, fol. 3–4: Copy ordinance V 3/40 issued by deputy Führer, Rudolf Hess, Munich, 30 January 1940. In order to secure the Nazi Party's influence on local government policy in the Protectorate, in late 1940 the Party Liaison Office proposed appointing all German mayors district or local commissioners of the Nazi Party for local government policy. In this way, the Nazi Party could bring them together for coordination meetings; ibid., fol. 21: Nazi Party Liaison Office, Office of the Reich Protector, Government Counsellor Dr Fritsche, Prague, to the Bavarian Eastern March Nazi Party Gauleitung, Bayreuth, 18 December 1940.
171. BA Berlin, NS 25/774, fol. 22+RS: Copy note Reich protector, Prague, 4 December 1940.
172. BA Berlin, NS 25/724, fol. 4–39: Draft articles of association and correspondence from January to December 1940.
173. Ibid., fol. 2: Copy Reich protector in Bohemia and Moravia, Office for Moravia, to the chief county commissioners in Brno, Olomouc, Moravian Ostrava and Jihlava, 6 December 1939.
174. BA Berlin, NS 25/774, fol. 48–55RS: 'Remarks on the Introduction of the German Municipal Code', statement by Government Commissar Dr Leo Engelmann, Jihlava, 22 April 1941.
175. Ibid., fol. 7–9: Copy circular Reich protector Bohemia and Moravia, Dr Mokry, Prague, to the Moravia Group and chief county commissioners, 30 December 1939. See ibid., fol. 18: Copy circular Reich protector Bohemia and Moravia, Prague, to the Moravia Group and chief county commissioners, 24 November 1939.
176. RGVA Moscow, 1488-1-25, fol. 99–100: Circular Reich protector to Groups, 13 March 1940, appendix, 'The Promotion of Germanity [Deutschtumsarbeit] in a Chief County Commissioner's District', March 1940, Chief County Commissioner Molsen, 7–8.
177. According to a report on the successful promotion of Germanity by the chief county commissioners, 5 October 1940, cited by Němec, 'Das tschechische Volk', 452.

178. Erich Später, *Villa Waigner: Hanns Martin Schleyer und die deutsche Vernichtungselite in Prag 1939–45* (Hamburg, 2009), 52–53.
179. Brandes, 'Nationalsozialistische Tschechenpolitik', 53–54; Bryant, *Prague in Black*, 110.
180. Bryant, *Prague in Black*, 163.
181. Report by the Foreign Office representative in the Office of the Reich Protector, 20 March 1940, in Mund, *Deutschland und das Protektorat*, doc. 232, 344–49. See Bryant, *Prague in Black*, 61.
182. BA Berlin, R 30/4c, fol. 2–3: Chief County Commissioner/Department III, Administrative report, 15th copy, secret, general political situation, Moravian Ostrava, 20 August 1940, 1–2; ibid., fol. 18: Chief County Commissioner/Department III, Administrative report, 15th copy, confidential, general political situation, Moravian Ostrava, 20 September 1940, 2.
183. Reference in Němec, 'Das tschechische Volk', 424–55, here 443–44; Bryant, *Prague in Black*, 116–25. Frank's memorandum is discussed in Report by the Foreign Office representative in the Office of the Reich Protector, 17 September 1940, in Mund, *Deutschland und das Protektorat*, doc. 301, 445–48. On Frank's Germanization plans, see Küpper, *Karl Hermann Frank*, 164–67.
184. Reference in Němec, 'Das tschechische Volk', 424–55, here 442.
185. USHMM Washington, RG 48.005M, reel 3 (Prague State Archive), no. 109, n.p.: Note Reich protector, 23 November 1940, 1–2. The Czech government passed a draft decree; ibid.: Draft government decree, 24 October 1940, 1–9.
186. Quoted in Note von Neurath, 23 September 1940, in Brandes, 'Nationalsozialistische Tschechenpolitik', 44. See Report by the Foreign Office representative in the Office of the Reich Protector, 5 October 1940, in Mund, *Deutschland und das Protektorat*, doc. 306, 453–54.
187. YV Jerusalem, O 7/55, fol. 152–53: Report by the Jewish Religious Community and the Prague Palestine Office on their activities in the first half of 1940, 13–14.
188. See Jan Láníček, 'The Czechoslovak Section of the BBC and the Jews during the Second World War', *Yad Vashem Studies* 38(2) (2010), 123–54.
189. Zdenka Fantlová, *My Lucky Star* (New York, 2001), 51–54.
190. YV Jerusalem, O 7/54, fol. 105: Weekly report Jewish Religious Community of Prague, 17–23 February 1940, 15.
191. Ibid., fol. 205: Monthly report Jewish Religious Community of Prague, 1–31 March 1940, 1.
192. Ibid., O 7/56, fol. 30: Weekly report Jewish Religious Community of Prague, 13–19 July 1940, 6.
193. See ibid., M 58/JM 11813, fol. 351–77: Minutes of the meetings of the Litomyšl Jewish Community from 1935 to 1940.
194. Frommer, 'Verfolgung durch die Presse', 140–41. The local authorities reacted in a variety of ways. Often they moved quickly to punish offenders, while in other cases they were more restrained. Charges were sometimes dismissed either because the individuals involved were not Jews or because they had acted with official permission; ibid., 141–147.
195. Frommer, 'Verfolgung durch die Presse', 142.
196. YV Jerusalem, O 7/54, fol. 90: Weekly report Jewish Religious Community of Prague, 10–16 February 1940, 14.
197. Max Mannheimer, *Spätes Tagebuch: Theresienstadt – Auschwitz. Warschau – Dachau* (Munich, 2009), 37; quoted in VEJ/3, 40.

198. The individual involved is likely to have been Marie Picková (1892–1942). On 9 January 1942 she was deported from Theresienstadt to Riga, where she died; VEJ/3, doc. 70, 206.
199. Law against Treacherous Attacks on the State and Party and for the Protection of Party Uniforms (Gesetz gegen heimtückische Angriffe auf Staat und Partei und zum Schutz der Parteiuniformen) of 20 December 1934, RGBl. 1934 I, 1269. See Bernward Dörner, 'Heimtücke': Das Gesetz als Waffe. Kontrolle, Abschreckung und Verfolgung in Deutschland 1933–1945 (Paderborn, 1998).
200. Copy of the article in VEJ/3, doc. 70, 206.
201. Staatsarchiv Chemnitz, 30071, no. 16731, fol. 7–10: Verdict of the Special Court at the German Regional Court (Landgericht) Prague, 12 July 1940, 1–7.
202. A reference to the partially aborted Nisko deportation. See above.
203. BA Berlin, R 30/4c, fol. 21: Chief County Commissioner/Department III, Administrative report, 15th copy, confidential, general political situation, Moravian Ostrava, 20 September 1940, 3. For a general account of such violations, see Frommer, 'Verfolgung durch die Presse', 141.
204. USHMM Washington, RG 48.005M, reel 4 (Prague State Archive), Shopping hours for Jews, carton, I-3b-5852, no. 2, n.p.: Nazi Party Head Party Liaison Office (Schroeter) to Reich protector, 28 November 1940. In Olomouc, when the authorities announced the introduction of restricted shopping hours, Czechs openly stated that they would make all purchases on Jews' behalf; RGVA Moscow, 1488-1-3, fol. 30: SD Headquarters (Leitabschnitt) Prague, Daily report (strictly confidential), 7 August 1940, 4.
205. Facsimile of a fat ration card (Fettkarte) of July 1940 in Grabowski and Haney, Kennzeichen 'Jude', 202.
206. The authorities resolved not to stimulate further immigration to Palestine and to prohibit the release of Polish Jews from concentration camps, even if they possessed emigration certificates; Paul Sauer (ed.), Dokumente über die Verfolgung der jüdischen Bürger in Baden-Württemberg durch das nationalsozialistische Regime 1933–1943 (Stuttgart, 1966), doc. no. 368, 125: RSHA decree in circular decree issued by the State Police Office (Stapoleitstelle) Karlsruhe, 3 May 1940.
207. Kurt Pätzold (ed.), Verfolgung, Vertreibung, Vernichtung: Dokumente des faschistischen Antisemitismus 1933–1942 (Leipzig, 1983), 350, doc. no. 320: Note Luther (Reich Ministry of Labour), 21 August 1942, on projects intended to facilitate a 'final solution to the Jewish problem'.
208. BA Berlin, R 8150, no. 45, fol. 178: Summons Secret State Police Office (Geheimes Staatspolizeiamt), 25 June 1940. See Gruner, Der Geschlossene Arbeitseinsatz, 146–47.
209. YV Jerusalem, O 7/56, fol. 212: Monthly report Jewish Religious Community of Prague, 1–30 July 1940, 11.
210. Note on summons from Eichmann, 3 July 1940, reference in Safrian, Eichmann's Men, 66; CZA Jerusalem, S 26, no. 1191g, n.p.: Report Israelite Religious Community of Vienna 1938–1944/45 (Löwenherz Report), 25.
211. Kulka believes both institutions were initiated within the Jewish community, with the latter acting autonomously; Kulka, 'History and Historical Consciousness', 72. On Germany and the Gestapo's determining influence on the foundation of the Reich Association, see Gruner, 'Poverty and Persecution'.

Chapter 6

Local versus Central Persecutory Initiatives

Efforts towards Centralization in the Protectorate

At the end of June 1940, 91,995 Jews still lived in the Protectorate of Bohemia and Moravia (see Table A.1 in the appendix). Since March 1939, 24,017 individuals of Jewish faith had emigrated and 2,453 had died, while just 155 births were recorded.[1] Persecution split up many families, whether through deportation, detention in camps, prison, emigration or violence.

The same year saw the proliferation of local initiatives, on the part of both Czech and German authorities, to separate Jews from the rest of the population. By this point, National Partnership had banned its members from associating with Jews. While the party expected Czechs to uphold its antisemitism, many did not and maintained contact with individual Jews, not so much because they were entirely free of antisemitic attitudes but because they were deeply hostile to the Germans.[2] Czech writers and publishers, for example, allowed Jewish colleagues to publish their literary works under their own names or pseudonyms.[3]

On 17 May, the Prague Police Directorate prohibited Jews from entering all public parks and gardens, prompting the Jewish Community to call for an easing of the ban.[4] In Olomouc the Nazi Party County Office (Kreisleitung) proposed the imposition of restricted shopping hours for Jews, compulsory armbands and the establishment of a ghetto, as the chief county commissioner notified the Reich protector.[5] In Holešov the Town Council, now packed with Nazi Party and Vlajka members, adopted a resolution banning Jews from public swimming pools,[6] while in Prague they were no longer allowed to use the steamboats on the Vltava.[7]

These local initiatives now provoked central regulations. On 9 July 1940, the Czech minister of the interior instructed the local authorities to prohibit Jews from shopping outside of specified daily hours. As far as possible, the minister underlined, they should avoid selecting the early hours of the morning so as to prevent Jews from benefiting from the delivery of scarce goods; the preferred times would be 10.30 a.m.–1 p.m. and 3 p.m.–5 p.m. Business owners must hang up clearly visible signs to this effect.[8] In Vienna such shopping hours had been in force since the beginning of the war, while in Berlin they were also introduced in July 1940.[9]

The Prague police chief carried out the Czech interior minister's instructions one month later: from 5 August 1940 onwards, Jews in the capital of the Protectorate were barred from patronizing 'Aryan' businesses except between 11 a.m. and 1 p.m. and 3 p.m. and 4.30 p.m.[10] According to news reports, this also applied to pharmacies and tobacconists, and allegedly even to Jewish businesses.[11] On 12 September, the Prague police issued an ordinance prohibiting Jews from visiting municipal markets on market days.[12] In August, meanwhile, the chief county commissioner of Moravian Ostrava had instructed the authorities to distribute ration cards to Jews only on specific days, supposedly in response to Jews' conduct. Shopping hours for Jews in the city were limited to just thirty minutes: from 11.30 a.m. to 12 p.m. They were no longer even allowed to patronize the rooms previously set aside for them in certain restaurants, but had to use entirely separate establishments.[13] Czechs in Moravian Ostrava sharply criticized the introduction of limited shopping times for the Jewish community.[14]

Due to the growing number of local initiatives restricting Jews' freedom of movement, as also described in the previous chapter, on 17 August 1940 the Commander of the Security Police in Prague sent a circular decree to all chief county commissioners. It stated critically: 'Because such ordinances often take account of purely local issues and are not geared towards issues in the rest of the Reich territory, not only does the standardized orientation of such measures suffer, but they often result in increased expenditure on welfare for the Jews affected and thus impose a heavy burden on the resources of the Emigration Fund'. The decree urged the chief county commissioners to implement anti-Jewish measures only in consultation with the Commander of the Security Police or Central Office for Jewish Emigration. The commander, the decree went on, had proposed to the Protectorate Government that it impose the following additional restrictions on Jews' freedom of movement: a ban on entering parks, attending sporting events and using dining or sleeping carriages on trains, controlling Jews' use of trams, the imposition of shopping hours and an end to mixed restaurants with extra rooms for Jews. The marking of Jews, as called for by the chief county commissioners, the establishment of ghettos or the concentration of Jews in specific dwellings or quarters could 'not be considered at the present time'.[15]

The example of shopping hours, in any event, shows beyond doubt that the Commander of the Security Police in Prague was not entirely in the picture about the measures the Czech authorities had now initiated. The same went for the abolition of mixed venues, which had been promulgated two days before, on 15 August 1940, in a circular decree issued by the Presidium of the State Authority in Prague and implemented one day earlier by the Prague Police Directorate. And the Prague Central Office, operating under the authority of the Commander of the Security Police, had long since (in May) decreed the restricted use of sleeping and dining carriages on Reich and Protectorate railways, as it had the ban on the use of hired cars (on 5 July).[16] With effect from 22 June, the Czech Interior Ministry had permitted the holding of sporting events only on the condition that Jews were barred and that this was publicly announced and displayed on posters.[17]

But Jews faced more than just official ordinances, with violence continuing to play a role in their everyday lives and leaving an imprint on individuals' memories to this day. In an interview, Alfred Dube tells of a pogrom in the summer of 1940 in his hometown of Pilsen, during which the synagogues and the cemetery were desecrated and vandalized.[18]

The Central Office's Plan for 'Jews' Houses' in Prague

Parallel campaigns thus continued to dominate within anti-Jewish policy, though the Central Office – in anticipation of the deportations – now pushed to gain control over broader swathes of Jews' lives, achieving, in its own terms, some success.

On 13 September 1940, the Central Office forbade Jews in the Protectorate from renting unoccupied dwellings. From now on, they were only allowed to move into those already being used by Jews.[19] Three days earlier, Eichmann had ordered the Jewish Community to submit to him a list of all properties occupied by Jews in Prague, broken down according to their Jewish or 'Aryan' ownership, size and number of residents, along with a map of the city integrating these findings.[20] In an exhausting special campaign, Jewish Community staff had to inspect and record every 'Jewish' home in Prague within a few days.[21]

The Jewish Community's Housing Service (Wohnungsfürsorge) had already faced major problems throughout the summer due to the skyrocketing number of Jewish renters in Prague receiving notice of cancelled rental contracts. At the same time, Jews struggled to find accommodation on the housing market, because private landlords were renting almost exclusively to 'Aryans'.[22] Nonetheless, for Housing Service staff the Central Office's directive was a profound turning point: they now saw it as their main task to support those families evicted from their homes and find accommodation for them subletting from other Jews.[23] As a rule, the latter entailed a tremendous loss of space, that is, a reduction from a home of several rooms to a single room per family. The Prague Accommodation Service thus had to try to find storage space for furniture while also developing and establishing rules governing the dividing up of apartments, the division of rental, electricity and gas bills and the use of kitchens.[24]

In Prague, the survey revealed 14,920 'Jewish dwellings', of which five thousand were to be vacated.[25] From 1 to 4 October, Community staff also registered Jewish homes in Brno.[26] In this context, the Reich protector had his staff contact Berlin to establish whether the Göring guidelines of late 1938 continued to apply; these provided for the concentration of Jews in 'Jews' houses' without stripping them of the legal protections normally enjoyed by tenants.[27]

The Reich protector supplemented the rules on renting with regulations on allocation in a decree of 7 October 1940. Henceforth, after the dissolving of rental agreements, flats previously rented to Jews could be leased to new tenants only with the approval of the Central Office.[28] This new measure adopted the policy, introduced after the pogrom, of concentrating Jewish families in German cities and in Vienna in ever smaller living quarters and exclusively in buildings owned by Jews, the so-called Jews' houses.[29]

These new circumstances inspired covetous thoughts, in the Prague city government for example. Deputy Primator Pfitzner concluded:

> A pleasing step in the right direction has been taken through an agreement between the Jewish Emigration Office and the Party on making available Jewish housing to German applicants. To this end the city has seconded its

official Dr Wuch to the municipal Housing Office (Wohnungsamt), where he is working on this entire set of issues in consultation with the Party.[30]

What was beginning to emerge in Prague was thus a concerted campaign to concentrate Jews in 'Jews' houses' and distribute their former homes to non-Jews, a process the city, the Central Office and the Nazi Party were all equally interested and involved in.[31]

Persecution and Isolation

The segregation, isolation and impoverishment of the Protectorate's Jewish population continued to accelerate. In October 1940, the Reich protector urged the Czech state president 'to prohibit civil servants in the Protectorate as well as members of the Government Troop (Regierungstruppe), the Gendarmerie, the Police and the Customs Service (Zolldienst) from associating with Jews'.[32]

Around this time, Jiří Orten from Prague wrote in his diary that the numerous prohibitions had left him unable to sleep. He was not allowed to leave his home after 8 p.m. and was barred from renting a flat himself. He could move only to Prague I or V and only as a subtenant. It was forbidden, he went on, to patronize wine restaurants, coffee houses (with a few exceptions), cinemas, theatres and concert performances, and the same went for visits to Prague's parks, public gardens and the municipal woods. He was not allowed to leave the city of Prague without permission from the Gestapo, could only use the final carriage of trams and could go shopping only at the brief, prescribed times. Jews could not perform in public, were barred from joining an association (Verein) and could not go to school; they were also banned from entering into contact with members of National Partnership.[33]

Since mid September 1940, the Prague city government or Police Directorate had barred Jews from visiting all hotels apart from two inns. They were also banned from all municipal markets and the municipal woods and faced restrictions on their use of municipal trams.[34] In the third quarter, a central directive dissolved the so-called 'Jewish sections in Aryan businesses', in other words the rooms reserved for Jews in restaurants. This was particularly hard for members of forced labour units, who could no longer provide themselves with food at their place of work as they were prevented from frequenting the nearby eateries.[35]

On 16 September the Reich protector reimposed the compulsory registration of securities, jewellery and art objects owned by Jews. The requirement to register with the Reich Protector II/1 3F Group in the

Czech Finance Ministry also applied to those associations that had not yet been disbanded, such as the Israelite Women's Association (Israelitischer Frauenverein) in Hranice na Moravě (Mährisch-Weißkirchen), which had taken out a 'unification loan' of five hundred crowns with the Städtische Sparkasse,[36] or the Israelite Burial Fraternity (Israelitische Beerdigungsbruderschaft) in Nové Strašecí (Neu-Straschitz), which had obtained two unification loans (Unifizierungsanleihen) to a total value of 5,500 crowns with the Stadtsparkasse at an interest rate of 4.5 per cent plus another of 1,000 crowns at a 3 per cent interest rate.[37]

Evidently, the SD Central Office instructed the Jewish Communities in the Protectorate to ensure that their members refrained from assembling in public on the Jewish feast days. This prompted the Moravian Ostrava Jewish Community to inform its members, when attending synagogue during the High Holy Days, to avoid gathering on the street in front of it; even during breaks in the service they were forbidden from standing around outside. Tellingly, due to lack of space but probably also to avoid the formation of large crowds of people, the Community suggested only to women to refrain entirely from attending Friday evening prayers, while bringing children along was also prohibited.[38] Such directives placed restrictions on Jews' ability to gather freely in their only remaining refuge, the synagogue.[39] Apparently, members of the local German community had complained that 'the Jews are conducting themselves in an intrusive manner in public streets and squares'.[40]

Emigration and Preparations for Emigration from mid 1940

As poverty and persecution made their living conditions increasingly unbearable, ever more Jews sought to leave Prague and the provinces for other countries and submitted applications for emigration to the Jewish Community. As most routes to that end were closed, the Community strove to make better use of those that remained open.

In July 1940, the Jewish Community and the Palestine Office referred 1,254 individuals to the Central Office, of whom 1,157 emigrated to Shanghai alone, while the figure for August was 1,175, with 1,124 going to Shanghai, and 872 in September, of whom 832 went to Shanghai. For purposes of emigration, along with the associated accommodation, official stamps and fees, the Community made available almost 404,000 crowns in July, 370,000 in August and around 304,000 in September.[41]

Thanks to the mediation of HAPAG's Prague bureau, Community officials managed to ensure that tickets for the Trans-Siberian Express to the Manchurian border could be paid in crowns rather than foreign currency, prompting them to reserve seats for those individuals earmarked for emigration up to September.[42] Some Jews, however, faced devastating news: the Jewish Community simply selected new candidates for emigration if the original applicants had been assigned to agricultural work teams and were considered unavailable during harvest time. The latter thus lost their chance to get out of the Protectorate.[43] In the second half of August, thirty emigrants managed to use the land route through Siberia to the Japanese puppet state of Manchukuo, of whom six travelled on to Shanghai, six to Ecuador and eight to the United States.[44] In mid September, meanwhile, the Jewish Community negotiated with the Soviet Union in an attempt to transport emigrants bound for Shanghai to Vladivostok on two special trains arranged by the Intourist state travel agency.[45]

Overall, at the end of the third quarter, the Jewish Community considered its efforts to have been successful: its officials had opened up new routes through negotiations with the consulates of neutral countries, provided the necessary foreign currency and managed to increase the number of emigrants. Through a concerted effort in collaboration with the Reich Association in Berlin and the Vienna Jewish Community, they had secured passage for emigrants on Japanese and American ships. While Japan issued transit visas enabling emigrants for the United States to depart from Japanese ports after difficult negotiations, talks with the relevant Soviet and Manchurian diplomats concerning the land route were initially beset by severe problems. But the Community managed to overcome them, allowing the departure of all emigrants for Shanghai and the United States.[46] In the third quarter of 1940, 3,305 individuals emigrated from the Protectorate, of whom 2,072 were men, but just 915 women and 314 children.[47]

Because Jews from the Greater German Reich could now obtain certificates for Palestine only if they had been living in neutral countries for an extended period, under Central Office supervision Jewish Community officials increasingly fostered illegal emigration to Palestine.[48] In December 1939, Egon Weiss had signed up for a transport consisting of revisionist Zionists. Departure having been delayed on a number of occasions, in early September 1940, carrying just a rucksack, he finally made the journey by train to Vienna and from there, via Bulgaria, by ship to Palestine.[49] He appears to have departed from Prague along with 651 other members of this 'Special Group' on 2 September.[50]

The Prague Jewish Community sought to enhance the prospects of emigration in multiple ways. In the first week of September, a variety of new retraining courses began in fields such as nursing, confectionery and conversational Hebrew, with more than one hundred participants in total. Existing courses were supplemented with new classes, in which sixty people studied such things as sewing, dry cleaning and cardboard box making.[51] While 140 girls and boys between the ages of fourteen and seventeen learned craft skills in the Youth Aliyah School (Jugend-Alijah-Schule), the Zionist HeHalutz organization concentrated on forging agreements with landowners, the aim being to get young people accustomed to working in forestry and agriculture through the deployment of 'closed groups'.[52]

While just over one thousand individuals were participating in work programmes at the beginning of July, 697 of them through the mediation of the HeHalutz, by the end of September the latter had already found work for 1,308 people, with a further 2,721 engaged in work programmes via the Jewish Employment Office.[53] The number of retraining courses run by the Prague Jewish Community increased from forty-three in early July, with 1,078 participants, to fifty courses, subdivided into eighty-seven classes attended by 1,211 individuals in August. By the end of September, the Community was running forty-eight courses, with almost 1,300 participants, half of them destitute.[54]

The Prague Jewish Community's Sisyphean Task

In July 1940, the Prague Jewish Community spent more than 2.7 million crowns on emigration, more than 1.7 million on cash welfare payments, 850,000 on food, 288,000 on health services, 217,000 on religious and educational needs and more than 550,000 on its employees' wages.[55]

That same month, the Community had a total staff of 812. The increase in comparison with the spring was due to its absorption of the employees of associations and foundations, such as those of the Laemmel Foundation (Laemmelstiftung) in late June, comprising a male administrator and (all females) a cook, a housekeeper, a janitor and five domestic servants. At the start of the second half of the year, 276 individuals worked in the various branches of the Jewish Community's administrative apparatus, 188 in welfare services, 165 in security, the telephone service, as janitors or labourers, 72 in religious, cemetery- or burial-related services, 53 in schools or retraining courses and 28 in the procurement of productive employment.[56]

The Jewish Community kept the Protectorate's Jews abreast of the latest developments through the *Jüdisches Nachrichtenblatt*, to which 8,311 individuals now subscribed. In July, the thirtieth issue, dedicated to topics connected with Eichmann's Central Office one year after its establishment, was published with a print run of 12,500 copies.[57]

In the first week of July 1940, the Social Department ministered to 7,317 people in need, while providing 3,770 individuals with support in the form of cash payments to a total value of 460,000 crowns. The Community's kitchens laid on 12,257 lunches and 7,757 evening meals costing almost 50,000 crowns, while the Clothing Service made available clothing, shoes and furniture to a value of 31,000 crowns. A total of 490 food parcels were distributed to children. Within the framework of its institutional welfare services, the Community looked after 684 Jews in eighteen homes.[58] By the first week of September, Community institutions already housed 738 individuals in seventeen homes and another forty-six in the 'Home for the Feeble-Minded', while providing support to a further fifty-seven individuals dependent on care. At the beginning of September, its noninstitutional services cared for 6,540 needy individuals and provided cash payments to 3,267 to a value of 418,000 crowns. The number of those dependent on such payments had fallen by five hundred over the previous two months, while the number of those registered as in need of support diminished by almost eight hundred. Emigration played an important role here, particularly the Special Group Transports of early September 1940, along with the growing deployment of closed work teams in agriculture and roadbuilding. Yet at the same time poverty surged. The Soup Kitchen now provided the needy with 12,238 lunches and 9,470 evening meals to a value of 69,000 crowns, while 515 children received food parcels. Both the number of meals and cash payments had thus increased (see Table A.3 in the appendix).[59]

In July, Jewish doctors lost their licence to practise, with only a very limited number, namely 140 in private practices and thirty-six in various institutions, allowed to continue to do so. This had an impact on the Jewish Community's health services, with many individuals losing their job and having to be replaced. The Out-Patient Clinic alone treated twenty-four thousand individuals in the third quarter. Due to the necessary reorganization, Jewish Community officials petitioned the Reich protector, but this resulted in partial solutions at best.[60]

On 7 August 1940, the Czech government decreed that Jewish children would be barred from attending Czech public schools starting the next school year.[61] As a result, in September some children between the ages of six and fourteen could not attend school as the Jewish Community lacked both premises and teachers,[62] prompting the Community to direct several petitions to the Department of Education and Culture (Abteilung Unterricht und Kultus) at the Office of the Reich Protector.[63] The Community not only had to dismiss its twelve

'Aryan' employees in September, but, in the course of the 'reorganization' of its administrative structure, also give notice to forty-one office workers with effect from the end of October. By the end of September, it had just 706 members of staff.[64]

At the behest of the Central Office, in autumn 1940 the Prague Jewish Community's Provincial Department reworked the administration of the Jewish Communities, with 129 of them being organized into eighteen districts, in each of which one Community took the lead on administrative matters. The goal was to ensure tighter centralization of the Communities and their finances.[65] Given the Prague Community's heavy burden of responsibilities – in addition to schools, welfare and emigration, it was also in charge of taxing its members and donations as well as the provincial Communities' administration and finances – centralization was an attempt to cut costs.

But Prague Community staff provided support in other ways too. In September 1940, for example, responding to a request from the Moravian Ostrava Jewish Community, they sent several crates of fruit, as it was near-impossible to obtain such unrationed goods there. They supplied other Jewish Communities with food as well.[66]

In the third quarter of 1940, the Jewish Social Institute noted that Community members who had until recently been making donations were now increasingly applying for welfare support, having used up their financial reserves due to lengthy periods of unemployment. While a family of three, even by the most modest of standards, spent 108 crowns a week, of which 39 went on food and drink and 32 on rent for a room with a kitchen, the Prague Social Institute could provide financial support of just 51 crowns, 37 in cash, 9.3 in the form of food and 5.4 in the form of clothing. The Jewish Community, then, could not even cover half of average consumption.[67] In 1940 alone, it thus provided one million meals in soup kitchens. It now operated five old people's homes, two orphanages and ten children's homes with a total of nine hundred residents, while also running two hospitals and a home for the mentally ill. Similar institutions were to be found in Brno and Moravian Ostrava.[68]

Decentralized Ghettoization in the Provinces

In July 1940, the chief county commissioner in Moravian Ostrava claimed to have learned 'by an indirect route' that:

> there is a plan to concentrate the old and infirm Jews from all over the Protectorate in care homes (Versorgungsanstalten) in Prague, Brno and

Moravian Ostrava. Moravian Ostrava is supposed to absorb all Jews from eastern Moravia. The younger Jews are meant to emigrate. Procuring the necessary accommodation will be difficult as this will require the provision of large properties, which are, however, currently unavailable.[69]

But for the time being this plan did not materialize.

In Prague, the Central Office had been regulating the housing market since September and had started to establish 'Jews' houses' in specific districts, but in the provinces the process of concentration had long since begun. The second half of 1940 then saw a dramatic increase in these decentralized efforts to expedite ghettoization. In July, the staff of the Jewish Communities did what they could to help those affected in, for example, Mladá Boleslav, Turnov, Hořice v Podkrkonoší and Jičín. In Březnice (Bresnitz) too, Jews had to vacate their homes at short notice due to a 'resettlement drive', among them the head of the local Jewish Community.[70] In Jičín and Mladá Boleslav the campaign was over by the end of July. Henceforth, 256 Jews from the latter town as well as from Mnichovo Hradiště and Bělá pod Bezdězem (Weißwasser) had to live in an old castle. In Hořice v Podkrkonoší, all the local Jews now lived either in the Hirsch factory or in a small house next to the synagogue, having vacated their homes and handed over the Jewish school as well. In Nové Benátky the Jewish community resided in the storeroom of the Silvia factory, while in Lysá nad Labem all the local Jews as well as those from the Byšicky (Bischitschek) district and Litol were accommodated in the Blaupunkt factory. In Turnov, on the other hand, the local Jews were forced to move into a street comprising a number of 'Jewish' buildings and one 'Aryan building'.[71]

In the district under the Königgrätz Chief County Commissioner's Office, the authorities were gearing up for a campaign, planned for late July, 'with the goal of concentrating Jewish homes', but the Prague Community lodged an objection with the Central Office, which blocked the plan.[72] In several other locations in the Protectorate, however, Jews had to vacate their houses or flats and move into dwellings inhabited by Jews.[73]

Prague Community officials also discussed these plans with representatives of the Communities affected. In Lysá nad Labem and Nové Benátky, the Prague functionaries investigated the implementation of the 'resettlement' policy and inspected the local families' new dwellings.[74] On 6 August, the head of the Prague Community's Provincial Department visited the town of Čáslav (Tschaslau), in order to discuss with local Jewish representatives and the relevant authorities the 'concentration of Jews in flats as decreed [there] or the mandated vacating of

Jewish flats and houses'.[75] Though Community officials lodged protests with the Central Office, the 'Housing campaign' in Čáslav continued until mid August.[76]

New 'resettlement campaigns' were also launched in the third week of August, in Nový Bydžov (Neu Bidschow) and Libochovice (Libochowitz) for example. The Jewish Communities intervened and at least succeeded in getting a number of deadlines extended.[77] In early September, Jews in Vyškov were supposed to abandon their homes, which the Jewish Community initially managed to prevent by appealing to the Central Office.[78] In the second week of September, meanwhile, the Jews of Holešov faced a 'resettlement campaign'; Jewish officials negotiated with the authorities concerning the number of homes to be vacated and their future designation. In Mělník (Melnik), the District Office ordered Jewish homeowners to sell their properties, though this directive was rescinded following intervention by the Central Office.[79] In mid September, 'resettlement campaigns' began in areas under the remit of the Jewish Communities of Benešov (Beneschau), Hořovice (Horschowitz), Hostomice (Hostomitz) and Kostel, as the Prague Community reported to the Central Office.[80] The Central Office put a stop to the resettlement drive in Vyškov but not in Sušice (Schüttenhofen).[81] In the third quarter of 1940, these ghettoization campaigns took place in more than twenty-five localities in total.[82]

In Prague, in early September 1940, the Housing Service provided help at short notice for 120 individuals who had arrived on transports from the provinces, housing some of them in private accommodation and others in the Jewish Community's own premises.[83] The acute situation was exacerbated by the fact that, as addressed above, in Greater Prague Jews were now allowed to patronize just two lodging houses, namely 'Fišer' and 'Star' in Prague II.[84]

In parallel to the ghettoization campaigns in the provinces, which often had local origins, the Central Office now sought to concentrate the Jewish population in Prague. In July 1940, by order of the Central Office, the Prague Jewish Community summoned one hundred individuals, who had to fill out forms transferring ownership of their homes, in District VII, to the 'Emigration Fund for Bohemia and Moravia'. The Community also procured the requisite cadastral forms.[85] This campaign dragged on until September, while another housing drive had already begun in Prague-Smichov.[86]

Paula Fröhlich and her husband were forced to vacate their original home in Prague in April 1940 and move into a four-room flat in an old building on Pařížská Street (Pariskastraße). In November they were then ordered to give up two rooms to two different families and later, in

February 1941, a third room to another family. The Fröhlichs suffered a massive reduction in the space available to them while also having to get rid of much of their furniture. Not only that, but the extremely overcrowded conditions and the shared use of the grossly inadequate sanitary and cooking facilities soon sparked interpersonal tensions.[87]

All over Prague, meanwhile, the authorities expropriated villas in particular to satisfy the needs of prominent buyers. In August 1940, Mr and Mrs Waigner lost their six-room property, featuring central heating and a bath, in District XII, which they had had built in 1923. Prior to the occupation, Emil Waigner had worked as a bank manager and was a member of several boards of directors. Despite being non-religious, as they had been declared Jews they had to make over their house to the Emigration Fund and vacate it immediately. New Prague residents Friedrich Klausing and his wife acquired the villa at far below its true value; Klausing had just been appointed professor of law and later became rector of Charles University.[88] Georgine Hyde's family had to abandon their house to make way for an officer in the Abwehr military intelligence service, who kept on all their domestic servants. They moved into a rented flat in the older part of Prague, where each Jewish family was allocated just one room.[89] In Brno, the process of concentrating Jews in 'Jews' houses' began in the last few months of 1940.[90]

'Aryanization'

Blackmail, ghettoization, the prospect of emigration and sheer hardship prompted an increasing number of Jews to quickly sell their properties. In November 1940, the chief county commissioner in Moravian Ostrava expressed his satisfaction in a report to the Office of the Reich Protector on the 'Aryanization' of real estate. It seemed, he wrote, that 'de-Judaization is now gaining greater momentum', as Jews were 'more willing to let go' (of their property).[91]

On 1 October 1940, after ten months' delay in order to avoid economic problems, the German authorities abolished the customs frontier between the Protectorate of Bohemia and Moravia and the German Reich.[92] This made it easier for Reich Germans to 'Aryanize' Jewish property, though much depended on the potential purchasers' contacts as well as local interests.[93] The termination of the customs frontier, however, did not mean the formal incorporation of the Protectorate into the Greater German Reich, because earlier, as Reichsführer-SS and head of the German Police, Himmler had mandated the establishment of a police border, to be secured by the Order Police on the German side and by the Czech police in the Protectorate.[94]

Around the same time, in early October, the Czech exile government in London received a report from Prague that included discussion of the massive 'wave of Aryanization'. The authors requested that radio broadcasts warn the Czech people to refrain from involvement in this theft while also announcing that after the war all expropriated property would be regarded as stolen and would have to be returned to its previous owners. Many Czechs, including no fewer than four hundred former officers, had in fact applied for trusteeships, but due to German dominance only a few such requests had been granted.[95]

However, by autumn 1940, the Böhmische Escompte-Bank, owned by the Dresdner Bank since February 1939, was already reporting to Otto Karl Kain, SS special commissioner (SS-Sonderbeauftragter), that there was 'no longer any significant de-Judaized property available for a new applicant'.[96] In March 1941, sources in Switzerland noted that all Jewish industrial and commercial enterprises in the Protectorate had either been liquidated or 'Aryanized', or functioned under trusteeship.[97]

Since March 1939, German businessmen and merchants, as well as individuals previously unfamiliar with their fields of activity, had been engaged in a race to acquire worthwhile 'Aryanization properties' in every economic sector in the Protectorate. By the beginning of 1941 – in addition to real estate, shops and firms – savings deposits, cash and foreign currency to a total value of around 1.8 billion crowns had been confiscated in the course of 'Aryanization'. Within eight months, German trustees had stripped local Jewish businesses of 2.5 million crowns. Most German trustees came from the Sudetenland; in the area under the administration of the Olomouc Chief County Commissioner's Office, for example, 188 of 195 trustees were Sudeten Germans.[98] The German banks, particularly the Dresdner Bank, made a substantial profit processing such transactions, which they arranged via their Czech business partners.[99]

This mass theft by no means occurred without public awareness. In autumn 1941, *Der Neue Tag* newspaper published information on the transfer of ownership, such as the document (Zustellungsurkunde) issued by the Pardubice chief county commissioner notifying Franz Kaufmann of the forced Aryanization of his carpet business in Hlinsko; one sent by the chief county commissioner in Jihlava instructing the absent Hermann Haas to sell his property; and one issued by the Reich protector advising shareholders with a stake in the Lomnitz textiles works and silk and woollen goods factories to sell their holdings, otherwise a trustee would be appointed in all cases.[100]

Often, the 'Aryanization' of factories and businesses brought the 'Aryanization' of housing in its wake. For example, in July 1941 – with reference to his 'Aryanization' of the Karl Diamant firm located on Prague's Wenceslas Square – a Reich German by the name of Koch, a former member of the Wehrmacht who had recently moved from Munich, asked the Central Administration in the Office of the Reich Protector to allocate him a flat on Sokolská (Sokolstraße), previously home to a Jewish tenant named Feigl. To step up the pressure, he had involved the Wehrmacht Housing Office (Wehrmachtswohnungsamt), part of the Prague Garrison Headquarters (Standortkommandantur).[101]

Group Deployment and Local Forced Labour

Though the forced labour deployment of Jews had long been practised in Germany and Austria and – as an element in their radicalized 'Jewish policy' – the Czech fascists went so far as to demand its implementation, it was never officially introduced in the Protectorate.[102] At the beginning of July 1940, 58 per cent of Jewish men in the Protectorate were unemployed, while the remaining 42 per cent were still working, a few of them in those free professions still permissible for Jews, perhaps 15 per cent in trade, commerce and crafts, and a little over 20 per cent in manual labour and other unskilled roles.[103]

The latter category included group deployments (Gruppeneinsatz) in agriculture and roadbuilding. As it had already done in the first half of the year, the Prague Jewish Community's Employment Office sought to place groups of unemployed individuals with private businesses, whether farmers or roadbuilding firms. To this end, it could draw on the so-called Occupational Index (Berufskartei), which by now held details on 18,167 men between the ages of sixteen and fifty with information on age, occupation, citizenship, capacity for work, employment and so on. By late September 1940, of those listed in the Index, 1,500 had looked for work themselves, 2,721 were placed in group deployments by the Jewish Employment Office or Jewish Communities and 1,308 were employed by the HeHalutz.[104] In finding work for the unemployed, the Jewish Employment Office aimed to endow them with practical knowledge of value to emigrants while also freeing the Jewish Welfare Service of the need to support them.[105]

Initially, in numerical terms the Jewish Employment Office was not particularly successful. In the first week of July, a group of eleven men made the trip to Lysá nad Labem to carry out street repairs, the firm Prášák & Co. again requested fifteen Jews for motorway building, while five men and two women were placed with the Xaver Estate near Březnice as seasonal workers.[106] In the second week of July, the Employment Office found work for just twenty more workers in roadbuilding in Lysá nad Labem and for six in seasonal positions at the Slavoňov (Slowoniow) estate near Mileŝov (Mileschau) in the District of Tábor (Tabor),[107] while in the third week it procured employment for forty men in motorway building.[108] By the end of July, 3,243 unemployed individuals had registered with the Jewish Employment Office, which had so far managed to find jobs for 1,025 of them, albeit often on a short-term basis.[109]

Despite the fact that the central authorities had as yet issued no directives of any kind concerning forced labour, amidst the general radicalization of anti-Jewish policy local administrations now implemented their own measures. The first major Jewish forced labour group in Prague was established in 1940 to work at the municipal refuse incineration plant; its members were former white-collar workers in receipt of state unemployment benefits.[110] In early July, the Holešov Town Council resolved to request permission from the District Authority to introduce 'compulsory labour for Jews'.[111] Regardless of the lack of central regulations, a form of forced labour comparable to that in Germany or Austria soon developed on the local level. In mid August, the towns of Klatovy and Jičín enlisted local Jews for labour deployment. While Klatovy quickly rescinded this measure, in Jičín twenty men had to report for duty by order of the chief county commissioner.[112]

At the same time, the Jewish Community continued to seek employment for groups of workers on estates and in roadbuilding, while also sounding out possible work in hop- and flax-picking by liaising with the Prague Labour Office. While the estate owner in Slavoňov had already laid off his Jewish workers by early August, the Fosista firm in Prague again requested twenty men for roadbuilding in Starý Vestec (Alt-Westetz) near Lysá nad Labem. Another business requested twenty Jews for motorway construction in Průhonice (Pruhonitz) near Prague. Meanwhile, the Jewish Employment Office negotiated with Ing. Belada & Co. on the possible dispatch of twenty men to work in the regulation of the Vltava in Braník (Branik).[113]

In early September, the head of the Jewish Community's Provincial Department discussed Jewish group deployment with the chief county commissioner in Mělník (Melnik) but the latter underlined that when it came to border districts under his authority, the 'labour deployment of Jews is not permitted'.[114] The Jewish Community continued to struggle to find jobs for more than a few work teams, comprising twenty-five individuals in the second week of September, of whom seventeen were women placed in Jewish households, with just eight men obtaining work in construction.[115] Towards the end of the month there was just one request for eighteen workers, namely from the kaolin factories in Horní Bříza (Ober-Birken). By this point in time, 3,611 unemployed individuals had registered with the Jewish Community.[116]

Max Mannheimer, who survived the Second World War, described his situation in 1940 near the Slovakian border as follows: 'I'm doing roadbuilding work now ... During the week my quarters are a wooden hut behind the toolshed. ... My work colleagues, all of whom are Czech, are friendly to me and treat me as an equal. ... The roadbuilding can't feed the family on its own. We've long since used up our reserves'.[117] So while the pay was very poor, in cases of closed labour deployment the authorities in the Protectorate did not enforce the separation of Jewish workers as strictly as in the rest of the Reich. This was both because the Jewish Community often arranged such deployments directly with firms and because, in cases where the German labour offices made the arrangements, they are likely to have viewed Czechs and Jews as similarly 'inferior' groups.[118]

Due to the exclusion of Jewish children from public schools, an increasing number of adolescents ended up in forced labour units.[119] Ruth Felix, who lived in the town of Stráznice (Straßnitz) in Moravia, was forced to leave her secondary school (Gymnasium) at the age of fifteen. Subsequently, until late 1940, she worked on agricultural estates owned by Germans, helping in the fields at harvest time and mucking out the stables.[120]

This period appears to have seen the creation of the first labour camps run by Jewish Communities, in other words similar to those maintained by the Reich Association in Germany.[121] In August, in Malokuncic (Klein Kuntschitz, District of Frýdava [Friedau]), the Moravian Ostrava Jewish Community established a 'labour camp', which became home to fifty-two Jews.[122] As in the Reich, in most cases this is likely to have been a matter of genuine labour deployment rather than training in preparation for emigration. The twenty men in the 'Hluboš Workers' Group', for example, carried out forestry work, supposedly in preparation for their emigration to Santo Domingo.[123]

In July 1940, the Central Office for Jewish Emigration tasked the Prague Jewish Community with providing a construction detail (Aufbaukommando) for a 'Linden (Lípa) school estate' near Německý Brod.[124] The Jewish Community negotiated with the Prague city authorities on the allocation of ration coupons to ensure the workers had the necessary equipment.[125] On 15 July an advance party of thirty Jewish workers, under the command of two construction specialists, arrived at the estate. With great rapidity, they levelled the terrain and erected three barracks for four hundred men.[126]

At the beginning of August, the Jewish Employment Office, which went so far as to assign a member of its staff specifically to procure workers for this estate, dispatched another eighty-six men.[127] The Jewish Community's Social Department was unable to provide those Jews sent in the third week of August with shoes and working clothes as it had run out of them. Upon arrival, therefore, the oldest member of the group was to draw up a list of individuals in need of such items and apply to the Central Office for ration coupons, after obtaining the countersignature of SS-Hauptscharführer (head squadron leader) Neubert.[128] In September, the Jewish Community took out accident insurance for 250 'retrainees'. This group comprised 200 men by the end of August, already reaching 304 by the end of September and 340 in October.[129]

From getting up in the morning through the midday break to the evening rollcall and going to sleep, the daily routine in the camp was governed by strict rules, which also regulated leisure time. The Jewish inmates worked in the estate's fields, garden, stables and workshops but also in railway construction and snow-clearing.[130] Under Austrian camp chief SS-Hauptscharführer Lederer, the 'retrainees' were not permitted to leave the premises and were required to repair storm damage and clear snow drifts on the local roads. Meagre provisions fuelled the

Figure 6.1. Inmates of the Linden SS Camp working in forestry, 1940. © USHMM Washington, Photo Archive, no. 51981.

hard work: coffee and a little bread in the morning, mostly potatoes at lunchtime and soup in the evening. Evidently, the Jewish inmates were regularly replaced by fresh workers after several months.[131]

In contrast to most other retraining camps in Germany and Austria, which were run by Jewish Communities or organizations, this camp was headed by a representative of the Central Office for Jewish Emigration in Prague. In this respect it resembled the Vienna Central Office's two so-called retraining camps of Doppl and Sandhof, which were in reality SS-run forced labour camps.[132] This may have been the main reason why the Prague Community struggled to repeatedly find three hundred men between the ages of eighteen and forty-five for three months of 'retraining' in Linden, as many of them regarded a stint at the camp as punishment.[133]

Following the issuance of another decree, on 14 September 1940, which ramped up the dismissal of Jewish employees,[134] in early December the Office of the Reich Protector in Bohemia and Moravia finally published an initial labour regulation that took its lead from the situation of Jewish forced labourers in Germany. This was a prohibition on Jews receiving paid leave during the statutory holidays at the turn of the year.[135] By way of contrast, however, in the first instance the authorities in the Protectorate did not introduce the special tax that had existed in Germany and Austria since the end of 1940, called the 'Social Equalization Tax for Jews' (Sozialausgleichsabgabe für Juden), because no comprehensive forced labour programme existed as yet.[136]

In Prague, as in other cities in the Greater German Reich, the authorities now began to deploy Jews to clear snow. Georgine Hyde's father was summoned to remove snow from a bridge, where he worked with a group of Jewish intellectuals.[137] During Christmas 1940, Petr Ginz's father slaved away for a total of five days at the airport in Kbely (Gbel), where the slush stood several decimetres high. He caught a cold while doing so.[138] The ongoing malnourishment suffered by Jews had left him highly susceptible to infection.

* * *

Towards the end of September 1940, the Jewish population in the Protectorate sank to 90,681 individuals (see Table A.1 in the appendix). While 24,998 Jews had managed to emigrate since the occupation began, 2,820 had died during this period, while the Jewish Communities registered just 189 births.[139] These figures are testimony both to an ageing Jewish population and to the consequences of anti-Jewish policy.

The second half of 1940 too was characterized by attempts to centralize such policy, which now took on a medium-term orientation, chiefly because the deportations had been kicked into the long grass. In

September, the Central Office for Jewish Emigration extended its remit to include the housing market and began to concentrate Jews in specific districts of Prague in so-called Jews' houses, cooperating to this end with the Prague city government and the local branch of the Nazi Party.

In August, the Commander of the Security Police tried to seize the initiative with respect to the segregation of Jews in public spaces. But he acted too late. In July 1940, in response to the local initiatives taken in the first half of the year, without his knowledge the Czech Interior Ministry, eager to ensure uniform regulations, had already decreed most of the measures demanded by the commander. The local authorities implemented these new rules at the ministry's behest, including special shopping hours for Jews, their exclusion from public schools and the prohibition on entering restaurants and parks.

The centralization drive, however, by no means gained the upper hand, as countless new local initiatives spawned during the second half of 1940 accelerated the isolation of the Jewish population. The intensified campaigns of ghettoization stood out here. In the third quarter of 1940 alone, twenty-five local authorities forced Jews to leave their homes and move into designated streets, abandoned factory buildings or old, deserted castles.

Many Jews tried to escape ghettoization and move to Prague. There, the Jewish Community's finances were increasingly stretched to breaking point, with outgoings far exceeding income. It spent vast sums on its renewed efforts to promote forced emigration – now possible, on a legal basis, almost exclusively to Shanghai and on an illegal one to Palestine – as well as on providing support to an increasingly impoverished Jewish population.

The Jewish Community's income, from both donations and taxes, diminished. Often, its compulsory members no longer drew a salary and had lost other forms of income due to the confiscation of their homes, as in Prague, or the 'Aryanization' of their property. By the end of 1940, the authorities regarded the 'Aryanization' of Jewish property – whose main beneficiaries were Germans and which encompassed not just real estate and businesses but also securities and the like – as essentially complete.

To support emigration but above all in order to stem its burgeoning welfare expenditure, the Prague Community organized more retraining programmes and continued to negotiate with labour offices and private businesses to facilitate the group deployment of Jewish workers, initially with limited success in numerical terms. The first municipal administrations now recruited Jews for local forced labour programmes, while the Central Office established the Linden forced labour camp.

Notes

1. YV Jerusalem, O 7/55, fol. 149: Report by the Jewish Religious Community and the Prague Palestine Office on their activities in the first half of 1940, Chart: 'Population movement among Jews in the Protectorate of Bohemia and Moravia'.
2. King, *Budweisers*, 181.
3. Rothkirchen, *Jews*, 211–13.
4. YV Jerusalem, O 7/55, fol. 56 and 58: Weekly report Jewish Religious Community of Prague, 11–17 May 1940, 5 and 7.
5. USHMM Washington, RG 48.005M, reel 4 (Prague State Archive), Marking of Jews, carton 389, I-3b-5851, no. 4, n.p.: Olomouc chief county commissioner to Reich protector, 13 June 1940.
6. Ibid., reel 4 (Prague State Archive), carton 389, I-3b-5850, no. 28, n.p.: Reich protector to chief county commissioner in Zlín, 10 July 1940. See Machala, 'Unbearable Jewish Houses of Prayer', 69.
7. YV Jerusalem, O 7/56, fol. 274: Report by the Jewish Religious Community and the Prague Palestine Office on their activities in the third quarter of 1940, submitted to the Central Office for Jewish Emigration, Prague, 37.
8. USHMM Washington, RG 48.005M, reel 1 (Prague State Archive, Interior Ministry: Jewish regulations), no. 44, n.p.: Circular decree issued by the Ministry of the Interior, Prague, to the State Authorities, 9 July 1940.
9. Gruner, *Zwangsarbeit und Verfolgung*, 127; Wolf Gruner, *The Persecution of the Jews in Berlin 1933–1945: A Chronology of Measures by Authorities in the German Capital*, translation of the second substantially extended and revised edition (Berlin, 2014), 137.
10. Report 'The Legal Position of Jews', in Krejčová, Svobodová and Hyndráková, *Židé v Protektorátu*, doc. 15, 246. See *Jüdisches Nachrichtenblatt*, Prague edition, 13 August 1940; Bondy, 'Chronik der sich schließenden Tore', 95.
11. YV Jerusalem, O 7/56, fol. 84: Weekly report Jewish Religious Community of Prague, 10–16 August 1940, 8.
12. Institute of Jewish Affairs, *Hitler's Ten-Year War*, 59.
13. BA Berlin, R 30/4c, fol. 3: Chief County Commissioner/Dept. III, Administrative report, 15th copy, secret, general political situation, Moravian Ostrava, 20 August 1940, 2. On supply policy in a specific district, see the dissertation soon to be published by Jan Vondráček (Wuppertal/Prague), 'Besatzungsherrschaft als soziale Praxis: Zwangsabgaben und Versorgung im Protektorat Böhmen und Mähren. Der politische Bezirk Kladno 1939–1945'.
14. BA Berlin, R 30/4c, fol. 156: Chief County Commissioner, Administrative report for the month of March 1941, general political situation, Moravian Ostrava, 20 March 1941, 9.
15. USHMM Washington, RG 48.005M, reel 3 (Prague State Archive), no. 60, n.p.: Circular decree Reich protector/BdS II 1305-6/40 (signed Frank), 17 August 1940.
16. Report 'The Legal Position of Jews', in Krejčová, Svobodová and Hyndráková, *Židé v Protektorátu*, doc. 15, 246–49. For more examples providing evidence of this, see Gruner, 'Das Protektorat Böhmen/Mähren', 42.
17. USHMM Washington, RG 45.005M, reel 1 (Prague State Archive, Ministry of the Interior), no. 42, n.p.: Copy Presidium Ministry of the Interior to Presidium State Authorities Prague and Brno, 22 June 1940; ibid., no. 1, n.p.: List of the legal

regulations issued by the Ministry of the Interior concerning Jews or Jewish halfbreeds (Mischlinge), 25 September 1940, 1.
18. USC SF/VHA, video interview, Alfred Dube, tape 2, min. 00:37–3:35.
19. Report 'The Legal Position of Jews', in Krejčová, Svobodová and Hyndráková, *Židé v Protektorátu*, doc. 15, 256. See also YV Jerusalem, O 7/56, fol. 153: Weekly report Jewish Religious Community of Prague, 7–13 September 1940, 7; Institute of Jewish Affairs, *Hitler's Ten-Year War*, 57.
20. YV Jerusalem, O 7/56, fol. 153: Weekly report Jewish Religious Community of Prague, 7–13 September 1940, 7.
21. Ibid., fol. 263: Report by the Jewish Religious Community and the Prague Palestine Office on their activities in the third quarter of 1940, 26; Report Jewish Religious Community of Prague 'Special Actions' (1942), in Krejčová, Svobodová and Hyndráková, *Židé v Protektorátu*, doc. 14, 227.
22. YV Jerusalem, O 7/56, fol. 41: Weekly report Jewish Religious Community of Prague, 20–26 July 1940, 3.
23. Ibid., fol. 227: Monthly report Jewish Religious Community of Prague, 1–30 September 1940, 4.
24. Ibid., fol. 187: Weekly report Jewish Religious Community of Prague, 21–27 September 1940, 3.
25. Sedláková, '"Burza" s židovskými byty', 208.
26. YV Jerusalem, O 7/56, fol. 263: Report by the Jewish Religious Community and the Prague Palestine Office on their activities in the third quarter of 1940, 26; Report Jewish Religious Community of Prague 'Special Actions' (1942), in Krejčová, Svobodová and Hyndráková, *Židé v Protektorátu*, doc. 14, 227.
27. USHMM Washington, RG 48.005M, reel 5 (Prague State Archive), I 3b-5800 carton 387, no. 5, n.p.: Note Reich protector I 3b, 26 September 1940. See Copy of the decree, 28 December 1939, in VEJ/2, doc. 215, 583–84.
28. Report 'The Legal Position of Jews', in Krejčová, Svobodová and Hyndráková, *Židé v Protektorátu*, doc. 15, 256. See Institute of Jewish Affairs, *Hitler's Ten-Year War*, 57. Facsimile of the copy of the decree in the *Jüdisches Nachrichtenblatt*, 18 October 1940, in Ruth Bondy, *Trapped: Essays on the History of the Czech Jews, 1939–1945* (Jerusalem, 2008), 26.
29. Gruner, 'Local Initiatives, Central Coordination', 275–76.
30. Report Pfitzner to Frank, 25 September to 28 October 1940, 31 October 1940, in Šustek, *Josef Pfitzner*, doc. 6, 89–90; cf. Report Pfitzner to Frank, 30 October to 5 December 1940, 6 December 1940, in ibid., doc. 7, 98.
31. Report 'The Legal Position of Jews', in Krejčová, Svobodová and Hyndráková, *Židé v Protektorátu*, doc. 15, 246–47; Institute of Jewish Affairs, *Hitler's Ten-Year War*, 59; according to the *Jüdisches Nachrichtenblatt*, Prague edition: Bondy, 'Chronik der sich schließenden Tore', 94–95.
32. See 'Report by the representative of the Foreign Office in the Office of the Reich Protector, 29 October 1940', in Mund, *Deutschland und das Protektorat*, doc. 315, 460–61.
33. Jiří Orten, Prague, Diary entry, 26 October 1940, reprinted in English in Garbarini et al., *Jewish Responses*, 311–12.
34. Report 'The Legal Position of Jews', in Krejčová, Svobodová and Hyndráková, *Židé v Protektorátu*, doc. 15, 246–47; Institute of Jewish Affairs, *Hitler's Ten-Year War*, 59; according to the *Jüdisches Nachrichtenblatt*, Prague edition: Bondy, 'Chronik der sich schließenden Tore', 94–95.
35. YV Jerusalem, O 7/56, fol. 275: Report by the Jewish Religious Community and the Prague Palestine Office on their activities in the third quarter of 1940, 38.

36. YV Jerusalem, M 58/JM 11812, fol. 441: Registration, 28 October 1940; ibid., O 7/56, fol. 174: Weekly report Jewish Religious Community of Prague, 14–20 September 1940, 9.
37. YV Jerusalem, M 58/JM 11814, fol. 122: Registration of assets of the Neu-Straschitz Israelite Burial Fraternity, 31 October 1940.
38. YV Jerusalem, M 58/JM 11816, fol. 244: Directive Jewish Religious Community of Moravian Ostrava, 27 September 1940.
39. On the basis of similar restrictions in Breslau in autumn 1939, as depicted in the diary of Willy Cohn; cf. Guy Miron's interesting remarks in '"Lately, Almost Constantly, Everything Seems Small to Me": The Lived Space of German Jews under the Nazi Regime', *Jewish Social Studies* 20(1) (Autumn 2014), 121–49, here 133–34.
40. BA Berlin, R 30/4c, fol. 21: Chief County Commissioner/Dept. III, Administrative report, 15th copy, confidential, general political situation, Moravian Ostrava, 20 September 1940, 3.
41. YV Jerusalem, O 7/56, fol. 202–3: Monthly report Jewish Religious Community of Prague, 1–30 July 1940, 1–2; ibid., fol. 217–18: Monthly report Jewish Religious Community of Prague, 1–31 August 1940, 1–2; ibid., fol. 224–25: Monthly report Jewish Religious Community of Prague, 1–30 September 1940, 1–2.
42. Ibid., fol. 64: Weekly report Jewish Religious Community of Prague, 3–9 August 1940, 1.
43. Ibid., fol. 77: Weekly report Jewish Religious Community of Prague, 10–16 August 1940, 9.
44. Ibid., fol. 111: Weekly report Jewish Religious Community of Prague, 24–30 August 1940, 1.
45. Ibid., fol. 165: Weekly report Jewish Religious Community of Prague, 14–20 September 1940, 1.
46. Ibid., fol. 237–42: Report by the Jewish Religious Community and the Prague Palestine Office on their activities in the third quarter of 1940, 3–7.
47. Ibid., fol. 245: Report by the Jewish Religious Community and the Prague Palestine Office on their activities in the third quarter of 1940, 10.
48. Ibid., fol. 242–44: Report by the Jewish Religious Community and the Prague Palestine Office on their activities in the third quarter of 1940, 7–9.
49. Egon Weiss, Diary, entry written in 1946, in Garbarini et al., *Jewish Responses*, 258–59.
50. YV Jerusalem, O 7/56, fol. 129: Weekly report Jewish Religious Community of Prague, 31 August to 6 September 1940, 1.
51. Ibid., fol. 132: Weekly report Jewish Religious Community of Prague, 31 August to 6 September 1940, 4.
52. Ibid., fol. 250: Report by the Jewish Religious Community and the Prague Palestine Office on their activities in the third quarter of 1940, 16.
53. Ibid., fol. 251–52: Report by the Jewish Religious Community and the Prague Palestine Office on their activities in the third quarter of 1940, Chart 'Deployment of Jewish Workers' and 17.
54. Ibid., fol. 220: Monthly report Jewish Religious Community of Prague, 1–31 August 1940, 4; ibid., fol. 250: Report by the Jewish Religious Community and the Prague Palestine Office on their activities in the third quarter of 1940, 16.
55. Ibid., fol. 215–16: Monthly report Jewish Religious Community of Prague, 1–30 July 1940, Appendix, 2–3: Overview of Income and Expenditure for the Month of July 1940.
56. Ibid., fol. 31: Weekly report Jewish Religious Community of Prague, 13–19 July 1940, 7.

57. Ibid., fol. 43: Weekly report Jewish Religious Community of Prague, 20–26 July 1940, 5.
58. Ibid., fol. 4: Weekly report Jewish Religious Community of Prague, 29 June to 5 July 1940, 3.
59. Ibid., fol. 131: Weekly report Jewish Religious Community of Prague, 31 August to 6 September 1940, 3.
60. Ibid., fol. 264–65, 274: Report by the Jewish Religious Community and the Prague Palestine Office on their activities in the third quarter of 1940, 27–28, 37.
61. Friedmann, 'Rechtsstellung', in Krejčová, Svobodová and Hyndráková, *Židé v Protektorátu*, 261 f.
62. YV Jerusalem, O 7/56, fol. 229: Monthly report Jewish Religious Community of Prague, 1–30 September 1940, 6.
63. Ibid., fol. 269: Report by the Jewish Religious Community and the Prague Palestine Office on their activities in the third quarter of 1940, 32.
64. Ibid., fol. 190–91: Weekly report Jewish Religious Community of Prague, 21–27 September 1940, 6–7; ibid., fol. 231: Monthly report Jewish Religious Community of Prague, 1–30 September 1940, 8.
65. Ibid., fol. 272: Report by the Jewish Religious Community and the Prague Palestine Office on their activities in the third quarter of 1940, 35.
66. Ibid., fol. 170–74: Weekly report Jewish Religious Community of Prague, 14–20 September 1940, 6–9.
67. Ibid., fol. 255–59: Report by the Jewish Religious Community and the Prague Palestine Office on their activities in the third quarter of 1940, 20–24.
68. According to the *Jüdisches Nachrichtenblatt*, 3 April 1941; Moskowitz, 'The Jewish Situation', 21–22.
69. BA Berlin, R 30/4b, fol. 144–45: Chief County Commissioner/II, General administrative report, economic issues, 15th copy, secret, Moravian Ostrava, 1 July 1940, 4–5.
70. YV Jerusalem, O 7/56, fol. 32: Weekly report Jewish Religious Community of Prague, 13–19 July 1940, 8.
71. Ibid., fol. 211: Monthly report Jewish Religious Community of Prague, 1–30 July 1940, 10.
72. Ibid., fol. 44–45: Weekly report Jewish Religious Community of Prague, 20–26 July 1940, 7–8; ibid., fol. 211: Monthly report Jewish Religious Community of Prague, 1–30 July 1940, 10.
73. Ibid., fol. 44–45: Weekly report Jewish Religious Community of Prague, 20–26 July 1940, 7–8.
74. Ibid., fol. 44–45: Weekly report Jewish Religious Community of Prague, 20–26 July 1940, 7–8.
75. Ibid., fol. 72: Weekly report Jewish Religious Community of Prague, 3–9 August 1940, 9.
76. Ibid., fol. 83: Weekly report Jewish Religious Community of Prague, 10–16 August 1940, 7.
77. Ibid., fol. 104: Weekly report Jewish Religious Community of Prague, 17–23 August 1940, 10.
78. Ibid., fol. 136: Weekly report Jewish Religious Community of Prague, 31 August to 6 September 1940, 8.
79. Ibid., fol. 152: Weekly report Jewish Religious Community of Prague, 7–13 September 1940, 6.
80. Ibid., fol. 173: Weekly report Jewish Religious Community of Prague, 14–20 September 1940, 8.

81. Ibid., fol. 232: Monthly report Jewish Religious Community of Prague, 1–30 September 1940, 9.
82. Ibid., fol. 272: Report by the Jewish Religious Community and the Prague Palestine Office on their activities in the third quarter of 1940, 35.
83. Ibid., fol. 131: Weekly report Jewish Religious Community of Prague, 31 August to 6 September 1940, 3.
84. Friedmann, 'Rechtsstellung', in Krejčová, Svobodová and Hyndráková, *Židé v Protektorátu*, 246; see also YV Jerusalem, O 7/56, fol. 153: Weekly report Jewish Religious Community of Prague, 7–13 September 1940, 7.
85. Ibid., fol. 26: Weekly report Jewish Religious Community of Prague, 13–19 July 1940, 2; ibid., fol. 40: Weekly report Jewish Religious Community of Prague, 20–26 July 1940, 2.
86. Ibid., fol. 166: Weekly report Jewish Religious Community of Prague, 14–20 September 1940, 2.
87. Letters by Paula Fröhlich, 7 April, (?) August and 8 November 1940, and 17 February 1941, in *Letters from Prague 1939–1941*, compiled by Raya Czerner Shapiro and Helga Czerner Weinberg (Chicago, 1991), 106, 118, 140 and 153.
88. Später, *Villa Waigner*, 52–57.
89. USC SF/VHA, video interview, Georgine Hyde, tape 2, min. 11:12–13:00.
90. USC SF/VHA, video interview, Helen Blenkins, tape 1, min. 8:54–10:00.
91. BA Berlin, R 30/4c, fol. 64: Chief County Commissioner/Dept. III, Administrative report, confidential, general political situation, Moravian Ostrava, 20 November 1940, 21.
92. BA Berlin, R 43II/1324b, fol. 34: Note Lammers (Reich Chancellery), 24 September 1940. On the delay, see unsigned note, 23 February 1940, in Mund, *Deutschland und das Protektorat*, doc. 220, 325–26; cf. ibid., doc. 226, 331–33.
93. See, for example, the negotiations on the acquisition by two Berlin-based Nazi Party Ortsgruppenleiter (local group leaders) of the Weiss & Sons jute spinning factory in Dvůr Králové nad Labem (Königinhof an der Elbe), which lasted from summer 1940 to August 1941 and involved both the Reich Ministry of the Economy and the Reich Chancellery; BA Berlin, R 43II/1325b, fol. 61–122.
94. BA Berlin, R 43II/1324b, fol. 36–37: Telex Reich Ministry of the Interior Stuckart to Reich protector in Prague, 27 September 1940. Furthermore, the abolition of the customs frontier did not engender the free movement of goods, as it was accompanied by a series of prohibitions on their consignment. These were intended to prevent economic upheaval and unrest in the Protectorate of the kind that might result from the 'sudden outflow of the remaining supplies into the Old Reich': even when the customs frontier had existed, a tremendous quantity of goods had drained out of the Protectorate. Ibid., fol. 38+RS: Express letter (copy) Reich Ministry of the Interior Stuckart to Reich Ministry for Food and Agriculture (Reichministerium für Ernährung und Landwirtschaft) and Reich Ministry of Economics, 1 October 1940; ibid., fol. 39–40: Telex (copy) Reich protector, on behalf of Frank, to Reich Ministry of the Interior Stuckart, 30 September 1940. See also 'Report by the representative of the Foreign Office in the Office of the Reich Protector, 16 September 1940', in Mund, *Deutschland und das Protektorat*, doc. 299, 443.
95. Rothkirchen, *Jews*, 107 and 176–77.
96. Letter, 2 October 1940, in *Europa unterm Hakenkreuz: Österreich und Tschechoslowakei*, doc. no. 82, 156–57.
97. According to the Swiss Office for the Development of Trade (Schweizerische Zentrale für Handelsförderung), Confidential communication, 3 April 1941, in Moskowitz, 'The Jewish Situation', 28.

98. Bryant, *Prague in Black*, 83.
99. For a detailed account, see Osterloh and Wixforth, 'Die "Arisierung" im Protektorat Böhmen und Mähren', 310–31.
100. *Der Neue Tag*, 20 September 1941, 10; ibid., 7 October 1941, 8; and ibid., 9 October 1941, 8.
101. NA Prague, Úřad říšského protektora [Office of the Reich Protector], signed Central Administration 1, carton 63, fol. 1: Koch to Garrison Headquarters Housing Office, 8 July 1941; ibid., fol. 3: Wehrmacht Housing Office to the Central Office in the Office of the Reich Protector, 9 July 1941. My thanks to Jan Vondráček (Wuppertal/ Prague) for alerting me to these documents.
102. RGVA Moscow, 1488-1-7, fol. 145: Cabinet Office to Reich protector, 30 January 1940, Appendix, Memorandum from the Czech fascists, n.d., 3.
103. Report by the Central Office, 2 October 1941, Appendix: Table 2, in *Deutsche Politik im 'Protektorat Böhmen und Mähren'*, 127, doc. no. 23.
104. YV Jerusalem, O 7/56, fol. 253–54: Report by the Jewish Religious Community and the Prague Palestine Office on their activities in the third quarter of 1940, 18–19.
105. Ibid., fol. 247 and 252: Report by the Jewish Religious Community and the Prague Palestine Office on their activities in the third quarter of 1940, 12 and 17.
106. Ibid., fol. 5: Weekly report Jewish Religious Community of Prague, 29 June to 5 July 1940, 4.
107. Ibid., fol. 16: Weekly report Jewish Religious Community of Prague, 6–12 July 1940, 4.
108. Ibid., fol. 29: Weekly report Jewish Religious Community of Prague, 13–19 July 1940, 5.
109. Ibid., fol. 55: Weekly report Jewish Religious Community of Prague, 27 July to 2 August 1940, 4.
110. Report by the Prague Jewish Community, 'Labour' (n.d., mid 1942), in Krejčová, Svobodová and Hyndráková, *Židé v Protektorátu*, doc. 5, 112.
111. USHMM Washington, RG 48.005M, reel 4 (Prague State Archive), carton 389, I-3b-5850, no. 28, n.p.: Reich protector to chief county commissioner in Zlín, 10 July 1940.
112. YV Jerusalem, O 7/56, fol. 83: Weekly report Jewish Religious Community of Prague, 10–16 August 1940, 7.
113. Ibid., fol. 68: Weekly report Jewish Religious Community of Prague, 3–9 August 1940, 5.
114. Ibid., fol. 136: Weekly report Jewish Religious Community of Prague, 31 August to 6 September 1940, 8.
115. Ibid., fol. 150: Weekly report Jewish Religious Community of Prague, 7–13 September 1940, 4.
116. Ibid., fol. 188: Weekly report Jewish Religious Community of Prague, 21–27 September 1940, 4.
117. LBI/A New York, Memoire Coll.: Max Mannheimer 'Von Neutitschen nach Dachau' (1969), 15.
118. Gruner, *Jewish Forced Labor*, 150.
119. YV Jerusalem, O 7/56, fol. 229: Monthly report Jewish Religious Community of Prague, 1–30 September 1940, 6.
120. Ruth Felix, *Diese Hölle überlebt: Ein jüdisches Familienschicksal aus Mähren 1924–1994. Mit einer Dokumentation*, ed. Erhard Roy Wiehn (Konstanz, 1995), 18.
121. See Gruner, *Der Geschlossene Arbeitseinsatz*, 228–49.
122. BA Berlin, R 30/4c, fol. 3: Chief County Commissioner/Dept. III, Administrative report, 15th draft, secret, general political situation, Moravian Ostrava, 20 August

1940, 2. See Excerpt from administrative report chief county commissioner Moravian Ostrava, 20 August 1940, in USHMM Washington, RG 48.005M, reel 4 (Prague State Archive), carton 389, I 3b 5850, no. 8, n.p.: Reich Protector I 1 a to Group I 3 b, Dr Mokry (n.d.).
123. Report by the Prague Jewish Community, 'Labour' (n.d., mid 1942), in Krejčová, Svobodová and Hyndráková, *Židé v Protektorátu*, doc. 5, 110.
124. Ibid.
125. YV Jerusalem, O 7/56, fol. 56: Weekly report Jewish Religious Community of Prague, 27 July to 2 August 1940, 5.
126. Report by the Prague Jewish Community, 'Labour' (n.d., mid 1942), in Krejčová, Svobodová and Hyndráková, *Židé v Protektorátu*, doc. 5, 115–16.
127. YV Jerusalem, O 7/56, fol. 68: Weekly report Jewish Religious Community of Prague, 3–9 August 1940, 5.
128. Ibid., fol. 80: Weekly report Jewish Religious Community of Prague, 10–16 August 1940, 4.
129. Report by the Prague Jewish Community, 'Labour' (n.d., mid 1942), in Krejčová, Svobodová and Hyndráková, *Židé v Protektorátu*, doc. 5, 115–16; YV Jerusalem, O 7/56, fol. 170: Weekly report Jewish Religious Community of Prague, 14–20 September 1940, 6; ibid., fol. 252: Report by the Jewish Religious Community and the Prague Palestine Office on their activities in the third quarter of 1940, 17.
130. Report by the Prague Jewish Community, 'Labour' (n.d., mid 1942), in Krejčová, Svobodová and Hyndráková, *Židé v Protektorátu*, doc. 5, 115–16.
131. USC SF/VHA, video interview, Martin Brauner, tape 1, min. 20:13–21:59; ibid., video interview, Alexander Singer, tape 3, min. 17:01–23:50; ibid., video interview, Martin Hilsenrath, tape 2, min. 7:02–11:58.
132. For detailed information on Sandhof and Doppl, see Gruner, *Zwangsarbeit und Verfolgung*, 178–87.
133. See Veselská, '"Sie müssen sich als Jude dessen bewusst sein, welche Opfer zu tragen sind ..."', 161–62.
134. Institute of Jewish Affairs, *Hitler's Ten-Year War*, 57.
135. BA Berlin, R 8150/12: fol. 158: List of legal regulations, here Decree issued by the Reich protector, 9 December 1940.
136. 2nd Decree on the implementation of the Decree on raising a Social Equalization Tax, 24 December 1940, RGBl. 1940 I, 1666. On the scope of this tax, see Gruner, *Der Geschlossene Arbeitseinsatz*, 199.
137. USC SF/VHA, video interview, Georgine Hyde, tape 2, min. 12:20–13:25.
138. Entry, 25 December 1941, in Ginz, *The Diary of Petr Ginz*, 55.
139. YV Jerusalem, O 7/56, fol. 246: Report by the Jewish Religious Community and the Prague Palestine Office on their activities in the third quarter of 1940, 11.

Chapter 7

Isolation, Forced Labour and Opposition

The Isolation of the Jews

In early 1941, around ninety thousand Jews still lived in the Protectorate. That year, on 28 February, German-language radio in Prague warned the people of the Protectorate that those continuing to maintain good relations with Jews would be regarded as enemies of the country (Landesfeinde) and punished accordingly. Some of the most senior leaders of National Partnership and other prominent figures were allegedly among those maintaining such contacts, as the Jewish Telegraphic Agency reported on 19 May 1941.[1] In line with this, during the previous year the Czech government had sought to have Czech Jews of outstanding merit in the worlds of art, science and sport excepted from the Germans' anti-Jewish laws. However, leading German actors, initially von Burgsdorff and later Frank, obstructed their efforts, until Heydrich shelved the idea in the autumn.[2]

By January 1941, the chief county commissioner in Moravian Ostrava was already complaining about the Czechs' mounting resistance. Czech shopkeepers, he asserted, had begun to treat Jewish customers better than German ones. They went about it so cleverly, however, that there was insufficient evidence to lodge official complaints.[3]

One initiative intended to divide Jewish from non-Jewish Czechs, however, was to prove successful. On 9 October 1940, on behalf of National Partnership, Josef Nebeský had – without German involvement – urged the Czech government to introduce a law 'to defend Czech Aryan honour and blood'. The government responded by drawing up a decree, which it submitted to the Reich protector in early November 1940, initially with no reaction from the German side. In a second letter of 3 April 1941, Eliáš again asked Deputy Reich Protector Frank for the German authorities' agreement. His government, he explained, had been criticized for the fact that in certain respects the Jewish question was yet to be resolved and that Jews were still able to marry non-Jews. It was to be some time before he got his wish, however, because the Nazi state had first to extend the Nuremberg laws to the Protectorate.[4] In July 1941, with retroactive effect from March 1939, the Reich Interior Ministry introduced the Law for the Protection of German Blood (Gesetz zum Schutz des deutschen Blutes) in the Protectorate.[5] It was only now, therefore, that the German Jews in the Protectorate were made de jure subject to the Nuremberg laws, though de facto their 'definition of a Jew' had already been in use since summer 1939.[6]

In order to complete the process of 'Aryanization', on 27 January 1941 the third 'Implementing Ordinance Concerning the Decree Issued by the Reich Protector to Eliminate Jews from the Economic Life of the Protectorate' (Durchführungserlaß zur Verordnung des Reichsprotektors zur Ausschaltung der Juden aus dem Wirtschaftsleben des Protektorats) ordered Jews to surrender all businesses still belonging to them by 31 March. Since 18 January, in accordance with an announcement by the Agriculture Ministry, Jews had been barred from purchasing apples. On 23 January, the Prague Police Directorate made it known that Jews had to hand in their driving licences and vehicle registration certificates within fourteen days, while also announcing that they were no longer permitted to take driving lessons.[7]

Even prior to the extension of the Nuremberg laws' sphere of application, in the first half of 1941 an unceasing flow of new directives had reinforced the separation of Jews from non-Jews in the Protectorate. On 31 January 1941, amending the decree issued the previous year, the Interior Ministry decided to restrict Jews' shopping hours to 3 p.m.–5 p.m. due to the 'issues [resulting from] Jews' use of Aryan shops in the morning'.[8] This was put into effect through a Prague police ordinance of 4 February 1941,[9] with the police in Brno following suit in March.[10] Reacting to the new guidelines, the Coal Sales Outlet (Kohlenverkaufsstelle) in Prague instructed its member firms to serve Jews only on Wednesdays between 1 p.m. and 5 p.m.[11] In late March, the

Prague police chief issued a directive allowing Jews to patronize banks and other financial institutions for just one hour a day, namely between 8 a.m. and 9 a.m.[12] The same soon applied to insurance companies.[13]

A diverse array of authorities now enacted anti-Jewish measures. In February 1941, the state president of Bohemia prohibited Jews from fishing, while the Czech Finance Ministry decreed that they must deposit their private stamp collections at a bank.[14] The Transport Ministry decided that Jews were to be deprived of their telephones by 28 February.[15] From 8 April 1941 onwards, on the orders of the Czech Finance Ministry, they were no longer permitted to buy tickets for the Protectorate's class lottery.[16] At the end of the same month, the Central Office instructed the Jewish Communities in the Protectorate to remove all Stars of David from synagogues and other buildings.[17] As in previous years, therefore, a number of institutions were responsible for radicalizing the persecution of Jews in the Protectorate.

Concentration and Ghettoization

On 5 February 1941, the Reich protector issued a decree on Jews' tenancies.[18] In the second week of that month, the Jewish Community had to submit to the Central Office a register of all homes of four rooms and more in Greater Prague.[19] In late March, it then provided the Central Office with another list, this time of all homes in the capital and their occupants.[20]

During this period, the authorities began to systematically concentrate an increasing number of Prague's Jewish residents in 'Jews' houses' in the city districts I and II. Of the 14,920 homes seized in October 1940, five thousand had to be vacated, as noted in Chapter 6. The Central Office also reached agreement with the Central Administration in the Office of the Reich Protector and the Nazi Party District Office, enabling the latter two institutions to allocate several hundred homes each.[21] The Central Administration was keen to provide Reich officials with homes freshly vacated by Jewish tenants, while the Nazi Party Commissioner for Housing Issues (Beauftragter für Wohnungsfragen) dedicated himself to the same task.[22] Staff in the Office of the Reich Protector went so far as to apply for homes still occupied by Jews, prompting the Central Administration to ask the Central Office to evict them and ready these properties for new tenants.[23] In the first half of 1941, Reich and ethnic Germans as well as Czechs employed in the justice system, media and German organizations requested that Jewish tenants be removed from suitable homes so they themselves could acquire them.[24]

In parallel to this, local administrations organized the systematic removal of the Jewish population from the smaller towns and villages in the various chief county commissioner districts and their resettlement in select cities. For example, Jews from Kyjov, Kostel and Holešov in the District of Zlín had to move to Uherský Brod. This, however, led to local conflicts of interest because every district aspired to 'avoid accommodating any Jews at all if possible. Their relocation from one area to another causes discontent among the Germans in reaction to the influx of Jews'. In the Chief County Commissioner District of Jihlava, the officials took the view that 'the Jews signify the strengthening of the Czechs'. A number of cities and local authorities refused to admit them. In Uherský Brod, some feared that once the Jews had been relocated from Kyjov, Kostel and Holešov the 'Aryan inhabitants' would find themselves confronted with a city made up of 'one third Jews'.[25]

In early March 1941, the Prague Jewish Community informed the SD Central Office that all 327 Jews had to leave the city of Jihlava by 1 May.[26] In Mladá Boleslav, meanwhile, the Jewish residents were forced from their homes and accommodated in a dilapidated castle outside the town. Only with the help of the Prague Jewish Community could this building, particularly its kitchens and bathrooms, be made inhabitable.[27] Towards the end of March 1941, the Reich protector decreed that the Göring directive of late 1938 concerning the concentration of Jews in 'Jews' houses', which was still in force in the Reich and aimed to prevent ghettoization, should be ignored in the Protectorate 'in light of the realities on the ground'. He thus gave the green light for ghettoization.[28]

In line with this, in May more Jews were compelled to relocate in a number of chief county commissioner districts.[29] In much the same way, in the Old Reich the Gestapo and the municipal authorities helped establish more than forty residential and labour camps in early summer, again mostly in dilapidated monasteries or abandoned hut camps, which were maintained on a makeshift basis and with costs covered by the Reich Association or the Jews forced to move there.[30] The SD in the Protectorate welcomed the 'resettlement of Jews': 'In the small premises allotted to them, which they must share with others of the same race, the Jews feel very confined and they would rather emigrate as soon as possible'.[31] This, however, was more a reflection of the SS's wishful thinking than the facts: there was no longer much prospect of emigration and many Jews had absolutely no funds for travel.

The Work, Structure and Relief Efforts of the Prague Jewish Community

The lot of the Jewish population continued to worsen dramatically. The Prague Jewish Community identified the main causes as Jews' elimination from the economy, the increasingly desperate housing shortage and the sweeping impoverishment of the Jewish middle class.[32] In response, it did what it could to find jobs for both men and women while also seeking to mitigate Jews' hardship. Around the end of 1940, within four days it provided financial support to the tune of more than 545,000 crowns to 3,420 individuals in need (see Table A.3 in the appendix).[33] In the first quarter of 1941, the Jewish Community's welfare services supported around seven thousand people in Prague per month to the amount of 5,700,000 crowns and more than 6,400 individuals in the provinces. During the same period the Soup Kitchen in Prague helped impoverished Jews by providing 104,000 lunches and 78,000 evening meals. By the end of March, Community-run institutions housed 877 individuals in Prague and 312 in the provinces. Five hundred applications for places in old people's homes had been received.[34] The Jewish Community operated five hospitals, four in Prague and one in Moravian Ostrava.[35]

Because Jewish children were barred from German and Czech schools in 1940, since the end of the holidays in January 1941, 566 of them had been attending the Jewish primary school and 318 the secondary school in Prague. Children in need, whether in school or not, received sandwiches, jam rolls and milk on a daily basis.[36] By the end of March, 898 pupils were attending the Prague primary and secondary school, 157 the primary school in Moravian Ostrava and 343 its counterpart in Brno, with 320 at the Realgymnasium (a secondary school with a focus on the sciences) in that city. While 1,718 Jewish pupils attended lessons, almost four thousand children of school age could not be schooled due to lack of space.[37]

At the end of 1940, the Prague Jewish Community had more than 420 white-collar employees (including officials, clerical and secretarial workers, school staff, researchers, doctors and religious staff), 108 auxiliary workers (telephone service staff, cooks and caretakers, among other things) and 53 labourers (in cemeteries and transport).[38] By the end of March 1941, the Community had to lay off one hundred salaried staff. This left 406 white-collar employees, 52 auxiliary workers and 42 labourers.[39] The Community still owned sixty-two million crowns' worth of cash funds and fixed assets entrusted to various banks.[40]

As the main source of information for the persecuted, at the end of 1940 the *Jüdisches Nachrichtenblatt* had 9,382 subscribers, with a total print run of 13,500.[41] Alongside the most important anti-Jewish decrees, it published reports on the prospects and problems of emigration, articles on retraining and appeals for donations of all kinds, particularly during the winter months.[42]

By this point there were 130 Jewish Communities left in the Protectorate.[43] In January 1941, the Prague Community passed on to all provincial Communities directives on domestic travel, tax assessment and the financing of Jewish labour deployment, welfare services and relocation.[44] If Jews wished to leave their places of residence in the Protectorate, they had to file applications with the Prague Community's Department for Domestic Travel (Abteilung für Inlandsreisen). In the month of January, the department approved 1,772 applications but rejected or shelved 553.[45]

On 1 February 1941, the Central Office requested from the Prague Jewish Community a list of all Jewish associations still in existence, all organizations dissolved by 1 December 1940 and all foundations and funds.[46] Meanwhile, the Prague Community replaced the heads of a number of smaller Moravian provincial Communities, while confirming others in office.[47] But it was by no means merely a subsidiary of the Central Office. Its employees tried to help Community members, mitigate the effects of persecution, oppose oppressive measures and sound out and exploit the available room for manoeuvre, which was often the result of the multiple initiatives pursued by different authorities and their varying responsibilities. In the second week of January 1941, the Prague Jewish Community submitted to the Finance Ministry's Auditing Department alone sixteen petitions relating to jewellery. Community staff also appeared at the Finance Ministry and the Currency Control Unit (Devisenschutzkommando).[48] Later, the Community filed seventeen applications with the Finance Ministry for retrospective approval of the registering or depositing of jewellery, which was required if individuals wished to leave the Protectorate.[49] In addition, in the second week of January 1941 alone, Community staff dispensed advice to 365 parties on legal and economic issues, composed fifty-three letters and thirteen petitions and submitted one complaint. In forty-four cases they interceded by contacting various authorities, above all with respect to matters of citizenship, taxation and pensions and in opposition to evictions. Two hundred and fifty individuals received advice in connection with the 'housing campaign', while sixty letters were sent out.[50] In the third week of January, Community officials helped 331 families and negotiated with various authorities on Jews' behalf on sixty-five occasions.[51]

Those seeking advice were particularly concerned with the consequences of new anti-Jewish measures, for example the recently published Third Implementing Ordinance to Eliminate Jews from the Economic Life of the Protectorate (Durchführungsverordnung zur Ausschaltung der Juden aus dem Wirtschaftsleben des Protektorats); among other things, they enquired about the liquidation and 'Aryanization' of businesses and pension-related matters. The fact that the implementing ordinance provided for 'Aryanization' with retroactive effect from 1 January 1941 had an adverse impact on the Jewish Community's collecting activities, in cases where firms' owners had already made regular contributions or donations to the Community prior to its issuance.[52]

In Moravian Ostrava, as the chief county commissioner reported, between 15 February and 15 March the authorities had 'Aryanized' seven businesses, three houses and one plot of land, in other words forced their owners to sell them, while closing another twenty-one businesses.[53] Over the course of the next four weeks, eleven businesses were 'Aryanized through purchase' and three were closed, while trustees still administered 119.[54] A few months later, the chief county commissioner stated that the transfer of 'Jewish business enterprises into German hands' was proceeding as planned. By mid July 1941, according to his report, 246 businesses had been closed and 146 sold to non-Jews. Ninety-eight were still being administered by trustees, while the fate of ninety-one was yet to be decided, though thirty-one of them had already been leased to 'Aryans'.[55]

In February, many individuals of Jewish faith sought information concerning the new prohibition on Jews having telephones.[56] Ultimately the Jewish Community submitted ninety requests to the Central Office from individuals wishing to keep their private telephone.[57] In March 1941, Community representatives tried to persuade the Prague city authorities to provide air-raid shelters for the Jewish population.[58]

Ghettoization in Prague and Other Cities

At the end of 1940, the Community's Legal Department advised 175 families who had lost their homes as a result of the housing campaigns in Prague districts I, V, VI and VII. With the authorities systematically scouring one district after the next, VIII and IX were about to face the same fate[59] and a similar campaign was in the pipeline in Brno. In January 1941, a bespoke department of the Prague Jewish Community facilitated the transfer of buildings to the Emigration Fund.[60] In the second week of January alone, the Central Registry (Zentralevidenz) thus had to update 1,147 addresses. In addition, Community officials drew up a list of all Jews of foreign citizenship for the SD Central Office.[61]

In February and March, one after another of Prague's districts fell victim to 'residential Aryanization'. By the end of March, eviction orders for 126 families had been issued in the city, all of which were supposed to find accommodation in a specific 'settlement area' (Einsiedlungsgebiet), leaving the Jewish Community facing serious logistical problems.[62] In Prague, therefore, the concentration or – to be more precise – ghettoization of the Jewish population had taken on a new quality and intensity. Meanwhile, the authorities were hatching similar plans for the Protectorate's other cities.

In mid March, on the instructions of the Central Office, the Prague Jewish Community had to prepare for a similar transfer of residential buildings in Moravian Ostrava and, one week later, in Pilsen.[63] A Community report described the conditions in the industrial city of Moravian Ostrava, population 200,000:[64] 'At present, the concentrated accommodating of Jews in a self-contained district – the creation of a ghetto – is throwing up a number of problems as a result of the associated resettlement of Aryans'. Jewish residents, the report stated, had had to vacate 2,680 flats to make way for 'Aryans'; 788 families remained in their old homes but the authorities had no interest in evicting them because their dwellings were in such dire condition; as a consequence of 'Aryanization' and the restrictions imposed on Jews, meanwhile, just four groceries, two general goods stores and two restaurants were left in the city to cater to the needs of the 3,600 Jews still living there (of 11,800 when the Protectorate was established). Jews, the report stated, faced a hopeless situation: 'Due to these circumstances Jews are suffering tremendous, mental distress. They have no means of engaging in any kind of activity of an intellectual or cultural nature, so the task facing the leaders of the Jewish Community was to raise the morale of the Jews entrusted to its care and ward off depression'. It was now clear that the 'Jews regard emigration from Europe as the only way of solving their problems'.[65]

Emigration and Preparations for Emigration at the Beginning of 1941

Because the authorities had yet to decide whether to carry out more deportations, the Prague Jewish Community focused a great deal of effort on supporting emigration. Though recently the prospects of leaving the Protectorate had greatly diminished, at the end of 1940 Community officials advised 391 families in person and 107 in writing within a five-day period alone.[66]

Community officials now mainly negotiated with the consulates of Slovakia, Spain, Portugal and Japan (the latter as a means of getting to Shanghai).[67] In the first week of 1941, 128 applicants completed the final stage of the Community's emigration process, of whom 121 were slated to travel to Shanghai, three to Argentina, two to the United States and one each to Hungary and Santo Domingo. One hundred and twenty-five applications were then passed on to the Central Office.[68] In the second week of January, 114 emigrants made it through the final document review, with 110 going to Shanghai and one each to Ecuador, Argentina, Finland and Hungary; the Central Office received 126 applications.[69]

In addition to regular emigration and the illegal Palestine transports, Jewish Community representatives pressed ahead with a number of other large-scale projects. In January 1941, the Community finally obtained the Joint's agreement concerning the planned settlement in Santo Domingo of 150 individuals from Prague, Vienna and Berlin. At the end of the month, thirty-one settlers from the Protectorate, who had already received their Dominican visas, made preparations for their trip to the Caribbean. The Jewish Community negotiated frantically with the Portuguese consulate to obtain the requisite transit papers.[70]

In the last week of January, the Community furnished 692 would-be emigrants with advice, with the figure surging to 1,451 in the third week of February. In the first week of March, 1,872 individuals obtained information on emigration; sadly, just sixteen made it out of the Protectorate, with ten going to Shanghai, five to Argentina and one to the United States.[71] In January, the Community passed on a total of five hundred applications for emigration to the Central Office, 474 of them for Shanghai, and another five hundred in February, 458 of them for Shanghai, 14 for the United States and 12 for Cuba; in March the figure was 421, 375 for Shanghai and 26 for the United States.[72]

Jewish Community officials found themselves facing acute challenges: the closure of the US and Japanese consulates, the reduction in available space aboard ships, new barriers in transit countries along emigrants' routes to various ports as well as difficulties arranging ship passages, obtaining foreign currency and finding the money for disembarkation fees. Japan's decision to cease issuing transit visas diminished the number of would-be emigrants for Shanghai referred to the Central Office to 108 in March 1941, following figures of 580 in February and 620 in January. Nonetheless, in the first quarter of that year the 1,308 individuals who made their way to Shanghai were the only group of emigrants of any significant size.[73]

In an attempt to improve potential emigrants' chances of leaving the Protectorate despite the greatly reduced prospect of immigration in many countries, Community officials set great store by occupational training, that is, so-called redeployment (Umschichtung). At the end of 1940, the HeHalutz alone operated twenty-three Group Retraining Sites in the Protectorate, catering to a total of 206 men and 43 women.[74] Such camps had been established, for example, in Lochkov (Lochkow) near Slivenec (Slowenetz), Hlohovice (Lohowitz), Čakovice (Tschakowitz) and on the estates of Obora and Liblin.[75] As in Germany, Jews undergoing 'redeployment' were not only trained in agriculture but were also put to work in forestry, snow-clearing or nearby industrial plants.[76] The 'Linden (Lípa) school estate', which came under the authority of the Central Office, regularly housed around three hundred workers, of whom one hundred were periodically replaced.[77]

Since the early deportation of October 1939, more Jewish women than men had lived in Moravian Ostrava. The city's Jewish Community organized a range of retraining courses in fields such as tailoring, photography, shoemaking, locksmithing and more, while also offering language courses in English, Hebrew, Spanish, French and Russian. Between February 1940 and May 1941, 921 individuals completed a retraining course financed by the Moravian Ostrava Jewish Community. Virtually every Community in the Protectorate put on such classes. At the beginning of May 1941, the Brno Community alone provided retraining for 420 individuals.[78]

Virtually unchanged over January 1941, in February the total number of individuals undergoing retraining was 1,350, of whom 984 were men and 366 women. Jewish Communities instituted eleven new courses with 183 participants.[79] In contrast to the position at the end of the first quarter of 1940, when there were 750 individuals undergoing retraining, by the end of the first quarter of 1941 there were 1,612, two thirds of them in courses in Prague and one third in the provincial Communities. That the number of retrainees had more than doubled resulted from the growing recognition, both among members of the Jewish population and the Communities, that there was very little prospect of emigration in the absence of occupational retraining. On the orders of the Central Office, the retraining courses or camps had to cover their own costs.[80] In effect, this meant that training had to play second fiddle to labour deployment. It would otherwise have been impossible to finance the camps, as too many potential retrainees had no income and were dependent on the Community's welfare services.

Retraining, placement in employment and group deployment, the latter chiefly in agriculture, were intended to take some of the pressure off the Jewish welfare services but also to help reduce the mass unemployment among Jews.[81] At the beginning of 1941, more than five thousand individuals had registered with the Central Jewish Employment Office, of whom fewer than 1,500 had so far been placed in work, though the Office had sent out enquiries to numerous private businesses.[82]

From Group Deployment to Forced Labour

In January 1941, the Jewish Community offered the Czech Labour Office men for snow shovelling. One hundred and ten Jews were soon clearing Prague's streets at the city authorities' behest. Meanwhile, the Labour Office informed the Central Jewish Employment Office that sixty-three Jews, who were in receipt of unemployment benefits, would be sent to work unpaid at the City of Prague's incineration plant in Vysočany (Wissotschan). They received neither health insurance, work clothes nor reduced-cost travel on the city's trams. In České Budějovice too, 190 men and women were already engaged in shovelling snow.[83] In the second week of January, 1,100 Jewish men and women were already clearing snow in fifty-three provincial locales.[84] Within the municipal area of Moravian Ostrava, in addition to one hundred Jews put to work in river regulation, due to heavy snow falls another one hundred had to shovel snow in segregated work details, though they received financial support from the city's Jewish Community.[85]

On 17 January 1941, the Prague Jewish Community unexpectedly received instructions from the SD Central Office to send between four and five hundred men to the Ruzin (Ruzyně) Airbase, located not far from the capital, to clear snow the next morning. More than two hundred Community members of staff, not just in the Jewish Employment Office but in the Palestine Office as well, delivered this summons during the night. On Saturday morning, 525 men reported for duty. The snow-clearing operation at the airbase took up the next two weeks, that is, until the end of the month. The 'Occupational Index' division (Berufskartei) supplied between 480 and 650 workers on a daily basis, amounting to a total of more than 7,600 individuals.[86] On Thursday 23 January, in addition the City of Prague asked the Jewish Community to provide it with men for work at a daily rate of thirty-seven crowns. For the next two days, the city authorities set a group of thirty-two men to work clearing snow under the supervision of a Jewish foreman.[87]

In February 1941, the Jewish Community again sent hundreds of men to work at Prague's Ruzin Airbase. Each worker had to complete a four-day stint, with between 528 and 746 Jews a day reporting for snow-shovelling work in the first week.[88] The city authorities' requirements remained the same for the second week of February, but they made no further requests after the 15th of that month. They did, however, request workers to help repair the Janáčkův (Janatschek) Bridge as an emergency measure, for which the Jewish Community made available a total of 126 men between 10 and 13 February. Three workers suffered accidents in the course of the arduous repair work. In the following days, the workers also had to remove chunks of ice that had washed ashore, a task performed by twenty men a day for between four and ten hours.[89] On 21 and 26 February 1941, the Jewish Employment Office received further requests for workers from the Ruzin Airbase. There, from 22 to 28 February, between 150 and 350 individuals were put to work clearing snow in the mornings and afternoons. During this period, the Prague city authorities also requested more Jews, around thirty-five men a day.[90] By this point, Jewish forced labourers were clearing snow in ninety-seven locations in the Protectorate.[91]

In an attempt to get more Jews into paid employment, the Prague Jewish Community had now entered into negotiations with a glove-making firm, the idea being to employ more women in production.[92] In March, meanwhile, in response to enquiries by the Jewish Employment Office, twelve roadbuilding firms requested 1,060 male workers, while nineteen landowners applied in advance for 180 labourers.[93] Instead of this contingency-dependent form of organization, however, the Protectorate authorities now decided to introduce the forced deployment in segregated work units (Geschlossener Arbeitseinsatz) operated so effectively by the labour offices in the Reich.[94]

In the absence of central regulations, by the beginning of 1941 the labour offices required Jewish men below the age of forty-five to work on a temporary basis in construction, roadbuilding or private firms.[95] Because the Reich had a growing need for workers[96] and the deportations announced for the Protectorate were repeatedly postponed, initially, on 10 January 1941, the Reich protector had prohibited Jews and Jewish businesses from engaging in virtually all forms of independent economic activity, for example in trade, the restaurant and hotel business, insurance firms, transport, tourism, banking, detective work, advertising, the stock market and the marriage business,[97] much as the Law to Amend the Regulations on Trades and Professions (Gesetz zur Änderung der Gewerbeordnung) of 6 July 1938 had done for Germany.[98] In the Protectorate, this freed up labour while also helping complete the process of 'Aryanization'. As a result, many Jews were now unemployed and without income.

On 23 January 1941, the Protectorate government issued the first Czech decree on the forced labour deployment of the Jewish population in Bohemia and Moravia. The obligation to work applied to all Jews between the ages of eighteen and fifty.[99] The decree stated:

> It is neither desirable nor reasonable for Jews fit for labour deployment to receive unemployment benefit and end up in perpetual receipt of support. It is thus imperative that all Jews who register as unemployed be given the opportunity to work as soon as possible. The main fields of activity in this respect are roadbuilding, earthworks, the laying out of grounds (parks) and the like, as people in every occupational field can be employed in this type of work and it is entirely welcome for Jews to engage in physical labour.[100]

When the Prague Jewish Community responded by making enquiries at the Office of the Reich Protector, Government Counsellor Dr Jaissle and Senior Inspector (Oberinspektor) Reinicke tasked the Community with making preparations for forced deployment on a centralized basis. All Jewish men in the Protectorate born between 1891 and 1923 were to undergo a medical examination as well as 'social screening' (to ascertain prior education, training and work experience); the results of the latter were to be noted in the Occupational Index in order to ensure a prompt and targeted response to requests for manpower.[101]

Now the labour offices began to deploy Jews registering as unemployed more systematically.[102] On 7 March 1941, *Der Neue Tag, Tageszeitung für Böhmen und Mähren* published an article[103] summarizing a report printed in the *Berliner Börsen-Zeitung* the previous day, entitled 'The Deployment of Jewish Workers: Provisional Regulations in Advance of the Upcoming Law'.[104] The Berlin publication presented the first official information on the forced labour of Jews as practised on a massive scale in Germany since 1939, while also serving to introduce to the public of the Greater German Reich the discriminatory rules developed to date, which were now to be extended to the Protectorate.[105]

While the Prague Jewish Community's Central Employment Office had already begun to register those fit for work in the preceding weeks, in March 1941, due to the amount of work involved, even the employees of the Central Zionist Union's Palestine Office had to assist in laying the ground for labour deployment.[106] At this point in time, the Occupational Index included information on all men born between 1893 and 1923. Towards the end of March, the Jewish provincial Communities received instructions to make preparations for forced labour deployment at the local level as well, and in particular to initiate the required fitness-for-work screening.[107] On 1 April, meanwhile, the Office of the Reich Protector (Department II) officially ordered the Jewish Community to begin the medical examinations required prior to labour deployment under file reference number 5431, the same used for forced labour in Germany and Austria since late 1938.[108] By now the Central Jewish Employment Office had registered 4,700 individuals.[109]

On 1 April 1941, 70 per cent of male Jews in the Protectorate between the ages of eighteen and fifty and fit for work were in some form of employment, for the Jewish Communities, in camps or retraining, in work details arranged by the Jewish Employment Office or, increasingly, performing forced labour organized by the labour offices.[110] Procedures were now to be brought into line with normal practice in the Reich. On 17 April, the Office of the Reich Protector wrote to the Ministry for Social and Health Administration in Prague informing it of this task and of the procedures prescribed by the Protector. He had instructed the Jewish Community 'to examine all Jews to establish their fitness for work', adding: 'To prevent special measures from disrupting the systematic labour deployment of Jews', the labour offices were to be exclusively responsible for selecting places of work, deploying Jews in separate groups. The Jewish Employment Office, the missive went on, would merely provide figures or the names of individuals fit for work and available. The 'Jewish work details' were to be headed by 'foremen' selected by the Jewish Religious Community.[111] The Reich protector thus brought to an end any influence the Jewish Employment Office might have had on the placing of workers and the conditions of labour deployment, for both of which the German labour offices now assumed responsibility.

From now on, therefore, forced labour in the Protectorate was the sole responsibility of the Labour Administration (Arbeitsverwaltung), entirely in line with the model implemented in the Old Reich and Austria. On 9 May 1941, the Czech Ministry for Social and Health Administration published updated regulations on forced deployment in segregated work units. These stipulated that the recruitment of Jews and the terms governing forced labour were to reflect joint instructions issued by the Office of the Reich Protector, the Central Office for Jewish Emigration and the ministry itself: such labour deployment would be arranged by the labour offices in accordance with the ministry's directives. The Central Office for Jewish Emigration retained control only over the approval of external deployments, that is, cases where men and women were to be taken to labour camps for Jews outside the cities.[112] The same day, the ministry published instructions for the Central

Jewish Employment Office, about which the Prague Jewish Community informed the SD Central Office a few days later.[113]

When the ministry had informed the labour offices as well, eleven of them immediately requested that the Prague Jewish Community provide 1,358 Jewish workers for seventeen firms.[114] In the course of this reorientation, in accordance with instructions issued by the Office of the Reich Protector, the ministry also reorganized agricultural labour deployment, approving the use of thirty-six separate Jewish groups made up of 376 men in total.[115]

At the end of March 1941, the City of Prague was still deploying a daily total of twenty Jewish workers to clear snow.[116] On 12 May, meanwhile, one hundred workers were again deployed at the Ruzin Airbase. The Jewish Labour Headquarters (Jüdische Arbeitszentrale, formerly the Central Jewish Employment Office) had also received requests from the Army Construction Office (Heeresbauamt) in Vyškov and from a firm named Konstruktiva for men to work in railway construction in Sázava (Sasau) near Německý Brod. Jewish officials inspected the deployment sites to assess the opportunities for board and lodgings.[117] By mid May, the Prague Community had placed 225 men in labour deployment, its Brno counterpart no fewer than 502.[118] During the month of May, a total of 1,157 Jews in the Protectorate performed work in external deployments.[119]

In the middle of that month, the Ministry for Social and Health Administration informed the Prague Jewish Community of the labour offices' increased requirements; they demanded, for example, 750 men in Brno and 80 in Pardubice.[120] Initially, the authorities in the Protectorate administered the segregation of forced labourers more loosely than in the Reich, because German officials regarded the Czechs as 'inferior' as well. Right from the start, however, they paid Jews less than Czechs, first unofficially and then officially from 1941 onwards, prompting the Jewish Communities to do their best to provide extra support.[121]

The forced labour organized by the German labour offices in the Protectorate quickly gathered pace. While the shortage of workers was considered acute, the available labour was yet to be exhausted. Now, in much the same way as in Germany since autumn 1940, the labour offices even required Jews to work in industry. In May 1941, the chief county commissioner in Moravian Ostrava reported that 'Jewish workers [are now] also [employed] on an increased scale in the metals industry, [practising] their professions in segregated gangs and isolated' from others. The Protectorate's forestry industry also suffered a growing shortage of workers.[122]

New Directions in Emigration and Retraining?

In spring 1941, at the behest of the Central Office for Jewish Emigration, various divisions of the Prague Jewish Community had to create card indexes. While, for example, the Central Jewish Employment Office ascertained the occupations and ability of those looking for work, the Schools Department (Schulreferat) compiled a list of all Jewish children and young people between the ages of three and eighteen living in the Protectorate; the Housing Department, meanwhile, drew up a list of all homes in Prague and their Jewish occupants.[123] On 17 March, SS-Hauptsturmführer Günther summoned all the Prague Jewish Community's leading staff to a meeting to inform them of their new responsibilities.[124] All private retraining courses had been prohibited three days earlier.[125] At the same time, the Reich Security Main Office in Berlin ordered the Reich Association and the Jewish Communities in Germany to implement extreme cost reductions and transfer all Jews undergoing retraining to the forced labour in segregated work units being organized by the labour offices.[126]

So, while in Germany all pre-emigration measures had been abruptly discontinued, in the Protectorate 1,348 individuals were still attending 116 retraining courses financed by the Jewish Communities in July 1941.[127]

The Prague Jewish Community also continued to promote emigration itself. At the end of March, over a six-day period, its Emigration Department advised 1,867 individuals. Its head travelled to Berlin and Vienna to negotiate with US and Japanese diplomats on emigration options and ship passages. With the Japanese, for example, she discussed the issuance of transit visas for travel to Ecuador and Shanghai. In total, 122 individuals' applications passed the Document Procurement Office's final review, 117 of them bound for Shanghai. The Jewish Community sent 135 completed emigration applications to the Central Office.[128] The situation grew more complicated towards the end of April because Portugal was no longer issuing transit visas, cutting off the route to the United States.[129] The Portuguese authorities, however, reversed this decision in mid May,[130] enabling forty-one individuals to travel to Lisbon via Berlin on a special transport.[131]

The Central Zionist Union's Palestine Office worked to obtain immigration certificates for Palestine. Its Workers' Transports Department (Abteilung Arbeitertransporte) prepared those who had been issued certificates for their group departure, pressing them to obtain the required documents and pay the necessary fees.[132] However, the German invasion of Yugoslavia scuppered the transport route used hitherto, prompting Jewish officials to consider journeys via Turkey and Russia.[133] Their efforts bore fruit in late April as a new route opened up via Budapest, Bucharest and Constanţa, with emigrants then travelling to Istanbul by ship before continuing on to Palestine by land.[134]

In the week of 10–16 May, the Prague Emigration Department furnished 2,103 individuals with advice.[135] A total of 113 would-be emigrants passed the Document Procurement Office's final review, ninety-one of them hoping to make it to Shanghai and fifteen to the United States. The Central Office received one hundred applications.[136] In the week of 24–30 May, Community staff helped 2,390 potential emigrants, brought 118 applications to completion, ninety-three of them for Shanghai and fifteen for the United States, again forwarding one hundred to the SD Central Office.[137] By this point, the only route to emigration was via Portugal or Spain.[138]

By 30 June 1941, 25,540 Jews had left the Protectorate. Of what had been a Jewish population of 118,310, a total of 88,686 still lived in Bohemia and Moravia (see Tables A.1 and A.2 in the appendix). In more than two years of occupation, the Prague Jewish Community recorded just 269 births as opposed to 4,353 deaths.[139] In Moravian Ostrava, the local Community registered just four births (compared to twenty-one in 1939) and fifty-four deaths in the first five months of 1941.[140] This gross disparity highlights the phenomenon of over-aging as a consequence of the emigration of younger Jews, while also underscoring individuals' dire lot as a result of what was now two years of persistent social, economic and psychological persecution.

In its half-year report for the SD Central Office, the Prague Jewish Community stated that all its activities were directed towards the 'ultimate objective that has been decided, namely the emigration of the Protectorate's Jewry in its entirety'. In a resigned tone, the report went on to state that the recognition that 'emigration [is] the only practicable means of definitively resolving the Jewish question in this country' had 'consolidated the desire to emigrate among the Jews of the Protectorate of Bohemia and Moravia to such an extent that while the difficulties arising as a result of the international situation may well slow the pace of emigration, they do nothing to change the general tendency'.[141]

On the Tasks of the Prague Jewish Community

At the beginning of April 1941, in the wake of the cost savings demanded by the authorities and in compliance with instructions issued by SS-Hauptsturmführer Günther of the Central Office on 17 March, the Prague Community laid off fifty employees, including thirty-five housemaids and cleaners. The total number of employees thus fell to 500, consisting of 406 white-collar workers, 52 auxiliary workers and 42 labourers.[142]

On 4 April, in response to a request from the Jewish Community, the Office of the Reich Protector approved the transfer of securities owned by the Jewish burial fraternities to the Community.[143] One day later, the Czech Finance Ministry even permitted the transfer of all the monetary and precious metal assets of these fraternities to a Community account, informing the Protectorate's financial institutions of its decision.[144] In May, the Prague Community informed its provincial counterparts that in light of the Reich protector's approval, all local Communities must immediately take possession of burial fraternities' assets, instructing the relevant financial institutions to make them over to the Prague Community and transfer them to its bank account.[145]

On 8 May 1941, the heads of the Jewish Community's various departments had to appear before SS-Hauptsturmführer Günther of the SD Central Office and report on their activities.[146] The Central Office was particularly interested in 'Jewish property', first because it had to avoid the financial collapse of the Jewish Communities and second because it was eager to advance preparations for the expropriation of such property. On 15 May, the Community submitted overviews of all the foundations and funds it administered and of the assets of all Jewish Communities and associations in the Protectorate.[147] Towards the end of May, the Central Office demanded that the Jewish Community draw up lists of 'Jewish estates in the Prague Chief County Commissioner District' and, on this basis, submit updated records of Jewish homes.[148] In Prague and the provinces, the transfer of Jewish-owned homes to the Emigration Fund continued at the behest of the Central Office. The local Communities in the Chief County Commissioner District of Zlín also started preparations for a transfer of this kind.[149] Their staff drew up lists of real estate, which they then sent to the Prague Jewish Community for submission to the Central Office.[150] Ultimately, the Prague Community provided the Central Office with lists of all villas belonging to Jews in Greater Prague, all Jews living in boarding houses and all 'Jewish buildings in Greater Prague containing Jewish residents'.[151]

Regardless of the problems plaguing the Jewish Communities, the Czech government began to lumber them with what had previously been the responsibilities of the state. With effect from 31 May 1941, the Czech Health Ministry instructed the Brno Pension Fund

(Brünner Pensionskasse) and the General Pensions Office (Allgemeine Pensionsanstalt) in Prague to cease paying Jewish women whose husbands lived abroad their pro rata pension. When his efforts in Brno proved fruitless, Salo Krämer of the Moravian Ostrava Jewish Community asked the Prague Community to contact the Pensions Office headquarters and the Health Ministry on behalf of one of his members, Helene Grünfeld, who had been left destitute by this measure.[152] Making the case for a number of women in this position, whose husbands had been deported to Nisko and from there across the border into the Soviet Union as a result of the 'relocations' of October 1939, Jewish Communities composed letters in which they argued that at the time the USSR had not been an enemy nation. Several petitions submitted by the Prague Jewish Community to the Pensions Office and the Czech Health Ministry, however, achieved nothing. Because the ministry had asked the Reich protector to settle this matter, the Prague Community considered appealing to him directly in order to 'bring about a rapid, favourable resolution of this issue'.[153]

While the burgeoning use of labour deployment lowered the number of Jews in need of welfare, worsening persecution had the opposite effect. As a result, in the first week of June the Prague Community paid out 655,000 crowns in welfare benefits to 3,451 individuals, which represented almost no change from the situation in the spring. While the Community welfare services had registered 6,927 individuals in need of support at the beginning of April, this number had fallen to 6,809 by the end of the month. In total, the Community paid out 2,103,000 crowns in welfare support in April in the form of cash payments, coal and rent subsidies.[154] In May, the number rose again to 6,872 individuals in need, who received support to a value of 1,900,000 crowns,[155] while in June, due to labour deployments, this figure fell to 6,621 individuals, who received benefits amounting to more than two million crowns.[156] In early June, the Jewish welfare services provided 7,882 lunches, 5,989 evening meals and, for children, five hundred food parcels (see Table A.3 in the appendix).[157]

Essentially, the Community now sought to 'support the elderly and those unable to work with cash payments and benefits in kind (Naturalbeihilfen) while placing younger and healthier people in labour deployment'. This strategy enabled the Community's welfare services to reduce the number of those fit for work but receiving benefits in the eighteen to fifty age range to 4.25 per cent.[158] Since the exclusion of Jews from the economy, only the forced labour deployment launched in April had prevented an overall rise in the number of those requiring benefits, as the Prague Community underlined in its half-year report.[159]

Through its institutional welfare services, the Community catered to 859 elderly people and individuals in need of care in Prague and 300 in the provinces. The vacating of institutions caused growing problems. The old people's home in Olomouc, for example, had to be abandoned, its residents dispersed to facilities in Moravian Ostrava and Brno. Also facing liquidation was the old people's home run by the Brecher Foundation (Brecher-Stiftung) in Prostějov (Proßnitz) in the District of Olomouc.[160] The Schools Department complained that 69 per cent of children could not attend school because the Jewish Communities generally lacked the capacity to educate them but, increasingly, also because school buildings had to be vacated. On 16 May, the Jewish secondary school in Brno was liquidated, its pupils incorporated into the eight-year primary school. The impoverishment of most parents, the Prague Community noted, ruled out the possibility of private lessons for their children.[161]

The disastrous economic situation engendered by persecution, the 'dire living conditions and difficulties in obtaining food products as a result of restricted shopping hours have weakened Jews' physical resilience, rendering them susceptible to socially-induced diseases in particular', as the Prague Community summed up the situation at the end of the first half of 1941.[162] While illnesses spread, just twenty-six doctors and ten dentists catered to the tens of thousands of Jews still living in Prague; in Brno the combined figure for doctors and dentists was sixteen. In 1930, prior to ostracization and the occupational bans, 3,450 Jews had worked in the health system.[163] According to the Community, there was no longer any 'potential for preventative measures through the promotion of a healthy lifestyle among Jews in order to stave off illnesses'. Jews now lived 'in cramped flats, crowded together without green spaces, with no access to open-air swimming pools and deprived of sunlight'.[164]

In January 1941, 1,023 'Jewish flats' were vacated, while the figures were 1,298 in February, 1,685 in March, 2,021 in April, 2,486 in May and 3,006 in June. The Prague Jewish Community's Housing Department had to find temporary quarters for thousands of evicted families, which generally meant subtenancies of one room per family. The number of those in search of accommodation increased from 1,441 in January to 4,131 in June, while the Community managed to place 1,032 tenants in new lodgings in January and 3,474 in June.[165]

The Jewish Community and Labour Deployment

In its half-year report to the Central Office, the Prague Jewish Community stated that – after all district and provincial Communities had been placed under its control – it had managed to centralize all administrative processes in such a way that it could steer the activities of the provincial Communities from the capital. This, the report explained, applied in particular to the field of labour deployment, which was now organized on a Protectorate-wide basis.[166]

Prior to every dispatch of a work detail to locations outside Prague, the Jewish Labour Headquarters notified the SD Central Office and solicited its approval.[167] At the beginning of April, 239 men and 46 women worked in group deployments at nineteen retraining sites run by the HeHalutz.[168] A number of agricultural assignments were delayed due to poor weather conditions. HeHalutz representatives, meanwhile, travelled throughout the Protectorate in an attempt to find more group workplaces for Jews.[169] Due to the reorganization of forced labour discussed above, in mid May just ninety-eight men and thirty-five women were engaged in agricultural work under the auspices of the Jewish Community. The SS retraining estate in Linden still had 330 inmates, but of these 121 men had already worked in agriculture the previous year, underlining the fact that here forced labour took priority over educational goals.[170] Conversely, at this point in time the Jewish Communities in the Protectorate still ran 159 retraining classes – more than half of them in Prague – attended by 2,788 individuals.[171]

At the end of May, the Jewish Labour Headquarters again counted almost three hundred individuals deployed in agriculture with the approval of the Ministry for Social and Health Administration, of which 227 were men and 68 women,[172] and in June more than four hundred, made up of 324 men and 87 women. A total of 163 men reported to the Linden camp for work assignments at regular intervals.[173] Several new groups having been placed at various estates, in mid June 498 individuals were already working in agriculture with the ministry's approval, consisting of 395 men and 103 women.[174] In the third week of June, the number climbed to more than six hundred individuals.[175]

In the month of June, the Jewish Labour Headquarters supervised a total of fifteen groups, made up of 528 individuals engaged in 'general labour deployment' (allgemeiner Arbeitseinsatz). Requests for 631 workers had already been received from various labour offices.[176] The fact that the Jewish Employment Office had to change its German name to Jewish Labour Headquarters in the second half of May 1941 by request of the Reich protector points to the growing significance of forced labour, which was to be organized by the German labour offices alone: the Jewish Labour Headquarters was allowed to continue using the same Czech name.[177]

The Expansion of Forced Labour in Summer 1941

In early April 1941, the Central Jewish Employment Office added the names of 234 individuals living in Prague and 252 resident in the provinces to the Occupational Index. By this point, Jewish officials had completed preparations for the 'medical examinations [required] for the Labour Service (Arbeitsdienst)' to be carried out on those between the ages of eighteen and fifty. The first seventy men were summoned to undergo these screenings from 7 April.[178] For the third week of April, the figure was already 590.[179] Of 1,228 men examined between 11 and 24 April, just sixty-two were assessed as unfit for work.[180] The heads of the district Communities now travelled to Prague to receive 'information and instructions pertaining to emigration and labour deployment'.[181]

Increasingly, as in Germany and Austria, the labour offices deployed Jewish forced labourers in dam construction, regardless of their earlier occupations.[182] By the end of June 1941, of the 9,578 men who had been evaluated as able bodied and capable of hard and moderately hard labour since April, the Jewish Labour Headquarters had placed almost 25 per cent in closed work units (geschlossener Gruppeneinsatz) – kept separate from 'Aryan workers' in compliance with the regulations – in road and railway construction and in agriculture.[183]

The Jewish Labour Headquarters helped arrange the deployment of several hundred Jewish workers: thirty-two men supplemented an existing group engaged in the construction of a complex of film studios for the Skorkowsky firm at a site in Barrandov, while fifteen men were placed in roadbuilding work in Zdiby (Zdib) for the Prague State Office. Fifty-four men completed the work detail engaged in the construction of the Helmowsky Dam for the Lanna Bau-Unternehmung AG Prag, which was founded in 1923 and subsisted on public construction contracts.[184]

At the beginning of July, with the approval of the Czech Ministry for Social and Health Administration, the Prague Community's Jewish Labour Headquarters sent a number of small groups to perform transport and construction work. Ten men began work in dam construction in Troja for Lanna AG, and another ten in Prague-Strážiště (Prag-Straschnitz) loading agricultural machines for the firm Hofherr Schrantz. Agricultural deployments, which took place at a number of estates as in previous years and in which 552 men and 130 women were engaged, now required the ministry's approval as well.[185] In the second week of July, thirty-three individuals reported to the Avia aircraft factory in Prague, opened in 1928, for construction work,[186] four to the firm Ing. Domanský in Cumbolds for motorway building, fifteen to the kaolin plant in Klumtschau, five to the City of Švihov (Schwiehau) for forestry work and six to the City of Turnov for construction tasks. A total of 567 men and 131 women now found themselves in agricultural labour deployment, while 328 Jews worked in the Linden camp.[187]

In mid July, the labour offices' requirements grew exponentially. While the ministry demanded forty-one workers for several firms, the labour offices in various cities requested the following numbers: twenty-five in Kladno, seventy-five in Německý Brod, thirty in Olomouc and twenty-one in Prague. Agricultural deployments, which included forestry, remained at about the same level.[188] One week later, a number of labour offices requested workers for a range of firms; the figures were twelve in Olomouc, ten in Pardubice, 146 in Jihlava and 190 in Prague. For railway construction in Sázava (Sasau)-Velká Losenice (Groß Lossenitz) near Německý Brod, officials discussed expanding labour deployment from eighty-five to two hundred individuals.[189]

Towards the end of July 1941, the Jewish Community had to make 250 workers available for the ministry, one hundred for the Olomouc Labour Office and thirty-eight for its counterpart in Kolín, while also providing smaller groups for the labour offices in Hradec Králové, Strakonice, Mladá Boleslav, Pilsen and Kladno. By this point, one hundred Jews were working for Lanna AG in Prague, seventeen at the Junkers Flugzeug- und Motorenwerke AG in Prague and twenty-one at brickworks in Stodůlky (Stodulek) and Záběhlice (Sabechlitz).[190] In early August, fifty-seven men began their group deployment in construction, transportation and brick production. The Jewish work details active in Prague were reinforced by sixty-six new members, while 159 men were employed at new sites in construction, forestry and brick production outside of Prague, in the Hradec Králové Municipal Forestry Administration for example. In addition, the Army Construction Office in Vyškov again recruited one hundred Jews for building work, while the Konstruktiva firm deployed thirty-seven men in Sázava in the same field. Labour offices had submitted further requests for seventy-five workers. By this point in time, 710 men and the same figure of 136 women were still working in agriculture and forestry; 123 Jews, now divided into ten groups, were deployed in forestry work alone.[191]

At this point in time, the Central Office ordered the Jewish Community to provide it with an overview of all Jewish work details in the Protectorate for the Reich protector and the Ministry for Social and Health Administration.[192] The ministry planned to publish guidelines on 'Jews' labour deployment', as follows. Once the Jewish Community had assessed the fitness for work of all those in the eighteen to fifty age range, the labour offices were to distribute workers to the vacant posts reported to them in agriculture, industry and commerce with a view to the group deployment of Jews in details of at least four individuals. However, the armaments industry would remain closed to Jews. If there was a lack of workers within a labour office's own district, it could request groups consisting of ten forced labourers each from other areas via the ministry. The Jews would be remunerated according to tariff as Jewish assets were reserved for emigration, so compulsory labour (Pflichtarbeit) or other forms of unpaid work were out of the question. Employers had to provide accommodation and wages and ensure the segregation of Jewish workers. The relocation of workers, meanwhile, required the approval of the Central Office for Jewish Emigration. These regulations were to apply only to unemployed Jews, while those employed on an individual basis in agriculture had to be reassessed.[193]

In mid August, in addition to construction work, soap factories in Prague such as those operated by Barton and Elba also employed Jews. While one group completed its work for the airbase command (Fliegerhorstkommandantur) in Ruzin, the Labour Office in Klatovy alone submitted a request for sixty men. By now, 1,020 individuals were already working in agriculture and forestry, 854 men and 166 women. Forestry work had doubled in size within a short period of time, now employing 198 individuals in nineteen groups. Jewish labour deployment had reached such a scale that the Czech Interior Ministry now informed all state offices and police directorates that the rules governing Jews' shopping hours required modification: Jewish forced labourers who could prove that their working hours came to an end after the restricted shopping hours for Jews would be allowed to shop between 5 p.m. and 7 p.m.[194]

By the end of August, more than two hundred additional workers had been placed at manufacturing sites in Prague. To take just one example, fifty Jews worked for Karl Kindl & Co at the Kobylisy firing range. New groups were deployed outside Prague as well, as other firms exploited an increasing number of Jewish workers. By now, 176 Jews were slaving away in railway construction in Sázava-Velká Losenice. By the end of the month, the labour offices in the Protectorate had requested another 250 men. Jewish officials compiled a numerical list for the Central Office detailing labour deployment in Prague and the provinces along with a list of the names of all Jews employed in the private sector, broken down according to trade, crafts and commerce.[195] In total, forty-four groups made up of 886 men, previously registered with the Jewish Labour Headquarters, were subject to general labour deployment. The Labour Headquarters' Occupational Index now included 6,364 individuals, of whom 78.39 per cent had earlier worked in trade and commerce, 16.19 per cent as labourers and craftsmen, and the remainder as doctors, lawyers and farmers. Now, at the behest of the Ministry for Social and Health Administration, the Jewish Labour Headquarters also registered those Jews who had started a job prior to the decree on forced labour, a total of 5,336 individuals.[196]

In August 1941, in parallel to the forced labour deployment of Jews in segregated work details, compulsory labour service was introduced for all Protectorate citizens fit for work.[197] Roadbuilding not essential to the war effort now stopped; it had been discontinued in Germany in autumn 1939 because of the war but until this point infrastructural adaptation to the German standard had remained a priority in the Protectorate.[198]

Of the 17,600 Jewish males between the ages of eighteen and fifty who had been examined to determine their fitness for work, only 2,170 were judged to be incapable of working. Of the more than fifteen thousand individuals thus considered able to perform light to heavy work, 11,700 were now subject to labour deployment, most of them in the labour office districts of Prague (5,452) and Brno (1,642). A total of 2,332 men worked in agriculture, 1,000 of them in work details, and 4,560 for construction firms, 3,000 of them in work details. A total of 4,300 still worked in business and commerce in enterprises for which they had worked earlier, but even here 581 of them were already deployed in work details. In the District of Brno, of the 2,038 Jews the Labour Office had registered, it deployed 866 in work details, 667 of them in large groups for construction firms.[199] For the District of Moravian Ostrava, the chief county commissioner reported that – with due regard to the 'guidelines published' by the ministry – all identifiable Jews fit for work had been deployed 'en bloc and in a state of isolation', mostly in 'earthworks'.[200]

The Jewish Community's Responses to Persecution

The Central Office increasingly looked to cut the costs of Jewish institutions: in July, the Prague Jewish Community's noninstitutional welfare services paid out the equivalent of more than two million crowns to the needy.[201] Certainly, growing labour deployment and, on a smaller scale, emigration cut the cost of welfare for the Community to a degree. For example, in the second week of August the Community registered thirty-seven additional welfare recipients who had been left destitute by persecution. But at the same time, sixty-four individuals ceased to receive support. The Protectorate-wide fundraising campaign known as 'Sacrifice – Construct – Live' also helped, bringing in more than 930,000 crowns in July and somewhat more than 1.1 million in August.[202]

However, in the second week of August alone, the Community's noninstitutional welfare services paid out almost 537,000 crowns in monetary benefits to the needy, while the Soup Kitchen prepared 629 breakfasts, 7,418 lunches and 5,110 evening meals, and also provided food parcels for five hundred children. A total of 848 individuals now lived in nineteen Community institutions.[203] In August, Community welfare services spent a total of almost 1.9 million crowns on financial support, while 642 individuals received clothing, shoes or furniture, and 392 had clothing or shoes repaired. Changes in the provision of welfare appeared to be in the offing: the Central Office demanded a list of the names of all those in receipt of welfare in the Protectorate, together with the monetary or in-kind benefits provided to each of them.[204]

It was at this of all times that the Reich protector palmed off the obligation to provide poor relief onto the Jewish Communities. From 1 September 1941, as had been the case in Germany and Austria since the end of 1938, Jews were thus excluded entirely from the state welfare system.[205]

Jews in the Protectorate learned of such official ordinances on a weekly basis in the *Jüdisches Nachrichtenblatt*, printed and distributed since September with a slightly diminished print run of 12,500 copies and now extending to just four pages.[206] Two months earlier, the publication had still run to ten pages.[207]

Although the Central Office continued to push emigration and the Prague Jewish Community's Emigration Department advised around one thousand would-be emigrants a week, very few escape routes remained.[208] In July, the Community transferred to the Central Office 461 emigration applications for 187 men, 227 women and 47 children. Of these, 427 were for Shanghai, 11 Cuba and 8 the United States.[209] In August, the Central Office received 422 applications from the Document Procurement Office, 389 of them for Shanghai. Twenty individuals, meanwhile, left the Protectorate on the so-called special transports.[210]

The number of people who managed to emigrate from the Protectorate remained negligible. While forty-five members of the Olomouc Jewish Community took their emigration folders to the Central Office in Prague in August alone,[211] between the beginning of May and the end of August just eleven individuals from this district managed to leave the Protectorate. In the same period, forty-seven individuals died there and there were four births for a total Jewish population of four thousand, of whom about 1,400 lived in Olomouc, 1,400 in Prostějov, 255 in Kroměříž, 250 in Hranice na Moravě, 230 in Přerov, 180 in Lipník nad Bečvou (Leipnik), 140 in Kojetín (Kojetein) and 100 in Loschik.[212]

In June, the authorities in the Chief County Commissioner District of Zlín announced plans for a resettlement campaign, prompting an official from the Prague Community's Provincial Department to travel to a number of locations, including Zlín, Holešov, Uherský Brod, Strážnice and Kyjov, to make preparations for it.[213] The campaign took place in late June.[214] From 26 June 1941, such campaigns were facilitated by the Czech government ordinance 248/41, which was actually intended to make it more difficult to evict people but excluded Jewish tenants from its provisions.[215]

The headquarters of the local Jewish Community was relocated to Uherský Brod when the authorities launched a resettlement campaign in Uherské Hradiště (Ungarisch-Hradisch).[216] Resettlement also intensified in Prague. Towards the end of July, the Prague Community had to vacate the old people's home in Dejvice (Dewitz), accommodating its thirty-nine charges in the so-called allocation area (Zuweisungsgebiet), where the situation grew increasingly dire. Jews who moved house not only had to register with the police but also required approval from the Central Office and the Jewish Community.[217] By this point, the Prague Community's Advice Centre on Legal and Economic Issues (Beratungsstelle in Rechts- und Wirtschaftsfragen) focused chiefly on locating records in order to effect the transfer of real estate to the Emigration Fund. It also compiled lists of property holdings in Prague and the provinces for the Central Office on the basis of new surveys.[218] In August, the Central Office in Prague evicted Jewish tenants from 324 flats, while the Trust Office (Treuhandstelle) instructed Jews to vacate another eighteen flats in confiscated buildings, leaving the Jewish Community with the extremely difficult task of accommodating those affected.[219]

At the beginning of August, the Central Office ordered the Prague Jewish Community to dissolve sixty-nine foundations it had administered hitherto, a further eighty-six in mid August and another 143 shortly afterwards. The assets of five foundations had already been transferred to the Emigration Fund for Bohemia and Moravia.[220] In total, by the end of August, 449 foundations controlled by the Prague Jewish Community had fallen victim to this policy.[221]

The Prague Jewish Community was still running an array of retraining courses. In the first week of July alone, for example, it admitted one hundred new students.[222] However, from September 1941, on the orders of the Central Office, all retraining measures were discontinued in the Protectorate. While this occurred several months later than in Germany, in the Protectorate too the decision was taken in light of the increased need for forced labour and intensified preparations for deportation.[223]

While it seemed as though the Central Office or the Reich protector had seized control of anti-Jewish measures, this was not the case. Local authorities continued to play a proactive role in radicalizing policy. On 26 June, the Prague Police Directorate instructed the Barbers' and Hairdressers' Cooperative (Genossenschaft der Raseure und Haarschneider) to serve Jews between 8 and 10 in the morning only.[224] In Brno, the same restricted hours applied to barbers and hairdressers from 5 July. On 21 July, the local police directorate prohibited Jews from entering all parks in the Greater Brno area and from sitting on the benches on Joštova ulice (Jodokstraße).[225] On 17 July, the Prague Police Directorate then prohibited Jews from entering all municipal and private woods in the Protectorate capital and the surrounding area[226] and, from 29 July, from frequenting either bank of the Vltava between the railway bridge in Smíchov (Smichow) and the Hlávka Bridge.[227]

Regardless of the circular decree of 17 August 1940, which sought to stop various authorities from implementing measures of their own, chief county commissioners, German government commissioners, Nazi Party offices and Czech district authorities continued to impose 'anti-Jewish measures of a proprietary or personal nature', such as local directives requiring Jews to hand over bicycles, typewriters or furniture or even prohibitions on leaving one's home or opening a window. On 31 July 1941, the Reich protector moved to stamp out this tendency by issuing another circular decree to the chief county commissioners, the Gestapo, the Nazi Party offices and the Central Office. The decree stated that a variety of agents were often pursuing personal interests under the guise of 'combating the Jews' (Judenbekämpfung), for example in the case of the theft or destruction of property. In Moravia, the decree asserted, there had been a number of cases in which the SA had acted in concert with Czechs.[228]

Here the Reich protector referred to incidents following Germany's invasion of the Soviet Union. Members of the Motorized SA (Motor-SA) had used the beginning of the attack as a pretext for looting and setting alight synagogues in southern Moravia, namely in Bzenec (Bisenz), Kyjov, Strážnice, Veselí nad Moravou (Wessely an der March) and Uherské Hradiště, aided by local residents, particularly Vlajka members.[229] Such individual actions must cease. Compliance with local anti-Jewish measures could only be guaranteed by the 'Protectorate executive', though, the decree underlined, it could hardly count on the support of a mostly 'Jew-friendly' populace. According to the Reich protector, as long as 'Jews are not required to don an external identifying mark, all prohibitions will be plagued by the shortcomings described above'. The 'Jewish problem [would] receive the utmost attention' from the Reich protector 'at all times', while policy would be coordinated with the Reich, such that the 'ground will already be laid for the far-reaching decisions imminent in this area upon the conclusion of the Eastern Campaign. Until then, however, the general political interests of the Reich must be borne in mind'. All future measures were to be presented for acceptance or rejection to the Commander of the Security Police.[230]

It was to these interests that Prague Jewish Community representatives appealed when they took up the cudgels against many of the proliferating local anti-Jewish measures and put their case to the Central Office. For example, in the second week of July they reported damage to synagogues in Kyjov, Bzenec, Strážnice and Uherské Hradiště as well as new restrictions imposed in Uherský Brod.[231] In the first week of August, the Community complained about official directives in the cities of Uherský Brod, Rakovník, Pilsen and Holešov, riots in Strážnice, an arson attack on a synagogue in Uherský Brod and food rationing in Olomouc.[232] For the period between 16 and 22 August, the Community reported to the Central Office house searches in Hodonín (Göding), cemetery damage in Pilsen and the confiscation of the Jewish Community library in Olomouc.[233] Towards the end of August, it once again reported house searches in Hodonín and tasks assigned by local authorities to the Jewish Communities in Olomouc and Strážnice.[234] Here the Prague Community sought to use the authority of Eichmann's Central Office to rein in the local authorities.

On 8 August 1941, all senior Prague Jewish Community functionaries were summoned to the Central Office to report on their activities, with SS-Hauptsturmführer Günther subsequently carrying out an inspection of the organization.[235] In July, the Central Office had instructed the Jewish Communities to register all the synagogues and cemeteries in the Protectorate, noting those no longer in use. Gatherings of attendees after services should be prevented.[236] In Moravian Ostrava, the local Jewish Community's Department of Cultural Affairs passed this on to Community members on 21 August; however, as in 1940, in anticipation of the High Holy Days, which attracted a greater number of worshippers, its directive was stricter than the original instructions.[237]

Jewish Resistance and Opposition

A 1939 publication in the *Jüdisches Nachrichtenblatt* had already warned the Jews of the Protectorate of the possible consequences for the Jewish community of any political action or other acts likely to incur the authorities' wrath. Nonetheless, many Jews refused to be cowed and continued to infringe anti-Jewish directives or even discuss politics in public, as Livia Rothkirchen established as early as 1981.[238]

The Special Court operated by the German State Court in Prague, for example, sentenced innkeeper Josef Herman, born in 1897, to two and a half years' imprisonment. Not only had he illicitly continued to run his own restaurant in Kutná Hora (Kuttenberg, District of Kolín) by obtaining a licence under the name of a non-Jewish straw person, but in February 1941, in the company of non-Jewish visitors, including a policeman and a municipal employee, he had made disparaging remarks about Hitler and polemicized against war and the persecution of Jews.[239]

In July, the chief county commissioner in Tábor reported to the Reich protector:

> Specific complaints have been made recently about the Jews' behaviour. Reports are coming in from all quarters according to which they are constantly infringing the curfews, while the Czech institutions dare not intervene. Though the Secret State Police have arrested a number of Jews, they cannot be everywhere. The Jews have once again become highly insolent and are engaging in agitation. I believe drastic measures will soon be imperative. In particular, the Jews in the countryside must be compelled to leave the villages and towns. ... The measures taken by the labour offices to bring Jewish men into the workforce cannot solve the problem in its entirety.[240]

With many Jews ignoring the official regulations, in articles and readers' letters a number of Protectorate newspapers publicly condemned specific cases of them frequenting markets, using bicycles, purchasing food without ration coupons or maintaining friendly relations with non-Jews. The *Arischer Kampf* urged non-Jews to report Jews to the authorities, avoid all contact with them and, above all, to refrain from helping them.[241] In many cases, such denunciations led to Jews' arrest by the Gestapo.

In some cases, Jewish representatives took pre-emptive action in an attempt to prevent negative consequences for members of the Jewish community. In Slaný (Schlan), numerous warnings from the Jewish Community had failed to dissuade Otto Löwy from flouting the evening curfew. Despite a written declaration promising to mend his ways, he attended a public boxing tournament, from which he was thrown out. When the *Arischer Kampf* newspaper denounced his actions, Community representatives sprang into action and registered him for the so-called Linden Retraining Camp in an attempt to get him off the authorities' radar.[242]

In the summer of 1941, the police chief in Hradec Králové imposed penalties on four Jewish men for violating a range of regulations: one received a five hundred-crown penalty notice because his son had been on the street after 8 p.m. and, moreover, had been riding a bicycle; another had to pay fifty crowns for violating the shopping hours; yet another was detained for three days for leaving his town without permission, while another member of the Jewish community suffered the same penalty for failing to comply with the curfew.[243]

In early June, the SD reported that Jews were increasingly infringing the persecutory regulations:

> Cinemas and restaurants have been virtually overrun by Jewish adolescents in recent times. In the realm of the economy, most working Jews no longer bother to comply with official regulations, particularly in the provinces; the stipulated shopping hours and the curfew are widely violated or evaded. In Jewish circles, it is often said that one can get away with more again now. Jews claim there are signs that Germany does not have victory in the bag, as more vigorous action would otherwise be taken against the Jews. The good relationship between Czechs and Jews remains unchanged. It has often been observed in recent times that a strikingly large number of Czechs, most of the population in some villages, have attended Jews' funerals, which came across as nothing more than a demonstration.[244]

In order to curb this tendency, State Secretary Karl Hermann Frank called for Jews in the Protectorate to be forced to wear an identifying mark: 'Jews' insolence is increasing on a daily basis. Constant violation of our Jewish ordinances is the order of the day. Reports are coming in from all quarters that Jews' anti-Reich activities are growing by the hour'.[245]

The Introduction of the 'Jewish Star' and Preparations for New Mass Deportations

The introduction of a 'Jewish star' within the borders of the Greater German Reich at the beginning of September 1941 signalled the authorities' transition to making concrete preparations for transports in Germany, Austria and the Protectorate.[246] The initiative to introduce a discriminatory badge, however, did not come from Berlin but arrived there in July from Prague via State Secretary Frank.[247]

The critical political situation in the Protectorate had revived the debate on forcing Jews to identify themselves with an external sign, a debate that had passed through several peaks and troughs. By spring 1941, an increasing number of prominent Czechs had declared their solidarity with the Jews. In May, news reached London that among the many Protectorate citizens who had been reported to the German authorities for maintaining relations with Jews were senior officials of National Partnership and other major figures in the territory's political, cultural and economic life. This occurred despite the fact that National Partnership had prohibited its members from associating with Jews the previous autumn. Demonstratively friendly behaviour towards Jews, reports stated, was one of the elements of national resistance to the Nazis. Many individuals had been denounced for such conduct by the German press or the Czech fascists, such as a National Partnership functionary in Příbram (Prebram) and the local police chief in Nova Cerekev (Neu Zerekwe).[248]

After Germany's attack on the Soviet Union in June 1941, the press in the Protectorate was instructed to launch a new anti-Jewish campaign in an attempt to reverse most Czechs' aversion to antisemitism. The German Reich, one Jewish Telegraphic Agency article stated, based its judgement as to whether the Czechs were genuinely willing to recognize the 'New Order' (Neue Ordnung) on their attitude towards the Jews. According to the *Venkov* newspaper, anti-Jewish measures must not only be implemented correctly but also inspired by the right spirit. The key slogan was: 'Let us resolve the Jewish question in our hearts'.[249]

Nonetheless, as we have seen, in the Protectorate it was above all Jews' attitudes that were regarded as 'challenging'. The war against the Soviet Union in particular changed the mood in the Jewish community. Many Czech Jews now placed their hopes in a Soviet victory, prompting them to act with greater self-confidence than at any time since the depressing defeat of France at the hands of the seemingly omnipotent Germans. Newspaper articles in the Protectorate criticized Jews' allegedly provocative behaviour, including the 'arrogance' of Jewish women, who ostentatiously rode bicycles and attended sporting events.[250]

In early July 1941, a report was circulated in the Office of the Reich Protector stating that complaints about Jews' insolent behaviour were piling up in every part of Bohemia and Moravia, while German circles frequently called for Jews to be forced to wear identifying armbands.[251] At this time the leadership of National Partnership was also discussing a proposal to introduce armbands, though with some caution as this came under the remit of the Czech government.[252]

State Secretary Frank now took the initiative. In the middle of July, he wrote to the head of the Reich Chancellery in Berlin, Reich Minister Hans Heinrich Lammers (1879–1962), stating that he believed the time had come to introduce armbands for Jews: they were becoming increasingly 'insolent and defiant in connection with the war against the Soviet

Union'. From a 'political and policing point of view', he underlined, 'the Czechs [must be] prevented from associating with Jews as far as possible'.[253] Lammers was eager to involve the Reich Interior Ministry. In late July, Frank pressed him to 'bring [the issue] to the Führer's attention so he can decide the matter', if necessary, once the Interior Ministry had released its statement. 'Marking the Jews in the Protectorate is a political imperative', Frank contended, one all the more urgently needed to 'pacify the Protectorate' as the food shortage became more acute, causing despair among the Czechs. The Jews were 'the agents of anti-German propaganda'. Marking them would set them apart from the Czech population and hamper the exchange of information.[254]

When Berlin failed to take action, on 10 August Frank also pressed Reich Protector von Neurath 'to immediately have the Jews in the Protectorate marked by armbands'.[255] Unbeknown to Frank, it was not until this date that Lammers conveyed his proposal to the Reich Interior Ministry, because it was 'responsible for dealing with the entire Jewish question'.[256] In the ministry, State Secretary Stuckart – in light of a political situation completely different from that pertaining in 1938 or 1940 – now believed the time had come to introduce the identificatory marking of Jews in the Protectorate. Foreign policy considerations, he contended, could be disregarded; after all, in the General Government and small parts of the incorporated territories such marking had long been in place.[257] However, it was important to examine 'whether there might, for example, be an increased outflow of Jewish workers from business enterprises in the Protectorate as a consequence of the marking of Jews', which might prove impossible to offset.[258] On 14 August, Reich Interior Minister Frick also made positive remarks, but he wanted to wait for a statement from the Foreign Office and for the results of the assessment of the impact on labour deployment in the Protectorate.[259]

Suddenly the debate in Berlin encompassed the rest of German territory as well. Once Goebbels had obtained Hitler's approval on 19 August 1941, the Reich Security Main Office drafted a corresponding police ordinance for the Greater German Reich,[260] Hitler having decided, in late July or early August, to resume the deportation of Jews from the Reich. The plan was that this would initially take the form of partial deportations from the major cities, including Prague, for which the identificatory marking of Jews was a key prerequisite.[261]

* * *

The year 1941 was distinguished by new, radical measures, many of them emanating from Eichmann's Central Office or the Office of the Reich Protector. They served mainly to cut the cost of state support for

Jews while also segregating Jewish from non-Jewish Czechs. On 31 May, the Reich protector transferred responsibility for supporting impoverished Jews from the state to the Jewish Communities, which were already under severe financial strain. He also facilitated the introduction of the Nuremberg laws in the Protectorate. The Czech government, meanwhile, restricted shopping hours and imposed other restrictions detrimental to the lives of Jews. In an attempt to quell resistance among Jews and diminish Czech solidarity, following Germany's attack on the Soviet Union Frank, as deputy to the Reich protector, proposed to Berlin that the Jews in the Protectorate be forced to wear an identificatory mark.

Nonetheless, the local authorities had by no means lost the initiative. In many smaller towns, but also in major cities such as Prague and Brno, they had pressed ahead with ghettoization before the Reich protector gave the concentration of Jews the green light in March 1941. Subsequently, it was chiefly the Central Office that pushed this agenda in Prague and other major cities. In the provinces, all the Jews in a given community were typically forced to move into a separate street or even a dilapidated castle, while in the major cities the tendency was to establish so-called 'Jews' houses' in specific districts. The Jewish Communities found themselves facing the virtually impossible task of quickly finding accommodation for hundreds of evicted families: the authorities now permitted only subtenancies in so-called 'Jews' houses'. The situation was exacerbated by the Central Office's efforts to accelerate the expropriation of buildings owned by Jews, and by the Reich protector's implementing decree on the exclusion of Jews from the economy, of spring 1941, which sought to complete the process of 'Aryanization'.

Although the Central Office exercised tight control over the Jewish Communities, when it came to matters of general policy this applied only to the fields of emigration, finances and housing. Even in these core areas, however, this did not mean that the Prague Jewish Community was fully domesticated as a mere organ of policy implementation. Community officials made interventions and lodged petitions with multiple agencies, demonstrating their efforts, some of them even successful, to resist oppression and alleviate the hardship of the Community's compulsory members. With respect to local restrictions or attacks, meanwhile, the Community sought to mobilize the Central Office on Jews' behalf.

At the start of 1941, local authorities, initially in Prague and Brno and later in a total of ninety-seven locations, began to recruit Jews to clear snow. While these workers were often poorly remunerated, Jewish representatives nonetheless viewed this development positively as a means of reducing the Prague Jewish Community's burgeoning welfare expenditure. The Community actively sought to get farmers, firms and public building contractors interested in Jewish work details. In January, April and May, several decrees issued by the Czech Ministry for Social and Health Administration then introduced forced labour for Jews in segregated work details in the Protectorate on the German model. Every Jew between the ages of eighteen and fifty had to submit to an examination, organized by the Jewish Communities, to determine his or her fitness for work. The new form of forced labour in segregated work gangs was organized by the German labour offices, guided by the directives of the Czech ministry. The Prague Jewish Community not only had to help arrange the fitness-for-work screening but also to provide lists of workers' names. The Reich protector was involved in rolling out the new policy, while the Central Office ensured that it too had a say when it came to external deployments, that is, those outside of Prague, because this touched on Jews' freedom of movement. The labour offices initially placed Jews mainly in agriculture and construction and later increasingly in industry and forestry. Henceforth, thousands of Czech Jews toiled for private companies and public agencies in civil engineering projects, river regulation, in industrial and craft businesses, on estates and in forestry. By early summer, of fifteen thousand Jewish men, more than 11,700 were subject to labour deployment, many of them in segregated work details.

Like the Central Office in the Protectorate, since the spring of 1941 the Reich Security Main Office had involved itself for the first time in forced labour and the concentration of Jews in 'Jews' houses' in Germany and Austria. The process of bringing forced labour deployment and the welfare system in the Protectorate into line with practices in Germany, the cessation of retraining and the debate on whether to force Jews to wear an identificatory sign reflect the authorities' efforts to centralize anti-Jewish policy in the Greater German Reich in light of the planned resumption of deportations.

Notes

1. Moskowitz, 'The Jewish Situation', 17–19 and fn 5.
2. Rothkirchen, *Jews*, 148.
3. BA Berlin, R 30/4c, fol. 114: Chief County Commissioner, Department II, Administrative report for January 1941, General political situation, Moravian Ostrava, 22 January 1941, 2.
4. USHMM Washington, RG 48.005M, reel 3 (Prague State Archive), no. 114, n.p.: Chairman of the government to State Secretary K.H. Frank in Prague, 3 April 1941.

On this discussion, see ibid., no. 109–12, n.p.: Note Reich protector, 23 November 1940 and 4 March 1941, also Letter BdS to Undersecretary of State von Burgsdorff, 5 April 1941. Cf. Rothkirchen, *Jews*, 149.
5. Third Decree on the Implementation of the Law on the Protection of German Blood and German Honour, 5 July 1941, RGBl. 1941 I, 384. Reprinted in VEJ/3, doc. 309, 732–33. See also *Verordnungsblatt des Reichsprotektors in Böhmen und Mähren*, 5 July 1941, 403; Němec, 'Das tschechische Volk', 446.
6. Moskowitz, 'The Jewish Situation', 17, fn 1.
7. YV Jerusalem, O 7/57, fol. 74: Weekly report by the Jewish Religious Community and the Prague Palestine Office on their activities, 18–24 January 1941, 13.
8. USHMM Washington, RG 48.005M, reel 4 (Prague State Archive), Shopping hours for Jews, carton, I-3b-5852, no. 5, n.p.: Interior Ministry to State Authorities in Prague and Brno, 31 January 1941.
9. YV Jerusalem, O 7/57, fol. 113a: Weekly report by the Jewish Religious Community and the Prague Palestine Office on their activities, 1–7 February 1941, 12; Institute of Jewish Affairs, *Hitler's Ten-Year War*, 59.
10. The Jewish Black Book Committee, *The Black Book*, 208.
11. YV Jerusalem, O 7/57, fol. 150: Weekly report by the Jewish Religious Community and the Prague Palestine Office on their activities, 15–21 February 1941, 12.
12. Ibid., fol. 233: Weekly report by the Jewish Religious Community and the Prague Palestine Office on their activities, 22–28 March 1941, 9.
13. Ibid., O 7/58, fol. 25: Weekly report by the Jewish Religious Community and the Prague Palestine Office on their activities, 5–11 April 1941, 8.
14. Ibid., O 7/57, fol. 131a: Weekly report by the Jewish Religious Community and the Prague Palestine Office on their activities, 8–15 February 1941, 13.
15. Ibid., fol. 321: Report by the Jewish Religious Community and the Prague Palestine Office on their activities in the first quarter of 1941, 35.
16. Ibid., O 7/58, fol. 115: Weekly report by the Jewish Religious Community and the Prague Palestine Office on their activities, 17–23 May 1941, 8.
17. Ibid., fol. 55: Weekly report by the Jewish Religious Community and the Prague Palestine Office on their activities, 19–25 April 1941, 8; ibid., fol. 189: Monthly report by the Jewish Religious Community of Prague, 1–30 April 1941, 11.
18. Institute of Jewish Affairs, *Hitler's Ten-Year War*, 57.
19. YV Jerusalem, O 7/57, fol. 127: Weekly report by the Jewish Religious Community and the Prague Palestine Office on their activities, 8–15 February 1941, 8.
20. Ibid., fol. 229: Weekly report by the Jewish Religious Community and the Prague Palestine Office on their activities, 22–28 March 1941, 5.
21. Brandes and Míšková, *Vom Osteuropa-Lehrstuhl ins Prager Rathaus*, 280; Monika Sedláková, 'Die Rolle der sogenannten "Einsatzstäbe" bei der Enteignung jüdischen Vermögens', in *Theresienstädter Studien und Dokumente* 2003, 275–305, here 282.
22. NA Prague, Úřad říšského protektora, sign. Central Administration 1, carton 63, fol. 22: Emil Walther to Reich protector/Central Administration, 2 August 1941; ibid., fol. 25: Reich protector/Central Administration to Central Office for Jewish Emigration, 1 August 1941.
23. Ibid., fol. 26: Wilhelmine Rispler to Reich protector/Central Administration, 4 August 1941; ibid., fol. 27: Reich protector/Central Administration to Central Office for Jewish Emigration, 14 August 1941. See Sedláková, 'Die Rolle der sogenannten "Einsatzstäbe"', 282.
24. NA Prague, Úřad říšského protektora, sign. Central Administration 1, carton 63, fol. 122: Hans Koeltzsch (Reichssender Böhmen [radio station]) to Reich protector/

Central Administration, 21 May 1941; ibid., fol. 169: Erich Füchte (German Higher Regional Court [Oberlandesgericht]) to Reich protector/Central Administration, 27 August 1941; ibid., fol. 311: Herbert Kunert to Masalsky (Reich protector/Central Administration), 16 May 1941; ibid., fol. 321: Maria Pfeiffer to Reich protector/ Central Administration, 19 August 1941; ibid., fol. 534: Radio dealer Kopecký to Reich protector/Central Administration, 27 March 1941. Dozens of other examples for the 1940–41 period can be found in the same file.

25. USHMM Washington, RG 11.001 M.23, reel 91 (OSOBI 1488-1-15), fol. 7: Copy SD Headquarters Prague, Monthly report March 1941, 57; ibid., RG 11.001 M.15, reel 83 (OSOBI 1322-2-391), fol. 44+49: Monthly report SD Headquarters Prague (May 1941), 1 June 1941, 41+46.
26. YV Jerusalem, O 7/57, fol. 183–84: Weekly report by the Jewish Religious Community and the Prague Palestine Office on their activities, 1–7 March 1941, 10–11.
27. Rothkirchen, *Jews*, 121.
28. USHMM Washington, RG 48.005M, reel 5 (Prague State Archive), I 3b-5800 carton 387, no. 7, n.p.: Note Dr von Burgsdorff, 26 March 1941.
29. Ibid., RG 11.001 M.23, reel 83 (OSOBI 1322-2-391), fol. 49: Monthly report SD Headquarters Prague (May 1941), 1 June 1941, 46.
30. For a detailed account, see chapter 2 of Gruner, *Jewish Forced Labor*, 61–74; cf. also Gruner, *Der Geschlossene Arbeitseinsatz*, 249–62.
31. USHMM Washington, RG 11.001 M.23, reel 91 (OSOBI 1488-1-15), fol. 7: Copy SD Headquarters Prague, Monthly report March 1941, 57.
32. YV Jerusalem, O 7/57, fol. 316: Report by the Jewish Religious Community and the Prague Palestine Office on their activities in the first quarter of 1941, 30.
33. Ibid., fol. 7: Weekly report by the Jewish Religious Community and the Prague Palestine Office on their activities, 27 December 1940 to 3 January 1941, 5.
34. Ibid., fol. 302a–303: Report by the Jewish Religious Community and the Prague Palestine Office on their activities in the first quarter of 1941, 18–19.
35. Ibid., fol. 304: Report by the Jewish Religious Community and the Prague Palestine Office on their activities in the first quarter of 1941, 20.
36. Ibid., fol. 249: Monthly report by the Jewish Religious Community and the Prague Palestine Office, 1–31 January 1941, 10.
37. Ibid., fol. 307: Report by the Jewish Religious Community and the Prague Palestine Office on their activities in the first quarter of 1941, 22.
38. Ibid., fol. 9: Weekly report by the Jewish Religious Community and the Prague Palestine Office on their activities, 27 December 1940 to 3 January 1941, 11.
39. Ibid., fol. 319: Report by the Jewish Religious Community and the Prague Palestine Office on their activities in the first quarter of 1941, 33.
40. Ibid., fol. 14: Weekly report by the Jewish Religious Community and the Prague Palestine Office on their activities, 27 December 1940 to 3 January 1941, Appendix: Summary as at 30 December 1940.
41. Ibid., fol. 8: Weekly report by the Jewish Religious Community and the Prague Palestine Office on their activities, 27 December 1940 to 3 January 1941, 10.
42. Bondy, 'Chronik der sich schließenden Tore', 92–98.
43. YV Jerusalem, O 7/57, fol. 309: Report by the Jewish Religious Community and the Prague Palestine Office on their activities in the first quarter of 1941, 24.
44. Ibid., fol. 253: Monthly report by the Jewish Religious Community and the Prague Palestine Office, 1–31 January 1941, 14.
45. Ibid., fol. 250: Monthly report by the Jewish Religious Community and the Prague Palestine Office, 1–31 January 1941, 11.

46. Ibid., fol. 106 and 112: Weekly report by the Jewish Religious Community and the Prague Palestine Office on their activities, 1–7 February 1941, 10.
47. Ibid., fol. 113–113a: Weekly report by the Jewish Religious Community and the Prague Palestine Office on their activities, 1–7 February 1941, 11–12.
48. Ibid., fol. 43: Weekly report by the Jewish Religious Community and the Prague Palestine Office on their activities, 11–17 January 1941, 2.
49. Ibid., fol. 63: Weekly report by the Jewish Religious Community and the Prague Palestine Office on their activities, 18–24 January 1941, 2.
50. Ibid., fol. 44–45: Weekly report by the Jewish Religious Community and the Prague Palestine Office on their activities, 11–17 January 1941, 3–4.
51. Ibid., fol. 65: Weekly report by the Jewish Religious Community and the Prague Palestine Office on their activities, 18–24 January 1941, 4.
52. Ibid., fol. 257: Monthly report by the Jewish Religious Community and the Prague Palestine Office, 1–28 February 1941, 2–3.
53. BA Berlin, R 30/4c, fol. 158: Chief County Commissioner, Administrative report for the month of March 1941, General economic situation, Moravian Ostrava, 20 March 1941, 11.
54. Ibid., fol. 169: Chief County Commissioner, Administrative report for the month of April 1941, confidential, General economic situation, Moravian Ostrava, 21 April 1941, 8.
55. BA Berlin, R 30/4d, fol. 51: Chief County Commissioner, Administrative report (confidential) for July 1941, Moravian Ostrava, 20 July 1941, 10.
56. YV Jerusalem, O 7/57, fol. 128: Weekly report by the Jewish Religious Community and the Prague Palestine Office on their activities, 8–15 February 1941, 9.
57. Ibid., fol. 164: Weekly report by the Jewish Religious Community and the Prague Palestine Office on their activities, 22–28 February 1941, 7.
58. Ibid., fol. 230: Weekly report by the Jewish Religious Community and the Prague Palestine Office on their activities, 22–28 March 1941, 6.
59. Ibid., fol. 5: Weekly report by the Jewish Religious Community and the Prague Palestine Office on their activities, 27 December 1940 to 3 January 1941, 3; ibid., fol. 65: Weekly report by the Jewish Religious Community and the Prague Palestine Office on their activities, 18–24 January 1941, 4.
60. Ibid., fol. 45: Weekly report by the Jewish Religious Community and the Prague Palestine Office on their activities, 11–17 January 1941, 4.
61. Ibid., fol. 51: Weekly report by the Jewish Religious Community and the Prague Palestine Office on their activities, 11–17 January 1941, 10; ibid., fol. 195: Weekly report by the Jewish Religious Community and the Prague Palestine Office on their activities, 8–14 March 1941, 4; ibid., fol. 212: Weekly report by the Jewish Religious Community and the Prague Palestine Office on their activities, 15–21 March 1941, 3.
62. Ibid., fol. 215: Weekly report by the Jewish Religious Community and the Prague Palestine Office on their activities, 15–21 March 1941, 6. The Community also had to compile lists of properties and almshouses owned by Jews in Prague and other cities in the Protectorate; ibid., fol. 198–99: Weekly report by the Jewish Religious Community and the Prague Palestine Office on their activities, 8–15 March 1941, 7–8.
63. Ibid., fol. 195: Weekly report by the Jewish Religious Community and the Prague Palestine Office on their activities, 8–14 March 1941, 4; ibid., fol. 212: Weekly report by the Jewish Religious Community and the Prague Palestine Office on their activities, 15–21 March 1941, 3.

64. *Der Neue Tag*, 8 October 1941, 9.
65. BA Berlin, R 30/4d, fol. 6–8: Chief County Commissioner, Administrative report (confidential) for May 1941, Moravian Ostrava, 20 May 1941, 6–8.
66. YV Jerusalem, O 7/57, fol. 3: Weekly report by the Jewish Religious Community and the Prague Palestine Office on their activities, 27 December 1940 to 3 January 1941, 1.
67. Ibid., fol. 21: Weekly report by the Jewish Religious Community and the Prague Palestine Office on their activities, 4–10 January 1941, 2.
68. Ibid.
69. Ibid., fol. 42–43: Weekly report by the Jewish Religious Community and the Prague Palestine Office on their activities, 11–17 January 1941, 1–2.
70. Ibid.; ibid., fol. 83: Weekly report by the Jewish Religious Community and the Prague Palestine Office on their activities, 25–31 January 1941, 1.
71. Ibid., fol. 83: Weekly report by the Jewish Religious Community and the Prague Palestine Office on their activities, 25–31 January 1941, 1; ibid., fol. 158: Weekly report by the Jewish Religious Community and the Prague Palestine Office on their activities, 22–28 February 1941, 1; ibid., fol. 174: Weekly report by the Jewish Religious Community and the Prague Palestine Office on their activities, 1–7 March 1941, 1.
72. Ibid., fol. 242: Monthly report by the Jewish Religious Community and the Prague Palestine Office, 1–31 January 1941, 2; ibid., fol. 255–56: Monthly report by the Jewish Religious Community and the Prague Palestine Office, 1–28 February 1941, 1–2; ibid., fol. 271: Monthly report by the Jewish Religious Community and the Prague Palestine Office, 1–31 March 1941, 2.
73. Ibid., fol. 284–85, 292: Report by the Jewish Religious Community and the Prague Palestine Office on their activities in the first quarter of 1941, 2–3, 8.
74. Ibid., fol. 6: Weekly report by the Jewish Religious Community and the Prague Palestine Office on their activities, 27 December 1940 to 3 January 1941, 4.
75. Ibid., fol. 25: Weekly report by the Jewish Religious Community and the Prague Palestine Office on their activities, 4–10 January 1941, 6; ibid., fol. 46: Weekly report by the Jewish Religious Community and the Prague Palestine Office on their activities, 11–17 January 1941, 5.
76. Ibid., fol. 25: Weekly report by the Jewish Religious Community and the Prague Palestine Office on their activities, 4–10 January 1941, 6.
77. Ibid., fol. 6: Weekly report by the Jewish Religious Community and the Prague Palestine Office on their activities, 27 December 1940 to 3 January 1941, 4.
78. According to reports on retraining measures in *Jüdisches Nachrichtenblatt*, 2 and 30 May 1941; Moskowitz, 'The Jewish Situation', 22.
79. YV Jerusalem, O 7/57, fol. 260: Monthly report by the Jewish Religious Community and the Prague Palestine Office, 1–28 February 1941, 6.
80. Ibid., fol. 296: Report by the Jewish Religious Community and the Prague Palestine Office on their activities in the first quarter of 1941, 10–12.
81. Ibid., fol. 298: Report by the Jewish Religious Community and the Prague Palestine Office on their activities in the first quarter of 1941, 14.
82. Ibid., fol. 6: Weekly report by the Jewish Religious Community and the Prague Palestine Office on their activities, 27 December 1940 to 3 January 1941, 4.
83. Ibid., fol. 26: Weekly report by the Jewish Religious Community and the Prague Palestine Office on their activities, 4–10 January 1941, 7.
84. Ibid., fol. 47: Weekly report by the Jewish Religious Community and the Prague Palestine Office on their activities, 11–17 January 1941, 6.

85. BA Berlin, R 30/4c, fol. 124: Chief County Commissioner, Department II, Administrative report for January 1941, Labour deployment and wages policy, Moravian Ostrava, 22 January 1941, 12.
86. YV Jerusalem, O 7/57, fol. 66–67: Weekly report by the Jewish Religious Community and the Prague Palestine Office on their activities, 18–24 January 1941, 5–6; ibid., fol. 83: Weekly report by the Jewish Religious Community and the Prague Palestine Office on their activities, 25–31 January 1941, 5.
87. Ibid., fol. 66–67: Weekly report by the Jewish Religious Community and the Prague Palestine Office on their activities, 18–24 January 1941, 5–6.
88. Ibid., fol. 106 and 108: Weekly report by the Jewish Religious Community and the Prague Palestine Office on their activities, 1–7 February 1941, 6.
89. Ibid., fol. 124–25: Weekly report by the Jewish Religious Community and the Prague Palestine Office on their activities, 8–15 February 1941, 5–6; ibid., fol. 143: Weekly report by the Jewish Religious Community and the Prague Palestine Office on their activities, 15–21 February 1941, 5.
90. Ibid., fol. 160–61: Weekly report by the Jewish Religious Community and the Prague Palestine Office on their activities, 22–28 February 1941, 3–4. In March too, several hundred Jewish men worked daily at the Ruzin Airbase in the mornings and afternoons, now engaged in earthworks; ibid., fol. 178: Weekly report by the Jewish Religious Community and the Prague Palestine Office on their activities, 1–7 March 1941, 5.
91. Ibid., fol. 301: Report by the Jewish Religious Community and the Prague Palestine Office on their activities in the first quarter of 1941, 16.
92. Ibid., fol. 160–61: Weekly report by the Jewish Religious Community and the Prague Palestine Office on their activities, 22–28 February 1941, 3–4.
93. Ibid., fol. 214: Weekly report by the Jewish Religious Community and the Prague Palestine Office on their activities, 15–21 March 1941, 5.
94. On forced labour in segregated work teams, see Gruner, *Der Geschlossene Arbeitseinsatz*.
95. LBI/A New York, Memoir Coll.: Max Mannheimer, 'Von Neutitschen nach Dachau' (1969), 17.
96. *Deutsche Politik im 'Protektorat Böhmen und Mähren'*, 123, doc. no. 23: Report by the Central Office, 2 October 1941.
97. *Jüdisches Nachrichtenblatt*, Prague edition, 21 February 1941; reprinted in English in Moskowitz, 'The Jewish Situation', 41. Cf. Osterloh and Wixforth, 'Die "Arisierung" im Protektorat Böhmen und Mähren', 310.
98. RGBl. 1938 I, 823.
99. BA Berlin, R 8150/12, fol. 158: Compilation of decrees. See Jewish Black Book Committee, *The Black Book*, 177; LBI/A New York, Memoir Coll.: Max Mannheimer, 'Von Neutitschen nach Dachau' (1969), 17.
100. Quoted in Report by the Jewish Religious Community of Prague, 'Labour' (n.d., mid 1942), in Krejčová, Svobodová and Hyndráková, *Židé v Protektorátu*, doc. 5, 105.
101. YV Jerusalem, O 7/57, fol. 301–2: Report by the Jewish Religious Community and the Prague Palestine Office on their activities in the first quarter of 1941, 16–17.
102. On Jewish forced labour in the Protectorate, see chapter 5 in Gruner, *Jewish Forced Labor*.
103. *Der Neue Tag*, 7 March 1941, 5.
104. *Berliner Börsen-Zeitung*, vol. 86, no. 110, 6 March 1941 (evening edition), 2.
105. For a detailed account, see Gruner, *Der Geschlossene Arbeitseinsatz*, 201–4.

106. YV Jerusalem, O 7/57, fol. 212: Weekly report by the Jewish Religious Community and the Prague Palestine Office on their activities, 15–21 March 1941, 3.
107. Ibid., fol. 232: Weekly report by the Jewish Religious Community and the Prague Palestine Office on their activities, 22–28 March 1941, 8.
108. Ibid., O 7/58, fol. 4–5: Weekly report by the Jewish Religious Community and the Prague Palestine Office on their activities, 29 March to 4 April 1941, 3–4.
109. Ibid., fol. 6: Weekly report by the Jewish Religious Community and the Prague Palestine Office on their activities, 29 March to 4 April 1941, 5.
110. Central Archives for the History of the Jewish People (CAHJP) Jerusalem, A/W no. 421, n.p.: Anonymous report on the 'Deployment of Jewish Workers', n.d., 3. Cf. Report by the Central Office, 2 October 1941, in *Deutsche Politik im 'Protektorat Böhmen und Mähren'*, 123, doc. no. 23; and appendix, table 2, in ibid., 127.
111. USHMM Washington, RG 48.005M, reel 4 (Prague State Archive), I 3b-5813 Treatment of Jews under Labour Law, no. 2, n.p.: Dr Bertsch (Reich protector/II 4 a 5431/41) to ministry, 17 April 1941, 1–3.
112. CAHJP Jerusalem, A/W no. 421, n.p.: Anonymous report on the 'Deployment of Jewish Workers', n.d., 1–3; cf. BA Berlin, R 8150/12, fol. 158: Compilation of decrees.
113. YV Jerusalem, O 7/58, fol. 97: Weekly report by the Jewish Religious Community and the Prague Palestine Office on their activities, 10–16 May 1941, 2.
114. Ibid., fol. 192: Monthly report by the Jewish Religious Community of Prague, 1–31 May 1941, 3.
115. Ibid., fol. 192: Monthly report by the Jewish Religious Community of Prague, 1–31 May 1941, 3.
116. Ibid., fol. 6: Weekly report by the Jewish Religious Community and the Prague Palestine Office on their activities, 29 March to 4 April 1941, 5.
117. Ibid., fol. 110: Weekly report by the Jewish Religious Community and the Prague Palestine Office on their activities, 17–23 May 1941, 3.
118. Ibid., fol. 98: Weekly report by the Jewish Religious Community and the Prague Palestine Office on their activities, 10–16 May 1941, 3.
119. Ibid., fol. 192: Monthly report by the Jewish Religious Community of Prague, 1–31 May 1941, 3.
120. Ibid., fol. 98: Weekly report by the Jewish Religious Community and the Prague Palestine Office on their activities, 10–16 May 1941, 3.
121. On forced labour in the Protectorate, see chapter 5 in Gruner, *Jewish Forced Labor*.
122. BA Berlin, R 30/4d, fol. 12: Chief County Commissioner, Administrative report (confidential) for May 1941, Moravian Ostrava, 20 May 1941, 12; ibid., fol. 37: Chief County Commissioner, Administrative report (confidential) for June 1941, Moravian Ostrava, 20 June 1941, 22.
123. YV Jerusalem, O 7/57, fol. 182: Weekly report by the Jewish Religious Community and the Prague Palestine Office on their activities, 1–7 March 1941, 9; ibid., fol. 227: Weekly report by the Jewish Religious Community and the Prague Palestine Office on their activities, 22–28 March 1941, 3–5.
124. Ibid., fol. 217a: Weekly report by the Jewish Religious Community and the Prague Palestine Office on their activities, 15–21 March 1941, 9.
125. Ibid., fol. 321: Report by the Jewish Religious Community and the Prague Palestine Office on their activities in the first quarter of 1941, 35.
126. Gruner, *Der Geschlossene Arbeitseinsatz*, 177–84.
127. YV Jerusalem, O 7/59, fol. 176: Monthly report by the Jewish Religious Community of Prague, 1–30 July 1941, 5.

128. YV Jerusalem, O 7/58, fol. 2–3: Weekly report by the Jewish Religious Community and the Prague Palestine Office on their activities, 29 March to 4 April 1941, 1–2; ibid., fol. 18: Weekly report by the Jewish Religious Community and the Prague Palestine Office on their activities, 5–11 April 1941, 1.
129. Ibid., fol. 48: Weekly report by the Jewish Religious Community and the Prague Palestine Office on their activities, 19–25 April 1941, 1.
130. Ibid., fol. 96: Weekly report by the Jewish Religious Community and the Prague Palestine Office on their activities, 10–16 May 1941, 1.
131. Ibid., fol. 190: Monthly report by the Jewish Religious Community of Prague, 1–31 May 1941, 1.
132. Ibid., fol. 4: Weekly report by the Jewish Religious Community and the Prague Palestine Office on their activities, 29 March to 4 April 1941, 3.
133. Ibid., fol. 20: Weekly report by the Jewish Religious Community and the Prague Palestine Office on their activities, 5–11 April 1941, 3.
134. Ibid., fol. 50: Weekly report by the Jewish Religious Community and the Prague Palestine Office on their activities, 19–25 April 1941, 3.
135. Ibid., fol. 96: Weekly report by the Jewish Religious Community and the Prague Palestine Office on their activities, 10–16 May 1941, 1.
136. Ibid.
137. Ibid., fol. 120: Weekly report by the Jewish Religious Community and the Prague Palestine Office on their activities, 24–30 May 1941, 1.
138. YV Jerusalem, M 58/JM 11808, fol. 424: Report by the Emigration Department of the Olomouc Jewish Religious Community, 1–31 May 1941, 3 June 1941.
139. YV Jerusalem, O 7/58, fol. 214: Report by the Jewish Religious Community of Prague on its activities in the first half of 1941, chart: Decline in the Jewish Population in the Protectorate of Bohemia and Moravia.
140. BA Berlin, R 30/4d, fol. 28: Chief County Commissioner, Administrative report (confidential) for June 1941, Moravian Ostrava, 20 June 1941, 13.
141. YV Jerusalem, O 7/58, fol. 212: Report by the Jewish Religious Community of Prague on its activities in the first half of 1941, 3.
142. Ibid., fol. 9: Weekly report by the Jewish Religious Community and the Prague Palestine Office on their activities, 29 March to 4 April 1941, 8; ibid., fol. 187: Monthly report by the Jewish Religious Community of Prague, 1–30 April 1941, 9.
143. YV Jerusalem, M 58/JM 11814, fol. 117: Copy letter Bing, Reich Protector, to Prague Jewish Religious Community, 4 April 1941.
144. Ibid., fol. 119: Partly translated copy of a decree issued by the Czech Finance Ministry, Prague to Jewish Religious Community of Prague, 5 April 1941.
145. YV Jerusalem, M 58/JM 11808, fol. 282: Translation of draft letter from the Jewish Religious Community of Prague to Jewish Communities, 21 May 1941.
146. YV Jerusalem, O 7/58, fol. 86: Weekly report by the Jewish Religious Community and the Prague Palestine Office on their activities, 3–9 May 1941, 6.
147. Ibid., fol. 102: Weekly report by the Jewish Religious Community and the Prague Palestine Office on their activities, 10–16 May 1941, 7.
148. Ibid., fol. 122: Weekly report by the Jewish Religious Community and the Prague Palestine Office on their activities, 24–30 May 1941, 3.
149. Ibid., fol. 132: Weekly report by the Jewish Religious Community and the Prague Palestine Office on their activities, 31 May to 6 June 1941, 2.
150. Ibid., fol. 144: Weekly report by the Jewish Religious Community and the Prague Palestine Office on their activities, 7–13 June 1941, 3.
151. Ibid., fol. 206: Monthly report by the Jewish Religious Community of Prague, 1–30 June 1941, 7.

152. YV Jerusalem, O 7/39, n.p.: Israelite Religious Community of Moravian Ostrava, Legal Department, Salo Krämer, to Jewish Community of Prague, Legal Department, 4 June 1941.
153. Ibid., n.p.: Note for leadership, Jewish Community of Prague, Legal advice, 19 June 1941.
154. YV Jerusalem, O 7/58, fol. 184: Monthly report by the Jewish Religious Community of Prague, 1–30 April 1941, 6; ibid., fol. 229: Report by the Jewish Religious Community of Prague on its activities in the first half of 1941, chart.
155. Ibid., fol. 195: Monthly report by the Jewish Religious Community of Prague, 1–31 May 1941, 6.
156. Ibid., fol. 205: Monthly report by the Jewish Religious Community of Prague, 1–30 June 1941, 6.
157. Ibid., fol. 135: Weekly report by the Jewish Religious Community and the Prague Palestine Office on their activities, 31 May to 6 June 1941, 5.
158. Ibid., fol. 222: Report by the Jewish Religious Community of Prague on its activities in the first half of 1941, 10.
159. Ibid., fol. 244: Report by the Jewish Religious Community of Prague on its activities in the first half of 1941, 21.
160. Ibid., fol. 225: Report by the Jewish Religious Community of Prague on its activities in the first half of 1941, 12.
161. Ibid., fol. 241: Report by the Jewish Religious Community of Prague on its activities in the first half of 1941, 19.
162. Ibid., fol. 225–26: Report by the Jewish Religious Community of Prague on its activities in the first half of 1941, 12–13.
163. *Jüdisches Nachrichtenblatt*, 20 June 1941; Moskowitz, 'The Jewish Situation', 29–30, fn 30.
164. YV Jerusalem, O 7/58, fol. 225–26: Report by the Jewish Religious Community of Prague on its activities in the first half of 1941, 12–13.
165. Ibid., fol. 235–36: Report by the Jewish Religious Community of Prague on its activities in the first half of 1941, 14 and chart: Constriction of Jews' Living Quarters in Prague.
166. Ibid., fol. 239–40: Report by the Jewish Religious Community of Prague on its activities in the first half of 1941, 17–18.
167. Ibid., fol. 110: Weekly report by the Jewish Religious Community and the Prague Palestine Office on their activities, 17–23 May 1941, 3.
168. Ibid., fol. 5: Weekly report by the Jewish Religious Community and the Prague Palestine Office on their activities, 29 March to 4 April 1941, 4.
169. Ibid., fol. 21: Weekly report by the Jewish Religious Community and the Prague Palestine Office on their activities, 5–11 April 1941, 4.
170. Ibid., fol. 99: Weekly report by the Jewish Religious Community and the Prague Palestine Office on their activities, 10–16 May 1941, 4.
171. Ibid., fol. 195: Monthly report by the Jewish Religious Community of Prague, 1–31 May 1941, 6.
172. Ibid., fol. 123: Weekly report by the Jewish Religious Community and the Prague Palestine Office on their activities, 24–30 May 1941, 4.
173. Ibid., fol. 145: Weekly report by the Jewish Religious Community and the Prague Palestine Office on their activities, 7–13 June 1941, 4.
174. Ibid., fol. 158: Weekly report by the Jewish Religious Community and the Prague Palestine Office on their activities, 14–20 June 1941, 4.
175. Ibid., fol. 170: Weekly report by the Jewish Religious Community and the Prague Palestine Office on their activities, 21–27 June 1941, 4.

176. Ibid., fol. 202: Monthly report by the Jewish Religious Community of Prague, 1–30 June 1941, 3.
177. Ibid., fol. 110: Weekly report by the Jewish Religious Community and the Prague Palestine Office on their activities, 17–23 May 1941, 3.
178. Ibid., fol. 4–5: Weekly report by the Jewish Religious Community and the Prague Palestine Office on their activities, 29 March to 4 April 1941, 3–4.
179. Ibid., fol. 20: Weekly report by the Jewish Religious Community and the Prague Palestine Office on their activities, 5–11 April 1941, 3.
180. Ibid., fol. 36: Weekly report by the Jewish Religious Community and the Prague Palestine Office on their activities, 1–18 April 1941, 4; ibid., fol. 51: Weekly report by the Jewish Religious Community and the Prague Palestine Office on their activities, 19–25 April 1941, 4.
181. Ibid., fol. 39: Weekly report by the Jewish Religious Community and the Prague Palestine Office on their activities, 12–18 April 1941, 7.
182. Ibid., fol. 133: Weekly report by the Jewish Religious Community and the Prague Palestine Office on their activities, 31 May to 6 June 1941, 3.
183. Ibid., fol. 221–22: Report by the Jewish Religious Community of Prague on its activities in the first half of 1941, 8–9 and table: Deployment of Jewish Workers.
184. Ibid., fol. 169: Weekly report by the Jewish Religious Community and the Prague Palestine Office on their activities, 21–27 June 1941, 3; see also *Das Protektorat Böhmen und Mähren im deutschen Wirtschaftsraum*, 77.
185. YV Jerusalem, O 7/59, fol. 4–5: Weekly report Jewish Religious Community of Prague, 28 June to 4 July 1941, 3–4.
186. *Das Protektorat Böhmen und Mähren im deutschen Wirtschaftsraum*, 61.
187. YV Jerusalem, O 7/59, fol. 17–18: Weekly report Jewish Religious Community of Prague, 5–11 July 1941, 3–4.
188. Ibid., fol. 30–31: Weekly report by the Jewish Religious Community of Prague, 12–18 July 1941, 3–4.
189. Ibid., fol. 43: Weekly report by the Jewish Religious Community of Prague, 19–25 July 1941, 3.
190. Ibid., fol. 56–56RS: Weekly report by the Jewish Religious Community of Prague, 26 July to 1 August 1941, 3–3RS.
191. Ibid., fol. 62–63: Weekly report by the Jewish Religious Community of Prague, 2–8 August 1941, 3–4.
192. Ibid.
193. USHMM Washington, RG 48.005M, reel 4 (Prague State Archive), I 3b-5813 Treatment of Jews under Labour Law, no. 4, n.p.: Circular note Reich protector/II 4 a 5431/41 (Dr Bertsch) to Groups in the Office of the Reich Protector, the Central Office and the BdS plus draft, 21 July 1941, 1–8.
194. YV Jerusalem, O 7/59, fol. 82–83: Weekly report by the Jewish Religious Community of Prague, 9–15 August 1941, 3–4.
195. YV Jerusalem, O 7/59, fol. 95–96: Weekly report by the Jewish Religious Community of Prague, 16–22 August 1941, 3–4; ibid., fol. 110: Weekly report by the Jewish Religious Community of Prague, 23–29 August 1941, 3.
196. Ibid., fol. 186–87: Monthly report by the Jewish Religious Community of Prague, 1–31 August 1941, 2–3.
197. Alfons Adam, 'Im Wettstreit um die letzten Arbeitskräfte: Die Zwangsarbeit auf dem Gebiet der Tschechischen Republik 1938–1945', in Dieter Pohl and Tanja Sebta (eds), *Zwangsarbeit in Hitlers Europa: Besatzung – Arbeit – Folgen* (Berlin, 2013), 115.

198. BA Berlin, R 30/4d, fol. 72: Chief County Commissioner, Administrative report (confidential) for August 1941, Moravian Ostrava, 22 August 1941, 14.
199. USHMM Washington, RG 48.005M, reel 2 (Prague State Archive), II-4-4055, carton 859, no. 1, n.p.: Labour Deployment Statistics, as at 1 September 1941. See also CAHJP Jerusalem, A/W no. 421, n.p.: Report on the 'Deployment of Jewish Workers', n.d., 3. Cf. Report by the Central Office, 2 October 1941, in *Deutsche Politik im 'Protektorat Böhmen und Mähren'*, 123, doc. no. 23; see also appendix: table 2, in ibid., 127.
200. BA Berlin, R 30/4d, fol. 74: Chief County Commissioner, Administrative report (confidential) for August 1941, Moravian Ostrava, 22 August 1941, 16.
201. YV Jerusalem, O 7/59, fol. 176RS: Monthly report by the Jewish Religious Community of Prague, 1–30 July 1941, 5RS.
202. Ibid., fol. 176: Monthly report by the Jewish Religious Community of Prague, 1–30 July 1941, 5; ibid., fol. 84: Weekly report by the Jewish Religious Community of Prague, 9–15 August 1941, 5; ibid., fol. 190: Monthly report by the Jewish Religious Community of Prague, 1–31 August 1941, 6.
203. Ibid., fol. 84: Weekly report by the Jewish Religious Community of Prague, 9–15 August 1941, 5.
204. Ibid., fol. 190: Monthly report by the Jewish Religious Community of Prague, 1–31 August 1941, 6.
205. Following publication on 22 August, the Reich protector's decree of 5 August 1941 came into force on 1 September 1941; USHMM, RG 48.005M, reel 4 (Prague State Archive), I 3b-5812 Poor relief for Jews, no. 2–3, n.p.: Handwritten notes on draft of the decree issued by the Reich protector, June 1941. See YV Jerusalem, O 7/59, fol. 115: Weekly report by the Jewish Religious Community of Prague, 23–29 August 1941, 8.
206. Ibid., fol. 126: Weekly report by the Jewish Religious Community of Prague, 30 August to 5 September 1941, 6; ibid., fol. 180: Monthly report by the Jewish Religious Community of Prague, 1–30 July 1941, 9.
207. YV Jerusalem, O 7/58, fol. 137: Weekly report by the Jewish Religious Community and the Prague Palestine Office on their activities, 31 May to 6 June 1941, 7.
208. The department advised 937 parties in the first week of July, with seventy-one individuals passing the Document Procurement Office's final review, sixty-six of them hoping to make it to Shanghai and five to Argentina. One hundred emigration applications were passed on to the Central Office. In the second week of July, department officials advised 925 parties, with 102 individuals passing the final review, 93 of them hoping to emigrate to Shanghai. One hundred applications were referred to the Central Office. The Emigration Department advised 1,068 parties in the following week alone. One hundred and one individuals submitted all the required documents, ninety of them aspiring to emigrate to Shanghai. Once again, the Central Office received one hundred applications; YV Jerusalem, O 7/59, fol. 2: Weekly report by the Jewish Religious Community of Prague, 28 June to 4 July 1941, 1; ibid., fol. 15: Weekly report by the Jewish Religious Community of Prague, 5–11 July 1941, 1; ibid., fol. 28–29: Weekly report by the Jewish Religious Community of Prague, 12–18 July 1941, 1–2.
209. Ibid., fol. 172+RS: Monthly report by the Jewish Religious Community of Prague, 1–30 July 1941, 1+RS.
210. Ibid., fol. 185–86: Monthly report by the Jewish Religious Community of Prague, 1–31 August 1941, 1–2.
211. YV Jerusalem, M 58/ JM 11808, fol. 403: List, 1 September 1941.

212. Ibid., fol. 382: Table on Movement of the Jewish Population in the Chief County Commissioner District of Olomouc, 1 May to 31 August 1941.
213. YV Jerusalem, O 7/59, fol. 8: Weekly report by the Jewish Religious Community of Prague, 28 June to 4 July 1941, 9.
214. YV Jerusalem, O 7/58, fol. 174: Weekly report by the Jewish Religious Community and the Prague Palestine Office on their activities, 21–27 June 1941, 8.
215. Sbírka zákonů a nařízení Protektorátu Čechy a Morava 248/41, in Lexa, *Anti-Jewish Laws*, 86; cf. Friedmann, 'Rechtsstellung', in Krejčová, Svobodová and Hyndráková, *Židé v Protektorátu*, 256, and YV Jerusalem, O 7/59, fol. 8: Weekly report by the Jewish Religious Community of Prague, 28 June to 4 July 1941, 9.
216. Ibid., fol. 48: Weekly report by the Jewish Religious Community of Prague, 19–25 July 1941, 8.
217. Ibid., fol. 46: Weekly report by the Jewish Religious Community of Prague, 19–25 July 1941, 6.
218. Ibid., fol. 3–4: Weekly report by the Jewish Religious Community of Prague, 28 June to 4 July 1941, 2–3.
219. Ibid., fol. 191–92: Monthly report by the Jewish Religious Community of Prague, 1–31 August 1941, 7–8; ibid., fol. 99: Weekly report by the Jewish Religious Community of Prague, 16–22 August 1941, 7.
220. Ibid., fol. 73: Weekly report by the Jewish Religious Community of Prague, 2–8 August 1941, 9; ibid., fol. 87: Weekly report by the Jewish Religious Community of Prague, 9–15 August 1941, 8; ibid., fol. 101: Weekly report by the Jewish Religious Community of Prague, 16–22 August 1941, 9.
221. Ibid., fol. 193: Monthly report by the Jewish Religious Community of Prague, 1–31 August 1941, 9.
222. Ibid., fol. 5: Weekly report by the Jewish Religious Community of Prague, 28 June to 4 July 1941, 4.
223. Ibid., fol. 190: Monthly report by the Jewish Religious Community of Prague, 1–31 August 1941, 6.
224. YV Jerusalem, O 7/58, fol. 174: Weekly report by the Jewish Religious Community and the Prague Palestine Office on their activities, 21–27 June 1941, 8; Friedmann, 'Rechtsstellung', in Krejčová, Svobodová and Hyndráková, *Židé v Protektorátu*, 249.
225. Friedmann, 'Rechtsstellung', in Krejčová, Svobodová and Hyndráková, *Židé v Protektorátu*, 249.
226. YV Jerusalem, O 7/59, fol. 35: Weekly report by the Jewish Religious Community of Prague, 12–18 July 1941, 8.
227. Quoted in Friedmann, 'Rechtsstellung', in Krejčová, Svobodová and Hyndráková, *Židé v Protektorátu*, 250.
228. USHMM Washington, RG 48.005M, reel 4 (Prague State Archive), Office of the Reich Protector, Jewish regulations, no. 18, n.p.: Circular decree Reich protector/ BdS I 2256/41 (von Burgsdorff), 31 August 1941, 1–3.
229. Machala, '"Unbearable Jewish Houses of Prayer"', 72.
230. USHMM Washington, RG 48.005M, reel 4 (Prague State Archive), Office of the Reich Protector, Jewish regulations, no. 18, n.p.: Circular decree Reich protector/ BdS I 2256/41 (von Burgsdorff), 31 August 1941, 1–3.
231. YV Jerusalem, O 7/59, fol. 22: Weekly report by the Jewish Religious Community of Prague, 5–11 July 1941, 8.
232. Ibid., fol. 73: Weekly report by the Jewish Religious Community of Prague, 2–8 August 1941, 9. On attacks on synagogues in Holešov and Uherské Hradiště, see Machala, '"Unbearable Jewish Houses of Prayer"', 73–74.

233. YV Jerusalem, O 7/59, fol. 102: Weekly report by the Jewish Religious Community of Prague, 16–22 August 1941, 10.
234. Ibid., fol. 115: Weekly report by the Jewish Religious Community of Prague, 23–29 August 1941, 8.
235. Ibid., fol. 74: Weekly report by the Jewish Religious Community of Prague, 2–8 August 1941, 10.
236. Ibid., fol. 180: Monthly report by the Jewish Religious Community of Prague, 1–30 July 1941, 9.
237. YV Jerusalem, M 58/JM 11816, fol. 245: Directive issued by Moravian Ostrava Jewish Religious Community, Department of Cultural Affairs, 21 August 1941.
238. Livia Rothkirchen, 'The Defiant Few: The Jewish and Czech "Inside Front" (1938–1942)', *Yad Vashem Studies* 14 (1981), 35–88, here 39.
239. StA Chemnitz, 30071 Zwickau Prison, no. 5281, fol. 14–20RS: Sentence by the Prague Special Court, 27 November 1941, 1–14. He died in prison on 3 November 1942; ibid., fol. 26: Note Zwickau Penal Institute (Strafanstalt Zwickau), 4 November 1942.
240. USHMM Washington, RG 48.005M, reel 4 (Prague State Archive), Office of the Reich Protector, Jewish regulations, no. 13, n.p.: Reich protector to Group I 3 plus Excerpt of administrative report by Tabor chief county commissioner (21 July 1941), 28 July 1941.
241. Frommer, *National Cleansing*, 169–73.
242. Frommer, 'Verfolgung durch die Presse', 147; Veselská, '"Sie müssen sich als Jude dessen bewusst sein, welche Opfer zu tragen sind ..."', 162.
243. Frommer, 'Verfolgung durch die Presse', 143.
244. USHMM Washington, RG 11.001 M.23, reel 83 (OSOBI 1322-2-391), fol. 49: Monthly report SD Headquarters Prague (May 1941), 1 June 1941, 46.
245. SS-Gruppenführer Frank to Neurath, 10 August 1941, in Celovsky, *Germanisierung und Genozid*, 270.
246. Police ordinance on the marking of Jews, 1 September 1941, RGBl. 1941 I, 547, Excerpt in *Europa unterm Hakenkreuz: Österreich und Tschechoslowakei*, doc. no. 102, 174.
247. Pätzold, *Verfolgung, Vertreibung, Vernichtung*, 294, doc. no. 269: State Secretary Frank to Lammers, 16 July 1941 (excerpt).
248. JTA, 'High Czech Officials Defy Nazis on Relations with Jews', 19 May 1941. See Report by the Foreign Office representative in the Office of the Reich Protector, 15 October 1940, in Mund, *Deutschland und das Protektorat*, doc. 311, 458; see also the examples from 1940/1941 in Brandes, '*Umvolkung, Umsiedlung, rassische Bestandsaufnahme*', 223–24.
249. JTA, 'New Press Campaign in Protectorate', 22 June 1941.
250. Rothkirchen, *Jews*, 122–23.
251. USHMM Washington, RG 48.005M, reel 4 (Prague State Archive), carton, I-3b-5851, no. 13, n.p.: Protectorate Group I to Group 1 3, for the attention of Ministerial Counsellor Dr Mokry, 2 July 1941.
252. RGVA Moscow, 1488-1-3, fol. 2: SD Headquarters Prague, Daily report (strictly confidential), 7 July 1941, 1.
253. Pätzold, *Verfolgung, Vertreibung, Vernichtung*, 294, doc. no. 269: State Secretary Karl Hermann Frank to Lammers, 16 July 1941. Cf. Küpper, *Karl Hermann Frank*, 182.
254. USHMM Washington, RG 48.005M, reel 4 (Prague State Archive), Marking of Jews, carton, I-3b-5851, no. 8, n.p.: State Secretary Frank to Lammers, 30 July 1941.

On the debate on the marking of Jews in the Protectorate, see also Kárný, 'The Genocide of the Czech Jews', 38.
255. SS-Gruppenführer Frank to Neurath, 10 August 1941, in Celovsky, *Germanisierung und Genozid*, 270.
256. BA Berlin, Case XI, no. 371, fol. 70–71: Lammers to Reich Interior Ministry, 10 August 1941 and Lammers to Frank (NG-1111).
257. See Gruner and Osterloh, *The Greater German Reich*, 359–60.
258. BA Berlin, Case XI, no. 371, fol. 72–73: Stuckart to Lammers, 14 August 1941 (NG-1111); cf. excerpt in Pätzold, *Verfolgung, Vertreibung, Vernichtung*, 302–3, doc. no. 276.
259. BA Berlin, Case XI, no. 371, fol. 74: Note Ficker on minister's statement, n.d. (NG-1111).
260. *Die Tagebücher von Joseph Goebbels.* Part II: *Diktate 1941–1945*, edited by Elke Fröhlich on behalf of the Institut für Zeitgeschichte and with the support of the Russian State Archive (Munich, 1996), vol. 1, 278: entry, 20 August 1941.
261. See Gruner, 'Von der Kollektivausweisung', 46–51.

CHAPTER 8

REPRESSION, DEPORTATION AND RESISTANCE

The Situation on the Eve of the New Mass Deportations

The introduction of the 'Jewish badge' signalled to the public at home and abroad the completion of the 'forced community' (Zwangsgemeinschaft) of Jews in the Greater German Reich.¹ By ensuring Jews' public identifiability through the stigmatizing yellow star and immobilizing them through the prohibition, anchored in the same decree, on leaving their place of residence without permission, the Nazi state created the prerequisites for the smooth execution of their mass deportation. The decree, which came into force on 19 September 1941, applied to all Jews of six years of age and above in Germany, Austria and the Protectorate of Bohemia and Moravia.²

On 13 September, the Prague newspaper *Der Neue Tag* justified the introduction of the 'yellow star' with the assertion that in the Eastern Campaign the German soldier had got to know 'the Jew in all his vileness and barbarity'. This marking, the newspaper went on, served to deprive Jews of the option of concealing themselves and 'thus violating those regulations that spare the German national comrades (Volksgenossen) contact with Jews'.³ With reference to the 'public marking of the Jews', *Der Neue Tag* wrote that it was readily apparent to every 'impartial observer' that 'the Jews continue to constantly infringe, for example, the regulations on shopping hours, their exclusion from parks, and the like'.[4]

What was the Jews' situation in September 1941? In the Protectorate, in order to secure a workforce and lay the ground for the deportations, a ban on emigration was in force for younger Jewish men capable of work; this was extended to Germany and Austria in early August 1941.[5] Marked with the yellow star, the Jews in Bohemia and Moravia found themselves excluded from economic and professional life as well as associations; their assets, under state control, were in blocked accounts; they were no longer permitted to own real estate or business assets, and were unable to use rental cars, sleeping or dining carriages on trains, steamboats or radios. Many public parks were now closed to them and they were even barred from walking along the banks of the Vltava. The authorities also prohibited them from frequenting entertainment and sports venues, public baths, theatres, cinemas and libraries as well as certain streets and squares, while imposing restricted shopping hours, an 8 p.m. curfew and segregation in trams, hospitals and post offices. In Prague, most Jews were concentrated within a limited area, with an average of twelve individuals penned up in just two rooms, and Jews had been ghettoized in many other cities as well. They could not move house or leave their place of residence without permission. Of the 137 Jewish organizations and 346 associations that had existed in the Protectorate, only fifteen organizations still operated, and not a single association. The Prague Jewish Community took over their responsibilities in addition to its own obligations, such as promoting emigration, welfare and schooling but, often, not their assets, which the Central Office controlled. The Community had already had to transfer 1,500 properties to the Emigration Fund for Bohemia and Moravia. Recruited by the labour offices, many Jews now performed forced labour.[6]

On 17 September, the Central Office for Jewish Emigration delivered the yellow badges to the Prague Jewish Community, with instructions to distribute them to all Jewish residents of the Protectorate.[7] The *Jüdisches Nachrichtenblatt* appeared the day before the decree on the stars came into force, with a total print run of fifteen thousand copies, 2,500 more than usual.[8] On the same day, representatives of all district Communities had to make the trip from the provinces to Prague in order to receive both the badges and related instructions from the Prague Community. They returned home the same day, with the heads of all remaining Jewish Communities within their jurisdiction waiting to receive the 'yellow stars' and instructions for their members.[9] The Přerov Jewish Community, for example, earmarked fifty crowns in its budget for fifty 'Jewish stars'.[10]

The staff of the Prague Community's Division for Non-Mosaic Jews, who advised 7,296 individuals in the third quarter of 1941, did their best to identify every individual regarded as Jewish in order to provide him or her with a star.[11] Earlier, on 31 March, the division had registered 12,680 Jews, of whom 5,600 described themselves as unaffiliated with any religion, more than 4,800 as Roman Catholic and more than 900 as Protestant.[12]

Writing about the day the decree came into force in his diary, thirteen-year-old Petr Ginz noted the sudden conspicuousness of the many star-bearing individuals passing through Prague's Old Market: 'It's foggy. The Jews have to wear a badge ... I counted sixty-nine sheriffs on the way to school, and then mummy saw more than a hundred. They're calling Dlouhá Avenue "The Milky Way"'.[13]

In its quarterly report, the Jewish Community commented on the significance of this act: 'Jews had already been almost entirely excluded from society by a range of measures. The introduction of the Jewish badge now signifies the Jews' complete isolation'.[14] Yet this was far from being the case. First of all, Jews themselves offered resistance. The chief county commissioner in Moravian Ostrava, for example, remarked later that the 'Jewish star' had sparked 'fierce resistance from the local Jews'. Widespread non-compliance, he went on, had begun to abate only after it had resulted in the arrest of several Jews.[15] Second, non-Jewish Czechs often showed solidarity with their Jewish counterparts, as Alfred Dube, eighteen years old at the time, remembered decades later. Upon seeing a Jew wearing a star, many had tipped their hat to show their respect.[16] According to historian Miroslav Kárný, some had donned home-made stars, while others had demonstratively associated with star-bearing Jews on the street.[17] The chief county commissioner in Moravian Ostrava bewailed the fact that when carrying out spot checks in the few restaurants still open to Jews, the police had found the vast majority of customers to be Czech miners who had ignored the rules on segregation.[18]

By way of contrast, the decree met with general approval among the German community, as evident in daily complaints by telephone or in writing to the authorities concerning Jews who had failed to don the star.[19] Yet even among Germans in the Protectorate, some must have taken a different view: in January 1942, the German-language local press felt the need to publish apologias on the historical precursors of the marking of Jews and other forms of discrimination.[20]

In addition to identificatory marking and the prohibition on Jews leaving their place of residence, other anti-Jewish regulations soon came into force that further restricted their freedom of movement.

In mid September 1941, the Prague Jewish Community submitted petitions to the authorities expressing its opposition to restrictions on Jews' use of the postal service in the Protectorate. In addition to Jewish residents themselves, this impacted in particular on the provincial Jewish Communities, which generally communicated with the Prague Community in writing.[21] In Moravian Ostrava, the Postal Administration (Postverwaltung) decided that Jews could patronize only Post Office 11 in Hrabůvka (Klein-Grabau) and only between 2 p.m. and 5 p.m.[22] On 24 September, meanwhile, the Postal Directorate (Post-Direktion) in the Protectorate capital decreed that Jews could use just one post office in the city, on 5 Inselgasse, Prague II, between 1 p.m. and 3 p.m.[23] An official announcement declared that in the major cities Jews would be allowed to patronize just one post office, while in smaller localities they would be permitted to use the local post offices for just a few hours.[24]

By 7 September, the Prague police chief had banned Jews from using public libraries and borrowing books.[25] On 11 September, the state president in Prague prohibited the playing, performance (on the radio or with audio devices) and dissemination (in the form of sheet music) of so-called 'Jewish music'.[26] All provincial Communities were now instructed to register bicycles and typewriters owned by Jews,[27] as well as cars.[28]

The Central Office ordered the Prague Jewish Community to procure records relating to properties in Prague and the provinces by 20 September. For months, the Community's Department for Legal and Economic Issues (Abteilung für Rechts- und Wirtschaftsfragen) had been collecting data on Jewish-owned real estate and its owners in order to compile overviews of Greater Prague and the Protectorate as a whole.[29] In addition, on 16 September the Central Office ordered the Community to centralize the registration of the members of all Jewish Communities (Matrikel) in Prague and, to this end, to have all registration books, more than two thousand of them, sent to Prague from the provinces, evidently in preparation for the deportations. The Community had received all of these registers by 25 September, with its Matriculation Department (Matrikelabteilung) taking up its work on 1 October.[30]

Regardless of the restrictions on Jews' freedom of movement, the Prague Jewish Community's Emigration Department continued to do its utmost to open up routes to emigration. In September, its officials advised 2,989 individuals in person and processed 360 written requests, while in 180 cases they petitioned the consulates of various countries on their clients' behalf. They also transferred four hundred complete applications to the Central Office, 383 of them for emigration to Shanghai.[31]

Because Jewish tenants were being driven from their homes, time and again Prague Community representatives had to intervene on their behalf at short notice. Jewish residents in the Chief County Commissioner District of Kladno, for example, were subjected to a campaign of resettlement.[32] At the same time, the Central Office terminated the tenancies of Jews living in 296 flats in Prague. The same fate also befell Jews resident in flats in (evidently Jewish-owned) buildings expropriated by the Trust Corporation (Treuhandgesellschaft), which the Prague Jewish Community had previously 'heavily occupied with subtenants' as directed. The vacating of five residential units alone affected fifty individuals. In total, 591 persons in search of accommodation registered with the Community during this month, among them an increasing number of Jews who had been forced to give up their 'subtenancy [by their] Aryan landlords'. The Community's monthly report to Eichmann referred to the tremendous difficulties involved in accommodating these people, which had only succeeded because the Community had made a 'monumental effort and overcome manifold difficulties', even disregarding sanitary concerns.[33] Within a year, the concentrating of Jewish tenants had halved the living space available per person, from 12.6 to 6.8 square metres.[34]

By this point in time, the Prague Jewish Community spent 57 per cent of the funds released by the Central Office on welfare, including support for the homeless, and 43 per cent on its other priorities such as emigration, administration, information, schools (while there were 1,598 Jewish pupils in the Protectorate, 3,889 children were still not attending school) and the SS estate of Linden.[35] In September 1941, the Jewish Community's noninstitutional welfare services paid out somewhat more than two million crowns in financial support for Jews in need, just 100,000 crowns more than in August, despite the fact that the state had shifted the entire burden of welfare provision onto its shoulders. It was only the burgeoning practice of forced labour around this time that helped the Community evade total financial collapse, as it absorbed many Jews previously in receipt of Community benefits.[36]

The Ramping Up of Forced Labour

Through a decree of 29 August 1941, the Czech Ministry for Social and Health Administration had extended forced labour deployment to all Jews between the ages of sixteen and sixty, who first had to be examined to establish their fitness for work. Article 1 of the decree underlined that Jews must be paid an adequate wage to spare the Jewish Community the need to provide additional support – suggesting that this is just what it had been doing. Responsibility for forced labour deployment was shared between the department of the Protectorate government known as Labour Deployment II, the above-mentioned Czech ministry and the Central Office.[37]

At the beginning of September, the Jewish Labour Headquarters arranged group deployments in Prague bookbinderies and carpentry and electricians' workshops. As a result of the new centralized control of forced labour, meanwhile, the state labour offices seamlessly placed Jews in new work as soon as their current deployment ended. The Brno Labour Office, for example, immediately found railway construction work in Brno-Tišnov for Jews formerly employed at the military training area in Vyškov.[38]

In September, the draftsmen of the Prague Community's Department of Economic Administration (Abteilung Wirtschaftsverwaltung) compiled nine sets of statistics on the significantly expanded Jewish labour deployment.[39] By modifying the age range subject to forced labour, the Protectorate's Labour Administration had succeeded in further intensifying it. In August 1941, of 741 Jewish men (between the ages of eighteen and fifty), the Olomouc Labour Office counted 333 subject to forced labour deployment. One month later, of the 1,079 Jews now registered (between the ages of sixteen and sixty), 472 were performing forced labour, while the figure for October had already climbed to 531.[40] In August, in the Labour Office District of Zlín, of 525 men, 366 were subject to forced labour, while the figure for September was 415 out of 579.[41] The Prague Labour Office's Department for Non-Aryans (Abteilung für Nichtarier) at Hollargasse 19, Prague XVI, registered 10,106 men in August, of whom 574 were compelled to work in agriculture and 2,206 in construction. In September, the number climbed to 15,710 registered men, of whom 5,405 had now been deployed as forced labourers.[42] Despite the regulations cited earlier, by this point Jews even worked in the armaments industry, such as the 215 men engaged in war production at the Avia aircraft factory.[43]

On 9 September 1941, the Ministry for Social and Health Administration issued the Labour Administration with an additional decree. Going beyond the modification of the age limits, this prohibited all individual deployments and required that Jews be put to work in segregated work gangs, the priority being to engage them in heavy construction work or in enterprises significant to the war effort.[44] In mid September, the Central Office demanded the creation of a card index of all men subject to labour deployment, their employers and the number of workers in each firm. In addition to work in construction and industry, 508 Jews in sixty-five groups were engaged in agriculture, while 190, divided into twenty groups, worked in forestry. Factoring in individual deployments for farmers approved by the ministry, agriculture and forestry employed 1,065 Jewish workers, 919 of them men and 146 women.[45]

In an effort to ensure that group deployments operated as smoothly and productively as possible, the Prague Jewish Community subjected candidates to 'psychotechnic examinations' to filter out 'psychopaths' and the 'feeble-minded', attempted to select appropriate foremen and sought to establish work details with members of a similar age. By now, the Prague Community noted, Jews had been shut out of economic life completely and integrated into (the predominantly manual) labour deployment.[46] In April 1941, just 23 per cent had been subject to group deployment, while a fair number had still worked in trades or had performed unskilled labour outside of group deployment. By the end of September 1941, however, 41 per cent of Jews fit for work were engaged in forced group labour (see Figure 8.1).[47]

In late October, the labour offices counted 11,949 Jewish men and 307 Jewish women subject to forced labour, that is, 12,256 in total (see Table A.4 in the appendix).[48] While this was only slightly more than in August, by this point employment on an individual basis had ceased almost entirely. What this meant was that between the end of August and the end of October 1941, the number of Jews performing forced labour had increased from just under seven thousand to more than twelve thousand, despite the mass deportations, beginning in mid October, of several thousand people.[49]

Many building projects were assigned to Jewish workers either from the provinces or Prague. In both cases, this involved the deployment of fairly large groups outside their normal place of residence and thus the establishment and maintenance of camps, most of them forgotten today. According to a report by the Jewish Community of Prague, among other things, Jewish forced labour units added a film studio to the famous Barrandov complex, worked at the airfield in Letňany (Letnian) near Prague, on the motorway in Strielek, at the electric power station in Srnojedy (Srnojed) and at the Mas factory in Sezimovo Ústí (Alt-Tabor). They were deployed in railway construction in Sázava, Velká Losenice, Nový Dvůr (Neuhof), Retschowits, Maloměřice (Malmeritz), Česká (Zinsendorf) and Neudorf, worked on the regulation of the River Ostravice (Ostrawitza) near Kunětice (Kunzendorf), the Elbe near Pardubice and the Vltava near Bavorovice (Baurowitz), and constructed the docks in Kolín, the Štěchovice (Stiechowitz) Dam and the lock near Velký Osek (Groß Ossek). Jews toiled in mining for the Horní

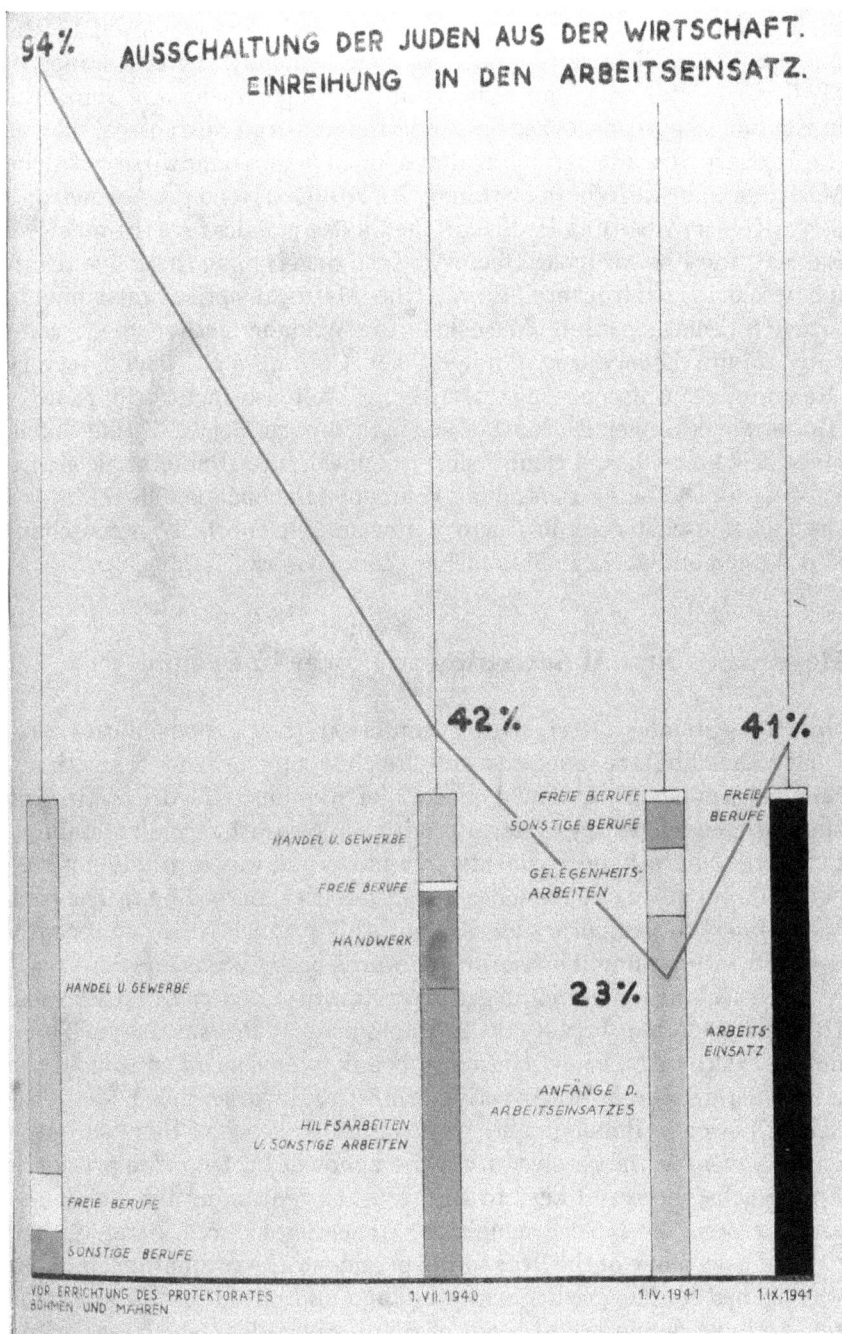

Figure 8.1. 'Exclusion of Jews from the Economy, Integration into Labour Deployment', September 1941. © YV Jerusalem, O 7/59, fol. 216: chart.

Bříza kaolin works and in Ledce (Ledetz) and were employed by the Südböhmische Elektrizitätswerke electric company, the coal mines in Mydlovary (Midlowar) and Kyjov, and the Prager Eisen AG ironworks in Kladno. They also worked for industrial and craft businesses, such as the Hofherr-Schrans agricultural machines plant (Landwirtschaftliche Maschinenfabrik Hofherr-Schrans), the Hrdlička wood processing company (Holzverarbeitung Hrdlička), the Baklax plastics firm (Kunststoffe Baklax), the Kos cardboard factory (Kartonagen Kos), the Pleva printing works (Buchdruckerei Pleva), the Matuška optical instruments firm (Optische Apparate Matuška), the Wildner leather goods company (Mann Lederwaren Wildner), the Chlumpschau kaolin factory (Kaolinfabrik Chlumpschau), the Singer suitcase factory in Klatovy (Kofferfabrik Singer Klattau), a sugar factory in Hejčín (Zuckerfabrik Hatschein), the Jiskra radio factory in Pardubice (Radiofabrik Jiskra Pardubitz), the Žaček roofing felt company (Dachpappenfabrik Žaček), the Tschemoschau ceramics factory (Keramische Fabrik Tschemoschau) and the cement works in Maloměřice (Zementwerke Malmeritz).[50]

Heydrich's Brutal Accession to Power in Prague

On 27 September 1941, Hitler conferred the responsibilities previously held by the allegedly 'ill' Reich Protector von Neurath on SS-Obergruppenführer and Police Chief Reinhard Heydrich. He was supposedly a temporary substitute, with von Neurath formally retaining his post.[51] Neurath, once considered a moderate, was certainly not suspended from office due to ideological differences. According to *The New York Times*' contemporary assessment, this staunch Nazi had recently behaved with profound intolerance towards both Czechs and Jews.[52]

As Hitler's new governor in the Protectorate of Bohemia and Moravia, Heydrich reported for duty on 28 September at Prague Castle. There he was welcomed by Karl Hermann Frank, who continued to hold the office of state secretary.[53] As acting protector, Heydrich now had a great deal of power in Bohemia and Moravia. Fully aware of this fact, later, on 19 November, he received from the hands of Protectorate president Emil Hácha the seven keys to the treasury containing the Bohemian kings' crown jewels in Prague's St. Wenceslas Church. After he had handed back three of the keys to the president, the coronation chamber was opened for Heydrich's inspection and appropriation.[54] There he is said to have donned the Crown of Saint Wenceslas, which, according to a legend probably conceived later, brings death to every illegitimate bearer.[55]

The main reason for the shakeup at the top of the German Protectorate administration was that the Germans believed Heydrich's uncompromising approach was vital to quelling the Czechs' resistance, which had intensified since Germany's attack on the Soviet Union. Acts of sabotage had proliferated, while industrial production had fallen by 20 per cent.[56] In the area under the jurisdiction of the Moravian Ostrava Police Directorate alone, Czechs carried out fifteen acts of sabotage in September.[57] Across the Protectorate, resistance included boycotting Nazi newspapers, attacks on railway carriages and the destruction of telephone lines.[58] This national wave of attacks even found reflection in the diary of the boy Petr Ginz. On 25 September 1941 he wrote: 'There was a fire engine in front of Denis Railway Station and smoke was billowing from it. Mummy heard a terrible bang and then a few smaller explosions. Probably sabotage again'.[59]

In August 1941, Himmler had received a detailed report on the Czechs' 'political sedition', allegedly fuelled by radio broadcasts from London and 'whispering campaigns'. These sources not only discussed the Allies' military successes but also rifts within the Nazi leadership. Hitler, dissatisfied with the progress of the war against the Soviet Union, had supposedly shot Göring dead. Other rumours held that Hitler himself was already dead, with a lookalike now acting in his stead, while Berlin had been hit by uprisings; Reich protector von Neurath, meanwhile, had also got himself a double for fear of the Czechs. Inspired by the Serbs' resistance, Czechs contemplated 'bloody revenge'. Beneš, according to German reports, had held out the prospect of liberation in the near future and instructed the Czechs to abandon all restraint towards the Germans.[60]

In Prague, Heydrich, just thirty-seven years old, took draconian measures to put a stop to this potentially dangerous development within the Greater German Reich. When Frank had called for such an approach ten days earlier, von Neurath had declined to act, which is what prompted Hitler to put him on forced leave. Heydrich immediately declared a state of emergency, which enabled the use of summary courts and the imposition of the death penalty; established two police drumhead courts martial at the State Police headquarters in Prague and Brno; launched a wave of arrests; closed cinemas and theatres and banned all public events. Further, he ordered the internment of Prime Minister General Eliáš, a step the Office of the Reich Protector had considered in the summer while planning a more radical occupation policy.[61]

The first six drumhead court martial verdicts were announced in Prague and Brno on 28 September for sabotage, treason and possession of weapons, with those convicted being executed, as announced in the press the following day.⁶² Just two days later, *Der Neue Tag* reported another fifty-eight executions by firing squad. Among those killed were at least six Jews resident in Prague, including Georg Spitzer and Leo Schwarz, accused by the occupation regime of membership in a resistance group, planning bomb attacks and carrying out arson attacks on crop reserves. According to the newspaper, 256 individuals had been handed over to the Gestapo.⁶³

On 2 October, the press announced that Czech Prime Minister Eliáš had been sentenced to death by the People's Court (Volksgerichtshof) for aiding the enemy and planning to commit high treason.⁶⁴ Rather than having him court-martialled and shot as originally planned, Heydrich had arranged a show trial before the People's Court. Following the preferral of charges by the State Police headquarters in Prague – rather than the public prosecutor (Oberstaatsanwalt) – on 1 October 1941, presided over by later Reich Justice Minister Otto Thierack, the judges of the First Senate of the People's Court (Erster Senat des Volksgerichtshofes), who had flown into Prague especially for this purpose, condemned Eliáš to death for acts of resistance, espionage and enemy propaganda. The German judges could certainly charge him as an accessory: files seized in Paris in 1940 had revealed his personal links with the Czech National Council in exile. Apart from that, he was aware of a number of acts of resistance though he was not actively involved in them himself. In light of this, the German court condemned Eliáš chiefly for supposedly being in cahoots with Dr Otakar Klapka, the primator of Prague, who had been arrested in July, accused of using municipal finances to support Czech refugees and the families they had left behind.⁶⁵ Prime Minister Eliáš undoubtedly maintained contact with opposition circles and, in light of the German occupation, discussed the possibility of resigning in summer 1941 with his inner circle, though without actually doing so.⁶⁶ Nonetheless, he played a key role in planning and implementing the anti-Jewish measures decreed by the Czech government, as set out in detail in previous chapters. In contrast to Klapka, who was sentenced the next day and executed on 4 October, initially the German authorities spared the prime minister's life because they wished to retain him as a hostage.⁶⁷

The same day Eliáš's death sentence was announced, the press reported another thirty-nine death penalties, with two Jews among those convicted. According to newspaper reports, they had already been executed, while 228 individuals had been handed over to the Gestapo.⁶⁸ The next day, readers learned that fifteen individuals had been executed by firing squad for economic sabotage, planning high treason and unauthorized possession of weapons, while three Jews had been hanged and 110 individuals transferred to the Gestapo.[69] On 4 October it was reported that another fifteen individuals had been executed. Among those killed were three Jews, two of them for alleged profiteering and one for membership of a communist youth organization. A total of 131 individuals had been handed over to the Gestapo.[70]

By 3 October, drumhead courts martial had already condemned between 150 and 200 individuals to death. By the end of November, Heydrich's new policy had resulted in 404 death sentences, 169 of them for alleged economic crimes, with a large number of Jews among the dead. More mass arrests were carried out, while transports took hundreds of individuals to concentration camps, mainly to Mauthausen. At the same time, Heydrich increased food rations and other forms of provisioning for Czech workers.[71] Among those subsequently executed – now mostly for economic offences – there were often Jews.[72] By the time the state of emergency was lifted on 20 January 1942, 486 individuals had lost their lives to execution. Of a total of five thousand individuals arrested, meanwhile, 2,242 were handed over to the Gestapo for admission to concentration camps.[73]

Heydrich's Rule and the Administration of the Protectorate

Heydrich now altered the Protectorate's administrative structure, cutting the number of chief county commissioners from fifteen to seven, based in Prague, České Budějovice, Pilsen, Hradec Králové, Brno, Jihlava and Moravian Ostrava (see Figure 8.2), while also reducing the Reich protector's staff and lessening the influence of the Nazi Party.[74]

Following the dissolution of the state authorities (Landesvertretungen) in 1940 and the appointment of German county commissioners, in the summer of 1941 Reich Protector von Neurath had declared that henceforth reference should no longer be made to 'Czech' authorities.[75] This, however, was essentially a case of German wishful thinking. By June 1941, of the 172 towns in the Chief County Commissioner District of Moravian Ostrava, only thirteen were led by Germans, mostly government commissioners. In some cases, mayors in the district had in fact been replaced by 'loyal' Czechs, while Czechs also retained half of the seventy-nine posts on the local councils.[76] The Olomouc government commissioner, Dr Fritz Cermak (1894–1966), a member of the German Bundestag in the 1950s, boasted of having increased the share of German municipal officials and employees from 7 per cent to 25 per cent of a total of 1,200 in just nine months. He took advantage

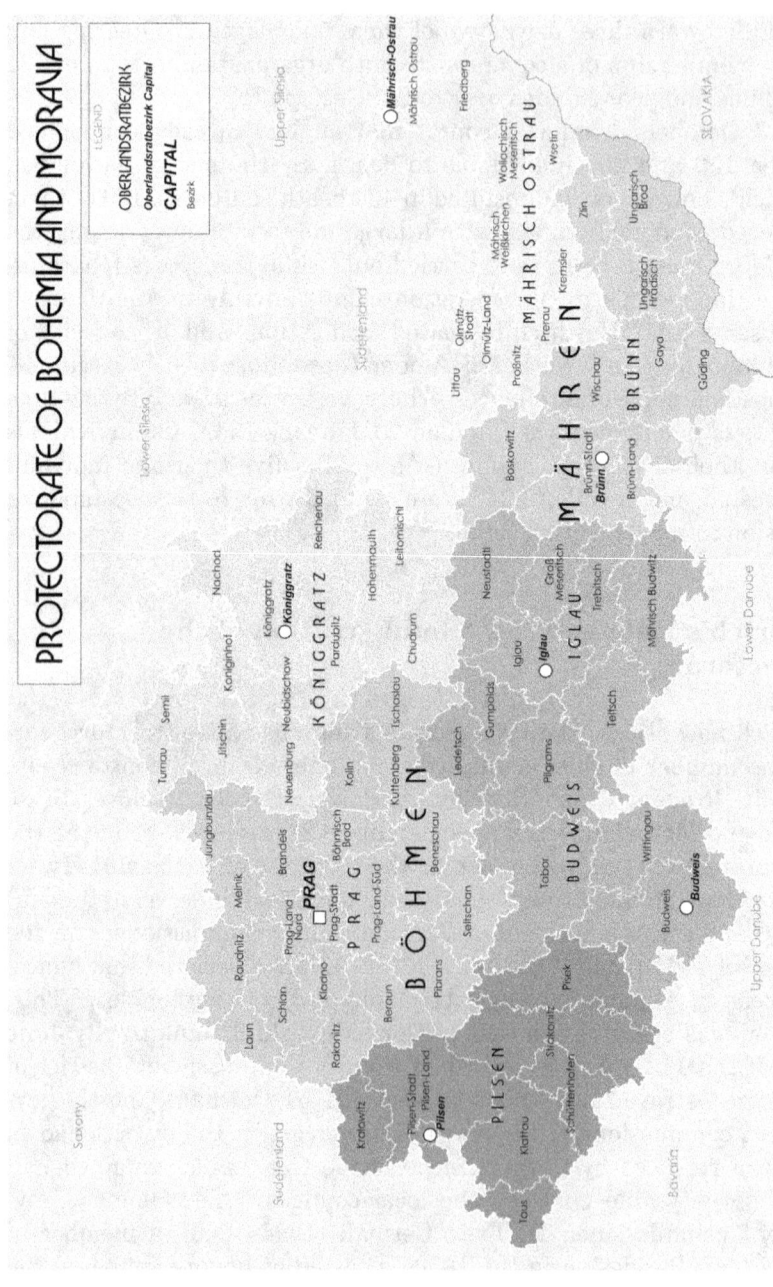

Figure 8.2. Protectorate administrative structure, featuring seven chief county commissioner districts, 1941. Wikimedia Commons.

of the process of bringing the Protectorate into line with the German Municipal Code (Gemeindeordnung) and reducing the number of municipal departments to place more fields of activity under German leadership. Germans made up 20 per cent of the city's inhabitants in 1939.[77] Many planned appointments, however, such as the directorship of the municipal savings bank in Pilsen, came to grief due to the lack of German personnel with the requisite competencies.[78]

Later, more than 6,800 German officials and employees worked in the Protectorate administration, more than four thousand of them for the Reich protector, chief county commissioners and other German agencies, though they generally remained dependent on Czech staff.[79] In total, around fifteen thousand Germans worked in the occupation and Czech authorities as opposed to around 400,000 Czech civil servants.[80] In Prague this disparity was still only too apparent by the end of 1942. The Protectorate capital's administrative apparatus employed 250 German but around 4,250 Czech officials, along with 143 German but more than eighteen thousand Czech white- and blue-collar workers.[81] These figures highlight both the weakness of German rule and the scale of Czech cooperation within the administration of the Protectorate.

In November 1941, senior officials in the Office of the Reich Protector were still discussing the need to reorganize the Czech administration with the goal of subverting 'Czech autonomy'.[82] They were keen to start at the very top. Under pressure from Berlin and Heydrich, in January 1942 President Hácha appointed a new government, reduced to seven posts and headed by former Justice Minister Jaroslav Krejčí as government chairman, while the role of prime minister was abolished.[83]

Henceforth, Colonel Emanuel Moravec – a revered war veteran and vocal opponent of concessions prior to the occupation, but later apologist for subjugation to the Germans and widely felt to personify the betrayal of the Czech people – headed the Ministry of Education and the new Office for Public Enlightenment (Amt für Volksaufklärung).[84] The Czech population responded with indignation to the appointment, to quote Petr Ginz, of 'Moravec, who writes the incendiary articles', as schools minister.[85] Dr Richard Bienert (1881–1949) became Interior Minister and Adolf Hrubý (1893–1951) Agriculture Minister, while Transport Minister (since 1941) Dr Jindřich Kamenický and Finance Minister (since 1939) Dr Josef Kalfus remained in post. Reich German Walter Bertsch (1900–52), previously responsible for labour deployment in the Office of the Protector,[86] took over the Ministry of Economy and Labour, which fused the Ministry of Social and Health Administration, the Ministry of Public Works and the Ministry of Industry, Trade and Commerce.[87]

Wilhelm Dennler, previously responsible for Social Affairs in the Office of the Reich Protector, became deputy to Bertsch.⁸⁸ He described his transfer as follows:

> While we could limit ourselves more to general directives and a supervisory role [in the Office of the Reich Protector], in our own ministry we ourselves have once again become the bearers of responsibility. ... Because there are only around 200 Germans among the approximately 2,000 officials in the ministry, our Czech colleagues naturally do the lion's share of the work, though their loyalty seems to me beyond all doubt.⁸⁹

Heydrich thus ruled with both carrot and stick in the Protectorate. Most ethnic Germans regarded him as an embodiment of the hope that now, at last, the authorities would take drastic measures against the Czechs.⁹⁰ Only a small number of 'reactionaries, aristocrats and those married to Czechs' along with a few officials and members of the Wehrmacht saw things differently, according to Heydrich in a letter to Lammers, head of the Reich Chancellery, of 9 October 1941.⁹¹

Heydrich also stepped up efforts to Germanize the Protectorate.⁹² Pilsen received a German mayor: Dr Walther Sturm, appointed by childhood friend State Secretary Frank.⁹³ In advance of the German National Day (Volkstag) in early September 1941, the city restored the German House (das Deutsche Haus) and the theatre at a cost of one million crowns, while also increasing the number of German schools from one to eleven.⁹⁴ An organization reminiscent of Strength Through Joy (Kraft durch Freude) was developed in the Protectorate, providing German-speakers between the ages of ten and eighteen with an obligatory physical, intellectual and moral education.⁹⁵

Heydrich's Accession to Power and Anti-Jewish Policy

In preparation for the resumption of mass transports of Jews, on 17 September Horst Böhme, Commander of the Security Police, sent out a circular in which he made the execution of all anti-Jewish measures in the Protectorate the sole preserve of his agency.⁹⁶ In advance of new deportations, the appointment of what was in effect a new Reich protector not only brought a more centralized but above all an intensified anti-Jewish policy in its wake.

This was just what the Jews of the Protectorate had feared ever since Heydrich's arrival, as the Jewish Telegraphic Agency reported across Europe on 30 September. They were particularly unnerved by the arrest of Eliáš, the agency explained, because he was considered to be one of those Czech politicians who had resisted the introduction of the Nuremberg laws. Jews, the JTA noted, feared attacks or repressive measures on Yom Kippur in particular, so synagogues would require special protection.[97]

On 29 September 1941, in one of his first official acts in the Protectorate, Heydrich changed the status of Jewish spouses in 'privileged mixed marriages' to match that of Jews in general. This meant that all restrictions also applied to this group, including the obligation to wear a 'Jewish star'.[98] This was somewhat watered down later on: in October, the Central Office decided to apply the rules in force in Germany in the Protectorate when it came to German-Jewish 'mixed marriages', such that a Jewish woman with an 'Aryan husband who is a citizen of the German Reich' was not required to wear a star but did have to comply with all other Jewish regulations; the same went for a Jewish man in 'a mixed marriage with an Aryan German', but only if they had non-Jewish children.[99]

In the same decree, Heydrich closed all synagogues and prayer rooms on the supposed grounds that they had long since ceased to serve religious purposes and instead served as 'sites of assembly for all subversive Jewish elements and the epicentres of illegal whispering campaigns'. He threatened 'Jewish sympathisers', in other words Czechs who associated with Jews on the street or in public venues in an 'ostentatiously friendly' manner, with Gestapo protective custody. In recent times, he contended, Czech circles had gone out of their way to demonstrate their 'pro-Jewish' attitudes, simultaneously evincing their hostility to the Reich.[100] Next came a propaganda campaign targeting relations between non-Jewish Czechs and their Jewish counterparts, focused in particular on Czechs' public donning of the Jewish star in solidarity with the Jews.[101] From this point forward, it took a great deal of courage for non-Jewish Czechs to help their Jewish fellows.[102] *Der Neue Tag* justified Heydrich's measure by asserting that to a singular degree the 'Jewish element in the Protectorate' was actively engaged 'in stirring up the population and organizing resistance'.[103]

One of the key provisions of the decree on the introduction of the Jewish star was the prohibition on leaving one's residential area without permission. The Prague Jewish Community informed the provincial Communities about the exceptions in a circular of 3 October 1941.[104] Within the Protectorate, the Central Office for Jewish Emigration alone gave approval for travel, though sometimes delegating the granting of permission for Jews to leave their residential areas to the district authorities. Generally speaking, such permission was granted only in cases of forced labour outside Prague, illnesses, the death of relatives, trips undertaken by Jewish officials and summons issued to Jews to present themselves at various agencies and authorities – and for deportations, now resuming for the first time since 1939.[105]

Even the centralization of Jewish policy and the presence of Heydrich did not stop some officials in the Protectorate from launching their own initiatives to further segregate Jews. In a submission to Prague's chief county commissioner, Deputy Primator Pfitzner suggested 'concentrating the Jews in a particular district in the manner of a ghetto after all', a proposal he repeated in his report of 1 October to Frank.[106] The City of Moravian Ostrava established a 'special work detail', supposedly consisting in the main of Jews with a criminal record, to carry out street cleaning and clearance work, prompting *Der Neue Tag* to refer to it as a penal gang.[107]

On 8 October, *Der Neue Tag* carried a report on a large-scale campaign by the Czech-language press, which was now calling for the immediate 'evacuation of the Jews' from the Protectorate's major cities. The newspaper *Národní politika*, the German publication stated, had claimed that the 'Czech public' was 'outraged' that 'they are forced to come into contact with the Jews on a daily basis and that the Jews ostentatiously mingle on the streets with the general population'.[108] National Partnership proposed to the Czech government that it 'congregate all Jewish individuals in one part of the city or somewhere near the city in order to regulate and control their lives completely and engage them in work beneficial to the community'.[109]

Subsequently, on 6 October 1941, President Hácha proposed to the Czech interior minister that the Jews be isolated in cordoned-off residential areas.[110] The latter rejected the idea, however, first because the Commander of the Security Police claimed to be in charge of all anti-Jewish measures and second because the deportations had already started.[111]

Laying the Ground for the New Mass Transports

Ever since the authorities in Berlin had decided, in late July or early August 1941, to restart the mass deportations,[112] their plans had included Jews living in the Protectorate of Bohemia and Moravia. On 23 September, Goebbels spoke to Hitler, who underlined that 'the Jews must be removed step-by-step from all of Germany. The first cities that should be made free of Jews are Berlin, Vienna and Prague'.[113] As a result, in the Protectorate as in Germany it was necessary to register the Jewish population once again on 1 October 1941. On the basis of Nazi criteria, around eighty-eight thousand Jews still lived in the Protectorate, half of them in Prague, as the Prague Central Office already reported by 2 October.[114] That same day, the Central Office called on the Czech government to cease issuing passports to Jews.[115] Four days later, at the Führer Headquarters (Führerhauptquartier), Hitler revealed that in future all 'Protectorate Jews' would be deported to the East rather than initially to Poland. At present, however, he contended, this was impossible because the armed forces desperately needed the requisite means of transport.[116]

On 10 October 1941, at Prague Castle, Heydrich met with Higher SS and Police Leader (Höherer SS- und Polizeiführer) Frank, Commander of the Security Police Horst Böhme, as well as Eichmann and other SS leaders to 'discuss measures that are becoming necessary to resolve the Jewish question primarily in the Protectorate and to some extent in the Old Reich' as well. Those in attendance heard that of the eighty-eight thousand Jews in the Protectorate, forty-eight thousand lived in Prague, ten thousand in Brno and ten thousand in Moravian Ostrava. The Gestapo, it was stated, planned to deport five thousand Jews from Prague beginning on 15 October. However, because of organizational problems, in the first instance the transports should roll only until 15 November, with due consideration being given to the authorities in Łódź (Litzmannstadt). The 'most troublesome Jews [must be] sought out' for the transports. Deportations to Minsk and Riga were to follow later.[117]

Those present went on to discuss the radical ghettoization, in just two or three locations, of those left behind in the Protectorate, with the only feasible candidates being an outlying suburb, a small village or a town with as little industry as possible. Initially, however, the Jews – including those living in scattered settlements in the countryside – were to be concentrated in the three major cities. Those present considered it appropriate to then establish two ghettos, one in Bohemia and one in Moravia, both of which would be divided into a work camp and supply camp. There the Jews could perform forced labour, either in the camp making items 'such as wooden shoes or straw mats for the Wehrmacht divisions in the North', or outside the camp, under guard and in segregated work details. For the forced labour deployments, the 'Council of Elders' (Ältestenrat) would receive the 'smallest possible amount of food containing the calculated minimum of vitamins, etc. (monitored by the Security Police)'. In Moravia the ghetto could be established in a small village, and in Bohemia either in the Hussite castle of Alt-Ratibor or, better, by the Central Office taking charge of Theresienstadt. Resettlement in ghettos would take place in accordance with the same principles as the deportations. From the outset, however, the Jews' time in the ghetto was envisaged as merely temporary, while the conditions, namely forced labour and minimal nutrition, were intended to be extremely harsh, as the next sentence in the minutes of the meeting demonstrates. Once the 'Jews have already been decimated' in the ghetto, they were to be transported to the East, while Theresienstadt would be developed into an exemplary German settlement. In general terms, Hitler wished 'the Jews to be removed from German territory as far as possible by the end of the year'.[118]

Before the day ended, Heydrich was pressing for the Czech government to finally enact the decree prohibiting marriages between Jewish and non-Jewish citizens of the Protectorate, which had been on ice since October 1940. This, he believed, would 'make it clear to the Czechs, through their own government, that in the Protectorate too a serious effort is being made to resolve the Jewish question'. Through segregation, Heydrich intended both to prevent solidarity and facilitate the deportation of Jews.[119]

Just two days after the meeting, Heydrich officially ordered the 'transfer' of Jewish assets during the process of 'evacuation', assigning this task to the Central Office for Jewish Emigration. The legal foundation for this Jewish property grab was the 'Second Decree issued by the Reich Protector in Bohemia and Moravia on the Supervision of the Jews and Jewish Organizations', which was signed by Heydrich.[120]

The practical execution of the mass transports was down to the local branches of the Security Police, while in Prague it fell to the Gestapo Headquarters in cooperation with the Central Office for Jewish Emigration. Since 10 October 1941, the Gestapo in Prague had been assembling the first Jews for 'evacuation' in the city's Exhibition Hall (Veletržní palác or Messepalast). That day, Petr Ginz noted: 'At school in the morning. Ehrlich from the parallel class is leaving on Monday with the first transport of five thousand Jews to Poland. Everyone is allowed to take along 50 kg of luggage, money, blankets, food, and insurance policies'.[121] Three days later, normal lessons were suspended because of Sukkot. Instead, like other pupils, Ginz received instructions to turn up at the school to fill sacks, which were delivered by two cars, with wood shavings. He and his fellows stuffed a total of 140 sacks, which were taken to the Exhibition Hall; these were to serve as sleeping bags for those awaiting transport there, as Ginz surmised in his diary.[122]

One week prior to the transport, Alfred Dube received a summons to report to the Exhibition Hall with fifty pounds of luggage. No one was entirely sure what was going on, Dube recalled; many thought they would travel to a work camp outside Prague.[123] Curt Allina turned up at the completely empty Exhibition Hall and saw people drawing squares on the floor in chalk for each family.[124] Alfred Dube remembers Eichmann receiving Jews in the hall by declaring that the Germans did not even need to kill the Jews as they would devour one another. Dube had to present himself at one table after the next, where officials divested Jews of their gold, rings, watches and so on. They had to hand over everything, just as they had their radios earlier on. The Gestapo demanded that he sign a form transferring his property to the government. The rest of his family, with the exception of his six-year-old sister Katie, who had not been ordered to attend and had stayed with an aunt in Prague, was deported to the East later on the second transport.[125]

On 12 October, articles appeared in the Protectorate press explaining the new policy to the general population. Citing the *České Slovo* newspaper, *Der Neue Tag* reported that the authorities would not stop at the 'marking of Jews' and would not allow the 'proposal to expel [the Jews] from the cities' to gather dust; the agencies of the Reich had now taken the 'Jewish question' out of the hands of the Protectorate authorities due to their alleged lack of initiative; the offices of the German Reich would be taking no half-measures; and it could be stated with 'total certainty ... that the Jews will be gradually isolated, that ghettos will be established for them, that they will be removed from the cities and that all of them will have to work to earn their crust'.[126]

Foreign observers, therefore, were aware of what was going on before the mass transports had occurred. Quoting articles in Prague newspapers of 14 October, the Jewish Telegraphic Agency reported that trains were being assembled to transport the Jews from Czech cities to unknown destinations. The press, the JTA stated, was calling this the 'first step towards a final solution to the Jewish problem' in the Protectorate. 'The yellow star will soon disappear from our cities', the *Národní Práce* newspaper had claimed.[127]

Two New Waves of Deportation

On 16 October 1941, officers of the German Order Police and the Czech Police escorted those slated for deportation from Prague from their point of assembly at the exhibition site to the train. A huge mass filled the street in front of the station. Men waved their hats in farewell and to show their respect and solidarity, while many women wept.[128] On this date the first special train left the Protectorate capital bound for Łódź, one day after the first train from Vienna and two days before the first from Berlin (see Table A.5 in the appendix).[129] Although the train from

Prague reached Łódź the next day, Alfred Dube remembered the journey taking far longer, two to three days, and nobody knew where the train was headed.[130]

In an attempt to ensure the smooth execution of the mass transports, on 24 October the Reich Security Main Office threatened all 'those of German blood' in the Reich with three months' detention in a concentration camp if they demonstrated 'friendly relations with Jews in public'. Goebbels discussed this decree in a newspaper editorial while also disseminating its message in radio broadcasts.[131]

At the same time, Jews in Prague were deployed to perform menial work at the exhibition site where those earmarked for deportation were forced to assemble. On the instructions of the Central Office for Jewish Emigration in Prague, since 23 October an on-call work detail had provided twelve men during each of three shifts to assist the Prague V Police Station day and night.[132] Petr Ginz noted in his diary that since the start of November his father had been working every day from 10 a.m. to 5 p.m. at the Exhibition Hall at the behest of the Jewish Religious Community. Meanwhile, his family had had to sign a form declaring that they would neither sell nor give away any of their possessions to 'Aryans'.[133]

Further deportation trains bound for the Łódź Ghetto left Prague on 21, 26 and 31 October as well as 3 November. In total, then, the first new partial operation, personally ordered by Hitler, entailed five transports carrying five thousand Jews.[134] The overall operation, of which this formed part, saw the removal of twenty thousand people from Berlin, Prague, Vienna and other major cities in the Greater German Reich, initially to the Warthegau.[135] Most of those deported from Prague had been members of the economic elite. They were housed in dilapidated buildings in the Łódź Ghetto and had to perform forced labour, with most of those unable to work gassed a year later, had they not already died of hunger and exhaustion.[136]

By this point, information on the deportation of Jews from the Protectorate had reached other countries. On 28 October 1941, in a prescient piece about the deportations from Germany entitled 'Nazi Drive to Remove All Jews from Europe', the *Washington Post* referred to an article in the *Krakauer Zeitung* that predicted the deportation of all the Jews in the cities and villages of the Protectorate in the near future.[137] Just two days later, with reference to the Berlin-based *Dienst aus Deutschland*, *The New York Times* carried similar reports. The former had mentioned the incipient deportation of forty-eight thousand Jews from Prague and the imminent removal of all Jews from the Protectorate.[138]

However, because the Łódź Ghetto lacked the space to absorb all the Jewish deportees, Hitler had selected Riga and Minsk as the next destinations, the specific and overriding goal being to remove ten thousand Jews each from Berlin, Vienna and Prague. The authorities planned to transport seventy-five thousand Jews in total by 4 December.[139] In addition to Jews resident in Prague, meanwhile, the second partial operation was also intended to deport those living in the Czech provinces. By 18 October, the Prague Jewish Community had already instructed the Communities in Bohemia and Moravia to draw up lists of names at the behest of the Central Office. They had to create and number card files providing details on their members, marking those receiving welfare benefits with a 'U' (for 'Unterstützung' or 'support').[140] The first transport of the second new partial operation left Brno on 16 November 1941 bound for Minsk, arriving there after no less than four days. Most of the roughly one thousand deportees were individuals in need of welfare, many of them refugees from Austria or of Polish origin. Now trains from Prague followed to Terezín, each carrying one thousand deportees on 30 November and on 4, 10 and 17 December, and from Brno on 2, 5 and 16 December. More than thirteen thousand Jews from the Protectorate had thus been relocated within two months.[141]

Anti-Jewish Measures Implemented by Various Authorities

In light of the recently launched mass transports departing from Prague, on 3 November 1941 Böhme reiterated to Czech Interior Minister Josef Ježek (1884–1969) that henceforth all measures to be taken against Jews would be the preserve of the Commander of the Security Police.[142] This, however, did not reflect realities on the ground: while the Gestapo had deported thousands of Jews to Poland since October, the labour offices nonetheless stepped up forced labour deployment – as we will see – while central and local authorities amplified their anti-Jewish policies.

On 30 October, the Commander of the Security Police pressed the Czech government to instruct all authorities, offices of the state, states and local authorities as well as public enterprises to lay down opening hours for Jews, which must be 'as short as possible' and uniform within a given location to stop 'the Jews from crowding the streets all day'.[143] In line with this, the Police Directorate in Brno restricted Jews' use of Protectorate agencies, institutions and enterprises to 8–9 a.m.[144]

On 2 November, the press published a warning to Jews: they were prohibited from selling their personal property, as they might use the proceeds to engage in hoarding. Due either to their 'well-known friendliness towards the Jews' or their acquisitiveness, it was claimed, Czechs helped Jews in this practice. The State Police would be taking action against sellers, buyers and those storing the goods involved. As if by chance, next to this announcement appeared an article concerning a gang of so-called economic saboteurs in Pilsen, that is, a grocer and her son, the latter employed in a printing works, who had been incited by the Jew Irma Hahn to steal thousands of ration cards. These they had sold to her at inflated prices, along with overpriced goods.[145]

Because Jews had supposedly bought too many goods, from 24 October a range of foodstuffs, including fruit of all kinds, poultry and fish but also tinned products, could no longer be sold or given to them. 'Aryans' were prohibited from shopping on their behalf.[146] On 31 October, meanwhile, the *Protectorate Law Gazette* published a decree outlawing the sale of cigarettes or other tobacco products to individuals wearing the yellow Jewish star.[147] In December, Jewish families did not receive ration cards to buy carp for the holidays.[148] The Czech Agriculture Ministry subsequently banned the sale of wine and spirits to Jews.[149] On 2 November, the Prague Tailors' Cooperative (Schneidergenossenschaft) called on its members to refuse to accept orders placed by Jews as a matter of principle.[150]

Further, by this point in time, the tens of thousands of Jews still resident in Prague were prohibited from using any of the public swimming pools in the city, having already been banned from patronizing swimming schools and public bathing facilities. For the time being, the only exception was the 'Koruna' baths, though this was only open to Jews on Tuesday mornings.[151] In Kroměříž, Jews were now banned from entering 'Aryan' businesses; they had earlier been prohibited from patronizing coffee houses and restaurants.[152] In early December, Klatovy banned them from entering marketplaces and a number of streets.[153] As Prague had already done, the City of Přerov enacted a ban on Jews visiting reading halls, exhibitions, galleries, archives and auctions of art and industrial products.[154]

New Europe-Wide Persecutory Plans

By now, the focus of the Nazi leadership had shifted from short-term partial deportation operations from Germany, Austria and the Protectorate to planning the removal of Jews from all of occupied Europe. In late

October 1941, the Jewish organizations in Berlin, Vienna and Prague had received the order to register the remaining Jewish population once again. This was intended to lay the ground for the conference to be held on the shores of the Großer Wannsee lake in Berlin, which was supposed to take place in early December, with Heydrich sending out the invitations on 29 November 1941; there he wished to coordinate these large-scale plans with the relevant Reich agencies.[155] While the plan was to deport all Jews, Nazi leaders continued to consider the potential for Germanization in the Protectorate.[156]

By mid November 1941, the Jewish Communities had provided the Reich Security Main Office with lists comparing the initial state of affairs in a given territory with the number of Jews at the end of October 1941. According to these statistics, in the Old Reich the number of Jews had fallen from 566,602 (1933) to 150,925 individuals, in Austria from 206,000 (1938) to 47,578 and in the Protectorate from 118,310 (1939) to 83,961. In Bohemia and Moravia, where, as in Germany, persecution involving forced emigration and deportation had caused a dramatic shift in what had been a balanced gender ratio, the remaining Jewish population consisted of 44,655 females and just 39,306 males. The trend towards the over-aging of the Jewish population was also similar in both cases. Nazi anti-Jewish policies had thus reduced the number of Jews in the Greater German Reich from 890,000 to 281,000.[157]

At the 'Wannsee Conference', originally planned for December but postponed until 20 January 1942 due to the United States' entry into the war,[158] Heydrich explained to the state secretaries in attendance: 'As we put the Final Solution (Endlösung) into effect we are combing through Europe from west to east. The territory of the Reich, including the Protectorate of Bohemia and Moravia, will have to be our first priority, simply because of the housing issue and other social policy necessities'. The Theresienstadt Ghetto was thus no longer to be merely a transit camp for the Protectorate but would also serve as an old-age ghetto for German and Austrian Jews.[159] The Nazi leadership in Berlin had thus made a decision that bound the fate of the Czech Jews even more tightly than before to that of their German brethren.

Ghettoization in Theresienstadt and Other Locations in the Protectorate

In the interim, the Commander of the Security Police had established a 'Jewish ghetto' in Theresienstadt, a garrison town sixty kilometres north-west of Prague founded in 1780.[160] Böhme had issued orders to this effect by early November 1941 at Heydrich's behest, announcing a meeting and inviting all groups (departments) within the Office of the Reich Protector, the Central Office (SS-Hauptsturmführer Günther) and the chief county commissioner in Kladno.[161]

New 'masters' (Herren) from Berlin had arrived 'to sort out the Jewish question in the Protectorate', as the representatives of the Olomouc Jewish Community learned on 25 November from Robert Redlich, who had just paid a visit to the Prague Jewish Community. The German authorities would now discuss 'preparations for evacuating the Prague Jews to Theresienstadt' and the problem of Jews of more than seventy years of age.[162]

On 24 November, 365 men were deported to Theresienstadt[163] to begin constructing the ghetto,[164] while the first large-scale transport to the new ghetto departed from Brno not long afterwards, on 30 November, carrying one thousand individuals.[165] In late November, meanwhile, many individuals in Prague were instructed to move to the ghetto, as Petr Ginz noted in his diary: 'Mr Mautner came to say good-bye. Mrs Mautnerova arrived shortly afterwards. Since 1 May they've been absolutely plagued by trouble. Emil was arrested, Karel was called up for labour deployment in Česká Lípa, and all their relatives are either in Poland or Theresienstadt'.[166] Mautner was evidently part of another workers' transport carrying one thousand individuals.[167]

When the preparatory work in Theresienstadt had advanced to the point that mass transports could be sent there, on 8 December 1941 the Commander of the Security Police issued the chief county commissioners in the Protectorate with guidelines detailing how the 'evacuation of the Jews' was to be executed.[168] Just four days earlier he had appointed a 'Council of Elders' for the ghetto, with Jakob Edelstein being made chairman of the 'autonomous Jewish administration' (jüdische Selbstverwaltung), which organized the inmates' accommodation, supplies and labour deployment. Edelstein saw it as his mission to make the prisoners' lives easier and save as many people as possible.[169]

Because her husband and father were already living in the ghetto, Mautner's wife volunteered to move to Theresienstadt along with his son. They had to be at the assembly point on 11 December, as Petr Ginz noted: 'The Mautners left early in the morning, with tears all around. They left the building like galley slaves with a number on their coats. Staff of the Jewish Religious Community carried their luggage for them ... The flat keys had to be handed over to the Germans. Mrs. Mautnerova was struck by one fit of weeping after another'.[170] Yet the genders were routinely separated upon arrival at the ghetto. Men were not allowed to have contact with women; married men were even prohibited from interacting with female members of their families. If men strayed from their places of work in order to meet women, the punishment was twenty-five lashes by cane, meted out by the SS guards.[171]

On 15 December 1941, Reinhard Heydrich himself signed another circular decree 'concerning the evacuation of Jews'. In parallel to the 'deportation of Jews to the ghettos in Litzmannstadt, Minsk and Riga', the decree stated, the authorities had now begun 'to send large-scale transports' to the Theresienstadt Ghetto. The Commander of the Security Police in Prague decided on the transportees' districts of origin and the order of the transports' departure, 'because only central control can [guarantee] due consideration for the needs of the economy, transport, labour deployment and the safeguarding of other general interests'. The composition of the group transports, the decree continued, was the responsibility of the Central Office for Jewish Emigration, which would also take possession of Jewish assets. This would be based on the victims' declaration of assets, handed over immediately before deportation. The Central Office would ensure that 'Jewish accommodation' was locked up and would deliver the keys to the relevant chief county commissioner; only in the chief county commissioner districts of Prague and Brno would they remain with the Central Office or in the latter case its Liaison Office. With the exception of Prague and Brno, the chief county commissioners, informed by the estimates provided by legally certified appraisers, would see to the sale of furniture and household goods as well as the allocation of accommodation in light of 'the needs of the German People (nach volkspolitischen Gesichtspunkten)'. Properties would be rented or sold with due regard for the interests of the Emigration Fund of Bohemia and Moravia, which would receive all the proceeds.[172]

In December 1941 alone, the Gestapo deported more than seven thousand people to Theresienstadt from Prague, Pilsen, Brno and other places. The point of assembly in Prague was once again the exhibition site, where those slated for deportation were accommodated in filthy wooden shacks devoid of sanitary facilities, guarded from the outside by Czech policemen and inside by the SS. There they had to hand over the keys to their homes, ration cards, money and personal documents, while also filling in a declaration of assets. In towns in the provinces, where the deportations to Theresienstadt began just under six months later, the Gestapo used schools, synagogues or municipal halls as assembly points.[173]

In parallel, Jews from the countryside were forced to resettle in the cities, now in preparation for the imminent transports. For example, by 19 December 1941, twenty-seven individuals living in the vicinity of

Prostějov were forced to move to that town, located eighteen kilometres from Olomouc.[174] For the District of Olomouc, the Jewish Community had to draw up lists of assets, including the real estate owned by all its members, by the end of the year. The Central Office also ordered the dissolution of old people's homes, forcing the residents of the Brecher Foundation to move from Prostějov to Olomouc.[175]

In the wake of the resumed deportations and Europe-wide planning, the authorities seized Jewish property with unprecedented vigour. Since 1 December, Jews had been required to hand over typewriters and bicycles to the Jewish Communities. In the District of Olomouc, removal companies transported these to the city, depositing them, as instructed by the Office of the Chief County Commissioner, in the gymnasium of the former Sokol gymnastics club, an organization dissolved by Heydrich on 12 October.[176] In Prague, Petr Ginz noted that by the end of the year Jews were forced to hand over 'all mouth organs and all other portable musical instruments, all thermometers and so on, as well as cameras and their accessories', while at least registering nonportable instruments.[177]

Jewish Resistance and Opposition

Though the Jewish community was gripped by depression and fear, as Mimi Berger described in her interview for the Shoah Foundation, Jews continued to resist persecution.[178] They sought to improve their dire social situation through banned forms of commerce, which above all meant infringing anti-Jewish restrictions on procuring victuals. When the Moravian Ostrava chief county commissioner heard from a number of sources that Jews had acquired fruit or vegetables in contravention of the regulations, he instructed the municipal authorities to undertake house searches in all '700 Jewish homes'. This operation, carried out on 14 October 1941 with the help of the SS, revealed the presence, 'in addition to preserved and pickled fruit … [of] foodstuffs, unused cloth goods and silk fabrics, as well as precious metals'. He instructed the municipal authorities to refer every infringement of the 'Jewish regulations' to the Gestapo and the 'largest-scale hoarding cases' to the Criminal Police, while dealing with the remaining incidents themselves. The National Socialist People's Welfare (Nationalsozialistische Volkswohlfahrt), the German Red Cross and the Miners' Soup Campaign (Suppenaktion der Bergarbeiter) received the confiscated foodstuffs, while textiles were sold, with the proceeds going to the Winter Relief (Winterhilfswerk) organization.[179]

Since the autumn, the semi-official daily newspaper *Der Neue Tag* had been publishing an increasing number of convictions and sentences imposed on Jews for infringing economic regulations, such as the case pursued by the District Authority in Strakonice, a town of ten thousand inhabitants,[180] against Rosa Fröhlich. For engaging in illicit and 'chain' trade (Kettenhandel),[181] she had been sentenced to three months in prison.[182] The District Authority of Nové Město nad Metují (Neustadt an der Mettau), meanwhile, had sentenced businessman Rudolf Kornfeld to four months in jail plus a fine of 150,000 crowns or three additional months in prison for concealing supplies of coffee and soap.[183] The Prague city authorities issued Alice Sarah Roubíček with a fine of ten thousand crowns and sentenced her to three days in prison for selling coffee and sausage at inflated prices in an attempt to eke out a living.[184] Earlier, in late August, six Jews had already been sentenced to between six weeks and twelve months in prison for assisting in 'chain' trading in furniture.[185] For 'chain' trading in textiles, in September Josef Lederer in Prague was sentenced to three months in prison and received a fifty thousand crown fine, while Erich Plowitz was detained for twenty-one days and Erich Fluß received a fine of twenty thousand crowns.[186] Every few days in the autumn, *Der Neue Tag* reported several similar sentences against Jews, which had often been imposed earlier, in July or August.[187]

Not just as dealers but also as buyers, Jews often faced severe punishment. Regina Lederer was sentenced to fourteen days in prison by the Strakonice District Authority for the 'unauthorized' purchase of butter and eggs, which were now prohibited goods for Jews.[188] In mid October in Prague, Leo Lehr received three months in prison for buying onions at inflated prices, while in November Ida Spira in Moravia Ostrava was sentenced to three months in prison and given a five thousand crown fine, again for the purchase of butter and eggs.[189]

On 9 October 1941, drumhead courts martial in Prague and Brno imposed ten death penalties for economic sabotage, with five of those hanged being Jews.[190] Of the latter, Ernst Uritz and Victor Ritter from Prague had violated war economy regulations, that is, they had hoarded and resold large quantities of leather gloves; Ernst Engelsrath from Prague had failed to register raw materials as required; while Ernst Prodavka and Ernst Weiß from Moravian Ostrava had bought and sold textile goods without ration coupons.[191] On 18 October, five of the twelve individuals condemned and executed by courts martial for 'repeated acts of economic sabotage' were again Jews.[192] The Prague Special Court later sentenced another four Jews and one non-Jewish Czech to death for illegally buying and reselling clothing ration cards, while the original non-Jewish sellers, including an official at the Seltchau District Authority, were sentenced to between eight and ten years in prison. *Der Neue Tag* emphasized that the Jew Rudolf Lustig, who had sold the coupons, had taken them to Prague without official authorization for his journey and then resold them.[193]

Courts also sentenced Jews to death during this period for sabotage or supposedly planning to commit treason. Walter Baß from Prague, who had urged German soldiers to desert, died by hanging on 22 November 1941.[194] One week later, the Prague drumhead court martial sentenced Georg Stricker to the same fate.[195] Around the same time, the Gestapo arrested Dr Karl Bondy for membership in a coordinating group of the Czech resistance. With the aid of Anna Pollertova, who had hidden crystal radio receivers in her flat, he had maintained contact with various cities in the Protectorate. Pollertova had also helped a paratrooper obtain false papers.[196]

It was above all the introduction of the Jewish star, the deportations to Poland and the transports to the Theresienstadt Ghetto, but also harassment and maltreatment, that sparked resistance among the persecuted Jews. On 14 December 1941, Petr Ginz noted: 'On the way we were warned that people (Jews, of course) are being struck on the street, so we tried to hide our stars. ... Jews weren't just being struck, but also beaten terribly. The browns (Vlajkaři) left many of them with their faces covered in blood'.[197]

A Gestapo official named Bankl had already made critical remarks to the Jewish Community of Olomouc in late September, because through 'peculiar ways of carrying bags, briefcases, furs, etc., [Jews] conceal the badges/Jewish stars'.[198] Towards the end of October, the Gestapo then informed the Jewish Community representatives once again of complaints that Jews in Olomouc and Prostějov 'are not wearing the Jewish badge as prescribed', and threatened to impose 'the severest of punishments'.[199] Six months later, the Gestapo warned Jewish officials that the stars had to be clean and, above all, firmly sewn on.[200] In Moravian Ostrava, the chief county commissioner criticized the alleged fact that 'the Jew [fights] the Jewish legislation whenever he finds it unpleasant and he has little at stake'. Seven Jews, he claimed, had refused to wear the star and had therefore been punished. Others had sewn on the star in such a way that they could cover it with their arm, for which twelve of them had been punished.[201]

By December 1941 several Jews had been arrested in Olomouc. In response to enquiries from the Jewish Community, a Gestapo official remarked to Robert Redlich and Dr Erwin Wechsner at one of their near-daily summonses that the State Police carried out arrests only in the most serious of cases. The Community must impress upon the Jews the need to comply stringently with all laws and ordinances in order to avoid further arrests.[202] The town of Prostějov in the District of Olomouc also saw a number of arrests 'due to various offences against the Jewish decrees'.[203] Previously, on several occasions the Gestapo had complained to the relevant Jewish representatives in Olomouc, without result, that a growing number of Jews in Prostějov were failing to comply with the provisions applying to them.[204] In early November, the Jewish inhabitants of Prostějov even signed a declaration confirming that they would comply henceforth with all regulations; failure to do so would result in the 'severest of measures'.[205]

Jews also refused to adhere to the restricted shopping hours introduced in various locations. In the District of Olomouc these applied between 3 p.m. and 5 p.m.[206] Ferdinand Ehrlich had violated this directive, prompting the Gestapo to inform the Jewish Community of Olomouc of its intention to arrest him in December 1941. Because Ehrlich, who was clearly of infirm mind, had been asked to make the purchases involved by one Hugo Spitzer, who had therefore been admonished 'most severely', the Gestapo was minded to drop the idea of arresting Ehrlich but only if the Jewish Community immediately placed him in an 'institution for the mentally defective' (Anstalt für Schwachsinnige).[207]

Jews also absconded from forced labour and transports. Moses Cimlichmann, born in 1911, had been forcibly deployed as a painter from April to the end of October 1941 in Trschepschein. He was then unemployed for two weeks until the Labour Office sent him to harvest beets on a large estate for three days in mid November. After that he worked for the Moravia firm in their Olomouc branch. One day in mid December he complained of pains and failed to turn up for work the next day. Assuming his absence was due to illness, it was not until the beginning of January 1942 that the foreman of the forced labour detail made enquiries at the local Jewish Community, but its staff did not know where he was either. Community officials reported his disappearance to the Police Directorate only on 5 January, in other words a few days later, justifying this to the Gestapo later on by stating that all staff members had had their hands full with the prescribed task of ensuring that the Jews in their district handed over goods of fur and wool as well as skis. At the same time, they sought to determine possible motives for his disappearance by questioning his roommates and other acquaintances. Cimlichmann, it emerged, had already left his room – as he did every weekend – on 20 December with a suitcase of dirty laundry and had not been seen since.[208]

It was not just individuals who put up resistance but also the representatives of the former Jewish Communities. During an inspection in Prostějov, Senior Secretary (Obersekretär) Bankl of the Olomouc Gestapo complained: 'I regard the compilation of a Czech circular [as a manifestation of] a pro-Czech stance on the part of the head of the Proßnitz [Prostějov] Jewish Community. [He went on to complain that,] together with the fact that the Jews speak Czech on the streets despite the fact that all of them can surely speak German very well, this clearly indicates the prevailing attitude among the Jews of Proßnitz'. He suggested that there would be a high price to pay for this, while also complaining that the Prostějov Jewish Community had been corresponding directly with its Prague counterpart, which was forbidden. If it failed to communicate via the Olomouc Community from now on, he would have its head arrested.[209] During an earlier visit in late November, he had already accused the leadership of the Prostějov Jewish Community of 'passive resistance to his directives'.[210] In another case, the local Jewish leader in Šumice (Schumitz) recruited a significant number of the Jews resident there into the illegal Communist Party, collecting seven hundred Reichsmarks from them.[211]

* * *

Describing the situation at the end of 1941, Petr Ginz wrote:

> Things that are commonplace now would undoubtedly have caused a stir in normal times. For example, the Jews have no fruit at all, no geese and absolutely no poultry or cheese, onions, garlic or other things. Prisoners, the mentally ill and Jews receive no tobacco ration coupons. They are not allowed to use the first carriage of trams or trolleybuses and are also banned from walking on the riverside promenade, etc., etc.[212]

Missing from Ginz's bleak list, alongside many other anti-Jewish measures, are the most significant developments of the previous few months: stigmatization through the compulsory wearing of the Jewish star, intensified ghettoization in the Protectorate and the resumption of the mass deportations. The main objective now was to segregate the Jewish from the non-Jewish population, primarily in order to prevent solidarity with Jews and resistance from Jews themselves.

As a result of resettlement and ghettoization, Jews often lost their personal possessions. House owners were forced to sign over their real estate to the Central Office and the Emigration Fund. Jews also had to hand over their bicycles and typewriters as well as musical instruments. While the first of these aimed at hindering Jews' mobility and the second at preventing any form of public protest via leaflets, the third must be understood as pure harassment.

The fourth quarter of 1941 saw the centralization of anti-Jewish policy in the Protectorate at the hands of the Reich protector and the Central Office along with the gradual adaptation to the policies implemented by Berlin in the rest of the Greater German Reich. Despite the increasing centralization of Jewish policy, regional and local authorities continued to play a proactive role: the Ministry of Agriculture denied Jews many foodstuffs, while local authorities – on the Reich protector's recommendation – barred them from public establishments or imposed restricted opening hours.

Nothing, however, embodies the Protectorate's special position more clearly than the intensified programme of forced labour. This was now organized by the labour offices in line with the norms developed in Germany and Austria, yet in the Protectorate it was extended to Jews between the ages of sixteen and sixty, exactly the same enlarged age range for Jewish forced labour as in the General Government.[213] Though forced labour in the Protectorate fell within the remit of the Czech Ministry for Social and Health Administration, the Reich protector and the Central Office were nonetheless involved. Forced labour saw rapid intensification beginning in the summer, while employment on an individual basis was prohibited in September. By October, twelve thousand mostly male Jews were already subject to segregated group deployment in road and railway construction, agriculture, forestry and industry.

In light of growing resistance among the Czechs, Hitler sent Heydrich to Prague to replace Neurath. Heydrich imposed a state of emergency. The Gestapo sent more than two thousand individuals to concentration camps, while drumhead courts martial imposed hundreds of death sentences, many of them on Jews for alleged sabotage, treason or economic offences.

In mid October, the authorities resumed mass transports of Jews to the East. Initially, the deportations consisted of two new partial operations: first to Łódź, then to Minsk. By November 1941, six thousand individuals had been deported to these locations. At the same time, the authorities in the Protectorate stepped up their efforts to concentrate Jews in major cities, followed by the first transports, carrying more than seven thousand people, to the way station of the ghetto in Theresienstadt. Hitler's decision to deport all Europe's Jews brought in its wake the decision to move certain groups of German and Austrian Jews to the Theresienstadt Ghetto the next year.

The increased repression by no means eliminated resistance and opposition among the Jewish population. Jews ignored the restricted shopping hours and the curfew, evaded restrictions on obtaining food and resisted countless local and central regulations. They absconded from forced labour sites and refused to wear the star. Even the rebukes delivered by the Gestapo to local Jewish representatives made very little difference. The Gestapo thus arrested many Jews, while others received severe sentences, in some cases the death penalty, for economic offences, sabotage or even treason.

Notes

1. Gruner, *Der Geschlossene Arbeitseinsatz*, 273.
2. Police ordinance on the marking of Jews, 1 September 1941, Reichsgesetzblatt. 1941 I, 547. See *Jüdisches Nachrichtenblatt*, no. 61, 12 September 1941, 1.
3. *Der Neue Tag*, 13 September 1941, 5.
4. *Der Neue Tag*, 17 September 1941, 3.
5. Memorandum by head of the Vienna Israelite Religious Community, 5 August 1941, in *Widerstand und Verfolgung in Wien 1934–1945*, Vol. 3: *1938–1945*, ed. Dokumentationsarchiv des österreichischen Widerstandes, 2nd ed. (Vienna, 1984), doc. no. 145, 276.
6. Report by the Central Office, 2 October 1941, in *Deutsche Politik im 'Protektorat Böhmen und Mähren'*, doc. no. 23, 123–26; and appendix, table 1, in ibid.; CAHJP Jerusalem, A/W no. 421, n.p.: Report on the 'Deployment of Jewish Workers', n.d., 3–6; VHA Prague, fonds 140, carton 19, no. 2, fol. 365: Report 'Impressions Arising from a Visit to the Prague Autumn Fair, 5–13 September 1941', 17 September 1941 (carbon copy), 3.
7. YV Jerusalem, O 7/59, fol. 211: Report by the Jewish Religious Community and the Prague Palestine Office on their activities in the third quarter of 1941, 1.
8. Ibid., fol. 151: Weekly report by the Jewish Religious Community of Prague, 13–19 September 1941, 7.
9. Ibid., fol. 152: Weekly report by the Jewish Religious Community of Prague, 13–19 September 1941, 8.
10. YV Jerusalem, M 58/JM 11812, fol. 607.
11. YV Jerusalem, O 7/59, fol. 239: Report by the Jewish Religious Community and the Prague Palestine Office on their activities in the third quarter of 1941, 22.
12. Ibid., fol. 315: Report by the Jewish Religious Community and the Prague Palestine Office on their activities in the first quarter of 1941, 29.
13. Entry of 19 September 1941, in Ginz, *The Diary of Petr Ginz*, 28. Translations of this diary amended throughout this chapter.
14. YV Jerusalem, O 7/59, fol. 211: Report by the Jewish Religious Community and the Prague Palestine Office on their activities in the third quarter of 1941, 1.
15. BA Berlin, R 30/4d, fol. 121: Chief county commissioner, administrative report (confidential) for November 1941, Moravian Ostrava, 22 November 1941, Appendix 1 Political status report, 4.
16. USC SF/VHA, video interview, Alfred Dube, tape 2, min. 26:00–27:20.
17. Kárný, 'The Genocide of the Czech Jews', 39–40.
18. BA Berlin, R 30/4d, fol. 139–40: Chief county commissioner, administrative report (confidential) for December 1941, Moravian Ostrava, 20 December 1941, Appendix 1 Political status report, 3–4.
19. But many reports, the commissioner contended, concerned foreign Jews, who made up a third of the 3,500 Jews still in his district; BA Berlin, R 30/4d, fol. 95–96:

Chief county commissioner, administrative report (confidential) for October 1941, Moravian Ostrava, 22 October 1941, 3–4.
20. 'Judenkennzeichnung in der Vergangenheit', *Brünner Tagesbote*, 4 January 1942, 3; 'Davidstern und andere Judenkennzeichen', *Brünner Tagesbote*, 6 May 1942, 3.
21. YV Jerusalem, O 7/59, fol. 138: Weekly report by the Jewish Religious Community of Prague, 6–12 September 1941, 7.
22. *Der Neue Tag*, 24 September 1941, 3.
23. YV Jerusalem, O 7/59, fol. 208: Monthly report Jewish Religious Community of Prague, 1–30 September 1941, 13.
24. *Der Neue Tag*, 27 September 1941, 5; JTA, 'Czechs Prohibited to Treat Jews to a Cigarette', 2 November 1941.
25. *Der Neue Tag*, 7 September 1941, 4; YV Jerusalem, O 7/59, fol. 139: Weekly report by the Jewish Religious Community of Prague, 6–12 September 1941, 8.
26. *Der Neue Tag*, 12 September 1941, 3.
27. YV Jerusalem, O 7/59, fol. 152: Weekly report by the Jewish Religious Community of Prague, 13–19 September 1941, 8.
28. YV Jerusalem, M 58/JM 11808, fol. 345: Note, Jewish Religious Community of Olomouc on visit to Gestapo, 9 October 1941, 1.
29. YV Jerusalem, O 7/59, fol. 147–48: Weekly report by the Jewish Religious Community of Prague, 13–19 September 1941, 3–4.
30. Ibid., fol. 151: Weekly report by the Jewish Religious Community of Prague, 13–19 September 1941, 7; ibid., no. 59, fol. 164: Weekly report by the Jewish Religious Community of Prague, 20–26 September 1941, 6; ibid., no. 64, fol. 28: Report by the Jewish Council of Elders, Prague, on the year 1944, 26.
31. YV Jerusalem, O 7/59, fol. 196: Monthly report by the Jewish Religious Community of Prague, 1–30 September 1941, 1.
32. Ibid., fol. 152: Weekly report by the Jewish Religious Community of Prague, 13–19 September 1941, 8.
33. Ibid., fol. 202–3: Monthly report by the Jewish Religious Community of Prague, 1–30 September 1941, 7–8.
34. Ibid., fol. 226–27: Report by the Jewish Religious Community and the Prague Palestine Office on their activities in the third quarter of 1941, 12 and chart.
35. Ibid., fol. 228–230: Report by the Jewish Religious Community and the Prague Palestine Office on their activities in the third quarter of 1941, 13–15.
36. Ibid., fol. 201: Monthly report by the Jewish Religious Community of Prague, 1–30 September 1941, 6.
37. CAHJP Jerusalem, A/W no. 421, n.p.: Report on the 'Deployment of Jewish Workers', n.d., 3–6; and Report by the Central Office, 2 October 1941, in *Deutsche Politik im 'Protektorat Böhmen und Mähren'*, doc. no. 23, 123–24. For an in-depth treatment of forced labour in the Protectorate, see chapter 5 in Gruner, *Jewish Forced Labor*.
38. YV Jerusalem, O 7/59, fol. 123: Weekly report by the Jewish Religious Community of Prague, 30 August to 5 September 1941, 3.
39. Ibid., fol. 150: Weekly report by the Jewish Religious Community of Prague, 13–19 September 1941, 6.
40. USHMM Washington, RG 48.005M, reel 2 (Prague State Archive), II-4-4055, carton 859, no. 1, n.p.: Labour deployment statistics, as at 1 September 1941; ibid., no. 1: Olomouc Labour Office, Statistics September 1941, 16 October 1941; ibid., no. 6, n.p.: Olomouc Labour Office, Statistics October 1941, 31 October 1941.
41. Ibid., no. 1, n.p.: Statistics on labour deployment of Jews in the Protectorate, as at 1 September 1941; ibid., no. 2, n.p.: Zlín Labour Office, Statistics for September 1941.

42. Ibid., no. 1, n.p.: Statistics on labour deployment of Jews in the Protectorate, as at 1 September 1941; ibid., no. 9, n.p.: Prague Labour Office, Statistics, September 1941.
43. Daily report Gestapo Headquarters, Prague, 30 September 1941, in *Deutsche Politik im 'Protektorat Böhmen und Mähren'*, doc. no. 18, 101.
44. Mentioned in USHMM Washington, RG 48.005M, reel 2 (Prague State Archive), II-4-4055, carton 859, no. 21, n.p.: Klatovy Labour Office to the Ministry for Social and Health Administration, 6 October 1941.
45. YV Jerusalem, O 7/59, fol. 161: Weekly report by the Jewish Religious Community of Prague, 20-26 September 1941, 3.
46. Ibid., fol. 214: Report by the Jewish Religious Community and the Prague Palestine Office on their activities in the third quarter of 1941, 3.
47. YV Jerusalem, O 7/59, fol. 216: Report by the Jewish Religious Community and the Prague Palestine Office on their activities in the third quarter of 1941, chart.
48. USHMM Washington, RG 48.005M, reel 2 (Prague State Archive), II-4-4055, carton 859, no. 22, n.p.: Statistics on labour deployment of Jews in the Protectorate, October 1941 (n.d.).
49. See the statement that more than 6,300 additional individuals were recruited during this period; CAHJP Jerusalem, A/W no. 421, n.p.: Report on the 'Deployment of Jewish Workers', n.d., 3-6; and Report by the Central Office, 2 October 1941, in *Deutsche Politik im 'Protektorat Böhmen und Mähren'*, doc. no. 23, 123-24.
50. Report by the Jewish Religious Community of Prague, 'Labour' (n.d., mid 1942), in Krejčová, Svobodová and Hyndráková, *Židé v Protektorátu*, doc. 5, 112-14.
51. Decree of 27 September 1941, in Mund, *Deutschland und das Protektorat*, doc. 395, 554. See *Der Neue Tag*, 28 September 1941, 1; *The New York Times*, 28 September 1941, 5. On what follows, see Gerwarth, *Hitler's Hangman*, 218-77; Lüdicke, *Constantin von Neurath*, 538-39.
52. *The New York Times*, 28 September 1941, 5. Küpper comes to the conclusion that there was virtually no difference between von Neurath and his state secretary, Frank, when it came, for example, to anti-Jewish policy; Küpper, *Karl Hermann Frank*, 179.
53. *Der Neue Tag*, 29 September 1941, 1.
54. *Der Neue Tag*, 20 November 1941, 1; see also *Der Neue Tag*, 21 November 1941, 3. On the significance of this act of taking possession, see also Gerwarth, *Hitler's Hangman*, 265.
55. On the myth and history of Charles IV, see Olaf B. Rader, *Kaiser Karl IV. (1316–1378): Eine Biographie* (Munich, forthcoming).
56. Gerwarth, *Hitler's Hangman*, 220-23; Rothkirchen, *Jews*, 205-6. On the supposed calm in the Protectorate, see Dennler, *Böhmische Passion*, 55-56.
57. BA Berlin, R 30/4d, fol. 94: Chief county commissioner, administrative report (confidential) for October 1941, Moravian Ostrava, 22 October 1941, 2.
58. Gerwarth, *Hitler's Hangman*, 221.
59. Entry of 25 September 1941, in Ginz, *The Diary of Petr Ginz*, 30.
60. BA Berlin, NS 19/2383, fol. 4-8: District president in Aussig (Ústí nad Labem), SS-Brigadeführer, honorary Gauleiter, to Heinrich Himmler, 19 August 1941, with addendum, 'Political Situation in General. Public Mood (among the Czechs)', 1-3.
61. Gerwarth, *Hitler's Hangman*, 225-27; Entry of 27 September 1941, in Ginz, *The Diary of Petr Ginz*, 30; *The New York Times*, 28 September 1941, 5; *Der Neue Tag*, 29 September 1941, 1-2; Dennler, *Böhmische Passion*, 57; Sládek, 'Standrecht und Standgericht', 331-32. On earlier plans, see Report by the Foreign Office

representative in the Office of the Reich Protector, 19 August 1940, in Mund, *Deutschland und das Protektorat*, doc. 285, 419–20.
62. *Der Neue Tag*, 29 September 1941, 1.
63. *Der Neue Tag*, 1 October 1941, 1–2; *Der Neue Tag*, 2 October 1941, 2.
64. *Der Neue Tag*, 2 October 1941, 1–2.
65. Heiber, 'Zur Justiz im Dritten Reich', 279–90. See also Gerwarth, *Hitler's Hangman*, 228–30. On Klapka's arrest, see Report by the Foreign Office representative in the Office of the Reich Protector, 11 July 1940, in Mund, *Deutschland und das Protektorat*, doc. 269, 401–2.
66. Rothkirchen, *Jews*, 152–53.
67. Heiber, 'Zur Justiz im Dritten Reich', 292; *Der Neue Tag*, 5 October 1941, 1. Cf. Brandes, 'Nationalsozialistische Tschechenpolitik', 45; Moskowitz, 'Three Years of the Protectorate', 373; Bryant, *Prague in Black*, 145.
68. *Der Neue Tag*, 2 October 1941, 1–2.
69. *Der Neue Tag*, 3 October 1941, 1.
70. *Der Neue Tag*, 4 October 1941, 1.
71. Gerwarth, *Hitler's Hangman*, 229–30, 237; Rothkirchen, 'Protectorate Government', 353; Rothkirchen, *Jews*, 206; Detlef Brandes, *Die Tschechen unter deutschem Protektorat. Part 2: Besatzungspolitik, Kollaboration und Widerstand im Protektorat Böhmen und Mähren von Heydrichs Tod bis zum Prager Aufstand (1942–1945)* (Munich, 1975), 10; Miroslav Kárný, 'Reinhard Heydrich als Stellvertretender Reichsprotektor in Prag', in *Deutsche Politik im 'Protektorat Böhmen und Mähren'*, 9–75, here 9–12; Bryant, *Prague in Black*, 129–43; *Der Neue Tag*, 4 and 5 October 1941, 1–2.
72. Two Jews were among the six individuals executed on 7 October 1941; *Der Neue Tag*, 8 October 1941, 1. Cf. *Der Neue Tag*, 12 October 1941, 1; *Der Neue Tag*, 14 October 1941, 1.
73. Celovsky, *Germanisierung und Genozid*, 42; Sládek, 'Standrecht und Standgericht', 332.
74. Bryant, *Prague in Black*, 160–61.
75. Brandes, *Tschechen unter deutschem Protektorat*, Part 1, 165–66.
76. BA Berlin, NS 25/776, fol. 141–43: Nazi Party Gauleitung Sudetenland, Gau Office for Local Government Policy, Reichenberg, to Nazi Party Reich Directorate, Main Office for Local Government Policy, Munich, 1 July 1941, with addendum: Report Moravian Ostrava County Office for Local Government Policy for the month of June, 26 June 1941.
77. Moskowitz, 'Three Years of the Protectorate', 361. Cf. BA Berlin, NS 25/776, fol. 148: Nazi Party Gauleitung Sudetenland, Gau Office for Local Government Policy, Reichenberg, to Nazi Party Reich Directorate, Main Office for Local Government Policy, Munich, 1 July 1941, with addendum: Political Administrative Report, 1 July 1941.
78. BA Berlin, NS 25/776, fol. 153: Nazi Party Gauleitung Sudetenland, Gau Office for Local Government Policy, Reichenberg, to Nazi Party Reich Directorate, Main Office for Local Government Policy, Munich, 1 July 1941, with addendum: Report County Office for Local Government Policy, Pilsen, Dr Wild, 19 June 1941; and ibid., fol. 149–52: Political Administrative Report, 1 July 1941.
79. Brandes, *Tschechen unter deutschem Protektorat*, Part 1, 165–66.
80. Brandes, 'Nationalsozialistische Tschechenpolitik', 52.
81. See chart: YV Jerusalem, Photo Archive, 19/5, 1939–1944. 5 years of wartime construction in the capital city of Prague, Prague 1944.
82. Celovsky, *Germanisierung und Genozid*, 286.

83. Report by the representative of the Foreign Office delegation in the Office of the Reich Protector, 20 January 1942, in Mund, *Deutschland und das Protektorat*, doc. 414, 586–87.
84. Brandes, 'Nationalsozialistische Tschechenpolitik', 45; Moskowitz, 'Three Years of the Protectorate', 373; Bryant, *Prague in Black*, 145; Rothkirchen, *Jews*, 153; Gerwarth, *Hitler's Hangman*, 239–40; Frommer, *National Cleansing*, 21–22.
85. Entry of 20 January 1942, in Ginz, *The Diary of Petr Ginz*, 64. On the Czechs' reaction, see Report by the Foreign Office representative in the Office of the Reich Protector, 23 February 1942, in Mund, *Deutschland und das Protektorat*, doc. 415, 588–89.
86. Walter Bertsch, administrative officer (Verwaltungsbeamter), lawyer, joined the Nazi Party in 1933 and the SS in 1938, head of Dept. II (Economy and Finances) in the Office of the Reich Protector, minister for economy and labour in the Protectorate (1942–45), SS-Brigadeführer (1944), arrested in 1945 and sentenced to life in prison by the Czechoslovak National Court in 1948, died in prison in Brno; see VEJ/3, 658.
87. Plans for a German to enter the Czech government had probably been in place since December 1941. This formed part of the planned administrative reform, which was also intended to establish a German Ministry of State, though it was not until 1943 that the latter appeared; Dennler, *Böhmische Passion*, 65–68.
88. Ibid.
89. Ibid., 71.
90. See Report by the Foreign Office representative in the Office of the Reich Protector, in Brandes, 'Nationalsozialistische Tschechenpolitik', 55.
91. Quoted in ibid.
92. For a detailed account, see Gerwarth, *Hitler's Hangman*, 244–56.
93. Sturm took office in October 1941; BA Berlin, NS 25/774, fol. 87–88: Performance report (Leistungsbericht) for 1942, Nazi Party County Office for Local Government Policy, Dr Wild, Pilsen, 4 January 1943. Sturm was arrested on 8 May 1945 and found dead in his cell the next morning; Frank, *Karl Hermann Frank*, 160.
94. 'Aufschwung des Deutschtums in Pilsen', *Der Neue Tag*, 4 September 1941, 3.
95. Rothkirchen, *Jews*, 153.
96. Jaroslava Milotová, 'Der Okkupationsapparat und die Vorbereitung der Transporte nach Lodz', in *Theresienstädter Studien und Dokumente* 1998, 40–69, here 41; Potthast, *Das jüdische Zentralmuseum*, 133.
97. JTA, 'Jews in Prague – Fear Increased – Terror under New Nazi Protector', 30 September 1941.
98. USHMM Washington, RG 48.005M, reel 4 (Prague State Archive), Marking of Jews, carton, I-3b5851, no. 21, n.p.: Circular decree Reich protector/BdS, 29 September 1941. Cf. *Deutsche Politik im 'Protektorat Böhmen und Mähren'*, doc. no. 14, 97. See also *Der Neue Tag*, 6 October 1941, 2; *The New York Times*, 8 October 1941, 8. Cf. Milotová, 'Okkupationsapparat', 57.
99. YV Jerusalem, M 58/JM 11808, fol. 323: Note, Jewish Religious Community of Olomouc on visit to Gestapo, 21 October 1941, 2.
100. USHMM Washington, RG 48.005M, reel 4 (Prague State Archive), Marking of Jews, carton, I-3b-5851, no. 21, n.p.: Circular decree Reich protector/BdS, 29 September 1941. Cf. *Deutsche Politik im 'Protektorat Böhmen und Mähren'*, 97, doc. no. 14; Celovsky, *Germanisierung und Genozid*, 270.
101. Institute of Jewish Affairs, *Hitler's Ten-Year War*, 59.
102. Rothkirchen, *Jews*, 222–23.

103. 'Verschärfte Maßnahmen gegen Juden im Protektorat', *Der Neue Tag*, 6 October 1941, 2; and *The New York Times*, 8 October 1941, 8. Cf. Milotová, 'Okkupationsapparat', 57; Gerwarth, *Hitler's Hangman*, 257.
104. YV Jerusalem, M 58/JM 11808, fol. 347: Note, Jewish Religious Community of Olomouc on visit to Gestapo, 7 October 1941, 1.
105. Ibid., fol. 337: Note, Jewish Religious Community of Olomouc on visit to Gestapo, 14 October 1941, 2.
106. Mentioned in Report Pfitzner to Frank, 1 October 1941, in Šustek, *Josef Pfitzner*, doc. 10, 149–50. Cf. Brandes and Míšková, *Vom Osteuropa-Lehrstuhl ins Prager Rathaus*, 276.
107. *Der Neue Tag*, 16 October 1941, 4. In November Jews also had to carry out other short-term assignments there. Due to an early frost, a 'closed brigade of Jews' was deployed to quickly unload large consignments of potatoes, the workers involved being withdrawn from earthworks on a temporary basis; BA Berlin, R 30/4d, fol. 114: Chief county commissioner, administrative report (confidential) for November 1941, Moravian Ostrava, 22 November 1941, 8.
108. 'Evakuierung der Juden gefordert', *Der Neue Tag*, 8 October 1941, 2.
109. Quoted in Milotová, 'Okkupationsapparat', 56.
110. Dr Josef Kliment to Josef Ježek (Ministry of the Interior), 6 October 1941, in *Deutsche Politik im 'Protektorat Böhmen und Mähren'*, doc. 24, 128. Cf. Milotová, 'Okkupationsapparat', 41.
111. Statement by the Ministry of the Interior, n.d., in *Deutsche Politik im 'Protektorat Böhmen und Mähren'*, doc. 24, 128–29.
112. For a detailed account of this and what follows, see Gruner, 'Von der Kollektivausweisung', 46–56.
113. *Die Tagebücher von Joseph Goebbels. Part II: Diktate 1941–1945*, vol. 1, 484–85: Entry of 24 September 1941.
114. Report by the Central Office, 2 October 1941, in *Deutsche Politik im 'Protektorat Böhmen und Mähren'*, doc. no. 23, 125; ibid., appendix: table 1; Anderl, 'Die "Zentralstellen für jüdische Auswanderung"', 294.
115. Milotová, 'Okkupationsapparat', 43.
116. Minutes of Hitler's remarks at table on the treatment of the Czechs, FHQ, 6 October 1941, in *Deutsche Politik im 'Protektorat Böhmen und Mähren'*, doc. no. 25, 130.
117. USHMM Washington, RG 48.005M, reel 3 (Prague State Archive), no. 1, fol. 77–81: Notes arising from the meeting on 10 October 1941 on the resolution of Jewish issues, 1–6, copy, in *Deutsche Politik im 'Protektorat Böhmen und Mähren'*, 137–41, doc. no. 29, and Peter Longerich (ed.), *Die Ermordung der europäischen Juden: Eine umfassende Dokumentation des Holocaust 1941–1945* (Munich, 1989), doc. no. 64, 172–76. Cf. Safrian, *Eichmann's Men*, 76–77.
118. USHMM Washington, RG 48.005M, reel 3 (Prague State Archive), no. 1, fol. 77–81: Notes arising from the meeting on 10 October 1941 on the resolution of Jewish issues, 1–6.
119. The decree was not enacted until March 1942; ibid., reel 3 (Prague State Archive), no. 123, n.p: Reich protector (signed Heydrich) to Undersecretary of State von Burgsdorff, 10 October 1941, 1–2.
120. Ibid., reel 3 (Prague State Archive), no. 9, n.p.: Circular decree Reich protector/BdS I 2776/41, 12 October 1941. Cf. Adler, *Der verwaltete Mensch*, 535–36; Anderl and Rupnow, *Die Zentralstelle für jüdische Auswanderung*, 335.
121. Entry of 10 October 1941, in Ginz, *The Diary of Petr Ginz*, 34.
122. Entry of 13 October 1941, in ibid., 35.

123. USC SF/VHA, video interview, Alfred Dube, tape 2, min. 10:30–15:00.
124. USC SF/VHA, video interview, Curt Allina, tape 2, seg. 127. Cf. ibid., video interview, Anna Grant, tape 2, min. 14:21–16:24.
125. USC SF/VHA, video interview, Alfred Dube, tape 2, min. 10:30–15:00.
126. 'Allmähliche Isolierung der Juden und Judenfreunde', *Der Neue Tag*, 12 October 1941, 3.
127. JTA, 'Nazis Assemble Trains for Transporting Czech Jews to Unknown Destination', 15 October 1941.
128. Rothkirchen, *Jews*, 124–25.
129. See https://www.bundesarchiv.de/gedenkbuch/chronicles.html?page=1 (accessed 26 June 2016); Krejčová, Svobodová and Hyndráková, *Židé v Protektorátu*, 364–66. Cf. Milotová, 'Okkupationsapparat', 60–61; Schmidt-Hartmann, 'Tschechoslowakei', 361; Rothkirchen, *Jews*, 125.
130. USC SF/VHA, video interview, Alfred Dube, tape 2, min. 15:00–15:49; cf. ibid., video interview, Curt Allina, tape 2, seg. 127.
131. BA Berlin, R 58/276, n.p. Cf. Peter Longerich, *'Davon haben wir nichts gewußt!' Die Deutschen und die Judenverfolgung 1933–1945* (Bonn, 2006), 181 and 399.
132. Report by the Jewish Religious Community of Prague, 'Labour' (n.d., mid 1942), in Krejčová, Svobodová and Hyndráková, *Židé v Protektorátu*, doc. 5, 110.
133. Entries of 1 and 3 November 1941, in Ginz, *The Diary of Petr Ginz*, 40–41.
134. See https://www.bundesarchiv.de/gedenkbuch/chronicles.html?page=1 (accessed 26 June 2016); Krejčová, Svobodová and Hyndráková, *Židé v Protektorátu*, 364–66. Cf. Schmidt-Hartmann, 'Tschechoslowakei', 361; Rothkirchen, *Jews*, 125.
135. Gruner, 'Von der Kollektivausweisung', 51–53. For a general account of this and what follows, see Adler, *Der verwaltete Mensch*, 168–204; Gottwaldt and Schulle, *Die 'Judendeportationen'*, 52–442.
136. Rothkirchen, *Jews*, 124–25.
137. *Washington Post*, 28 October 1941, 5.
138. *The New York Times*, 30 October 1941, 6.
139. Gruner, 'Von der Kollektivausweisung', 54–56.
140. Hájková, 'Erfassung', 54; Milotová, 'Okkupationsapparat', 46; Potthast, *Das jüdische Zentralmuseum*, 135.
141. See https://www.bundesarchiv.de/gedenkbuch/chronicles.html?page=1 (accessed 26 June 2016); Krejčová, Svobodová and Hyndráková, *Židé v Protektorátu*, 364–66. Cf. Hájková, 'Erfassung', 54; Milotová, 'Okkupationsapparat', 46; Schmidt-Hartmann, 'Tschechoslowakei', 361; Rothkirchen, *Jews*, 125.
142. Meeting between Ježek and Böhme, 3 November 1941, in *Deutsche Politik im 'Protektorat Böhmen und Mähren'*, doc. no. 44, 174. Cf. Milotová, 'Okkupationsapparat', 42; Potthast, *Das jüdische Zentralmuseum*, 133.
143. USHMM Washington, 45.005M, reel 1 (Prague State Archive, Commander Security Police and SS [BdS]), no. 1, n.p.: Copy BdS Böhme to the deputy prime minister in Prague, 30 October 1941, 1.
144. *Der Neue Tag*, 11 December 1941, 4.
145. *Der Neue Tag*, 2 November 1941, 5.
146. *Der Neue Tag*, 25 October 1941, 6.
147. JTA, 'Czechs Prohibited to Treat Jews', 2 November 1941.
148. *Der Neue Tag*, 26 November 1941, 5.
149. Announcement of 2 December 1941; *Der Neue Tag*, 4 December 1941, 3.
150. *Der Neue Tag*, 2 November 1941, 5.
151. *Der Neue Tag*, 7 November 1941, 3; *Brünner Tagesbote*, 7 November 1941, 4.
152. *Der Neue Tag*, 5 November 1941, 3.

153. *Der Neue Tag*, 7 December 1941, 5.
154. *Der Neue Tag*, 21 December 1941, 4.
155. On the invitation, see the document in Kurt Pätzold and Erika Schwarz, *Tagesordnung: Judenmord. Die Wannseekonferenz am 20. Januar 1942. Eine Dokumentation zur Organisation der 'Endlösung'* (Berlin, 1992), no. 10–11, 88–90.
156. King, *Budweisers*, 186.
157. BA Berlin, R 8150/31, fol. 32: Table 'Age Structure of Jews, 14 November 1941'.
158. For different takes on the goals of the conference, see, for example, Pätzold and Schwarz, *Tagesordnung: Judenmord*, 44–46; Longerich, *Politik der Vernichtung*, 466–72; Christian Gerlach, 'Die Wannsee-Konferenz, das Schicksal der deutschen Juden und Hitlers politische Grundsatzentscheidung, alle Juden Europas zu ermorden', *Werkstatt-Geschichte* 18 (1997), 7–44; Mark Roseman, *The Villa, the Lake, the Meeting: Wannsee and the Final Solution* (London, 2002).
159. Minutes of the conference, 20 January 1942, in Pätzold and Schwarz, *Tagesordnung: Judenmord*, doc. no. 24, 102–12.
160. For a detailed account of what follows, see Adler, *Theresienstadt*; Wolfgang Benz, *Theresienstadt: Eine Geschichte von Täuschung und Vernichtung* (Munich, 2013); and the forthcoming essential account based on the as yet unpublished dissertation by Anna Hájková, 'The Prisoner Society in Terezín Ghetto, 1941–1945'.
161. USHMM Washington, RG 48.005M, reel 3 (Prague State Archive), no. 11, n.p.: Circular decree BdS (Böhme) I 498/41, 4 November 1941.
162. YV Jerusalem, M 58/JM 11808, fol. 255: Note, Jewish Religious Community of Olomouc on visit to Gestapo, 25 November 1941, 2.
163. On all those deported, see *Terezín Memorial Book: A Guide to the Czech Original* (Prague, 1996); *Theresienstädter Gedenkbuch: Die Opfer der Judentransporte aus Deutschland nach Theresienstadt 1942–1945*, ed. Institut Theresienstädter Initiative (Prague, 2000).
164. YV Jerusalem, O 7/264, fol. 52: Statement on the files, 23 November 1945 (carbon copy). Cf. Report by the Jewish Religious Community of Prague, 'Labour' (n.d., mid 1942), in Krejčová, Svobodová and Hyndráková, *Židé v Protektorátu*, doc. 5, 108. On the construction detail and the status of these men in the later ghetto hierarchy, see Anna Hájková, 'Die fabelhaften Jungs aus Theresienstadt: Junge tschechische Männer als dominante soziale Elite im Theresienstädter Ghetto', in Christoph Dieckmann and Babette Quinkert (eds), *Im Ghetto 1939–1945: Neue Forschungen zu Alltag und Umfeld* (Beiträge zur Geschichte des Nationalsozialismus, vol. 25) (Göttingen, 2009), 116–35.
165. YV Jerusalem, O 7/264, fol. 52: Statement on the files, 23 November 1945 (carbon copy).
166. Entries of 28 and 30 November 1941, in Ginz, *The Diary of Petr Ginz*, 46.
167. Report by the Jewish Community of Prague, 'Labour' (n.d., mid 1942), in Krejčová, Svobodová and Hyndráková, *Židé v Protektorátu*, doc. 5, 108.
168. Mentioned in USHMM Washington, RG 48.005M, reel 3 (Prague State Archive), no. 3, n.p.: Note Group I 3 b in the Office of the Reich Protector, 10 December 1941.
169. Rothkirchen, *Jews*, 235.
170. Entry of 11 December 1941, in Ginz, *The Diary of Petr Ginz*, 49.
171. YV Jerusalem, O 7/265, fol. 59: Events in Theresienstadt on 21 December 1941 (carbon copy).
172. USHMM Washington, RG 48.005M, reel 3 (Prague State Archive), no. 10, n.p.: Circular decree Reich protector/BdS I 3098/41 (signed Heydrich), 15 December 1941, 1–8.

173. Vojtěch Blodig, *Theresienstadt in der 'Endlösung der Judenfrage' 1941–1945: Führer durch die Dauerausstellung des Ghetto-Museums in Theresienstadt* (Terezín, 2003), 32–33; Schmidt-Hartmann, 'Tschechoslowakei', 362; Rothkirchen, *Jews*, 127–28; Bartož, 'Arisierung', 293.
174. YV Jerusalem, M 58/JM 11808, fol. 200: Note, Jewish Religious Community of Olomouc on visit to Gestapo, 19 December 1941; ibid., fol. 349: Note, Jewish Religious Community of Olomouc on visit to Gestapo, 4 October 1941, 1.
175. Ibid., fol. 201: Note, Jewish Religious Community of Olomouc on visit to Gestapo, 19 December 1941.
176. Ibid., fol. 238–39: Note, Jewish Religious Community of Olomouc on visit to Gestapo, 1 December 1941. On the dissolution of Sokol, see *Der Neue Tag*, 12 October 1941, 2; BA Berlin, R 43 II/1326, fol. 29: Telex Heydrich to Lammers, 9 October 1941.
177. Entry of 23 December 1941, in Ginz, *The Diary of Petr Ginz*, 55.
178. USC SF/VHA, video interview, Mimi Berger, tape 1, min. 11:17.
179. BA Berlin, R 30/4d, fol. 96–97: Chief county commissioner, administrative report (confidential) for October 1941, Moravian Ostrava, 22 October 1941, 4–5.
180. *Der Neue Tag*, 8 October 1941, 9.
181. According to Duden, the leading German dictionary, *Kettenhandel* is an economically unjustified form of intermediate trade that increases the final price unnecessarily. During the war it meant buying up scarce goods from retailers in order to sell them on at a high price.
182. *Der Neue Tag*, 20 September 1941, 10. Cf. a similar case in Pilsen, where Kitty Klauber received a twenty thousand crown fine and one month in prison; ibid., 22 December 1941, 7.
183. *Der Neue Tag*, 27 September 1941, 10. Cf. similar cases: *Der Neue Tag*, 29 December 1941, 6–7.
184. *Der Neue Tag*, 3 October 1941, 8.
185. *Der Neue Tag*, 9 October 1941, 8.
186. *Der Neue Tag*, 10 October 1941, 8. For more cases of this kind, see *Der Neue Tag*, 11 October 1941, 11; 24 December 1941, 7; 30 December 1941, 7.
187. *Der Neue Tag*, 16 October 1941, 10; 22 October 1941, 9. See also later: *Der Neue Tag*, 29 December 1941, 6–7; 30 December 1941, 7.
188. *Der Neue Tag*, 20 September 1941, 10.
189. *Der Neue Tag*, 29 October 1941, 9; 11 November 1941, 9. See also *Der Neue Tag*, 24 December 1941, 7.
190. *Der Neue Tag*, 10 October 1941, 1.
191. *Der Neue Tag*, 11 October 1941, 2.
192. *Der Neue Tag*, 19 October 1941, 1.
193. *Der Neue Tag*, 8 November 1941, 6. In December two Jews were sentenced to several years in prison, having bought and sold on clothing ration cards from non-Jewish dealers in stolen goods; *Der Neue Tag*, 14 December 1941, 5.
194. *Der Neue Tag*, 23 November 1941, 1; 25 November 1941, 2.
195. *Der Neue Tag*, 29 November 1941, 1; 30 November 1941, 2.
196. RSHA report, 14 November 1941, in Celovsky, *Germanisierung und Genozid*, 290.
197. Entry of 14 December 1941, in Ginz, *The Diary of Petr Ginz*, 50.
198. YV Jerusalem, M 58/JM 11808, fol. 356: Note, Jewish Religious Community of Olomouc on visit to Gestapo, 29 September 1941, 2.
199. Ibid., fol. 318: Note, Jewish Religious Community of Olomouc on visit to Gestapo, 23 October 1941, 2.
200. YV Jerusalem, M 58/JM 11809, fol. 195: Note, Jewish Religious Community of Prague/Olomouc Branch on visit to Gestapo, 21 April 1942, 2.

201. BA Berlin, R 30/4d, fol. 139–40: Chief county commissioner, administrative report (confidential) for December 1941, Moravian Ostrava, 20 December 1941, Appendix 1 Political status report, 3–4.
202. YV Jerusalem, M 58/JM 11808, fol. 235: Note, Jewish Religious Community of Olomouc on visit to Gestapo, 5 December 1941.
203. Ibid., fol. 209: Note, Jewish Religious Community of Olomouc on visit to Gestapo, 17 December 1941.
204. Ibid., fol. 265: Note, Jewish Religious Community of Olomouc on visit to Gestapo, 21 November 1941; ibid., fol. 295: Note, Jewish Religious Community of Olomouc on visit to Gestapo, 5 November 1941.
205. Ibid., fol. 303: Note, Jewish Religious Community of Prostějov on telephone conversation with the Jewish Religious Community of Olomouc, 5 November 1941.
206. Ibid., fol. 102: Economic Group on Retail/Olomouc District Office to Jewish Religious Community of Olomouc, 9 December 1941.
207. Ibid., fol. 75: Note by Jewish Religious Community of Olomouc, 17 December 1942.
208. Ibid., fol. 50–56: Notes by Jewish Religious Community of Olomouc, 16–22 January 1942.
209. Ibid., fol. 232: Note Jewish Religious Community of Prostějov on visit from Chief Secretary (Obersekretär) Bankl of the Olomouc Gestapo, 9 December 1941.
210. Ibid., fol. 243: Note, Jewish Religious Community of Olomouc on visit to Gestapo, 28 November 1941, 2.
211. RSHA report, 11 March 1942, in Celovsky, *Germanisierung und Genozid*, 304.
212. Entry of 1 January 1942, in Ginz, *The Diary of Petr Ginz*, 58.
213. On Jewish forced labour in the General Government, see Gruner, *Jewish Forced Labor*, 230–75.

CHAPTER 9

TRANSPORTS, THEFT, FORCED LABOUR AND FLIGHT

The Concentration of Czech Jews in Theresienstadt

By the end of 1941, the Gestapo had already deported well over ten thousand Jews from the Protectorate. On 6 January 1942, the Jewish Telegraphic Agency reported from London that the same fate now awaited the ninety thousand Jews still living there. Going by the available incomplete information on the first transports, the agency concluded that men between the ages of sixteen and fifty would be subject to forced labour, while those over fifty, along with women and children (including a number of elderly women of more than eighty years of age), would be sent to camps in eastern Poland and occupied Russia. From there, however, the agency stated, very little news was getting out; the little that did spoke of unimaginable suffering due to the lack of food and accommodation. The dire sanitary conditions had caused epidemics.[1]

The systematic deportations from the cities of the Protectorate to the Theresienstadt Ghetto began in mid January 1942 in Pilsen, from which two transports departed carrying one thousand people each, plus another with 604 (see Figure 9.1; cf. Table A.5 in the appendix).[2] Hana Beer recalls that her family had to report to a gym hall, where they spent one or two nights sleeping on the floor before their transport with passenger-carrying coaches left. Rumours were their sole source of information on the destination – either camps in Poland or a place called Theresienstadt that nobody had heard of.³

There followed a train carrying one thousand individuals from Brno, three transports from Prague with a total of three thousand individuals on board and, by mid February, another two trains from Kladno transporting 1,623 individuals in total (see Table A.5 in the appendix).⁴ Petr Ginz noted in his diary: 'A huge number of our friends have been called up for the new transport: Bardach, Mr. Mautner (an acquaintance of Uncle Karel), Hirschová, who used to go for walks with Eva, and many others'.⁵

While more than 8,200 individuals from the Protectorate had thus arrived at the ghetto within a month, on 9 and 15 January the first two trains, together carrying two thousand Czech Jews, had already left Terezín for Riga; the ghetto had, after all, been conceived from the outset as a transit camp for Czech Jews.⁶ But even as a temporary solution, the former fortress was unable to absorb a sufficient number of them. As a result, by 16 February the Reich protector had dissolved the local municipality in light of 'measures concerning the accommodating of Jews in closed settlements', while the plan for a second ghetto in Kyjov was shelved around the same time.⁷

The seven thousand inhabitants of the town of Terezín thus had to abandon their homes. The German population was to leave the town.

Figure 9.1. Deportation in Pilsen, probably January 1942. © YV Jerusalem, Photo Archive, no. 82DO2.

For their now expropriated homes, they were compensated by the 'Emigration Fund for Bohemia and Moravia', which drew on confiscated Jewish assets.[8] The Central Office made available to the resettlers from Terezín vacated flats formerly occupied by Jewish tenants in Prague, which they were to claim by contacting the Nazi Party housing commissioner (Wohnungsbeauftragter). In other districts the chief county commissioners were responsible for this task.[9]

The entire town, then, was now transformed into a ghetto.[10] By mid 1942, tens of thousands of Czech Jews had been taken to Terezín.[11] As in the Reich, Jews in 'mixed marriages', so-called *Mischlinge*, as well as Jewish functionaries, were initially excepted from deportation.[12] However, children resulting from 'mixed marriages' who had reached the age of fourteen could be deported. This fate befell Petr Ginz, for example, in October, while his father remained behind in Prague;[13] the local Jewish Communities had to draw up relevant lists for the Gestapo.[14] By September, sixty thousand individuals lived in the ghetto, among them thousands of German Jews of more than sixty-five years of age, who had been brought to Theresienstadt since the summer on special transports, to what was also known as the old-age ghetto (Altersghetto).[15]

The press echoed the German perspective: *České slovo* welcomed the steps taken to isolate Jews in the 'interests of the peaceful and working Czech population', because the Jews had 'failed to temper their insolence', and underlined the tremendous advantages that would result from the 'cleansing of the Protectorate of the Jews for the entire Aryan Czech population'. The German-influenced *Lidové noviny* explained the removal of Jews to a 'closed settlement zone' in light of their alleged support for both whispering campaigns and illicit trade, while the *A-Zet* stated that the 'Jewish ghetto' would rid the Czech people 'definitively of its worst enemies'.[16]

While the SS Main Economic and Administrative Office (SS-Wirtschafts- und Verwaltungshauptamt) in Berlin managed all concentration camps, the Central Office for Jewish Emigration in Prague would be in charge of the Theresienstadt Ghetto.[17] The Central Office for Jewish Emigration and its asset holder, the public fund called the 'Emigration Fund for Bohemia and Moravia', were supervised by the Commander of the Security Police in Prague. According to the Supreme Auditing Office of the German Reich (Rechnungshof des Deutschen Reiches), in mid 1941 the Emigration Fund's assets amounted to around ninety-five million Reichsmarks, while it had debts of around seventy-seven million.[18] At the beginning of 1942, the Prague Central Office had a staff of around fifty and cash assets of several million Reichsmarks, deposited at the Böhmische Escompte-Bank. At the

Emigration Fund for Bohemia and Moravia, twenty-five members of staff worked with mobile assets of around twenty million Reichsmarks, while its Administrative and Property Disposal Office (Verwaltungs- und Verwertungsstelle) employed seventy-five white-collar workers. In 1945, the Emigration Fund had three accounts in the name of the 'Jewish Autonomous Administration of Theresienstadt' (Jüdische Selbstverwaltung Theresienstadt) at the Böhmische Unionsbank in Prague, with a total balance of 905 million crowns. As the Central Office's property administrator, it was the 'Emigration Fund' that financed the ghetto, so it was stolen Jewish property, additional income from agriculture, horticulture and the inmates' forced labour (in the camp or for private firms and various agencies) that paid for the upkeep of the ghetto.[19] All those between the ages of sixteen and sixty-five incarcerated at the Terezín ghetto were subject to compulsory labour. Women slaved away in the kitchens, gardens and sick rooms, while also keeping the roads and barracks clean, the men working in a variety of wood, machining and textile workshops.[20]

Winter Deployment in the Protectorate

Since November 1941, all citizens of the Protectorate had had to report to the Labour Office upon taking up a job, while employment record books (Arbeitsbücher) were issued by the health insurance providers for those in permanent employment.[21] In December, following the two waves of deportations, the labour offices in the Protectorate registered just 43,122 available Jews (21,227 men and 21,895 women) between the ages of sixteen and sixty. A total of 13,030 Jews were now subject to forced labour deployment, 12,071 men and 959 women. Despite the mass deportations, the labour offices had again placed an additional one thousand individuals in forced labour over the previous month (see Table A.4 in the appendix). A total of 4,267 Jews were now considered fit for work but unemployed, including 1,927 Jewish women, a reflection of the fact that women were now being assessed for their fitness for work.[22]

In late 1941, the Czech Ministry of Social Affairs ceased to pay Jews Christmas and end-of-year bonuses in the Protectorate.[23] During the winter months, a variety of construction projects, where Jews performed forced labour, were temporarily halted. Nonetheless, in January 1942, in the Labour Office District of Hradec Králové, of 343 registered Jews, 299 were subject to labour deployment. For the seven forced labourers laid off by Ing. Kindl in Předměřice nad Labem (Predmeritz) due to seasonal factors, the Labour Office immediately found work at the municipality of Hradec Králové.²⁴ Hradec Králové was one of the last labour office districts in which, even in February, neither men between the ages of sixteen and eighteen and between fifty and sixty, nor any women at all, had been screened for their fitness to work.²⁵

In parallel to the general allocation of forced labourers by the local labour offices, the Jewish Communities often had to make workers available for various employers at short notice. By early December 1941, 630 men in Prague had begun to clear snow, under the supervision of municipal staff, using wheelbarrows, brooms, rakes and shovels, much as had happened the year before (see Figure 9.2).²⁶ On 24 December, Petr Ginz noted: 'Daddy, Uncle Miloš and Uncle Sláva were notified that they must be ready to clear snow whenever it falls'.²⁷ On 2 January

Figure 9.2. Jewish forced labourers clearing snow in Prague, 1941/1942. © YV Jerusalem, Photo Archive, no. 7E01.

1942, as arranged by the Jewish Labour Headquarters in Prague, two hundred men reported to the Ruzin airbase for winter clearing work.[28]

At this point in time, under the supervision of the Jewish Community, 250 individuals, divided into twenty-seven details, were working in forestry, 429 individuals in fifty-four details in agriculture and, employed on an individual basis with the ministry's approval, 326 Jews. A total of 298 men lived at the so-called retraining camp of Linden (Lípa).[29] By the end of January, there were thirty-three groups working in forestry, consisting of a total of 347 individuals, for example for the Forestry Office of the Municipality of Soběslav (Sobieslau), while thirty-eight groups, consisting of 288 individuals, were deployed in agriculture, for a big landowner in Velká Bystřice (Groß Wisternitz) for example. Including authorized employment on an individual basis, 839 men and 101 women worked in the countryside (see Table A.4 in the appendix).[30]

Further, in the second half of January, the Prague Jewish Community's Labour Headquarters established an on-call service consisting of fifty men, who would provide emergency auxiliary services for the deportation transports. The Prague Labour Office's Department for Non-Aryans, which was responsible for Jews' forced labour, established nine groups consisting of 125 Jewish forced labourers under the supervision of the Jewish Labour Headquarters. In total, the latter was now in charge of one hundred groups consisting of a total of 860 workers.[31]

For the Prague city authorities alone, one hundred men now worked a daily total of ten hours each.[32] As on previous days, on 26 January the Jewish Labour Headquarters again provided workers for snow clearing, 357 men on this occasion. The prohibition, which had just been imposed, on Jews using trams made it hard for the men to reach the various municipal courtyards where they were to report for clearing work, until the Jewish Religious Community was able to procure special certificates for them. The number of workers needed on a daily basis increased to almost six hundred by 29 January. This required calling up men up to sixty years of age.[33] Petr Ginz noted: 'Uncle Slavá has been forced to shovel snow for many days already; he doesn't even have proper shoes and he's freezing'.[34]

In the first week of February, the Prague municipality instructed the Jewish Labour Headquarters to provide an additional three hundred men. On 1 February, 625 men were working clearing snow, a figure that had already risen to 980 men by 3 February.[35] In addition, 360 Jews carried out various forms of hard menial work at the behest of the Jewish Religious Community, for example at the exhibition site where the deportation transports were assembled.[36] The snow-clearing work dragged on and by mid February was being performed by around seven hundred men on a daily basis. In its report to the Central Office, the Jewish Religious Community noted that the City of Prague had now been employing many of these Jews for three weeks non-stop, even at weekends, yet they had received no coupons for extra bread. In Olomouc, Kojetín and Loštice (Loschitz), smaller groups of Jews also cleared snow for the municipal authorities.[37] In the districts of Tábor and Kolín, the municipal authorities increasingly recruited Jewish women to clear snow and perform other forms of heavy physical labour.[38] In Prague, at the end of February a daily total of between six hundred and seven hundred men continued to perform snow-clearing work, while at the Ruzin airfield up to one hundred rather than the previous fifty men worked on a daily basis.[39] On 22 March, Petr Ginz noted: 'Uncle Miloš also has to sweep snow despite having periostitis of the arm. Uncle Slavá has been doing this for eight weeks already and he has huge calluses and terribly cracked hands'.[40]

In February, only 38,195 Jews were still available, 18,709 men and 19,486 women. A total of 13,567 men and 754 women were considered employed, making a combined total of 14,321, and thus, despite further deportations, 1,200 more than at the end of 1941 (see Table A.4 in the appendix). While the labour offices placed very few workers in agriculture or construction for seasonal reasons, more than two thousand newly employed individuals were put to work in other economic sectors, presumably industry.[41]

Anti-Jewish Measures and Systematic Deportations

The Prague-based *Jüdisches Nachrichtenblatt* increasingly became an organ for announcing anti-Jewish measures. In January 1942 it ran to just two pages but with a print run of eleven thousand copies.[42] In order to restrict their access to information, in the third week of January Jews in the Protectorate were banned entirely from buying Czech daily newspapers.[43] In March, Petr Ginz observed a sign in the public display cases of the *Politika* newspaper in Prague declaring that Jews were not permitted to read newspapers.[44] Beginning in May, Jews were also banned from buying German newspapers.[45]

The Ministry of Agriculture prohibited Jews in the Protectorate from buying garlic in mid January 1942,[46] pork on 15 January,[47] oranges and mandarins on 24 January[48] and dried onions in May.[49] In the spring, the Jews of Prague faced such a dire lack of alimentation that every source of nutrition became acceptable, as we learn from the diary of Petr Ginz: 'You are allowed to make sausages out of dog meat. Bloch's acquaintances had roasted crow!'.[50] In an attempt to better control the wartime supply situation in the Protectorate, on 27 May the Ministry of Agriculture and Forestry introduced new buyer cards to regulate the distribution of unrationed foodstuffs and luxury food, but these were denied to Jews.[51]

The authorities decided to introduce compulsory identity cards in the Protectorate for Jews of German citizenship, which had existed in Germany since 1938, with relevant decrees appearing in the Reich protector's Official Gazette in mid January 1942. Only the date of implementation remained undetermined.[52] In every sphere of daily life, the broadest range of institutions amplified the segregation of the Jewish population. With a few exceptions, in January Prague's municipal electric companies barred Jews from using trams.[53] On 7 February, the Post Office prohibited those bearing the Jewish star from making use of public telephones.[54] On 20 February, the Prague Police Directorate then announced a ban on Jews patronizing launderettes.[55] In Mladá Boleslav, Jews were prohibited from attending exhibitions or using public reading halls and similar facilities from January onwards.[56] On 24 April, the Police Directorate in Brno banned Jews from entering certain streets: Pellicova (Pellicogasse), Lužánská (Augartengasse) between Neugasse and Alleegasse and Mozartova (Mozartgasse).[57] The Central Office for Jewish Emigration in Prague prohibited Jews from entering barbershops and hairdressing salons as well as from having 'Aryan' barbers and hairdressers come to their homes.[58]

Towards the end of February 1942, the Central Office instructed the Prague Jewish Community to draw up a list of the names of all Jews receiving welfare benefits.[59] Evidently, as in the Reich, the plan was to deport them first in order to cut welfare expenditure.[60] Between mid March and early April, the Gestapo then emptied the District of Brno using six special trains that removed a total of 5,923 individuals to the Bohemian ghetto (see Table A.5 in the appendix).[61] From Theresienstadt, meanwhile, two trains departed in March carrying more than two thousand Jews destined for Izbica, while on 1 April another transport left for Piaski.[62]

On 27 March 1942, the Central Office for Jewish Emigration informed the Prague Jewish Community that all the provincial Communities had been dissolved as independent organizations.[63] While the Jewish Religious Community of Prague had been forced to take charge of the provincial Communities since the spring of 1940, henceforth their remnants existed only as subunits of the Prague institution, that is, as local or branch offices. On the one hand this reflected the goal of the ongoing deportations, namely the concentration of the Jews and their organizations, while on the other it helped centralize Jewish affairs in Prague. Above all, however, it facilitated the transfer of the properties owned by these Jewish Communities to the Emigration Fund, a project the authorities had been working on for several months.

The Activities of the Prague Jewish Community in the New Circumstances

In the first week of January 1942, the Prague Community laid the ground for Jews to surrender their fur and woollen goods, as they had been ordered to do throughout the Reich.[64] On 11 January, in the Protectorate capital, Petr Ginz noted: 'We received orders to hand in fur coats, everything made of fur, wool undergarments, pullovers, etc. Only one set of such clothes is allowed per person'.[65] Olomouc Jewish Community officials, meanwhile, received a phone call on 14 January 1942 instructing them to hand over items, submitted from a number of locations in the surrounding area, to the local Gestapo that same day.[66]

The registration of all Jews in the Protectorate was carried out in Prague. Meanwhile, in the second week of January, the Jewish Community sent members of staff to Pilsen in order to process Jews' declarations of assets in preparation for the deportations there.[67] In February, employees of virtually every department helped process the transports.[68] At this point in time, the Prague Jewish Community still had a staff of 414 white-collar workers, fifty-two auxiliary workers and thirty-four labourers, that is, a total of five hundred individuals. The threat of layoffs to come, however, loomed on the horizon: the Central Office had demanded a list of all employees, broken down by department.[69]

Because the transports from the provinces were taking an increasing number of Jews to the Theresienstadt Ghetto, the Prague Jewish Community sent old crockery, kitchen furnishings and other necessary articles of daily use there. By February the Community had already dispatched two railway wagons containing workshop components, kitchen furnishings and religious objects.[70] In March, with the Central Office's approval, it sent five wagons containing medical equipment.[71] On 12 and 13 March alone, three wagons crammed full of bathtubs, ovens, kitchen utensils and ladders arrived in Terezín, while the dispatch of the component parts of former retraining workshops was underway.[72] A few days later there followed two additional wagons loaded with various forms of equipment.[73]

Like those transported to Theresienstadt, Jews taken to the ghettos in Łódź and Lublin received support from the Prague Jewish Community, chiefly in the form of food parcels.[74] In the first week of January 1942, the Prague Community's noninstitutional welfare services provided just under 794,000 crowns to Jews in need, while seventeen Community institutions cared for 770 individuals.[75] In the first week of February, meanwhile, the Community only paid out just under 300,000 crowns in welfare support (see Table A.3 in the appendix).[76]

In February 1942, welfare payments for impoverished Jews cost 1,565,000 crowns in total. The Soup Kitchen provided 1,040 breakfasts, 14,919 lunches and 9,607 evening meals, while 552 individuals received clothing or furniture, and food parcels were distributed to 921 children in exchange for food ration cards.[77] In March, welfare payments came to almost the same amount, but due to the dreadful food supply situation for Jews, the number of meals provided increased to 1,169 breakfasts, 15,933 lunches and 10,173 evening meals.[78] In April, the cash payments provided by the Community's noninstitutional welfare services amounted to 1,670,000 crowns; the Soup Kitchen distributed 1,202 breakfasts, 15,227 lunches and 9,818 evening meals. The increase in these figures, despite the ongoing mass deportations and resulting forced departure of hundreds of needy clients, is testimony to the rapid impoverishment of the Jewish population, in significant part a result of the resettlements from the provinces described in what follows. In total, 464 impoverished Jews ceased to receive welfare support over the course of April, while fifty-four were signed up. A total of 1,139 individuals received second-hand clothing, shoes or furniture, that is, twice as many as in February. Children received 569 food parcels, only half as many as in February.[79] In May, 474 fewer Jews received support while only thirty were signed up. Nonetheless, the Community's noninstitutional welfare services paid out 1,376,000 crowns in support, while the Soup Kitchen provided poor Jews with 1,191 breakfasts, 10,343 lunches and 8,169 evening meals. A total of 687 Jews in need received clothing and so on, while 970 children were given food parcels.[80] The Community's institutional services now cared for 793 individuals in seventeen institutions and homes.[81] In June its noninstitutional services paid out 1,409,000 crowns, with the Soup Kitchen distributing 2,012 breakfasts, 12,749 lunches and 8,509 evening meals. A total of 888 Jews in need received clothing, shoes or furniture, while 942 food parcels were distributed to children. A total of 433 needy Jews ceased to receive regular welfare payments over the course of June, with just thirty-eight new recipients being signed up.[82]

Further Transports and New Anti-Jewish Measures

On 3 March 1942, at the behest of the Reich Ministry of the Interior, Heydrich decreed that all residents of the Protectorate, including Jews, must carry an identity card. This clearly signalled the end of the Protectorate's semiautonomous status and the incorporation of non-Aryan residents into the Greater German Reich's central policies.[83] A government decree of 7 March extended the so-called Blood Protection Regulations (Blutschutzbestimmungen) to Czechs in the Protectorate, meaning that marriage and sexual relations between Jews and Czechs were now prohibited.[84] Meanwhile, the day before, at a meeting in the Reich Security Main Office, Eichmann had announced that soon another twenty thousand people would be 'evacuated' from Prague.[85]

In March, evictions and resettlements increased again, as a result of which a total of 137 Jews from Benešov (Beneschau) were forced to move to various locations in the District of Tábor.[86] The Jewish residents of Neveklov were also 'resettled'.[87] Since the beginning of the second quarter, the Prague Jewish Community had once again had to register the Jews in every chief county commissioner district to lay the ground for the transports to Terezín. In late March, its staff began with the District of Budějovice, followed by the District of Tábor between 7 and 14 April.[88] The process of registration had been completed in the District of Kolín by 24 April 1942, with the Jewish Community officials' efforts subsequently focused on the District of Jihlava.[89] The first transport bound for the ghetto had already left Budějovice on 18 April, carrying 909 individuals, while five transports with a total of five thousand people on board had departed from Prague by 12 May.

Next came Třebíč, where two trains carrying a total of 1,370 individuals had left by 22 May (see Table A.5 in the appendix). Many people quickly had to leave the Theresienstadt Ghetto soon after their arrival. Between 18 and 31 April, trains deported six thousand individuals from there to occupied Poland: to Piaski, Warsaw, Zamość and other locations. On 9 May, the first special transport, carrying one thousand individuals, left for the Sobibor extermination camp. On 17 and 25 May, meanwhile, two trains carrying one thousand ghetto inmates each made the trip to Lublin in the General Government.[90]

Since 27 April 1942, Jewish assets could be confiscated on the basis of the decree of 4 October 1939.[91] On 3 April, the Czech Ministry for Economy and Labour had prohibited the sale to Jews of all leather goods such as suitcases, rucksacks, briefcases, bags, purses and wallets.[92] In May, Jewish Community staff had to register all motorbikes in the private possession of Jews for the Central Office as well as all books owned by the former local Jewish Communities.[93] By decree of the electric companies of Prague, henceforth Jews had to leave overcrowded trams, thus losing their tickets, in order to make way for 'Aryan' passengers.[94] In late May, meanwhile, the Finance Ministry enshrined in law the payment of a 'Jewish tax' (Judensteuer) to the Central Office.[95]

On 8 May 1942, the Prague Jewish Community initiated the registration of the Jews still living in the District of Olomouc in preparation for their mass transport, while the same work began in the District of Pardubice on 19 May, and in the District of Hradec Králové on 27 May.[96] Ever more Prague Community employees had to dedicate their efforts to processing the deportations, from the registration of all Jews, the recording of Jewish-owned property and preparing the transports to processing the disposal of property extorted from Jews and correcting the Occupational Index. They also had to devote time and energy to providing the ghetto with various forms of equipment, often involving several wagonloads a week, while also processing the postal traffic to and from Terezín.[97]

Forced Labour against the Backdrop of the Transports

Following subsequent transports, at the beginning of March 1942 the labour offices had on their books just 35,941 Jews between the ages of sixteen and sixty, 17,707 men and 18,234 women. Of these, 13,854 men and 595 women were subject to forced labour deployment by the end of March. While this was only slightly more people than in the previous month, it included almost all available men. Thousands, moreover, had been deported by the Gestapo (see Table A.4 in the appendix).[98]

In the second week of March, the Prague city authorities deployed a daily total of between 630 and 710 men to clear snow, while the Ruzin airfield discontinued the snow-clearing work being performed by more than one hundred Jews on the eighth of that month.[99] Until 20 March, the number of Jews clearing snow for the City of Prague on a daily basis remained constant, before falling to around four hundred men, who were dismissed by the City on 27 March.[100] In Brno as well, more than one hundred Jews a day had performed winter work for the authorities of the Moravian state capital. This work was halted not due to the weather but because of the deportations. According to its own statements, however, the Brno Labour Office at least managed to spare Jews deployed in mining 'from the Jewish transports for the time being' given the 'extraordinary importance of coal extraction'. In the Pilsen area, as a result of the deportations to the Theresienstadt Ghetto the number of employed Jews also fell significantly.[101]

By this point in time, the Jewish Labour Headquarters in Prague was cooperating with the Ghetto Council of Elders, sending fitness-for-work certificates to the Labour Headquarters in Terezín for the men and women deported on the new transports from Kladno, for example.[102] It was not just in Terezín itself that Jews performed forced labour. Hundreds of ghetto inmates were sent to various parts of the Protectorate to carry out construction or mining – ironically, for example, back to Kladno to 'increase coal extraction'. According to the plans made by the Labour Office there, the 250 men who arrived from Terezín in March 1942 were to be followed by another 160 in April. The performance of the Jewish workers employed so far, according to the Labour Office, was satisfactory and although 'the deployment of Jews seems undesirable from a long-term perspective', all reservations had to take a back seat; the authorities must make full use of these workers given the lack of alternatives.[103] In April 1942, more than one thousand ghetto inmates planted trees in the District of Rakovník.[104] They worked there, divided into groups, until June, and were mostly accommodated in the meeting halls of inns, though the larger work details stayed in barracks.[105] Some of these prisoners' work crews existed until autumn 1943.[106]

Independent of the deployment of ghetto inmates in various locations, in late March the Prague Jewish Labour Headquarters carried out instructions to prepare for the forced labour deployment of two hundred men to work on the road between Prague and Karlštejn (Karlstein), who were to be accommodated in a camp consisting of three barracks beginning in April.[107] At the same time, the staff of the Occupational Index completed a statistical survey of all those subject to forced labour and yet to be deported along with an overview of all Jews fit for work. The department sent a list of unemployed men born between 1891 and 1923, destined for the Prague Labour Office's Department for Non-Aryans, to the SD Central Office first for approval.[108] In April, the Jewish Community then had to arrange medical examinations for all those between the ages of sixteen and sixty-five.[109]

In addition, the Prague Central Office ordered the Jewish Labour Headquarters to put together a work detail of one hundred men to dig slit trenches (see Figure 9.3) at the German Order Police camp on Prague's Letenská Street (Sommerbergstraße), starting on 3 April. By now there were ninety-six work details in Prague consisting of a total of 952 men, while 228 individuals were engaged in menial work. While the Jewish Labour Headquarters assessed the fitness for work of entire age groups, it also drew up a list of Jewish 'specialists' at short notice for the Central Office, which needed to provide this information to the Labour Office in Prague. The list detailed their earlier occupations such as chemical scientist or turner, which could be relevant to the war effort, regardless of their current engagement in forced labour.[110]

For seasonal reasons, requests for labour from agriculture and forestry now increased sharply. The Vyškov Army Forestry Administration (Heeresforstverwaltung) alone asked for two hundred men and women for the Hammer Labour Camp. While the number of Jewish forced labourers working in agriculture and forestry had been around seven hundred on average during the winter, this surged to 1,081 in the second half of April, chiefly due to forestry deployment. By this point in time, thirty-three work details consisting of a total of 288 individuals were engaged in agriculture and thirty-seven details made up of 571 individuals in forestry, while 202 individuals were working on an individual basis with official approval. In mid April, there were ninety-eight work details consisting of 1,078 forced labourers in Prague. In addition, 255 Jews worked there with the approval of the ministry or the Labour Office, 189 of them performing unskilled labour and seventy-six in casual employment. In the provinces, eleven work details consisting of 375 Jewish forced labourers operated under the supervision of the Jewish Labour Headquarters (see Table A.4 in the appendix). Seventy-three men, meanwhile, began their deployment in roadbuilding in Kozolupy (Kosolup) in the west of the Protectorate.[111]

The two uncles of Petr Ginz, who had previously spent weeks shovelling snow in Prague in dire conditions, left the city on 17 April to work on the motorway in Křivoklát (Pürglitz). As they were no longer needed there after just a few days, the Labour Office immediately sent them to work in roadbuilding in Mořina (Groß Morschin) near Karlštejn. Their experience there was dreadful. The labour camp lacked running water, which the inmates had to collect from a considerable distance away. The leaky barracks let in the rain, resulting in one uncle catching a cold, while the other injured his hand pounding gravel.[112]

With the help of the transport lists, the Prague Jewish Community's Labour Headquarters constantly had to eliminate the names of all deportees from the Occupational Index in order to keep it as up to date as possible and thus facilitate the placement of forced labourers.[113] By the end of April, the number of work details in the provinces had increased exponentially: there were now 111 groups consisting of 2,120 Jewish forced labourers, of whom 2,001 were men and 119 women; agriculture and forestry employed 1,229 forced labourers, made up of 938 men and 291 women; and 303 Jews lived and worked in the SS camp in Linden (see Table A.4 in the appendix). The Central Office now

Figure 9.3. Construction of a slit trench in Prague. © YV Jerusalem, Photo Archive, Album 19, fol. 77 (Report by the City of Prague).

demanded ever more forced labourers to meet its own needs. For example, in late April it requested five men for painting jobs in its building and eight to work in its garden, along with thirty-six men needed by the local Waffen-SS.[114] Other agencies also acted on their own behalf. In the District of Olomouc, on 25 April the Jewish Community received a phone call from the Gestapo official responsible for it requesting that it send ten strong men to the 'Villa Carmen', located in Plumlov (Plumenau) in the vicinity of a dam.[115]

As a consequence of new deportations, at the beginning of April the labour offices in the Protectorate now had just 35,014 Jews between the ages of sixteen and sixty on their books. Nonetheless, due to seasonal deployments in agriculture and construction, by the end of the month the labour offices had again increased the total number of Jewish forced labourers by just under 1,300 more than in the previous month, to a total of 15,747 individuals (see Table A.4 in the appendix). By the end of April, there were just 1,868 unemployed but fit-for-work Jews.[116]

At the beginning of May, of the 3,953 Jews living in the Chief County Commissioner District of Olomouc, 779 were subject to forced labour, eleven of them in the Linden camp.[117] They slaved away, for example, in the Durit brickworks in Bystrovany (Bistrowan), for Master Bricklayer Edmund Klemm in Olomouc, at Josef Niesner & Co, at a sugar factory in Olomouc, a distillery in Loštice, various market gardens in Olomouc, Prostějov and the surrounding area, for the municipal authorities in Olomouc and Prostějov, a number of farmers and big landowners, the Gestapo in Plumlov and the Vyškov Army Forestry Administration in the Scherowitz-Hammer Camp.[118]

The Olomouc Labour Office had placed Jewish forced labourers, 113 men and seventy-one women between the ages of sixteen and sixty, at the Hammer Labour Camp, thirteen kilometres from Prostějov, where they planted trees for the Žárovice (Scherowitz) Army Forestry Administration. During an inspection by a delegation of Jewish Community representatives, Dr Ernst Wald (Prostějov Local Office) and Robert Redlich (Olomouc Branch Office) noted that the forced labourers were also carrying out other forms of strenuous forest work. Only men of fitness category I were supposed to do work of this kind. The food, provided by the Army Forestry Office (Heeresforstamt) at a cost of eighteen crowns a day, deducted from the forced labourers' wages, was far from adequate given the taxing nature of the work and the long distances the workers had to travel to their worksites, which often required a journey of up to three hours on foot. The workers had to rise at five in the morning, according to the Camp Commandant (Lagerführer) Forester (Forstmeister) Hanowetz, with breakfast at six consisting of coffee and a small piece of spread bread; work began at half past six. At 7.30 p.m. the workers would return to the camp, where they would receive a bowl of soup. During the day the workers would eat bread, receiving 1.8 kg for every four days. The hygienic and sanitary conditions left a great deal to be desired. With the only available barrack grossly overcrowded with two hundred people, illnesses proliferated. The workers had access to just one washing area, with a kettle the only means of obtaining hot water. The remainder of the wages (Restlöhne) was not paid but instead transferred to the Emigration Fund of Bohemia and Moravia, while the forced labourers' families received no support.[119]

In the wake of such visits, the local Jewish Communities tried to help out the Jewish inmates, only to be prohibited from doing so by the Gestapo, as had occurred again and again, for example, in the Hammer-Scherowitz Camp in May. In the labour camps of the Protectorate, Jewish forced labourers thus always lived in a state of extreme isolation. Due to the mass deportations, by this point in time the authorities had already announced the deployment of Jews 'related to Aryans' ('arisch Versippte'), i.e. those living in 'mixed marriages' or 'Mischlinge'.[120]

The labour deployment of Jews organized by the Prague Jewish Community – independent of the Labour Administration as in Germany and Austria – in agriculture and forestry also reached its apogee. This form of deployment was regarded as so-called retraining and, very much in line with the Austrian model, was strictly supervised by the Security Police.[121] At the end of 1941, 1,300 Jews were subject to this type of deployment but after a seasonal dip this figure had already climbed to more than 1,900 Jews by May 1942, including three hundred individuals in the Linden camp, employed in 110 work details on estates and in various forestry districts.[122] In addition, in Prague ninety-two work details existed consisting of 942 Jews along with 701 engaged in manual labour and thirty-seven individuals performing casual work. In the provinces, 144 work details made up of 2,371 Jews, 139 of them women, were by now subject to labour deployment (see Table A.4 in the appendix).[123]

Despite the deportation of a further four thousand individuals, by May 1942 the forced labour of Jews in the Protectorate had grown to encompass more than fifteen thousand men and almost one thousand women, that is, a little over sixteen thousand individuals in total.[124] The Labour Administration had thus reached the zenith of Jewish forced labour in the Protectorate and exhausted completely the pool of Jews fit for work and aged between sixteen and sixty.[125] The forced labour programme now incorporated the last of those not subject to deployment. For example, in Moravian Ostrava the Labour Office managed to chase down Ervin Krumholz, born in 1924: having failed to don the identificatory star, he was working in a firm where he had begun an apprenticeship. Henceforth he would be engaged along with other Jews in river construction outside the city.[126]

The Flight and Resistance of Czech Jews

Many Jews responded to their impending deportation to the ghetto by fleeing or committing suicide, as evident in the case of the residents of the small town of Prostějov alone. Dr Paul Katzer, born in 1891, had lived in the town since 1931, where he worked until 1934 as secretary of the Industrial Association/Clothing Industry Division (Industriellen-Verband/Fachgruppe für Konfektionsindustrie) and then, until 1939, as a lawyer. Later he performed forced labour in Olšany (Olschan), working on the road between Prostějov and Olomouc, where he was arrested for unknown reasons. Having served the prison sentence meted out to him in court, in April 1942 he was dismissed and immediately subjected to forced labour in forestry in Žárovice, until the camp there was disbanded in June. Katzer fled from Prostějov shortly afterwards.[127] The Frankl family, meanwhile, had already escaped the town. Former furrier Samuel Frankl, born in 1902, his wife Helene, born in 1908, and their two sons, Josef and Karl, born in 1932 and 1936, all vanished together prior to 23 May on the pretext of a hospital visit due to illness.[128] In Moravian Ostrava too, Jews evaded the looming deportation to Terezín by, for example, fleeing to Prague.[129]

In Prostějov, Marie Bock, born in 1885, had been forced to leave her own house a few months earlier, moving into the home of Leo Beer as subtenant. Summoned to Olomouc for a transport on 22 June 1942, she packed her bags and told her co-residents she was going to visit the cemetery first. Instead she went to the house she owned in Prostějov, where she committed suicide by taking poison. It was several days before her body was discovered.[130] In late July, Therese and Bruno Winter, again of Prostějov, also took their own lives.[131] Around this time, in the district under the remit of the Olomouc Jewish Community alone, another five Jews evaded transport either through flight or suicide.[132]

Jews continued to resist, on an individual or collective basis, the wide range of discriminatory regulations in the Protectorate. Senior Secretary Bankl of the Gestapo, for example, informed Community representatives that Jews would face serious consequences if they violated the prohibition on entering the Adolf-Hitler Ring in Olomouc.[133] At the beginning of December 1941, in two towns in the District of Olomouc, the Provisioning Office (Wirtschaftsamt) restricted Jews' use of the local shops to just one each for milk, groceries and meat. This made life extraordinarily difficult for 365 families in Hejčín and 285 families in Chvalkovice (Chwalkowitz).[134] Through negotiations with the Economic Group Retail Trade (Wirtschaftsgruppe Einzelhandel), the Olomouc Jewish Community managed to ensure that Jews could at least buy food in the stores specified for their use all day rather than only at restricted times, albeit in separate rooms.[135] In Prostějov, meanwhile, four extra sales outlets were established 'in order to prevent problems from arising'.[136] In June 1942, the Olomouc Branch Office managed to persuade the Gestapo that it needed to be able to purchase items for the Jewish Community throughout the day. As a result, a local shop was tasked with procuring all the goods requested by the Community, which could then be picked up at any time by two delivery men.[137]

In 1941, a Gestapo official complained that Jewish workers engaged in marsh regulation in Olomouc were talking politics with Czechs and listening to the radio rather than working.[138] In May of the next year, Kriminalsekretär Hüntgen of the Gestapo complained to the Olomouc Jewish Community that, time and again, Jews had been observed 'gathering in mobs and discussing politics ... in the Soup Kitchen (Volksküche) and Middle Class Kitchen (Mittelstandsküche)'. Should this conduct continue, he threatened a new round of arrests.[139] In summer 1942, for the umpteenth time the Olomouc Gestapo instructed the Jewish Community to make members of the Jewish forced labour details aware that if they wished to avoid the most severe punishment, they 'must conduct themselves inconspicuously and respectably and avoid doing anything that might attract the attention and sympathy of passers-by'.[140]

Evidently, in view of the growing unrest among what was left of the Jewish population, the Gestapo was keen to avert resistance or acts of desperation. In an operation in mid June, therefore, the authorities collected all hitting and stabbing weapons, from clubs to sabres. Jews who failed to hand in these items would face the firing squad.[141] Due to surveillance, repression, terror and fear of deportation, no organized group resistance emerged within the Jewish population. Nonetheless, many Jews, particularly students, intellectuals, leftists, Zionists and members of the Maccabi sports organization, were involved in various groups in the Czech resistance, that is, communist and left-wing groupings, those working for the exile government and independent circles. While some of them issued regulations barring Jews due to the risks involved, many were admitted. Up to 1941/1942, Jews certainly played a role in acts of resistance and sabotage; this then changed as a result of the repressive measures that began under Heydrich and the deportations.[142]

As reported abroad, the Nazis went so far as to justify the execution of Czechs in light of the underground activities of Jews. In January 1942, an article in the pro-German newspaper *České slovo* claimed that the Jews were 'to blame for Czech tears'. The Jewish Telegraphic Agency commented that the efforts to undermine the Czechs' sympathy for the Jews had failed miserably.[143] Irrespective of such statements, there is only meagre evidence in the documents produced by the Czech resistance of any sympathy for persecuted Jews. Some groups even held positive views about Nazi antisemitism. In Prague, one underground report addressed to the exile government stated that the prevailing view among the general population was that the Jews deserved their fate.[144]

Meanwhile, in London, what was initially known as the Czech National Committee and only in 1941, following lengthy negotiations, officially recognized by the United Kingdom, United States and Soviet Union as the government in exile under President Beneš, had already concluded an agreement with the French government in autumn 1939 to develop a Czech exile army. More than 1,200 Jews registered as volunteers and trained in North Africa. Furthermore, in 1940 a Czech Jewish Battalion was established in Palestine.[145] Despite this, the Czech government in exile tended towards an antisemitic tone when discussing the 'Jewish question', particularly when looking ahead to the postwar period.[146] As Beneš put it to Jewish representatives as early as 1941, if Palestine was to be established as a Jewish state, this would eliminate the issue of minority rights for Jews; all Jews would then have to opt either for Palestine or for assimilation in their home country. In 1943, he went so far as to declare that the prewar approach to minorities had failed. Moreover, Beneš discounted the growing number of reports of the systematic mass murder of Jews by the Nazi state. He responded to requests to intervene dismissively until the reality of genocide had been confirmed by the Allies in late 1942.[147]

In London, Beneš had likely been laying the ground for the attempt to assassinate Heydrich ever since his accession as acting Reich protector, partly in order to neutralize British and Soviet accusations of negligible resistance in Czechoslovakia. Ignoring warnings of potential repressive measures, two men, symbolically one Czech and one Slovak, parachuted into Bohemia. After months of preparation, together with a third man who had managed to smuggle himself into the country, on 27 May 1942 in Prague the pair attempted to assassinate Heydrich, injuring him severely. A furious Hitler instructed Heydrich's deputy Frank to retaliate by having ten thousand Czechs put to death by firing squad. Before the next day had dawned, Himmler first ordered the arrest of ten thousand individuals, above all members of the Czech intelligentsia, as well as the immediate execution of one hundred prominent hostages. The next day, Frank persuaded Hitler that the mass shooting of ten thousand Czechs would be counterproductive, merely generating one hundred thousand new resistance fighters. In an attempt to capture the assassins, therefore, the German authorities offered a reward of ten million crowns to anyone providing intelligence leading to their arrest, while threatening to shoot anyone accommodating or helping them along with their entire families. Frank declared martial law in the Protectorate. All Czechs of sixteen years of age or older had to collect new papers from the chief county commissioner offices within two days. Henceforth, anyone caught without papers risked being shot. Theatres and cinemas were closed, the transportation system was brought to a standstill and a curfew imposed. Enraged by the attack, ethnic Germans attacked Czech shops.[148] Of the 541 individuals arrested during the first night of a security crackdown carried out jointly by the SS, SA, Wehrmacht and Protectorate Police, 111 were handed over to the Gestapo. Among them were several Jews accused of 'racial defilement'

(Rassenschande), one Jew who had left his home without permission and another carrying anti-German materials on his person.[149]

Reprisals against Jews

Following the assassination attempt, Heydrich lay seriously injured in hospital for several days. Just a few days earlier, there had been an arson attack in central Berlin on the anti-Soviet propaganda exhibition *Das Sowjetparadies* (The Soviet Paradise), which had previously opened in Prague in late February;[150] it had been carried out by a Jewish resistance group centred on Herbert Baum.[151] As a result, before the day of the assassination attempt ended, the head of the Prague Jewish Community and his deputy had been ordered to travel to Berlin.[152] On 29 May 1942, two representatives each from the Jewish Communities of Prague (Franz Weidmann and Franz Friedmann) and Vienna (Josef Löwenherz and Benjamin Murmelstein) along with six representatives of the Reich Association and the Berlin Jewish Community (Leo Baeck, Paul Eppstein, Moritz Henschel, Phillip Kozower, Leo Kreindler and Arthur Lilienthal) reported to the Reich Security Main Office. There, the ten men first had to wait for six hours lined up in front of a wall. When this torture was over, in the presence of Eichmann, Gestapo Chief Müller personally informed the summoned Jewish representatives of the detention of five hundred Berlin Jews as hostages due to the participation of five Jews in the arson attack. Two hundred and fifty Jews, he stated, had been shot and 250 transferred to a concentration camp. One hundred and fifty-four of the victims had already been executed in Berlin, and ninety-six later in the Sachsenhausen concentration camp. Should Jews perform similar acts in future, Müller threatened to carry out more shootings, a fact the Jewish officials from Prague, Berlin and Vienna must convey to the Jewish population.[153] Eichmann then informed them that the 'total evacuation of the Jews from the Old Reich, Austria and the Protectorate' was a fait accompli. All Jews of less than sixty-five years of age would be transported east, while their older and war-injured counterparts would become 'permanently resident' in Theresienstadt.[154] Weidmann and Friedmann returned to Prague with this depressing news on 31 May.[155] There, information about the attack in the capital of the Third Reich, the shooting of 250 Jewish hostages and the admittance of another 250 to the concentration camp spread like wildfire the next day, as Petr Ginz noted in his diary.[156]

Heydrich succumbed to his injuries on 4 June 1942. While Frank had persuaded Hitler to refrain from shooting the ten thousand hostages, the Führer insisted that the assassins be captured promptly.[157] The Protectorate Police stepped up its manhunt, the Wehrmacht got involved and the reward was increased to twenty million crowns.[158] The Gestapo used the raids that followed to arrest large numbers of Jews, often because of trivial items they found in their homes. One Jew, for example, had failed to hand in a decorative, wall-mounted antique sabre.[159]

Hitler now appointed Kurt Daluege, chief of the Order Police in the German Reich, as the new deputy Reich protector. Himmler immediately accompanied him to Prague. There they imposed draconian repressive measures, such as executions by order of courts martial, and carried out more than thirteen thousand arrests. In České Budějovice the synagogue was blown up and the cemetery levelled. Many of those directly involved in the assassination but also hundreds who were not were shot dead, such as Prime Minister Eliáš, who had been imprisoned since the previous year. In the village of Lidice, 173 or according to other sources 199 men over the age of fifteen were brutally murdered, the roughly two hundred women transported to concentration camps or the Terezín Police Prison, and most of the eighty-eight children killed, with a small number going to children's homes or unknown families. In the village of Ležáky (Ležak), the Germans burned down all the houses, shot dead thirty-three men and women, and handed over the children to the German authorities. This wave of reprisals in the Protectorate claimed several thousand lives, with Jewish Czechs making up between one third and one half of the victims.[160]

While the Czech people feared further reprisals from the Germans, according to SD situation reports, the reaction among Germans in the Protectorate was initially one of despondency and shock, but this soon mutated into outrage and hatred towards the Czechs. As they had done when the assassination attempt was made public, following Heydrich's death they called for 'the severest of measures to liquidate the Czech problem'.[161] Many went so far as to welcome the terror in Lidice, with just a few expressing sorrow for the victims.[162] It was not until autumn 1942 that the Reich protector lifted martial law.[163]

The news of the attempt to assassinate Heydrich and his subsequent death 'caused panic' among the Jewish population 'because it was initially feared that some Jew or other might have been involved'. The SD cynically commented that typically Jews holding such views 'almost universally wish to get out of Bohemia and Moravia'.[164] Their concerns seemed justified, as the German occupation authorities were clearly using the opportunity to target Jews who had shown any form of resistance or infringed anti-Jewish decrees. On 7 June, the Jewish

Telegraphic Agency reported that, according to official statements from the Czech government, the number of executions ordered by courts martial had now reached 153, including twenty-nine women. Six of these women were Jews, two of whom had been executed at the weekend just past. In Prague, Dr Max Sachs, fifty-nine years of age, lost his life for defying the authorities' segregation efforts and living in the house of a non-Jewish Czech hairdresser without permission. In Brno, three Jews, the 57-year-old Moric Abelas, 46-year-old Ivan Waltig and 50-year-old Moric Judenberg, were shot dead because they had 'welcomed the attack on Heydrich'. The Jewish Telegraphic Agency believed this wave of reprisals had claimed even more Jewish victims.[165]

The temporarily tightened restrictions on Prague Jews' freedom of movement were due to the preparations underway for the memorial events marking Heydrich's death. On 5 June 1942, the Police Directorate announced that Jews were banned from entering Wenceslas Square, Na příkopě, Národní třída (Viktoriastraße) and Hybernska (Hibernergasse) as well as the streets abutting the main railway station between 3 p.m. on Saturday and 8 a.m. on Monday.[166]

The official memorial ceremonies took place on 7 June, with Heydrich's body lying in state in the courtyard of Prague Castle. The public could lay flowers and wreaths from 8 a.m. onwards. In the afternoon came the changing of the Guard of Honour, which now included, among others, his SS comrades Franz Alfred Six, Arthur Nebe and Bruno Streckenbach. The castle courtyard was then closed to the public. The guests of honour, among them President Hácha, now arrived. At 6 p.m., Reichsführer SS Heinrich Himmler began the official funeral service with a speech. One hour later, the funeral procession started, its route taking it from the castle across the Charles Bridge and through Wenceslas Square to the main railway station. From there, a train took the coffin directly to the Anhalter station in the capital of the Third Reich.[167]

On 9 June 1942, the day when Heydrich was buried in Berlin, Hitler received Hácha and the Czech government, declaring that nothing would prevent him from 'resettling a few million of the Czechs of Bohemia and Moravia, should they reject the option of peaceful coexistence'.[168] For a while, the repressive measures and Hitler's threat reduced the number of acts of resistance and sabotage, which did not occur again on a large scale until near the end of the war.[169]

At the same time, Hitler now pressed for the rapid deportation of all Jews, above all from Germany.[170] The decision that Theresienstadt would function henceforth as a ghetto for old and privileged German Jews affected the Czech Jews directly. Increasingly they were deported east from the former fortress in order to make way for their German counterparts.[171] Concurrently, those Protectorate districts whose Jewish residents had not yet been transported to the ghetto were to be systematically cleared (see Figure 9.4).

Anti-Jewish Policies in the Summer of 1942

Following the attack on Heydrich and in the context of anti-Jewish policies in general, the Nazi leadership made the decision to accelerate and intensify the deportation of Jews in the Greater German Reich. The systematic transports eastwards from Theresienstadt would reduce the Jewish population in the Protectorate from 61,320 (51.83 per cent of the 1939 figure) to 48,273 (40.8 per cent) during the second quarter of 1942 (see Table A.1 in the appendix and Figure 9.4).[172]

In retaliation for the assassination, on 10 June 1942 the Gestapo sent the next transport from a Protectorate district, carrying one thousand people, not to the Bohemian ghetto as usual but directly to Poland, to the Lublin area. Two trains, each with one thousand people on board, then left the ghetto in rapid succession on 12 and 13 June for the Sobibor extermination camp. Meanwhile, the first small-scale transport carrying 'privileged' or older Jews from Reich territory had arrived in Terezín from Berlin on 5 June. Subsequently, groups of fifty to one hundred individuals arrived from the Reich capital and other German cities at short intervals throughout the month. The first large-scale transports from Cologne and Vienna reached the Bohemian ghetto on 15 and 21 June. By the end of August, the Gestapo had sent three more trains from the ghetto, carrying just under three thousand individuals in total, to the occupied Soviet Union, two to Minsk and one to Baranavichy.[173]

In June and July, the Central Office deported Jews from more Protectorate districts, notably including Prague. Three transports bound for Terezín left Kolín carrying around 2,400 Jews between 5 and 13 June,[174] followed by four special trains with 3,445 individuals on board from Olomouc between 26 June and 8 July. In addition, between 10 June and 7 August a variety of transports from Prague arrived at the ghetto, carrying a total of fourteen thousand individuals (see Tables A.5 and A.6 in the appendix).[175] Jewish Community officials made preparations for deportations from the other regions, registering Jews, at the behest of the Central Office, in the Chief County Commissioner District of Jičín in early June, followed by those in the District of Mladá Boleslav in the second week of the month and in the District of Klatovy on 16

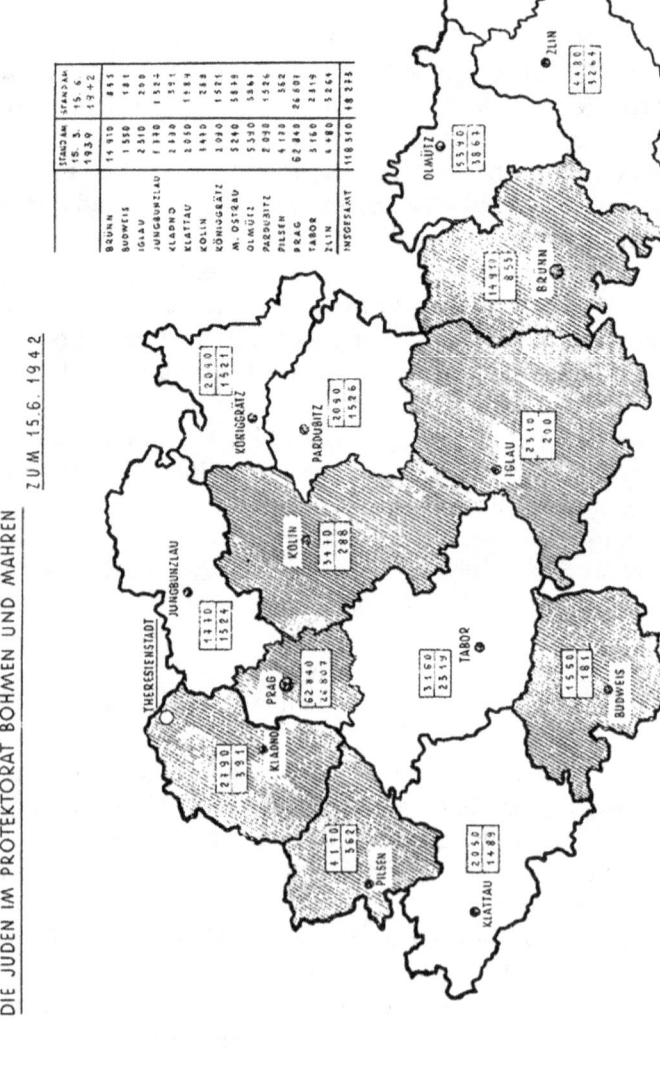

Figure 9.4. Contemporary map showing the distribution of the Jewish population in the Protectorate, 15 June 1942. Source: Helena Krejčová, Jana Svobodová, and Anna Hyndráková (eds). Židé v Protektorátu. Hlášení Židovské náboženské obce v roce 1942. Dokumenty. Ústav pro soudobé dějiny AV ČR, 1997, p. 56. © Maxdorf Publishing.

June.[176] Jews in the District of Moravian Ostrava were registered on 26 June.[177]

To pave the way for these clearances, new directives were issued concerning the property of the Jewish population. As in the Old Reich and Austria, Jews were forced to hand over all their pets. While their seizure was one of the bitterest moments in the run-up to deportation for many families and is mentioned in many autobiographical accounts, until now it was unclear where the animals were surrendered or what became of them.

For the first time we are in a position to answer these questions. In Germany, the Gestapo had already imposed a ban on keeping pets on 15 May 1942 and an obligation to register them by 20 May,[178] but while the Prague Jewish Community was instructed to register all animals, initially no ban was imposed. On 1 June it published bilingual leaflets explaining that all star-bearers must complete a form listing all dogs, cats, birds and other pets, either in person at the Jewish Community of Prague or by post, by the ninth of the month. Those attempting to give away or sell an animal prior to registration risked severe punishment.[179] One month later, the Central Office for Jewish Emigration in Prague ordered the surrender of 'pets owned by Jews or the Aryan relatives of Jews'.[180] In mid July, the Prague Jewish Community then instructed all its branch offices, in other words the former Jewish provincial Communities, to contact the local animal welfare organizations so they could make preparations for the surrender of Jews' pets.[181]

We now have evidence that Jews in Prague surrendered their privately owned dogs, cats and birds to the local animal welfare association on 23 and 24 July.[182] Towards the end of July, Jewish Community staff visited the branch offices in Mladá Boleslav, Pardubice and Hradec Králové to lay the ground for the surrender of pets to the animal welfare associations. Similar preparations were made in other provincial localities.[183] In early August, the local Jewish Community offices in the chief county commissioner districts of Mladá Boleslav, Hradec Králové and Pardubice then surrendered pets in the various district capitals, while animals in the districts of Tábor and Klatovy were taken to Tábor.[184] As prescribed, in the second week of August pets in the districts of Jihlava and Brno were taken to Brno, while those in the districts of Olomouc and Zlín were transported to Zlín. The surrender of pets in Moravian Ostrava initially faced a delay until 19 and 20 August.[185] After the Jews in Moravian Ostrava had handed in their pets as scheduled, on 22 August the local animal welfare association already started to sell them to non-Jewish residents of the city and nearby Vítkovice. The buyers had to fill in a form confirming that they were not resident in a household containing 'Jews required to wear the badge'.[186] This shows that the animals were not killed, as sometimes assumed, but were in fact sold to non-Jews, including their previous owners' neighbours. Tragic events ensued, as Katherine Kral recalled: surrendered dogs, for example, sometimes tried to return to their former owners, who might live a considerable distance away.[187]

With effect throughout the Reich, meanwhile, on 9 June Jews were ordered to hand over without compensation 'all articles of clothing not necessary for a modest lifestyle', though they had had no opportunity to acquire new items since the beginning of the war.[188] In the Protectorate, 'old clothes and old woven goods' were then collected at the local Community offices over the course of June and transferred to Prague at the behest of the Central Office.[189] Beginning on 19 June, Jews in the Protectorate were also required to turn in without compensation all optical and electrical appliances, including electric bowl fires, hotplates, vacuum cleaners and duplicating machines, in addition to typewriters and bicycles.[190] They had in fact already been instructed to hand over the latter two items at the end of the previous year.

After the Old Reich imposed a total ban on education, closed Jewish schools and reported pupils of fourteen years and above to the Labour Office for forced labour on 26 June 1942,[191] a month later, on 24 July, the Central Office for Jewish Emigration in Prague decreed the closure of all Jewish schools in the Protectorate. All public or private instruction for Jewish children was prohibited, while 'Mischlinge' could no longer attend public schools.[192] On 27 July, a directive issued by the Czech Ministry of Education enshrined this prohibition in law.[193]

The Prague Jewish Community and the Provisioning of the Jews

As the *Manchester Guardian* later reported, up to forty thousand mostly elderly Jews lived in Theresienstadt in mid August 1942, in addition to seven thousand younger Jews who had constructed the camp. The inmates, the newspaper stated, had had to leave behind all their worldly goods and now had no possessions at all. The sanitary conditions were horrendous. Sixty thousand Czech Jews had so far passed through the camp en route to the ghettos in the East, where they carried out forced labour, according to the paper. Several thousand of them had been taken directly to the Upper Silesian labour camps.[194]

While the process of registering Jews for deportation in Moravian Ostrava got underway, one transport each made the trip from Prague and Olomouc to Terezín. The Jewish Religious Community of Prague continued to try to improve living conditions in the ghetto. In addition to sending the medical appliances of deported doctors and the office equipment of the former Jewish Communities of Kolín, Budějovice and Olomouc, in early July it organized the transport of sixteen thousand straw sack sleeves directly from a factory in Dvůr Králové nad Labem (Königinhof).[195] In mid July, the Community sent an additional ten thousand straw sack sleeves (another ten thousand were already on order) and two more wagons carrying utensils and materials to the ghetto.[196] In preparation for the coming winter, it also ordered one thousand ovens and filling material for straw sacks.[197]

In August 1942, the Gestapo deported Jews from the ghetto to Riga and Minsk, while transports concurrently left Germany and Austria bound for both Riga and Terezín.[198] Many desperate cries for help were directed at the consul general of the Czech exile government, Jaromír Kopecký, in Geneva, from those seeking to get out of the Protectorate, save people from the deportations or help starving deportees in ghettos or labour camps in the Warthegau and the Lublin area. Via neutral Switzerland, the exile government in London launched a campaign to provide parcels for the deportees in occupied Poland. Later, via Portugal, it sent sixty-six thousand of these charitable gifts to Terezín and even sent more than twelve thousand parcels to Auschwitz.[199]

In the month of July, the Prague Jewish Community's noninstitutional welfare services paid out benefits to needy Jews to the amount of 1,365,000 crowns. While forty-two individuals signed up, 1,198 individuals ceased to receive benefits as a result of the mass transports. The Soup Kitchen still distributed 1,517 breakfasts, 10,353 lunches and 6,374 evening meals. A total of 1,072 needy individuals received clothing, shoes or furniture, while food parcels were distributed to 449 children.[200] In August, the Community's welfare services paid out just 803,000 crowns in cash benefits, as more than five hundred needy Jews ceased to receive support due to new transports. The Soup Kitchen distributed just eleven thousand meals.[201] In September, Community welfare payments amounted to almost nine hundred thousand crowns. While forty-five new individuals registered for such benefits, 448 ceased to receive them. The Soup Kitchen now distributed just 7,914 meals.[202] The dramatic drop in the number of meals shows clearly the impact of the district-by-district deportations, which affected Prague in particular during the summer.

A large proportion of the residents of the Community's old people's homes now had to move to the ghetto. With the same goal in mind, the Central Office also demanded details of all so-called mentally ill

(Geisteskranke) and feeble-minded (Schwachsinnige) individuals both in the provinces and Prague.[203] The deportations had thus also reached the residents of Community-run institutions. At the beginning of July 1942, 537 individuals lived in the seventeen institutions still operating, just over half the highest figure. The Prague Community then began to merge these homes.[204] The number of those living within Community-run institutions had fallen to 255 by the beginning of September, 209 by the end of September and just 170 by the end of October.[205]

As a result of the deportations from the provincial Communities, some synagogues were now sold. For example, the Nazi Gymnastics Community (Turngemeinde) in Dvůr Králové nad Labem acquired the local Jewish house of worship.[206] In Kroměříž, the German government commissioner, an Austrian named Hans Humplik appointed in autumn 1941 to replace the old municipal council, bought the synagogue from the Central Office with municipal funds, the Jewish residents having already been deported during the summer. He had the building demolished completely in November 1942, though it had been in good condition save for a few broken windows. In Holešov, meanwhile, in March 1942, in other words prior to the removal of the Jewish residents, the town council had already had the rubble of the synagogue – destroyed in the summer of 1941 – levelled to make way for a park.[207]

In Prague, the Jewish Community put together six railway wagons for Theresienstadt packed with equipment in September 1942, along with another containing chlorinated lime and several more carrying filling material for straw sacks. As in the previous months, the local Community offices affected by the deportations also sent equipment to the ghetto. For example, in September the Olomouc Branch Office sent six wagons and its counterpart in Kolín one. In addition, a number of branch offices sent hearses to the ghetto.[208]

As its membership shrank due to the deportations, in late July the Prague Jewish Community reduced the print run of the *Jüdisches Nachrichtenblatt*, which had long remained constant, initially to 10,000 copies, then to 9,500 in the second half of August, 9,000 on 4 September and 8,000 on 11 September.[209]

To the 'Central Office for Jewish Emigration', which had adopted the telling name 'Central Bureau for the Regulation of the Jewish Question in Bohemia and Moravia' (Zentralamt für die Regelung der Judenfrage in Böhmen und Mähren) on 12 August 1942,[210] in August alone the Prague Jewish Community submitted forty-one petitions and reports, eighteen in the first week of September alone and twenty-six in the final week of September.[211] While some of them were reports requested by the Central Bureau, the rest dealt with the problems arising from persecution and the deportations. The renaming of this persecutory institution highlights the authorities' new priorities, the ultimate goal being to eliminate the Jewish population in the Protectorate entirely.

The Consequences of the Transports for Forced Labour Deployment

The deportations started to have a detrimental impact on forced labour, prompting the authorities to factor into their planning both the labour market and the war effort. In line with this, in mid June 1942 the Jewish Labour Headquarters provided the Central Office with a list of the names of all Jews employed in industrial enterprises along with an overview that recorded 9,045 Jews subject to forced labour of a total Jewish population that had dropped to 48,273 as at 15 June. Evidently, this referred to the forced labour organized by the labour offices, without including the group deployment arranged by the Jewish Labour Headquarters.[212]

The labour deployment supervised by the Jewish Labour Headquarters in Prague now began to diminish due to the transports, falling slightly in July to eight-nine groups made up of 940 workers, 242 of them women. A total of 389 people worked on an individual basis with the approval of the ministry, 972 were now engaged in manual labour and forty-two were performing casual work. In the provinces, however, labour deployment had grown to encompass 142 groups made up of 2,367 Jewish workers, 178 of whom were women, while the number of those engaged in agriculture and forestry had reached its highest ever level, at 1,884 individuals (see Table A.4 in the appendix).[213]

While mass labour deployment had long since passed its peak in Germany, it reached its high point in the Protectorate in spring 1942, prompting the authorities to consider whether to legalize forced labour and, in line with conditions in the Old Reich, create a special labour law for Jews. In early May, a draft put together by the Ministry for Economy and Labour, now headed by Reich German Walter Bertsch, circulated in the Office of the Reich Protector. This provided for the adoption of the Reich labour regulations for Jews introduced in October of the previous year.[214] In contrast to Germany, however, the draft added a form of partial discrimination against Jews in 'mixed marriages'.[215] Group I 3 in the Office of the Reich Protector, informed by the 'perspective of Jewish policy in general', pushed for 'privileged' Czech Jews in 'mixed marriages' to be given the same status as other Jewish forced labourers, backing up its case by pointing to Heydrich's Protectorate directive of 29 September 1941.[216]

On 30 June 1942, the Ministry for Economy and Labour published an announcement on the new rules governing the employment conditions of Jewish labourers.[217] The 'Government Decree on the Treatment of Jews under Labour Law in the Protectorate of Bohemia and Moravia' (Regierungsverordnung über die arbeitsrechtliche Behandlung der Juden im Protektorat Böhmen und Mähren) appeared on 17 July and, devoid of the exemption clauses for 'privileged' Jews, came into force on 1 August 1942.[218] As had applied in Germany since 31 October 1941, Jews in the Protectorate thus lost the right to social insurance, overtime pay, holidays and other benefits enjoyed by non-Jewish Czech workers.[219] Decree 260, which legalized forced labour in analogy to the decree issued in Germany of 3 October 1941, appeared at the end of July 1942, stipulating that 'Jews placed in work [are subject to] employment of a special kind'.[220]

While these regulations legalized the forced labour controlled by the labour offices, the SS began to avail itself more and more of the cheap labour force in the Protectorate. In mid July, SS-Obersturmführer Karl Denk ordered the Prague Jewish Community to make available thirty able-bodied Jews through its Brno Branch Office for four to five weeks. However, all the men there were already performing forced labour, prompting the Brno Labour Office to explain that the freeing up of Jews already in employment would require a directive from a higher authority.[221] The Central Office even ordered the deployment of Jews living in 'mixed marriages', at the behest, for example, of the district head in Třebíč, for whom the local Jewish branch office had to make available between eight and ten men 'married to Aryans' for late July to help process deportees' property.[222] In August, one hundred Jewish women had to help out, often for several days at short notice, with the collection and sorting of the second-hand clothing compulsorily surrendered by Jews (Spinnstoffsammlung or Woven Goods Collection), the processing of Jewish property in the Trust Office's depots and the cleaning of the exhibition site following transports.[223] At the beginning of August, the Jewish Telegraphic Agency reported that 1,200 Jews had been dispatched to carry out forced labour in the coal mines of Moravian Ostrava and nearby Karviná (Karvin). There they slaved away for twelve hours a day for 15 per cent of the standard wage, but instead of money they merely received overpriced food and government securities to be redeemed after the war.[224]

Due to the ongoing deportations, ever fewer Jews were available for forced labour deployment in the Protectorate. The number of work details in Prague fell dramatically from eighty-nine at the beginning of July to seventy-eight at the beginning of August, consisting of just 738 Jews, 182 of them women. In the provinces, over the same period the number dropped from 142 to 109 details consisting of 2,266 Jews, of whom, again, 182 were women. Not including the SS camp of Linden, where 292 men now worked, the number of groups engaged in agriculture had fallen from seventy-four to just fifty-one, made up of 637 individuals, while the number of labour details working in forestry decreased from forty-two to just thirty-five, consisting of 440 individuals.[225]

A new form of forced labour began at the Prague Jewish Community's newly established Monuments Department (Denkmalsreferat). In accordance with the guidelines issued by the Central Office, for the benefit of the 'Jewish Central Museum' (Jüdisches Zentralmuseum) its expert staff had to select and prepare the numerous ritual objects initially secured in the synagogues and Jewish institutions in the provinces and then transferred to Prague. For this purpose, staff members gave the High Synagogue in Prague a new coat of paint and created a storeroom in the Pinkas synagogue.[226]

An inspection tour by the head of the Jewish Labour Headquarters revealed that municipal authorities and private firms paid their Jewish forced labourers miserably or not at all, often employing them under poor conditions. Of the sixteen Jews working for the Pelhřimov Municipal Office and the eighteen employed by the Weiner firm in Pacov (Patzau), most had in fact been allocated to category IV, whose members were supposed to be spared from working, including women with children to look after or in 'mixed marriages' with households to run. When the local labour office requested one hundred men from the Jewish Community Branch Office in Pardubice for the railway construction being carried out by the Gebrüder Preus firm in Rakovník, there were no longer enough men available in categories I and II, prompting the municipality to report forty men in category III, who were in fact ineligible for deployment. Earlier it had sent a group of sixty men to various worksites in Moravian Ostrava. At the behest of the Waffen-SS, the Prague Labour Office removed thirty-two men from a construction site in Karlštejn to build a firing range in Prostějov, accommodating the forced labourers there in a pigsty and providing them with grossly inadequate victuals. The Prague Jewish Community reported all these problems to the Central Bureau for the Regulation of the Jewish Question in Bohemia and Moravia. The Community also expressed concern that in Třebíč, Brno, Vyškov, Olomouc and Kolín the district authorities had enlisted Jews to clear the flats of their deported brethren. In the

District of Kladno, meanwhile, workers had received no payment upon completing their work. The Prague Jewish Community requested that in future remuneration and health insurance be governed by uniform regulations.[227]

At the end of August 1942, the Jewish Labour Headquarters registered a vastly smaller number of forced labourers in Prague, namely 606 Jews, of whom 158 were women, divided into just seventy work details, while in the towns of the provinces forced labour reached its peak, with 103 work details and 2,416 forced labourers, 211 of them women. In agriculture and forestry, the number of those in work details supervised by the Prague Jewish Community also diminished.[228] In total, as a consequence of the massive deportations, Jewish labour deployment in segregated work teams in the Protectorate now comprised just 8,948 Jews, 6,687 men and 2,261 women, that is, seven thousand fewer workers than at the end of May (see Table A.4 in the appendix).[229]

Finally, in the second half of September 1942, the Jewish Labour Headquarters summoned women to assess their employment status. Drawing on existing work gangs, it augmented the group working at the SS Motor Pool (Kraftfahrzeugpark) at 10 Passauer Strasse in Prague XVI by ten men, making a total of thirty. Another group finished their work for the Order Police and took up a new assignment at a teacher training college. In the capital of the Protectorate and in the provinces, the number of workers barely fell in September. In agriculture and forestry, the number of Jewish workers dropped to 1,383, including 389 women, again only a minor change, despite the fact that, since the issuance of the new decrees, individual employment was no longer possible even with official approval (see Table A.4 in the appendix).[230]

In early October, the forced labour group at the SS Motor Pool mentioned above was augmented further to make a new total of forty men.[231] At the end of the month, the forced labour details in Karlštejn were dissolved, with the exception of one consisting of eight Jews living in 'mixed marriages' from the district of the Kladno Labour Office. At the same time, the Smíchov branch of the Prague Labour Office instructed the Jewish Labour Headquarters to make as many Jews as possible, but at least thirty men, available for construction work for the Avia firm in Letňany.[232] In October 1942, the total number of Jews subject to deployment organized by the Jewish Labour Headquarters and controlled by Eichmann's Central Office remained roughly stable in Prague and in agriculture and forestry, while the number of forced labourers decreased by two hundred in the provinces.[233] Nonetheless, despite increased recruitment of women, due to the deportations the total number of Jews performing forced labour in segregated work teams organized by the labour offices in the Protectorate fell again by almost one thousand (see Table A.4 in the appendix).[234]

The Last Mass Deportations

Until the end of 1942, anti-Jewish directives were still issued by a wide variety of agencies in the Protectorate. Even by this late point in time, then, it would be wrong to think in terms of a consistently regulated, central 'Jewish policy'. On 4 August, for example, the Protectorate's Ministry for Internal Affairs published a decree on the treatment of Jewish patients,[235] while on 26 August the Bohemian Doctors' Association announced a prohibition on the treatment of sick Jews by non-Jewish doctors other than in emergencies, along with the segregation of Jewish and 'Aryan' patients.[236] On 10 August, the Czech Ministry for Agriculture and Forestry issued a ban on supplying Jews with previously announced foodstuffs,[237] the items in question evidently being all types of vegetables, fruit and mushrooms.[238]

In August, the Central Bureau demanded lists of 'Jewish flats in Aryan buildings', prompting the Jewish Community to initially submit lists for Prague and Kladno. The assumption that such flats still existed in large numbers tells us a good deal about the objectives and limits of the authorities' segregation efforts by this point in time.[239] Not long afterwards, the Central Bureau asked for lists detailing the property of former foundations and associations as well as lists of real estate in various chief county commissioner districts.[240] In September, the Central Bureau received lists of 'Jewish flats' in the North and South districts on the periphery of Prague and, in October, of Jews in 'mixed marriages' living in the homes of 'Jewish main tenants who have emigrated'.[241]

On 7 October, the Presidium of the Bohemian State Authority prohibited Jews from using taxis, while three days later the Central Bureau for the Regulation of the Jewish Question set about restricting Jews' use of trams. On 1 December, the Prague Police Directorate banned Jews from patronizing the Fišer hotel, the last one they had been permitted to stay in.[242] The next day, the Czech Ministry for Agriculture and Forestry imposed further restrictions on Jews' acquisition of unrationed foodstuffs: as in the Reich since mid September, now Jews could no longer obtain meat or eggs. Jewish children received milk ration cards only until the age of six. Jewish forced labourers, meanwhile, received bonuses for overtime and night work but none for heavy labour. Only veterans of the First World War could apply for an exemption.[243]

As in the rest of the Reich, the Gestapo organized the deportations locally. At the beginning of August, for example, it deported M. Zwicker, the eighty-year-old president of the Brno Jewish Community, to Terezín.[244] In Moravian Ostrava, the local Gestapo expected the deportation of Jews to Terezín to take place in September or October. In preparation for this, however, in the summer it already drew up a list of all Jews who 'have drawn attention for political or criminal reasons but who were not dealt with through protective custody or referral to a court in light of the imminent evacuation'. The Gestapo proposed their 'immediate evacuation' to the Central Office, which eventually complied.[245]

Piecemeal deportations from Moravian Ostrava to the ghetto thus increased.[246] The district head complained that the local Gestapo had seized the deportees' possessions, such as home furnishings, pointing out that according to the decrees issued by the Reich protector and the Commander of the Security Police on 12 January and 8 May, only the chief county commissioner, but since June the District Head/ Administration (Bezirkshauptmann/Reichsauftragsverwaltung), was authorized to liquidate Jewish property.[247] The Gestapo defended itself, claiming that it had merely made the items from the inventory of the Jewish Community available to the SS and Wehrmacht on loan.[248]

Following the completion of the transports from Brno, 'resettlement' was to begin in the Chief County Commissioner District of Moravian Ostrava, as the local Gestapo learned in late August, ironically from the local Jewish Community rather than through official channels in Brno or Prague.[249] While the State Police Headquarters in Brno had no information and pointed to the previous cooperation between the Prague Central Office/Central Bureau and chief county commissioners, the Gestapo in Moravian Ostrava received more detailed information from the Central Bureau on 2 September, presumably at a meeting: 3,610 Jews would be 'evacuated' on four transports (on 18, 22, 26 and 30 September); only those 'related to Aryans' (Versippte) would stay behind, with a decision on their fate to be made later, along with those incapable of being transported; the deportees were forbidden from taking jewellery or securities along with them and had to fill out a declaration of property; an assembly camp was to be established for every transport for a four-day period in a local school, where the deportees' luggage would be checked; and the Prague Jewish Community had been instructed to detail forty to fifty men to help with these tasks.[250] According to the State Police Headquarters in Brno, men who had returned from the Nisko deportation and had been deployed in forced labour programmes were now to be incorporated into the transports at the behest of the RSHA, while 'evacuation lists' were to be sent to Brno following every transport.[251]

Because a number of Jews had fled prior to the departure of the first train, carrying 860 people, on 18 September 1942, the State Police Headquarters in Brno had demanded their names the same day in order to put out an alert for them. Should the Gestapo in Moravian Ostrava discover fugitives following the completion of the 'evacuation', according to the command from Brno it must send them to a concentration camp.[252] The second transport, which departed on 21 September with 860 individuals on board, was also missing two fugitive Jews, while another two had committed suicide.[253]

By the end of the month, a further two transports, each carrying 860 Jews, had made the trip from Moravian Ostrava to the ghetto, while three transports from Prague, each with one thousand individuals on board, had already arrived there in the first half of September (see Table A.6 in the appendix). In addition, by the end of September three special trains, each carrying one thousand inmates, had left Theresienstadt for Raasiku or Minsk (or Maly Trostenets on the outskirts of that city), as had four trains bound for the Treblinka extermination camp, each carrying around two thousand individuals.[254]

Some of those still remaining in the districts of Kladno, Budějovice and Pilsen were now instructed to join a transport to Terezín and present themselves on 5 October at the assembly point established at the Prague exhibition site. The Jewish Community's local offices in these three areas had to dissolve themselves, appointing a so-called *Vertrauensmann* as their final representative. Prior to the departure of the Jewish officials, documentary material and all religious objects were secured for the Central Museum in Prague.[255]

The Theft and Utilization of Deportees' Property

In accordance with Heydrich's above-mentioned decree of 12 October 1941, the Central Bureau, formerly the Central Office for Jewish Emigration, could 'take over the liquidation of the property of emigrating Jews upon receipt of a written request from the holder of the right of disposal'. As described in the previous chapter, all Jews had to formally apply for the transfer of their property upon arrival at the assembly point and prior to departure. Their property was then made over to the Emigration Fund.[256]

Vacated homes were registered and reported to the Central Office, which stored their keys. The Prague Housing Office received notice of homes seized by the Gestapo or transferred to the Emigration Fund, passing the information on to the Office of the Reich Protector. Together with the Nazi Party commissioner for housing issues, it was these three institutions to which those in Prague working for a Reich agency could turn to help them find a home, while circumventing the free market.[257] In addition, the new German tenants could buy the deported Jews' furniture.[258]

In the provinces it was the district head who locked up the homes previously occupied by Jews with the help of the local Protectorate Police. According to the Moravian Ostrava Gestapo, the Nazi Party should stay invisible as the 'Jews' homes [that were] becoming available' were allocated. Furniture and other items were to be sold first to Germans, with the days of the sale being announced in leaflets produced by the National Socialist People's Welfare.[259]

When the deportations began, a so-called Trust Office was established at the Prague Jewish Community, headed by Salo Krämer, former president of the Moravian Ostrava Jewish Community. It employed several hundred people, including many craftsmen. At the behest of the Central Office, these forced labourers had to sort, clean and prepare for sale the vast 'estate' of tens of thousands of deportees: books, pianos, furniture, crockery, carpets and clothing. Name tags and initials were removed, any damage repaired and value assessed.[260] Zuzana Podmelova, twenty years old at the time, was forced to catalogue the belongings Jews had left behind. She soon felt so psychologically battered by this task that she got herself transferred to a desk job.[261]

These workers had to process not only the material left behind by the deportees but also those items Jews had been forced to surrender by the authorities, such as musical instruments, thermometers and cameras.[262] On 26 February 1942, for example, Professor Karl Weinfeld handed over a Pilat violin and a viola owned by his son to the Prague Jewish Community's Olomouc Branch Office, which it immediately sent to the Gestapo by courier.[263] The Trust Office had already been instructed to establish special depots the previous year, with fifty-seven bespoke depots being set up in the capital of the Protectorate alone. By the end of 1942, the Trust Office administered 8,730 homes in the city and within a radius of fifty kilometres. A total of 3,221 complete sets of home furniture were removed. In March 1943, the Trust Office depots contained more than 1.2 million textiles, 621,909 glasses and china cups, 21,008 carpets, 55,454 paintings, 778,195 books, 9,943 art objects and 603 pianos, to a total value of more than twenty-three million crowns.[264] The Trust Office then either sold – in the Protectorate – the linen, furniture and other items formerly owned by Czech Jews or sent them to the Reich, for example to the Ruhr area.[265] Because the 'utilization' of such vast quantities of stolen property required a great deal of time, in 1944 fifty-four large, packed depots still existed in former synagogues or Jewish institutions (see Figure 9.5).[266]

While more than two thousand synagogues in Germany had fallen victim to the pillaging of the November pogrom, in the Protectorate the majority of Jewish houses of prayer, along with their ritual objects, had so far made it through the occupation unscathed – though, as set out in chapter 2, several synagogues were demolished or set on fire by German or Czech fascists at the beginning of the occupation. By January 1942, the Prague Jewish Community had already provided the Central Office with a list of all synagogues that had been transferred to the Emigration Fund of Bohemia and Moravia.[267] Synagogues that now stood empty following the deportation of Jewish inhabitants and the dissolution of Jewish Communities, along with Jewish cemeteries, however, faced a high risk of looting and destruction. Between the end of March and the end of April, for instance, the Prague Jewish Community reported to the Central Office the destruction of Jewish cemeteries in Kyjov, Kostel, Zámostí (Samost) and Roudnice nad Labem (Raudnitz an der Elbe) as well as attacks on synagogues in Jindřichův Hradec (Neuhaus), Eisenz, Mladá Vožice (Jung Woschitz) and Dobříš (Doberschich).[268]

In order to save valuable books and ritual objects, the Prague Jewish Community proposed to the Central Office that they be accumulated in Prague. At the same time, Community officials sought to use this assignment to protect those members of staff needed to collect and register items from transport. The SS, meanwhile, used the material amassed in Budějovice, Klatovy, Pilsen and other locations as the basis for the so-called Central Museum, established in the summer of 1942, to document the 'dying Jewish race'. Jewish Community staff, however, not only collected more than one hundred thousand objects of religious and art-historical importance but – as a form of resistance – also sought to record the condition of the synagogues photographically for posterity prior to their destruction.[269]

A decree issued by the Reich protector for Bohemia and Moravia of 14 June 1940 had also authorized the Emigration Fund of Bohemia and Moravia to acquire Jewish real estate. In Brno alone, the Fund acquired five hundred houses.[270] It also took possession of the assets of the remaining Jewish associations and foundations that were liquidated by order of the Central Office at the end of 1941.[271] For example, the Israelite Women's Association (Israelitischer Frauenverein) in Hranice na Moravě received notification that it would be dissolved on 31 December and its assets made over to the Emigration Fund. On 21

Figure 9.5. Furniture stored by the Trust Office in a synagogue, first half of 1944. © YV Jerusalem, Photo Archive, FA-155, fol. 126: Report by the Trust Office, first half of 1944.

January 1942, its chairwoman Regine Singer then transferred what was left of its assets of a little over 1,100 crowns to the Israelite Religious Community of Hranice na Moravě.[272] By the end of January, the Central Office had already liquidated 60 associations, 783 foundations and 144 endowment funds. Plans existed to wind up a further 3,526 foundations and 53 associations.[273]

The Security Police also seized the funds Czech Jews had paid into insurance policies. In July 1942, the Prague Gestapo had already confiscated policies to a repurchase value of 54.4 million crowns, of which 20.1 million was held by the Generali and 13.8 million by the Victoria insurance firms. The Czech Slavia insurance company, meanwhile, held Jewish policyholder funds to the amount of 2.1 million crowns.[274]

In contrast to the rest of the Reich territory, then, in the Protectorate it was the Prague Central Office that was responsible for the administration and utilization of Jewish assets. Due to the use made of these assets, the Reich Supreme Auditing Office (Reichsrechnungshof), which was still asserting wide-ranging authority to audit Eichmann's Central Office at the start of 1942, sharply criticized this practice, asserting that Jewish property ought to be utilized – 'in accordance with the regulations' – to the benefit of the Reich and not that of Nazi Party offices or 'slush funds'.[275]

When it became apparent that the mass deportations in the Protectorate would soon be over, in order to finance the Theresienstadt Ghetto over the long term the property assets of the Emigration Fund of Vienna (around 982,000 Reichsmarks in cash and bank accounts and – with an estimated value of around 1.4 million Reichsmarks in total – unutilized Jewish real estate holdings and the SS-run Austrian 'retraining camp' for Jews in Sandhof)[276] were transferred free of charge to the 'Emigration Fund for Bohemia and Moravia', a step taken 'in the interests of the Reich'. In addition to the assets stolen in the Protectorate, this Prague-based Emigration Fund also acquired those of dissolved Jewish entities in Berlin (around 120 million Reichsmarks) and Vienna (8 million Reichsmarks).[277]

The Jewish Community and the Transports to Theresienstadt

As a consequence of the ongoing transports, the number of those in care at Prague Community institutions fell to 163 in October 1942. At the same time, an increasing number of those resident in old people's homes or in makeshift homes in the areas affected by the deportations had to be rehoused in Prague.[278] During the same month, the Jewish Community required just 651,000 crowns for cash welfare payments. Forty-seven new welfare recipients were signed up, compared to 111 individuals who ceased to receive benefits. In November, the cash total fell to 580,000 crowns, while there were forty-nine new recipients and 154 individuals left the welfare system. In December, the total amount of cash benefits fell to 500,000 crowns. Forty-nine needy Jews were integrated into the welfare system while 237 left it, with the number of meals distributed by the Soup Kitchen falling from 7,334 in October to 7,046 in December (see Figure 9.6).[279]

Every week during this period, Prague Jewish Community staff loaded a number of railway wagons with materials and equipment for the ghetto. In the final week of October alone, at least two wagons a day departed from Prague, now mostly carrying either household goods made available by the Trust Office or filling material for straw sacks.[280] While the Trust Office prepared twenty-two wagons packed with furniture and household goods for the ghetto in October, the Jewish Community sent nine wagons loaded with equipment, two containing ten thousand straw sack sleeves and several more carrying filling material for said sacks. In November, the Trust Office sent twenty-nine wagons carrying furniture and household goods and the Jewish Community seven containing medical and other items as well as 120 tonnes of filling material for straw sacks and twenty thousand straw sack sleeves.[281] By the end of 1942, materials from the various dissolved Jewish Communities had been taken to Theresienstadt in more than twenty wagons, in addition to household goods and now, above all because of the winter, another seventy tonnes of filling material for straw sacks and wood for heating.[282] Between July 1942 and March 1943, the Jewish Communities loaded a total of 409 wagons with goods for Terezín.[283] At the end of 1942, of the just under fifty thousand prisoners there, only half hailed from the Protectorate.[284]

By mid November, in the course of the clearing and dissolving of the local Jewish Communities, more than twenty-seven thousand items for the Central Museum had arrived at the Prague Jewish Community's Monuments Department (see Figure 9.7).[285] In Olomouc, for example, Community staff packed nine hundred books from the collection of the Rabbi Berthold Oppenheim into four crates.[286] By now their counterparts in Prague had sorted most of the books in the High Synagogue, while also pressing ahead with the preservation of the religious objects in the Pinkas synagogue. By early December, Community staff had catalogued more than thirty-one thousand artefacts, with the number increasing to almost thirty-nine thousand by the end of that month.

Figure 9.6. Providing an impoverished population with meals, 1943. © YV Jerusalem, Photo Archive, FA-156, fol. 27: Report on the Year 1943, Council of Elders of the Jews.

Other Jews, meanwhile, carried out maintenance and painting work in the Klaus synagogue in preparation for an exhibition.[287]

In an attempt to organize their tasks as effectively as possible, on 23 October 1942 the heads of all the Jewish branch offices got together for a meeting in Prague.[288] Since September, the Central Bureau in Prague had summoned all individuals 'related to Aryans', in other words Jews in 'mixed marriages' and 'Mischlinge', to assess their status, a process that encompassed hundreds of people every week. They had to provide an accredited transcript or accredited German translation of their documents. Because many of them were not in a position to do so, the Jewish Religious Community provided the certification.[289] In the second week of November alone, Jewish Community staff certified 2,468 translations into German for 418 parties.[290] The assessments of a weekly total of five hundred individuals continued until the end of the year.[291] Apparently, the SS incorporated those who failed to prove their status into the ongoing transports.

While two large-scale transports from Vienna and one from Berlin reached the ghetto at the start of October, five major transports with more than 7,300 individuals on board left for Treblinka, and another at the end of the month carrying 1,866 people for Auschwitz.[292] In mid November, Jews in the Protectorate were even prohibited from moving within their authorized residential communities.[293] Meanwhile, Prague Jewish Community staff too were now taken to Theresienstadt on the 'Cc' transport.[294] By mid November, two trains from Tábor with 650 and 617 inmates on board made the trip to Terezín, followed by two from Klatovy carrying 650 and 619 individuals and two from Prague each carrying one thousand people by the end of November. In December, the final transports left from Pardubice (1,256 people), Hradec Králové (1,198) and Prague (1,000) (see Table A.6 in the appendix). Concurrently, since the end of October every few days smaller special trains, each carrying up to one hundred deportees from Berlin and other German cities, arrived at the ghetto.[295]

Due to the mass deportations of the Czech Jews from the ghetto to Poland, before long they were soon outnumbered in Theresienstadt by their German and Austrian counterparts. By late summer 1942, the ghetto was already considered severely overcrowded, with just 1.6 square metres available for each person. This led not only to illnesses and an increased death rate but also to tensions between the mostly younger Czech and almost always older Reich German inmates. A number of Germans and Austrians were co-opted into the Ghetto Council. The most radical change was that experienced by the Council of Elders on 13 January 1943, with the arrival of the senior officials from the Jewish

Figure 9.7. Sorting consignments from the provinces in Prague, 1943.
© YV Jerusalem, Photo Archive, FA-156, fol. 31: Report on the Year 1943, Council of Elders of the Jews.

Community of Vienna and the Reich Association. Henceforth, along with Jakob Edelstein, this body was headed by Benjamin Murmelstein (Vienna) and Paul Eppstein (Berlin).[296]

Though deportations to the East had been ongoing for months, it was not until 2 November 1942 that State Secretary Stuckart, on behalf of the Reich Interior Ministry, issued a 'Decree on the Loss of Protectorate Citizenship' (Verordnung über den Verlust der Protektoratsangehörigkeit) for Jews.[297] Borrowing from the German 11th Decree on the Reich Citizenship Law, issued a year earlier,[298] which already applied to German citizens in the Protectorate but not to Protectorate citizens,[299] this stipulated that those resident abroad would automatically lose their Protectorate citizenship. Their assets would thus be forfeited to the German Reich and serve 'to further all objectives linked with the resolution of the Jewish question'.[300] On the basis of this decree, all deported Czech Jews could be stripped of their property, with the exception of those taken to Auschwitz, as this extermination camp was located within Reich territory. In this case, as throughout the Greater German Reich, deportees were designated as enemies of the people or state and their property confiscated on this basis.[301]

The Dwindling of Forced Labour Deployment

At the beginning of November 1942, the Ministry for Economy and Labour provided the labour offices in the Protectorate with new guidelines stating that Jews in 'privileged mixed marriages', who wore no star, were excepted from group deployment. They could be deployed everywhere, other than in the armaments industry, as individual employees without special approval.[302] Despite the mass transports, the forced labour deployment controlled by the Central Office via the Jewish Labour Headquarters had long maintained the same numerical level, but fell in November from 4,106 to 4,044 individuals, and even further to 3,317 by the end of December (see Table A.4 in the appendix). Many of these forced labourers presumably lived in 'mixed marriages', given that with the exception of Prague, Mladá Boleslav and Uherský Brod, the deportations had been completed.[303]

At the end of the year, the Gestapo in the Protectorate once again had all Jews registered and now all 'Mischlinge' as well, even those not considered to be Jews.[304] In the Protectorate, outside of the ghetto there now lived just 15,550 individuals classified as Jews.[305] For example, during the summer, the deportations had reduced the number of Jews in the district of the Olomouc Jewish Community from almost four thousand to a few hundred. On 17 December 1942, the latter Jewish Community counted just 260 'full Jews' ('Volljuden'), seventy-nine 'Mischlinge' who were considered Jews, forty-five prisoners, ten camp inmates in Linden and eleven 'missing persons' ('Abgängige'), in other words fugitives.[306] This, however, also meant that after more than two years of ghettoization and deportation, hundreds of Jews continued to live even in small towns.

* * *

In contrast to the Old Reich, in the Protectorate ghettoization began in the provinces. Following partial ghettoization in a number of cities, since early 1942 and prior to their later transport to the East, most Jews were temporarily concentrated in Theresienstadt. Proceeding from one district to the next, at the behest of the Central Office/Central Bureau, Prague Jewish Community staff registered all Jewish residents of the Protectorate in preparation for their removal.

Though tens of thousands of men and women were deported district by district to the Theresienstadt Ghetto or from there to Poland, the Labour Administration intensified forced labour deployment. Initially, as in the previous year, labour deployment consisted mostly of winter work, before swiftly transitioning into coordinated group deployment in construction, industry, agriculture and forestry. Often, forced labour took place in camps under dreadful conditions that left Jews ill or in need of welfare benefits. At its zenith in May 1942, more than sixteen thousand individuals between the ages of sixteen and sixty, most of them men, were subject to forced labour. The authorities had thus largely exhausted the pool of available able-bodied Jews.

In the Protectorate, forced labour was governed by the Ministry for Social and Health Administration and organized by the Labour Administration but, in contrast to the territory of the Reich, it was the SD Central Office – renamed the Central Bureau in summer 1942 – in Prague that was in charge of non-urban deployment, which made up a large chunk of overall deployment in the Protectorate. Many work details were also arranged directly by the Jewish Labour Headquarters in Prague. Several elements, such as the recruitment of Jews between the ages of sixteen and sixty and Central Office control, were reminiscent of the form of forced labour introduced for the Jewish population immediately after the establishment of the General Government. This lent Jewish forced labour in the Protectorate of Bohemia and Moravia something of a transitory quality.[307] While the labour offices and the Jewish Labour Headquarters could initially expand forced labour despite the deportations, the number of Jewish forced labourers fell during the summer. This period saw the recruitment of a greater number of women and Jews scarcely capable of working.

Although many Jews performed forced labour, they continued to require welfare benefits, either because they were not paid or because they were paid so miserably. The burden on the Jewish welfare services thus barely diminished despite the fact that thousands of Jews ceased to receive benefits as a result of their deportation. It was only when the clearing of the districts gradually drew to a close in the autumn of 1942 – following the summer transports from Prague – that the number of cash payments and meals distributed fell dramatically. Furthermore, the Prague Jewish Community did its best to supply Jews in the Theresienstadt Ghetto with materials and equipment, sending dozens of wagonloads there each month.

While Jews had already had to surrender their last articles of nonessential clothing, following the attack on Heydrich and the decision to rapidly deport all Jews from the Greater German Reich, the central authorities launched a final raid on what was left of their individual possessions in the summer of 1942. Jews working at the Property Utilization Office (Vermögensverwertungsstelle) established by the Prague Jewish Community had to sort through, repair and estimate the value of thousands upon thousands of objects prior to their sale; these were stored in more than fifty depots, some of them repurposed synagogues. Local animal welfare organizations received the pets owned by Jews. The animals were not killed as has often been assumed, but simply sold on to non-Jewish neighbours. The theft of Jews' assets comprised individuals' movable and immovable possessions, while the decree issued in November stripped every deported Jew resident in the Protectorate of his or her property. Associations were dissolved and their assets transferred to the Emigration Fund.

Though central measures increasingly held sway in 1942, a variety of authorities and agencies at the Protectorate, district and local level continued to play a role in shaping the persecution of Jews, including municipal authorities, police directorates, Czech ministries, the Reich protector and the Central Office. An astonishingly large number of Jews in the Protectorate put up resistance to the diverse range of persecutory measures, through flight, suicide, a refusal to comply with measures such as the compulsory donning of a star and active sabotage. This is illustrated by the many arrests, court sentences and Gestapo complaints.

Eichmann's Central Office and other authorities forced the staff of the Prague Jewish Community and its branch offices to contribute to the organization of forced labour, help pave the way for the deportations and facilitate the theft of Jewish property.[308] While their activities were strictly controlled, Jewish Community representatives managed to resist, intervening through countless submissions and petitions to various authorities and the Gestapo in an attempt to mitigate particularly onerous burdens. Seeking to counter measures imposed by local authorities, they tried to get the Central Office/Central Bureau involved, with occasional success.

By the end of 1942, the Security Police had 'evacuated' a total of 69,677 individuals from the Protectorate. Just 15,550 Jews, 6,211 of them in 'mixed marriages', lived in this territory outside of Terezín and the concentration camps, 13 per cent of the original figure.[309]

Notes

1. JTA, Report from London, 6 June 1942: 'Nazis Resume Deportation of Czech Jews to Occupied Poland and Ukraine', 7 January 1942.
2. Krejčová, Svobodová and Hyndráková, *Židé v Protektorátu*, 364–66.
3. USC SF/VHA, video interview, Hana Beer, tape 2, min. 10:08–13:20.
4. Data in Krejčová, Svobodová and Hyndráková, *Židé v Protektorátu*, 364–66.
5. Entry of 5 February 1942, in Ginz, *The Diary of Petr Ginz*, 69.
6. Blodig, *Theresienstadt*, 32–33; Schmidt-Hartmann, 'Tschechoslowakei', 362; Rothkirchen, *Jews*, 127–28. On the fate of the transport, see Andrej Angrick and Peter Klein, *Die 'Endlösung' in Riga: Ausbeutung und Vernichtung 1941–1944* (Darmstadt, 2006), 232, 235–37.
7. Official Gazette of the Reich Protector in Bohemia and Moravia, no. 7/1942, 28 February 1942, 38; facsimile in *Europa unterm Hakenkreuz: Österreich und Tschechoslowakei*, fig. 22. In the typewritten draft of the decree of 1941 the municipality of Gaya (Kyjov) still appeared, but had been scored through by hand in the version of 16 February 1942; USHMM Washington, RG 48.005M, reel 3 (Prague State Archive), no. 2, n.p.: Circular decree Reich protector, assigned to carry out executive functions (Heydrich), 16 February 1942, 1; cf. ibid., no. 4: Note Reich protector, I3b 6569, 17 December 1941.
8. Official Gazette of the Reich Protector in Bohemia and Moravia, no. 7/1942, 28 February 1942, 38. Facsimile in *Europa unterm Hakenkreuz: Österreich und Tschechoslowakei*, fig. 22. Cf. Heydrich to Frick on decree of 16 February 1942, in *Deutsche Politik im 'Protektorat Böhmen und Mähren'*, doc. no. 82, 237. On the Emigration Fund of Bohemia and Moravia, see chapter 7 of this book.
9. Brandes, *'Umvolkung, Umsiedlung, rassische Bestandsaufnahme'*, 226–27.
10. *Deutsche Politik im 'Protektorat Böhmen und Mähren'*, 237, doc. no. 82: Heydrich to Frick on decree of 16 February 1942; cf. Institute of Jewish Affairs, *Hitler's Ten-Year War*, 57.
11. Institute of Jewish Affairs, *Hitler's Ten-Year War*, 60.
12. Rothkirchen, *Jews*, 127. On policies concerning 'mixed marriages' in the Old Reich, see Gruner, *Widerstand in der Rosenstraße*, 85–102.
13. Ginz, *The Diary of Petr Ginz*, 124.
14. YV Jerusalem, M 58/JM 11808, fol. 35: Note, Jewish Religious Community of Olomouc, 13 March 1942.
15. On the society in the ghetto, see the forthcoming work by Anna Hájková, 'The Prisoner Society in Terezín Ghetto, 1941–1945' (unpublished dissertation). See also Anna Hájková, 'To Terezín and Back: Czech Jews and their Bonds of Belonging between Theresienstadt and Postwar Czechoslovakia', *Dapim. Studies on the Holocaust* 28(1) (2014), 38–48.
16. Report by the Foreign Office representative in the Office of the Reich Protector, 18 March 1942, in Mund, *Deutschland und das Protektorat*, doc. 418, 593–95.

17. Anderl and Rupnow, *Die Zentralstelle für jüdische Auswanderung*, 334. On the SS Main Economic and Administrative Office, see Jan Erik Schulte, *Zwangsarbeit und Vernichtung: Das Wirtschaftsimperium der SS. Oswald Pohl und das SS-Wirtschafts-Verwaltungshauptamt 1933–1945* (Paderborn, 2001).
18. Anderl and Rupnow, *Die Zentralstelle für jüdische Auswanderung*, 248.
19. Ibid., 250–51, 321 and 336.
20. Rothkirchen, *Jews*, 235–36. H.G. Adler greatly advanced the research on Terezín. See Adler, *Theresienstadt 1941–1945*; Adler, *Die verheimlichte Wahrheit*.
21. *Der Neue Tag*, 8 November 1941, 5.
22. USHMM Washington, RG 48.005M, reel 2 (Prague State Archive), II-4-4055, carton 859, no. 64, n.p.: Statistics on the Labour Deployment of Jews in the Protectorate, December 1941 (n.d.).
23. Ordinance, 22 November 1941; *Der Neue Tag*, 23 November 1941, 4.
24. USHMM Washington, RG 48.005M, reel 2 (Prague State Archive), II-4-4055, carton 859, no. 74, n.p.: Hradec Králové Employment Office to Ministry for Social and Health Administration, 2 February 1942.
25. Ibid., no. 96, n.p.: Hradec Králové Employment Office to Ministry for Social and Health Administration, 2 March 1942.
26. *Der Neue Tag*, 6 December 1941, 5.
27. Entry of 24 December 1941, in Ginz, *The Diary of Petr Ginz*, 55. Translation amended.
28. YV Jerusalem, O 7/60, fol. 3–4: Weekly report Jewish Religious Community of Prague, 27 December 1941 to 2 January 1942, 2–3.
29. Ibid., fol. 3–4: Weekly report Jewish Religious Community of Prague, 27 December 1941 to 2 January 1942, 2–3.
30. Ibid., fol. 47: Weekly report Jewish Religious Community of Prague, 24–30 January 1942, 4.
31. Ibid., fol. 33: Weekly report Jewish Religious Community of Prague, 17–23 January 1942, 2.
32. Ibid., fol. 150: Monthly report Jewish Religious Community of Prague, 1–30 January 1942, 3.
33. Ibid., fol. 45–46: Weekly report Jewish Religious Community of Prague, 24–30 January 1942, 2–3.
34. Entry of 29 January 1942, in Ginz, *The Diary of Petr Ginz*, 66.
35. YV Jerusalem, O 7/60, fol. 57: Weekly report Jewish Religious Community of Prague, 31 January to 6 February 1942, 2.
36. Ibid., fol. 58: Weekly report Jewish Religious Community of Prague, 31 January to 6 February 1942, 3.
37. Ibid., fol. 69–70: Weekly report Jewish Religious Community of Prague, 7–13 February 1942, 2–3.
38. Ibid., fol. 80–81: Weekly report Jewish Religious Community of Prague, 14–20 February 1942, 2–3.
39. Ibid., fol. 92–93: Weekly report Jewish Religious Community of Prague, 21–27 February 1942, 2–3; ibid., fol. 103: Weekly report Jewish Religious Community of Prague, 28 February to 6 March 1942, 2; ibid., fol. 80–81: Weekly report Jewish Religious Community of Prague, 14–20 February 1942, 2–3.
40. Entry of 22 March 1942, in Ginz, *The Diary of Petr Ginz*, 93. Translation amended.
41. USHMM Washington, RG 48.005M, reel 2 (Prague State Archive), II-4-4055, carton 859, no. 108, n.p.: Statistics on the Labour Deployment of Jews in the Protectorate, February 1942 (n.d.). According to reports by the county Communities in the Protectorate, on 28 February 12,790 Jews were subject to labour deployment; YV

Jerusalem, O 7/60, fol. 103: Weekly report Jewish Religious Community of Prague, 28 February to 6 March 1942, 2.
42. Ibid., fol. 5: Weekly report Jewish Religious Community of Prague, 27 December 1941 to 2 January 1942, 4.
43. JTA, 'Sale of Czech Newspapers to Jews Prohibited in the Protectorate by Nazi Order', 23 January 1942.
44. Entry, 12 March 1942, in Ginz, *The Diary of Petr Ginz*, 82.
45. According to Friedmann, 'Rechtsstellung', in Krejčová, Svobodová and Hyndráková, *Židé v Protektorátu*, 261.
46. YV Jerusalem, O 7/60, fol. 27: Weekly report Jewish Religious Community of Prague, 10–16 January 1942, 7.
47. Ibid., fol. 38: Weekly report Jewish Religious Community of Prague, 17–23 January 1942, 7.
48. Ibid., fol. 51: Weekly report Jewish Religious Community of Prague, 24–30 January 1942, 8.
49. According to Friedmann, 'Rechtsstellung', in Krejčová, Svobodová and Hyndráková, *Židé v Protektorátu*, 261.
50. Entry of 14 April 1942, in Ginz, *The Diary of Petr Ginz*, 98.
51. According to Friedmann, 'Rechtsstellung', in Krejčová, Svobodová and Hyndráková, *Židé v Protektorátu*, 261.
52. YV Jerusalem, O 7/60, fol. 38: Weekly report Jewish Religious Community of Prague, 17–23 January 1942, 7.
53. Ibid., fol. 38: Weekly report Jewish Religious Community of Prague, 17–23 January 1942, 7.
54. Ibid., fol. 75: Weekly report Jewish Religious Community of Prague, 7–13 February 1942, 8.
55. Ibid., fol. 97: Weekly report Jewish Religious Community of Prague, 21–27 February 1942, 7.
56. JTA, 'Sale of Czech Newspapers to Jews Prohibited in the Protectorate by Nazi Order', 23 January 1942.
57. According to Friedmann, 'Rechtsstellung', in Krejčová, Svobodová and Hyndráková, *Židé v Protektorátu*, 250.
58. According to ibid., 249.
59. YV Jerusalem, O 7/60, fol. 106: Weekly report Jewish Religious Community of Prague, 28 February to 6 March 1942, 5.
60. Gruner, 'Von der Kollektivausweisung', 57.
61. Krejčová, Svobodová and Hyndráková, *Židé v Protektorátu*, 364–66.
62. See https://www.bundesarchiv.de/gedenkbuch/chronicles.html?page=1 (accessed 26 June 2016); Krejčová, Svobodová and Hyndráková, *Židé v Protektorátu*, 364–66.
63. YV Jerusalem, O 7/60, fol. 180: Monthly report Jewish Religious Community of Prague, 1–31 March 1942, 11.
64. Ibid., fol. 15: Weekly report Jewish Religious Community of Prague, 3–9 January 1942, 5.
65. Entry of 11 January 1942, in Ginz, *The Diary of Petr Ginz*, 63. Translation amended.
66. YV Jerusalem, M 58/JM 11808, fol. 93: Note, Jewish Religious Community of Olomouc, 14 January 1942.
67. YV Jerusalem, O 7/60, fol. 16: Weekly report Jewish Religious Community of Prague, 10–16 January 1942, 1.
68. Ibid., fol. 60+63: Weekly report Jewish Religious Community of Prague, 31 January to 6 February 1942, 5+8.

69. Ibid., fol. 167: Monthly report Jewish Religious Community of Prague, 1–28 February 1942, 9.
70. Ibid., fol. 165–66: Monthly report Jewish Religious Community of Prague, 1–28 February 1942, 7–8.
71. Ibid., fol. 175: Monthly report Jewish Religious Community of Prague, 1–31 March 1942, 6.
72. Ibid., fol. 119: Weekly report Jewish Religious Community of Prague, 7–13 March 1942, 6; ibid., fol. 131: Weekly report Jewish Religious Community of Prague, 14–20 March 1942, 6.
73. Ibid., fol. 142: Weekly report Jewish Religious Community of Prague, 21–27 March 1942, 6.
74. Rothkirchen, *Jews*, 130.
75. YV Jerusalem, O 7/60, fol. 13–14: Weekly report Jewish Religious Community of Prague, 3–9 January 1942, 3–4.
76. Ibid., fol. 59: Weekly report Jewish Religious Community of Prague, 31 January to 6 February 1942, 4.
77. Ibid., fol. 163–64: Monthly report Jewish Religious Community of Prague, 1–28 February 1942, 4–5.
78. Ibid., fol. 173: Monthly report Jewish Religious Community of Prague, 1–31 March 1942, 4.
79. YV Jerusalem, O 7/61, fol. 143: Monthly report Jewish Religious Community of Prague, 1–30 April 1942, 3.
80. Ibid., fol. 153: Monthly report Jewish Religious Community of Prague, 1–31 May 1942, 4.
81. Ibid., O 7/61, fol. 135: Weekly report Jewish Religious Community of Prague, 20–26 June 1942, 3.
82. Ibid., fol. 162: Monthly report Jewish Religious Community of Prague, 1–30 June 1942, 3.
83. Announcement concerning the decree on identity cards, 3 March 1942, RGBl. 1942 I, 100.
84. YV Jerusalem, O 7/60, fol. 133: Weekly report Jewish Religious Community of Prague, 14–20 March 1942, 8. The government decree involved had existed since autumn 1940, as described above, but could only be enacted following the introduction of the Nuremberg laws in July 1941. In autumn 1941, Heydrich had pushed for segregation to be expedited in order to facilitate the deportations; USHMM Washington, RG 48.005M, reel 3 (Prague State Archive), no. 123, n.p.: Reich protector (signed Heydrich) to Undersecretary of State von Burgsdorff, 10 October 1941.
85. Report Gestapo Düsseldorf, 9 March 1942, on meeting of 6 March 1942 at Office IV B 4, in *Deutsche Politik im 'Protektorat Böhmen und Mähren'*, doc. no. 85, 241.
86. YV Jerusalem, O 7/60, fol. 141: Weekly report Jewish Religious Community of Prague, 21–27 March 1942, 5; ibid., fol. 142a: Weekly report Jewish Religious Community of Prague, 21–27 March 1942, 7.
87. Entry of 7 April 1942, in Ginz, *The Diary of Petr Ginz*, 88.
88. YV Jerusalem, O 7/61, fol. 8: Weekly report Jewish Religious Community of Prague, 28 March to 3 April 1942, 7; ibid., fol. 14: Weekly report Jewish Religious Community of Prague, 3–10 April 1942, 1.
89. Ibid., fol. 41: Weekly report Jewish Religious Community of Prague, 18–24 April 1942, 7.
90. See https://www.bundesarchiv.de/gedenkbuch/chronicles.html?page=1 (accessed 26 June 2016); Krejčová, Svobodová and Hyndráková, *Židé v Protektorátu*, 364–66.
91. Lexa, 'Anti-Jewish Laws', 80.

92. According to Friedmann, 'Rechtsstellung', in Krejčová, Svobodová and Hyndráková, *Židé v Protektorátu*, 260.
93. YV Jerusalem, O 7/61, fol. 158: Monthly report Jewish Religious Community of Prague, 1–31 May 1942, 9.
94. According to Friedmann, 'Rechtsstellung', in Krejčová, Svobodová and Hyndráková, *Židé v Protektorátu*, 248.
95. Decree no. 42, 29 May 1942; in Lexa, 'Anti-Jewish Laws', 89.
96. YV Jerusalem, O 7/61, fol. 74: Weekly report Jewish Religious Community of Prague, 9–15 May 1942, 6; ibid., fol. 85: Weekly report Jewish Religious Community of Prague, 16–22 May 1942, 6; ibid., fol. 91: Weekly report Jewish Religious Community of Prague, 23–29 May 1942, 1.
97. Ibid., fol. 47–55: Weekly report Jewish Religious Community of Prague, 25 April to 1 May 1942, 1–8.
98. USHMM Washington, RG 48.005M, reel 2 (Prague State Archive), II-4-4055, carton 859, no. 129, n.p.: Statistics on the Labour Deployment of Jews in March 1942.
99. YV Jerusalem, O 7/60, fol. 115–16: Weekly report Jewish Religious Community of Prague, 7–13 March 1942, 2–3.
100. Ibid., fol. 127: Weekly report Jewish Religious Community of Prague, 14–20 March 1942, 2; ibid., fol. 138: Weekly report Jewish Religious Community of Prague, 21–27 March 1942, 2.
101. USHMM Washington, RG 48.005M, reel 2 (Prague State Archive), II-4-4055, carton 859, no. 129, n.p.: Excerpt from the employment offices' situation reports, March 1942.
102. YV Jerusalem, O 7/60, fol. 117: Weekly report Jewish Religious Community of Prague, 7–13 March 1942, 4.
103. USHMM Washington, RG 48.005M, reel 2 (Prague State Archive), II-4-4055, carton 859, no. 129, n.p.: From the employment offices' situation reports, March 1942.
104. Kárný, 'Zur Statistik der jüdischen Bevölkerung', 16. Cf. USC SF/VHA, video interview, Eva Rozvoda Wölfler.
105. Adam, 'Im Wettstreit um die letzten Arbeitskräfte', 114.
106. Kárný, 'Zur Statistik der jüdischen Bevölkerung', 16.
107. YV Jerusalem, O 7/60, fol. 138: Weekly report Jewish Religious Community of Prague, 21–27 March 1942, 2.
108. Ibid., fol. 139: Weekly report Jewish Religious Community of Prague, 21–27 March 1942, 3.
109. YV Jerusalem, O 7/61, fol. 148: Monthly report Jewish Religious Community of Prague, 1–30 April 1942, 8.
110. Ibid., fol. 3–4: Weekly report Jewish Religious Community of Prague, 28 March to 3 April 1942, 2–3.
111. Ibid., fol. 24–25: Weekly report Jewish Religious Community of Prague, 11–17 April 1942, 2–3; ibid., fol. 37: Weekly report Jewish Religious Community of Prague, 18–24 April 1942, 3.
112. Entries of 17, 20 and 25 April 1942, in Ginz, *The Diary of Petr Ginz*, 99–101.
113. YV Jerusalem, O 7/61, fol. 24–25: Weekly report Jewish Religious Community of Prague, 11–17 April 1942, 2–3; ibid., fol. 37: Weekly report Jewish Religious Community of Prague, 18–24 April 1942, 3.
114. Ibid., fol. 48–49: Weekly report Jewish Religious Community of Prague, 25 April to 1 May 1942, 2–3.
115. YV Jerusalem, M 58/JM 11808, fol. 476: Note, Jewish Religious Community of Olomouc, 26 April 1942.

116. USHMM Washington, RG 48.005M, reel 2 (Prague State Archive), II-4-4055, carton 859, no. 150, n.p.: Statistics on the Labour Deployment of Jews in the Protectorate, April 1942 (n.d.).
117. YV Jerusalem, M 58/JM 11809, fol. 116–17: Report Jewish Religious Community of Prague/Olomouc Branch, 24 May 1942, 1–2.
118. Ibid., fol. 135–36: Report on labour deployment, 15 May 1942, 1–2.
119. Ibid., fol. 196–98: Note, Jewish Religious Community of Prague/Prostějov Local Office on visit to Scherowitz labour camp, 20 April 1942, 1–3. Cf. Report by the Jewish Religious Community of Prague, 'Labour' (n.d., mid 1942), in Krejčová, Svobodová and Hyndráková, Židé v Protektorátu, doc. 5, 111.
120. YV Jerusalem, M 58/JM 11809, fol. 111: Emanuel Drattler, Hammer-Scherowitz, to Jewish Religious Community of Prostějov, 28 May 1942, 1.
121. On similar deployment in camps run by the Reich Association in Germany, see chapter 2 of Gruner, *Jewish Forced Labor*. On Austria, see Gruner, *Zwangsarbeit und Verfolgung*, 177–87.
122. Report by the Jewish Religious Community of Prague, 'Labour' (n.d., mid 1942), in Krejčová, Svobodová and Hyndráková, Židé v Protektorátu, doc. 5, 111. At the end of May, the number of forced labourers in agriculture and forestry was 1,114 men and 487 women; YV Jerusalem, O 7/61, fol. 93: Weekly report Jewish Religious Community of Prague, 23–29 May 1942, 3.
123. YV Jerusalem, O 7/61, fol. 93: Weekly report Jewish Religious Community of Prague, 23–29 May 1942, 3; ibid., fol. 102–3: Weekly report Jewish Religious Community of Prague, 30 May to 5 June 1942, 2–3.
124. USHMM Washington, RG 48.005M, reel 2 (Prague State Archive), II-4-405, carton 8, no. 171, n.p.: Statistics on the Labour Deployment of Jews in the Protectorate in May 1942 (n.d.).
125. Gruner, *Jewish Forced Labor*, 170–72.
126. USC SF/VHA, video interview, Ervin Krumholz, tape 1, min. 16:20.
127. YV Jerusalem, M 58/JM 11808, fol. 546–47: Notes, Jewish Religious Community of Olomouc, 16 July 1941 and 18 August 1941.
128. YV Jerusalem, M 58/JM 11809, fol. 121: Note, Jewish Religious Community of Prague/Prostějov Local Office, 23 May 1942.
129. See USC SF/VHA, video interview, Paul Brichta.
130. YV Jerusalem, M 58/JM 11808, fol. 534: Note, Jewish Religious Community of Prague/Prostějov Local Office (n.d., June 1942); ibid., fol. 592: Note, Jewish Religious Community of Prague/Prostějov Local Office, 22 June 1942.
131. Ibid., fol. 572: Note, Jewish Religious Community of Olomouc on visit to Gestapo, 27 July 1942.
132. Ibid., fol. 574: Note, Jewish Religious Community of Olomouc on visit to Gestapo, 25 July 1942.
133. YV Jerusalem, M 58/JM 11809, fol. 146: Report Jewish Religious Community of Prague/Olomouc Branch Office on visit to Gestapo, 9 May 1942, 1.
134. YV Jerusalem, M 58/JM 11808, fol. 106: Government commissioner/Olomouc Provisioning Office to Jewish Religious Community of Olomouc, 2 December 1941; ibid., fol. 224: Note, Jewish Religious Community of Olomouc on visit to chief county commissioner and Provisioning Office on 12 December 1941.
135. Ibid., fol. 102: Economic Group Retail Trade/Olomouc District Office to Jewish Religious Community of Olomouc, 9 December 1941.
136. Ibid., fol. 265: Note, Jewish Religious Community of Olomouc on visit to Gestapo, 21 November 1941.

137. YV Jerusalem, M 58/JM 11809, fol. 4: Note, Jewish Religious Community of Prague/Olomouc Branch Office on visit to Gestapo, 17 June 1942, 1.
138. YV Jerusalem, M 58/JM 11808, fol. 360: Note, Jewish Religious Community of Olomouc on visit to Gestapo, 25 September 1941, 2.
139. YV Jerusalem, M 58/JM 11809, fol. 139: Report Jewish Religious Community of Prague/Olomouc Branch Office on visit to Gestapo, 18 May 1942, 2.
140. YV Jerusalem, M 58/JM 11808, fol. 571: Note, Jewish Religious Community of Olomouc on visit to Gestapo, 1 August 1942.
141. YV Jerusalem, M 58/JM 11809, fol. 69: Note, Jewish Religious Community of Olomouc on visit to Gestapo, 12 June 1942, 2; ibid., fol. 73: Note, Jewish Religious Community of Olomouc on the confiscation of cutting and stabbing weapons, 11 June 1942.
142. With plenty of details on activities and names, see Rothkirchen, 'The Defiant Few'. See also Rothkirchen, *Jews*, 187–89; Erich Kulka, 'The Importance of Documenting the Role of Jews in the Czechoslovak Anti-Nazi Resistance', *Review of the Society for the History of Czechoslovak Jews* 5 (1992–93), 63–67.
143. JTA, 'Sale of Czech Newspapers to Jews Prohibited in the Protectorate by Nazi Order', 23 January 1942.
144. Hahn, 'Verdrängung und Verharmlosung', 147.
145. Rothkirchen, *Jews*, 162–69; cf. Wein, 'The Czechoslovak Exile in London', 141–42.
146. See Wein, 'The Czechoslovak Exile in London', 138–46; Jan Láníček, *Czechs, Slovaks and the Jews, 1938–48: Beyond Idealization and Condemnation* (Houndmills, 2013), 42–145.
147. Rothkirchen, *Jews*, 173–75, 180–81.
148. For general information on the assassination attempt and its consequences, see Vojtech Šustek, *Atentát na Reinharda Heydricha a druhé stanné právo na území tzv. protektorátu Čechy a Morava: Edice historickych dokumentu*, vol. 1 (Prague, 2012); entries of 27–31 May 1942, in Ginz, *The Diary of Petr Ginz*, 99–101; Report Prague Gestapo and Himmler telegram of 27 May 1942, along with Report Frank on visit to Hitler on 28 May 1939, in Celovsky, *Germanisierung und Genozid*, 316–17. See also Küpper, *Karl Hermann Frank*, 268–71; Gerwarth, *Hitler's Hangman*, 1–10; Bryant, *Prague in Black*, 167–72.
149. Report Prague Gestapo on operation of 27 May 1942, in Celovsky, *Germanisierung und Genozid*, 317.
150. It had 150,000 visitors in March 1942 according to Report by the Foreign Office representative in the Office of the Reich Protector, 18 March 1942, in Mund, *Deutschland und das Protektorat*, doc. 418, 593–94. See also Entry of 3 March 1942, in Ginz, *The Diary of Petr Ginz*, 79.
151. On the operation and the Baum group, see Wolfgang Scheffler, 'Der Brandanschlag im Berliner Lustgarten im Mai 1942 und seine Folgen', in *Berlin in Geschichte und Gegenwart: Jahrbuch des Landesarchivs Berlin* (Berlin, 1984), 91–118; Eric Brother, *Berlin Ghetto: Herbert Baum and the Anti-Fascist Resistance* (Stroud, 2012), 161–74.
152. YV Jerusalem, O 7/61, fol. 159: Monthly report Jewish Religious Community of Prague, 1–31 May 1942, 10.
153. BA Berlin, R 8150/8, fol. 109: Note Reich Association, 29 May 1942; CZA Jerusalem, S 26, no. 1191g, n.p.: Report Israelite Religious Community of Vienna, 1938–1944/45 (Löwenherz Report), 41. See also Hildesheimer, *Jüdische Selbstverwaltung*, 221–31.
154. CZA Jerusalem, S 26, no. 1191g, n.p.: Report Israelite Religious Community of Vienna, 1938–1944/45 (Löwenherz Report), 41; cf. Note on visit to RSHA, 29–30

May 1942; quoted in Safrian, *Eichmann's Men*, 117–18; Gruner, *Der Geschlossene Arbeitseinsatz*, 300.
155. YV Jerusalem, O 7/61, fol. 159: Monthly report Jewish Religious Community of Prague, 1–31 May 1942, 10.
156. Entry of 1 June 1942, in Ginz, *The Diary of Petr Ginz*, 109.
157. On this and what follows, see Küpper, *Karl Hermann Frank*, 270–79; Gerwarth, *Hitler's Hangman*, 10–13, 278–87.
158. VHA Prague, fonds SS-Panzergrenadier Training and Replacement Battalion 10, carton 9, no. 12, n.p.: Special issue no. 2, *Polizeianzeiger für das Protektorat Böhmen und Mähren*, 5 June 1942 (print), 1–2; ibid.: Note by the Wehrmacht commissioner in the Office of the Reich Protector in Bohemia and Moravia, 10 June 1942, 1–2. Cf. *Politika*, 20 June 1942, facsimile in Grabowski and Haney, *Kennzeichen 'Jude'*, 208.
159. USC SF/VHA, video interview, Katherine Kral, tape 3, min. 23:18–25:30. Cf. another case of the failure to hand over a collection of weapons: ibid., video interview, Gertrude Pfeiffer, tape 2.
160. Gerwarth, *Hitler's Hangman*, 280–85; Küpper, *Karl Hermann Frank*, 272–73; King, *Budweisers*, 187; Rothkirchen, *Jews*, 155; Bryant, *Prague in Black*, 167–72. The RSHA report of 24 June 1942 refers to 1,148 arrests and 695 death sentences; Celovsky, *Germanisierung und Genozid*, 47, 326–28. Sládek assumes a total of five thousand victims, including three thousand Jews, during the 'Heydrichiade'; Sládek, 'Standrecht und Standgericht', 332–33.
161. BA Berlin, R 58/172, fol. 218: Report no. 290, 11 June 1942, 4. Reprinted in *Meldungen aus dem Reich*, vol. 10, 3804–5.
162. According to German reports referred to in Brandes, 'Nationalsozialistische Tschechenpolitik', 55–56.
163. Dennler, *Böhmische Passion*, 94.
164. BA Berlin, R 58/172, fol. 219: Report no. 290, 11 June 1942, 5. Reprinted in *Meldungen aus dem Reich*, vol. 10, 3805.
165. JTA, 'Four More Jews Executed by Nazis in Retaliation for Heydrich's Death', 7 June 1942.
166. According to Friedmann, 'Rechtsstellung', in Krejčová, Svobodová and Hyndráková, *Židé v Protektorátu*, 250.
167. VHA Prague, fonds SS-Panzergrenadier Training and Replacement Battalion 10, carton 9, no. 12, n.p.: Order for funeral procession and transfer of the deceased SS-Obergruppenführer and Police Chief Heydrich, 1–6; Programme of the memorial ceremonies for the deceased SS-Obergruppenführer and Police Chief Heydrich on Sunday, 7 June 1942, 1–5.
168. Quoted in Minutes from memory, K.H. Frank, in Brandes, 'Nationalsozialistische Tschechenpolitik', 47. Cf. Gerwarth, *Hitler's Hangman*, 280.
169. Rothkirchen, *Jews*, 159. Nonetheless, there were subtler forms of resistance. See Chad Bryant, 'The Language of Resistance? Czech Jokes and Joke-Telling under Nazi Occupation, 1943–45', *Journal of Contemporary History* 41(1) (2006), 133–51.
170. *Die Tagebücher von Joseph Goebbels*. Part II: *Diktate 1941–1945*, vol. 7, 405: Entry, 30 May 1942.
171. Institute of Jewish Affairs, *Hitler's Ten-Year War*, 60.
172. Krejčová, Svobodová and Hyndráková, *Židé v Protektorátu*, doc. 2, 51.
173. See https://www.bundesarchiv.de/gedenkbuch/chronicles.html?page=1 (accessed 26 June 2016); Krejčová, Svobodová and Hyndráková, *Židé v Protektorátu*, 364–66.
174. See Krejčová, Svobodová and Hyndráková, *Židé v Protektorátu*, 364–66.
175. See ibid.

176. YV Jerusalem, O 7/61, fol. 101: Weekly report Jewish Religious Community of Prague, 30 May to 5 June 1942, 1; ibid., fol. 117: Weekly report Jewish Religious Community of Prague, 6–12 June 1942, 6; ibid., fol. 123: Weekly report Jewish Religious Community of Prague, 13–19 June 1942, 1.
177. YV Jerusalem, O 7/61, vol. 133: Weekly report Jewish Religious Community of Prague, 20–26 June 1942, 1.
178. *Jüdisches Nachrichtenblatt* (Berlin), 1942, no. 20, 15 May 1942, 1.
179. YV Jerusalem, O 7/40, fol. 1–2: Instruction sheet, Jewish Community of Prague, 1 June 1942. On 13 June, the Jewish Community representatives presented the local Gestapo with the results of the registration of all pets in the area under the administration of the Olomouc chief county commissioner; ibid., M 58/JM 11809, fol. 59: Memorandum, Jewish Religious Community of Olomouc on visit to Gestapo, 13 June 1942, 1.
180. According to Friedmann, 'Rechtsstellung', in Krejčová, Svobodová and Hyndráková, *Židé v Protektorátu*, 261.
181. YV Jerusalem, O 7/62, fol. 39: Weekly report Jewish Religious Community of Prague, 18–24 July 1942, 6.
182. Ibid.
183. Ibid., fol. 48: Weekly report Jewish Religious Community of Prague, 25–31 July 1942, 5.
184. Ibid., fol. 59–60: Weekly report Jewish Religious Community of Prague, 1–7 August 1942, 6–7.
185. Ibid., fol. 71: Weekly report Jewish Religious Community of Prague, 8–14 August 1942, 7.
186. YV Jerusalem, O 7/40, fol. 3–5: Several signed forms, 22 August 1942.
187. USC SF/VHA, video interview, Katherine Kral, tape 3, min. 14:27–15:20.
188. *Jüdisches Nachrichtenblatt* (Berlin), 9 June 1942.
189. YV Jerusalem, O 7/61, fol. 167: Monthly report Jewish Religious Community of Prague, 1–30 June 1942, 8.
190. *Jüdisches Nachrichtenblatt* (Berlin), 19 June 1942.
191. BA Berlin, R 8150/7, fol. 138: Reich Association circular, 26 June 1942.
192. Lexa, 'Anti-Jewish Laws', 87; see also Friedmann, 'Rechtsstellung', in Krejčová, Svobodová and Hyndráková, *Židé v Protektorátu*, 262; YV Jerusalem, O 7/62, fol. 39: Weekly report Jewish Religious Community of Prague, 18–24 July 1942, 6.
193. Lexa, 'Anti-Jewish Laws', 87.
194. *Manchester Guardian*, 17 September 1942, 4. On the forced labour camps in Upper Silesia, see Gruner, *Jewish Forced Labor*, 214–29.
195. YV Jerusalem, O 7/62, fol. 6–7: Weekly report Jewish Religious Community of Prague, 27 June to 3 July 1942, 5–6.
196. Ibid., fol. 28: Weekly report Jewish Religious Community of Prague, 11–17 July 1942, 5.
197. Ibid., fol. 70: Weekly report Jewish Religious Community of Prague, 8–14 August 1942, 6.
198. See https://www.bundesarchiv.de/gedenkbuch/chronicles.html?page=1 (accessed 26 June 2016); Krejčová, Svobodová and Hyndráková, *Židé v Protektorátu*, 364–66.
199. See various letters from 1942–44, in VHA Prague, fonds 140, carton 59, no. 101, fol. 1–92. On the parcel campaign, see Jan Láníček, 'Arnost Frischer und seine Hilfe für Juden im besetzten Europa (1941–1945)', in *Theresienstädter Studien und Dokumente* 2007, 11–91, here 37–47.
200. YV Jerusalem, O 7/62, fol. 312–14: Monthly report Jewish Religious Community of Prague, 1–31 July 1942, 3–5.

201. A total of 462 people received shoes, clothing or furnishings, while food parcels were distributed to 240 children: YV Jerusalem, O 7/62, fol. 322: Monthly report Jewish Religious Community of Prague, 1–31 August 1942, 4.
202. Ibid., fol. 333: Monthly report Jewish Religious Community of Prague, 1–30 September 1942, 4.
203. Ibid., fol. 312–14: Monthly report Jewish Religious Community of Prague, 1–31 July 1942, 3–5.
204. Ibid., fol. 15: Weekly report Jewish Religious Community of Prague, 4–10 July 1942, 3; ibid., fol. 27: Weekly report Jewish Religious Community of Prague, 11–17 July 1942, 4; ibid., fol. 36: Weekly report Jewish Religious Community of Prague, 18–24 July 1942, 3.
205. Ibid., fol. 101: Weekly report Jewish Religious Community of Prague, 29 August to 4 September 1942, 4; ibid., fol. 134: Weekly report Jewish Religious Community of Prague, 15–24 September 1942, 4; ibid., fol. 345: Monthly report Jewish Religious Community of Prague, 1–31 October 1942, 5.
206. Ibid., fol. 17: Weekly report Jewish Religious Community of Prague, 4–10 July 1942, 5.
207. Machala, '"Unbearable Jewish Houses of Prayer"', 73–85.
208. YV Jerusalem, O 7/62, fol. 337: Monthly report Jewish Religious Community of Prague, 1–30 September 1942, 8.
209. Ibid., fol. 47: Weekly report Jewish Religious Community of Prague, 25–31 July 1942, 4; ibid., fol. 79: Weekly report Jewish Religious Community of Prague, 15–21 August 1942, 4; ibid., fol. 102: Weekly report Jewish Religious Community of Prague, 29 August to 4 September 1942, 5; ibid., fol. 112: Weekly report Jewish Religious Community of Prague, 5–11 September 1942, 4.
210. Anderl and Rupnow, *Die Zentralstelle für jüdische Auswanderung*, 282–83. Following the renaming of the Prague Central Office as the 'Central Bureau for the Regulation of the Jewish Question in Bohemia and Moravia', the Department of the Commander of the Security Police in the Office of the Reich Protector (Abteilung des Befehlshabers der Sicherheitspolizei beim Reichsprotektor) was divided into departments I–V: the Central Bureau for the Regulation of the Jewish Question in Bohemia and Moravia, the Theresienstadt Office (Dienststelle Theresienstadt), the Emigration Fund for Bohemia and Moravia (Auswandererfonds für Böhmen und Mähren), the SD Headquarters Prague (SD-Leitabschnitt Prag) and the Commander of the Security Police (Kommandeur der Sicherheitspolizei) in Prague and in Brno; BA Berlin, R 70/14, n.p.: Chart Structure BdS Prague (n.d.).
211. YV Jerusalem, O 7/62, fol. 329: Monthly report Jewish Religious Community of Prague, 1–31 August 1942, 11; ibid., fol. 115: Weekly report Jewish Religious Community of Prague, 5–11 September 1942, 7; ibid., fol. 137: Weekly report Jewish Religious Community of Prague, 15–24 September 1942, 7.
212. YV Jerusalem, O 7/61, fol. 124: Weekly report Jewish Religious Community of Prague, 13–19 June 1942, 2; Krejčová, Svobodová and Hyndráková, *Židé v Protektorátu*, doc. 2, 51. Four weeks later, as the Jewish Labour Headquarters reported to the Central Office, just 8,365 people were subject to labour deployment (though the District of Olomouc had submitted no figures due to the ongoing transports); YV Jerusalem, O 7/62, fol. 25: Weekly report Jewish Religious Community of Prague, 11–17 July 1942, 2.
213. Seventy-four groups consisting of a total of 884 individuals were engaged in agriculture and forty-two groups made up of 575 workers in forestry, while 123 Jews were employed on an individual basis and 302 lived in the SS camp of Linden;

YV Jerusalem, O 7/62, fol. 13–15: Weekly report Jewish Religious Community of Prague, 4–10 July 1942, 1–3.
214. On Germany, see Gruner, *Der Geschlossene Arbeitseinsatz*, 273–86.
215. Jewish women, for example, were to be deprived of maternity benefit; USHMM, RG 48.005M, reel 4 (Prague State Archive), I 3b-5813 Treatment of Jews under Labour Law, no. 8–9, n.p.: Circular Reich Protector II 4 to Groups within the Office, BdS and to the Party Liaison Office in the Office of the Reich Protector II 4, 8 May 1942, 1–3.
216. Ibid.: Reich protector I 3 b to Group II 4, 21 May 1942.
217. Official Gazette (Amtsblatt) no. 159, 9 July 1942; in Friedmann, 'Rechtsstellung', in Krejčová, Svobodová and Hyndráková, *Židé v Protektorátu*, 255.
218. USHMM, RG 48.005M, reel 4 (Prague State Archive), I 3b-5813 Treatment of Jews under Labour Law, no. 8–9, n.p.: Reich protector II 4 b to Group I 3 b, 16 October 1942. See Compendium of Laws and Decrees, 28 July 1942, no. 122, in Friedmann, 'Rechtsstellung', in Krejčová, Svobodová and Hyndráková, *Židé v Protektorátu*, 255–56.
219. Institute of Jewish Affairs, *Hitler's Ten-Year War*, 58. See Implementing decree concerning the decree on the employment conditions of Jews, RGBl. 1941 I, 681.
220. YV Jerusalem, O 7/62, fol. 49: Weekly report Jewish Religious Community of Prague, 25–31 July 1942, 6. Cf. Decree on the employment conditions of Jews, RGBl. 1941 I, 675.
221. YV Jerusalem, O 7/62, fol. 24: Weekly report Jewish Religious Community of Prague, 11–17 July 1942, 1.
222. Ibid., fol. 44: Weekly report Jewish Religious Community of Prague, 25–31 July 1942, 1.
223. Ibid., fol. 320: Monthly report Jewish Religious Community of Prague, 1–31 August 1942, 2.
224. JTA, 'Jewish Men and Women Sent to Forced Labor in Coal Mines in Czech Protectorate', 9 August 1942. Cf. with the incorrect figure of twelve thousand, The Jewish Black Book Committee, *The Black Book*, 178.
225. Including deployment on an individual basis, this made 1,212 Jews, 376 of them women; YV Jerusalem, O 7/62, fol. 55: Weekly report Jewish Religious Community of Prague, 1–7 August 1942, 2.
226. Ibid., fol. 57: Weekly report Jewish Religious Community of Prague, 1–7 August 1942, 4; ibid., fol. 102: Weekly report Jewish Religious Community of Prague, 29 August to 4 September 1942, 5. See Magda Veselská, 'Der Mann, der niemals aufgab: Die Geschichte des Josef Polák, Hauptkurator des Jüdischen Zentralmuseums in Prag zur Zeit des Zweiten Weltkrieges', in *Theresienstädter Studien und Dokumente* 2006, 14–61, here 56–59.
227. YV Jerusalem, O 7/62,, fol. 87: Weekly report Jewish Religious Community of Prague, 22–28 August 1942, 2.
228. Sixty-two groups consisting of 758 workers were engaged in agriculture, thirty-four work details made up of 459 workers in forestry, a total of 1,217 forced labourers, 799 men and 418 women; ibid., fol. 320–21: Monthly report Jewish Religious Community of Prague, 1–31 August 1942, 2–3.
229. Ibid., fol. 100: Weekly report Jewish Religious Community of Prague, 29 August to 4 September 1942, 3.
230. In Prague there were still sixty-seven forced labour details consisting of 596 Jews, ninety-three of them women. In the provinces there were ninety-three work details made up of 2,368 Jews, 205 of them women. Sixty-one forced labour groups

consisting of 718 Jews were engaged in agriculture, while twenty-six groups encompassing a total of 374 individuals still worked in forestry; ibid., fol. 132–33: Weekly report Jewish Religious Community of Prague, 15–24 September 1942, 2–3; cf. ibid., fol. 332: Monthly report Jewish Religious Community of Prague, 1–30 September 1942, 3.

231. Ibid., fol. 156: Weekly report Jewish Religious Community of Prague, 3–9 October 1942, 2.
232. Ibid., fol. 191–92: Weekly report Jewish Religious Community of Prague, 24–30 October 1942, 2–3; ibid., fol. 344: Monthly report Jewish Religious Community of Prague, 1–31 October 1942, 4.
233. In Prague, sixty-seven work details still existed consisting of a total of 598 forced labourers, sixty-eight of them women, while in the provincial towns there were still ninety-two groups made up of 2,146 forced labourers, 197 of them women; agriculture and forestry engaged 1,362 forced labourers, of whom 418 were women (sixty-one groups in agriculture encompassing 712 workers in total and twenty-six forestry groups made up of 370 workers); ibid., fol. 191–92: Weekly report Jewish Religious Community of Prague, 24–30 October 1942, 2–3; ibid., fol. 344: Monthly report Jewish Religious Community of Prague, 1–31 October 1942, 4.
234. Ibid., fol. 204: Weekly report Jewish Religious Community of Prague, 31 October to 6 November 1942, 3.
235. Lexa, 'Anti-Jewish Laws', 79.
236. Ibid.
237. Sbírka zákonů a nařízení Protektorátu Čechy a Morava 133/42, in Lexa, 'Anti-Jewish Laws', 85.
238. JTA, 'Sale of Fruits and Vegetables Prohibited to Jews in Czech Protectorate', 26 August 1942.
239. YV Jerusalem, O 7/62, fol. 329: Monthly report Jewish Religious Community of Prague, 1–31 August 1942, 11.
240. Ibid., fol. 331: Monthly report Jewish Religious Community of Prague, 1–30 September 1942, 2.
241. Ibid., fol. 335: Monthly report Jewish Religious Community of Prague, 1–30 September 1942, 6; ibid., fol. 346: Monthly report Jewish Religious Community of Prague, 1–31 October 1942, 6.
242. Lexa, 'Anti-Jewish Laws', 78.
243. YV Jerusalem, O 7/62, fol. 282: Weekly report Jewish Religious Community of Prague, 12–18 December 1942, 8.
244. JTA, 'Jewish Men and Women Sent to Forced Labor in Coal Mines in Czech Protectorate', 9 August 1942.
245. BA Berlin, R 70/10, n.p.: Note Gestapo II B 2, undated draft (likely July) 1942 and draft of letter to Central Office, 25 July [1942].
246. Ibid.: Draft letter Gestapo II B 2 to mayor of Moravian Ostrava, sent 14 August 1942.
247. Ibid.: District head in Friedberg to head of Gestapo Moravian Ostrava, 5 August 1942.
248. Ibid.: State Police Headquarters Brno, Field Office Moravian Ostrava to district head in Friedberg, 18 August 1942.
249. Ibid.: Telex State Police Headquarters Brno, Field Office Moravian Ostrava to State Police Headquarters Brno, 31 August 1942; cf. ibid.: Telex State Police Headquarters Brno, Field Office Moravian Ostrava to State Police Headquarters Brno, 2 September 1942.

250. Ibid.: Note, Gestapo Moravian Ostrava, 2 September 1942; ibid.: Telex State Police Headquarters Brno, Field Office Moravian Ostrava to State Police Headquarters Brno, 2 September 1942.
251. Ibid.: Telex State Police Headquarters Brno to State Police Headquarters Brno, Field Office Moravian Ostrava, 19 September 1942.
252. Ibid.: Telex State Police Headquarters Brno to State Police Headquarters Brno, Field Office Moravian Ostrava, 18 September 1942.
253. Ibid.: Telex State Police Headquarters Brno, Field Office Moravian Ostrava, to State Police Headquarters Brno, 22 September 1942.
254. See https://www.bundesarchiv.de/gedenkbuch/chronicles.html?page=1 (accessed 26 June 2016); Krejčová, Svobodová and Hyndráková, *Židé v Protektorátu*, 364–66.
255. YV Jerusalem, O 7/62, fol. 155–61: Weekly report Jewish Religious Community of Prague, 3–9 October 1942, 1–7.
256. Quoted in Adler, *Der verwaltete Mensch*, 535; Anderl and Rupnow, *Die Zentralstelle für jüdische Auswanderung*, 335–36.
257. Sedláková, '"Burza" s židovskými byty', 208–12.
258. Brandes and Míšková, *Vom Osteuropa-Lehrstuhl ins Prager Rathaus*, 284.
259. BA Berlin, R 70/10, n.p.: Note, Gestapo Moravian Ostrava, 2 September 1942; ibid.: Telex State Police Headquarters Brno, Field Office Moravian Ostrava to State Police Headquarters Brno, 2 September 1942.
260. Rothkirchen, *Jews*, 129; Sedláková, '"Burza" s židovskými byty', 208; Adler, *Der verwaltete Mensch*, 536–38.
261. USC SF/VHA, video interview, Zuzana Podmelova, tape 1, seg. 10.
262. Entry of 23 December 1941, in Ginz, *The Diary of Petr Ginz*, 55.
263. YV Jerusalem, M 58/JM 11808, fol. 34: Note, Jewish Religious Community of Olomouc for Gestapo Olomouc, 26 February 1942.
264. Potthast, *Das jüdische Zentralmuseum*, 213.
265. In 1943, wagons from Prague loaded with furniture arrived in the Ruhr area, while others took second-hand linen to Cologne; Götz Aly, *Hitlers Volksstaat: Raub, Rassenkrieg und nationaler Sozialismus* (Frankfurt a. M., 2005), 150.
266. Rothkirchen, *Jews*, 129.
267. YV Jerusalem, O 7/60, fol. 15: Weekly report Jewish Religious Community of Prague, 3–9 January 1942, 5.
268. YV Jerusalem, O 7/61, fol. 8: Weekly report Jewish Religious Community of Prague, 28 March to 3 April 1942, 7; ibid., fol. 20: Weekly report Jewish Religious Community of Prague, 3–10 April 1942, 7; ibid., fol. 29: Weekly report Jewish Religious Community of Prague, 11–17 April 1942, 7; ibid., fol. 57: Weekly report Jewish Religious Community of Prague, 25 April to 1 May 1942, 6.
269. Veselská, 'Der Mann, der niemals aufgab', 46–59; Rothkirchen, *Jews*, 213–15; Kulka, 'History and Historical Consciousness', 85. On the museum, see Potthast, *Das jüdische Zentralmuseum*.
270. According to Rainer Weinert, *'Die Sauberkeit der Verwaltung im Kriege': Der Rechnungshof des Deutschen Reiches 1938–1946* (Opladen, 1993), 127–28, quoted in Anderl and Rupnow, *Die Zentralstelle für jüdische Auswanderung*, 248.
271. YV Jerusalem, O 7/60, fol. 6: Weekly report Jewish Religious Community of Prague, 27 December 1941 to 2 January 1942, 5.
272. YV Jerusalem, M 58/JM 11812, fol. 447: Minutes, 21 January 1942.
273. YV Jerusalem, O 7/60, fol. 157: Monthly report Jewish Religious Community of Prague, 1–30 January 1942, 10.
274. Gerald D. Feldman, *Die Allianz und die deutsche Versicherungswirtschaft 1933–1945* (Munich, 2001), 421.

275. Anderl and Rupnow, *Die Zentralstelle für jüdische Auswanderung*, 282–83.
276. On this camp, see Gruner, *Zwangsarbeit und Verfolgung*, 177–80.
277. Anderl and Rupnow, *Die Zentralstelle für jüdische Auswanderung*, 321–22.
278. YV Jerusalem, O 7/62, fol. 182: Weekly report Jewish Religious Community of Prague, 17–23 October 1942, 4; ibid., fol. 365: Monthly report Jewish Religious Community of Prague, 1–31 December 1942, 4.
279. Ibid., fol. 344: Monthly report Jewish Religious Community of Prague, 1–31 October 1942, 4; ibid., fol. 354: Monthly report Jewish Religious Community of Prague, 1–30 November 1942, 4; ibid., fol. 365: Monthly report Jewish Religious Community of Prague, 1–31 December 1942, 4.
280. Ibid., fol. 195–96: Weekly report Jewish Religious Community of Prague, 24–30 October 1942, 6–7.
281. Ibid., fol. 348: Monthly report Jewish Religious Community of Prague, 1–31 October 1942, 8; ibid., fol. 358: Monthly report Jewish Religious Community of Prague, 1–30 November 1942, 8; cf. ibid., fol. 232: Weekly report Jewish Religious Community of Prague, 14–20 November 1942, 6.
282. Ibid., fol. 256: Weekly report Jewish Religious Community of Prague, 28 November to 4 December 1942, 6; ibid., fol. 369: Monthly report Jewish Religious Community of Prague, 1–31 December 1942, 8.
283. Report Council of Elders, 1 April 1943, in Krejčová, Svobodová and Hyndráková, *Židé v Protektorátu*, doc. 20, 380.
284. Kárný, 'Zur Statistik der jüdischen Bevölkerung', 11.
285. YV Jerusalem, O 7/62, fol. 219: Weekly report Jewish Religious Community of Prague, 7–13 November 1942, 5.
286. YV Jerusalem, M 58/JM 11808, fol. 513: Note, Jewish Religious Community of Olomouc, 4 November 1942.
287. YV Jerusalem, O 7/62, fol. 219: Weekly report Jewish Religious Community of Prague, 7–13 November 1942, 5; ibid., fol. 255: Weekly report Jewish Religious Community of Prague, 28 November to 4 December 1942, 5; ibid., fol. 302: Weekly report Jewish Religious Community of Prague, 26 December 1942 to 1 January 1943, 4. Cf. Veselská, 'Der Mann, der niemals aufgab', 56–59.
288. YV Jerusalem, O 7/62, fol. 196: Weekly report Jewish Religious Community of Prague, 24–30 October 1942, 7.
289. Ibid., fol. 143: Weekly report Jewish Religious Community of Prague, 25 September to 2 October 1942, 1; ibid., fol. 155: Weekly report Jewish Religious Community of Prague, 3–9 October 1942, 1; ibid., fol. 179: Weekly report Jewish Religious Community of Prague, 17–23 October 1942, 1; ibid., fol. 190: Weekly report Jewish Religious Community of Prague, 24–30 October 1942, 1.
290. Ibid., fol. 215: Weekly report Jewish Religious Community of Prague, 7–13 November 1942, 1.
291. Ibid., fol. 239: Weekly report Jewish Religious Community of Prague, 21–27 November 1942, 1; ibid., fol. 251: Weekly report Jewish Religious Community of Prague, 28 November to 4 December 1942, 1; ibid., fol. 288: Weekly report Jewish Religious Community of Prague, 18–25 December 1942, 1.
292. See https://www.bundesarchiv.de/gedenkbuch/chronicles.html?page=1 (accessed 26 June 2016); Krejčová, Svobodová and Hyndráková, *Židé v Protektorátu*, 364–66.
293. YV Jerusalem, O 7/62, fol. 222: Weekly report Jewish Religious Community of Prague, 7–13 November 1942, 8.
294. Ibid., fol. 358: Monthly report Jewish Religious Community of Prague, 1–30 November 1942, 8.

295. See https://www.bundesarchiv.de/gedenkbuch/chronicles.html?page=1 (accessed 26 June 2016); Krejčová, Svobodová and Hyndráková, *Židé v Protektorátu*, 364–66.
296. Rothkirchen, *Jews*, 239–44.
297. This decree had already been discussed in the summer; Note from the Foreign Office, 17 August 1942, in Mund, *Deutschland und das Protektorat*, doc. 429, 603.
298. 11th Decree on the Reich Citizenship Law of 25 November 1941, RGBl. 1941 I, 722.
299. YV Jerusalem, M 58/JM 11808, fol. 86: Jewish Religious Community of Prague to Jewish Religious Community of Olomouc, 15 January 1942.
300. Determining the forfeiture of property would be the responsibility of the BdS, while the Finance Office (Vermögensamt) in the Office of the Reich Protector would be responsible for administering the property itself; RGBl. 1942 I, 637.
301. Law on the Seizure of Communist Assets (Gesetz über die Einziehung kommunistischen Vermögens), 26 May 1933 and Law on the Seizure of the Assets of Enemies of the People and State (Gesetz über die Einziehung volks- und staatsfeindlichen Vermögens), 14 July 1933; RGBl. 1933 I, 293 and 479. Cf. Gruner and Osterloh, *The Greater German Reich and the Jews*, 364–65.
302. YV Jerusalem, O 7/62, fol. 215: Weekly report Jewish Religious Community of Prague, 7–13 November 1942, 1.
303. In Prague, sixty-six work details still existed, made up of 617 Jews, 57 of them women, while in the provincial localities there were still ninety-three groups consisting of 2,161 Jews, including 185 women. Fifty-six groups consisting of 606 workers were engaged in agriculture, twenty-eight groups with a total of 381 members worked in forestry (987 individuals, 348 of them women) and 279 Jews lived and worked at the SS estate of Linden; YV Jerusalem, O 7/62, fol. 353: Monthly report Jewish Religious Community of Prague, 1–30 November 1942, 3. Towards the end of December, there were sixty-six work details in Prague made up of 588 individuals, including 61 women, while in the provinces there were just eighty-one groups consisting of 1,709 workers, 154 of them women; 752 Jews, 264 of them women, still worked in agriculture and forestry and 268 continued to toil at the Linden estate; ibid., fol. 289–90: Weekly report Jewish Religious Community of Prague, 19–25 December 1942, 2–3.
304. YV Jerusalem, M 58/JM 11808, fol. 504: Note, Jewish Religious Community of Olomouc, 12 December 1942.
305. Kárný, 'Zur Statistik der jüdischen Bevölkerung', 11.
306. YV Jerusalem, M 58/JM 11808, fol. 510: Note, Jewish Religious Community of Olomouc, 21 December 1942.
307. For a comparative look at Germany, the Protectorate and the General Government, see Gruner, *Jewish Forced Labor*.
308. On the similar situation in Germany, see Meyer, *A Fatal Balancing Act*.
309. LBI/A New York, Microfilms: Wiener Library London, 500 series, no. 526: The Final Solution to Europe's Jewish Problem (Die Endlösung der Europäischen Judenfrage). Statistical report, as at 1 April 1943, 5. Cf. The Jewish Black Book Committee, *The Black Book*, 178.

CHAPTER 10

THOSE LEFT BEHIND AND THE END OF THE WAR

The Last Jews in Prague and Theresienstadt

In January and February 1943, small-scale special transports, generally with one hundred people on board, reached the Bohemian ghetto every few days from Vienna, Berlin and other cities. The last large-scale transports from the Protectorate also arrived: three trains from Uherský Brod carrying 2,837 individuals and two from Mladá Boleslav with a total of 1,041 on board (see Table A.5 in the appendix). During the same period, five large transports left the ghetto bound for Auschwitz, two of them carrying two thousand people each and three with one thousand people each on board.[1] Apart from six hundred men and three hundred women, all those deported to Auschwitz were gassed after the completion of a selection process.[2]

As in Vienna, in Prague the impending end of the deportations also meant the end of the Jewish Religious Community of Prague as it had existed hitherto. The Commander of the Security Police renamed it the 'Council of Elders of the Jews' (Ältestenrat der Juden) on 28 January, while the last remaining representatives of the old Jewish Religious Community, Weidmann, Kahn and Friedmann, were sent to Theresienstadt. Salo Krämer, who had headed the Property Utilization Office, was now appointed chairman of the Council of Elders, with

Herbert Langer as his deputy. The functionaries in the branch offices and the final representatives or *Vertrauensmänner* continued their work as before.³

Against the background of the mass transports, Prague Radio warned the Czechs against providing Jews with help of any kind. And there was no mistaking the message addressed to other European countries, namely that those of them still supporting the Jews, and thus the enemy, would meet with the same fate that had befallen – and continued to befall – the Jews themselves.⁴

In February, the *Manchester Guardian* learned from sources in Geneva that the German authorities were putting plans in place to complete the deportations from the Protectorate by 31 March in a push to make the territory 'Jew-free', with a similar plan in the pipeline for Berlin.⁵ While in the Reich dozens of small-scale transports left for Theresienstadt from a variety of cities up until June, the last major transport from Prague, carrying 1,021 individuals, left for the Bohemian ghetto on 6 March, with another three smaller transports making the trip by the end of the month (see Table A.5 in the appendix).⁶

Those remaining in Prague, like those incarcerated in Theresienstadt, urgently needed help from abroad.⁷ By this point, the ghetto Council of Elders' own capacity to actively help people was extremely limited. Nonetheless, two key tasks lay close to its members' hearts: getting help to the inmates by every means possible and preserving the legacy of the Bohemian and Moravian Jewry.⁸ Those Jews remaining behind in the former Jewish local Communities also did all they could to help former Community members. In the summer of 1943, for example, Jews in Lysá nad Labem still managed to send fifty Reichsmarks a month, exchanged for 532 crowns at the Town Treasurer's Office (Stadtkasse), to Georg and Bertha Arnstein, who had been deported to the Litzmannstadt Ghetto with the third transport from Prague in 1941.⁹

While small and medium-sized transports, chiefly from Germany, continued to arrive at the Theresienstadt Ghetto, the Gestapo also sent transports from the latter to Poland. In the early summer of 1943, many inmates of the Theresienstadt Ghetto died as a result of the dreadful conditions, particularly older individuals. Jakob Edelstein of the Council of Elders was arrested and deported in November 1943 for trying to cover up the flight of fifty-five prisoners.¹⁰

The final deportation train is said to have left Prague, carrying officials from the old Jewish Religious Community and their families, in June 1943;¹¹ among those deported to Theresienstadt was Salo Krämer, chairman of the Prague Council of Elders.¹² The 13th Decree on the Reich Citizenship Law came into force in the Greater German Reich on 1 July, stripping Jews of all their remaining rights and making their punishable acts subject to police law. Their estate was now automatically forfeited to the Reich upon their death. The decree made all Jews of German origin in the Protectorate subject to police law, while the forfeiture of assets applied to all Jews.[13]

It was at this very moment, no less than five years after the annexation of Austria and four years after the occupation of Bohemia and Moravia but right after the official end of the mass deportations from Germany and Austria and the total isolation of the remaining Czech Jews in the ghetto, that Hitler demanded that he be referred to henceforth as the 'Führer of the Greater German Reich' in all diplomatic communications. His vision of a 'Greater German Reich' thus came to fruition only when virtually all Jews had been banished.[14]

As so often with the Nazis, however, this was wishful thinking: Jews still lived in the territory of the Reich and in the Protectorate. In June, the Prague Council of Elders thus gained new leaders: František Friedmann (1897–1945), a prominent Prague-based Zionist, and Erich Kraus. Both lived in 'mixed marriages' and were tasked with looking after the interests of the 8,695 Jews remaining outside the ghetto in the Protectorate, most of whom were protected by the same marital status, as well as so-called half-Jews and 1,081 'borderline cases' (Zweifelsfälle).[15]

Flight and Resistance

At the end of 1942, 260 'full Jews' and seventy-nine 'Mischlinge' who were considered to be Jews still lived in the District of Olomouc. Another forty-five Jews were in prison and eleven were 'missing', that is, had fled.[16] By the end of June 1943, the Olomouc Branch Office of the Prague Council of Elders counted 292 'full Jews' in the district, 240 of them in 'mixed marriages', along with ninety 'Geltungsjuden', that is, individuals deemed to be Jews; a further twenty-three Jews were now imprisoned, while thirteen were on the run.[17] These statistics reveal that as late as the end of 1942, one in five of the remaining Jews had carried out acts of open resistance, either by violating anti-Jewish regulations, resulting in their imprisonment, or through flight. The true number will have been higher as these figures only reflect those cases known to the Gestapo. By the summer of 1943, the figures decreased somewhat.

During this period, once again the Gestapo held Robert Redlich, head of the Olomouc Jewish Community, personally liable for ensuring that Jews did in fact wear the yellow star visibly on their clothing in public. He was also to warn the Jewish forced labourers working for the Reich Contract Administration (Reichsauftragsverwaltung) to conduct themselves in a 'quiet and inconspicuous' way.[18]

Flight and efforts to aid those fleeing were important elements of Jewish resistance in the Protectorate during this phase. For example, in March 1943 the Prague Special Court convicted a group for helping Jews flee. This eighteen-member group included five Jews who received the death penalty for evading deportation. With the support of the other members of this resistance group, they had helped other Jews flee and provided them with money before the Gestapo managed to smash the network in November 1942.[19] The same court imposed the death penalty on a similar group in July 1943, including four Jewish Czechs who had attempted to escape the deportations. Six non-Jewish Czechs, including Marianne Goltz, the group leader, who had helped them find work and shelter, were also convicted. All were beheaded in Pankrac Prison the day the trial ended. Further, in 1943 the occupying power imposed more than a dozen death sentences on Czechs in Prague alone for furnishing Jews with forged papers or providing them with shelter.[20]

In October 1943, the Gestapo arrested four Jews, namely Dr Otokar Weisel (b. 1912), Dr Jan Veleminsky (b. 1914), Dr Georg Veleminsky (b. 1912) and Zdenek Veleminsky (b. 1918), for involvement in the resistance movement.[21] In 1943 and 1944, Protectorate courts imposed further death sentences on Jews, above all those participating in the organized resistance against the Nazi occupation, such as Milan Weiss, who procured weapons for a group, and Jiři Kohn, who coordinated a number of illegal cells.[22]

The Protectorate within the Greater German Reich

The wartime situation and the seeming consolidation of the Greater German Reich had a direct impact on the administration of the Protectorate. In mid August 1943, Hitler released Daluege from his duties as deputy Reich protector and, finally, von Neurath following his prolonged leave of absence.[23] He appointed Reich Interior Minister Frick the new Reich protector and Karl Hermann Frank German Minister of State for Bohemia and Moravia (Deutscher Staatsminister für Böhmen und Mähren), a new office whose occupant enjoyed the same rank as a Reich minister. From 1939 until the end of the war, therefore, Frank, who had long focused his efforts on the Germanization of the Czech lands, personified the backbone of German Protectorate policy. Every

Reich ministry and authority, with the exception of the Wehrmacht, received its own office in his German State Ministry (Deutsches Staatsministerium),[24] thus gaining indirect representation and a voice in the Protectorate.[25]

The year 1943 also advanced the debate on long-planned appointments. For example, Rudolf Jung (1882–1945), president of the State Labour Office for Central Germany (Landesarbeitsamt Mitteldeutschland) in Erfurt, was eager to succeed Klapka – executed during the phase of violent persecution following Heydrich's arrival – as primator of Prague. Jung had long been the ideological leader of the Sudeten German Nazis in Czechoslovakia. Initially, however, for reasons of foreign policy, Hitler had put off appointing a German to this crucial post in the Protectorate capital; for the same reasons, at the end of 1943, State Minister Frank was still expressing opposition to the idea at a meeting in the Reich Chancellery, despite Jung's vigorous efforts to obtain the post he had been promised.[26]

Over the course of the same year, in communication with Martin Bormann and Lammers, Frank argued in favour of raising the salaries of officials in the Protectorate in particular and improving the social situation of the Czech population in general. Presenting this as a 'burning political problem', he demanded that the Reich Chancellery enable him to inform Hitler about the issue in person, as the Reich Finance Ministry was slowing things down with its audits. He threatened to act on his own should he fail to gain access to Hitler.[27] Frank's potential concessions, however, solely resulted from Germany's ever-worsening military predicament, particularly on the eastern front, and aimed at forestalling Czech resistance.

Forced Labour until the End of the War

Since the end of 1942, the major concentration camps of Flossenbürg, Auschwitz and Groß-Rosen had erected a total of thirty-eight sub-camps dedicated to the construction of armaments factories in the Protectorate and the Sudeten region (less at risk of aerial bombardment than Germany). At the end of the war, twenty thousand prisoners toiled there, including many Jews previously deported from the Greater German Reich.[28] While the armaments industry in the Protectorate had already employed 317,000 people in the spring of 1942, 105,000 of them in Prague alone, from 1943 at the latest it suffered a lack of labour.[29]

Most Jews in the Protectorate who were not incarcerated in the Theresienstadt Ghetto lived in 'mixed marriages'. Both the labour offices and the SS now recruited them to perform forced labour (see Figure 10.1). In March 1943, at the behest of the Central Office, the Council of Elders issued summons to all Jews in 'mixed marriages'[30] to report to the Gestapo in Prague, which now designated them 'full Jews' and subjected them to forced labour, as Berta Landré related. Forced labourers were used to clear out and renovate the homes of deported Jews. In the various large depots, meanwhile, men and women worked registering, sorting and repairing the furniture and other objects left behind.[31] It was only now, at the beginning of May 1943, that the Czech government introduced the 'Social Equalization Tax for Jews', which had existed in the Old Reich since late 1940 and transferred to the state 15 per cent of Jews' meagre wages as forced labourers.[32]

In 1943, 64.9 per cent of the Jews in the Protectorate outside the ghetto performed forced labour; in 1944 this increased to 83.4 per cent, requiring the Prague Council of Elders to expand the Jewish Labour Headquarters. The remaining 16.6 per cent of Jews were considered incapable of working. In the spring, the Central Bureau for the Regulation of the Jewish Question in Bohemia and Moravia evidently took over responsibility for forced labour from the civil labour offices, ordering the Jewish Labour Headquarters to assume total responsibility for the organizational aspects of forced labour. In May 1944, the latter received 9,300 information cards (Evidenzkarten) from the Prague Labour Office's Department for Non-Aryans. At the end of the year, the labour offices in the provinces also handed over their index cards and responsibilities. Controlled by the Central Bureau, the Jewish Labour Headquarters now took care of all formalities relating to labour law, monitored working conditions and amended forced labourers' employment records. The Central Bureau then ordered all Jewish women in Prague and the provinces to submit to an examination in preparation for segregated group work splitting mica.[33] In the first half of the year, meanwhile, several hundred Jewish men in 'mixed marriages' were sent to labour camps outside Prague.[34]

In July 1944, the Central Bureau for the Regulation of the Jewish Question in Bohemia and Moravia ordered the registration of Jewish 'grade 1 and 2 Mischlinge':[35] the Prague Council of Elders registered 3,500 male and 3,230 female 'grade 1 Mischlinge' along with the 'Aryan' relatives of Jews.[36] As in Germany, in parallel the labour offices in the Protectorate organized a special deployment for '*jüdisch versippte Arier* and Jewish Mischlinge', that is, non-Jewish spouses in 'mixed marriages' and children resulting from 'mixed marriages'.[37] One thousand individuals were soon constructing training grounds for SS troops at special camps in Tršovice, Uhlířské Janovice (Kohljanowitz) and

Figure 10.1. Jews marked with a star engaged in roadbuilding, 1943. © YV Jerusalem, Photo Archive, FA-156, fol. 13: Report on the Year 1943, Council of Elders of the Jews.

Bystřice. Evidently, after completing this work their number fell to two hundred by the end of September, with these Jews slaving away on the construction of a railway station.[38] Sixty Prague 'Mischlinge', who performed forced labour for the Červený Hrádek (Rothenhaus) Forestry Administration, were quartered in two local inns.[39]

At the behest of the Central Bureau, the Jewish Labour Headquarters then summoned all fit-for-work Jews to Prague, with the first contingent arriving on 17 September 1944.[40] For example, Jaroslav Lederer from the District of Olomouc received a telegram ordering him to Hagibor Square (Hagiborplatz) in the Protectorate capital. He was required to present himself there on 20 September with work clothes, ration cards, two sets of bedlinen as well as blankets, a bowl and cutlery.[41] Women in particular soon arrived from the Czech provinces at the hut camp erected on the former sports grounds of the Jewish 'Hagibor' association, where they later had to work twelve-hour days, together with Jewish women from Prague, splitting mica into wafer-thin sheets.[42]

The barrack camp for the forced labourers was built on what had been the Hagibor Association's football field and its two tennis courts. On 10 July 1944, assisted by the construction workers from the Council of Elders' Technical Department (Technische Abteilung), the erection of two barracks had begun. By September, five residential and two labour barracks had been put up, plus one more of each kind by the end of November (see Figures 10.2–10.4).[43] In total, the camp had 1,644 beds equipped with 1,700 straw sacks. Much of the equipment and furniture was provided by the Council of Elders from the holdings of the Trust Office, in other words from the property left behind by Jewish deportees.[44]

In total, at the end of 1944 1,304 individuals, 607 men and 697 women, lived at the Hagibor Square camp. The Jewish Labour Headquarters had exempted around three hundred people due to illness. In the grounds of the camp, 836 women, 484 of them from the provinces, and 46 men now performed the strenuous work of splitting mica.[45] More than one hundred Jewish women resident in Prague and living in 'mixed marriages', who were not resident in the camp, thus performed this work as well.[46]

As the authorities saw it, Jewish women from 'mixed marriages' were deployed at Hagibor Square to perform 'segregated manual work'.[47] In December 1944, meanwhile, well over one hundred Jewish men from Prague living in 'mixed marriages' were sent to work in camps in the Komotau area (Sudeten region). From then on, they lived in wooden barracks in Kalek.[48] At the same time, however, numerous forced labour camps in the provinces were dissolved, with the Jews who had been working there being transferred to Prague to build air-raid shelters. This reallocation served to enhance the authorities' control

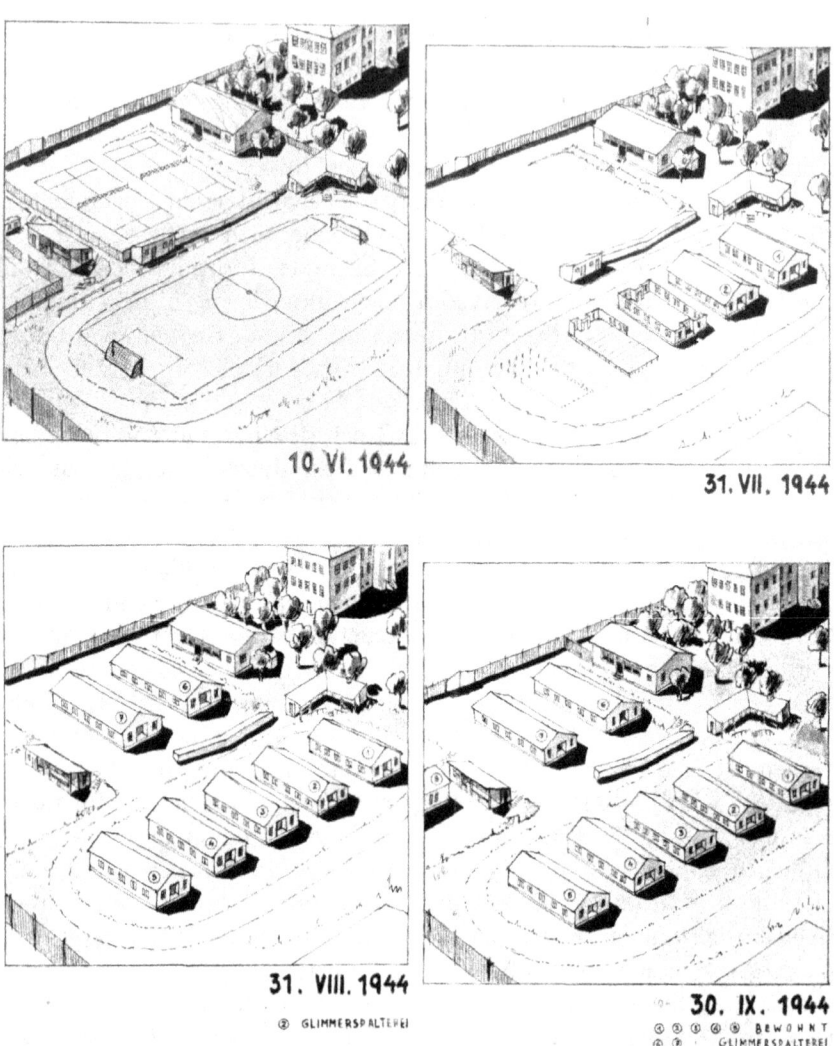

Figures 10.2 and 10.3. Phases in the construction of the labour camp at Hagibor Square, 1944. © YV Jerusalem, Photo Archive, FA-156, fol. 60A, aA.

over forced labour. Two camps still existed at this point in time, namely the SS estate of Linden, with just seventy-two inmates, and one in Oslavany (Oslawan) housing seventy-eight men.[49]

The Prague Council of Elders supervised a diverse range of forced labour groups encompassing more than one thousand individuals in total, who received a monthly salary of 884 crowns. To the benefit

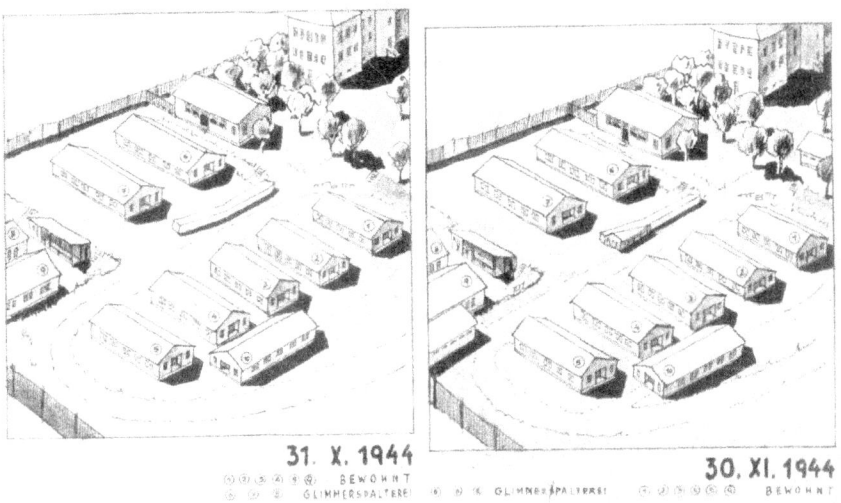

Figure 10.4. Phases in the construction of the labour camp at Hagibor Square, 1944. © YV Jerusalem, Photo Archive, FA-156, fol. 60bA.

of other forced labour projects, the number of staff working for the Council of Elders had been reduced to 1,210 individuals by the end of 1944 (compared with 1,923 individuals at the end of 1943), equating to about 60 per cent of women and roughly 29 per cent of men. Most of those dismissed, 202 women and 210 men, were placed in forced labour, while others were deported. A total of 121 members of staff of Jewish Communities in the provinces also had to be laid off and begin forced labour in Prague at Hagibor Square.[50] In early March 1945, forced labourer Albert Unterstab wrote to his family in Prague from Special Camp A (Sonderlager A) in Bystřice u Benešova (Bistritz bei Beneschau): 'Got card of 28 Feb. Nice. Cold. No doubt you have to make a lot of trips down to the cellar to fetch coal now. ... Parcel: only what you can spare. Got enough footwraps. Yours, Albert'.[51]

The Persecution of 'Mixed Marriages' until the End of the War

Until the end of the war, Jews remaining in the Protectorate outside the ghetto had to submit to periodic assessments to determine whether they were still in the exceptional categories that spared them deportation.

In other words, for Jews in 'mixed marriages' the key issue was whether their 'Aryan' partners still lived with them. The Gestapo put tremendous pressure on the latter to divorce their husbands or wives, but only a few of them did so. In this way, most of them saved their spouses' lives until the war was over.[52]

In Prague, the Central Bureau concentrated the remaining Jews in the so-called Allocation Area (Einweisungsgebiet) in 1944. Jewish tenants from Jewish flats on the left bank of the Vltava, from centrally heated flats and from those whose main tenants the Gestapo had deported, had to move, affecting 625 families made up of a total of 1,262 individuals. The Council of Elders' Housing Office (Wohnungsamt) once again registered all apartments in Prague with Jewish occupants by district as well as those in the provinces.[53]

In Olomouc, in June 1944 the Gestapo ordered the clearing of the homes of a number of couples in 'mixed marriages' and then forced two couples into one flat.[54] Evidently, the Gestapo had also instructed the remaining branch offices of the Council of Elders to move into smaller premises. In Olomouc this relocation ran into trouble in early February when the owner of the shop earmarked for the new office withdrew her agreement.[55]

By the end of 1943, 16,581 buildings and plots of land had been made over to the Emigration Fund.[56] One year later, the Fund had already swallowed up more than twenty thousand properties: 11,854 buildings previously owned by Jews, including 9,646 privately owned ones, 514 under the ownership of Jewish Religious Communities and 112 owned by Jewish organizations and associations, in addition to 8,737 plots of land.[57]

During this period, the Council of Elders' Welfare Department (Fürsorgeabteilung) did its best to deal with the multitude of problems thrown up by the intensification of forced labour (this alone required more than five thousand fit-for-work examinations), such as the growing deployment of so-called *jüdisch Versippte* (the husbands of Jewish wives), as well as deportations, illnesses and the transfer of parents to camps. Overall, the Council of Elders noted a 'steady worsening in the general state of health', at a time when the care of the sick had to be limited to the most urgent cases due to a lack of resources. Pulmonary diseases, particularly tuberculosis, increased from 230 cases in January 1944 to 660 in December. The middle-class kitchens provided for just under six thousand individuals at the start of 1944, but for thirteen thousand by the end of the year. This was a result of the intensification of forced labour, to which the Gestapo contributed with its own demands.[58] The Olomouc Gestapo, for instance, ordered the sick and unfit-for-work Siegfried Tauber to report for duty at 7 a.m. every morning for making careless remarks. Only after the intervention of Jewish representatives did the relevant Kriminalsekretär rescind Tauber's punishment.[59] The mortality rate among Jews in the Protectorate now stood at 44 per 1,000, compared to a rate of just 15 per 1,000 for the rest of the population.[60]

The Council of Elders had to send all stamps for parcels to Theresienstadt, process the mail to and from the ghetto and deliver durable goods there – more than seventy-four wagons' worth in 1944 alone.[61] While additional small-scale transports from various German cities continued to arrive in the Theresienstadt Ghetto, large-scale special transports left the ghetto bound for the Auschwitz death camp at regular intervals in 1943 and 1944: one large transport carrying 2,500 individuals in September 1943, one in October with 1,249 inmates on board and one carrying 2,500 people in December.[62] These deportations, however, were dealt with quite differently than the earlier ones. Rather than carrying out a 'selection' and dividing up families, the SS transported everyone to the so-called separate Family Camp (Familienlager) in Birkenau. Each group of these deportees was murdered only six months after their arrival.[63] Three large-scale transports, each carrying 2,500 individuals, left the ghetto in mid May 1944; late September saw the departure of one transport carrying 1,500 people and another with 2,500 individuals on board; while seven trains, each carrying 1,500 people, left in October, with another two, carrying 1,700 and 2,500 people respectively, departing towards the end of the same month.[64]

In parallel, the deportations of Jews to the ghetto from various locations in the Protectorate continued. These chiefly affected adolescents of fourteen years of age and above and widowers and divorcees formerly in 'mixed marriages'.[65] Fourteen collective transports (Sammeltransporte) deported 441 Jews, 143 on 9 January 1944 alone as a direct consequence of the decree issued by Gestapo Chief Müller, who had ordered the deportation of the previously protected spouses in 'mixed marriages' that no longer existed. Families consisting of couples in 'mixed marriages' with non-Jewish children were now deported from Prague as well.[66] By the end of the year, officially there were just 6,795 Jews still living in the Protectorate, while other sources suggest around eight thousand.[67]

As in the Reich, at the start of 1945 the Gestapo revoked the protected status for 'mixed marriages' in the Protectorate. Transports thus made their way to Theresienstadt on 31 January and 4 February 1945, while the authorities were already preparing for the next transport, of 913 individuals, slated for 11 February.[68] The corresponding summons for a supposed 'labour deployment in Theresienstadt' issued by the Council of Elders to Jewish men from 'mixed marriages' underlined that children considered Jews must be taken along as well, but claimed that since this was not ghettoization there was no need for these Jews to report their impending departure on the 11 February transport to the police. Nonetheless, those earmarked for deportation had to report with a minimum of luggage to a number of assembly points, including Hagibor Square, on threat of punishment.[69]

The day of departure saw dreadful scenes at the assembly points, where panic held sway. Children failed to recognize their fathers, some of whom had spent two years apart from their families performing forced labour outside the city. Some of those ordered to report for transport took their own lives. Just 2,803 Jews were allowed to remain in Prague. The Gestapo deported a total of 3,570 individuals to Theresienstadt in January and February 1945, including the members of the Prague Council of Elders.[70]

The Theresienstadt Ghetto, which was led, following Eppstein's murder in 1944, by Murmelstein and Leo Baeck, the Berlin Rabbi and former president of the Reich Association of Jews in Germany, was now home to Jews from the Netherlands, Denmark and Slovakia as well. While more than one thousand prisoners received permission to travel to Denmark and Switzerland at the last minute following negotiations with Himmler, ever more Jews arrived at the ghetto following 'evacuation marches' from other camps. All of this happened in light of the nearing front; this was to bring liberation, in May 1945, to a ghetto heralded by the Nazis as a 'showpiece camp' (Vorzeigelager).[71]

The End of the Protectorate and the Birth of the Third Republic

The Allied bombing of Prague began in February 1945. The Czech uprising, which occurred against the backdrop of the threatening approach of the Soviet and American armies, finally drove the German occupiers from the Czech capital in early May.[72] Fully aware of their reign of terror, before fleeing the staff of the German Protectorate Authority burned their classified files on the orders of German State Minister and SS-Obergruppenführer Frank.[73] Ignoring reality, after the war Wilhelm Dennler, senior official at the Protectorate Authority, laid all the blame for persecutory policies at the door of the Gestapo and the SD: they had made 'mistakes, perhaps even committed crimes'. The 'hands of all other Germans' had supposedly 'remained clean'; they had never 'laid a hand on even one of the seven million Czechs and have never defiled themselves with the blood of their Czech fellow citizens'.[74]

The Czechs saw things differently and put prominent figures in the German occupation authorities on trial when the war was over. It is no coincidence that as early as September 1945 one of the newly established people's courts, which dealt with the crimes committed during the occupation, put Josef Pfitzner, the German deputy to the mayor of Prague, on trial. He was sentenced to death and publicly hanged.[75] His policy of Germanization in the capital was notorious and his execution drew tens of thousands of spectators.[76] This early trial and its outcome is testimony to the significance ascribed by contemporaries to

Figure 10.5. The execution of Karl Hermann Frank in Prague, 22 May 1946. © YV Jerusalem, Photo Archive, no. 81GO6.

the persecutory policies pursued by the Prague city authorities, long overlooked by historians.

Not long afterwards, the man who had been the second most powerful figure in the Protectorate, Karl Hermann Frank, also stood trial, the Americans having handed him over to the Czech authorities in July 1945.[77] In keeping with his convictions as described above, Dennler appeared as a witness for the defence in the trial of his former boss.[78] On 22 May 1946, the Prague People's Court sentenced Frank to death by hanging as the leading representative of German policy in the Protectorate and as 'executioner of the Czech nation'. Frank, responsible for deportations and repressive measures as senior SS and police chief, remained a diehard Nazi; for him, the Theresienstadt Ghetto had been a resort for Jews. During the execution Frank is said to have called out: 'Long live the German people! Long live the German spirit!' (see Figure 10.5).[79]

The new beginning, however, also meant that the Czechs had to make a clean break with the past. The new government thus initiated one of the most rigorous programmes of 'national cleansing' in Europe in an effort to punish all those Czechs who had cooperated with the Germans.[80] Several members of the Czech Protectorate government were arrested. Moravec had already shot himself on 5 May 1945 in light of the uprising. Hácha died in the prison infirmary. While former Finance Minister Kalfus's guilt was an established fact, he was acquitted by the People's Court in the summer of 1946 since he had cooperated with the resistance movement. In contrast, former Interior Minister Bienert was sentenced to three years in prison, former Transport Minister Kamenický to ten years, former Justice Minister and later Head of Government Krejčí to twenty-five years and former Agriculture Minister Hrubý to life in prison, all for collaborating with the Nazi occupiers.[81] Particularly in the first few months after the war, rapidly established drumhead courts martial condemned many Germans and Czechs to death, while later the people's courts sentenced many to prison for cooperating with the occupation authorities or denouncing their fellow citizens.[82]

On 5 April 1945, in liberated Košice, Beneš had proclaimed a binational Czech-Slovak state that would enjoy freedom of religion and equal rights for all citizens and that would also be free of race-based discrimination.[83] Yet in Prague just a month later he announced the expulsion of Germans and Hungarians in order to achieve a united Czechoslovak state.[84] Violence and mass arrests were the order of the day. Some of the measures that the Nazis had imposed on the Jews were now applied to those Germans who had not fled. They were required to wear armbands and perform forced labour, were not allowed to use the pavement and received reduced rations. Some of the local 'national committees' that had now been established even decreed these measures for Czechs married to Germans.[85]

The tale of the 'imitation Crown of St Wenceslas', which did the rounds in November 1945, is symbolic of the actual and felt subjugation and plundering of Bohemia and Moravia by the Germans. The story was that the government in Prague had established that the Nazis had stolen the most precious historical regalia from St Vitus Cathedral. Heydrich, it was said, had had the Crown of St Wenceslas and the crown jewels taken to Germany and sold. Forgeries had been brought to Prague to replace them; following Heydrich's death, the proceeds of the sale had ended up in the pockets of his successor, Karl Hermann Frank.[86]

On the first anniversary of the founding of the republic in October 1945, Beneš, freshly re-elected as president at the first sitting of the provisional National Assembly, publicly declared that the German and Hungarian minorities would be 'expelled with all due consideration'. The republic would confiscate German property, regarding this as part of the 'reparations' it was owed.[87] Most Germans and Hungarians were then transferred to their 'home countries' and in this way the new state was ethnically homogenized. Czechs and Slovaks soon made up more than 94 per cent of the population.[88]

At the end of the war, just twenty-four thousand Jews had survived persecution, forced labour, deportation and murder in Bohemia and Moravia.[89] The International Red Cross had taken charge of the Theresienstadt Ghetto at the beginning of May.[90] Those who had survived Theresienstadt and now returned home, such as Hana Beer, looked for their relatives and friends. They needed food and accommodation. Completely destitute, they relied upon soup kitchens and charitable donations.[91]

As almost everywhere in Europe, quite soon some of the few survivors began to document the persecution and annihilation on the territory of the former Czechoslovakia 'in memoriam of the victims of the Nazi terror'. Some of the Zionists among them founded the so-called Documentation Campaign (Dokumentationsaktion) and sought to arouse the interest of Jewish institutions abroad, such as the Central Zionist Archives in Jerusalem and the World Jewish Congress.[92] They organized the transfer of original documents to Palestine and appealed for funds to support their documentation work, which focused on Theresienstadt, particularly for photographic work, until their office had to make way for a different organization, which also collected the testimony of survivors, in the spring of 1946.[93] In its detailed forms, which asked about persecution, ghettoization, the deportations and annihilation, the Jewish Agency only raised two questions relating to resistance, namely what preventative measures Jews had taken individually or collectively to oppose the anti-Jewish decrees and whether some Jews had attempted to escape from the ghetto.[94]

Czech actors suppressed the fate of the Jews in their own way. Before the war was over, some had even demanded that Jews be subjected to a strict process if they were to regain their citizenship. Communists in particular demanded that the 'Aryanized' property of industrial and financial magnates such as Petschek, Weinmann and Rothschild should not be restituted in order to end capitalist exploitation. Hence the Czechoslovak state no longer recognized a Jewish nationality. Jews had to declare their allegiance either to the Czech or Slovak nationality.[95]

The few returning German Jews who had survived the mass murder were often declared Germans: they received white armbands, were stripped of their citizenship and their property was confiscated. Like most Germans, they faced the prospect of expulsion. Only in response to international protest were they allowed to apply for repatriation. Those Jews interned in camps as Germans were released in late autumn 1945 following appeals by the Prague Jewish Community. Interventions by the newly constituted Council of the Jewish Religious Communities in Bohemia and Moravia allowed two thousand Jews classified as Germans to obtain Czech citizenship. In September 1946, a decree then spared German Jews from the transports on which hundreds of thousands of Sudeten Germans were deported to occupied Germany. These victims, however, received no special assistance.[96]

The property of persecuted and murdered Jews confiscated and expropriated by the Germans, whether furniture, books or religious objects, passed to the new state as a consequence of a general edict.[97] Portions of the deportees' property, such as clothing, shoes, crockery, tools and carpets, were still stored at three sites in Prague. These were either to be returned to the few returnees or sold to other survivors for a small fee, with the proceeds being distributed among the survivors.[98] The survivors and the Jewish representatives often struggled to reclaim formerly personal or Community property, though in several edicts issued in 1945 and 1946 the new state had criminalized the Nazi confiscation of property and expressed support for restitution.[99] Communists and extreme nationalists wanted to nationalize Jewish property, particularly businesses, and it was not until May 1946 that a restitution law regulating the return of property first saw the light.[100] In many cases, however, Jews did not get their property back. Of sixteen thousand claims, just three thousand had met with a positive response by the end of 1947.[101] In 1952, the republic finally rejected the claim lodged by surviving family members for restitution of the Prague villa – Aryanized in 1940 and rapidly made state property in 1945 – previously owned by Mr and Mrs Waigner, who were murdered during the war.[102]

Jewish returnees were traumatized, having often lost both their families and neighbourly support. They felt isolated in the new society.[103] Some of the anti-Semites said: 'It's a shame Hitler didn't kill you'.[104] Many Jews heard such comments.[105] Often returnees, such as Hana Beer and Mimi Berger, were unable to return to their flats, now occupied by non-Jewish Czechs, while in other cases, such as those of Anna Grant and Mimi Berger, Czechs failed to return the valuables left with them for safekeeping. Moreover, Jews received very little help from the authorities.[106] Up until autumn 1947, a growing number of attacks occurred on Jewish cemeteries. Anti-Jewish riots occurred in thirty-one towns or cities.[107]

Understandably, just a third of émigré Jews wished to return to their old homeland, while at the same time many of the survivors from the camps quickly left the country.[108] In the next two years, almost nineteen thousand people emigrated to Palestine: Beneš supported the development of a Jewish state, which his successor President Klement Gottwald already recognized in 1948. The initially close relations between the two countries rapidly cooled when the communists failed to live up to expectations in the Israeli elections.[109]

* * *

By the spring of 1943, the Gestapo had completed the deportations from the districts of the Protectorate to Theresienstadt. From there, transports departed for the death camps in the East. Potential victims attempted to flee or to resist in other ways. Soon, only Jewish representatives, the so-called *Vertrauensleute*, were left in the provinces, though in a few locations branch offices of the Prague Jewish Community, renamed the Council of Elders, still existed.

In the summer of 1943, following the completion of the mass transports from the Greater German Reich, Reich Interior Minister Frick was made Reich protector, while Karl Hermann Frank, the linchpin of the German Protectorate administration since 1939 as state secretary, was appointed German minister of state. The Prague Central Office received the new name 'Central Bureau for the Regulation of the Jewish Question'.

The latter took over responsibility for the forced labour of Jews in the Protectorate from the Labour Administration in 1944, while the Czech government ministry continued to lay the legal foundation for anti-Jewish labour policy, as with the introduction of the Social Equalization Tax in 1943. The Central Bureau tasked the Jewish Labour Headquarters with organizing the forced labour of the last remaining Jews, most of whom were in 'mixed marriages'. While all able-bodied Jews had to move to Prague in the autumn of 1944, henceforth the women lived in the newly established camp on Hagibor Square, performing the arduous work of mica splitting. Many of the men, however, slaved away in labour camps outside the city. Forced labour – mostly in labour camps dedicated to the construction of SS training grounds – now also encompassed the 'Mischlinge and those married to Jews' newly registered in the summer of 1944. In a parallel process, couples in 'mixed marriages' were concentrated in flats in a single district of Prague. In January and February 1945, the deportations of Jewish spouses in 'mixed marriages' to Theresienstadt began everywhere in the Greater German Reich, leaving just a few Jews in the Protectorate outside the ghetto.

When the war was over, Czech people's courts convicted Frank and Pfitzner for the crimes they had committed during the occupation. The pair represented the two poles of German responsibility for the persecution of Jews, namely the Office of the Reich Protector (together with the Security Police) and the German mayors. But the Czech ministers were held responsible for their actions too.

The new Czechoslovak state implemented a strict policy of ethnic homogenization, while many perpetrators continued to live in the society. The surviving Jews, who quickly took steps to document the persecution, were initially discriminated against as Germans and often failed to regain their property even when recognized as Czechs. Many of them thus left their homeland, earlier regarded as the European country least inclined towards antisemitism.

Notes

1. See https://www.bundesarchiv.de/gedenkbuch/chronicles.html?page=1 (accessed 26 June 2016); Krejčová, Svobodová and Hyndráková, *Židé v Protektorátu*, 364–66.
2. VHA Prague, fonds 140, carton 23, no. 97, fol. 71: 'Factual report by a returnee Jew deported from Slovakia', March 1944, 21.
3. Rothkirchen, *Jews*, 130; YV Jerusalem, M 58/JM 11809, fol. 317: Note Olomouc, 15 February 1943. On Vienna, see Gruner, *Zwangsarbeit und Verfolgung*, 264–71.
4. JTA, 'Nazi Radio Warns Non-Jews in Occupied Europe to Refrain from Helping Jews', 5 January 1943.
5. *Manchester Guardian*, 13 February 1943, 6.

6. See https://www.bundesarchiv.de/gedenkbuch/chronicles.html?page=1 (accessed 26 June 2016); Krejčová, Svobodová and Hyndráková, *Židé v Protektorátu*, 364–66.
7. Letter from Heinz Schuster and Lazar Moldovan, 20 May 1943, to Palestine, in Rothkirchen, *Jews*, 131–32. The letter was smuggled out of Prague and consisted in part of information in code.
8. Rothkirchen, *Jews*, 135.
9. YV Jerusalem, M 58/JM 11814, fol. 59–65: Postal orders of 21 June, 17 July and 13 August 1943, receipts of delivery Litzmannstadt Ghetto of 25 June and 22 July 1943 and receipts of purchase from the Lysá nad Labem Town Treasurer's Office of 1 June, 1 July and 4 August 1943.
10. Rothkirchen, *Jews*, 239–44.
11. The train that departed in June supposedly had four thousand people on board; see Bryant, *Prague in Black*, 151 and Gerwarth, *Hitler's Hangman*, 287. The figure seems far too high. The transport does not appear in the official list of deportations in the Memorial Book. See https://www.bundesarchiv.de/gedenkbuch/chronicles.html.de?page=1 (accessed 30 October 2015).
12. He was deported from there to Auschwitz in 1944. See 'Ghetto Theresienstadt. Theresienstadt 1941–1945. Ein Nachschlagewerk' at http://www.ghetto-theresienstadt.info/pages/k/kraemers.htm (accessed 5 July 2015). The following website refers to 15 July as the day of deportation: http://www.holocaust.cz/en/database-of-victims/victim/102257-salo-kr-mer/ (accessed 25 June 2016).
13. RGBl. 1943 I, 372.
14. For more detail on this vision and its realization, see Wolf Gruner, 'Greater Germany', in Peter Hayes and John Roth (eds), *The Oxford Handbook of Holocaust Studies* (New York, 2010), 293–309.
15. Rothkirchen, *Jews*, 130; Kárný, 'Zur Statistik der jüdischen Bevölkerung', 11.
16. YV Jerusalem, M 58/JM 11808, fol. 510: Note Jewish Religious Community of Olomouc, 21 December 1942.
17. YV Jerusalem, M 58/JM 11809, fol. 284: Statistical overview, 30 April 1943.
18. Ibid., fol. 280: Note Jewish Religious Community of Olomouc on visit to Gestapo, 7 May 1943.
19. Später, *Villa Waigner*, 85.
20. Rothkirchen, *Jews*, 224–26.
21. RSHA report, 15 October 1943, in Celovsky, *Germanisierung und Genozid*, 386–87.
22. Rothkirchen, 'The Defiant Few', 79.
23. Hitler to von Neurath, 22 August 1943, in Mund, *Deutschland und das Protektorat*, doc. 439, 619–20.
24. According to Wilhelm Dennler, the German Ministry of State under Frank's leadership was already an element in an administrative reform planned in December 1941, which was intended to divest the Reich protector of administrative responsibilities. See Dennler, *Böhmische Passion*, 65.
25. On the Ministry of State and Frank, see René Küpper, 'Karl Hermann Frank als Deutscher Staatsminister für Böhmen und Mähren', in Glettler, Lipták and Míšková, *Geteilt, besetzt, beherrscht*, 31–52; Küpper, *Karl Hermann Frank*, 313–72.
26. BA Berlin, R 43II/1328b, fol. 67: Note Reich Chancellery, 13 December 1943. On Rudolf Jung, see, for example, Osterloh, *Nationalsozialistische Judenverfolgung*, 45, 66–72.
27. BA Berlin, R 43/3518, n.p.: Copy telex German Ministry of State, Frank, Prague to head of Reich Chancellery, Lammers, 7 December 1943; ibid.: Copy Reich Finance Ministry to head of Reich Chancellery, 15 December 1943.

28. Adam, 'Im Wettstreit um die letzten Arbeitskräfte', 106. With reference to the Todt/ Einsatzgruppe VII organization – which, however, included Silesia – Stefan Laube quotes the figure of thirty-eight thousand prisoners, most of them Jews, at the end of 1944. See Stefan Laube, 'Technik, Arbeit und Zerstörung: Die Organisation Todt in Prag (1944–1945)', *Bohemia* 40(2) (1999), 387–416, here 405.
29. Adam, 'Im Wettstreit um die letzten Arbeitskräfte', 116.
30. Adler, *Der verwaltete Mensch*, 304.
31. Berta Landré, 'Jüdische Zwangsarbeit in Prag', *Zeitgeschichte* 9(11/12) (Vienna, 1982), 365–77.
32. Government decree (119/43), 3 May 1943, re. imposition of a tax to achieve social equalization in the Protectorate of Bohemia and Moravia for Jews, Poles and Gypsies, in Lexa, 'Anti-Jewish Laws', 86.
33. YV Jerusalem, O 7/64, fol. 3–4: Report by the Council of Elders of the Jews in Prague on the year 1944, 2–3.
34. Ludomír Kocourek, 'Das Schicksal der Juden im Sudetengau im Licht der erhaltenen Quellen', in *Theresienstädter Studien und Dokumente* 1997, 86–104, here 96; Rothkirchen, *Jews*, 157.
35. USHMM Washington, RG 48.005M, reel 5 (Prague State Archive), I 3b-5800, carton 387, no. 39, n.p.: Office of the Reich Protector to the State Authorities in Prague and Brno, 7 July 1944.
36. YV Jerusalem, O 7/64, fol. 22+24: Report by the Council of Elders of the Jews in Prague on the year 1944, 21+23.
37. On deployment in Germany, see chapter 3 of Gruner, *Jewish Forced Labor*, 83–102.
38. Rothkirchen, *Jews*, 157; Adam, 'Im Wettstreit um die letzten Arbeitskräfte', 115.
39. Kocourek, 'Schicksal', 96.
40. YV Jerusalem, O 7/64, fol. 5, 68: Report by the Council of Elders of the Jews in Prague on the year 1944, 4, 65.
41. YV Jerusalem, M 58/JM 11809, fol. 349: Telegram from the Council of Elders in Prague, 18 September, received 19 September 1944.
42. Landré, 'Jüdische Zwangsarbeit in Prag'. On the splitting of mica, see USC SF/ VHA, video interview, Margaret Lukas, tape 4, min. 12:10–16:35.
43. YV Jerusalem, Photo Archive FA-165, fol. 60A, aA, bA: Hagibor operation and camp.
44. YV Jerusalem, O 7/64, fol. 43, 56–60: Report by the Council of Elders of the Jews in Prague on the year 1944, 41, 55–58; cf. illustrations in the album: ibid., Photo Archive E, 156/53A–61A: Hagibor operation and camp.
45. YV Jerusalem, O 7/64, fol. 5–7, 67–68: Report by the Council of Elders of the Jews in Prague on the year 1944, 4–6, 64–65.
46. See Landré, 'Jüdische Zwangsarbeit in Prag'.
47. YV Jerusalem, O 7/64, fol. 67: Report by the Council of Elders of the Jews in Prague on the year 1944, 64.
48. Kocourek, 'Schicksal', 96.
49. YV Jerusalem, O 7/64, fol. 4, 39, 67: Report by the Council of Elders of the Jews in Prague on the year 1944, 3, 37, 64.
50. Ibid., fol. 4+39: Report by the Council of Elders of the Jews in Prague on the year 1944, 3+37.
51. LAMOTH/A Los Angeles, RG-72.08.36, n.p.: Postcard from Albert Unterstab in Bystřice u Benešova to Karl Unterstab in Prague, 4 March 1945.
52. Rothkirchen, *Jews*, 130. For an overview of the situation of Jews in 'mixed marriages' in Germany, France and the Netherlands, see Gruner, *Widerstand in der Rosenstraße*.

53. YV Jerusalem, O 7/64, fol. 14, 23, 35: Report by the Council of Elders of the Jews in Prague on the year 1944, 13, 22, 33.
54. YV Jerusalem, M 58/JM 11809, fol. 205: Note, Jewish Religious Community of Olomouc on visit to Gestapo, 6 June 1944.
55. YV Jerusalem, M 58/JM 11808, fol. 9: Note, Jewish Religious Community of Olomouc, 7 February 1944.
56. YV Jerusalem, Photo Archive FA-156, fol. 4: Report on the year 1943, Council of Elders of the Jews.
57. YV Jerusalem, O 7/64, fol. 33: Report by the Council of Elders of the Jews in Prague on the year 1944, 31.
58. Ibid., fol. 16–18: Report by the Council of Elders of the Jews in Prague on the year 1944, 15–17.
59. YV Jerusalem, M 58/JM 11809, fol. 208: Note, Jewish Religious Community of Olomouc on visit to Gestapo, 19 February 1944.
60. YV Jerusalem, O 7/64, fol. 20: Report by the Council of Elders of the Jews in Prague on the year 1944, 19.
61. Ibid., fol. 38: Report by the Council of Elders of the Jews in Prague on the year 1944, 36.
62. See https://www.bundesarchiv.de/gedenkbuch/chronicles.html?page=1 (accessed 26 June 2016).
63. VHA Prague, fonds 140, carton 23, no. 97, fol. 78–82: 'Factual report by a returnee Jew deported from Slovakia', March 1944, 27–31.
64. See https://www.bundesarchiv.de/gedenkbuch/chronicles.html?page=1 (accessed 26 June 2016).
65. YV Jerusalem, O 7/64, fol. 50: Report by the Council of Elders of the Jews in Prague on the year 1944, 48.
66. Ibid., fol. 51, 67: Report by the Council of Elders of the Jews in Prague on the year 1944, 49, 64. For a detailed account of the development of policies on 'mixed marriages' and for more on the Müller decree, see Gruner, *Widerstand in der Rosenstraße*, 178–89.
67. Rothkirchen, *Jews*, 133; Kárný, 'Zur Statistik der jüdischen Bevölkerung', 11.
68. Rothkirchen, *Jews*, 133.
69. Státní Zidovské Museum Prague, DP, carton 15, n.p.: Instruction leaflet 'Summons for Journey Number ...' published by the Council of Elders of the Jews in Prague (n.d.). My thanks to Jörg Osterloh for making me aware of this document.
70. Rothkirchen, *Jews*, 133.
71. Ibid., 246.
72. Frommer, *National Cleansing*, 28.
73. Order Frank, 1 March 1945, in Celovsky, *Germanisierung und Genozid*, 410. Cf. Dennler, *Böhmische Passion*, 153.
74. Dennler, *Böhmische Passion*, 200.
75. *Das Volk. Tageszeitung der sozialdemokratischen Partei Deutschlands*, 9 September 1945, 2. On the establishment of the special courts, their legal foundations and the comparatively fair administration of justice, see Frommer, *National Cleansing*, 78–97.
76. For an account featuring a relevant picture, see Frommer, *National Cleansing*, 97–99.
77. *Das Volk*, 15 July 1945, 2.
78. Dennler, *Böhmische Passion*, 220–29.
79. On the trial and execution, see Küpper, *Karl Hermann Frank*, 397–402 (quotation 402); Frommer, *National Cleansing*, 233–37.

80. Benjamin Frommer sheds light on this in his study and argues that there was much more to this postwar process than just a communist purge; Frommer, *National Cleansing*, 2–8.
81. Ibid., 37, 277–91. See also the photograph of the ministers in Prague Prison, in ibid., 281. Cf. Dennler, *Böhmische Passion*, 218–20, 236–37.
82. Frommer, *National Cleansing*, 41–185.
83. Rothkirchen, *Jews*, 185.
84. Frommer, *National Cleansing*, 42.
85. Ibid., 49–59; Dennler, *Böhmische Passion*, 155–214.
86. *Der Tagesspiegel*, 10 November 1945, 1.
87. *Der Tagesspiegel*, 30 October 1945, 2; *Das Volk*, 31 October 1945, 1.
88. Rothkirchen, *Jews*, 185–86, 287–88; Frommer, *National Cleansing*, 31. Frommer points out that many Germans avoided legal prosecution through the expulsion; ibid., 254–57.
89. Rothkirchen, *Jews*, 185–86, 287–88.
90. Erich Kessler, 'Ein Theresienstädter Tagebuch: Der Theresienstädter 20. April 1945 und die Tage danach ...', in *Theresienstädter Studien und Dokumente* 1995, 306–24, here 315.
91. USC SF/VHA, video interview, Hana Beer, tape 3, min. 21:00–22:00.
92. YV Jerusalem, O 7/265, fol. 44: Zeev Scheck to Dr Georg Herlitz, Central Zionist Archives, Jerusalem, 29 October 1945 (carbon copy). For an account of documentation efforts in Europe, though one that does not consider the case of Czechoslovakia, see Laura Jockusch, *Collect and Record! Jewish Holocaust Documentation in Early Postwar Europe* (New York, 2012).
93. YV Jerusalem, O 7/265, fol. 66–67: Zeev Scheck to Dr Georg Herlitz, Central Zionist Archives, Jerusalem, 5 December 1945 (carbon copy); ibid., fol. 111: Confidential note Documentační akce, 3 May 1946.
94. YV Jerusalem, O 7/264, fol. 78–85: Jewish Agency, Documentation Division, n.d. (c. beginning 1946) (carbon copy), 1–5.
95. Láníček, *Czechs, Slovaks and the Jews*, 126–86; Rothkirchen, *Jews*, 207–8, 284–85; Hájková, 'To Terezín and Back', 48–50.
96. Jan Láníček, 'What Did It Mean to Be Loyal? Jewish Survivors in Post-War Czechoslovakia in a Comparative Perspective', *Australian Journal of Politics and History* 60(3) (2014), 384–404, here 392–403; Hahn, 'Verdrängung und Verharmlosung', 144; Dennler, *Böhmische Passion*, 217; Christa Schikorra, 'Rückkehr in eine sich neu konstituierende Gesellschaft: Jüdische Remigrantinnen in der Tschechoslowakei', in *Theresienstädter Studien und Dokumente* 2006, 364–98, here 373.
97. YV Jerusalem, O 7/264, fol. 62–64: Zeev Scheck, Dr Robert Weinberger, Documentační akce, to the rector of the Hebrew University, 28 January 1946 (carbon copy). For a general account of restitution policy, see Eduard Kubů and Jan Kuklík Jr., 'Reluctant Restitution: The Restitution of Jewish Property in the Bohemian Lands after the Second World War', in Dean, Goschler and Ther, *Robbery and Restitution*, 223–39.
98. Dennler, *Böhmische Passion*, 241.
99. YV Jerusalem, O 7/264, fol. 62–64: Zeev Scheck, Dr Robert Weinberger, Documentační akce, to the rector of the Hebrew University, 28 January 1946 (carbon copy). On the edicts issued by the Czech government in 1945/46 and Jews' struggle to regain property, see Kubů and Kuklík, 'Reluctant Restitution', 225–27; Sedláková, 'Die Rolle der sogenannten "Einsatzstäbe"', 297–98.
100. Kubů and Kuklík, 'Reluctant Restitution', here 228; Rothkirchen, *Jews*, 285.

101. Schikorra, 'Rückkehr', 371; Kubů and Kuklík, 'Reluctant Restitution', here 229–34.
102. Später, *Villa Waigner*, 85.
103. Schikorra, 'Rückkehr'; Hájková, 'To Terezín and Back', 48–55.
104. Schikorra, 'Rückkehr', 375–88 (quotation 383).
105. See Láníček, 'What Did It Mean to Be Loyal?', 389.
106. Hana Beer on her return to Pilsen: USC SF/VHA, video interview, Hana Beer, tape 3, min. 25:36–26:30. Mimi Berger on her return to Prague, ibid., video interview, Mimi Berger, tape 1, min. 24:34–26:30, tape 3, 12:11–21:00; ibid., video interview, Anna Grant, tape 2, min. 8:30–10:00.
107. Hájková, 'To Terezín and Back', 50.
108. Hahn, 'Verdrängung und Verharmlosung', 147; Láníček, *Czechs, Slovaks and the Jews*, 186.
109. Láníček, *Czechs, Slovaks and the Jews*, 126–29, 186; Rothkirchen, *Jews*, 185–86, 287–88; Schikorra, 'Rückkehr', 374.

Conclusion

Only around fourteen thousand of the approximately 118,000 Jews who had lived in Bohemia and Moravia in 1938 were there to see the end of the war.[1] Historians estimate that around eighty thousand Jews from the Protectorate of Bohemia and Moravia were murdered. Because the Security Police had initially prohibited the emigration of Jews from the Protectorate for several months after the occupation began and the war then rapidly hampered the emigration of more people, only about twenty-five thousand Jews had managed to flee the Protectorate by October 1941. If we factor in the other parts of the pre-occupation state such as Slovakia, 265,000 of the 350,000 Jews who had lived in what had been Czechoslovakia lost their lives. They represented more than three-quarters of all Czech victims of the German occupation.[2]

Who, however, was responsible for persecution in the Protectorate of Bohemia and Moravia? The present study shows in detail that, as in Germany and Austria, in the Protectorate too a diverse range of institutions on all levels of the state were actively involved in the persecution of Jews. As early as March 1939, immediately after the occupation of rump Czechoslovakia and the proclamation of the Protectorate as a semiautonomous territory, Hitler had formulated the goal of ostracizing the Jews. Yet he assigned this task to the Czech government because here, for the first time, the Reich had absorbed a territory with a non-German majority. The Czech government continued to exist, as did the Czech administrative system and Czech law. As late as the end of 1939, in its situation report, the SS Security Service noted that the Reich had not 'intervened directly' to 'solve the Jewish problem in Bohemia and Moravia'.[3]

Though this statement is not entirely correct, its core message – contrary to previous assumptions – is surprisingly accurate. The Czech government along with its ministries, the district offices and municipalities as well as private Czech clubs and associations sought to exclude Jews, initially from economic and cultural life and later from the public sphere in its entirety. Through acts of violence, street rallies, newspaper propaganda and petitions, Czech fascist organizations put public and internal pressure on the Czech government and administrative system, particularly in the spring of 1939 and in 1941. On the German side, Reich Protector Konstantin Freiherr von Neurath, his state secretary Karl Hermann Frank and later Reinhard Heydrich together with the officials in the Office of the Reich Protector, Security Police and Central Office for Jewish Emigration certainly developed anti-Jewish measures. Yet with the exception of the economic realm and 'Aryanization', these often lagged behind Czech policies. Until the deportations began in 1941, Berlin intervened only in a small number of exceptional cases.

How does the active role of the Czech government and its local administrative apparatus in the persecution of Jews fit with two key beliefs prevalent among historians, namely, first, that after the First World War antisemitism was a marginal phenomenon in the first Czechoslovak Republic in comparison to other European countries and, second, that the German occupation regime was behind anti-Jewish policies in the Protectorate? On the first point: while the Czechoslovak Republic, formed in 1919 from part of the former Habsburg Empire, was soon considered less antisemitic than most other countries in postwar Europe, here too anti-Jewish incidents occurred amid the nationbuilding undertaken by the new Czechoslovak state. As I have shown in the present book with the help of USC Shoah Foundation video interviews, in some places Jews certainly experienced antisemitism in their daily lives. Nonetheless, in the 1920s and 1930s most of Czechoslovakia's roughly 350,000 Jewish inhabitants were well integrated and assimilated. It took the model of the Nazi regime and the Nazi Party's influence on both the Germans living in the republic (particularly the Sudeten region) and Czech fascists to trigger the growth of antisemitism in Czechoslovakia in the 1930s, though the democratic government took steps to combat it.

Only with the formation of the Second Republic, a mere rump state stripped of the Sudeten territory following the Munich Agreement of October 1938, did this policy drastically change. The violence that accompanied the German occupation of the Sudetenland produced a flood of refugees from the German Reich, including Austria, into the increasingly authoritarian Czech Republic. The refugees, most of them Czechs, were welcomed, though this applied less to Jews, who were often regarded as German. For some politicians and propagandists, the humanitarian and economic problems resulting from the arrival of hundreds of thousands of people provided a welcome opportunity to mobilize prejudices against Jews.

From November 1938 onwards, governmental actors discussed anti-Jewish measures. The education minister suspended Jewish professors in December. At the start of 1939, the government under Beran imposed anti-Jewish measures on specific occupational groups and on Jews who had immigrated after 1914. Professional bodies and sections of the civil service began to introduce 'Aryan clauses' or to suggest to Jews that they take a leave of absence. Antisemitism, therefore, had already become part of the rump Czech Republic's government programme months before the German occupation, laying the ground for the anti-Jewish initiatives soon to be pursued by the Czech Protectorate authorities.

German troops occupied what was left of the Czech Republic in mid March 1939, after Slovakia split off and President Emil Hácha gave in to the immense political and military pressure exercised by Hitler and abandoned the republic without a fight. Then came the task forces of the SS and Security Police as well as SS-*Totenkopfverbände*. Following Hitler's speedy proclamation of the Protectorate of Bohemia and Moravia, the Czech government retained authority over everything apart from foreign and defence policy, while the German army, via the heads of the civil administrations in Bohemia and Moravia, started to control the Czech administrative apparatus and police.

Notably, Josef Bürckel, head of the Civil Administration in Moravia, had already gained broad experience of persecutory measures as Reich commissioner for the reintegration of the Saarland and for the reunification of Austria with the Reich. Together with the staff he had brought with him, he now drew on this background as the German authorities proceeded with the occupation of the new region; much the same can be said of Walter Stahlecker, also from Vienna, now head of the Security Police. By March 1939, the Sudeten German Gauleiter Konrad Henlein and Josef Bürckel, as heads of the civil administrations, issued the first decrees limiting Jews' right of disposal over their own property, while – after negative experiences in Austria with 'unruly Aryanization' – Hermann Göring in Berlin made an early intervention to steer the sale of banks and businesses so as to benefit the German state. In Berlin, State Secretary Stuckart in the Reich Interior Ministry monitored the introduction of the Reich laws and the adaptation of the Protectorate administration to Reich structures.

When German sovereign power passed to Reich Protector Konstantin Freiherr von Neurath and his authority in April 1939, the Czech government gained autonomy in many fields, though it had to involve the Reich protector in its decisions. Otherwise, regardless of a concerted effort by Czech fascists, who pressed him to take a tougher German-style approach, Hitler personally ensured that the formulation of anti-Jewish policies was left entirely in the hands of the Czech government.

The first anti-Jewish initiatives thus came from the Czech Cabinet under Hácha. The first anti-Jewish decree had already been issued by mid March 1939, followed by others. In May, the Czech government, now led by General Alois Eliáš and replete with familiar faces from the Second Republic, such as Agriculture Minister Feierabend, Finance Minister Kalfus and Transport Minister Havelka, even drew up a comprehensive law to exclude Jews from public life. Only when the Office of the Reich Protector had evaluated this draft legislation as insufficiently radical did the Reich protector disregard the independent role in 'Jewish policy' granted to the Czech government, issuing a decree in June. While this included a stricter 'definition of a Jew' consonant with the Nuremberg laws, its main goal was in fact the 'Aryanization' of Jewish property.

The period of transition following the occupation opened up opportunities for radical Germans but also Czechs to unleash violence against Jews. Between March and June, synagogues, cafes and other establishments were attacked in several towns and cities. The local administration responded to the new situation in a variety of ways. In some places the chief county commissioners ordered the marking of Jewish businesses, while in others they had such signs, put up by antisemites, removed.

The local attacks were accompanied by a wave of arrests by the Gestapo targeting the Germans' political opponents but also prominent Jews. As had happened a year earlier in Vienna, Jewish institutions, including the welfare services, had to close for several weeks before the Gestapo allowed them to reopen under strict supervision. Every form of support, therefore, whether welfare or help for would-be emigrants, abruptly if temporarily ceased to exist. Many Jews fled from the terror across the border, for example into Poland or Slovakia, or went into hiding within the country. However, at variance with the previous official policy of forced expulsion – and in contrast to the decision made a year earlier in Vienna – in May 1939 Heydrich, head of the Security Police, stopped all Jewish emigration from the Protectorate and initially refrained from establishing a bespoke agency of the Security Police or SS Security Service devoted to Jewish emigration. Because options for emigrating to other countries had diminished rapidly around this time, the authorities wished to prevent emigration from the Protectorate occurring at the expense of the expulsion of Jews from Germany.

It was not until the summer that Heydrich suddenly changed his view, lifting the ban on emigration for Czech Jews. As war with Poland had become increasingly likely, expelling the Jews from every part of the Greater German Reich now became the top priority. However, the Central Office for Jewish Emigration in Prague was founded at the end of July 1939 not by the SS but by the Reich protector in consultation with the Czech government, as a state institution. On the Vienna model, the Prague Central Office, here too led by Stahlecker with Eichmann ultimately in charge, supervised the largest local Jewish Community along with its finances at the local level, while centralizing all state agencies with responsibility for Jewish emigration – including all Czech ones – in its headquarters. Immediately after the establishment of this body, Adolf Eichmann informed the Prague Jewish Community that thirty thousand Jews had to emigrate by the end of 1939, and no fewer than seventy thousand by the summer of 1940. Because the Central Office was initially responsible only for Prague and the surrounding areas, in order to better organize forced emigration, Jews from the Bohemian and Moravian provinces were to be resettled in the Protectorate capital. Local authorities took advantage of this, with at least six of them forcing local Jewish residents to move to Prague.

The expulsion of such large numbers of Jews points to the German authorities' increasingly firm plans to Germanize the Protectorate. To this end, the local administration, especially in the 'German language islands' and in the cities, received a major injection of German personnel. This Germanization of the administration also directly bolstered the German influence on 'Jewish policy' in the Protectorate. Though the Prague Central Office gained more power in 1940 than its sister organization in Vienna, by no means – as I have been able to show here for the first time – was it the 'decision-making body for all matters affecting the fate of the Protectorate's Jewish population' as historians have often wrongly assumed.[4]

So how did the various parties influence the persecution of Jews in concrete terms? It was mainly the Czech government as well as the chief county commissioners, district offices, police headquarters and municipalities that initiated persecutory policies. Beginning in the summer of 1939, mayors and chief county commissioners prohibited Jews from using public institutions before either the Czech government or the German occupation authorities imposed central regulations to this effect on the Protectorate. While the German side focused on finances and 'Aryanization', the Czech government and its ministries began to segregate Jews within the public realm, for example in stores, restaurants and schools. Czech fascists, meanwhile, put increasing pressure on the government in Prague. The Czech government's July ordinance excluding Jews from a range of occupations worsened the impoverishment and sense of hopelessness among the Jewish population. The Prague Jewish Community – in an attempt to more effectively counter the growing poverty and enhance its ability to cope with the influx from the provinces – responded by integrating Jewish agencies responsible for emigration, welfare and schooling into its own structures.

Following the occupation of Poland, Germany radicalized its plans for the Jewish population within the Greater German Reich and for a brief period central measures dominated, such as the curfew for Jews. In the Protectorate, the German police were now considered solely responsible for the Jews, with all German administrative organs being made subordinate to the Reich protector. In mid September, when the Jewish Communities had carried out their instructions to provide a statistical survey of Jews in the Protectorate, Hitler and his senior Nazi colleagues made the strategic decision – in view of the rapid victory over Poland – to deport all less well-off Jews, in other words the majority of them, from the Greater German Reich to the eastern portion of the territory under German occupation. To this end, all so-called racial Jews had to register anew with the Jewish Communities, including those in the Protectorate, by the end of September.

Because the long-term plan was to Germanize the Protectorate – in other words to 'purge' it of all non-Germans – the Nazi leadership incorporated Jews from the Protectorate into its new plans to create reserves for Jews and deport them from the 'Greater German Reich'. As a result, Czech Jews were among the first victims of the mass deportations to occupied Poland, which Eichmann centrally planned and steered in his new post in the Reich Security Main Office in Berlin.

In mid October, the first mass transports, coordinated by Eichmann, of Jews from the border regions of the Protectorate and Upper Silesia as well as from major cities in the Protectorate and Austria left for Nisko in eastern Poland. A number of researchers have perceived this as a local Eichmann operation stopped by Berlin after just a few days. But given that Eichmann planned the transports in Berlin and then monitored them locally, this explanation is far from persuasive.

Following a first transport from Moravian Ostrava, against which Czech residents had protested, Eichmann's superior Müller put transports from the Protectorate to the back of the queue behind those from Vienna, a reordering of priorities that has often been misunderstood as an abrupt change of policy. In fact, however, small-scale transports continued to roll from Brno and Prague. Of those Jews deported to Nisko, near Lublin, beginning in the second half of October, 1,800 were from Moravian Ostrava, Brno and Prague, the largest Czech cities with the greatest number of Jewish residents. Five thousand Jews from the Greater German Reich having been deported, in early November Himmler suspended the deportations until February 1940 for technical reasons.

This interruption, of several months, influenced the medium-term planning of Jewish policy in the Protectorate. The Prague Central Office, which had been closed at the start of the war, was now reopened in order to expedite the mass expulsion of all Jews by the summer of 1940. The *Jüdisches Nachrichtenblatt*, planned for some time and intended to promulgate anti-Jewish decrees, finally saw the light of day two weeks after the suspension of the transports. Those responsible saw both measures as temporary: at the time, no one in the Protectorate had the remotest idea that it would take two years for the mass transports to resume.

While the Reich Security Main Office in Berlin centrally organized the deportations from the Protectorate as elsewhere, other fields of Jewish policy remained within the ambit of local or regional authorities. The Jewish Communities sought to counter the impoverishment rooted in mass unemployment by trying to organize their work more effectively. The Prague Jewish Community integrated numerous Jewish organizations and institutions into its own structures, as evident in its weekly reports – analysed in the present book for the first time – to Eichmann's Central Office. The Jewish Religious Community organized the provisioning of the growing number of impoverished Jews, children, old people and those who had recently arrived from the provinces, all of them in need of support. This was a mammoth task on which it was soon spending more than twice its income.

Because Stahlecker, Commander of the Security Police in the Office of the Reich Protector, expected the deportations (suspended until February 1940) to resume soon, on 29 January he extended the authority of the Central Office for Jewish Emigration beyond Greater Prague to the entire Protectorate. Henceforth, the Central Office oversaw all Jewish Communities. In February, however, Heydrich suspended the mass transports for an unspecified period. Over the medium term, the authorities in the Protectorate thus worked on the assumption that the Jewish population would remain there.

In March 1940, the Central Office thus made the Prague Jewish Community responsible for supervising all Jewish Communities in the Protectorate, while at the same time transforming it into a compulsory organization, with all 'racial Jews' forced to become members. As I have shown here for the first time, although the Office of the Reich Protector had discussed the founding of a 'Reich Association' since autumn 1939, in other words emulating the German model, those responsible ultimately preferred the Vienna paradigm, that is, making the largest Jewish Community responsible for all Jews rather than creating new structures. Because the Prague Jewish Community now had to cater to the needs of 'racial Jews' as well, it established a Division for 'Non-Mosaic Jews'.

While the suspension of the mass transports in the spring of 1940 brought a number of strategic decisions in its wake in the Protectorate, at the same time these decisions laid the ground for the transports' resumption. The fact that the authorities did not introduce forced labour for Czech Jews also provides indirect evidence that the transports were still expected to resume before long. Heydrich's February ban on the emigration of fit-for-work Jews to other European countries, meanwhile, highlights the significance of Jewish forced labour in the rest of the Greater German Reich.

By this point, most Jews were eager to leave the Protectorate sooner rather than later due to persecution and destitution, with the Jewish Community of Prague advising thousands of would-be emigrants a week. However, in the first half of 1940 – with the exception of Shanghai – there were very few options for escape left, while the cost of emigration grew. The incipient ghettoization in the Protectorate also increased the Jews' desire to leave. Rather than in 1941, as earlier research assumed, or in the summer of 1940, a period recently emphasized by Sedláková, it was in fact as early as the spring of 1940 that local agencies and authorities, particularly in towns, put pressure on Jewish residents to abandon their homes – as I have shown here for the first time. While some local authorities forced their Jewish residents to move to cities, others forcibly relocated them to specific streets, old castles or vacant factories in the local area. Ghettoization, therefore, which Czech fascists were calling for as early as 1939, began in the spring of 1940 in the Czech provinces before it took off in the cities and, in fact, prior to the establishment of ghettos in certain parts of occupied Poland.

The separation of families as a consequence of emigration, relocation or expulsion from provincial towns led to the rapid impoverishment of many Jews. New decrees issued by the Reich protector to eliminate Jews from the economy at the start of 1940 worsened the situation, as did the 'Aryanization' of businesses, factories and real estate. In March, all Jews in the Protectorate had to hand over their shares, securities, precious metals, jewels and pearls to a foreign exchange licensed bank. From April onwards, the Protectorate capital evicted Jewish tenants from city-owned property.

At the behest of the Reich interior minister, the Reich protector had tasked Albert Hoffmann – who had already held the post of so-called liquidation commissar in Austria and the Sudetenland – with 'restructuring' organizations in the Protectorate. His authority rapidly liquidated both Jewish and non-Jewish associations in an attempt – by destroying infrastructure and seizing assets – to weaken political and 'racial' opponents and secure German hegemony.

These measures had a disastrous financial impact on the provisioning of the Jewish population, while the number of people supported by the Prague Jewish Community's Welfare Department increased week on week. Hence, new retraining measures in skilled crafts and in agriculture now served both to prepare Jews for emigration and to relieve some of the burden on overstretched welfare institutions. In July 1940, the Central Office ordered the establishment of the so-called retraining camp of Linden. Much like the camps of Doppl and Sandhof in Austria, this was officially run by the Prague Jewish Community. In reality, for its inmates, usually numbering around three hundred, it was an SS-run forced labour camp until near the end of the war. In addition, the Jewish Employment Office made direct contact with farmers, estate owners and businesspeople to encourage them to take on unemployed Jews. A total of 90,681 Jews still lived in the Protectorate in late September 1940, while 24,998 had emigrated since the occupation began.

In August 1940, the Commander of the Security Police attempted to seize the initiative with respect to the segregation of Jews in the public realm. Unbeknown to him, however, due to the growing number of local initiatives, in July the Czech Interior Ministry had already instructed the local authorities to implement most of his demands on a uniform basis, whether restricted shopping hours, exclusion from public schools or bans on entering restaurants and parks. The Central Office for Jewish Emigration, meanwhile, extended its control to the Prague housing market in September and, with the help of the city authorities and the Nazi Party, began to concentrate the Jewish population in 'Jews' houses' in specific districts. It also regulated the dissolution of Jewish organizations, foundations and provincial Communities and the transfer of their assets to the so-called Emigration Fund of Bohemia and Moravia.

Nonetheless, the drive for centralization by no means gained the upper hand: the second half of 1940 saw countless new local initiatives aimed at isolating Jews. The rapid decentralized ghettoization is a particularly striking phenomenon: in the third quarter of 1940 alone, local authorities in twenty-five locations forced Jewish residents to leave their homes and move into abandoned factory buildings or vacant castles. Many Jews fled to Prague. The Prague Community's intensified efforts to facilitate forced emigration, which was now possible on a legal basis almost exclusively to Shanghai and on an illegal basis to Palestine, and its rapidly growing expenditure on an increasingly impoverished population, were immensely expensive, as evident in its weekly reports, while its revenues fell as its compulsory members often no longer had an income. By the end of 1940, the 'Aryanization' of Jewish property, which encompassed not just real estate and businesses but also securities and so on, and from which Germans profited above all, was considered largely complete.

In an attempt to reduce its burgeoning expenditure on welfare, the Prague Jewish Community increasingly negotiated with labour offices and private businesses regarding the group deployment of Jews, initially with little numerical success. At the start of 1941, municipal administrations, initially in Prague and Brno and later in a total of ninety-seven localities, began to recruit Jewish workers to clear snow. While they often received meagre wages, Jewish Community representatives were nonetheless positive about such deployment as it took at least a little of the pressure off the Religious Community's budget, severely strained due to skyrocketing welfare costs.

As there was no longer any prospect of a rapid resumption of the deportations, in January, April and May 1941, through a number of decrees, the Czech Ministry for Social and Health Administration introduced forced labour in segregated work details for Jews in the Protectorate on the German-Austrian model. The labour offices organized forced labour, while the Reich protector was also involved and the Central Office ensured it too had a say when it came to deployments outside the Protectorate capital, as this related to Jews' freedom of movement. In contrast to the Old Reich, here the Jewish Communities themselves had to examine all male Jews between the ages of eighteen and fifty to establish their fitness for work. Initially, the German labour offices placed Jews chiefly in agriculture and construction, later shifting focus to industry and forestry. Henceforth, thousands of Czech Jews slaved away for private firms and public agencies in civil engineering projects and railway construction, river regulation, industry and craft businesses, on estates and in forestry. By early summer, of 15,000 male Jews, more than 11,700 were already deployed in labour programmes, many of them in segregated work details.

The year 1941 saw new, radical measures, many of them emanating from Eichmann's Central Office or the Office of the Reich Protector. On the one hand they served to lower the state's expenditure on Jews, while on the other separating Jewish from non-Jewish Czechs. On 31 May, the Reich protector transferred responsibility for the welfare of impoverished Jews from the state to the Jewish Communities, whose finances were already in a desperate state. He also arranged for the introduction of the Nuremberg laws in the Protectorate. The Czech government, meanwhile, restricted shopping hours for Jews and imposed other restrictions.

Just as in the Reich, in the Protectorate too local authorities, police chiefs, chief county commissioners and mayors continued to forge ahead with anti-Jewish initiatives. In the Protectorate, however, there was no institution comparable to the German Council of Municipalities to standardize and disseminate local anti-Jewish proposals. Hence, in light of the contradictory policies emerging from such local prohibitions, in summer 1941 the Czech government adopted several restrictions and standardized them across the entire Protectorate. The fact that the Czech government pre-empted the German Reich protector, who presented it with similar proposals, by more than a month, is testimony to the continuing autonomy enjoyed by the Czech authorities and to the lack of coordination of anti-Jewish policy in occupied Bohemia and Moravia. In the Protectorate too, therefore, we observe local, regional and central persecutory measures feeding into one another and reinforcing their mutual momentum.

Like the Central Office in the Protectorate, since spring 1941 the Reich Security Main Office had for the first time involved itself in issues of forced labour and the concentration of Jews in 'Jews' houses' in Germany and Austria. The process of bringing forced labour deployment and welfare practices in the Protectorate into line with those in the Old Reich, the end of retraining and the debate on forcing Jews to wear an identificatory badge are emblematic of the efforts made to achieve the general centralization of anti-Jewish policy in the Greater German Reich in light of the planned resumption of the deportations.

Nonetheless, the local authorities had by no means lost the initiative. They had already forged ahead with the ghettoization of Jews in the towns by the time the Reich protector gave the green light for the concentration of Jews in March 1941. While in the provinces all Jews in particular towns were quartered in separate streets or dilapidated castles, in Prague and other cities they were now concentrated in 'Jews' houses' or particular districts under the supervision of the Central Office. The Jewish Communities had to find new living quarters for hundreds of homeless families at short notice. This was a near-impossible task: Jews were only permitted to hold subtenancies in so-called Jews' houses, while the Central Office constantly expropriated Jewish-owned buildings.

Nothing illustrates the Protectorate's special status with regard to anti-Jewish policy better than the intensified programme of forced labour. On the one hand, at the behest of the Czech Ministry for Social and Health Administration, this was organized by the labour offices in accordance with German norms, while on the other – just as in the General Government – since summer 1941 it had encompassed Jews between the ages of sixteen and sixty. Beginning in September, work on an individual basis was prohibited and in October twelve thousand mostly male Jews were already subject to group deployment in segregated work details. Though initially very few women were affected, they too were now examined to establish their fitness for work.

When Heydrich was invested with the powers of the Reich protector in September 1941, he immediately planned the concentration of the remaining Jews in a small number of cities in the Protectorate and in temporary ghettos prior to their deportation. Following the introduction of the 'Jewish star', more than thirteen thousand Jews were deported by the end of the year. First, two partial operations relocated six thousand people to Łódź and Minsk. Second, the authorities intensified the concentration of Jews in the cities and the first transports from Prague and Brno, with 7,365 Jews on board, made their way to the interim ghetto of Theresienstadt.

The main goal of anti-Jewish measures was now to separate the Jewish and non-Jewish population, above all in order to prevent non-Jews from developing a sense of solidarity with their Jewish fellows and to forestall resistance among the Jews themselves. Following Heydrich's arrival in the Protectorate in September, drumhead courts martial imposed hundreds of death sentences, many of them on Jews who had put up resistance and were accused of sabotage, treason and economic crimes.

While the Reich protector and the Central Office – against the backdrop of the mass deportations – attempted to centralize anti-Jewish policy in the hands of the German Security Police, Czech ministries and local authorities remained proactive players in the persecution of Jews. The Agriculture Ministry prohibited Jews from acquiring many foodstuffs, and municipal authorities banned them from various public institutions or restricted the times at which they could present themselves at various public offices, upon the recommendation of the Reich protector. The German influence had increased within the local political sphere as a result of the large-scale appointment of Germans as mayors, though they always relied on Czech officials and employees. In January 1942, following the arrest of Head of Government Eliáš, Germans also took up ministerial posts in the Czech government, now headed by former justice minister and Nazi sympathizer Jaroslav Krejčí.

The great mass of Jewish residents of the Protectorate were concentrated in the Theresienstadt Ghetto, a total of 73,608 individuals by 1945, many only to be deported from there to the East soon after. As early as the start of 1942, however, the Reich authorities had selected Theresienstadt as an 'old-age ghetto' for tens of thousands of German and Austrian Jews, which resulted in the increased transportation of Czech Jews to the annihilation camps. Theresienstadt was also a forced labour camp. The inmates' labour within and outside of the ghetto helped it finance itself, supplemented by the utilization of Jewish assets. Furniture, tools and office equipment in the ghetto came from the dissolved Jewish provincial Communities as well as from Jews' private property.

District by district, at the behest of the Central Office, Prague Jewish Community staff registered all Jewish residents in 1942 before the Gestapo transported thousands at a time to Theresienstadt. Regardless of the ongoing mass deportations, the Protectorate Labour Administration intensified forced labour in every district. Initially, as in the previous year, winter work predominated, soon to be replaced by coordinated group deployment in construction, industry, agriculture and forestry. The Czech Ministry for Social and Health Administration supervised two forms of forced labour: first, labour deployment in segregated work details for Jews at meagre rates of pay organized by the German labour offices and, second, the so-called group labour, demanded by the Central Office to relieve the welfare burden and regulated by the Jewish Labour Headquarters; the latter generally involved the deployment of Jews outside Prague in agriculture, forestry, construction and industry. In contrast to Germany and Austria, where Jewish forced labour reached its peak in the summer of 1941 prior to the resumption of the mass deportations, in the Protectorate it did not peak until May 1942, encompassing more than sixteen thousand people, most of them men. This was also reflected in the late legalization of forced labour and the adoption, in the summer of 1942, of the discriminatory labour regulations introduced in Germany in October 1941. Many Jews fell ill as a consequence of insufficient nutrition and dire working conditions. Because the mass transports depleted the workforce, the number of Jewish forced labourers now fell, while at the same time more women and those less suited to heavy labour were recruited.

An ever-growing number of Jews subject to forced labour required support from the Jewish welfare services, either because they received no pay or because their meagre wages failed to cover their or their families' needs. As a result, the burden on the Prague Jewish Community remained virtually unchanged despite the fact that thousands of Jews no longer received regular welfare payments because they had been deported. It was only when the 'clearing' of the districts of their Jewish residents gradually came to an end in the autumn, following the massive summer transports from Prague, that the amount of cash benefits paid out and the number of meals distributed by the Prague Jewish Community decreased dramatically. At the same time, however, the Community now had to do what it could to provision the tens of thousands of ghetto inmates in Theresienstadt.

The German authorities now focused on confiscating Jews' property, including mobile goods, as with the handing in, demanded only in the Protectorate, of musical instruments in December 1941 or the Reich-wide surrender of winter clothing in January 1942. In more than fifty depots, Jews working for the Property Utilization Office established by the Jewish Religious Community of Prague had to sort, repair and estimate the value of many thousands of objects, including those left behind by the deportees, prior to their sale. Following the assassination attempt on Heydrich in late May 1942 and the subsequent decision to deport the Jews rapidly and completely from the Greater German Reich, the central authorities made a final push to seize the remaining possessions of those families yet to be transported, forcing them to hand in electrical goods and all pets. Here for the first time I have shown that Jews had to surrender their dogs, cats and birds to animal welfare organizations. However, following this brutal invasion of Jews' family life, their animals were not killed but instead sold on to neighbours or other interested parties. Beginning in November 1942, a decree stipulated that every deported Jew with Protectorate citizenship would automatically lose his or her property.

By the end of 1942, outside the Theresienstadt Ghetto and concentration camps, only 15,550 Jews still lived in the Protectorate, 6,211 of them in 'mixed marriages', just 13 per cent of the original figure. By the spring of 1943, the Gestapo had completed the deportations from the districts of the Protectorate to Theresienstadt. Some victims tried to flee or put up resistance in other ways. Soon the only Jews left in the provinces were the *Vertrauensleute*, that is, the final representatives of the Jewish Communities, while in a small number of places there were still branch offices of the Prague Jewish Community, now renamed the Council of Elders. Following the completion of the mass transports from the Greater German Reich, in the summer of 1943 Reich Interior Minister Frick took over as Reich protector. Karl Hermann Frank became German minister of state in the Protectorate government, while the Prague Central Office was renamed the 'Central Bureau for the Regulation of the Jewish Question'.

While in Poland the SS had largely taken control of Jewish policy by 1942, it did so in the Protectorate only in 1943 and, when it came to forced labour, not until 1944. In contrast to Germany, where the labour offices retained their authority until the end of the war, the Prague Central Bureau now gained responsibility for forced labour in the Protectorate, tasking the Prague Council of Elders' Jewish Labour Headquarters with the practical organization of forced labour, with most of the Jews involved in 'mixed marriages'. In autumn 1944, able-bodied Jews had to move to Prague. In excess of 1,300 individuals lived in the newly established camp on Hagibor Square, where they had to split mica. Many men slaved away in labour camps outside Prague. Forced labour was now also extended to the 'Mischlinge and those married to Jews' newly registered in summer 1944, in other words a year later than in Germany, most of them in labour camps dedicated to the construction of SS training grounds. In parallel, couples in 'mixed marriages' were concentrated in homes in a single district of Prague; they were then deported to Theresienstadt in January or February 1945, as were Jews throughout the Greater German Reich.

Because of the general lack of interinstitutional conflict and the absence of central guidelines, in the Protectorate of Bohemia and Moravia the Czech government as well as the chief county commissioners, district offices and municipalities had considerable room for manoeuvre when it came to anti-Jewish policy until well into the war. This fact opened up to both German and Czech officials broad scope for individual engagement and thus also for personal responsibility. As in Germany and Austria, in the Protectorate too regional and local actors, who often implemented measures pre-empting German policy emanating from Berlin or Prague, were a major driving force of the persecutory process that historians have tended to underestimate. Up until 1941 – and in fact often later as well – they played a leading role in the formulation of anti-Jewish policy and thus moulded the victims' experience of persecution. This is clearly evident, among other things, in the prosecution of Czech ministers and other Czechs for so-called collaboration after the war.

A considerable proportion of anti-Jewish policy in the Protectorate, therefore, was developed locally in Prague and the Czech provinces. The vast majority of local forms of discrimination, which had a crucial impact on Jews' everyday lives, originated in municipal and regional administrations and less often in the Nazi Party or Gestapo. The different times at which municipal restrictions were introduced point to the generally substantial room for manoeuvre enjoyed by city administrations within the 'Greater German Reich'. While the ghettoization of Jewish residents in towns had already begun in the Warthegau and in the Protectorate by 1940, in Germany this process of concentration did not start until the summer of 1941 with the establishment of the labour and residential camps. By way of contrast, the first 'Jews' houses' had appeared in Dresden and Leipzig by the summer of 1939 but not until autumn 1940 in Prague and Brno.[5]

We can also discern autonomous developments in the Protectorate in the organization of other fields of persecution, which deviated from policies in Germany and/or Austria. As in Austria, a Central Office for Jewish Emigration controlled the Jewish Communities, but only in Prague did it establish a so-called Emigration Fund to rob the Jewish population. Rather than creating an institution similar to the Reich Association in Germany in the Protectorate, as initially planned, the authorities adopted the Vienna model for Prague in the spring of 1940, that is, the Jewish Community in the capital of the annexed territory was made responsible for all Communities and all their compulsory members, who were defined in racial terms. This also occurred because, following the discontinuation of the first deportations in autumn 1939, most actors expected the mass transports to quickly resume. For the same reason, in contrast to Germany, Austria and Poland but comparable to the Warthegau, the authorities initially saw it as unnecessary to introduce forced labour in the Protectorate, but then, in early 1941, decided to do so after all when the deportations were delayed.

Anti-Jewish policy in Bohemia and Moravia, therefore, was neither – as assumed previously – formulated solely in Berlin nor did it consist in the application of German laws. On the one hand, it was advanced by the Czech government and influenced by the German Protectorate authorities, while on the other it was dictated by specific temporal, persecutory and economic factors along with the political and social interests of the various authorities and officials involved. While there were often only fairly minor differences in the views of anti-Jewish policy among the key German actors, whether Reich Protector von Neurath, his State Secretary Frank, the chief county commissioners, the officials in the Office of the Reich Protector, the Security Police or the Central Office for Jewish Emigration, this is less true of the Czech side. President Hácha and General Eliáš, specific ministers and mayors and other municipal officials drove persecution forward more than other actors. Future studies might usefully delve into the background and individual motives of the Czechs involved, whether ministers or local officials. In general terms, it would be valuable to take a closer look at how such radical anti-Jewish policies managed to emerge in the territory with the lowest incidence of antisemitism in interwar Europe, policies that in many ways did not emanate from the occupying power or that preempted its plans. As in Germany, material gain, careers and loyalties no doubt constituted key motives for individuals in this regard.[6]

Historians need to break the habit of underestimating the significance of the Protectorate of Bohemia and Moravia to the Nazi state's anti-Jewish policies. This applies both to its independent radicalization as well as the influence of Protectorate measures on the overall development of the Nazi persecution of Jews. Certain initiatives emanating from the Protectorate encouraged decisions made at the centre of the German Reich, such as the Czech Finance Ministry's freezing of Jews' bank accounts in 1939 or the marking of Jews with an identificatory badge in 1941. The Protectorate thus took on an important intermediary role with respect to the persecution of Jews between Germany, Austria and the Sudeten area, the annexed Polish territories and the other occupied areas of Poland. The present study helps to clarify the importance of the periphery vis-à-vis the centre, in this case the role of regional policy in relation to decisions made centrally regarding the persecution of Europe's Jews.

The present work also contributes to other fundamental debates. It shows that Jewish forced labour should not be seen as a step on the way to annihilation, let alone as annihilation itself. In the Protectorate, forced labour was intensified regardless of the incipient mass deportations, a result of the economic and social interests prevailing at the time.

Finally, with the help of a comprehensive corpus of previously unnoticed sources, this study also documents the fact that individual Jewish resistance to persecution not only existed but occurred in a wide variety of forms. Often, this involved direct responses to the plethora of measures, implemented by the various local authorities, which made up the contradictory anti-Jewish policy in the Protectorate.[7]

How did the functionaries and staff of the Jewish Religious Communities respond to such an unpredictable anti-Jewish policy?

After the reopening of the Jewish Communities, which had been closed at the start of the occupation, their work and their leading officials, such as Emil Kafka, Franz Weidmann, Jakob Edelmann and Franz Friedmann, were strictly controlled by the Security Police and the rapidly established Central Office for Jewish Emigration. The representatives of the Prague Jewish Community searched frantically for emigration options. They advised thousands regarding emigration and new anti-Jewish measures issued by the broadest range of authorities both in the Protectorate and the Greater German Reich. Responsible for the entire Protectorate from March 1940 onwards, the biggest problem facing the Jewish Community was the extreme impoverishment of its compulsory members. In response to the increasing unemployment among the Jewish population and growing poverty, the Community expanded retraining opportunities both in the countryside and in the city, while augmenting welfare services by establishing new homes for the elderly and children. Jewish representatives sought to alleviate the Community's ever more troubling financial situation, caused by falling income and rising expenditure on emigration and welfare, through the 'Sacrifice – Construct – Live' fundraising campaign. They negotiated with towns and cities, labour offices, estate owners and businessmen in an attempt to procure employment for the large number of unemployed Jews. Despite the strict surveillance to which it was subject in all matters relating to emigration, finances, housing and labour deployment outside of Prague, the Prague Jewish Community did not allow Eichmann's Central Office to turn it into a mere organ of policy implementation. Representatives of the Prague Jewish Community and the provincial Jewish Communities intervened in countless attempts to help individual Jews in difficulty or the Jewish community as a whole, addressing their concerns to Czech and German agencies as well as the Central Office. Here they exploited the contradictions of anti-Jewish policy and played various organs of the Protectorate administration off against one another, sometimes successfully.

The present study has also documented that in many cases individual Jews put up resistance and protested, triggering a harsh response from police and courts: they refused to comply with local and central regulations in many places, ignored restrictions on shopping hours and the centrally ordained curfew, evaded restrictions on foodstuffs and traded in forbidden goods. They politicized against the Germans, fraternized with non-Jewish Czechs, refused to wear the star and absconded from forced labour sites or fled prior to deportation. Some helped other Jews to flee, while others participated in the Czech resistance. While hundreds of Jews were punished for their opposition with fines and prison sentences or were sent to concentration camps, many paid for their resistance with their lives. This study thus shows that Jews by no means – as is often wrongly assumed – merely suffered persecution passively. On the contrary, it portrays Jews, whether as individuals or as representatives of their communities, as active agents in the face of extreme repression.

Notes

1. Hahn, 'Verdrängung und Verharmlosung', 136.
2. Kárný, 'Die tschechischen Opfer', 152–53.
3. Quoted in Celovsky, *Germanisierung und Genozid*, 208.
4. For the view of the Central Office as the key decision-making body, see Schmidt-Hartmann, 'Tschechoslowakei', 359, and Anderl, 'Zentralstellen', 279.
5. On Germany, see Gruner, 'NS-Judenverfolgung und Kommunen', 117–19.
6. For a discussion in light of the example of the municipal officials with responsibility for welfare, see Gruner, *Öffentliche Wohlfahrt*, 325–27.
7. A point recently highlighted by Veselská, '"Sie müssen sich als Jude dessen bewusst sein, welche Opfer zu tragen sind ..."', 156–57.

Appendix

Table A.1. Report by the Jewish Religious Community of Prague: 'The Jews in the Protectorate of Bohemia and Moravia, 15 March 1939 to 15 June 1942'.

Overall Development

The overall development of the Jewish population in the Protectorate of Bohemia and Moravia is characterized by constant decline. The following table provides an overview of the extent of this decline in the periods specified below:

	Jewish population	% of the figure as at 15 March 1939
15 March 1939	118,310	100.00%
31 July 1939	108,898	92.94%
30 September 1939	103,878	87.80%
31 December 1939	97,961	83.70%
31 March 1940	94,741	80.08%
30 June 1940	91,995	77.76%
30 September 1940	90,681	76.65%
31 December 1940	90,041	76.11%
31 March 1941	89,338	75.51%
30 June 1941	88,686	75.37%
30 September 1941	88,105	74.96%
30 December 1941	74,190	62.71%
31 March 1942	61,320	51.83%
15 June 1942	48,273	40.80%

It is thus evident that in the period from 15 March 1939 to 15 June 1942 the number of Jews in the territory of the Protectorate of Bohemia and Moravia decreased by 59.20 per cent from 118,310 to 48,273.

The total decrease for the period from 15 March 1939 to 15 June 1942 breaks down as follows:

1	Emigration	25,860
2	Flight	7,000
3	Admission to the ghetto	31,153
4	Due to natural change	6,024
	Total decrease in the period from 15 March 1939 to 15 June 1942	70,037

Source: Krejčová, Svobodová and Hyndráková, Židé v Protektorátu, doc. 2, 51.

Table A.2. Jewish emigration from the Protectorate of Bohemia and Moravia, 15 March 1939–1 March 1941.

Destination area	Age				Total number
	<18	18–45	45–60	>60	
North America	246	799	269	111	1,425
South America	922	3,163	489	79	4,653
Central America	68	445	75	14	602
Africa	20	111	29	5	165
Asia excluding Palestine	530	2,620	788	90	4,028
Europe	2,317	7,466	1,823	602	12,208
Australia	16	114	33	13	176
Palestine	799	885	362	71	2,117
Total					25,374

Source: YV Jerusalem, O 7/57, fol. 293: Report by the Jewish Religious Community and the Prague Palestine Office on their activities in the first quarter of 1941, 9.

Table A.3. Support for impoverished Jews provided by the Religious Community, 1939–42.

Jewish religious community of Prague	Noninstitutional welfare services	Soup Kitchen		
	Number of needy individuals in receipt of support	Lunch	Supper	Breakfast
1939				
End July	3,564	4,214		
Start August	3,869	3,305		
Mid August	2,989	4,749		
19 August	3,305	5,178		
End August	3,926	5,281		
First week of September	4,303	6,560		
First week of October	5,536	8,468		
First week of December	5,705	10,970		
1940				
First week of January	5,567	9,422		
Second week of January	6,158	9,370	726	
Third week of January	6,765	9,957	2,467	
End January	7,139	10,004	3,665	
First week of April	7,204	9,882	4,765	
Start May	7,243	10,323	5,264	
Start June	7,353	9,595	5,670	
First week of July	7,317	12,257	7,757	
Start September	6,540	12,238	9,470	
1941				
First week of January		7,301	5,690	
Start April	6,927			
End April	6,809			

(*continued*)

Table A.3. Continued.

Jewish religious community of Prague	Noninstitutional welfare services	Soup Kitchen		
	Number of needy individuals in receipt of support	Lunch	Supper	Breakfast
Start June		7,882	5,989	
Second week of August		7,418	5,110	629
1942				
First week of January		4,113	2,418	277

Sources: YV Jerusalem, O 7/53, fol. 2: Weekly report by the Jewish Religious Community of Prague, 23–29 July 1939, 1; ibid., fol. 4: Weekly report by the Jewish Religious Community of Prague, 30 July to 5 August 1939, 1; ibid., fol. 6: Weekly report by the Jewish Religious Community of Prague, 6–12 August 1939, 1; ibid., fol. 10: Weekly report by the Jewish Religious Community of Prague, 13–19 August 1939, 1; ibid., fol. 13: Weekly report by the Jewish Religious Community of Prague, 20–25 August 1939, 2; ibid., fol. 29: Weekly report by the Jewish Religious Community of Prague, 2–8 September 1939, 2; ibid., fol. 184–85: Monthly report by the Jewish Religious Community of Prague, 1–30 November 1939, 2–3; YV Jerusalem, O 7/54, fol. 5: Weekly report by the Jewish Religious Community of Prague, 1–6 January 1940, 4; ibid., fol. 17: Weekly report by the Jewish Religious Community of Prague, 7–12 January 1940, 4; ibid., fol. 31: Weekly report by the Jewish Religious Community of Prague, 13–19 January 1940, 5; ibid., fol. 56: Weekly report by the Jewish Religious Community of Prague, 27 January to 2 February 1940, 5; ibid., fol. 5: Weekly report by the Jewish Religious Community of Prague, 1–6 January 1940, 4; ibid., fol. 17: Weekly report by the Jewish Religious Community of Prague, 7–12 January 1940, 4; ibid., fol. 31: Weekly report by the Jewish Religious Community of Prague, 13–19 January 1940, 5; ibid., fol. 56: Weekly report by the Jewish Religious Community of Prague, 27 January to 2 February 1940, 5; ibid., fol. 174: Weekly report by the Jewish Religious Community of Prague, 23–29 March 1940, 5: YV Jerusalem, O 7/53, fol. 89: Weekly report by the Jewish Religious Community of Prague, 28 October to 2 November 1939, 2; YV Jerusalem, O 7/55, fol. 45: Weekly report by the Jewish Religious Community of Prague, 4–10 May 1940, 3; ibid., fol. 7: Weekly report by the Jewish Religious Community of Prague, 30 March to 5 April 1940, 7; ibid., fol. 45: Weekly report by the Jewish Religious Community of Prague, 4–10 May 1940, 3; ibid., fol. 77: Weekly report by the Jewish Religious Community of Prague, 29 June to 5 July 1940, 3; ibid., fol. 131: Weekly report by the Jewish Religious Community of Prague, 31 August to 6 September 1940, 3; YV Jerusalem, O 7/58, ibid., fol. 7: Weekly report by the Jewish Religious Community and the Prague Palestine Office on their activities, 27 December 1940 to 3 January 1941, 5; YV Jerusalem, O 7/58, fol. 184: Monthly report by the Jewish Religious Community of Prague, 1–30 April 1941, 6; ibid., fol. 229: Report by the Jewish Religious Community of Prague on its activities in the first half of 1941, submitted to the Central Office for Jewish Emigration, Prague, chart; ibid., O 7/60, fol. 13–14: Weekly report by the Jewish Religious Community of Prague, 3–9 January 1942, 3–4.

Table A.4. Forced labour deployment of Jews in the Protectorate.

	Total number of Jews	Forced labour organized by labour offices			Group deployment organized by Jewish Labour Headquarters					
		Men	Women	Total	Agriculture	Forestry	Individual employment agriculture	Linden camp	City of Prague	Provinces
30 September 1941	88,105			11,700						
31 October 1941		11,949	307	12,256						
31 December 1941	74,190	12,071	959	13,030	429	250	326	298		
31 January 1942					288	347	305			
28 February 1942		13,567	754	14,321						
31 March 1942	61,320	13,854	595	14,449	288	571	202		1,078	375
30 April 1942		14,809	938	15,747		1,229		303		2,120
31 May 1942	48,273	c. 15,000	c. 1,000	c. 16,000		1,600		300	942	2,371
10 July 1942					884	575	123	302	940	2,367
31 August 1942		6,687	2,261	8,948	758	459	0	292	606	2,416
24 September 1942					718	374		291	596	2,368
30 October 1942		5,978	1,334	7,312	712	370		280	598	2,146
30 November 1942					606	381		279	617	2,161

(continued)

Table A.4. Continued.

Sources: CAHJP Jerusalem, A/W no. 421, n.p.: Report on the 'Deployment of Jewish Workers', n.d., 3. Cf. *Deutsche Politik im 'Protektorat Böhmen und Mähren'*, 123, doc. no. 23: Report by the Central Office, 2 October 1941; and ibid., 127, appendix: Plate 2; USHMM Washington, RG 48.005M, reel 2 (Prague State Archive), II-4-4055, carton 859, no. 1, n.p.: Labour deployment statistics, as at 1 September 1941; ibid., no. 22, n.p.: Statistics on the labour deployment of Jews in the Protectorate, October 1941 (n.d.); ibid., no. 64, n.p.: Statistics on the labour deployment of Jews in the Protectorate, December 1941 (n.d.); ibid., no. 108, n.p.: Statistics on the labour deployment of Jews in the Protectorate, February 1942 (n.d.); ibid., no. 129, n.p.: Statistics on the labour deployment of Jews, March 1942; ibid., no. 150, n.p.: Statistics on the labour deployment of Jews in the Protectorate, April 1942 (n.d.). Data for May partially illegible: ibid., no. 171, n.p.: Statistics on the labour deployment of Jews in the Protectorate, May 1942 (n.d.); YV Jerusalem, O 7/60, fol. 3–4: Weekly report by the Jewish Religious Community of Prague, 27 December 1941 to 2 January 1942, 2–3; ibid., fol. 47: Weekly report by the Jewish Religious Community of Prague, 24–30 January 1942, 4; YV Jerusalem, O 7/61, fol. 24–25: Weekly report by the Jewish Religious Community of Prague, 11–17 April 1942, 2–3; ibid., fol. 37: Weekly report by the Jewish Religious Community of Prague, 18–24 April 1942, 3; ibid., fol. 48–49: Weekly report by the Jewish Religious Community of Prague, 25 April to 1 May 1942, 2–3; ibid., fol. 93: Weekly report by the Jewish Religious Community of Prague, 23–29 May 1942, 3; ibid., fol. 102–3: Weekly report by the Jewish Religious Community of Prague, 30 May to 5 June 1942, 2–3; YV Jerusalem, O 7/62, fol. 13–15: Weekly report by the Jewish Religious Community of Prague, 4–10 July 1942, 1–3; ibid., fol. 320–21: Monthly report by the Jewish Religious Community of Prague, 1–31 August 1942, 2–3; ibid., fol. 100: Weekly report by the Jewish Religious Community of Prague, 29 August to 4 September 1942, 3; ibid., fol. 132–33: Weekly report by the Jewish Religious Community of Prague, 15–24 September 1942, 2–3; cf. ibid., fol. 332: Monthly report by the Jewish Religious Community of Prague, 1–30 September 1942, 3; ibid., fol. 191–92: Weekly report by the Jewish Religious Community of Prague, 24–30 October 1942, 2–3; ibid., fol. 344: Monthly report by the Jewish Religious Community of Prague, 1–31 October 1942, 4; ibid., fol. 204: Weekly report by the Jewish Religious Community of Prague, 31 October to 6 November 1942, 3; ibid., fol. 353: Monthly report by the Jewish Religious Community of Prague, 1–30 November 1942, 3.

Table A.5. Report by the Jewish Community of Prague on the transports of Jews in the Protectorate of Bohemia and Moravia in 1941–42.

No	Designation	From	Report on	Departure	Figure	Total
1	A	Prague	13 October 1941	16 October 1941	1,000	1,000
2	B	Prague	18 October 1941	21 October 1941	1,000	2,000
3	C	Prague	23 October 1941	26 October 1941	1,000	3,000
4	D	Prague	28 October 1941	31 October 1941	1,000	4,000
5	E	Prague	31 October 1941	3 November 1941	1,000	5,000
6	F	Brno	13 November 1941	16 November 1941	1,000	6,000
7	AK 1	Prague		24 November 1941	365	6,365
8	G	Prague	27 November 1941	30 November 1941	1,000	7,365
9	H	Brno	29 November 1941	2 December 1941	1,000	8,365
10	J	Prague	1 December 1941	4 December 1941	1,000	9,365
11	K	Brno	2 December 1941	5 December 1941	1,000	10,365
12	L	Prague	7 December 1941	10 December 1941	1,000	11,365
13	M	Prague	11 December 1941	14 December 1941	1,000	12,365
14	N	Prague	17 December 1941	17 December 1941	1,000	13,365
15	R/P1	Pilsen	13 January 1942	17 January 1942	1,000	14,365
16	S/P2	Pilsen	18 January 1942	21 January 1942	1,000	15,365
17	T/P3	Pilsen	22 January 1942	25 January 1942	604	15,969
18	U	Brno	25 January 1942	28 January 1942	1,000	16,969
19	V	Prague	27 January 1942	30 January 1942	1,000	17,969
20	W	Prague	5 February 1942	8 February 1942	1,000	18,969
21	X	Prague	9 February 1942	12 February 1942	1,000	19,969
22	Y/K1	Kladno	18 February 1942	22 February 1942	800	20,769

(*continued*)

Table A.5. Continued.

No	Designation	From	Report on	Departure	Figure	Total
23	Z/K2	Kladno	23 February 1942	26 February 1942	823	21,592
	Aa					
	Ab					
24	Ac	Brno	16 March 1942	19 March 1942	1,000	22,592
25	Ad	Brno	20 March 1942	22 March 1942	1,000	23,592
26	Ae	Brno	24 March 1942	29 March 1942	1,000	24,592
27	Af	Brno	28 March 1942	31 March 1942	1,000	25,592
	Ag					
28	Ah	Brno	1 April 1942	4 April 1942	1,000	26,592
29	Ai	Brno	5 April 1942	8 April 1942	923	27,515
30	Ak	České Budějovice	14 April 1942	18 April 1942	909	28,424
	Al					
31	Am	Prague	21 April 1942	24 April 1942	1,000	29,424
	An					
32	Ao	Prague	25 April 1942	28 April 1942	1,000	30,424
	Ap					
	Ar					
	As					
33	At	Prague	4 May 1942	7 May 1942	1,000	31,424
34	Au	Prague	9 May 1942	12 May 1942	1,000	32,424
35	Au 1	Prague	12 May 1942	15 May 1942	1,000	33,424
36	Av	Třebíč	14 May 1942	18 May 1942	720	34,144
37	Aw	Třebíč	19 May 1942	22 May 1942	650	34,794
	Ax					
	Ay					
	Az					

38	AAa	Brno	26 May 1942	81	34,875
39	AAb	Kolín	1 June 1942	744	35,619
40	AAc	Kolín	6 June 1942	724	36,343
41	AAh	Prague	7 June 1942	1,000	37,343
42	Aad	Kolín	10 June 1942	734	38,077
43	AAe	Prague	15 June 1942	1,000	39,077
Special transports until			20 June 1942	83	39,160

Source: Report by the Jewish Community of Prague, 'Record of Jews, Registration, Transports' (1942), in Krejčová, Svobodová and Hyndráková, *Židé v Protektorátu*, doc. 10, 172–75.

Table A.6. Report by the Council of Elders of the Jews, Prague, on the transports of Jews in the Protectorate of Bohemia and Moravia in 1942.

Designation	from	Report on	Departure on	Figure	Total
Aaf	Olomouc	23 June 1942	26 June 1942	900	40,060
Aag	Olomouc	27 June 1942	30 June 1942	900	40,960
Aah	Prague	7 June 1942	10 June 1942	1,000	41,960
Aai					
Aak					
Aal	Prague	26 June 1942	2 July 1942	1,000	42,960
Aam	Olomouc	1 July 1942	4 July 1942	900	43,860
Aan	Prague	3 July 1942	6 July 1942	1,000	44,860
Aao	Olomouc	5 July 1942	8 July 1942	745	45,605
Aap	Prague	6 July 1942	9 July 1942	1,000	46,605
AAqu	Prague	10 July 1942	13 July 1942	1,000	47,605
Aar	Prague	13 July 1942	16 July 1942	1,000	48,605
Aas	Prague	17 July 1942	20 July 1942	1,000	49,605
Aat	Prague	20 July 1942	23 July 1942	1,000	50,605
Aau	Prague	24 July 1942	27 July 1942	1,000	51,605
Aav	Prague	27 July 1942	30 July 1942	1,000	52,605
Aaw	Prague	31 July 1942	3 August 1942	1,000	53,605
Aax					
Aay					
Aaz					
Ba	Prague	7 August 1942	10 August 1942	1,460	55,065
Bb					
Bc					
Bd	Prague	1 September 1942	4 September 1942	1,000	56,065
Be					

Bf	Prague	5 September 1942	8 September 1942	1,000	57,065
Bg	Prague	9 September 1942	12 September 1942	1,000	58,065
JB	Prague		14 September 1942	51	58,116
Bh	Moravian Ostrava	15 September 1942	18 September 1942	860	58,976
Bi	Moravian Ostrava	19 September 1942	22 September 1942	860	59,836
Bk					
Bi	Moravian Ostrava	23 September 1942	26 September 1942	860	60,696
Bm	Moravian Ostrava	27 September 1942	30 September 1942	862	61,558
Bn					
Bo					
Bp					
Bqu					
Br					
Bs					
Bt					
Bu					
Bv					
Bw					
Bx					
By					
JB II	Prague		17 October 1942	10	61,568
Bz	Tábor	9 November 1942	12 November 1942	650	62,218
Ca	Prague	21 October 1942	24 October 1942	1,000	63,218
Cb	Tábor	13 November 1942	16 November 1942	617	63,835
Cc	Prague	17 November 1942	20 November 1942	1,000	64,835
Cd	Klatovy	23 November 1942	26 November 1942	650	65,485
JBIII	Prague		26 November 1942	3	65,488
Ce	Klatovy	27 November 1942	30 November 1942	619	66,107

(*continued*)

Table A.6. Continued.

Designation	From	Report on	Departure on	Figure	Total
Cf	Pardubice	2 December 1942	5 December 1942	650	66,757
Cg	Pardubice	6 December 1942	9 December 1942	606	67,363
Ch	Hradec Králové	14 December 1942	17 December 1942	650	68,013
Ci	Hradec Králové	18 December 1942	21 December 1942	548	68,561
Ck	Prague	19 December 1942	22 December 1942	1,000	69,561
Cl	Mladá Boleslav	10 January 1943	13 January 1943	550	70,111
Cm	Mladá Boleslav	13 January 1943	16 January 1943	491	70,602
Cn	Uherský Brod	19 January 1943	22 January 1943	1,000	71,602
Co	Uherský Brod	23 January 1943	26 January 1943	1,000	72,602
Cp	Uherský Brod	27 January 1943	30 January 1943	837	73,439
Cqu					
Cr					
Cs					
Ct					
Cu					
Cv	Prague	3 March 1943	6 March 1943	1,021	74,460
Cv 2	Prague		8 March 1943	13	74,473
Cw	Prague	8 March 1943	9 March 1943	84	74,557
Cx	Prague	20 March 1943	22 March 1943	51	74,608
Special transports until			24 March 1943	137	74,745

Source: Report by the Council of Elders of the Jews, Prague, 'Development and Activities' (April 1943), in Krejčová, Svobodová and Hyndráková, *Židé v Protektorátu*, doc. 20, 364–66.

BIBLIOGRAPHY

Unprinted Sources

Bundesarchiv (BA) Berlin
- R 30 Reichsprotektor in Böhmen und Mähren
- R 43II Reichskanzlei
- R 58 Reichssicherheitshauptamt
- R 70 Böhmen und Mähren
- R 8150 Reichsvereinigung
- NS 19 Persönlicher Stab Reichsführer-SS
- NS 25 NSDAP Reichsleitung, Hauptamt für Kommunalpolitik

Central Archives for the History of the Jewish People (CAHJP) Jerusalem
- A/W Archiv der Israelitischen Kultusgemeinde Wien

Central Zionist Archives (CZA) Jerusalem
- S 26 Rescue Committee

Landesarchiv (LA) Berlin
- A Rep. 355 Sondergericht Berlin

Leo Baeck Institute Archives (LBI/A) New York
- Memoir Coll.

Los Angeles Museum of the Holocaust/Archive (LAMOTH/A)
- RG-23 Atrocities and Perpetration, Collection of Photo documents
- RG-66 Bundesarchiv, Collection of Photo documents
- RG-72 Ed Victor Papers

Národní Archiv (NA) Prague
- Úřad říšského protektora

Österreichisches Staatsarchiv-Archiv der Republik (ÖStA/AdR) Wien
- Bürckel-Materie

Rossiiskii gosudarstvennyi voennyi arkhiv (Russian State Military Archive or RGVA), Moscow
- Fonds 500 Reichssicherheitshauptamt
- Fonds 1488 Büro des Reichsprotektors in Böhmen und Mähren, Prague

Sächsisches Hauptstaatsarchiv (S-HStA) Dresden
- Nachrichtenstelle der Staatskanzlei-Zeitungsausschnittssammlung

Staatsarchiv (StA) Chemnitz
- 30071 Zuchthaus Zwickau

Staatsarchiv (StA) Freiburg im Breisgau
- Mühlheim County Commissioner's Office (Landratsamt)

Státní Zidovské Museum Prague
- DP Persecution Documents

University of Southern California Shoah Foundation/Visual History Archive (USC SF/ VHA) Los Angeles
- Video Interview Curt Allina
- Video Interview Yehudah Bakon
- Video Interview Hana Beer
- Video Interview Hilda Beran
- Video Interview Mimi Berger
- Video Interview Helen Blenkins
- Video Interview Martin Brauner
- Video Interview Paul Brichta
- Video Interview Alfred Dube
- Video Interview Oskar Felcer
- Video Interview Anna Grant
- Video Interview Martin Hilsenrath
- Video Interview Georgine Hyde
- Video Interview Fred Klein
- Video Interview Katherine Kral
- Video Interview Ervin Krumholz
- Video Interview Margaret Lukas
- Video Interview Anny Maass
- Video Interview Gertrude Pfeiffer
- Video Interview Zuzana Podmelova
- Video Interview Alexander Singer
- Video Interview Eva Rozvoda Wölfler

US Holocaust Memorial Museum (USHMM) Washington, DC
- RG 11.001M OSOBI Moscow
- RG 48.005M Selected Records from the Czech State Archives
- RG 48.008M Uřad říšského protektora (Central State Archives in Prague)

Vojenský Historický Archiv (VHA) Prague
- Fonds SS-Panzergrenadier Ausbildungs- und Ersatzbattaillon 10
- Fonds Führer SS Totenkopfstandarten und Konzentrationslager
- Fonds 117 Concentration Camps
- Fonds 140 J. Kopecky Papers

Yad Vashem (YV) Jerusalem
Archive
- O 3 Yad Vashem Collection of Testimonies
- O 7 Czechoslovakia Collection
- O 30 Austria Collection
- O 51 Nazi Documentation
- M 58 Archives in the Czech Republic

Photo Archive

Contemporary Newspapers and Periodicals

Berliner Börsen-Zeitung 1941
Brünner Tagesbote 1939–42
CV-Zeitung 1938
Das Volk. Tageszeitung der Sozialdemokratischen Partei Deutschlands 1945
Der Neue Tag. Tageszeitung für Böhmen und Mähren 1941
Der Tagesspiegel 1945–46
Deutsches Nachrichtenbüro (news service) 1938–40
Egerer Zeitung 1938
Jüdisches Nachrichtenblatt, Berlin 1942
Leitmeritzer Zeitung 1938
Marienbader Zeitung 1938
Reichsgesetzblatt (RGBl.) 1939–43
The Jewish Chronicle 1938
The Jewish Telegraphic Agency 1939–43
The Los Angeles Times 1940
The Manchester Guardian 1939–43
The New York Times 1939–41
The Washington Post 1939–41
Verordnungsblatt für Böhmen und Mähren/Verordnungsblatt des Reichsprotektors in Böhmen und Mähren 1939–1942

Primary Sources

Adler, H.G. (ed.). *Die verheimlichte Wahrheit: Theresienstädter Dokumente.* Tübingen, 1958.
Alexander, Manfred. *Deutsche Gesandtschaftsberichte aus Prag. Innenpolitik und Minderheitenprobleme in der Ersten Tschechoslowakischen Republik. Teil III: Von der Regierung unter Svehla bis zum Vorabend der nationalsozialistischen Machtergreifung in Deutschland 1926–1932.* Munich, 2009.
Beneš, Vojta, and R.A. Ginsburg. *10 Million Prisoners (Protectorate Bohemia and Moravia).* Chicago, 1940.
Čapek, Emanuel. 'Racial and Social Aspects of the Czechoslovak Census'. *The Slavonic and East European Review* 12(36) (1934), 596–610.
Čechoslovakische Statistik, vol. 9, series VI (Census 1). Part I: Census in the Czechoslovak Republic of 15 February 1921. Prague, 1924.
Čechoslovakische Statistik, vol. 98, series VI (Census 7). Part I: Census in the Czechoslovak Republic of 1 December 1930. Prague, 1934.
Celovsky, Boris. *Germanisierung und Genozid: Hitlers Endlösung der tschechischen Frage. Deutsche Dokumente 1933–1945.* Dresden, 2005.
Das Protektorat Böhmen und Mähren im deutschen Wirtschaftsraum: Überreicht von der Deutschen Bank. Berlin, 1939.
Die Tagebücher von Joseph Goebbels. Part II: *Diktate 1941–1945.* Edited by Elke Fröhlich on behalf of the Institut für Zeitgeschichte and with the support of the Russian State Archive. 15 vols. Munich, 1993–96.
Dennler, Wilhelm. *Sozialpolitik im Protektorat Böhmen und Mähren.* Berlin, 1940.
Dennler, Wilhelm. *Die Böhmische Passion.* Freiburg im Breisgau, 1953.
Deutsche Politik im 'Protektorat Böhmen und Mähren' unter Reinhard Heydrich 1941–1942: Eine Dokumentation. Edited by Miroslav Kárný, Jaroslava Milotová and Margita Kárná. Berlin, 1997.

Deutschland-Berichte der Sozialdemokratischen Partei Deutschlands (Sopade) 1934–1940. Edited by Klaus Behnken. Salzhausen, 1989.
Dolezel, Heidrun, and Stephan Dolezel (eds). *Vom Vorabend der Machtergreifung in Deutschland bis zum Rücktritt von Präsident Masaryk 1933–1935: Berichte des Gesandten Koch, der Konsuln von Bethusy-Huc, von Druffel, von Pfeil und des Gesandtschaftsrates von Stein. Deutsche Gesandtschaftsberichte aus Prag.* Part 4. Munich, 1991.
Domarus, Max (ed.). *Hitler: Reden und Proklamationen 1932–1945.* Vol. I, 2nd half-volume 1935–38. Munich, 1965.
Domarus, Max (ed.). *Hitler: Reden und Proklamationen 1932–1945.* Vol. II, 1st half-volume 1939–40. Munich, 1965.
Erdely, Eugen V. *Germany's First European Protectorate: The Fate of the Czechs and Slovaks.* London, 1942.
Europa unterm Hakenkreuz: Die faschistische Okkupationspolitik in Polen (1939–1945). Document selection and introduction by Werner Röhr. With the assistance of Elke Heckert et al. Berlin (East), 1989.
Europa unterm Hakenkreuz: Die faschistische Okkupationspolitik in Österreich und der Tschechoslowakei (1938–1945). Document selection and introduction by Helma Kaden. With the assistance of Ludwig Nestler et al. Berlin (East), 1988.
Fantlová, Zdenka. *My Lucky Star.* New York, 2001.
Felix, Ruth. *Diese Hölle überlebt: Ein jüdisches Familienschicksal aus Mähren 1924–1994. Mit einer Dokumentation.* Edited by Erhard Roy Wiehn. Konstanz, 1995.
Garbarini, Alexandra et al. (eds). *Jewish Responses to Persecution: Vol. II 1938–1940.* Lanham, MD, 2011.
Gedye, George E.R. *Fallen Bastions: The Central European Tragedy.* 7th edition. London, 1940.
Ginz, Petr. *The Diary of Petr Ginz 1941–1942.* Edited by Chava Pressburger, translated from the Czech by Elenea Lappin. New York, 2007.
Hartmann, Georg. 'Die Judenfrage in der Tschechoslowakei'. *Volk und Reich. Politische Monatshefte,* ed. Friedrich Heiß, 14(3) (1938), 180–98.
Henlein, Konrad. 'The German Minority in Czechoslovakia'. *International Affairs* 15(4) (1936), 561–72.
Institute of Jewish Affairs (ed.). *Hitler's Ten-Year War on the Jews.* New York, 1943.
Jacoby, Gerhard. *Racial State: The German Nationalities Policy in the Protectorate of Bohemia and Moravia.* New York, 1944.
The Jewish Black Book Committee (ed.). *The Black Book: The Nazi Crime against the Jewish People.* New York, 1946.
Kárný, Miroslav, and Jaroslava Milotová (eds). *Anatomie okupační politiky hitlerovského Německa v 'Protektorátu Čechy a Morava': Dokumenty z období říšského protektora Konstantina von Neuratha.* Prague, 1987.
Kárný, Miroslav, and Jaroslava Milotová (eds). *Protektorátní politika Reinharda Heydricha.* Prague, 1991.
Kessler, Erich. 'Ein Theresienstädter Tagebuch: Der Theresienstädter 20. April 1945 und die Tage danach ...'. *Theresienstädter Studien und Dokumente* 1995, 306–24.
Krejčová, Helena, Jana Svobodová, and Anna Hyndráková (eds). *Židé v Protektorátu: Hlášení Židovské náboženské obce v roce 1942. Dokumenty.* Prague, 1997.
Kulka, Otto Dov, and Eberhard Jäckel (eds). *The Jews in the Secret Nazi Reports on Popular Opinion in Germany, 1933–1945.* New Haven, CT, 2010 (German original 2004).
Lemkin, Raphael. *Axis Rule in Occupied Europe: Laws of Occupation, Analysis of Government, Proposals for Redress* (reprint of original 1944). Clark, NJ, 2008.

Letters from Prague 1939–1941. Compiled by Raya Czerner Shapiro and Helga Czerner Weinberg. Chicago, 1991.
Longerich, Peter (ed.). *Die Ermordung der europäischen Juden: Eine umfassende Dokumentation des Holocaust 1941–1945*. Munich, 1989.
Mannheimer, Max. *Spätes Tagebuch. Theresienstadt – Auschwitz. Warschau – Dachau*. Munich, 2009.
Meldungen aus dem Reich 1938–1945: Die geheimen Lageberichte des Sicherheitsdienstes der SS. Edited and with an introduction by Heinz Boberach. 17 vols. Herrsching, 1984.
Moskowitz, Moses. 'The Jewish Situation in the Protectorate of Bohemia and Moravia'. *Jewish Social Studies* 4(1) (January 1942), 17–44.
Moskowitz, Moses. 'Three Years of the Protectorate of Bohemia and Moravia'. *Political Science Quarterly* 57(3) (September 1942), 353–75.
Mund, Gerald (ed.). *Deutschland und das Protektorat Böhmen und Mähren: Aus den deutschen diplomatischen Akten von 1939 bis 1945*. Göttingen, 2014.
Osud Židů v protektorátu 1939–1945. Edited by Milena Janišová. Prague, 1991.
Pätzold, Kurt (ed.). *Verfolgung, Vertreibung, Vernichtung: Dokumente des faschistischen Antisemitismus 1933–1942*. Leipzig, 1983.
Pätzold, Kurt, and Erika Schwarz. *Tagesordnung: Judenmord. Die Wannseekonferenz am 20. Januar 1942. Eine Dokumentation zur Organisation der 'Endlösung'*. Berlin, 1992.
Sauer, Paul (ed.). *Dokumente über die Verfolgung der jüdischen Bürger in Baden-Württemberg durch das nationalsozialistische Regime 1933–1943*. Stuttgart, 1966.
Seton-Watson, Robert William. 'The German Minority in Czechoslovakia'. *Foreign Affairs* 16(4) (1938), 651–66.
Shirer, William L. *Berlin Diary: The Journal of a Foreign Correspondent 1934–1941*. London, 1942.
Sobota, Emil. 'Czechs and Germans: A Czech View'. *The Slavonic Review* 14(41) (1936), 301–20.
Šustek, Vojtěch. *Josef Pfitzner a protektorátní Praha v letech 1939–45*. Vol. 2. Prague, 2001.
Die Tagebücher von Joseph Goebbels. Part I: Aufzeichnungen 1923–1941. Edited by Elke Fröhlich. 9 vols. Munich, 1998–2006.
Tartakower, Arieh, and Kurt R. Grossmann. *The Jewish Refugee*. New York, 1944.
Terezín Memorial Book: A Guide to the Czech Original. Prague, 1996.
Theresienstädter Gedenkbuch: Die Opfer der Judentransporte aus Deutschland nach Theresienstadt 1942–1945. Edited by Institut Theresienstädter Initiative. Prague, 2000.
Utermöhle, Walther, and Herbert Schmerling. *Die Rechtsstellung der Juden im Protektorat Böhmen und Mähren*. (n.p.), 1940.
Die Verfolgung und Ermordung der europäischen Juden durch das nationalsozialistische Deutschland 1933–1945 [VEJ]. Vol. 2: *Deutsches Reich, 1938–August 1939*. Edited by Susanne Heim. Munich, 2009.
Die Verfolgung und Ermordung der europäischen Juden durch das nationalsozialistische Deutschland 1933–1945 [VEJ]. Vol. 3: *Deutsches Reich und Protektorat, September 1939–September 1941*. Edited by Andrea Löw. Munich, 2012.
Widerstand und Verfolgung in Wien 1934–1945. Vol. 3: *1938–1945*. Edited by Dokumentationsarchiv des österreichischen Widerstandes. 2nd edition. Vienna, 1984.
Wildt, Michael (ed.). *Die Judenpolitik des SD 1935–1938: Eine Dokumentation*. Munich, 1995.

Wiskemann, Elizabeth. 'Czechs and Germans after Munich'. *Foreign Affairs* 17(2) (1939), 291–304.

Secondary Literature

Adam, Alfons. 'Im Wettstreit um die letzten Arbeitskräfte: Die Zwangsarbeit auf dem Gebiet der Tschechischen Republik 1938–1945', in Dieter Pohl and Tanja Sebta (eds), *Zwangsarbeit in Hitlers Europa: Besatzung – Arbeit – Folgen* (Berlin, 2013), 105–28.

Adam, Uwe-Dietrich. *Judenpolitik im Dritten Reich*. Düsseldorf, 1972.

Adler, H.G. *Theresienstadt 1941–1945. Das Antlitz einer Zwangsgemeinschaft: Geschichte, Soziologie, Psychologie*. Tübingen, 1955.

Adler, H.G. *Der verwaltete Mensch: Studien zur Deportation der Juden aus Deutschland*. Tübingen, 1974.

Aly, Götz. *'Final Solution': Nazi Population Policy and the Murder of the European Jews*. London, 1999 (German original 1995).

Aly, Götz. *Hitlers Volksstaat: Raub, Rassenkrieg und nationaler Sozialismus*. Frankfurt a. M., 2005.

Anderl, Gabriele. 'Die "Zentralstellen für jüdische Auswanderung" in Wien, Berlin und Prag – ein Vergleich'. *Tel Aviver Jahrbuch für deutsche Geschichte* 23 (1994), 276–99.

Anderl, Gabriele, and Dirk Rupnow. *Die Zentralstelle für jüdische Auswanderung als Beraubungsinstitution*. Nationalsozialistische Institutionen des Vermögensentzuges 1. *Veröffentlichungen der Österreichischen Historikerkommission*. With the editorial assistance of Alexandra-Eileen Wenck. Vienna, 2004.

Angrick, Andrej, and Peter Klein. *Die 'Endlösung' in Riga: Ausbeutung und Vernichtung 1941–1944*. Darmstadt, 2006.

Bajohr, Frank. *'Aryanisation' in Hamburg: The Economic Exclusion of Jews and the Confiscation of Their Property in Nazi Germany*. New York, 2002 (German original 1997).

Balcar, Jaromír. *Panzer für Hitler – Traktoren für Stalin: Großunternehmen in Böhmen und Mähren 1938–1950*. Munich, 2014.

Banken, Ralf. *Edelmetallmangel und Großraubwirtschaft: Die Entwicklung des deutschen Edelmetallsektors im 'Dritten Reich' 1933–1945*. Berlin, 2009.

Bartož, Josef. 'Die Arisierung jüdischen Vermögens in Olmütz im Jahre 1939'. *Theresienstädter Studien und Dokumente* 2000, 282–96.

Benda, Jan. 'Okupace pohraničí a nucená imigrace v letech 1938–1939'. *Český Časopis Historický* 110(2) (2012), 329–47.

Benz, Wolfgang. *Theresienstadt: Eine Geschichte von Täuschung und Vernichtung*. Munich, 2013.

Blodig, Vojtěch. *Theresienstadt in der 'Endlösung der Judenfrage' 1941–1945: Führer durch die Dauerausstellung des Ghetto-Museums in Theresienstadt*. Terezin, 2003.

Bodensieck, Heidrich. 'Das Dritte Reich und die Lage der Juden in der Tschecho-Slowakei nach München'. *Vierteljahrshefte für Zeitgeschichte* 9(3) (1961), 249–61.

Boesch, Ina. *Grenzfälle: Von Flucht und Hilfe. Fünf Geschichten aus Europa*. Zürich, 2008.

Bondy, Ruth. 'Chronik der sich schließenden Tore: Jüdisches Nachrichtenblatt – Židovské Listy (1939–1945)'. *Theresienstädter Studien und Dokumente* 2000, 86–103.

Bondy, Ruth. *Trapped: Essays on the History of the Czech Jews, 1939–1945*. Jerusalem, 2008.

Borák, Mečislav. *Transport to TMY: První deportace evropských Židů*. Ostrava, 1994.

Boyer, Christoph. *Nationale Kontrahenten oder Partner? Studien zu den Beziehungen zwischen Tschechen und Deutschen in der Wirtschaft der ČSR (1918–1938)*. Munich, 1999.
Brade, Laura. 'Networks of Escape: Jewish Flight from the Bohemian Lands, 1938–1941'. Dissertation, University of North Carolina-Chapel Hill, 2017.
Brandes, Detlef. *Die Tschechen unter deutschem Protektorat.* Part 1: *Besatzungspolitik, Kollaboration und Widerstand im Protektorat Böhmen und Mähren bis Heydrichs Tod (1939–1942)*. Edited by Vorstand des Collegium Carolinum, Forschungsstelle für die böhmischen Länder. Munich, 1969.
Brandes, Detlef. *Die Tschechen unter deutschem Protektorat.* Part 2: *Besatzungspolitik, Kollaboration und Widerstand im Protektorat Böhmen und Mähren von Heydrichs Tod bis zum Prager Aufstand (1942–1945)*. Munich, 1975.
Brandes, Detlef. *Die Sudetendeutschen im Krisenjahr 1938*. Munich, 2008.
Brandes, Detlef. 'Nationalsozialistische Tschechenpolitik im Protektorat Böhmen und Mähren', in Detlef Brandes and Václav Kural (eds), *Der Weg in die Katastrophe: Deutsch-tschechoslowakische Beziehungen 1938–1947* (Essen, 1994), 39–56.
Brandes, Detlef. *'Umvolkung, Umsiedlung, rassische Bestandsaufnahme': NS-'Volkstumspolitik' in den böhmischen Ländern*. Munich, 2012.
Brandes, Detlef, and Alena Míšková (eds). *Vom Osteuropa-Lehrstuhl ins Prager Rathaus: Josef Pfitzner 1901–1945*. Essen, 2013.
Brandes, Detlef, and Václav Kural (eds). *Der Weg in die Katastrophe: Deutsch-tschechoslowakische Beziehungen 1938–1947*. Essen, 1994.
Brenner, Michael, Andreas Gotzmann and Yfaat Weiss (eds). 'Germans – Jews – Czechs: The Case of the Czech Lands'. Special Issue, *Bohemia* 46(1) (2005).
Brother, Eric. *Berlin Ghetto: Herbert Baum and the Anti-Fascist Resistance*. Stroud, 2012.
Browning, Christopher. *The Origins of the Final Solution: The Evolution of Nazi Jewish Policy, September 1939–March 1942*. Lincoln, NE, 2004.
Buchholz, Marlies. *Die hannoverschen Judenhäuser: Zur Situation der Juden in der Zeit der Ghettoisierung und Verfolgung 1941 bis 1945*. Hildesheim, 1987.
Bryant, Chad. 'The Language of Resistance? Czech Jokes and Joke-Telling under Nazi Occupation, 1943–45'. *Journal of Contemporary History* 41(1) (2006), 133–51.
Bryant, Chad. *Prague in Black: Nazi Rule and Czech Nationalism*. Cambridge, MA, 2007.
Čapková, Kateřina. 'Czechs, Germans, Jews – Where Is the Difference? The Complexity of National Identities of Bohemian Jews, 1918–1938'. *Bohemia* 46(1) (2005), 7–14.
Čapková, Kateřina. *Czechs, Germans, Jews? National Identity and the Jews of Bohemia*. New York, 2012.
Čapková, Kateřina, and Michal Frankl. *Unsichere Zuflucht: Die Tschechoslowakei und ihre Flüchtlinge aus NS-Deutschland 1933–1938*. Vienna, 2013 (Czech original 2008).
Cesarani, David. *Becoming Eichmann: Rethinking the Life, Crimes and Trial of a 'Desk Murderer'*. Cambridge, 2004.
Cesarani, David. *Final Solution: The Fate of the Jews 1933–1949*. London, 2016.
Crowhurst, Patrick. *Hitler and Czechoslovakia in World War II: Domination and Retaliation*. London, 2013.
Dean, Martin. *Robbing the Jews: The Confiscation of Jewish Property in the Holocaust, 1933–1945*. Cambridge, 2008.
Dean, Martin, Constantin Goschler and Philipp Ther (eds). *Robbery and Restitution: The Conflict over Jewish Property in Europe*. New York, 2007.

Dieckmann, Christoph, and Babette Quinkert (eds). *Kooperation und Verbrechen: Formen der 'Kollaboration' im östlichen Europa 1939–1945* (Beiträge zur Geschichte des Nationalsozialismus, vol. 19). Göttingen, 2003.
Dillmann, Hans Ulrich, and Susanne Heim. *Fluchtpunkt Karibik: Jüdische Emigranten in der Dominikanischen Republik.* Berlin, 2009.
Dörner, Bernward. *'Heimtücke': Das Gesetz als Waffe. Kontrolle, Abschreckung und Verfolgung in Deutschland 1933–1945.* Paderborn, 1998.
Feldman, Gerald D. *Die Allianz und die deutsche Versicherungswirtschaft 1933–1945.* Munich, 2001.
Frank, Ernst. *Karl Hermann Frank: Staatsminister im Protektorat.* 2nd expanded edition. Heusenstamm, 1971.
Frankl, Michal. *'Prag ist nunmehr antisemitisch': Tschechischer Antisemitismus am Ende des 19. Jahrhunderts.* Berlin, 2011.
Frankl, Michal. 'Prejudiced Asylum: Czechoslovak Refugee Policy, 1918–60'. *Journal of Contemporary History* 49(3) (2014), 477–90.
Friedländer, Saul. *Nazi Germany and the Jews: The Years of Persecution, 1933–1939.* New York, 1997.
Friedländer, Saul. *The Years of Extermination: Nazi Germany and the Jews, 1939–1945.* New York, 2007.
Frommer, Benjamin. *National Cleansing: Retribution against Nazi Collaborators in Postwar Czechoslovakia.* New York, 2005.
Frommer, Benjamin. 'Verfolgung durch die Presse: Wie Prager Bürokraten und die tschechische Polizei halfen, die Juden des Protektorats zu isolieren', in Andrea Löw, Doris Bergen and Anna Hájková (eds), *Alltag im Holocaust: Jüdisches Leben im Großdeutschen Reich 1941–1945* (Munich, 2013), 137–50.
Frommer, Benjamin. *The Ghetto without Walls: The Identification, Isolation, and Elimination of Bohemian and Moravian Jewry, 1938–1945* (forthcoming).
Gall, Lothar et al. *Die Deutsche Bank 1870–1995.* Munich, 1995.
Gallas, Elisabeth. '"Facing a Crisis Unparalleled in History": Jüdische Reaktionen auf den Holocaust aus New York 1940 bis 1945'. *S:I.M.O.N. Shoah: Intervention. Methods. Documentation* 2 (2014), 5–14.
Gebel, Ralf. *'Heim ins Reich!': Konrad Henlein und der Reichsgau Sudetenland (1938–1945).* Munich, 1999.
Gerlach, Christian. 'Die Wannsee-Konferenz, das Schicksal der deutschen Juden und Hitlers politische Grundsatzentscheidung, alle Juden Europas zu ermorden'. *Werkstatt-Geschichte* 18 (1997), 7–44.
Gerlach, Christian. *The Extermination of the European Jews.* Cambridge, 2016.
Gerwarth, Robert. *Hitler's Hangman: The Life of Heydrich.* New Haven, CT, 2011.
Glettler, Monika, Ľubomir Lipták and Alena Míšková (eds). *Geteilt, besetzt, beherrscht. Die Tschechoslowakei 1938–1945: Reichsgau Sudetenland, Protektorat Böhmen und Mähren, Slowakei.* Essen, 2004.
Goldhagen, Daniel J. *Hitler's Willing Executioners: Ordinary Germans and the Holocaust.* New York, 1996.
Goshen, Seev. 'Eichmann und die Nisko-Aktion im Oktober 1939', *Vierteljahrshefte für Zeitgeschichte* 29(1) (1981), 74–96.
Gottwaldt, Alfred, and Diana Schulle. *Die 'Judendeportationen' aus dem Deutschen Reich 1941–1945: Eine kommentierte Chronologie.* Wiesbaden, 2005.
Grabowski, Hans-Ludwig, and Wolfgang Haney (eds). *Kennzeichen 'Jude'. Antisemitismus – Entrechtung – Verfolgung – Vernichtung. Dokumentation basierend auf Belegen der zeitgeschichtlichen Sammlung Wolfgang Haney.* Regenstauf, 2014.

Gruner, Wolf. *Der Geschlossene Arbeitseinsatz deutscher Juden: Zwangsarbeit als Element der Verfolgung 1938–1943*. Berlin, 1997.
Gruner, Wolf. 'Poverty and Persecution: The Reichsvereinigung, the Jewish Population, and the Anti-Jewish Policy in the Nazi-State, 1939–1945'. *Yad Vashem Studies* 27 (1999), 23–60.
Gruner, Wolf. 'The German Council of Municipalities and the Coordination of Anti-Jewish Local Policies in the Nazi State'. *Holocaust and Genocide Studies* 13(2) (1999), 171–99.
Gruner, Wolf. 'Die NS-Judenverfolgung und die Kommunen: Zur wechselseitigen Dynamisierung von zentraler und lokaler Politik 1933–1941'. *Vierteljahrshefte für Zeitgeschichte* 48(1) (2000), 75–126.
Gruner, Wolf. *Zwangsarbeit und Verfolgung: Österreichische Juden im NS-Staat 1938–1945*. Innsbruck, 2000.
Gruner, Wolf. *Öffentliche Wohlfahrt und Judenverfolgung: Wechselwirkungen lokaler und zentraler Politik im NS-Staat (1933–1942)*. Munich, 2002.
Gruner, Wolf. 'Von der Kollektivausweisung zur Deportation der Juden aus Deutschland (1938–1945): Neue Perspektiven und Dokumente', in Beate Meyer and Birthe Kundrus (eds), *Die Deportation der Juden aus Deutschland: Pläne, Praxis, Reaktionen 1938–1945* (Beiträge zur Geschichte des Nationalsozialismus, vol. 20) (Göttingen, 2004), 21–62.
Gruner, Wolf. 'Local Initiatives, Central Coordination: German Municipal Administration and the Holocaust', in Gerald D. Feldman and Wolfgang Seibel (eds), *Networks of Nazi Persecution: Bureaucracy, Business, and the Organization of the Holocaust* (New York, 2005), 269–94.
Gruner, Wolf. 'Protektorát Čechy a Morava a protižidovská politika v letech 1939–1941'. in *Terezinske Studie a Dokumenty* 2005 (Prague, 2005), 25–58 (German: 'Das Protektorat Böhmen/Mähren und die antijüdische Politik 1939–1941: Lokale Initiativen, regionale Maßnahmen und zentrale Entscheidungen im "Großdeutschen Reich"', *Theresienstädter Studien und Dokumente* 2005, 27–62).
Gruner, Wolf. *Widerstand in der Rosenstraße: Die Fabrik-Aktion und die Verfolgung der 'Mischehen' 1943*. Frankfurt a.M., 2005.
Gruner, Wolf. *Jewish Forced Labor under the Nazis: Economic Needs and Racial Aims (1938–1944)*. New York, 2006.
Gruner, Wolf. 'Von Wien nach La Paz: Der Lebensweg von Max Schreier'. in Stiftung Jüdisches Museum Berlin and Stiftung Haus der Geschichte der Bundesrepublik (eds), *Heimat und Exil: Emigration der deutschen Juden nach 1933* (Frankfurt a.M., 2006), 161–63.
Gruner, Wolf. 'Greater Germany', in Peter Hayes and John Roth (eds), *The Oxford Handbook of Holocaust Studies* (New York, 2010), 293–309.
Gruner, Wolf. '"The Germans Should Expel the Foreigner Hitler": Open Protest and Other Forms of Jewish Defiance in Nazi Germany'. *Yad Vashem Studies* 39(2) (2011), 13–53.
Gruner, Wolf. *The Persecution of the Jews in Berlin 1933–1945: A Chronology of Measures by Authorities in the German Capital*. Translation of the second substantially extended and revised edition. Berlin, 2014.
Gruner, Wolf. 'Verweigerung, Opposition und Protest: Vergessene jüdische Reaktionen auf die NS-Verfolgung in Deutschland', in Alina Bothe, Monika Schärtl and Stefanie Schüler-Springorum (eds), *Shoah: Ereignis und Erinnerung* (3. Jahrbuch Zentrum Jüdische Studien Berlin-Brandenburg) (Berlin, 2019), 11–30.
Gruner, Wolf, and Jörg Osterloh (eds). *The Greater German Reich and the Jews: Nazi Persecution Policies in the Annexed Territories 1935–1945*. New York, 2015 (German original 2010).

Hahn, Eva. 'Verdrängung und Verharmlosung: Das Ende der jüdischen Bevölkerungsgruppe in den böhmischen Ländern nach ausgewählten tschechischen und sudetendeutschen Publikationen', in Detlef Brandes and Václav Kural (eds), *Der Weg in die Katastrophe: Deutsch-tschechoslowakische Beziehungen 1938–1947* (Essen, 1994), 135–50.

Hájková, Alena. 'Erfassung der jüdischen Bevölkerung des Protektorats'. *Theresienstädter Studien und Dokumente* 1997, 50–62.

Hájková, Anna. 'Die fabelhaften Jungs aus Theresienstadt: Junge tschechische Männer als dominante soziale Elite im Theresienstädter Ghetto', in Christoph Dieckmann and Babette Quinkert (eds), *Im Ghetto 1939–1945: Neue Forschungen zu Alltag und Umfeld* (Beiträge zur Geschichte des Nationalsozialismus, vol. 25) (Göttingen, 2009), 116–35.

Hájková, Anna. 'To Terezín and Back: Czech Jews and Their Bonds of Belonging between Theresienstadt and Postwar Czechoslovakia'. *Dapim. Studies on the Holocaust* 28(1) (2014), 38–55.

Hallama, Peter. *Nationale Helden und jüdische Opfer: Tschechische Repräsentationen des Holocaust*. Göttingen, 2015.

Hampel, Jens. 'Das Schicksal der jüdischen Bevölkerung der Stadt Iglau 1938–1942'. *Theresienstädter Studien und Dokumente* 1998, 70–99.

Haslinger, Peter. *Nation und Territorium im tschechischen politischen Diskurs 1880–1938*. Munich, 2010.

Heiber, Helmut. 'Zur Justiz im Dritten Reich: Der Fall Eliáš'. *Vierteljahrshefte für Zeitgeschichte* 3 (1955), 275–96.

Heimann, Mary. *Czechoslovakia: The State That Failed*. New Haven, CT, 2011.

Heinemann, Isabel. *'Rasse, Siedlung, deutsches Blut': Das Rasse- und Siedlungshauptamt der SS und die rassenpolitische Neuordnung Europas*. Göttingen, 2003.

Heumos, Peter. 'Flüchtlingslager, Hilfsorganisationen, Juden im Niemandsland: Zur Flüchtlings- und Emigrationsproblematik in der Tschechoslowakei im Herbst 1938'. *Bohemia* 25(2) (1984), 245–75.

Hilberg, Raul. *The Destruction of the European Jews*. Chicago, 1961.

Hilberg, Raul. *Die Vernichtung der europäischen Juden*. Vol. 1. Frankfurt a.M., 1990.

Hildesheimer, Esriel. *Die Jüdische Selbstverwaltung unter dem NS-Regime: Der Existenzkampf der Reichsvertretung und Reichsvereinigung der Juden in Deutschland*. Tübingen, 1994.

Hoensch, Jörg K. et al. (eds). *Judenemanzipation – Antisemitismus – Verfolgung in Deutschland, Österreich-Ungarn, den Böhmischen Ländern und in der Slowakei*. Essen, 1999.

James, Harold. *The Deutsche Bank and the Nazi Economic War against the Jews: The Expropriation of Jewish-Owned Property*. New York, 2001.

Jančik, Drahomír. 'Die "Arisierungsaktivitäten" der Böhmischen Escompte Bank im Protektorat Böhmen und Mähren 1939–1945,' in Dieter Ziegler (ed.), *Banken und 'Arisierungen' in Mitteleuropa während des Nationalsozialismus* (Stuttgart, 2002), 143–73.

Jančik, Drahomír, and Eduard Kubů. 'Ein abartiges Monopol: "Hadega" Handelsgesellschaft m. b.H. und ihr Geschäft mit Edelmetallen und Edelsteinen während des Zweiten Weltkrieges'. *Theresienstädter Studien und Dokumente* 2001, 305–72.

Jančik, Drahomír, and Eduard Kubů. *'Arizace' a arizátoři: Drobný a střední židovský majetek v úvěrech Kreditanstalt der Deutschen (1939–1945)* ['Aryanization' and Aryanizers: Small- and Medium-Sized Jewish Property in the Loans Issued by the Kreditanstalt der Deutschen]. Prague, 2005.

Jančik, Drahomír, Eduard Kubů and Jiří Šouša, with the assistance of Jiří Novotný. *Arisierungsgewinnler: Die Rolle der deutschen Banken bei der 'Arisierung' und Konfiskation jüdischer Vermögen im Protektorat Böhmen und Mähren (1939–1945)*. Wiesbaden, 2011.
Jasch, Hans-Christian. *Staatssekretär Wilhelm Stuckart und die Judenpolitik: Der Mythos von der sauberen Verwaltung*. Munich, 2012.
Jockusch, Laura. *Collect and Record! Jewish Holocaust Documentation in Early Postwar Europe*. New York, 2012.
Kaiserová, Kristina, Eduard Niznanský and Martin Schulze Wessel (eds). *Religion und Nation: Tschechen, Deutsche und Slowaken im 20. Jahrhundert*. Essen, 2015.
Kaplan, Marion A. *Dominican Haven: The Jewish Refugee Settlement in Sosúa, 1940–1945*. New York, 2008.
Kárný, Miroslav. 'Die "Judenfrage" in der nazistischen Okkupationspolitik'. *Historica* 21 (1982), 137–92.
Kárný, Miroslav. 'Zur Statistik der jüdischen Bevölkerung im sogenannten Protektorat'. *Judaica Bohemiae* 22(1) (1986), 9–19.
Kárný, Miroslav. *'Konecné resení': Genocida ceských zidu v nemecké protektorátní politice*. Vol. 1. Prague, 1991.
Kárný, Miroslav. 'Die Protektoratsregierung und die Verordnungen des Reichsprotektors über das jüdische Vermögen'. *Judaica Bohemiae* XXIX (1993), 54–66.
Kárný, Miroslav. 'Die tschechischen Opfer der deutschen Okkupation', in Detlef Brandes and Václav Kural (eds), *Der Weg in die Katastrophe: Deutsch-tschechoslowakische Beziehungen 1938–1947* (Essen, 1994), 151–64.
Kárný, Miroslav. 'The Genocide of the Czech Jews', in *Terezín Memorial Book: Jewish Victims of Nazi Deportations from Bohemia and Moravia 1941–1945* (Terezin, 1996), 27–88.
Kárný, Miroslav. 'Reinhard Heydrich als Stellvertretender Reichsprotektor in Prag', in *Deutsche Politik im 'Protektorat Böhmen und Mähren' unter Reinhard Heydrich 1941–1942: Eine Dokumentation*, edited by Miroslav Kárný, Jaroslava Milotová and Margita Kárná (Berlin, 1997), 9–75.
Kárný, Miroslav. 'Auswahlbibliographie der Arbeiten von Miroslav Kárný 1971–2001'. *Theresienstädter Studien und Dokumente* 2002, 33–44.
Kieval, Hillel J. *The Making of Czech Jewry: National Conflict and Jewish Society in Bohemia, 1870–1918*. New York, 1988.
King, Jeremy. *Budweisers into Czechs and Germans: A Local History of Bohemian Politics, 1848–1948*. Princeton, NJ, 2005.
Kocourek, Ludomír. 'Das Schicksal der Juden im Sudetengau im Licht der erhaltenen Quellen'. *Theresienstädter Studien und Dokumente* 1997, 86–104.
Köhler, Ingo. 'Werten und Bewerten: Die "kalte" Technik der Arisierung', in Hartmut Berghoff, Jürgen Kocka and Dieter Ziegler (eds), *Wirtschaft im Zeitalter der Extreme. Beiträge zur Unternehmensgeschichte Österreichs und Deutschlands. Im Gedenken an Gerald D. Feldman* (Schriftenreihe zur Zeitschrift für Unternehmensgeschichte, vol. 20) (Munich, 2010), 316–36.
Koeltzsch, Ines. 'Antijüdische Straßengewalt und die semantische Konstruktion des "Anderen" im Prag der Ersten Republik'. *Judaica Bohemiae* 46(1) (2011), 73–99.
Koeltzsch, Ines. *Geteilte Kulturen: Eine Geschichte der tschechisch-jüdisch-deutschen Beziehungen in Prag (1918–1938)*. Munich, 2012.
Kokoška, Stanislav. 'Resistance, Collaboration, Adaptation … Some Notes on the Research of the Czech Society in the Protectorate'. *Czech Journal of Contemporary History* 1 (2013), 54–76.

Kolár, Pavel. 'Die Geschichtswissenschaft an der Deutschen Universität Prag 1882–1938: Entwicklung der Lehrkanzeln und Institutionalisierung unter zwei Regimen', in Hans Lemberg (ed.), *Universitäten in nationaler Konkurrenz: Zur Geschichte der Prager Universitäten im 19. und 20. Jahrhundert* (Munich, 2003), 85–114.

Kosta, Jiří, Jaroslava Milotová and Zlatica Zudová-Lešková (eds). *Tschechische und slowakische Juden im Widerstand 1938–45*. Berlin, 2008.

Krejčová, Helena, and Alena Mišková. 'Anmerkungen zur Frage des Antisemitismus in den Böhmischen Ländern Ende des 19. Jahrhunderts', in Jörg K. Hoensch et al. (eds), *Judenemanzipation – Antisemitismus – Verfolgung in Deutschland, Österreich-Ungarn, den Böhmischen Ländern und in der Slowakei* (Essen, 1999), 55–62.

Krejčová, Helena, and Alena Mišková. 'Die antijüdischen bzw. antideutschen Kundgebungen und Demonstrationen in Böhmen und Mähren (1899)', in Jörg K. Hoensch et al. (eds), *Judenemanzipation – Antisemitismus – Verfolgung in Deutschland, Österreich-Ungarn, den Böhmischen Ländern und in der Slowakei* (Essen, 1999), 63–84.

Krejčová, Helena, and Jana Svobodová. *Postavení a osudy židovského obyvatelstva v Čechách a na Moravě v letech 1939–1945: sborník studií*. Prague, 1998.

Kreutzmüller, Christoph, and Jaroslav Kučera. 'Die Commerzbank und die Vernichtung der jüdischen Gewerbetätigkeit in den böhmischen Ländern und den Niederlanden', in Ludolf Herbst and Thomas Weihe (eds), *Die Commerzbank und die Juden 1933–1945* (Munich, 2004), 173–222.

Kubů, Eduard. 'Die Verwaltung von konfisziertem und sequestriertem Vermögen – eine spezifische Kategorie des "Arisierungs-Profits": Die Kreditanstalt der Deutschen und ihre Abteilung "F."', in Dieter Ziegler (ed.), *Banken und 'Arisierungen' in Mitteleuropa während des Nationalsozialismus* (Stuttgart, 2002), 175–210.

Kubů, Eduard, and Jan Kuklík Jr. 'Reluctant Restitution: The Restitution of Jewish Property in the Bohemian Lands after the Second World War', in Martin Dean, Constantin Goschler and Philipp Ther (eds), *Robbery and Restitution: The Conflict over Jewish Property in Europe* (New York, 2007), 223–39.

Kučera, Jaroslav. *Minderheit im Nationalstaat: Die Sprachenfrage in den tschechisch-deutschen Beziehungen 1918–1938*. Munich, 1999.

Kučera, Jaroslav, and Volker Zimmermann. 'Zum tschechischen Forschungsstand über die NS-Besatzungsherrschaft in Böhmen und Mähren: Überlegungen anlässlich des Erscheinens eines Standardwerkes'. *Bohemia* 49(1) (2009), 164–83.

Kulka, Erich. 'The Importance of Documenting the Role of Jews in the Czechoslovak Anti-Nazi Resistance'. *Review of the Society for the History of Czechoslovak Jews* 5 (1992–93), 63–67.

Kulka, Otto Dov. 'History and Historical Consciousness: Similarities and Dissimilarities in the History of the Jews in Germany and the Czech Lands 1918–1945'. *Bohemia* 46(1) (2005), 68–86.

Kuller, Christiane. *Bürokratie und Verbrechen: Antisemitische Finanzpolitik und Verwaltungspraxis im nationalsozialistischen Deutschland*. Munich, 2013.

Küpper, René. 'Karl Hermann Frank als Deutscher Staatsminister für Böhmen und Mähren', in Monika Glettler, L'ubomir Lipták and Alena Míšková (eds), *Geteilt, besetzt, beherrscht. Die Tschechoslowakei 1938–1945: Reichsgau Sudetenland, Protektorat Böhmen und Mähren, Slowakei* (Essen, 2004), 31–52.

Küpper, René. *Karl Hermann Frank (1898–1946): Politische Biographie eines sudetendeutschen Nationalsozialisten*. Munich, 2010.

Kwiet, Konrad. 'Forced Labour of German Jews in Nazi Germany'. *Leo Baeck Institute Year Book* XXXVI (1991), 389–407.

Landré, Berta. 'Jüdische Zwangsarbeit in Prag'. *Zeitgeschichte* 9(11/12) (Vienna 1982), 365–77.
Láníček, Jan. 'Arnost Frischer und seine Hilfe für Juden im besetzten Europa (1941–1945)'. *Theresienstädter Studien und Dokumente* 2007, 11–91.
Láníček, Jan. 'The Czechoslovak Section of the BBC and the Jews during the Second World War'. *Yad Vashem Studies* 38(2) (2010), 123–54.
Láníček, Jan. *Czechs, Slovaks and the Jews, 1938–48: Beyond Idealization and Condemnation*. Houndmills, 2013.
Láníček, Jan. 'What Did It Mean to Be Loyal? Jewish Survivors in Post-War Czechoslovakia in a Comparative Perspective'. *Australian Journal of Politics and History* 60(3) (2014), 384–404.
Laube, Stefan. 'Technik, Arbeit und Zerstörung: Die Organisation Todt in Prag (1944–1945)'. *Bohemia* 40(2) (1999), 387–416.
Lexa, John G. 'Anti-Jewish Laws and Regulations in the Protectorate of Bohemia and Moravia', in Avigdor Dagan (ed.), *The Jews of Czechoslovakia: Historical Studies and Surveys*, vol. 3 (Philadelphia, 1984), 75–103.
Lichtenstein, Tatjana. '"Making" Jews at Home: Zionism and the Construction of Jewish Nationality in Inter-War Czechoslovakia'. *East European Jewish Affairs* 36(1) (June 2006), 49–71.
Lichtenstein, Tatjana. 'Racializing Jewishness: Zionist Responses to National Indifference in Interwar Czechoslovakia'. *Austrian History Yearbook* 43 (April 2012), 75–97.
Lichtenstein, Tatjana. *Zionists in Interwar Czechoslovakia: Minority Nationalism and the Politics of Belonging*. Bloomington, IN, 2016.
Lilla, Joachim. 'Die Vertretung des "Reichsgaus Sudetenland" und des "Protektorats Böhmen und Mähren" im Großdeutschen Reichstag'. *Bohemia* 40(2) (1999), 436–71.
Longerich, Peter. *'Davon haben wir nichts gewußt!' Die Deutschen und die Judenverfolgung 1933–1945*. Bonn, 2006.
Longerich, Peter. *Holocaust: The Nazi Persecution and Murder of the Jews*. New York, 2010 (German original 1998).
Lüdicke, Lars. *Constantin von Neurath: Eine politische Biographie*. Paderborn, 2014.
Machala, Jan. '"Unbearable Jewish Houses of Prayer": The Nazi Destruction of Synagogues Based on Examples from Central Moravia'. *Judaica Bohemiae* 49(1) (2013), 59–87.
Majer, Diemut. *'Non-Germans' under the Third Reich: The Nazi Judicial and Administrative System in Germany and Occupied Eastern Europe with Special Regard to Occupied Poland, 1939–1945*. Baltimore, MD, 2003 (German original 1981).
Mallmann, Klaus-Michael. 'Menschenjagd und Massenmord: Das neue Instrument der Einsatzgruppen und -kommandos 1938–1945', in Gerhard Paul and Klaus-Michael Mallmann (eds), *Die Gestapo im Zweiten Weltkrieg: 'Heimatfront' und besetztes Europa* (Darmstadt, 2000), 291–316.
Marek, Michaela, Dusan Kovác, Jirí Pesek et al. (eds). *Kultur als Vehikel und als Opponent politischer Absichten: Kulturkontakte zwischen Deutschen, Tschechen und Slowaken von der Mitte des 19. Jahrhunderts bis in die 1980er Jahre*. Essen, 2010.
Maršálek, Pavel. *Protektorát Čechy a Morava: Státoprávní a politické aspekty nacistického okupačního režimu v českých zemích 1939–1945* [The Protectorate of Bohemia and Moravia: Constitutional and Political Aspects of the Nazi occupation Regime in the Bohemian Lands 1939–1945]. Prague, 2002.
Mazower, Mark. *Hitler's Empire: Nazi Rule in Europe*. New York, 2008.
Meyer, Beate. *A Fatal Balancing Act: The Dilemma of the Reich Association of Jews in Germany, 1939–1945*. New York, 2013 (German original 2011).

Milotová, Jaroslava. 'Die Zentralstelle für jüdische Auswanderung in Prag: Genesis und Tätigkeit bis zum Anfang des Jahres 1940'. *Theresienstädter Studien und Dokumente* 1997, 7–30.

Milotová, Jaroslava. 'Der Okkupationsapparat und die Vorbereitung der Transporte nach Lodz'. *Theresienstädter Studien und Dokumente* 1998, 40–69.

Milotová, Jaroslava. 'Zur Geschichte der Verordnung Konstantin von Neuraths über das jüdische Vermögen'. *Theresienstädter Studien und Dokumente* 2002, 75–115.

Miron, Guy. '"Lately, Almost Constantly, Everything Seems Small to Me": The Lived Space of German Jews under the Nazi Regime'. *Jewish Social Studies* 20(1) (Autumn 2014), 121–49.

Mohn, Volker. *NS-Kulturpolitik im Protektorat Böhmen und Mähren: Konzepte, Praktiken, Reaktionen*. Essen, 2014.

Mommsen, Hans. *Beamtentum im Dritten Reich: Mit ausgewählten Quellen zur nationalsozialistischen Beamtenpolitik*. Stuttgart, 1966.

Moser, Jonny. *Nisko: Die ersten Judendeportationen*. Vienna, 2011.

Murdock, Caitlin E. *Changing Places: Society, Culture, and Territory in the Saxon-Bohemian Borderlands, 1870–1946*. Ann Arbor, 2010.

Němec, Petr. 'Die Lage der deutschen Nationalität im Protektorat Böhmen und Mähren unter dem Aspekt der "Eindeutschung" dieses Gebiets'. *Bohemia* 32(1) (1991), 39–59.

Němec, Petr. 'Das tschechische Volk und die nationalsozialistische Germanisierung des Raumes'. *Bohemia* 32(2) (1991), 424–55.

Nižňanský, Eduard. 'Die Aktion Nisko, das Lager Sosnowiec (Oberschlesien) und die Anfänge des Judenlagers in Vyhne (Slowakei)'. *Jahrbuch für Antisemitismusforschung* 11 (2002), 325–35.

Novotný, Jiří, and Jiří Šouša. 'Die Nationalbank in den Jahren 1939–1945 und die "Arisierung" im Protektorat Böhmen und Mähren', in Dieter Ziegler (ed.), *Banken und 'Arisierungen' in Mitteleuropa während des Nationalsozialismus* (Stuttgart, 2002), 119–42.

Oprach, Marc. *Nationalsozialistische Judenpolitik im Protektorat Böhmen und Mähren: Entscheidungsabläufe und Radikalisierung*. Hamburg, 2006.

Orzoff, Andrea. *Battle for the Castle: The Myth of Czechoslovakia in Europe 1914–1948*. New York, 2009.

Osterloh, Jörg. *Nationalsozialistische Judenverfolgung im Reichsgau Sudetenland 1938–1945*. Munich, 2006.

Osterloh, Jörg. 'Religionsgemeinschaft oder Nation? Der Weg zur Anerkennung einer jüdischen Nationalität in den böhmischen Ländern', in Martin Schulze Wessel, Kristina Kaiserová and Eduard Nižňanský (eds), *Religion und Politik: Deutsche, Tschechen und Slowaken im 20. Jahrhundert* (Essen, 2015), 91–109.

Osterloh, Jörg. '"… gegen den jüdischen Rektor Steinherz": Antisemitische Proteste an der Deutschen Universität in Prag 1922/23', in Pavel Kocman, Milan Řepa and Helmut Teufel (eds), *'Avigdor, Beneš, Gitl' – Juden in Böhmen, Mähren und Schlesien im Mittelalter: Samuel Steinherz zum Gedenken (1857 Güssing–1942 Theresienstadt)* (Essen, 2016), 415–26.

Osterloh, Jörg, and Harald Wixforth. 'Die "Arisierung" im Protektorat Böhmen und Mähren: Rahmenbedingungen und gesetzliche Vorgaben', in Harald Wixforth, with the assistance of Johannes Bär et al., *Die Expansion der Dresdner Bank in Europa* (Munich, 2006), 306–48.

Pawlowsky, Verena, Edith Leisch-Prost and Christian Klösch. *Vereine im Nationalsozialismus: Vermögensentzug durch den Stillhaltekommissar für Vereine, Organisationen und Verbände und Aspekte der Restitution in Österreich nach 1945*. Vienna, 2004.

Petrův, Helena. *Právní postavení židů v Protektorátu Čechy a Morava (1939–1941)*. Prague, 2000.
Pohl, Dieter. *Nationalsozialistische Judenverfolgung in Ostgalizien 1941–1944*. Munich 1996.
Pohl, Dieter. 'Die Holocaust-Forschung und Goldhagens Thesen'. *Vierteljahrshefte für Zeitgeschichte* 45 (1997), 1–48.
Potthast, Jan Björn. *Das jüdische Zentralmuseum der SS in Prag: Gegnerforschung und Völkermord im Nationalsozialismus*. Frankfurt a.M., 2002.
Přibyl, Lukáš. 'Das Schicksal des dritten Transports aus dem Protektorat nach Nisko'. *Theresienstädter Studien und Dokumente* 2000, 297–342.
Rader, Olaf B. *Kaiser Karl IV. (1316–1378): Eine Biographie*. Munich, forthcoming.
Reitlinger, Gerald. *The Final Solution: The Attempt to Exterminate the Jews of Europe 1939–1945*. London, 1952.
Roseman, Mark. *The Villa, the Lake, the Meeting: Wannsee and the Final Solution*. London, 2002.
Rosenkranz, Herbert. *Verfolgung und Selbstbehauptung: Die Juden in Österreich 1938 bis 1945*. Vienna, 1978.
Rothkirchen, Livia. 'Czech Attitudes toward the Jews during the Nazi Regime'. *Yad Vashem Studies* 13 (1977), 287–329.
Rothkirchen, Livia. 'The Defiant Few: The Jewish and Czech "Inside Front" (1938–1942)'. *Yad Vashem Studies* 14 (1981), 35–88.
Rothkirchen, Livia. 'The Protectorate Government and the "Jewish Question", 1939–1941'. *Yad Vashem Studies* 27 (1999), 331–62.
Rothkirchen, Livia. *The Jews of Bohemia and Moravia: Facing the Holocaust*. Lincoln, NE, 2005.
Rothkirchen, Livia. 'Der Jüdische Widerstand im Protektorat', in Jiří Kosta, Jaroslava Milotová and Zlatica Zudová-Lešková (eds), *Tschechische und slowakische Juden im Widerstand 1938–45* (Berlin, 2008), 20–60.
Safrian, Hans. *Eichmann's Men*. Cambridge, 2009 (German original 1993).
Sandkühler, Thomas. *'Endlösung in Galizien': Der Judenmord in Ostpolen und die Rettungsinitiativen von Berthold Beitz 1941–1944*. Bonn, 1996.
Scheffler, Wolfgang. 'Der Brandanschlag im Berliner Lustgarten im Mai 1942 und seine Folgen', in *Berlin in Geschichte und Gegenwart: Jahrbuch des Landesarchivs Berlin* (Berlin, 1984), 91–118.
Schikorra, Christa. 'Rückkehr in eine sich neu konstituierende Gesellschaft: Jüdische Remigrantinnen in der Tschechoslowakei'. *Theresienstädter Studien und Dokumente* 2006, 364–98.
Schmidt-Hartmann, Eva. *Thomas G. Masaryk's Realism: Origins of a Czech Political Concept 1882–1914*. Munich, 1984.
Schmidt-Hartmann, Eva. 'Tschechoslowakei', in Wolfgang Benz (ed.), *Dimension des Völkermords: Die Zahl der jüdischen Opfer des Nationalsozialismus* (Munich, 1991), 353–79.
Schulte, Jan Erik. *Zwangsarbeit und Vernichtung: Das Wirtschaftsimperium der SS. Oswald Pohl und das SS-Wirtschafts-Verwaltungshauptamt 1933–1945*. Paderborn, 2001.
Schulze Wessel, Martin. 'Czech Anti-Semitism in the Context of Tensions between National and Confessional Programs, and the Foundation of the Czechoslovak National Church'. *Bohemia* 46(1) (2005), 102–7.
Sedláková, Monika. 'Die Rolle der sogenannten "Einsatzstäbe" bei der Enteignung jüdischen Vermögens'. *Theresienstädter Studien und Dokumente* 2003, 275–305.
Sedláková, Monika. '"Burza" s židovskými byty – součást protektorátní bytové politiky', in *Documenta Pragensia XXVI. Evropská velkoměsta za druhé světové války*

Každodennost okupovaného velkoměsta. Praha 1939–1945 v evropském srovnání (Prague, 2007), 205–20.
Shlain, Margalit. 'Jakob Edelsteins Bemühungen um die Rettung der Juden aus dem Protektorat Böhmen und Mähren von Mai 1939 bis Dezember 1939'. *Theresienstädter Studien und Dokumente* 2003, 71–94.
Shumsky, Dimitry. 'Introducing Intellectual and Political History to the History of Everyday Life: Multiethnic Cohabitation and Jewish Experience in Fin-de-Siecle Bohemia'. *Bohemia* 46(1) (2005), 39–67.
Sládek, Oldřich. 'Standrecht und Standgericht: Die Gestapo in Böhmen und Mähren', in Gerhard Paul and Klaus-Michael Mallmann (eds), *Die Gestapo im Zweiten Weltkrieg: 'Heimatfront' und besetztes Europa* (Darmstadt, 2000), 317–39.
Später, Erich. *Villa Waigner: Hanns Martin Schleyer und die deutsche Vernichtungselite in Prag 1939–45*. Hamburg, 2009.
Spector, Scott. 'Mittel-Europa? Some Afterthoughts on Prague Jews, "Hybridity", and Translation'. *Bohemia* 46(1) (2005), 28–37.
Spitzer, Leo. *Hotel Bolivia: The Culture of Memory in a Refuge from Nazism*. New York, 1998.
Stone, Dan (ed.). *The Historiography of the Holocaust*. Houndmills, 2004.
Šustek, Vojtech. 'Die nationalsozialistische Karriere eines sudetendeutschen Historikers', in Alena Míšková and Vojtěch Šustek, *Josef Pfitzner a protektorátní Praha v letech 1939–45* [Josef Pfitzner and Prague under the Protectorate 1939–1945], vol. 1 (Prague, 2000), 71–109.
Šustek, Vojtech. 'Bemühungen um die Germanisierung Prags während der NS-Okkupation: Aus den Berichten des Stellvertretenden Primators Josef Pfitzner', in Monika Glettler, Ľubomir Lipták and Alena Míšková (eds), *Geteilt, besetzt, beherrscht. Die Tschechoslowakei 1938–1945: Reichsgau Sudetenland, Protektorat Böhmen und Mähren, Slowakei* (Essen, 2004), 53–66.
Šustek, Vojtech. *Atentát na Reinharda Heydricha a druhé stanné právo na území tzv. protektorátu Čechy a Morava: Edice historickych dokumentu*. Vol. 1. Prague, 2012.
Tulechov, Valentina von. *Tomas Garrigue Masaryk: Sein kritischer Realismus in Auswirkung auf sein Demokratie- und Europaverständnis*. Göttingen, 2011.
Uhlíř, Jan Boris. *Ve stínu říšské orlice: Protektorát Čechy a Morava, odboj a kolaborace* [In the Shadow of the Imperial Eagle: The Protectorate of Bohemia and Moravia, Resistance and Collaboration]. Prague, 2002.
Umbreit, Hans. *Deutsche Militärverwaltungen 1938/39: Die militärische Besetzung der Tschechoslowakei und Polens*. Stuttgart, 1977.
Universalisierung des Holocaust? Erinnerungskultur und Geschichtspolitik in internationaler Perspektive. Edited by Jan Eckel and Claudia Moisel (Beiträge zur Geschichte des Nationalsozialismus, vol. 24). Göttingen, 2008.
Veselská, Magda. 'Der Mann, der niemals aufgab: Die Geschichte des Josef Polák, Hauptkurator des Jüdischen Zentralmuseums in Prag zur Zeit des Zweiten Weltkrieges'. *Theresienstädter Studien und Dokumente* 2006, 14–61.
Veselská, Magda. '"Sie müssen sich als Jude dessen bewusst sein, welche Opfer zu tragen sind …": Handlungsspielräume der jüdischen Kultusgemeinden im Protektorat bis zum Ende der großen Deportationen', in Andrea Löw, Doris Bergen and Anna Hájková (eds), *Alltag im Holocaust: Jüdisches Leben im Großdeutschen Reich 1941–1945* (Munich, 2013), 151–66.
Vierling, Birgit. *Kommunikation als Mittel politischer Mobilisierung: Die Sudetendeutsche Partei (SdP) auf ihrem Weg zur Einheitsbewegung in der Ersten Tschechoslowakischen Republik (1933–1938)*. Marburg, 2014.

Wein, Martin. 'The Czechoslovak Exile in London and the Jews 1938–1945', in Jan Láníček and James Jordan (eds), *Governments-in-Exile and the Jews during the Second World War* (Middlesex, 2013), 135–50.

Wein, Martin J. 'Zionism in Interwar Czechoslovakia: Palestino-Centrism and Landespolitik'. *Judaica Bohemiae* 44(1) (April 2009), 5–47.

Wildt, Michael. *An Uncompromising Generation: The Nazi Leadership of the Reich Security Main Office*. Madison, 2009 (German original 2002).

Willems, Susanne. *'Der entsiedelte Jude': Albert Speers Wohnungsmarktpolitik für den Berliner Hauptstadtbau*. Berlin, 2002.

Wingfield, Nancy. *Flag Wars and Stone Saints: How the Bohemian Lands Became Czech*. Cambridge, MA, 2007.

Wixforth, Harald. *Die Expansion der Dresdner Bank in Europa*. With the assistance of Johannes Bär et al. Munich, 2006.

Wolf, Gerhard. *Ideologie und Herrschaftsrationalität: Nationalsozialistische Germanisierungspolitik in Polen*. Hamburg, 2012.

Wünschmann, Kim. *Before Auschwitz: Jewish Prisoners in the Prewar Concentration Camps*. Cambridge, MA, 2015.

Zarusky, Jürgen, and Martin Zückert (eds). *Das Münchener Abkommen von 1938 in europäischer Perspektive*. Munich, 2013.

Ziegler, Dieter (ed.). *Banken und 'Arisierungen' in Mitteleuropa während des Nationalsozialismus*. Stuttgart, 2002.

Zimmermann, Volker. *Die Sudetendeutschen im NS-Staat: Politik und Stimmung der Bevölkerung im Reichsgau Sudetenland (1938–1945)*. Essen, 1999.

Zückert, Martin. *Zwischen Nationsidee und staatlicher Realität: Die tschechoslowakische Armee und ihre Nationalitätenpolitik 1918–1938*. Munich, 2006.

INDEX OF NAMES

Abelas, Moric 316
Adam, Uwe-Dietrich 2
Adler, H. G. 7
Allina, Curt 26, 53, 270
Anderl, Gabriele 7
Arnstein, Bertha 357
Arnstein, Georg 357
Auschwitz, extermination and
    concentration camp 321, 336, 338,
    356, 360, 367
Austria 1–3, 9–10, 13–5, 26, 32–4, 42, 53,
    57–8, 63, 66, 68, 71, 73–4, 91, 97, 109,
    110, 114–7, 119–20, 125, 137, 139,
    148, 154–5, 191, 192, 195, 217, 225,
    229, 234, 238, 252–3, 273–5, 283, 310,
    314, 319, 321, 358, 380, 382, 385, 388,
    390, 392, 394–6

Baeck, Leo 314, 368
Bakon, Yehudah 112
Bankl [Gestapo official] 280, 282, 311
Baranavichy 317
Baß, Walter 280
Bauer [Protectorate Jew], 124
Bauer, Yehuda 4
Baum, Herbert 314
Bavorovice (Baurowitz) 258
Beck, Rudolf 161
Beer, Hana 294, 373
Beer, Leo 311
Beer, Ludwig 120
Běla pod Bezdězem (Weißwasser) 187

Belgium 60, 163
Beneš, Eduard 36
Beneš, Vojta 5
Benešov (Beneschau) 188, 304, 365
Beran, Hilda 26, 60
Beran, Rudolf 37, 39, 42, 59, 63
Berger, Mimi 32, 278, 373
Berlin 1, 3, 5–11, 13–6, 24, 40, 52, 56,
    65, 74, 85, 98–100, 109, 111, 113–7,
    122–3, 125, 135, 138, 148, 150, 154–5,
    163, 178, 180, 183, 212, 216, 219,
    234–7, 261, 265, 268, 271–3, 275–6,
    283, 296, 314, 316–7, 333, 336, 338,
    356–7, 368, 381–3, 385–6, 394–5
Beroun (Beraun) 152
Bertsch, Walter 265
Best, Dr. Werner 110
Biček, František 60
Bielitz (Bielsko) 113
Bienert, Dr. Richard 265
Birkenau, Auschwitz concentration camp
    367
Blenkins, Helen 26
Bock, Marie 311
Böhme, Horst 266, 269
Bolivia 135, 147, 149
Bondy, Dr. Karl 280
Bormann, Martin 360
Boschan [JKG official] 111
Brandes, Detlef 5, 7
Braník 192
Brauchitsch, Walther von 31

Breslau 56
Březnice (Bresnitz) 187
Brno (Brünn) 26, 28, 34, 37–42, 53–4, 56, 61–2, 67, 73, 86, 95–6, 113–4, 117, 123–5, 134, 141, 153–7, 180, 186, 189, 205, 208, 210, 213, 218, 223–3, 228, 231, 237, 257, 261, 263, 269, 273, 276–7, 279, 295, 301, 305, 316, 319, 324–5, 328–9, 331, 386, 389, 391, 395
Brunner, Alois 85
Bucharest 220
Buchenwald, concentration camp 160
Budapest 220
Bukovina 27
Bulgaria 183
Bürckel, Joseph 4, 53, 56, 61, 64, 74, 382
Burgsdorff, Dr. Curt von 61, 74, 158, 204
Byšicky (Bischitschek) 187
Bystřice u Benešova (Bistritz bei Beneschau) 365
Bystrovany (Bistrowan) 309
Bzenec (Bisenz) 231–2

Čakovice (Tschakowitz) 213
Carpatho-Ukraine 24, 26–7, 29, 36
Čáslav (Caslau), 150
Cermak, Dr. Fritz 263
Cesarani, David 2
Česká (Zinsendorf) 258
Česka Lipa 276
Česke Budějovice (Böhmisch-Budweis) 54, 68, 86, 90–1, 96, 150, 154, 214, 263, 315
Česky Těšin (Teschen) 117, 151
China 118–9, 147, 149
Chvalkovice (Chwalkowitz) 111
Chvalkowsky, František 41
Cimlichmann, Moses 281
Constanta 220
Cumbolds 225
Czech Republic 5, 7, 36, 38, 60, 382
Czechoslovakia 2–3, 7, 10, 13, 23–43, 51, 60, 96, 313, 360, 371, 380–1

Dachau, concentration camp 56, 68
Daluege, Kurt 53, 315, 359
Dejvice (Dewitz) 230
Denk, Karl 324
Denmark 147, 163, 368
Dennler, Wilhelm 266, 368
Diamant, Karl 191

Dobříš (Doberschich) 331
Domažlice (Taus) 150
Doppl, Camp 89, 195, 388
Drazda, František 93
Dresden 395
Dube, Alfred 25–6, 28, 32, 120, 179, 254, 270–2

Ecuador 119, 183, 219
Edelstein, Jakob 86, 87, 111, 118, 135, 139, 276, 338, 357
Eger (Cheb) 35, 57, 60
Egerland 35
Ehrlich, Ferdinand 281
Eichmann, Adolf 4, 10, 11, 13, 15, 85–90, 99, 100, 108–9, 111–14, 116, 118, 121, 125, 135, 139, 145, 149, 163–4, 179, 185, 232, 236, 256, 269, 271, 304, 314, 326, 333, 340, 384–6, 390, 397
Eicke, Theodor 56
Eisenz 331
Elbe River 258
Eliaš, Alois 59, 69, 70, 84, 205, 261, 262, 266, 315, 383, 392, 396
Engelsrath, Ernst 279
England 38, 162–3
Eppstein, Paul 314, 338, 368
Erfurt 360
Europe 3–6, 8, 23, 28, 33, 34, 108, 158, 163–4, 211, 266, 272, 274–5, 278, 283, 370–1, 381, 396

Falkenau (Falknov nad Ohří) 67
Fantlova, Zdenka 160
Feierabend, Dr. Ladislav 41, 58, 383
Felix, Ruth 193
Fiechtner [Senior County Commissioner] 107
Fiehler, Dr. Karl 156
Fischer, Dr. Ottokar 41
Flossenbürg, concentration camp 56, 360
Fluß, Erich 279
Foltar, Ing. Karl 54
France 35, 37, 90, 158, 163, 235
Frank, Karl Hermann 7, 57, 71, 124, 158, 204–5, 234–7, 260–1, 266, 268–9, 313, 314, 359–60, 368–71, 373–4, 381, 394, 396
Frankfurt am Main 56
Frankl, Helene 311
Frankl, Josef 311
Frankl, Karl 311

Index of Names

Frankl, Samuel 311
Franzensbad (Františkovy Lázně) 37
Freiburg im Breisgau 6
Frick, Wilhelm 53–4, 236, 359, 373, 394
Friedländer, Saul 2
Friedmann, Dr. Franz (František) 86, 314, 356, 358, 397
Friedmann, Richard 111
Fröhlich, Paula 188
Fröhlich, Rosa 279
Frýdava (Friedau) 193
Frýdek-Místek (Friedeck) 52

Gajda, Radola 39, 67
Galicia 27, 108
Geneva 321, 357
Gerlach, Christian 2
Germany 1, 3, 5–6, 9, 10, 11–4, 23–4, 26, 28, 30–3, 35, 37, 52, 59, 64, 69, 71, 74, 75, 90, 94, 97, 110, 117, 119–20, 125, 137–8, 143, 154, 163–4, 191–3, 195, 213, 215–9, 225, 228–31, 234–5, 237–8, 252–3, 261, 267–8, 272, 274–5, 283, 301, 310, 316, 319, 321, 323–4, 331, 357–8, 360–1, 368, 371–2, 380, 384–5, 390, 392, 394–6
Gerwarth, Robert 7
Ginsburg, Roderick 5
Ginz, Petr 1, 195, 254, 261, 265, 270, 272, 276, 278, 280, 282, 295–6, 298–300, 302, 307, 314
Goebbels, Joseph 1, 54, 57, 59, 236, 268, 272
Goltz, Marianne 359
Göring, Hermann 57, 61, 63–4, 74, 106, 134, 180, 207, 261, 382
Gottberg, Curt von 158
Gottwald, Klement 373
Grant, Anna 26, 373
Grazer, Dr. Oskar 61
Greater German Reich 1–2, 8, 11, 14, 52–4, 65, 110–1, 117, 122, 125, 135, 163, 183, 189, 195, 216, 234, 236, 238, 252, 261, 272, 275, 283, 304, 317, 338, 340, 357–60, 373–4, 384–7, 390, 393–5, 397
Groß-Rosen, concentration camp 360
Groß, Theodor 158
Grün [Jewish Community official] 111
Grünfeld, Helene 222
Günther, Hans 85, 111, 113–4, 141, 219, 221, 232, 276

Haas, Hermann 190
Hácha, Emil 3, 37, 52, 56, 58–9, 67, 69, 70, 73, 93, 95–6, 142, 162, 260, 265, 268, 316, 370, 382–3, 396
Hahn, Irma 274
Hanowetz, Forester (Forstmeister) 309
Hartmann, Georg 33,
Havelka, Dr. Jiří 41, 58, 383
Havlíčkův Brod 90
Hechter, Wilhelm 115–6
Heinemann, Isabel 6
Hejčín (Hatschein), 260, 311
Henlein, Konrad 30–2, 35, 56, 64, 382
Henschel, Moritz 314
Herman, Josef 233
Hermann [Government Counsellor] 108
Heß, Rudolf 156
Heydrich, Reinhard 4, 7, 12, 68, 75, 84, 99, 107–8, 110, 134, 156, 163–4, 204, 260–70, 275–8, 283, 304, 312–7, 340, 381, 384, 386–7, 391, 393
Hilberg, Raul 2
Himmler, Heinrich 11, 53, 56–7, 61, 73, 110, 116–7, 125, 189, 261, 313, 315–6, 368, 386
Hitler, Adolf 2, 6, 8, 11, 28, 31–2, 35, 37, 41, 43, 51–7, 64–5, 69–70, 73–4, 97, 108, 110, 124–5, 156–9, 162, 233, 235–6, 260–1, 268–70, 272–3, 283, 311, 313–6, 358–60, 373, 380, 382, 383, 385
Hlinka, Andrej 32, 37
Hlinsko 190
Hlohovice (Lohowitz) 213
Hloubětín (Tiefenbach) 145, 153
Hodonín (Göding), 232
Hoffmann, Albert 91, 388
Hoffmann, Camill 53
Holešov (Holleschau) 25, 62, 178, 188, 192, 207, 230, 232, 322
Hopf, Volkmar 124
Hořice v Podkrkonoší (Horschitz) 142, 187
Horní Bříza (Ober-Birken) 193, 258, 260
Hořovice (Horschowitz) 188
Hostomice (Hostomitz) 188
Hrabůvka (Klein-Grabau) 255
Hradec Králové (Königgrätz) 68, 95, 187, 226, 233, 263, 297–8, 305, 319, 331, 336
Hrotovice (Hrottowitz) 62
Hruby, Adolf 265, 370

Hulice (Hulitz) 154
Humplik, Hans 322
Humpolec (Humpoletz) 91
Hüntgen [Gestapo official] 311
Hyde, Georgine 26, 189, 195

Israel 8, 15, 373
Istanbul 220
Izbica 301

Jacoby, Gerhard 5
Jaissle, Dr. [Government Counsellor] 216
Janovice (Janowitz) 361
Ježek, Josef 273
Jičin (Jitschin) 142–3, 187, 192, 317
Jihlava (Iglau) 54, 56, 60, 95–6, 107, 155–6, 190, 207, 226, 263, 304, 319
Jindřichův Hradec (Neuhaus) 331
Judenberg, Moric 316
Jung, Rudolf 360
Jury, Dr. Hugo 156

Kafka, Dr. Emil 37, 66, 86–7, 397
Kain, Otto Karl 190
Kalek 263
Kalfus, Dr. Josef 41, 58, 265, 370, 383
Kamenice nad Lípou (Kamnitz an der Linde) 91
Kamenicky, Dr. Jindřich 265, 370
Kapras, Dr. Jan 39
Karlsbad (Karlovy Vary) 31, 35, 38, 57
Karlštejn (Karlstein) 306–7, 325–6
Kárný, Miroslav 7, 254
Karvin (Karvina) 324
Kattowitz (Katowice) 108, 11–4, 117
Katzer, Dr. Paul 310–1
Kaufmann, Franz 190
Kbely (Gbel) 195
Kennan, George 66
Kladno 68, 123, 226, 256, 260, 276, 295, 306, 326–7, 329
Klapka, Dr. Otakar 59, 262, 360
Klatovy (Klattau) 60, 162, 192, 227, 260, 274, 317, 319, 331 336
Klausing, Friedrich 158, 189
Klein, Fred 32
Klemm, Edmund 309
Klumpar, Dr. Vladislav 96
Klumtschau 226
Kobylisy (Kobilis) 154, 227
Kohn, Jiři 359
Kojetín (Kojetein) 229, 300

Kolín 140, 152, 226, 233, 258, 304, 317, 321–2, 325
Komotau (Chomutov) 161, 363
Königsberg an der Eger (Kynšperk nad Ohří) 60
Königshütte (Chorzów) 113
Kopecky, Jaromir 321
Kornfeld, Rudolf 279
Koryčany 153
Košice 370
Kostel 188, 207, 331
Kozolupy (Kosolup) 307
Kozower, Phillip 314
Krakau 111, 114
Kral, Katherine 26, 320
Krämer, Salo 222, 330, 356–7
Kraus, Erich 358
Kreindler, Leo 314
Krejčí, Jaroslav 59, 265, 370, 392
Křivoklat (Pürglitz) 307
Kroměřiž (Kremsier) 62, 67, 229, 274, 322
Krumholz, Ervin 310
Kulka [Protectorate citizen] 124
Kulka, Otto Dov 164
Kulm (Chlumec) 67
Kundt, Ernst 54
Kuněticе (Kunzendorf) 258
Küpper, René 7
Kutná Hora (Kuttenberg) 152
Kyjov (Gaya) 62, 207, 230–2, 260, 295, 331

Lammers, Hans Heinrich 235–6, 266, 360
Landre, Berta 361
Langer, Herbert 357
Ledce (Ledetz) 260
Leděč nad Sázavou 91
Lederer [SS-Hauptscharführer] 194
Lederer, Dr. Edvard 28
Lederer, Dr. Rudolf 35
Lederer, Jaroslav 5
Lederer, Josef 279
Lederer, Regina 279
Lehr, Leo 279
Leipzig 395
Leitmeritz (Litoměřice) 35, 161
Lemkin, Raphael 6
Letňany (Letnian) 258, 326
Ležáky (Ležak) 315
Libeň (Lieben) 145
Liblin 213

Index of Names 433

Libochowitz (Libochovice) 188
Lidice (Liditz) 315
Lilienthal, Arthur 314
Linden (Lípa), camp 193–6, 213, 224, 226, 233, 256, 299, 307–8, 310, 325, 339, 364, 388
Linz 56
Lipník nad Bečvou (Leipnik) 229
Lisbon 219
Litol 187
Lochkov (Lochkow) 213
Łódź (Litzmannstadt), ghetto 122, 269, 271–3, 283, 303, 391
Lomnitz 190
London 39, 87, 93, 160, 234, 261
Longerich, Peter 2
Los Angeles 16
Loštice (Loschitz) 300, 309
Louny (Laun) 141
Löw, Arthur 31
Löwenherz, Josef 314
Löwy, Otto 233
Lublin 111, 115–7, 122, 303–4, 317, 321, 386
Ludwig, Siegfried 73
Luhačovice (Luhatschowitz) 161
Lustig, Rudolf 280
Lysá nad Labem (Lissa an der Elbe) 142, 187, 191–2, 357

Maass, Anny 25–6
Mährisch-Weißkirchen (Hranice na Moravě) 182, 229, 331, 333
Malokuncic (Klein Kuntschitz) 193
Maloměřice (Malmeritz) 260
Maly Trostinec 329
Mandelik, Robert 72
Mannheimer, Max 161, 193
Margulies, Dr. Emil 35
Marienbad 35
Masaryk, Tomáš G. 3, 25, 34, 42
Mauthausen, concentration camp 263
Mautner [Prague Jew] 276, 295
Mautnerova [Prague Jew] 276
Meckel, Dr. Rudolf 54
Meissner, Dr. Alfréd 28
Meissner, Lotte 147
Melnik (Mělnik) 188, 192
Merin, Moshe 116
Milešov (Mileschau) 192
Minsk 269, 273, 277, 283, 317, 321, 329, 391

Mladá Boleslav (Jungbunzlau) 140, 142–3, 187, 207, 226, 301, 317, 319, 338, 356
Mladá Vožice (Jung Woschitz) 331
Mokry [Ministerial Counsellor] Dr. 139
Molsen [Senior County Commissioner] 157
Moravec, Emanuel 265, 370
Moravian Ostrava (Moravská Ostrava, Mährisch-Ostrau) 25–8, 33, 37–8, 40, 52, 60–1, 66–7, 95–6, 108–9, 111–7, 121, 125, 136, 151, 156, 158, 162, 178, 182, 186–7, 189, 204, 208, 210–11, 213–4, 218, 220, 222–3, 228, 232, 254, 261, 263, 268–9, 278–80, 310–1, 319–20, 328–30, 386
Moravské Budějovice (Mährisch-Budwitz) 61–2
Morawetz, Margit 29
Mořina (Groß Morschin) 307
Moscow 16, 33
Müller, Heinrich 108–9, 111, 113–5, 117, 314, 367, 386
Münchengrätz (Mnichovo Hradiště) 142
Munich 2, 6, 10, 35–6, 42, 124, 191
Murmelstein, Benjamin 111, 314, 338, 368
Mydlovary (Midlowar) 260

Náchod 67
Nebe, Arthur 316
Německy Brod (Deutsch-Brod) 90–1, 119, 152, 193, 218, 226
Netherlands, The 163, 368
Neubert, SS-Hauptscharführer 194
Neudorf 258
Neurath, Freiherr Konstantin von 55, 57, 69, 84–5, 92, 97, 107, 137–9, 158, 236, 260–1, 263, 283, 359, 381, 383, 396
Neveklov (Neweklau) 304
New York 16
Niesner, Josef 309
Nisko am San 111–2, 114, 116, 118, 125, 151, 222, 328, 385–6
Norway 163
Nova Cerekev (Neu-Cerekee) 235
Nove Benatky (Neu-Benatek) 142
Nové Strašecí (Neu-Straschitz) 182
Novotna, Serafine 38
Nový Bydžov (Neubidschow) 150, 188
Nový Dvůr (Neuhof) 258
Nuremberg 35, 39, 54, 69–71, 44, 141, 158, 205, 237, 267, 283, 390

Obora 213
Old Reich 9, 36, 58, 66, 97, 107, 109–10, 117–8, 120, 148, 163, 207, 217, 269, 275, 315, 319–20, 324, 339, 361, 389–90
Olomouc (Olmütz) 15, 28, 38, 40, 53, 60–1, 67, 72–3, 95–6, 123, 147, 156–7, 177, 190, 223, 226, 229, 232257, 263, 276, 278, 280–2, 300, 302, 305, 308–12, 317, 319, 321–2, 325, 330, 334, 339, 358, 363, 366
Olšany (Olschan) 310
Opletal, Jan 123
Oppenheim, Berthold 334
Oprach, Marc 8
Orten, Jiři 181
Oslavany (Oslawan) 364
Osterloh, Jörg 8, 14
Ostrava-Karvinna 63
Ostravice (Ostrawitza) River 258
Oświęcim 116

Pacov (Patzau) 325
Palestine 28, 81, 107, 147, 183, 196, 212, 313, 371, 373, 389
Pardubice (Pardubitz) 67, 93, 95, 190, 218, 226, 258, 260, 305, 319, 325, 336
Paris 87, 90, 262
Pelhřimov 91, 325
Petschek, Julius 68, 372
Pfitzner, Josef 59, 180, 268, 369, 374
Piaski 301, 304
Pick, Marie 161
Pilsen (Plzeň) 25–6, 28, 32, 68, 93, 140, 156, 160, 179, 211, 226, 232, 263, 265, 274, 277, 294–5, 302, 305, 329, 331
Plowitz, Erich 279
Plumlov (Plumenau) 308
Podmelova, Zuzana 26, 330
Polak, Leopold 60
Polak, Rudolf 60
Poland, 1–3, 13–15, 33, 60–1, 75, 106–8, 111–3, 116–8, 111–3, 116–8, 122, 125, 142–3, 151, 154, 269–70, 273, 276, 280, 294–5, 304, 317, 321, 338–9, 357, 383–5, 387, 394–6
Pollertova, Anna 280
Prague 24, 148, 151, 158, 181, 214, 218, 300, 305, 308
Předměřice nad Labem (Predmeritz) 297
Prerau (Přerov) 73, 229, 253, 274
Příbram (Prebram) 235

Prodavka, Ernst 279
Prostějov (Proßnitz) 223, 229, 278, 280–2, 309–11, 325
Pruhonitz (Průhonice) 192

Raasiku 329
Radvansky, Artur 61
Radwanitz 61
Rakovnik (Rakonitz) 152, 232, 306, 325
Rasch, Dr. Otto 56, 58
Ravensbrück, concentration camp 160
Redlich, Robert 276, 280, 309, 358
Reichenberg (Liberec) 40
Retschowits 258
Ribbentrop, Joachim von 53
Riefenstahl, Leni 123
Riga 269, 273, 277, 295, 321
Ritter, Victor 279
Rothkirchen, Livia 8, 233
Rothschild, Baron Robert de 87
Roubiček, Alice Sarah 279
Roudnice nad Labem (Raudnitz an der Elbe) 331
Rufeisen, Dr. Josef 28
Ruzin (Ruzyně) 214–5, 218, 227, 299–300, 305
Rys, Jan Roszevac 67

Sachs, Dr. Max 316
Sachsenhausen, concentration camp 56, 123, 314
Sadek, Dr. Vlastimil 41
Sandhof, camp 89, 195, 333, 388
Santo Domingo 135, 148–9, 154, 193, 212
Sázava (Sasau) 218, 226
Sázava (Sasau)-Velká Losenice (Groß Lossenitz) 226–7, 258
Scherowitz 309
Schmidt-Hartmann, Eva 5
Schmolka, Dr. Marie 60, 66
Schwabe [Brno Police Chief] 61
Schwarz, Leo 262
Seltchau 280
Semily (Semil) 142
Seyß-Inquart, Arthur 53
Sezimovo Ústí (Alt-Tabor) 258
Shanghai 118–9, 147–9, 164, 182–3, 196, 212–3, 219–20, 229, 255, 387, 389
Siegel, Dr. Raimund 54
Silesia 24, 27, 34, 36, 109, 116–7, 125, 155, 320, 385

Index of Names 435

Singer, Dr. Oskar 122
Singer, Regine 333
Six, Franz Alfred 316
Slaný (Schlan) 233
Slavoňov (Slowoniow) 192
Slivenec (Slowenetz), 213
Slovakia 26–7, 35–7, 368, 382
Smíchov (Smichow) 231
Soběslav (Sobieslau) 299
Sobibor, extermination camp 304, 317
Sosnowitz 116
Soviet Union (USSR) 149, 183, 222, 235, 237, 312
Spira, Ida 279
Spitzer, Georg 262
Spitzer, Hugo 281
Srnojedy 258
Stahlecker, Dr. Franz Walter 56, 58, 71, 74, 77, 84–5, 99, 108, 111, 134, 139, 382, 384, 386
Starý Vestec (Alt-Westetz) 192
Štěchovice (Stechowitz) 154, 258
Stein, Arnold 38
Steinherz, Samuel 25
Stier, Dr. Rudolf 73
Stodůlky (Stodulek) 226
Stone, Dan 2
Storfer [Jewish Community official] 111
Strakonice (Strakonitz) 150
Stránský, Prof. Jaroslav 42
Stráznice (Straßnitz) 193
Streckenbach, Bruno 316
Streicher, Julius 67
Stricker, Georg 280
Strielek 258
Stuckart, Wilhelm 9, 53, 56, 64, 97–8, 236, 338, 383
Sturm, Dr. Walther 266
Stuttgart 56
Sudetenland 2, 30–2, 34–38 42, 51, 54, 56–8, 60, 66, 7391, 156, 190, 360, 363, 381–2, 388
Šumice (Schumitz) 282
Sušice (Schüttenhofen) 188
Švihov (Schwiehau) 226
Syrovy, General 36

Tábor 152, 155, 192, 233, 300, 304, 319, 336
Tauber, Siegfried 367
Taus 150
Teplitz (Teplice) 35

Theresienstadt (Terezín) 2, 4, 7, 13–15, 269–70, 273, 275–77, 280, 283, 294–7, 301–4, 305–6, 311, 314–7, 328–9, 333–4, 336, 339–41, 356–7, 360, 367–8, 370–1, 373–4, 391–4
Thierack, Otto 262
Tišnov (Tischnowitz) 153–4, 257
Třebíč (Trebitsch) 62, 304, 324–5
Trěbichovice (Trebichowitz) 154
Treblinka, extermination camp 329, 336
Třešť (Triesch) 147
Troja 225
Troper, Morris C. 87
Trschepschein 281
Tršovice 361
Tschaslau 187
Turnov (Turnau) 142, 187, 226

Uhlířske Janovice (Kohljanowitz) 361
Ungarisch-Brod (Uhersky Brod) 147, 202, 230, 232, 338, 357
Ungarisch-Hradisch (Uherske Hradišti) 230–2
United Kingdom (UK) 35, 37, 312
United States (US) 5–6, 33, 42, 66, 148, 183, 212, 219, 312, 327
Untermöhle [Reich Bank Counsellor] 118
Unterstab, Albert 365
Uritz, Ernst 279

Valašske Meziřiči (Walachisch-Meseritsch) 62
Veleminsky, Dr. Georg 359
Veleminsky, Dr. Jan 359
Veleminsky, Zdenek 359
Velká Bystřice (Groß Wisternitz) 299
Velký Osek (Groß Ossek) 258
Veseli nad Moravou (Wessely an der March) 231
Vienna 7, 9, 26, 53, 55–6, 58, 60, 63, 69, 74, 84–100, 109, 111–9, 122 125 135, 151, 163–4, 178, 180, 183, 195, 212 268, 271–3, 275, 314, 317, 333, 336, 338, 356, 382–4, 386–7, 395
Vítkovice (Witkowitz) 57, 67, 319
Vladivostok 183
Vltava River 41, 53, 154, 178, 192, 231, 253, 258, 366
Vsetin (Wsetin) 60–2
Vyškov (Wischau) 180, 218, 226, 257, 307, 309, 325

Waigner, Emil 189
Waltig, Ivan 316
Warsaw 304
Weimar 160
Weisel, Dr. Otokar 359

Yokohama 149
Yugoslavia 147, 220

Záběhlice (Sabechlitz) 226
Zabřeh (Hohenstadt), 68
Zamość 304
Zámostí (Samost) 331
Zdiby (Zdib) 225
Zlín 124, 155, 207, 221, 230, 257, 319

Index of Subjects

Agricultural University 37
agriculture 24, 28, 40, 58, 90, 119, 149, 152–3, 184–5, 191, 205, 213–4, 224–8, 238, 257–8, 265, 274, 283, 297, 299–301, 307, 308, 310, 323, 325–7, 329, 339, 370, 383, 388, 89, 91, 92
Allies 25, 261, 313, 368, 381
annexation 5, 9, 10–1, 34, 42, 51, 53, 74, 358
annihilation 2, 4, 93, 371–2, 392, 396
anti-Jewish laws 1–15, 32, 34, 36–43, 58–61, 63–6, 69–70, 73–75, 92–7, 98–9, 118–9, 121–3, 134–5, 147, 149, 160, 163, 164, 179, 192, 195, 204, 206, 209–10, 231–3, 235, 238, 254, 262, 266, 268, 273, 275, 278, 282–3, 300, 304, 315, 317, 327, 358, 372–3, 381–3, 386, 390–1, 394–7
antisemitism 3, 10, 25, 26, 29, 32–3, 37, 38, 41–2, 57, 67–8, 160, 177, 235, 312–3, 374, 381–3, 396
armaments 34, 227, 257, 338, 360
arson 67, 232, 262, 314
Aryanization 9–10, 12, 61, 63–4, 67, 72–4, 85, 91, 98, 100, 107, 120, 136–7, 144, 150–1, 155, 157, 165, 189–91, 196, 205, 210–1, 216, 237, 372–3, 381–3, 385, 388–9
assimilation 26–8, 42, 155, 158, 313, 381

birth rates 24, 27, 145, 177, 195, 220, 229
boycotts 34, 96, 261

Catholicism 26, 37, 58, 254
Central Office for Jewish Emigration 10–3, 15, 68–9, 84–92, 94, 99–100, 107, 117–8, 122, 134–5, 137, 139–41, 143, 145, 147–50, 160, 164, 179, 181–3, 185, 187–88, 193–6, 206–7, 209–10, 212, 214, 217–21, 224, 226–32, 235, 237–8, 253, 255–7, 267, 269–70, 272, 276–8, 282–3, 296, 301–2, 305–7, 317, 319–24, 326, 329, 331, 333, 337–40, 373, 381, 384, 386–92, 394–7
centralization 12, 121, 139, 141, 164, 177, 186–7, 195–6, 216, 224, 238, 255, 257, 266, 268, 283, 302, 384, 389–91
Charles University in Prague 25, 27, 39, 42, 123, 158, 189
Chief County Commissioners 6, 10, 16, 58–9, 61–2, 71–2, 74, 95, 107, 116, 124, 136, 143, 149, 151, 155–8, 162, 178–9, 186–7, 189–90, 192, 204, 207, 210, 218, 221, 230–1, 233, 254, 256, 263–5, 268, 276–8, 280, 296, 304, 308, 313, 317, 319, 327–8, 383–5, 390, 394, 396
communism 4, 7, 26, 32, 36, 60, 263, 282, 312, 372–3
Communist Party 36, 282
concentration 9, 12–3, 86, 88, 90, 108–9, 142, 146, 179–81, 186–9, 196, 206–7, 211, 237–8, 253, 256, 268, 269, 283, 294–6, 301, 339, 366, 374, 388, 390–2, 394–5

concentration camps 51–2, 56, 60, 68, 89, 122–3, 160, 165, 263, 272, 283, 296, 314–5, 329, 341, 360, 393, 398
courts 31, 41, 60, 62, 70, 115, 124, 151, 160–2, 233, 261–3, 279–80, 283, 299, 310, 315–6, 328, 340, 359, 369–70, 374, 391, 397
curfews 107, 125, 161, 233–4, 253, 283, 313, 385, 397
Czech Ministry of Agriculture and Forestry 40–1, 58, 119, 205, 258, 265, 274, 283, 300–1, 327, 370, 383, 391
Czech Ministry of Commerce and Crafts 58
Czech Ministry of Economy and Labor 265, 304, 307, 338
Czech Ministry of Education and Culture 39–40, 42, 58, 92, 138, 265, 320, 382
Czech Ministry of Finance 41, 58, 63, 72, 136, 182, 206, 209, 221, 265, 305, 383, 396
Czech Ministry of Foreign Affairs 41, 52
Czech Ministry of Industry, Trade, and Commerce 41, 73, 90, 265
Czech Ministry of the Interior 41, 58, 94, 96, 134, 138, 141, 150, 156, 161, 178–9, 196, 227, 265, 268, 273, 370, 388
Czech Ministry of Internal Affairs 327
Czech Ministry of Justice 28, 58–9, 146, 265, 370, 392
Czech Ministry of Public Works 58, 265
Czech Ministry of Social and Health Administration 12, 89, 96, 153, 217–8, 221–2, 224–6, 228, 238, 256–7, 265, 283, 339, 391–2
Czech Ministry of Social Affairs 297
Czech Ministry of Transport 41, 58, 206, 265, 370, 383
Czechoslovak National Democracy 30
Czechoslovak National Socialist Party 30
Czechoslovak People's Party 30
Czechoslovak Social Democratic Workers' Party 30

death penalty 12, 123, 261–2, 279, 283–4, 359, 369, 391
demographics 5, 10, 26, 51
demonstrations 25, 35, 37, 41, 59, 67, 72, 123, 158, 234
deportations 2–4, 11–13, 33–4, 37, 107–26, 134–5, 151, 155, 158, 163–5, 177, 179, 195, 211, 213, 215, 22, 230, 234, 236, 238, 252–3, 255, 258, 266, 268–83, 294–312, 316–31, 333, 335, 338–40, 356–61, 363, 365–74, 381, 385–6, 389–97
doctors 39–40, 42, 63, 66, 89, 93, 112, 143, 146, 185, 208, 223, 228, 321, 327
donations 121, 186, 196, 209–10, 371

emigration 4, 7, 9, 11–12, 37, 51, 60, 65, 68–9, 75, 84–90, 98–100, 107, 10, 116, 118–20, 122, 125, 134—6, 138–9, 40–1, 144–52, 154, 160, 163–5, 177, 182–4,, 186, 189, 193, 196, 207, 209–13, 219–20, 225, 227–9, 237, 253, 255–6, 275, 380–1, 384–5, 387–9, 397
Emigration Fund for Bohemia and Moravia 139, 178, 188–9, 210, 221, 230, 253, 277, 282, 296–7, 302, 309, 329–31, 333, 340, 366, 389, 395
expropriation 66, 221, 237
extermination camps 3, 304, 317, 329, 338
eviction 142, 165, 180, 206, 209, 211, 223, 230, 237, 304, 388

fascism 1, 25, 39, 42, 64, 67, 74, 93, 100, 158, 191, 235, 331, 381, 383, 385, 387
First World War 10, 23, 25, 42, 57, 61, 116, 328, 381
forestry 119, 152–4, 184, 193–4, 213, 218, 226–7, 238, 258, 283, 299, 301, 307, 309–10, 323, 325–7, 339, 363, 389–90, 392
forced emigration 11–2, 86, 100, 126, 196, 275, 384, 389
forced labour 2, 4, 12–3, 51, 112, 181, 191–6, 214, 222, 224–5, 227–8, 230, 238, 253, 256–8, 267, 269–73, 281–4, 294, 297–9, 305–10, 312, 320, 323–30, 338–40, 359, 361, 363–6, 368, 370–4, 387–97
freedom of movement 141, 178–9, 238, 255, 316, 389

Gajda [fascist organization] 64, 67
Gauleiter (Nazi party district leader) 53, 58, 113, 156, 382
German Agrarian Party 30
German Christian Social People's Party 30, 32

Index of Subjects

German Democratic Republic (GDR) 4, 6
German National Party of Bohemia 30–1, 57
German National Socialist Workers' Party (Deutsche Nationalsozialistische Arbeiterpartei or DNSAP) 30
German–Polish Accord 34
German Social Democratic Party 30
Germanization 4, 24, 33, 54, 73, 95–6, 100, 154–5, 158–9, 266, 275, 359, 369, 384–5
Gestapo (Secret State Police) 9–11, 15, 35, 56, 60–1, 66, 68–9, 72–4, 85–6, 89–91, 99, 106–117, 120–3, 136–7, 138, 141, 160–1, 163, 181, 207, 231, 233, 262–3, 267, 269–71, 273, 277–8, 280–4, 294, 296, 301–2, 305, 308–9, 311–15, 317, 319, 321, 328–30, 333, 338, 340–1, 357–9, 361, 366–8, 373, 383, 392–3, 395
ghettos 4, 211, 268–70, 272–3, 275–6, 283, 294–7, 301, 304–6, 310, 316–7, 321, 328, 333–5, 336, 338–40, 356–8, 360–1, 365, 367–8, 370–1, 391–3
ghettoization 2, 12–3, 67, 134, 141, 143, 164–5, 186–9, 196, 206–7, 210–1, 237, 253, 269, 275, 282, 339, 368, 371, 387, 389–90, 395

Habsburg Empire 3, 24, 381
HeHalutz organization 148–9, 184, 191, 213, 224
HICEM 33, 60, 88

immigration 27, 32–3, 37, 40–1, 69, 89, 213, 219, 382
impoverishment 4, 11–12, 66, 68, 84, 98–100, 110, 119–21, 126, 143, 145, 146, 152, 165, 181–2, 185, 196, 208, 223, 237, 303, 335, 385–7. 389–90, 397
industry (general) 24, 28, 39, 63, 73–4, 90, 218, 227, 238, 258, 269, 283, 300, 339, 389–90, 392

Jewish businesses (firms) 10, 25, 34–5, 36, 38, 61–3, 66–7, 71–4, 93–5, 136, 144, 150–1, 157, 178, 190, 210, 215, 383
Jewish children 90, 92, 99, 113, 116, 119–121, 126, 145–7, 149, 182–3, 185–6, 193, 208, 219, 222–3, 229, 256, 267, 294, 296, 303, 315, 320–1, 325, 328, 361, 368, 386, 397

Jewish elderly 36, 120–1, 126, 145–6, 153, 155, 186, 208, 222–3, 230, 278, 294, 320–1, 333, 386, 397
Jewish mentally infirm 186, 281–2, 321–2
Jewish Party 29, 36
Jewish property 2, 5, 9, 13, 36, 63–4, 66, 71, 73–4, 91–2, 110, 117, 119–20, 136–7, 158, 189, 196, 221, 270, 278, 297, 324, 328, 333, 341, 372, 383, 389
Jewish Question 33, 37, 39–41, 64–5, 68–9, 93, 97–8, 135, 163, 205, 220, 235–6, 269, 270–1, 276, 313, 322, 325, 327, 338, 361, 373, 394
Jewish Relief Committee 32–3
Jewish Religious Communities (general), 4, 8–9, 11–13, 15–6, 27, 32, 37, 59, 66, 74, 86, 90, 93, 107–9, 117, 125, 135, 139–43, 148, 150–1, 157, 160, 164–5, 182, 186–8, 191, 193, 195, 206, 209, 213, 216–9, 221–5, 229, 232, 237–8, 253, 255, 267, 273, 275, 278, 282, 296, 298, 301–2, 305, 309, 314, 319, 321–2, 331, 334, 336, 357, 365–6, 372, 385–98
Jewish Religious Community of Brno 154, 213, 218, 324, 328, 389
Jewish Religious Community of Moravian Ostrava 33, 111–3, 121, 182, 186, 193, 213, 220, 222–3, 232, 328, 330
Jewish Religious Community of Olomouc 15, 229, 276, 278, 280–2, 302, 309, 310–2, 324, 330, 339, 358
Jewish Religious Community of Prague 9, 11–2, 13, 15–6, 27, 37, 60, 66, 85–7, 89–91, 98–100, 107, 111, 115, 118–22, 126, 135, 137, 139–54, 160–1, 164, 177, 179, 180, 182–8, 191–6, 206–26, 228–30, 232–3, 237–8, 253–8, 267, 272–3, 276, 299–308, 314, 319, 321–2, 324–5, 328, 330–1, 333–4, 339–41, 356–7, 372–3, 384–9, 392–5, 397.
Jewish Religious Community of Vienna 85–7, 89, 111, 135, 183, 338
Jewish star, 1, 12, 142, 234, 252–4, 267, 271, 274, 280, 282, 284, 301, 310, 319, 338, 340, 359, 362, 391, 397
Jews' houses 143, 179–81, 187, 189, 196, 206–7, 237–8, 388, 390–1, 395
Joint Distribution Committee (the Joint) 33, 87, 144, 148, 212

kindertransport 90

labour camps, 112, 193, 195–6, 207, 217, 307, 309, 321, 362–5, 374, 387, 392, 394
law 1, 4, 5, 8–9, 24, 27, 35, 39–42, 54–5, 58, 61–2, 64–5, 69–71, 73–4, 93, 106, 110, 122–4, 136–8, 141, 146, 158, 189, 204–5, 215–6, 237, 267, 274, 281, 305, 313, 315, 320, 323–4, 338, 357–8, 361, 372, 381, 383, 390, 395
lawyers 35, 40–1, 63, 66, 93, 119, 146, 228, 310
liquidation 71, 91, 121, 136–40, 146, 157, 190, 210, 223, 315, 328–9, 331, 333, 388
looting 9, 25, 231, 331

marriage 13, 27, 65, 158–9, 215, 267, 270, 296, 304, 309, 323–7, 336, 338, 341, 358, 360–1, 363, 365–8, 374, 393–4
Marxism 36, 59, 68
mayors 10, 59–60, 96, 155–7, 263, 266, 369, 374, 285, 390, 392, 396
Munich Agreement (Diktat), 2, 10, 35, 36, 42, 381

nationalism 25, 29, 32, 142, 372
National Coordination Committee 33
National Partnership 58–9, 69–70, 72, 142, 158, 177, 181, 204–5, 235, 268
National Socialism 30–1, 42, 53, 57, 67, 91, 93
Nazi Party (NSDAP), 5, 40, 54, 58, 67, 115, 156–7, 177–8, 181, 196, 206, 231, 263, 296, 330, 333, 381, 388, 395
Non-Mosaic (non-religious) Jews 141, 164, 254
Nuremberg Race Laws 39, 69, 71, 74, 141, 158, 205, 237, 267, 383, 390

Orthodox Jews 26–28

Palestine Office 87, 111, 118–9, 135, 139, 143, 147–8, 182, 214, 216, 219–20
Party of National Unity 39–41
pogroms 25, 34, 36, 68–9, 179, 180, 331
propaganda 32–3, 42, 59, 78, 123, 155, 158, 236, 262, 266, 314, 381
protests 25, 40, 68, 73, 96, 113, 115, 121–3, 125, 145–6, 160, 188, 282, 372, 386, 397

rabbis 26–7, 61, 334, 368
racial Jews 11, 108, 110, 125, 164, 385, 387

radicalization 3, 9, 10, 14, 41, 125, 141, 191–2, 206, 231, 285, 396
refugees 10, 27, 32–4, 36–8, 40, 42, 60, 66, 86, 120, 262, 273, 382
Reich Association of Jews in Germany 9, 119, 135, 138, 148, 150, 158, 163–4, 183, 193, 207, 219, 314, 338, 368, 387, 395
Reich Ministry of Finance 110, 360
Reich Ministry of Foreign Affairs 55
Reich Ministry of Justice 262
Reich Ministry of the Economy 63–4, 73
Reich Ministry of the Interior 9, 51, 53–4, 57, 64–65, 91, 95, 97–8, 156, 205, 236, 304, 338, 359, 373, 383, 394
Reich Protector of Bohemia and Moravia 1–2, 5–8, 10, 55, 58–9, 64–5, 69, 71, 73–4, 85, 91–2, 95–99, 107, 107, 110–1, 136–9, 141–2, 146, 150, 155–8, 162, 165, 180–1, 189–91, 195, 205–7, 215, 217, 221–2, 224, 226, 229, 231–2, 235–8, 260–1, 263, 265–6, 270, 270, 283, 295, 315, 328, 331, 339, 359, 374, 381, 383–4, 387–91, 396
Reich Security Main Office (RSHA) 11, 115, 117, 219, 329
Republican Party of Farmers and Peasants 30
resettlement 12, 27, 90–1, 98, 116–8, 120, 143, 148, 159, 163, 187–8, 207–8, 211, 230, 256, 269, 277, 282, 296, 303–4, 316, 328, 384
resistance 4, 7, 12–4, 51, 61, 110, 122, 124, 156–7, 160–1, 165, 204, 232, 235, 237, 252, 254, 261–2, 267, 278, 280, 282–3, 310, 312–6, 331, 340, 358–60, 370, 372, 391, 393, 396–8
retraining 12, 85, 89, 90, 99, 112, 114, 119, 122, 148–51, 164, 183–5, 195–6, 209, 213–4, 217, 219, 224, 230, 233, 238, 299, 302, 310, 333, 388, 390, 397
reunification 6, 53, 74, 382
riots 8, 34, 60, 232, 373
roadbuilding 12, 154, 161, 185, 191–3, 215–6, 225, 228, 307, 362

sabotage 4, 13, 123–4, 261–2, 279–80, 283–4, 312, 316, 340, 391
schools 1, 9, 11, 24–6, 28–9, 32, 39, 42, 70, 90, 92, 95–6, 99–100, 108, 112, 123, 138, 148, 157, 181, 184–7, 193, 196,

208, 213, 219, 223, 253–4, 236, 265–6, 270, 274, 277, 320, 328, 385, 388
Second Czecho-Slovak Republic 3, 10, 13, 52
Security Police (Sicherheitspolizei), 4, 10, 51–2, 56–7, 68, 71, 73–4, 84–5, 97, 99, 107–8, 113, 117, 134, 138–9, 142, 178–9, 196, 232, 266, 268–70, 273, 275–7, 296, 310, 328, 333, 341, 356, 374, 380–2, 384, 386, 388, 391, 396–7
segregation 6, 10, 12, 74, 94, 97, 100, 181, 196, 214–5, 217–9, 227–8, 236, 238, 353–4, 257, 268–70, 282–3, 301, 316, 326–7, 301, 363, 385, 388–92
shopping hours 162, 177–9, 196, 205, 223, 227, 234, 237, 253, 381, 283, 388, 390, 397
Slovak People's Party 37
Social Institute 66, 98–9, 145, 152–3, 186
solidarity 122, 124, 234, 237, 254, 267, 270–1, 282, 392
SS (Schutzstaffel), 3, 6, 10, 35, 56–7, 60, 65, 69, 73, 85, 89, 106–9, 11–6, 123, 141, 151, 154, 158, 190, 224, 356, 369, 277, 296, 307, 316, 324–6, 328, 336, 361, 364, 367, 370, 374, 381–2, 384, 394
SS Death's Head Units 56, 73
SS Race and Settlement Main Office 6, 158
SS Security Service (SD) 10, 35–6, 56–7, 69, 72, 85–6, 97, 109, 112–4, 116, 124, 150, 182, 207, 211, 214, 218, 220–1, 224, 234, 306, 315, 339 381, 384
SS Task Forces 3, 56, 73, 114, 382
students 25, 28, 37, 40, 54, 92, 123, 148, 230, 312
Sudeten German 7, 24, 31, 34–5, 56, 59–60, 155, 190, 360, 372, 382
Sudeten German Free Corps 31
Sudeten German Home Front 3
Sudeten German Party (SdP) 31–2, 57
synagogues 26, 36, 60–2, 67–8, 74, 95, 137, 151, 179, 182, 187, 206, 231–2, 267,

277, 315, 322, 325, 331–2, 334, 336, 340, 383

taxes 89, 139, 141, 144, 161, 186, 195–6, 209, 305, 309, 327, 361, 374
theft 7, 13, 64, 190, 231, 294, 297, 329, 331, 333, 340–1, 371
transports 2, 24, 41, 57–9, 90, 107, 109, 11–8, 122–5, 136, 138, 148, 150–1, 183, 185, 188, 206, 208, 212, 215, 219–20, 225–6, 229, 234, 263, 265–6, 268–73, 276–8, 280–1, 283, 294–6, 299, 301–7, 311, 313–5, 317, 319–21, 323–4, 328–9, 333, 336, 338–40, 356–7, 367–8, 370, 372–3, 385–7, 391–5

unemployment, 4, 12, 120, 216, 152–3, 186, 192, 214, 216, 386, 397
universities 25, 28, 39, 123–4, 158
University of Brno 42
University of Frankfurt 158
University of Freiburg 6

vandalism 25, 35, 179
visas 41, 107, 148–9, 183, 212, 219
Volkstum 7, 136, 155
vote 24, 31, 97, 305, 384

weapons 65, 97, 261–2, 312, 359
Wehrmacht 51–2, 56–7, 60, 63–4, 95–6, 106, 109, 115, 155, 191, 266, 269, 313, 315, 328, 360
welfare 4, 9, 11–2, 27–8, 53, 58, 66, 90, 99, 100, 108, 120, 122, 138, 141, 144, 146, 152, 158, 164–5, 178, 184–6, 191, 196, 208–9, 213–4, 222–3, 228–9, 238, 253, 256, 273, 278, 301, 303, 319, 321, 330, 334, 339–40, 366, 383, 383, 388–90, 392–3, 397

Zionism 16, 26, 28, 30, 35, 37, 86, 143, 183–4, 216, 219, 312, 358, 371

www.ingramcontent.com/pod-product-compliance
Lightning Source LLC
Chambersburg PA
CBHW070041120526
44589CB00035B/2022